T0192013

Lecture Notes in Computer Science 13011

Aditya Ghose · Jennifer Horkoff ·
Vítor E. Silva Souza · Jeffrey Parsons ·
Joerg Evermann (Eds.)

Conceptual Modeling

40th International Conference, ER 2021
Virtual Event, October 18–21, 2021
Proceedings

 Springer

Editors
Aditya Ghose ⓘ
School of Computing and IT
University of Wollongong
Wollongong, NSW, Australia

Vítor E. Silva Souza ⓘ
Universidade Federal do Espírito Santo
Vitória, Brazil

Joerg Evermann
Faculty of Business Administration
Memorial University of Newfoundland
St. John's, NL, Canada

Jennifer Horkoff ⓘ
Department of Computer Science
and Engineering
Chalmers | University of Gothenburg
Gothenburg, Sweden

Jeffrey Parsons ⓘ
Faculty of Business Administration
Memorial University of Newfoundland
St. John's, NL, Canada

ISSN 0302-9743 ISSN 1611-3349 (electronic)
Lecture Notes in Computer Science
ISBN 978-3-030-89021-6 ISBN 978-3-030-89022-3 (eBook)
https://doi.org/10.1007/978-3-030-89022-3

LNCS Sublibrary: SL3 – Information Systems and Applications, incl. Internet/Web, and HCI

This Springer imprint is published by the registered company Springer Nature Switzerland AG
The registered company address is: Gewerbestrasse 11, 6330 Cham, Switzerland

Preface

ER 2021 is the premiere international conference on conceptual modeling, its foundations and applications. Conceptual models are essential for the development of software and the appropriate structuring of data. They promote reuse, integration, and integrity. Furthermore, conceptual models are also suitable for supporting the use of software. They help to open the black box, as to which software often presents itself, and thus contribute to transparency and user empowerment.

This year, ER celebrates its 40th instance as a conference. The first ER conference was held in 1979 in Los Angeles, then held every two years until 1985, when the conference became an annual event. Thus, we celebrate 42 years and 40 events dedicated to the science, methods, and practice of conceptual modeling. During its 40 instances, the conference has been held in 18 countries on five continents. We are proud to be a part of and continue to enable such an international scientific community.

The overall theme of ER 2021 is conceptual modeling in an age of uncertainty. Conceptual modeling has never been more important in this age of uncertainty. As individuals, organizations, and nations face new and unexpected challenges, software and data must be developed that can cope with and help address this new uncertainty in an ever-faster changing world. Conceptual modeling can be used to describe, understand and cope with increasing levels of uncertainty in our world.

ER 2021 was held in the beautiful and vibrant city of St. John's, Canada, as well as virtually from around the world. This is the third time that ER has been hosted in a Canadian city, with the first time being hosted in the Maritime provinces of Canada.

Despite the continued COVID-19 situation, the conference timelines were upheld as expected, with standard submissions, reviews, and notification periods. The review process was successful, with most reviews received on time, despite the added pressures of virtual science and education. This is the second time ER was organized with a virtual option, with ER 2020 being the first virtual event, and all previous ER conferences being held in person. We express our gratitude to the organizers of ER 2020 for paving the way for the virtual ER conference experience. Particularly, we have the challenge of finding a schedule that would accommodate the many time zones in which the participants would be located at during the conference. Our hybrid solution was adopted from the ER 2020 program.

In terms of paper submissions, we received 95 abstracts, 85 final submissions, and desk rejected 6 submissions. Each paper was reviewed by three Program Committee (PC) members, and the paper discussions were moderated by senior PC members. We were able to accept 14 high-quality full papers. We also accepted 18 short papers, all of which were submitted as camera-ready files and appeared in the conference as well as the proceedings. Looking at the full papers only, this renders an acceptance rate of 16.5%, lower than in previous conference instances.

This year brings some unprecedented situations. It is the first year where submitting authors are aware of the virtual or hybrid nature of the conference, and where we continued to deal with greatly restricted travel. Although COVID-19 cases in St. John's are low, the international nature of the conference makes it challenging for many to travel to. With virtual conferences becoming the norm, many attendees sadly lack many in-person networking opportunities, or the chance to visit a beautiful new location. As such, the submission rate for ER 2021 was lower than in past years, but the acceptance rate was also lower, keeping the quality of the papers high. We also see a slightly more than normal number of accepted short papers, with the submission of many great ideas and evaluations which were not quite ready to be accepted in their full form. In order to maintain and increase paper quality, this year, a small number of selected papers were conditionally accepted as full papers, allowing the PC Chairs to check that the authors satisfied certain conditions set out by the paper reviewers and moderators. This allowed us to ensure both that the papers were of high final quality and that the conference included many interesting presentations of ongoing work in conceptual modeling. The accepted papers cover a broad spectrum of innovative topics, including business process modeling, goals and requirements, modeling IOT, social aspects of conceptual modeling, enterprise modeling, ontologies, and data modeling. This wide range of topics underlines the importance and attractiveness of research on conceptual modeling. We hope that the papers will be of interest to you and wish you an inspiring read.

Finally, we would like to thank the authors, whose contributions made the conference possible, the many reviewers for their outstanding commitment in preparing more than 200 expert opinions, and last, but not least, the senior PC members without whose support we would not have been able to handle the evaluation of the expert opinions.

The resilience of the international scientific community remains as impressive as ever. The scientific endeavor continues apace, despite the significant challenges posed by the pandemic.

September 2021

Aditya Ghose
Jennifer Horkoff
Vítor E. Silva Souza
Jeffrey Parsons
Joerg Evermann

Organization

General Chairs

Jeffrey Parsons   Memorial University of Newfoundland, Canada
Joerg Evermann   Memorial University of Newfoundland, Canada

Program Committee Chairs

Aditya Ghose   University of Wollongong, Australia
Jennifer Horkoff   University of Gothenburg and Chalmers University
           of Technology, Sweden
Vítor E. Silva Souza   Federal University of Espírito Santo, Brazil

Steering Committee

Peter P. Chen   Louisiana State University, USA
Isabelle Wattiau   ESSEC and CNAM, France
Karen Davis   Miami University, USA
Ulrich Frank   Universität Duisburg-Essen, Germany
Giancarlo Guizzardi   Free University of Bozen-Bolzano, Italy, and
           University of Twente, The Netherlands
Matthias Jarke   RWTH Aachen University, Germany
Paul Johannesson   Royal Institute of Technology, Sweden
Gerti Kappel   Vienna University of Technology, Austria
Alberto Laender   Universidade Federal de Minas Gerais, Brazil
Stephen W. Liddle   Brigham Young University, USA
Tok Wang Ling   National University of Singapore, Singapore
Hui Ma   Victoria University of Wellington, New Zealand
Heinrich Mayr   Alpen-Adria-Universität Klagenfurt, Austria
Antoni Olivé   Universitat Politècnica de Catalunya, Spain
José Palazzo Moreira de   Universidade Federal do Rio Grande do Sul, Brazil
   Oliveira
Jeffrey Parsons   Memorial University of Newfoundland, Canada
Oscar Pastor   Universidad Politécnica de Valencia, Spain
Sudha Ram   University of Arizona, USA
Motoshi Saeki   Tokyo Institute of Technology, Japan
Peretz Shoval   Ben-Gurion University, Israel
Il-Yeol Song   Drexel University, USA
Veda Storey   Georgia State University, USA

Juan Carlos Trujillo	University of Alicante, Spain
Yair Wand	The University of British Columbia, Canada
Carson Woo	The University of British Columbia, Canada
Eric Yu	University of Toronto, Canada

Senior Program Committee

Jacky Akoka	CEDRIC-CNAM and IMT-TEM, France
Paolo Atzeni	Università Roma Tre, Italy
Silvana Castano	University of Milan, Italy
Stefano Ceri	Politecnico di Milano, Italy
Roger Chiang	University of Cincinnatti, USA
Dolors Costal	Universitat Politècnica de Catalunya, Spain
Karen Davis	Miami University, USA
Gill Dobbie	The University of Auckland, New Zealand
Xavier Franch	Universitat Politècnica de Catalunya, Spain
Giancarlo Guizzardi	Free University of Bozen-Bolzano, Italy, and University of Twente, The Netherlands
Sven Hartmann	Clausthal University of Technology, Germany
Matthias Jarke	RWTH Aachen University, Germany
Manfred Jeusfeld	University of Skövde, Sweden
Paul Johannesson	Royal Institute of Technology, Sweden
Gerti Kappel	Vienna University of Technology, Austria
Alberto Laender	Universidade Federal de Minas Gerais, Brazil
Mong Li Lee	National University of Singapore, Singapore
Stephen W. Liddle	Brigham Young University, USA
Sebastian Link	The University of Auckland, New Zealand
Heinrich C. Mayr	Alpen-Adria-Universität Klagenfurt, Austria
John Mylopoulos	University of Ottawa, Canada
Antoni Olivé	Universitat Politècnica de Catalunya, Spain
Oscar Pastor Lopez	Universidad Politécnica de Valencia, Spain
Zhiyong Peng	Wuhan University, China
Barbara Pernici	Politecnico di Milano, Italy
Sudha Ram	University of Arizona, USA
Colette Rolland	Paris 1 Panthéon-Sorbonne University, France
Motoshi Saeki	Tokyo Institute of Technology, Japan
Peretz Shoval	Ben-Gurion University, Israel
Pnina Soffer	University of Haifa, Israel
Veda Storey	Georgia State University, USA
Juan Trujillo	University of Alicante, Spain
Isabelle Wattiau	ESSEC and CNAM, France
Carson Woo	The University of British Columbia, Canada
Eric Yu	University of Toronto, Canada

Program Committee

Mara Abel	Universidade Federal do Rio Grande do Sul, Brazil
Joao Paulo Almeida	Federal University of Espírito Santo, Brazil
Joao Araujo	Universidade NOVA de Lisboa, Portugal
Fatma Başak Aydemir	Boğaziçi University, Turkey
Fernanda Baião	Pontifical Catholic University of Rio de Janeiro, Brazil
Wolf-Tilo Balke	TU Braunschweig, Germany
Ladjel Bellatreche	LIAS, ENSMA, France
Devis Bianchini	University of Brescia, Italy
Sandro Bimonte	INRAE, France
Dominik Bork	TU Wien, Austria
Shawn Bowers	Gonzaga University, USA
Stephane Bressan	National University of Singapore, Singapore
Robert Andrei Buchmann	Babeş-Bolyai University of Cluj Napoca, Romania
Jordi Cabot	Universitat Oberta de Catalunya, Spain
Cinzia Cappiello	Politecnico di Milano, Italy
Luca Cernuzzi	Universidad Católica, Paraguay
Suphamit Chittayasothorn	King Mongkut's Institute of Technology Ladkrabang, Thailand
Tony Clark	Aston University, UK
Sergio de Cesare	University of Westminster, UK
Johann Eder	Alpen Adria Universität Klagenfurt, Austria
Vadim Ermolayev	Zaporizhzhia National University, Ukraine
Rik Eshuis	Eindhoven University of Technology, The Netherlands
Bernadette Farias Lóscio	Federal University of Pernambuco, Brazil
Michael Fellmann	University of Rostock, Germany
Hans-Georg Fill	University of Fribourg, Switzerlands
Frederik Gailly	Ghent University, Belgium
Ming Gao	East China Normal University, China
Yunjun Gao	Zhejiang University, China
Faiez Gargouri	Institut Supérieur d'Informatique et de Multimédia de Sfax, Tunisia
Aurona Gerber	University of Pretoria, South Africa
Mohamed Gharzouli	Constantine 2 University, Algeria
Asif Qumer Gill	University of Technology Sydney, Australia
Cesar Gonzalez-Perez	Incipit CSIC, Spain
Georg Grossmann	University of South Australia, Australia
Esther Guerra	Universidad Autónoma de Madrid, Spain
Renata Guizzardi	University of Twente, The Netherlands
Simon Hacks	University of Southern Denmark, Denmark
Martin Henkel	Stockholm University, Sweden
Hao Huang	Wuhan University, China
Shareeful Islam	University of East London, UK
Mohammad Ali Jabbari Sabegh	Queensland University of Technology, Australia

Manuel Wimmer   Johannes Kepler University Linz, Austria
Robert Wrembel   Poznan University of Technology, Poland
Apostolos Zarras   University of Ioannina, Greece
Jelena Zdravkovic   Stockholm University, Sweden
Xiangmin Zhou   RMIT University, Australia
Xuan Zhou   Renmin University of China, China

Additional Reviewers

Victorio Albani Carvalho   Nico Grohmann
Mario Berón   Karamjit Kaur
Hitesh Dhiman   Fabienne Lambusch
Ghada El-Khawaga   Denis Martins
Jan Everding   Mario Peralta
Hao Feng   Matt Selway
Hao Feng   Johannes Wagner
Marco Franceschetti

Contents

Enterprise Modeling

Goals and Requirements

Modeling the Internet of Things

Ontologies

Social Aspects of Conceptual Modeling

Business Process Modeling

Conceptualizing Bots in Robotic Process Automation

Maximilian Völker[(✉)] and Mathias Weske

Hasso Plattner Institute, University of Potsdam, Potsdam, Germany
{maximilian.voelker,mathias.weske}@hpi.de

Abstract. Promising automation of repetitive tasks and release of manpower, Robotic Process Automation (RPA) continues to be a fast-growing market in the IT industry. The industry-driven advancement also comes with disadvantages. Each vendor established their own terminology and ecosystem, impeding communication, integration, and comparisons between RPA systems. In consequence, terminology and concepts are heterogeneous and not well understood. As a result, the scientific exchange lacks a consistent vocabulary. This paper proposes a vendor-independent conceptualization of RPA robots, their constituent parts and the relationships between those. It aims at providing a conceptual foundation for the further scientific investigation of RPA robots.

Keywords: Robotic process automation · Ontology · Conceptualization

1 Introduction

In times of unforeseeable developments in dynamic markets, we can witness the high value of creative human labor. As a result, organizations are facing the challenge to reduce the working time employees spend on repetitive and time-consuming tasks. With the electronic representation of business data, many data processing tasks are largely simplified. It might come as a surprise that the amount of human labor to process these data, actually, did not change much. Besides the shift from paper sheets to virtual files on computers, data still needs to be extracted from documents, transferred between systems and matched with other data sources.

Robotic Process Automation (RPA) promises to relieve workers from such repetitive tasks by offering a software solution that primarily simulates the interactions of a human user with the computer [2]. With the advancement of technology, activities that previously had to be performed manually can now be automated. Today, RPA is not only capable of simulating mouse clicks and keyboard interactions, but offers deep integration with many applications and, by using artificial intelligence techniques, acquires more and more human abilities, such as making decisions and processing unstructured data autonomously, which opens up entirely new use cases for automation [3,5,13,19].

© Springer Nature Switzerland AG 2021
A. Ghose et al. (Eds.): ER 2021, LNCS 13011, pp. 3–13, 2021.
https://doi.org/10.1007/978-3-030-89022-3_1

Triggered by its success in industry, RPA has only recently gained momentum in research. With missing conceptual underpinning of RPA and increasing complexity of the tools, the RPA vendors diverged in terms of concepts and terminology [13]. The lack of a shared understanding and conceptual foundation [9,10,17] hinders an overall comparison and overview, as well as the exchange of new ideas and approaches.

This paper aims at increasing the understanding of RPA by providing a conceptual basis for RPA bots, including their composition and their general capabilities. A vendor-independent ontology of RPA operations as well as the underlying concepts are introduced, categorized, and put into context. Furthermore, usage scenarios based on this conceptualization are presented, and its limitations are discussed.

The remainder of this paper is structured as follows. Section 2 presents related work from the field of robotic process automation. In Sect. 3, preliminary remarks about the underlying ontology are provided and basic RPA definitions are introduced. In Sect. 4, the conceptualization of RPA robots is presented, for which different usage scenarios are described in Sect. 5. The paper is concluded in Sect. 6, which includes points for future extension and research on this topic.

2   Related Work

Robotic Process Automation is increasingly attracting attention in research, which is expected to continue to grow in the upcoming years [10]. This technology utilizes "software agents called 'bots' that mimic the manual path taken by a human through a range of computer applications" [17]. However, there appears to be no generally accepted definition so far [10]. According to more traditional definitions, RPA is particularly suited for automating repetitive, well-structured, and rule-based workflows [1,2,11]. Other definitions, for example, also take capabilities of artificial intelligence into account, attributing RPA more flexible and complex characteristics [10,17].

Current research in this area is aimed at different aspects, ranging from case studies (e.g., [2,16]), to organizational considerations (e.g., [11]), to studying individual phases of the RPA lifecycle as introduced by Enriquez et al. [5]. However, there has been little focus on characterizing and classifying elementary concepts of RPA bots. Martínez-Rojas et al. [13] address a part of this problem by introducing a taxonomy of RPA components, i.e., building blocks, that rely on artificial intelligence. Motivated by the different naming schemes established by RPA software vendors, they propose a classification of such RPA components based on their capabilities using a unified terminology and link the corresponding vendor implementations to these concepts.

In this work, we do not focus on a specific technology such as AI in RPA, but want to provide a solid conceptual basis of RPA while abstracting from the concepts and the terminology used by specific vendors. For this purpose, a conceptualization of RPA bots is introduced.

3 Preliminaries

In the following, we introduce the foundations for the conceptualization of RPA bots presented in this paper and propose essential definitions for RPA.

Conceptualizations are often captured and formalized in ontologies to enable a common understanding of terms and concepts in the conceptualized domain [8]. In the domain of software, ontologies have a variety of applications, such as for identifying the nature of software errors [4] or for capturing the concepts and their interplay of software processes [6].

For the conceptualization presented in this work, the Core Software Ontology (CSO) introduced by Oberle et al. [14] will be used as a basis. This core ontology defines common, general terms in the software domain like `Data`, `Class`, and `Interface`. It is based on the foundational ontology DOLCE and some of its extensions such as the Ontology of Plans (OoP) and the Ontology of Information Objects (OIO) [7]. In the following, elements reused from this ontology are denoted by the prefix `CSO:`.

As discussed above, the term *RPA* is typically defined in a loose manner, often with different focal points. It is important to observe that RPA technology consists of several building blocks. This is similar to business process automation, with business processes, activities, and execution constraints as its components.

So far, the building blocks of RPA have rarely been defined or even identified explicitly, making it difficult to establish common ground for discussions and research. To overcome this problem, this section proposes definitions for the building blocks of RPA and outlines their respective characteristics. To continue the analogy with business process automation, RPA also has an equivalent of business processes—RPA bots (cf. Definition 1)—as well as activities—RPA operations (cf. Definition 2).

Based on the general definitions of RPA presented in the literature, the following definition of an RPA bot is introduced.

Definition 1 (RPA bot). An RPA bot is a machine-executable sequence of instructions consisting of RPA operations to automate interactions of human users with computer systems.

Definition 2 (RPA operation). An RPA operation is an atomic step in an RPA bot. It represents a single action performed on the system to be automated, usually, but not limited to, via cursor and keyboard interactions on the user interface level.

These RPA operations represent the smallest building blocks of RPA bots and are, to a large extent, already predefined by the respective RPA vendors.

Examples of RPA operations are manifold and range from internal operations of the RPA software, such as a variable assignment, to a mouse click on a button, to text extraction from documents. RPA operations should not be limited solely to interactions on the user interface, since RPA is capable of much more, such as performing database queries or calling web-services [9], and it is very likely that it will further evolve.

4   An Ontology of RPA Operations

Over the last few years, a number of RPA vendors have entered the market [1] and established their own terminologies [13]. However, most of the RPA functionality offered by these vendors does not differ much [9]. The conceptualization proposed in this paper captures and categorizes the concepts of RPA operations, i.e., the building blocks of RPA bots, in a vendor-independent manner. For building the ontology, the methodology introduced by Uschold and Gruninger [18] is applied.

4.1   Goal of Ontology and Competency Questions

The main goal of the proposed ontology is to provide a normative model [18] to create a shared understanding of RPA bots and RPA operations. Thus, reducing ambiguities and enabling researchers and practitioners to communicate without prior agreement on a vendor-specific terminology. The ontology is intended to provide a scaffold for later refinement and extension. This is important because RPA still evolves, such as through novel combinations with AI [13,19].

The following informal competency questions (CQ) guided the development.

CQ 1: What is an RPA bot?
CQ 2: Which types of RPA operations exist?
CQ 3: Which types of software can be automated by a given RPA operation?
CQ 4: What is the needed input/output data for an RPA operation?
CQ 5: What kinds of operations can be applied to a certain file type?
CQ 6: What kinds of operations can be used to automate a given software?
CQ 7: Are there potential prerequisites for executing an RPA operation?

4.2   Ontology Capture

To capture the concepts in RPA, prominent and obvious terms are recorded first. Subsequently, concrete RPA operations, especially from the tools UiPath[1] and Automagica[2], are analyzed to further specialize and group the concepts.

Main Concepts. Besides the fundamental concepts of RPA bots and RPA operations defined in the previous section, data plays a crucial role for RPA (see also CQ 4 and 5). RPA bots are capable of extracting information from documents, they transfer data between different computer systems and can check and validate data [11,17]. Another important facet to consider is the software that is automated using RPA (cf. CQ 3 and 6).

Both concepts, data and software, are already defined in the Core Software Ontology (CSO) and are reused here. CSO:Software is defined as a kind of CSO:Data, with the difference that software expresses a certain plan that defines

---

[1] https://www.uipath.com/ (accessed 27.04.2021).
[2] https://github.com/automagica/automagica/tree/ae8a1846f2 (latest open-source version, accessed 27.04.2021).

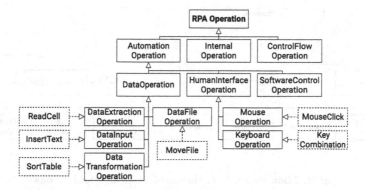

Fig. 1. Taxonomy of the concept RPAOperation. Terms framed with dashed lines are possible members of the concept and are not exhaustive.

a sequence of CSO:ComputationalTasks (cf. [14, 15]). We furthermore introduce Files for referring to CSO:Data that is not executable.

In the context of RPA, RPABots are a special kind of CSO:Software, which complies with the definition of RPA bots given in Definition 1, including the sequence of certain tasks or operations, respectively. Consequently, RPAOperations are a special kind of CSO:ComputationalTasks representing the smallest building blocks of software, just as RPAOperations are the building blocks of RPABots.

Specializations. To be able to answer more specific competency questions, such as CQ 2 or CQ 3, these main concepts are further subdivided.

In terms of software, there are different types that usually are automated using RPA. Besides the RPABot itself, the most prominent and obvious type are Applications, like browsers or office applications. They are the traditional target of RPABots and are usually automated by simulating mouse and keyboard inputs or, if available, via an API. Additionally, many RPA vendors allow the use of Services in RPABots to add a certain capability to the bot. A prominent example for a Service in RPA is optical character recognition (OCR) to retrieve text from images or documents. Also, basic operations on the OperatingSystem itself can be automated, like accessing the clipboard, stopping processes, or moving files.

To address CQ 2, operations are, as depicted in Fig. 1, further subdivided into AutomationOperations, InternalOperations, and ControlFlowOperations.

ControlFlowOperations are used to steer the sequence of operations within the bot, e.g., using *if/else* instructions or *loops*. InternalOperations do not access any data or software outside the bot, but mainly operate on internal variables, like matching a variable with a regular expression or adding a log message. AutomationOperations are the more apparent parts of a bot, they, for example, access external data, operate on applications, or call services.

AutomationOperations are further subdivided into three main concepts. DataOperations in general mark operations that access CSO:Data and are again

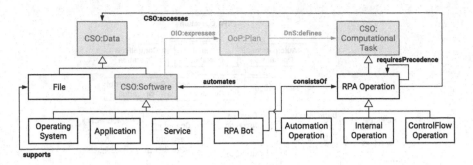

Fig. 2. Main elements of the ontology of RPAOperations

divided into different types (see Fig. 1), distinguishing whether data is read, written, transformed, or the file itself is manipulated. HumanInterfaceOperations identify operations that are usually independent of concrete CSO:Software and CSO:Data. They simulate the input of a human user, such as mouse clicks and key presses, and partly rely on so-called computer vision capabilities to locate elements on the UI. The third type, SoftwareControlOperations, label operations that manage software beyond the scope of data, i.e., they do not access data, but, for example, start or terminate Applications or RPABots.

Relations. Important relations between the concepts are introduced in the following. In general, RPAOperations can be used to automate a certain CSO:Software and to CSO:access CSO:Data.

To express how operations can be used to manipulate files, CSO:access is further specialized into read, write, and transform (the combination of the former two). These relations are a shortcut for the roles CSO:Input and CSO:Output in combination with the relations CSO:inputFor and CSO:outputFor, i.e., if an operation reads a certain kind of CSO:Data, this data plays the role of a CSO:Input for this operation (cf. [14,15]). In the case of DataOperations, the type of operation already implies what kind of CSO:access takes places, e.g., DataExtractionOperations read CSO:Data (CQ 4), which is therefore an input for the respective operation.

The automate relation between RPAOperations and CSO:Software expresses that an operation utilizes or triggers a certain functionality offered by the software. While in some cases no distinct relation can be established, e.g., for generic UI operations, for software-specific operations, the automate relation can indicate for which type of software the operation can be used (CQ 3 and 6).

In most cases, applications and data are independent as well. This connection is expressed by the supports relation, defining that an Application supports a certain File (can be inferred from CSO:accesses and automates).

Lastly, the relation requiresPrecedence is used to express constraints on the order of RPAOperations (cf. CQ 7), e.g., to express that the open operation needs to be executed before the application can be automated.

The described main concepts and their relations are depicted in Fig. 2.

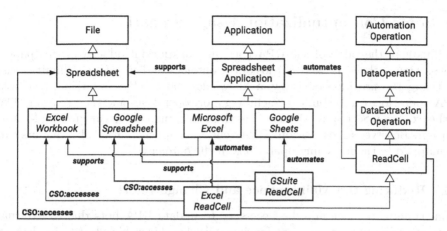

Fig. 3. Exemplary sub-concepts and *instances* related to the concept of reading a cell in a spreadsheet

Example. Figure 3 illustrates an example for the concept of the RPAOperation ReadCell, a DataExtractionOperation. Using the ontology, it can be expressed that this operation CSO:accesses (reads) data from Spreadsheet Files and that it can be used to automate SpreadsheetApplications. A concrete instance realizing the concept of reading a cell in a spreadsheet is *ExcelReadCell*. It is related to the Spreadsheet's instance *ExcelWorkbook*, which in turn is *supported* by the specific SpreadsheetApplication *MicrosoftExcel*.

4.3 Consideration of the Competency Questions

For evaluating ontologies, the research methodology proposes to review the competency questions in regard to the created ontology [18]. Table 1 lists the previously raised competency questions along with elements from the ontology that can be used to answer the respective question; it shows that all posed questions can be answered with the help of the concepts introduced.

Table 1. Review of the competency questions

CQ		Satisfied by
1	Nature of RPA bots	Type of CSO:Software that consistsOf RPAOperations
2	Types of operations	Taxonomy of RPA operations (see Fig. 1)
3	Automatable software	Taxonomy of software with automates relation
4	Input/output data	CSO:accesses with the types read, write, transform
5	Processable file types	Inverse of CSO:accesses relation
6	Operations for software	Inverse of automates relation
7	Prerequisites of operations	requiresPrecedence between RPA operations

5   Some Conceptualization Usage Scenarios

To illustrate the value of the RPA conceptualization introduced in this paper, this section outlines usage scenarios of the ontology and addresses its limitations.

Using the provided ontology, a knowledge base (KB) comprising available RPA operations can be built by including more operations and their relations like in the example (Sect. 4.2). Moreover, as the conceptualization captures real-world concepts observed across various RPA vendors, implementations by vendors can be mapped to the matching operations in the ontology.

5.1   Reducing the Maintenance and Change Effort

From time to time, it may be necessary to update RPA bots due to external changes or for improvements. So far, it required considerable effort to implement these changes, especially with the increasing number of automated software and RPA bots. Two conceivable scenarios should be highlighted here, the replacement of a software system automated using RPA and the change of the RPA vendor.

Replacing Software Systems. Continuing the example introduced in Fig. 3, we assume that *Microsoft Excel* is to be replaced by *Google Sheets*. In general, such a change makes any RPA bot inoperative, as the user interfaces differ.

By traversing the relations in the ontology, the required changes to the bots can, at least partly, be applied automatically. First, each operation used is checked whether it is affected by the change. In the example, the operation *ExcelReadCell* is linked to the affected software via the `automates` relation and thus must be replaced. Second, using the included taxonomies and relations, for each affected operation, the new appropriate operation, that realizes the same concept as before, must be identified. Here, the operation for reading a cell in *Google Sheets* must be found. By analyzing the `automates` relation of all instances of `ReadCell`, the operation *GSuiteReadCell* can be identified as the suitable replacement. Of course, this does not address any reconfiguration that may be required.

Changing an RPA Vendor. Provided that the aforementioned mapping of vendor-specific implementations to the knowledge base exists, the previously time-consuming and thus improbable switching of RPA providers can be facilitated. Figure 4 shows an example for such a mapping. Here, *ExcelReadCell*, an instance in the KB, is linked to matching implementations by vendors. The KB with the vendor mapping can automatically provide the appropriate, functionally equal operation of the new vendor to replace the old one. This approach not only allows to translate already implemented RPA bots between existing vendors, but also enables to first model bots independent of a vendor by using the

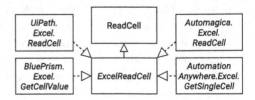

Fig. 4. Mapping of vendor implementations to an instance in the knowledge base

instances present in the KB which can later be translated to a specific vendor implementation using the mapping.

5.2 Enabling Automatic Documentation of RPA Bots

Interviews with RPA practitioners showed that despite the graphical modeling interfaces offered by most RPA software, RPA bots often have to be documented additionally. A reason for this could be that RPA operations are very narrow in scope, resulting in extensive models whose intent is difficult to grasp.

Using the introduced taxonomies, a simplified view on modeled RPA bots for documentation and communication purposes could be created. Assuming proper rules for abstraction, related, similar operations could be combined into an abstract activity. In addition, certain internal or preparatory operations could be removed in the documentation to further improve the clarity.

Moreover, the presented ontology could be used to replace vendor-specific, inexpressive labels by more informative and consistent names from the ontology.

Overall, the ontology and a resulting knowledge base could be used not only to (re)design bots, but also to enable an automated documentation, further reducing the overall implementation effort.

5.3 Limitations

This work focuses on RPA bots, their operations, and related software and data. Therefore, many other aspects of RPA are not covered here, such as management and methodological aspects, the execution or operating environment of bots, such as how exactly an application is automated, internal aspects like variables, or further configurations required for execution.

While the used core ontology already provides a formalized foundation, the degree of formality of the presented ontology could be further increased by using a more formal language to code the ontology and basing all relations on existing ones. This would be especially beneficial for a more automated processing, e.g., to realize the application ideas presented in this section.

6 Conclusion

This paper presents a conceptualization of RPA bots and their operations, revealing connections to data and applications that can be automated. Additionally, some potential applications were discussed, such as an abstracted, human-readable representation of bots, or the translation between different RPA vendors.

Furthermore, the ontology, especially when extended to a knowledge base, could prove useful in combination with existing approaches, like for providing possible labels for the analysis of textual process descriptions proposed by [12], or as an intermediate layer for implementations or research prototypes.

Besides, the ontology and its concepts could and should be extended as well. Here, several aspects are conceivable, like adding information on configurations of operations, i.e., more operational information, or adding information on the user interface elements automated by operations. This would eventually allow new RPA bots to be modeled using the knowledge base and later translated into vendor-specific bots with only minor adjustments, thus decoupling the modeling process from individual vendors.

References

1. van der Aalst, W.M.P., Bichler, M., Heinzl, A.: Robotic process automation. Bus. Inf. Syst. Eng. **60**(4), 269–272 (2018)
2. Aguirre, S., Rodriguez, A.: Automation of a business process using robotic process automation (RPA): a case study. In: Figueroa-García, J.C., López-Santana, E.R., Villa-Ramírez, J.L., Ferro-Escobar, R. (eds.) WEA 2017. CCIS, vol. 742, pp. 65–71. Springer, Cham (2017). https://doi.org/10.1007/978-3-319-66963-2_7
3. Chakraborti, T., et al.: From robotic process automation to intelligent process automation. In: Asatiani, A., et al. (eds.) BPM 2020. LNBIP, vol. 393, pp. 215–228. Springer, Cham (2020). https://doi.org/10.1007/978-3-030-58779-6_15
4. Duarte, B.B., Falbo, R.A., Guizzardi, G., Guizzardi, R.S.S., Souza, V.E.S.: Towards an ontology of software defects, errors and failures. In: Trujillo, J.C., et al. (eds.) ER 2018. LNCS, vol. 11157, pp. 349–362. Springer, Cham (2018). https://doi.org/10.1007/978-3-030-00847-5_25
5. Enriquez, J.G., Jimenez-Ramirez, A., Dominguez-Mayo, F.J., Garcia-Garcia, J.A.: Robotic process automation: a scientific and industrial systematic mapping study. IEEE Access **8**, 39113–39129 (2020)
6. Falbo, R.D.A., Bertollo, G.: A software process ontology as a common vocabulary about software processes. IJBPIM **4**(4), 239–250 (2009)
7. Gangemi, A., Borgo, S., Catenacci, C., Lehmann, J.: Task taxonomies for knowledge content: Metokis deliverable D07 (2004)
8. Gruber, T.R.: Toward principles for the design of ontologies used for knowledge sharing. Int. J. Hum. Comput. Stud. **43**(5–6), 907–928 (1995)
9. Hofmann, P., Samp, C., Urbach, N.: Robotic process automation. Electron. Mark. **30**(1), 99–106 (2020)
10. Ivančić, L., Suša Vugec, D., Bosilj Vukšić, V.: Robotic process automation: systematic literature review. In: Di Ciccio, C., et al. (eds.) BPM 2019. LNBIP, vol. 361, pp. 280–295. Springer, Cham (2019). https://doi.org/10.1007/978-3-030-30429-4_19
11. Lacity, M.C., Willcocks, L.P.: A new approach to automating services. MIT Sloan Manage. Rev. Fall (2017). http://eprints.lse.ac.uk/68135/
12. Leopold, H., van der Aa, H., Reijers, H.A.: Identifying candidate tasks for robotic process automation in textual process descriptions. In: Gulden, J., Reinhartz-Berger, I., Schmidt, R., Guerreiro, S., Guédria, W., Bera, P. (eds.) BPMDS/EMMSAD -2018. LNBIP, vol. 318, pp. 67–81. Springer, Cham (2018). https://doi.org/10.1007/978-3-319-91704-7_5
13. Martínez-Rojas, A., Barba, I., Enríquez, J.G.: Towards a taxonomy of cognitive RPA components. In: Asatiani, A., et al. (eds.) BPM 2020. LNBIP, vol. 393, pp. 161–175. Springer, Cham (2020). https://doi.org/10.1007/978-3-030-58779-6_11

14. Oberle, D., Grimm, S., Staab, S.: An ontology for software. In: Staab, S., Studer, R. (eds.) Handbook on Ontologies. IHIS, pp. 383–402. Springer, Heidelberg (2009). https://doi.org/10.1007/978-3-540-92673-3_17
15. Oberle, D., Lamparter, S., Grimm, S., Vrandečić, D., Staab, S., Gangemi, A.: Towards ontologies for formalizing modularization and communication in large software systems. Appl. Ontol. 1(2), 163–202 (2006)
16. Penttinen, E., Kasslin, H., Asatiani, A.: How to choose between robotic process automation and back-end system automation? In: ECIS 2018 (2018)
17. Syed, R., et al.: Robotic process automation: contemporary themes and challenges. Comput. Ind. 115, 103162 (2020)
18. Uschold, M., Gruninger, M.: Ontologies: principles, methods and applications. Knowl. Eng. Rev. 11(2), 93–136 (1996)
19. Viehhauser, J.: Is robotic process automation becoming intelligent? Early evidence of influences of artificial intelligence on robotic process automation. In: Asatiani, A., et al. (eds.) BPM 2020. LNBIP, vol. 393, pp. 101–115. Springer, Cham (2020). https://doi.org/10.1007/978-3-030-58779-6_7

Freezing Sub-models During Incremental Process Discovery

Daniel Schuster[1,2](✉) ⓘ, Sebastiaan J. van Zelst[1,2] ⓘ,
and Wil M. P. van der Aalst[1,2] ⓘ

[1] Fraunhofer Institute for Applied Information Technology FIT,
Sankt Augustin, Germany
{daniel.schuster,sebastiaan.van.zelst}@fit.fraunhofer.de
[2] RWTH Aachen University, Aachen, Germany
wvdaalst@pads.rwth-aachen.de

Abstract. Process discovery aims to learn a process model from observed process behavior. From a user's perspective, most discovery algorithms work like a *black box*. Besides parameter tuning, there is no interaction between the user and the algorithm. Interactive process discovery allows the user to exploit domain knowledge and to guide the discovery process. Previously, an incremental discovery approach has been introduced where a model, considered to be under "construction", gets incrementally extended by user-selected process behavior. This paper introduces a novel approach that additionally allows the user to *freeze* model parts within the model under construction. Frozen sub-models are not altered by the incremental approach when new behavior is added to the model. The user can thus steer the discovery algorithm. Our experiments show that freezing sub-models can lead to higher quality models.

Keywords: Process mining · Process discovery · Hybrid intelligence

1 Introduction

Executing business processes generates valuable data in the information systems of organizations. *Process mining* comprises techniques to analyze these *event data* and aims to extract insights into the executed processes to improve them [1]. This paper focuses on *process discovery*, a key discipline within process mining.

Conventional process discovery algorithms use observed process behavior, i.e., event data, as input and return a process model that describes the process, as recorded by the event data. Since event data often have quality issues, process discovery is challenging. Apart from modifying the input (event data), the algorithm's settings, or the output (discovered model), there is no user interaction.

To overcome this limitation, the field of *interactive process discovery* has emerged. The central idea is to exploit the domain knowledge of process participants within process discovery in addition to the standard input of event data.

An extended version is available online: https://arxiv.org/abs/2108.00215.

A. Ghose et al. (Eds.): ER 2021, LNCS 13011, pp. 14–24, 2021.
https://doi.org/10.1007/978-3-030-89022-3_2

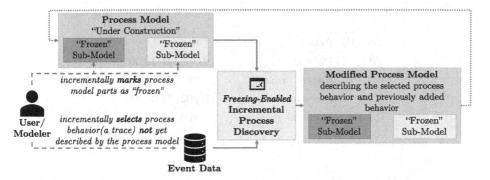

Fig. 1. Overview of the proposed freezing option extending *incremental* process discovery. A user incrementally selects traces from the event log and optionally freezes sub-models that should not get altered in the model "under construction"

Several techniques have been proposed. However, most existing approaches only attempt to use additional inputs besides the event data. Thus, a user still has only limited options to interact with the algorithm during the actual discovery phase, and the algorithm remains a black box from a user's perspective.

In [11], we have introduced an incremental process discovery algorithm, allowing a user to incrementally add process behavior to a model under construction. This allows the user to control the algorithm by interactively deciding which process behavior to add next. In this context, we propose in this paper a novel way to interact with a discovery algorithm as a user. During the discovery phase, we allow a user to freeze sub-models of the model under construction. By marking sub-models as frozen, the incremental discovery approach does not alter these frozen model parts during the incremental discovery. Figure 1 summarizes the proposed approach that can be applied with any incremental discovery algorithm.

There are many use cases where freezing sub models during incremental process discovery is beneficial. For instance, it enables a user to combine *de jure* and *de facto* models [1]. De jure models describe how a process should be executed (normative), and de facto models describe how a process was executed (descriptive). A user might freeze a model part because, from the user's perspective, the sub-model to be frozen is already normative. Therefore, a user wants to protect this sub-model from being further altered while incrementally adding new behavior to the model under construction. Thus, the proposed freezing approach allows combining process discovery with modeling. Our conducted experiments show that freezing sub-models can lead to higher quality models.

This paper is structured as follows. Section 2 presents related work while Sect. 3 presents preliminaries. Section 4 presents the proposed freezing approach. Section 5 presents an evaluation, and Sect. 6 concludes this paper.

Table 1. Example of an event log from an e-commerce process

Case-ID	Activity	Timestamp	$\cdots$
151	Place order (p)	10/03/21 12:00	$\cdots$
153	Cancel order (c)	10/03/21 12:24	$\cdots$
152	Place order (p)	11/03/21 09:11	$\cdots$
151	Payment received (r)	11/03/21 10:00	$\cdots$
$\cdots$	$\cdots$	$\cdots$	$\cdots$

2   Related Work

For an overview of process mining and conventional process discovery, we refer to [1]. Hereinafter, we mainly focus on interactive process discovery.

In [7], the authors propose to incorporate precedence constraints over the activities within process discovery. In [4], an approach is presented where an already existing process model is post-processed s.t. user-defined constraints are fulfilled. In [10], an approach is presented where domain knowledge in form of an initial process model is given. Compared to our extended incremental process discovery, all approaches remain a black-box from a user's perspective since they work in a fully automated fashion. In [5], an interactive Petri net modeling approach is proposed in which the user is supported by an algorithm.

Related work can also be found in the area of process model repair [6]. However, the setting of model repair, which attempts to make the repaired model as similar as possible to the original, differs from incremental process discovery. In [2] an interactive and incremental repair approach is proposed.

3   Preliminaries

We denote the power set of a set X by $\mathcal{P}(X)$. We denote the universe of multi-sets over a set X by $\mathcal{B}(X)$ and the set of all sequences over X as X^*, e.g., $\langle a, b, b \rangle \in \{a, b, c\}^*$. Given two sequences σ and σ', we denote their concatenation by $\sigma \cdot \sigma'$, e.g., $\langle a \rangle \cdot \langle b, c \rangle = \langle a, b, c \rangle$. We extend the $\cdot$ operator to sets of sequences, i.e., let $S_1, S_2 \subseteq X^*$ then $S_1 \cdot S_2 = \{\sigma_1 \cdot \sigma_2 \mid \sigma_1 \in S_1 \wedge \sigma_2 \in S_2\}$. For sequences σ, σ', the set of all interleaved sequences is denoted by $\sigma \diamond \sigma'$, e.g., $\langle a, b \rangle \diamond \langle c \rangle = \{\langle a, b, c \rangle, \langle a, c, b \rangle, \langle c, a, b \rangle\}$. We extend the $\diamond$ operator to sets of sequences. Let $S_1, S_2 \subseteq X^*$, $S_1 \diamond S_2$ denotes the set of interleaved sequences, i.e., $S_1 \diamond S_2 = \bigcup_{\sigma_1 \in S_1, \sigma_2 \in S_2} \sigma_1 \diamond \sigma_2$.

For $\sigma \in X^*$ and $X' \subseteq X$, we define the projection function $\sigma_{\downarrow_{X'}} : X^* \to (X')^*$ with: $\langle \rangle_{\downarrow_{X'}} = \langle \rangle$, $(\langle x \rangle \cdot \sigma)_{\downarrow_{X'}} = \langle x \rangle \cdot \sigma_{\downarrow_{X'}}$ if $x \in X'$ and $(\langle x \rangle \cdot \sigma)_{\downarrow_{X'}} = \sigma_{\downarrow_{X'}}$ otherwise.

Let $t = (x_1, \ldots, x_n) \in X_1 \times \cdots \times X_n$ be an n-tuple over n sets. We define projection functions that extract a specific element of t, i.e., $\pi_1(t) = x_1, \ldots, \pi_n(t) = x_n$, e.g., $\pi_2((a, b, c)) = b$.

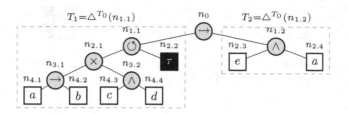

Fig. 2. Process tree $T_0 = (\{n_o, \ldots, n_{4.4}\}, \{(n_o, n_{1.1}), \ldots, (n_{3.2}, n_{4.4})\}, \lambda, n_o)$ with $\lambda(n_o) = \to, \ldots, \lambda(n_{4.4}) = d$

3.1 Event Data and Process Models

The data that are generated during the execution of (business) processes are called *event data* [1]. Table 1 shows an example of an event log. Each row represents an event. Events with the same case-id belong to the same process execution often referred to as a *case*. The sequence of executed activities for a case is referred to as a *trace*, e.g., the partial trace for case 151 is: $\langle p, r, \ldots \rangle$.

Process models allow us to specify the control flow of a process. In this paper, we use process trees [1], e.g., see Fig. 2. Leaves represent activities and τ represents an unobservable activity, needed for certain control flow patterns. Inner nodes represent operators that specify the control flow among their subtrees. Four operators exist: *sequence* ($\to$), *excl. choice* ($\times$), *parallel* ($\wedge$), and *loop* ($\circlearrowleft$).

Definition 1 (Process Tree Syntax). *Let $\mathcal{A}$ be the universe of activities with $\tau \notin \mathcal{A}$. Let $\bigoplus = \{\to, \times, \wedge, \circlearrowleft\}$ be the set of process tree operators. We define a process tree $T = (V, E, \lambda, r)$ consisting of a totally ordered set of nodes V, a set of edges $E \subseteq V \times V$, a labeling function $\lambda : V \to \mathcal{A} \cup \{\tau\} \cup \bigoplus$, and a root node $r \in V$.*

- *$(\{n\}, \{\}, \lambda, n)$ with $\lambda(n) \in \mathcal{A} \cup \{\tau\}$ is a process tree*
- *given $k > 1$ trees $T_1 = (V_1, E_1, \lambda_1, r_1), \ldots, T_k = (V_k, E_k, \lambda_k, r_k)$ with $r \notin V_1 \cup \cdots \cup V_k$ and $\forall i, j \in \{1, \ldots, k\}(i \neq j \Rightarrow V_i \cap V_j = \emptyset)$ then $T = (V, E, \lambda, r)$ is a tree s.t.:*
  - *$V = V_1 \cup \cdots \cup V_k \cup \{r\}$*
  - *$E = E_1 \cup \cdots \cup E_k \cup \{(r, r_1), \ldots, (r, r_k)\}$*
  - *$\lambda(x) = \lambda_j(x)$ for all $j \in \{1, \ldots, k\}, x \in V_j$*
  - *$\lambda(r) \in \bigoplus$ and $\lambda(r) = \circlearrowleft \Rightarrow k = 2$*

We denote the universe of process trees by $\mathcal{T}$.

Note that every operator (inner node) has at least two children except for the loop operator which always has exactly two children. Next to the graphical representation, any process tree can be textually represented because of its totally ordered node set, e.g., $T_0 \hat{=} \to (\circlearrowleft (\times (\to (a, b), \wedge (c, d)), \tau), \wedge (e, a))$.

Given two process trees $T_1, T_2 \in \mathcal{T}$, we write $T_1 \sqsubseteq T_2$ if T_1 is a *subtree* of T_2. For instance, $T_1 \sqsubseteq T_0$ and $T_1 \not\sqsubseteq T_2$ in Fig. 2. The child function $c^T : V \to V^*$

≫	≫	≫	a	b	≫	≫	≫	≫	≫	c	≫	f	≫	≫	≫
$(n_{1.1},$ open$)$	$(n_{2.1},$ open$)$	$(n_{3.1},$ open$)$	$(n_{4.1},$ a$)$	$(n_{4.2},$ b$)$	$(n_{3.1},$ close$)$	$(n_{2.1},$ close$)$	$(n_{2.2},$ $\tau)$	$(n_{2.1},$ open$)$	$(n_{3.2},$ open$)$	$(n_{4.3},$ c$)$	$(n_{1.4+},$ $(n_{4.4},$ d$)$		$(n_{3.2},$ close$)$	$(n_{2.1},$ close$)$	$(n_{1.1},$ close$)$

Fig. 3. Optimal alignment $\gamma = \langle (\gg, (n_{1.1}, open)), \ldots, (\gg, (n_{1.1}, close)) \rangle$ for the trace $\langle a, b, c, f \rangle$ and the process tree T_1 (Fig. 2)

returns a sequence of child nodes according to the order of V, i.e., $c^T(v) = \langle v_1, \ldots, v_j \rangle$ s.t. $(v, v_1), \ldots, (v, v_j) \in E$. For instance, $c_0^T(n_{1.1}) = \langle n_{2.1}, n_{2.2} \rangle$. For $T = (V, E, \lambda, r) \in \mathcal{T}$ and $v \in V$, $\triangle^T(v)$ returns the with root node v. For example, $\triangle^{T_0}(n_{1.1}) = T_1$.

For $T = (V, E, \lambda, r)$ and nodes $n_1, n_2 \in V$, we define the *lowest common ancestor (LCA)* as $LCA(n_1, n_2) = n \in V$ such that for $\triangle^T(n) = (V_n, E_n, \lambda_n, r_n)$ $n_1, n_2 \in V_n$ and the distance (number of edges) between n and r is maximal. For example, $LCA(n_{4.4}, n_{2.2}) = n_{1.1}$ and $LCA(n_{4.4}, n_{2.3}) = n_0$ (Fig. 2).

Next, we define running sequences and the language of process trees.

Definition 2 (Process Tree Running Sequences). *For the universe of activities $\mathcal{A}$ (with $\tau, open, close \notin \mathcal{A}$), $T = (V, E, \lambda, r) \in \mathcal{T}$, we recursively define its running sequences $\mathcal{RS}(T) \subseteq (V \times (\mathcal{A} \cup \{\tau\} \cup \{open, close\}))^*$.*

- *if $\lambda(r) \in \mathcal{A} \cup \{\tau\}$ (T is a leaf node): $\mathcal{RS}(T) = \{\langle (r, \lambda(r)) \rangle\}$*
- *if $\lambda(r) = \rightarrow$ with child nodes $c^T(r) = \langle v_1, \ldots, v_k \rangle$ for $k \geq 1$:*
  $\mathcal{RS}(T) = \{\langle (r, open) \rangle\} \cdot \mathcal{RS}(\triangle^T(v_1)) \cdot \ldots \cdot \mathcal{RS}(\triangle^T(v_k)) \cdot \{\langle (r, close) \rangle\}$
- *if $\lambda(r) = \times$ with child nodes $c^T(r) = \langle v_1, \ldots, v_k \rangle$ for $k \geq 1$:*
  $\mathcal{RS}(T) = \{\langle (r, open) \rangle\} \cdot \{\mathcal{RS}(\triangle^T(v_1)) \cup \ldots \cup \mathcal{RS}(\triangle^T(v_k))\} \cdot \{\langle (r, close) \rangle\}$
- *if $\lambda(r) = \wedge$ with child nodes $c^T(r) = \langle v_1, \ldots, v_k \rangle$ for $k \geq 1$:*
  $\mathcal{RS}(T) = \{\langle (r, open) \rangle\} \cdot \{\mathcal{RS}(\triangle^T(v_1)) \diamond \ldots \diamond \mathcal{RS}(\triangle^T(v_k))\} \cdot \{\langle (r, close) \rangle\}$
- *if $\lambda(r) = \circlearrowright$ with child nodes $c^T(r) = \langle v_1, v_2 \rangle$:*
  $\mathcal{RS}(T) = \{\langle (r, open) \rangle \cdot \sigma_1 \cdot \sigma_1' \cdot \sigma_2 \cdot \sigma_2' \cdot \ldots \cdot \sigma_m \cdot \langle (r, close) \rangle \mid m \geq 1 \wedge \forall 1 \leq i \leq m$
  $(\sigma_i \in \mathcal{RS}(\triangle^T(v_1))) \wedge \forall 1 \leq i \leq m-1 (\sigma_i' \in \mathcal{RS}(\triangle^T(v_2)))\}.$

Definition 3 (Process Tree Language). *For given $T \in \mathcal{T}$, we define its language by $\mathcal{L}(T) := \{(\pi_2^*(\sigma))_{\downarrow_{\mathcal{A}}} \mid \sigma \in \mathcal{RS}(T)\} \subseteq \mathcal{A}^*$.*

For example, consider the running sequences of T_2 (Fig. 2), i.e., $\mathcal{RS}(T_2) = \{\langle (n_{1.2}, open), (n_{2.3}, e), (n_{2.4}, a)), (n_{1.2}, close) \rangle, \langle (n_{1.2}, open), (n_{2.4}, a), (n_{2.3}, e), (n_{1.2}, close) \rangle\}$. Hence, this subtree describes the language $\mathcal{L}(T_2) = \{\langle e, a \rangle, \langle a, e \rangle\}$.

3.2   Alignments

Alignments quantify deviations between observed process behavior (event data) and modeled behavior (process models) [3]. Figure 3 shows an alignment for the trace $\langle a, b, c, f \rangle$ and T_1 (Fig. 2). Ignoring the skip-symbol $\gg$, the first row of an alignment always corresponds to the trace and the second row to a running sequence of the tree. In general, we distinguish four alignment move types.

1. **synchronous moves** (shown light-gray in Fig. 3) indicate *no* deviation
2. **log moves** (shown black in Fig. 3) indicate a *deviation*, i.e., the observed activity in the trace is not executable in the model (at this point)
3. **visible model moves** (shown dark-gray in Fig. 3) indicate a *deviation*, i.e., an activity not observed in the trace must be executed w.r.t. the model
4. **invisible** ($\tau, open, close$) **model moves** (shown white in Fig. 3) indicate *no* deviation, i.e., opening or closing of a subtree or an executed τ leaf node

Since multiple alignments exist for a given tree and trace, we are interested in an *optimal alignment*, i.e., the number of log and visible model moves is minimal.

4   Freezing-Enabled Incremental Process Discovery

In Sect. 4.1, we formally define the problem of freezing sub-models during incremental discovery. Then, we introduce the proposed approach in Sect. 4.2.

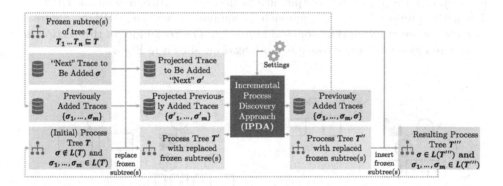

Fig. 4. Overview of the proposed freezing-enabled IPDA approach

4.1   Problem Definition

Reconsider Fig. 1 showing the overall framework of our proposal. A user incrementally selects subtrees from a process tree "under construction" and a trace σ from an event log. Both, the tree with frozen subtree(s) and the trace, are the input for an *freezing-enabled* incremental process discovery algorithm, which returns a modified tree that contains the frozen subtree(s) and accepts the selected trace. Next, we define an Incremental Process Discovery Algorithm (IPDA).

Definition 4 (IPDA). $\alpha \colon \mathcal{T} \times \mathcal{A}^* \times \mathcal{P}(\mathcal{A}^*) \nrightarrow \mathcal{T}$ *is an IPDA if for arbitrary* $T \in \mathcal{T}$, $\sigma \in \mathcal{A}^*$, *and previously added traces* $\mathbf{P} \in \mathcal{P}(\mathcal{A}^*)$ *with* $\mathbf{P} \subseteq \mathcal{L}(T)$ *it holds that* $\{\sigma\} \cup \mathbf{P} \subseteq \mathcal{L}\big(\alpha(T, \sigma, \mathbf{P})\big)$. *If* $\mathbf{P} \nsubseteq \mathcal{L}(T)$, α *is undefined.*

Starting from an (initial) tree T, a user incrementally selects a trace σ not yet described by T. The algorithm alters the process tree T into T' that accepts σ and the previously selected/added traces. T' is then used as input for the next incremental execution. For a specific example of an IPDA, we refer to our previous work [11]. Next, we formally define a freezing-enabled IPDA.

Definition 5 (Freezing-Enabled IPDA). $\alpha_f \colon \mathcal{T} \times \mathcal{A}^* \times \mathcal{P}(\mathcal{A}^*) \times \mathcal{P}(\mathcal{T}) \nrightarrow \mathcal{T}$
is a freezing-enabled IPDA if for arbitrary $T \in \mathcal{T}$, $\sigma \in \mathcal{A}^*$, previously added traces $\mathbf{P} \in \mathcal{P}(\mathcal{A}^*)$ with $\mathbf{P} \subseteq \mathcal{L}(T)$, and $n \geq 0$ frozen subtrees $\mathbf{T} = \{T_1, \dots, T_n\} \in \mathcal{P}(\mathcal{T})$ s.t. $\forall i, j \in \{1, \dots, n\}(T_i \sqsubseteq T \wedge i \neq j \Rightarrow T_i \not\sqsubseteq T_j)$ it holds that $\{\sigma\} \cup \mathbf{P} \subseteq \mathcal{L}\big(\alpha_f(T, \sigma, \mathbf{P}, \mathbf{T})\big)$ and $\forall T' \in \mathbf{T}(T' \sqsubseteq \alpha_f(T, \sigma, \mathbf{P}, \mathbf{T}))$.
If $\mathbf{P} \not\subseteq \mathcal{L}(T)$ or $\exists i, j \in \{1, \dots, n\}(T_i \not\sqsubseteq T \vee i \neq j \Rightarrow T_i \sqsubseteq T_j)$, α_f is undefined.

4.2 Approach

This section presents the proposed freezing approach, i.e., a freezing-enabled IPDA, that is based on an arbitrary, non-freezing-enabled IPDA. The central idea is to modify the input and output artefacts of an non-freezing-enabled IPDA. Thus, the proposed freezing approach is compatible with any IPDA. Figure 4 provides an overview of the proposed approach. The remainder of this section is structured along the input/output modifications shown in Fig. 4.

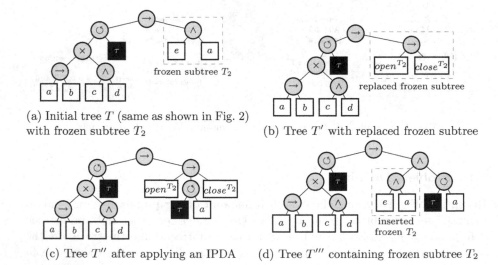

(a) Initial tree T (same as shown in Fig. 2) with frozen subtree T_2

(b) Tree T' with replaced frozen subtree

(c) Tree T'' after applying an IPDA

(d) Tree T''' containing frozen subtree T_2

Fig. 5. Running example of the freezing approach. Previously added traces: $\{\sigma_1 = \langle d, c, a, b, a, e \rangle, \sigma_2 = \langle a, b, e, a \rangle\}$. Trace to be added next: $\sigma = \langle c, d, a, e, a, a, e \rangle$

Replacing Frozen Subtrees. As shown in Fig. 4, we assume an (initial) tree T with frozen subtrees $T_1, \dots, T_n \sqsubseteq T$ and return a modified tree T'. For example, Fig. 5a shows the tree T (same as in Fig. 2) with the frozen subtree T_2. To replace

T_2, we choose two unique labels which are neither in the event log nor in the tree, e.g., $open^{T_2}$ and $close^{T_2}$. Next, we replace T_2 by $\rightarrow(open^{T_2}, close^{T_2})$ and get T' (Fig. 5b). Semantically, $open^{T_2}$ represents the opening and $close^{T_2}$ the closing of T_2. In general, we iteratively replace each frozen subtree.

Projecting Previously Added Traces. The set of previously added traces $\{\sigma_1, \ldots, \sigma_m\}$ (Fig. 4), which fits the tree T, does not fit T' because of the replaced frozen subtree(s). Thus, we have to modify the traces accordingly.

We replay each trace $\{\sigma_1, \ldots, \sigma_m\}$ on T and mark when a frozen subtree is *opened* and *closed*. Next, we insert in these traces the corresponding replacement label whenever a frozen subtree was opened/closed and remove all activities in between that are replayed in a frozen subtree. Other activities remain unchanged. For example, reconsider T (Fig. 5) and its frozen subtree T_2 that was replaced by $\rightarrow(open^{T_2}, close^{T_2})$. Assume the traces $\{\sigma_1 = \langle d, c, a, b, a, e \rangle, \sigma_2 = \langle a, b, e, a \rangle\}$. Below, we show the running sequence of σ_1 on T and the projected trace σ_1'.

extract of the running sequence for σ_1 on $T = T_0$ (see Fig. 2):
$\langle \ldots (n_{4.4}, d), (n_{4.3}, c) \ldots (n_{4.1}, a), (n_{4.2}, b) \ldots (n_{1.2}, open), (n_{2.4}, a), (n_{2.3}, e), (n_{1.2}, close) \ldots \rangle$

projected trace σ_1' based on above running sequence:					
$\langle d,$	$c,$	$a,$	$b,$	$open^{T_2},$	$close^{T_2} \rangle$

We transform $\sigma_1 = \langle d, c, a, b, a, e \rangle$ into $\sigma_1' = \langle d, c, a, b, open^{T_2}, close^{T_2} \rangle$ (and σ_2 into $\sigma_2' = \langle a, b, open^{T_2}, close^{T_2} \rangle$). Note that $\sigma_1', \sigma_2' \in \mathcal{L}(T')$ since $\sigma_1, \sigma_2 \in \mathcal{L}(T)$.

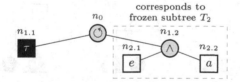

(a) Abstraction tree A used to detect full executions of frozen tree T_2 (Fig. 2)

move index		1	2	3	4	5	6	7	8	9	10	11	12	13	14
trace		c	d	≫	≫	a	e	≫	≫	≫	a	a	e	≫	≫
model		≫	≫	$(n_0,$ open$)$	$(n_{1.2},$ open$)$	$(n_{2.2},$ $a)$	$(n_{2.1},$ $e)$	$(n_{1.2},$ close$)$	$(n_{1.1},$ $\tau)$	$(n_{1.2},$ open$)$	$(n_{2.2},$ $a)$	≫	$(n_{2.1},$ $e)$	$(n_{1.2},$ close$)$	$(n_0,$ close$)$

(b) Optimal alignment of $\sigma = \langle c, d, a, e, a, a, e \rangle$ and abstraction tree A

Fig. 6. Detecting full executions of T_2 (Fig. 2) in $\sigma = \langle c, d, a, e, a, a, e \rangle$

Projecting Trace to Be Added Next. The idea is to detect full executions of the frozen subtree(s) within the trace to be added next and to replace these full executions by the corresponding replacement labels.

Reconsider Fig. 5 and the trace to be added next $\sigma = \langle c, d, a, e, a, a, e \rangle$. To detect full executions of the frozen subtree $T_2 \,\widehat{=}\, \wedge(e, a)$ independent from the entire tree T, we align σ with the abstraction tree $A \,\widehat{=}\, \circlearrowleft(\tau, \wedge(e, a))$, cf. Fig. 6a. The alignment (cf. Fig. 6b) shows that T_2 is twice fully executed, i.e., 4–7 and 9–13 move. Thus, we project σ onto $\sigma' = \langle c, d, open^{T_2}, close^{T_2}, open^{T_2}, a, close^{T_2} \rangle$.

Reinserting Frozen Subtrees. This section describes how the frozen sub-
tree(s) are reinserted into T''', returned by the IPDA (Fig. 4). Note that T'' can
contain the replacement label for opening and closing of a frozen subtree multiple times because the IPDA may add leaf nodes having the same label. Thus, we
have to find appropriate position(s) in T'' to insert the frozen subtree(s) back.

For example, reconsider Fig. 5c. We receive $T'' \widehat{=} \rightarrow (\wedge(\times(\rightarrow(a,b), \wedge(c,d)), \tau),$
$\rightarrow(open^{T_2}, \circlearrowleft(\tau, a), close^{T_2}))$. We observe that between opening ($open^{T_2}$) and
closing ($close^{T_2}$) of T_2, a loop on a was inserted. First, we calculate the LCA
of $open^{T_2}$ and $close^{T_2}$, i.e., the subtree $\rightarrow(open^{T_2}, \circlearrowleft(\tau, a), close^{T_2})$. Next, we do
a semantic analysis of this subtree to determine how often $open^{T_2}$ and $close^{T_2}$
can be replayed. This analysis is needed because the IPDA changes the tree
and $open^{T_2}$ or $close^{T_2}$ could be now skipped or executed multiple times. In T'',
$open^{T_2}$ and $close^{T_2}$ must be executed exactly once. Hence, we apply the case
$\{1\}$ visualized in Fig. 7b where T_i represents the frozen subtree and T'_c the LCA
subtree after removing nodes labelled with $open^{T_2}$ and $close^{T_2}$. We obtain T''''
(Fig. 5d) that contains the frozen subtree T_2 and accepts the traces $\{\sigma, \sigma_1, \sigma_2\}$.

In general (cf. Fig. 4), we iteratively insert the frozen subtrees $\{T_1, \ldots, T_n\}$
back. For $T_i \in \{T_1, \ldots, T_n\}$, we calculate the LCA from all nodes in T'' that are
labeled with the replacement label of T_i. Next, we do a semantic analysis of
the LCA to determine how often T_i has to be executed. This semantic analysis

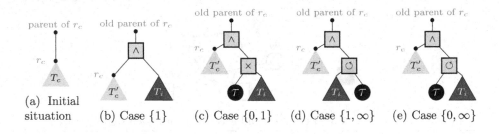

(a) Initial
situation   (b) Case $\{1\}$ (c) Case $\{0,1\}$ (d) Case $\{1,\infty\}$ (e) Case $\{0,\infty\}$

Fig. 7. Four cases showing how to insert a frozen subtree T_i back

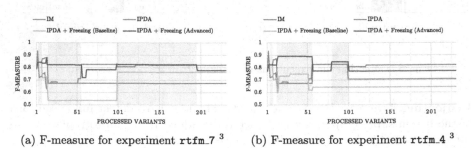

(a) F-measure for experiment `rtfm_7` [3]   (b) F-measure for experiment `rtfm_4` [3]

Fig. 8. F-measure for a real-life event log [9] using two different initial process models,
each with a different frozen subtree. We refer to the proposed approach in this paper
as *IPDA + Freezing (Advanced)*. Highlighted segments indicate that the proposed approach outperforms the other evaluated algorithms

results in one of the four cases shown in Fig. 7, which specify how the frozen subtree needs to be inserted back into T''.

5 Evaluation

This section presents an experimental evaluation. We compare four different discovery approaches: the Inductive Miner (a conventional discovery algorithm) [8], an IPDA [11], a baseline freezing approach (described in the extended version of this paper) using the IPDA in [11], and the proposed freezing approach (Sect. 4.2) using the IPDA in [11]. All four approaches guarantee replay fitness, i.e., traces given to the algorithm are accepted by the resulting tree. We use a publicly available event log [9]. We use the same initial model for all IPDA approaches per run. Further, we do not change the frozen subtree during incremental discovery. More detailed data of the experiments are available online[1].

Figure 8 shows the F-measure of the incremental discovered trees based on the entire event log. We observe that the proposed advanced freezing approach clearly dominates the baseline freezing approach in both runs. Further, we observe that the advanced freezing approach outperforms the other approaches in the highlighted areas (Fig. 8a). Note that in reality, *incorporating all observed process behavior is often not desired* because the event data contains noise, incomplete behavior and other types of quality issues. For instance, after integrating the first 17 most frequent trace-variants of the RTFM log, the process model covers already 99% of the observed process behavior/traces. Comparing IPDA with the proposed advanced freezing approach (Fig. 8), we observe that the advanced freezing approach clearly dominates IPDA in most segments. In general, the results indicate that freezing subtrees during incremental process discovery can lead to higher quality models since we observe that the advanced freezing approach dominates the other algorithms in many segments.

6 Conclusion

This paper introduced a novel option to interact with a process discovery algorithm. By being able to freeze parts of a process model during incremental process discovery, the user is able to steer the algorithm. Moreover, the proposed approach combines conventional process discovery with data-driven process modeling. In the future, we plan to explore strategies that recommend appropriate freezing candidates to the user. Further, we plan to integrate the proposed approach into the incremental process discovery tool *Cortado* [12].

References

1. van der Aalst, W.M.P.: Process Mining - Data Science in Action. Springer, Heidelberg (2016). https://doi.org/10.1007/978-3-662-49851-4

---

[1] https://github.com/fit-daniel-schuster/Freezing-Sub-Models-During-Incr-PD.

2. Armas Cervantes, A., van Beest, N.R.T.P., La Rosa, M., Dumas, M., García-Bañuelos, L.: Interactive and incremental business process model repair. In: Panetto, H., et al. (eds.) OTM 2017. LNCS, vol. 10573, pp. 53–74. Springer, Cham (2017). https://doi.org/10.1007/978-3-319-69462-7_5

3. Carmona, J., van Dongen, B.F., Solti, A., Weidlich, M.: Conformance Checking - Relating Processes and Models. Springer, Heidelberg (2018). https://doi.org/10.1007/978-3-319-99414-7

4. Dixit, P.M., Buijs, J.C.A.M., van der Aalst, W.M.P., Hompes, B.F.A., Buurman, J.: Using domain knowledge to enhance process mining results. In: Ceravolo, P., Rinderle-Ma, S. (eds.) SIMPDA 2015. LNBIP, vol. 244, pp. 76–104. Springer, Cham (2017). https://doi.org/10.1007/978-3-319-53435-0_4

5. Dixit, P.M., Verbeek, H.M.W., Buijs, J.C.A.M., van der Aalst, W.M.P.: Interactive data-driven process model construction. In: Trujillo, J.C., et al. (eds.) ER 2018. LNCS, vol. 11157, pp. 251–265. Springer, Cham (2018). https://doi.org/10.1007/978-3-030-00847-5_19

6. Fahland, D., van der Aalst, W.M.P.: Repairing process models to reflect reality. In: Barros, A., Gal, A., Kindler, E. (eds.) BPM 2012. LNCS, vol. 7481, pp. 229–245. Springer, Heidelberg (2012). https://doi.org/10.1007/978-3-642-32885-5_19

7. Greco, G., Guzzo, A., Lupia, F., Pontieri, L.: Process discovery under precedence constraints. ACM Trans. Knowl. Discov. Data 9(4), 1–39 (2015). https://doi.org/10.1145/2710020

8. Leemans, S.J.J., Fahland, D., van der Aalst, W.M.P.: Discovering block-structured process models from event logs - a constructive approach. In: Colom, J.-M., Desel, J. (eds.) PETRI NETS 2013. LNCS, vol. 7927, pp. 311–329. Springer, Heidelberg (2013). https://doi.org/10.1007/978-3-642-38697-8_17

9. de Leoni, M., Mannhardt, F.: Road traffic fine management process (2015). https://doi.org/10.4121/uuid:270fd440-1057-4fb9-89a9-b699b47990f5

10. Rembert, A.J., Omokpo, A., Mazzoleni, P., Goodwin, R.T.: Process discovery using prior knowledge. In: Basu, S., Pautasso, C., Zhang, L., Fu, X. (eds.) ICSOC 2013. LNCS, vol. 8274, pp. 328–342. Springer, Heidelberg (2013). https://doi.org/10.1007/978-3-642-45005-1_23

11. Schuster, D., van Zelst, S.J., van der Aalst, W.M.P.: Incremental discovery of hierarchical process models. In: Dalpiaz, F., Zdravkovic, J., Loucopoulos, P. (eds.) RCIS 2020. LNBIP, vol. 385, pp. 417–433. Springer, Cham (2020). https://doi.org/10.1007/978-3-030-50316-1_25

12. Schuster, D., van Zelst, S.J., van der Aalst, W.M.P.: Cortado—an interactive tool for data-driven process discovery and modeling. In: Buchs, D., Carmona, J. (eds.) PETRI NETS 2021. LNCS, vol. 12734, pp. 465–475. Springer, Cham (2021). https://doi.org/10.1007/978-3-030-76983-3_23

Modeling Adaptive Data Analysis Pipelines for Crowd-Enhanced Processes

Cinzia Cappiello, Barbara Pernici, and Monica Vitali(✉)

Department of Electronics, Information, and Bioengineering,
Politecnico di Milano, Milan, Italy
{cinzia.cappiello,barbara.pernici,monica.vitali}@polimi.it

Abstract. Information from social media can be leveraged by social scientists to support effective decision making. However, such data sources are often characterised by high volumes and noisy information, therefore data analysis should be always preceded by a data preparation phase. Designing and testing data preparation pipelines requires considering requirements on cost, time, and quality of data extraction. In this work, we aim to propose a methodology for modeling crowd-enhanced data analysis pipelines using a goal-oriented approach, including both automatic and human-related tasks, by suggesting the kind of components to include, their order, and their parameters, while balancing the trade-off between cost, time, and quality of the results.

Keywords: Data analysis pipeline modeling · Crowd-enhanced processes · Human-in-the-loop processes · Goal-oriented process improvement

1 Introduction

Social media analysis can be very effective to support decision processes in citizen science [5,6]. However, the sources of data are not totally reliable and are characterised by high volume and high heterogeneity, also lacking relevant metadata that might help to identify the items that are actually significant for the decision process. Extracting and selecting relevant data for a specific goal from social media can be very challenging and time consuming. This process can be facilitated and improved by adopting a human-in-the-loop approach, in which the relevance of the data is validated by experts and/or volunteers. Existing approaches combine automatic tools with crowdsourcing and automatic classification techniques to make the data extraction from social media process more efficient and reliable. However, including crowdsourcing in the process generates some challenges both from the cost and time perspectives. In this paper we propose a methodology for improving crowd-enhanced pipelines, modeling their requirements and constraints and the pipeline components and their characteristics. The paper is organized as follows. Related work and research directions in the field are discussed in Sect. 2. Section 3 defines the data preparation

© Springer Nature Switzerland AG 2021
A. Ghose et al. (Eds.): ER 2021, LNCS 13011, pp. 25–35, 2021.
https://doi.org/10.1007/978-3-030-89022-3_3

pipeline and its main components. Section 4 provides a model for the adaptive pipeline definition. Section 5 describes the methodology for a goal-oriented pipeline design. An application of the approach is illustrated in Sect. 6.

2   Related Work

Recently, representing and analyzing data science life cycles has received more and more attention. Characterizing machine learning processes, proposing a maturity model and emphasizing the need of assessing the accuracy of the results of a pipeline, is discussed in [1]. The NIST Big Data Reference Architecture [4] proposes a framework in which activities for the big data life cycle management are defined and a system orchestrator enables the execution of different processes. The data science life cycle presented in [12] is analysed focusing on the main steps and their possible infrastructure components, and a customization for specific projects is advocated according to the data sets and the purpose of the data collection. The choices made in the selection of parameters and their motivations are to be considered in the workflow documentation. In [9], several aspects of the data preparation process, defined as "black art" in the paper, are emphasized. In particular a significant issue is the cost of labeling, performed by crowdsourcing. The fact that different data preprocessing pipelines may lead to different analysis results has been also highlighted in [3], where the author proposes the Learn2Clean method to identify the optimal sequence of tasks for the maximization of the quality of the results. In this approach the feasibility of the pipeline in term of cost and execution time has not been considered.

Pipelines for social good projects are analyzed in [11]. In particular the paper discusses the problems of data collection and integration and of managing a large number of annotators in crisis events. In emergency situations, when awareness about the ongoing event is derived also from social media, the data preparation phase is particularly critical as the total workload of emergency operators and involved emergency support online communities is constrained. Some studies analyze the correlation between workload and recall of highest ranked alerts [10]. In [6] the use of social media posts for emergencies has been studied, focusing on extracting images for awareness purposes. In this case, social media data is usually very noisy, with a limited number of relevant information, so automatic filtering must be used for reducing the number of irrelevant posts [2]. In [8] we presented a pipeline in which the preparation phases is augmented with some automatic ML-based filters to remove non-relevant images in a generic way. The present work is motivated by the need of designing such pipelines in a systematic way, considering the specific goals of the collection and analysis pipeline.

3   Components for Adaptive Pipelines

Data analysis always requires the definition of a pipeline in which the different steps show the way in which data are processed throughout their lifecycle.

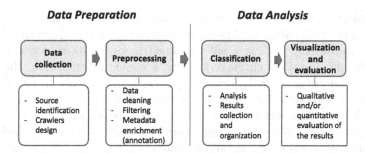

Fig. 1. High level social media pipeline

The high level pipeline is composed of two main phases (Fig. 1): (i) *Data preparation*, related to the definition of the data to collect and to the preprocessing activities needed to transform the data before their analysis and (ii) *Data analysis*, which focuses on the specific analysis (a crowdsourcing task in the considered scenario) to perform and on the visualization and evaluation of the obtained results. Focusing on the preprocessing phase, we aim to build the most appropriate pipeline along the analysis requirements. The pipeline will be built by considering different components. The *preprocessing components* include:

- *Cleaning tasks*: they (i) identify and correct errors and anomalies; (ii) eliminate duplicates; (iii) eliminate inappropriate and useless data.
- *Semantic filters*: they reduce the volume of data to consider on the basis of their value or characteristics. For example, tweets can be selected on the basis of their content (e.g., presence of images) or on the basis of the tweet metadata (e.g., posting time, geolocation data, popularity of the post).
- *Selectors (or Sampling filters)*: they reduce the number of values to analyze. They are characterized by a reduction rate, i.e., the ratio between the output and the input data sets. In our approach, we use the simple random sampling.
- *Metadata enrichment/Annotation tasks*: they add important metadata such as location, topic, image description. Metadata can be simply extracted from the available information (e.g., gather the location of a tweet from the text) or derived from a more complex content analysis, such as a classification of the available images into photos and non-photos, like diagrams or memes.

Most of the preprocessing tasks can be performed automatically or manually, e.g., assigning them on crowdsourcing platforms. Crowdsourcing is also used as a classifier in the data analysis phase since the use of a human-in-the-loop approach can guarantee better results compared to a ML classifier.

There are various components that can be employed to perform preprocessing activities. Selecting a proper combination for a specific data set and a specific goal is not trivial also for expert users and several trials are often needed to find an effective pipeline. Here we focus on this issue by proposing a semi-automatic approach to support data scientists in composing the pipeline for their tasks.

A **Pipeline** $\mathcal{P}$ is a process composed of a set of input sources $\mathcal{S}$, a set $\mathcal{C}$ of components, which are the elementary work units that collectively achieve the process objective O_i, within a set of requirements (goals and constraints) $\mathcal{R}$ and a collection of results Res. In this paper we consider only sequential processes.

A **Component** $c_i \in C$ is a self-contained module that performs a specific step of the pipeline. It is characterized by a name, a description, the type of inputs IN_i and outputs OUT_i (e.g., text, image), the fan-in FI_i, i.e., the maximum number of input values allowed, the set of non functional criteria C_i associated with the component (e.g., estimated cost, time, quality), the set IQ_i that describes the impact of the component on the quality criteria described in next section, and the set of configuration parameters $Conf_i$ (e.g., the reduction rate for selectors or the confidence threshold for semantic filters).

4   Adaptive Pipeline Model Definition

In this paper, we propose a methodology for supporting users in the definition of a pipeline and its improvement using a requirement-aware adaptive approach. We introduce a set of criteria to evaluate a pipeline (Sect. 4.1) and we introduce the concept of requirements to express the expected or desired behaviour (Sect. 4.2).

4.1   Evaluation Criteria

We consider three main criteria for assessing the performance of a pipeline and comparing different configurations: (i) cost, (ii) time, and (iii) quality.

Cost. The cost of execution of a pipeline depends on the amount of resources required for processing all the items of the data set. At the component level, the cost can be computed depending on the type of component we are considering:

- the computational cost: in case of automatic components, the cost is related to the computational resources needed for its execution. It depends on the processing capability of the component, expressed by the parameter FI, and on the amount of data items that it has to process;
- the crowd cost: it is the cost of human-in-the-loop components. It depends on the number of items submitted to the crowd. Defining the price per task, that is the amount of money owed to each crowdworker who executes it is a complex and ethical related issue[1] that might affect the quality of the result [7]. Here, we assume that a price, as well as the crowdsourcing platform, has been predefined by the user.

Given the cost of each component, the overall cost of the pipeline $cost_P$ is the sum of the costs of each component according to the number of items that each component has to analyze.

---

[1] https://medium.com/ai2-blog/crowdsourcing-pricing-ethics-and-best-practices-8487fd5c9872.

Time. The time of execution of the pipeline contributes to the efficiency of the process. The time depends on the features of the components as well as on the number of items to analyze. As discussed in Sect. 3, each component is characterised by an estimated average execution time per item. The overall execution time of the pipeline $time_P$ can be computed as the sum of the expected computation time of each component given the expected number of items to process. It is worth noticing that the order in which the components are executed can affect the overall time of execution. This is due to the fact that each component is characterised by a time for processing an item. Also, some components can reduce the size of items in output (reduction rate). Thus, postponing the execution of time expensive components to when the items to be analysed are reduced after several filters can be a strategy to reduce the overall execution time.

Quality. Quality is a criteria that contributes to the effectiveness of the pipeline, measuring the relevance of the items in input of the data analysis phase. More precisely, the quality of the pipeline can be expressed with the following metrics: precision, recall, population completeness, and volume. Considering an input set $\mathcal{I}$ with $m \leq |\mathcal{I}|$ relevant items and an output set $\mathcal{I}'$ with $n \leq |\mathcal{I}'|$ relevant items and $\mathcal{I}' \subset \mathcal{I}$ we can define precision and recall as follows.

Precision p is a metric measuring the ability to select only items that are relevant for the task and is measured as $p = \frac{n}{|\mathcal{I}'|}$. For the filtering components, the average precision at component level is known based on their characteristics, while precision at pipeline level is not known before the pipeline is instantiated. In order to estimate the likely precision of the overall pipeline, we can refer to some precision related metrics at the pipeline level like the maximum, minimum, and average precision of the components of the pipeline.

Recall r is a metric measuring the the the ability to keep items that are relevant to the task and is measured as $r = \frac{n}{m}$. As for precision, recall at pipeline level is not known before the pipeline is instantiated. As before, we can refer to some recall related metrics at the pipeline level like the maximum, minimum, and average recall of the components of the pipeline.

Population Completeness d measures the number of data items in the data set belonging to the different classes that the user aims to represent. It ensures the presence of a sufficient number of items for all the classes of interest.

Volume measures the size of the data set in input or output. The volume is the cardinality of the data set $|\mathcal{I}|$. Volume, measured at the pipeline level, ensures that enough data are available for executing the analysis tasks.

4.2 Requirements: Goals and Constraints

When a task is defined, the user defines a set of requirements that the pipeline is expected to achieve, based on the three criteria presented in Sect. 4.1. These criteria are not independent. In fact, high quality negatively affects cost and time. Similarly, reducing time might affect the cost (more resources need to be employed) or quality (same resources are employed thus components have to reduce their precision). Finally, reducing cost might increase the execution time and/or reduce the quality. According to this, not all the three criteria can be optimised, but a trade-off between them is required. We split requirements in constraints to be satisfied (e.g., maximum cost and time available for computation) and goals to be optimized (e.g., maximize precision and recall) for a pipeline.

The pipeline is associated with a set $\mathcal{R}$ of requirements (see Sect. 3).

A **constraint** $n \in \mathcal{R}$ expresses a desired behaviour measurable through an evaluation criteria. An example of constraint could be "*precision* > 0.9".

A **goal** $g \in \mathcal{R}$ expresses a desired achievement of the pipeline measurable through an evaluation criteria. An example of goal could be "*minimize(cost)*". A goal can be associated with a weight expressing the importance of the criteria satisfaction. For the general assessment of a pipeline, we consider the overall optimization function as the weighted sum of all the goals expressed by the user.

5   Methodology for Pipeline Improvement

In this section, we describe the methodology for supporting the user in improving the pipeline. The users willing to extract relevant information from a data source, define a preliminary pipeline based on the task that they are willing to execute. The preliminary pipeline is evaluated according to the criteria. Based on the results, a modification of the pipeline is suggested to the user according to some preliminary knowledge: (i) a set of predefined actions that can be applied to generate a modified version of the pipeline (Sect. 5.1) and (ii) the expected outcome of the applied action on the evaluation criteria (Sect. 5.2). The modified version is also evaluated and a new modification is proposed until a satisfactory solution has been found. In this section we are going to define the actions that can be applied to modify the pipeline and their impact on the evaluation criteria.

5.1   Actions

The pipeline can be modified changing its components or their configuration. Each modification can affect the evaluation criteria, positively or negatively. Here, we introduce two different classes of actions, structural and configuration actions, and their effects on the three identified criteria.

Structural Actions affect the composition of the pipeline. Possible structural actions are: (i) add component; (ii) remove component; (iii) switch components.

The **add component** action AC affects the set of components $\mathcal{C}$ of the pipeline by adding an additional component c. This action potentially affects all the criteria, positively or negatively according to the contribution of the added component. For instance, adding a semantic filter can affect positively the quality if it is able to discard not relevant elements while keeping relevant ones. Having less items, even though the component itself requires time and computational resources to be executed, positively affects the following components of the pipeline reducing their execution time and cost. The **remove component** action RC affects the set of components $\mathcal{C}$ of the pipeline by removing a component c. This action improves the pipeline if the removed component was not relevant or had a limited impact, thus improving quality as well as time and cost. However, removing a relevant component might negatively affect the three criteria. The **switch components** action SC affects the order of two components $c_i, c_j \in \mathcal{C}$ of the pipeline. For filtering components, this action has not an effect on the overall quality, since in the end the steps executed will be the same. However, executing a most effective component before a less effective one in filtering out not relevant items might affect the time and the cost of the execution.

Configuration Actions affect the pipeline without changing its structure. They act on the data input (fan-in) or output (fan-out) volume of a single component.

The **increase fan-in** action FI_I affects a component c by reducing the reduction rate parameter of the selector preceding it. The effect is positive on quality since less items are discarded (randomly) before the component execution, but it affects time and cost increasing the load for the component. The **decrease fan-in** action FI_D increases the reduction rate of the selector. It negatively affects quality while reduces time and/or cost.

For changing the fan-out we can instead change the confidence threshold used by a semantic filter component for classifying relevant and not relevant items. The **increase fan-out** action FO_I affects a component c by decreasing its confidence threshold parameter. It improves the recall but decreases the precision, since uncertain items (e.g., false negatives and false positives) are not discarded. It also affects time and cost negatively since a higher volume of items has to be processed by following components. The **decrease fan-out** action FO_D increases the confidence threshold parameter of the component. It reduces time and cost, while negatively affecting the recall and improving the precision.

5.2   Requirements and Impact

Each action affects the requirements in some way (Sect. 4.2). As an example, the relationship that we qualitatively discussed in Sect. 5.1 is summarized in Table 1 referring to the semantic filter components. These effects represent a

Table 1. Actions effect on criteria for semantic filters components

Action	Description	Quality	Cost	Time
AC	Add component	− recall/volume/completeness, + precision	+, −	+, −
RC	Remove component	+ recall/volume/completeness, − precision	+, −	+, −
SC	Switch components	No effect	+, −	+, −
FI_I	Increase fan-in	+	−	−
FI_D	Decrease fan-in	−	+	+
FO_I	Increase fan-out	+ recall/volume/completeness, − precision	−	−
FO_D	Decrease fan-out	− recall/volume/completeness, + precision	+	+

general case, however each pipeline will have specific effects according to the components considered and to the task. We define the **impact** $i_{a,e} \in [+, -, n]$ as the effect of an action a on a criteria e. The impact is positive (negative) if the evaluation criteria e improves (gets worse) after the enactment of action a and neutral if no significant change is observed. As it can be observed, for structural actions it is difficult to define an overall effect on cost and time since it depends both on the execution time and the reduction rate of the component. As an example, adding a component implies reducing the number of items to be analysed by the following components. However, the execution time and cost for the component itself have to be considered.

6   Validation

Figure 2 shows how different components have been combined to design a pipeline for extracting visual information from social media. The pipeline execution is supported by the VisualCit tool environment illustrated in [8]. Data preparation phase includes data cleaning, semantic filtering, and enrichment component types (selectors are not shown in the figure). For each type of component, several alternatives can be selected, as listed in the figure.

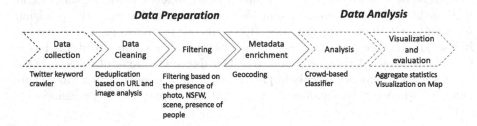

Fig. 2. VisualCit pipeline, revisited from [8]

In this section we briefly discuss two case studies applying the proposed methodology. We start from a general knowledge of the available components and their main characteristics, as shown in Fig. 3. We assume that each component is preceded by a selector in order to control its fan-in.

In the first case study, the goal is to improve an existing data analysis pipeline for providing awareness after a natural disaster. We consider a dataset of images posted in tweets related to the earthquake that stroke Albania on November 26, 2019. The data set consists of 900 images that result from another data analysis pipeline using automatic damage grading classifier components, derived from research at Qatar University [13]. In order to compare human evaluation and automatic classification for damage grading, we used crowdsourcing, in particular 10 annotators, for evaluating the relevance of the images for the analysis task. With the design of an initial data analysis pipeline composed of some filters to select relevant tweets we still noticed a high percentage of non relevant

	person detector	photo detector	NSFW detector	public/private scene	geolocation enrichment	native location
reduction rate	0,21	0,35	0,92	0,80	0,59	0,03
precision	95,81	99,77	99,38	91,81	84,00	100,00
recall	97,15	94,67	98,77	97,26		
time / image (sec)	0,99	0,58	0,33	0,34	10	0,01

Fig. 3. Examples of components parameters

images (80% precision, considering relevance as a parameter for its evaluation), after the filtering provided by the initial data analysis pipeline. Therefore, we apply our methodology to assess if some of the available filtering tools presented in Fig. 3 can improve the quality of the result, retaining a sufficient number of images for the analysis, which is set as $V_{output} > 500$. A combination of NSFW, Photo, Public filters to improve the precision of the result appears a good candidate, considering both the semantics of the filters and their precision and recall characteristics. The application of the filters shows an increase to 90% for precision, while recall decreases by 19%. To further improve the pipeline another candidate component is the geolocation enrichment component since it increases the population completeness. Applying a semantic filter based on location (Albania) after the automatic enrichment with the geolocation enrichment component, only images located in the area of interest (Albania) are considered. However, this component lowers too much the recall (yielding in this case only 200 images) violating the volume constraint needed for the analysis phase.

The second case study concerns extracting visual information on the behavioral impact of COVID-19, described in detail in [8]. Differently from the first case study, this case study is characterized by a very high number of images to be analyzed (approx 1,500,000 per week). Constraints are the computational resources and the size of the crowd, as well as the total time for preprocessing (set to max 12 h), with $5,000 < V_{output} < 6,000$ to make the image analysis manageable for a small community crowd (3–10 persons) and to get a number of tweets that would provide some minimal information at country level. A first proposal, and typical approach for a social media pipeline in which post location is needed, is to consider the native geolocation metadata of the tweets to select the items of the initial data set as a first step, and then apply the photo, NSFW, public, persons filter in the order, considering their reduction rate. However, even starting with 1,500,000 tweets, the final estimated volume is 1,516 due to the high selectivity of the native location selector. Time constraints are also not satisfied (15 h). A possible action to modify the pipeline is to remove the native geolocation selector at the beginning of the preprocessing pipeline, which is too restrictive (native geolocation metadata in posts are limited to only 3% of tweets). To provide the needed information, we add an enrichment component for the geolocation. Considering the high computational requirements of the component (see Fig. 3), it should be placed at the end of the preprocessing pipeline. To fulfill the time requirement, we add a selector at the beginning of the pipeline to reduce the number of items to be analysed. With a 1/6 reduction, the resulting volume is in the desired range. To additionally fulfill the time requirement, we need to assign additional resources to the enrichment component, thus reducing its computational time while increasing costs.

7 Conclusion and Future Work

In this paper we propose a systematic approach to design a data science process, providing an adaptive way to combine different possible alternative components in a pipeline. We addressed this issue by providing a goal-oriented approach for pipeline definition and improvement, proposing a set of evaluation criteria and a set of improvement actions. There is still need of developing this research further in several directions. In particular, there is a need to investigate on methods for classification and characterization of components in specific domains, and to define how the different components can be combined, with respect to the compatibility between them, as proposed in [3].

Acknowledgements. This work was funded by the European Commission H2020 Project Crowd4SDG, #872944.

References

1. Akkiraju, R., et al.: Characterizing machine learning processes: a maturity framework. In: Fahland, D., Ghidini, C., Becker, J., Dumas, M. (eds.) BPM 2020. LNCS, vol. 12168, pp. 17–31. Springer, Cham (2020). https://doi.org/10.1007/978-3-030-58666-9_2
2. Barozzi, S., Fernandez-Marquez, J.L., Shankar, A.R., Pernici, B.: Filtering images extracted from social media in the response phase of emergency events. In: Proceedings of ISCRAM (2019)
3. Berti-Équille, L.: Learn2Clean: optimizing the sequence of tasks for web data preparation. In: Proceedings of WWW Conference, pp. 2580–2586. ACM (2019)
4. Chang, W.L., Boyd, D., NBD-PWG NIST big data public working group: NIST big data interoperability framework: volume 6, big data reference architecture [version 2] (2019)
5. Fritz, S., et al.: Citizen science and the united nations sustainable development goals. Nat. Sustain. **2**(10), 922–930 (2019)
6. Havas, C., et al.: E2mC: improving emergency management service practice through social media and crowdsourcing analysis in near real time. Sensors **17**(12), 2766 (2017)
7. Iren, D., Bilgen, S.: Cost of quality in crowdsourcing. Hum. Comput. **1**(2), 283–314 (2014)
8. Negri, V., et al.: Image-based social sensing: combining AI and the crowd to mine policy-adherence indicators from Twitter. In: ICSE, Track Software Engineering in Society, May 2021
9. Polyzotis, N., Roy, S., Whang, S.E., Zinkevich, M.: Data lifecycle challenges in production machine learning: a survey. SIGMOD Rec. **47**(2), 17–28 (2018)
10. Purohit, H., Castillo, C., Imran, M., Pandey, R.: Ranking of social media alerts with workload bounds in emergency operation centers. In: Proceedings of Conference on Web Intelligence (WI), pp. 206–213. IEEE (2018)

11. Scheunemann, C., Naumann, J., Eichler, M., Stowe, K., Gurevych, I.: Data collection and annotation pipeline for social good projects. In: Proceedings of the AAAI Fall 2020 AI for Social Good Symposium (2020)
12. Stodden, V.: The data science life cycle: a disciplined approach to advancing data science as a science. Commun. ACM **63**(7), 58–66 (2020)
13. Zahra, K., Imran, M., Ostermann, F.O.: Automatic identification of eyewitness messages on twitter during disasters. Inf. Process. Manag. **57**(1), 102107 (2020)

Ontology-Based Process Modelling - Will We Live to See It?

Carl Corea[1]([✉]), Michael Fellmann[2], and Patrick Delfmann[1]

[1] University of Koblenz-Landau, Koblenz, Germany
{ccorea,delfmann}@uni-koblenz.de
[2] University of Rostock, Rostock, Germany
michael.fellmann@uni-rostock.de

Abstract. In theory, ontology-based process modelling (OBPM) bares great potential to extend business process management. Many works have studied OBPM and are clear on the potential amenities, such as eliminating ambiguities or enabling advanced reasoning over company processes. However, despite this approval in academia, a widespread industry adoption is still nowhere to be seen. This can be mainly attributed to the fact, that it still requires high amounts of manual labour to initially create ontologies and annotations to process models. As long as these problems are not addressed, implementing OBPM seems unfeasible in practice. In this work, we therefore identify requirements needed for a successful implementation of OBPM and assess the current state of research w.r.t. these requirements. Our results indicate that the research progress for means to facilitate OBPM are still alarmingly low and there needs to be urgent work on extending existing approaches.

Keywords: OBPM · Ontologies · Research agenda

1 Introduction

In the scope of Business Process Management, *process models* have evolved as central artifacts for the design, enactment and analysis of company processes [19]. Many modelling languages, such as the Business Process Model and Notation[1], are available and have received widespread adoption in practice. While these standards offer support for the *representation* of company processes, the actual *content* of the model is still the responsibility of the modeller. That is, process models are designed by human modellers, often times also in a collaborative and incremental manner. In this setting, modelling errors can occur frequently [5, 13]. For example, humans might accidentally model a non-compliant sequence of activities or use ambiguous activity labels.

To conquer such modelling problems, there is a broad consensus in academia that business process models should be extended with an additional conceptual layer, namely *ontologies* [5]. Ontologies are artifacts that can be used to formally

---

[1] https://www.omg.org/bpmn/.

A. Ghose et al. (Eds.): ER 2021, LNCS 13011, pp. 36–46, 2021.
https://doi.org/10.1007/978-3-030-89022-3_4

conceptualize a domain of interest [3]. As shown in Fig. 1, *ontology-based process models* can thus be created by extending process models with ontologies, which allows to define unambiguous semantics of process models and create a shared understanding of business processes for humans and machines alike. To clarify, the ontologies addressed in this works are limited to models that are coded in description logics, e.g., OWL-ontologies linked to process models.

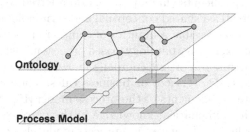

Fig. 1. Exemplary ontology-based process model.

Many works have discussed the potential benefits of OBPM, e.g. eliminating ambiguous process descriptions or advanced compliance reasoning using ontology-based reasoning [3,5]. Still, industry adoptions are sparse. Based on reports such as [13], this can be mainly attributed to the problems in creating the ontology-based process models themselves. First, ontologies must initially be created. As this requires a high expertise in knowledge representation, this is currently still a difficult task for companies. Second, even given an ontology, the ontology has to be annotated to the process model. As finding the connections between ontology- and process model elements is a complex task, manual annotation can be seen as highly unfeasible in practice [13].

While there have been works proposing initial means for the problems raised above, the lack of industry adoptions suggests that companies need more support in implementing OBPM. In this report, we therefore investigate what methods and results are still missing to support companies in implementing OBPM and leverage industry adoption. Here, our contributions are as follows:

- **Requirements for OBPM.** We identify requirements needed for implementing and maintaining ontology-based process models for companies.
- **Literature Analysis.** We identify the state-of-the-art of OBPM research based on a literature review and assess to which extent current results support the identified requirements.
- **Research Agenda.** We identify current research gaps and distill a research agenda to guide future research and tool development.

This work is structured as follows. In Sect. 2, we provide preliminaries and raise requirements for implementing OBPM. In Sect. 3, we analyze the state-of-the-art on OBPM research and identify research gaps, from which we distill a corresponding research agenda in Sect. 4. We conclude in Sect. 5.

2 Preliminaries

2.1 Ontology-Based Process Models

Ontology-based process models [15] allow to define the semantics of business process model elements by extending traditional process models with an additional ontology-layer. To this aim, elements of business process models can be annotated to ontology concepts via mappings, also referred to as *semantic annotation* [6,13]. This creates a shared conceptual and terminological understanding and defines a machine-accessible semantics of company processes.

Figure 1 shows an exemplary ontology-based process model. A company ontology can be used to define important company knowledge, e.g., concepts such as organizational units, tasks, services or business rules. These ontology concepts can then be annotated to elements of the process model [15]. Technically, this is performed by creating axiomatical knowledge in the ontology, i.e., instances of ontology concepts, which each represent a process model element. In this way, the semantics and relations of the process model elements can be formalized.

Regarding ontology-based process models, the potential advantages are clear from an academic standpoint [4,5,8,9,13,15]. Such artifacts foster a shared semantic understanding for humans and machines and allow for advanced reasoning capabilities over process models for companies. Still, a widespread industry adoption cannot be observed. As this could be attributed to companies having problems implementing OBPM, we therefore investigate requirements of implementing OBPM in the following to gain an understanding about whether there could be any obstacles impeding industry adoption.

2.2 Requirements for Implementing OBPM

On a high-level, implementing OBPM can be distinguished into ensuring three components: *an ontology, a process model* and *a mapping between the ontology and the process model.* This might seem trivial, however, to anticipate the results of our literature analysis, there was no approach that supported companies in creating and maintaining all three of these components. For example, virtually all existing approaches assume "ready-to-go" ontologies that can be used as a basis for extending process models. Here, following works such as [7], we argue that this assumption might not be plausible in an enterprise setting, an rather, companies must also be supported in the initial creation of ontologies (R1). Also, following woks such as [13], both the ontology- and process model labels should be initially standardized, as a basis for extending process models (R2).

Furthermore, companies must be able to create mapping of ontologies and process models. Here, there is a broad consensus that companies should be supported by means of mapping- and annotation techniques (R3) [4,13].

When mappings are created, these mappings between ontology concepts and process model element have to be checked for plausibility. A problem here is that the mappings are mostly created based on terminological similarity between ontology concepts and process model elements. This however means that the semantic contexts of these elements are mostly disregarded, which in turn can lead to implausible mappings. For instance, consider the example in Fig. 2. On the ontology level, the company has defined departments and activities, both of which are mutually exclusive. Furthermore, we see a specialized review department. Given a linguistic-based mapping approach matches the ontology concept *Review department* with the activity *Review department* (this would be highly sensible based on various linguistic-based similarity measures), this would result in a case where a process element is both an activity and a department, which, as defined in the ontology, is not possible.

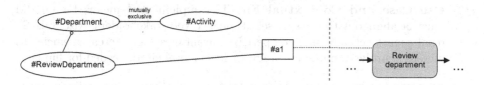

Fig. 2. Exemplary linguistic-based annotation leading to incoherent mappings.

Thus, while the mapping might be sensible from a terminological viewpoint, from a global perspective, the ontology-based process model is inconsistent, i.e., it cannot be instantiated. In the field of ontology matching, this problem is referred to as *mapping incoherence* (i.e., mappings that induce inconsistencies) and is widely acknowledged as a challenging task [11]. Further challenges are also mappings that are simply implausible in a real-life sense, e.g., mapping a process model activity from a sales process to an ontology concept describing a purchase process if they have similar labels. An annotation verification is therefore necessary during modelling to ensure the plausibility of annotations (R4).

Soundness checks are especially relevant in the scope of model evolution. For instance, given an annotated process model, if either the underlying ontology or process is edited, the corresponding counterpart should be altered as well to ensure consistent co-evolution. Here, companies need to be supported in co-evolving ontologies and process models in a synchronized manner through an automatic application of change patterns, e.g. deleting something in the ontology if a corresponding element is deleted in the process model (R5).

Only if the requirements R1–R5 are met, the ontology-based process model can and should be used for ontology-based reasoning. For example, the process model can be verified for compliance by means of ontology-based reasoning (R6).

Withal, an important requirement of implementing OBPM is that the capabilities w.r.t. R1–R6 have to be tailored to the skill set of the stakeholders involved in the respective companies' business process management. Otherwise, it cannot be ensured that the technical capabilities can even be used correctly. Therefore, an important aspect of implementing OBPM are means for assessing the actual usability of the underlying technical capabilities (R7).

Consequently, we raise the following requirements for implementing OBPM:

R1. Ontology Support: Support to create ontologies.

R2. Terminological Standardization: Support to standardize ontologies and process models.

R3. Annotation Support: Support to create semantic annotations.

R4. Annotation Verification: Support to verify soundness (consistency, plausibility) of annotations.

R5. Evolution Support: Support to further evolve and maintain ontology-based models (in a synchronized manner).

R6. Ontology-based reasoning: Support to exploit the ontology-based process model, e.g., reasoning about process model, ontology-based recommendations during modelling.

R7. Use Case and Contextual Fit: The implemented means for OBPM must be aligned with the skill set of the involved stakeholders. Also, OBPM results must actually offer competitive advantages, e.g., increased efficiency, increased understanding accuracy, or less mental effort needed for humans.

Our requirements catalogue is an extension of [20] who raise initial requirements regarding the implementation of modelling and analysis in OBPM (here: R5 and R6). As discussed, all the identified requirements must be met, as otherwise, it can be expected that OBPM can not be successfully implemented (e.g., the OBPM cannot be created without an ontology, etc.). In the following, we therefore assess the state-of-the-art on OBPM research, in order to verify whether there exist sufficient means to meet these requirements.

3 OBPM "State-of-the-Art" Analysis

3.1 Method

To assess the current state-of-the-art on OBPM research w.r.t. the requirements proposed in Sect. 2.2, we conducted a literature review following the standard literature review method in [17]. First, we conducted brief searches to gain an initial overview, as suggested in [14]. We then used concept-mapping techniques to derive suitable keywords for a keyword-based search, as proposed by [17]. We utilized the keyword combination of "Ontolog*" AND "Process Model*", and "Semantic" AND "Process Model*". In iterative pre-testing, we found that these keywords are suitable to retrieve a feasible amount of relevant work. We queried 6 pertinent databases, i.e., ACM digital library, AISel, IEEE, Emeralds Publishing, INFORMS Pubs, Science Direct and Springer Link. This resulted in a total of 434 identified works. We then conducted a screening in two phases, as suggested by [2]. In review phase I, we eliminated duplicates and filtered out irrelevant articles based on title and abstract. Then, in review phase II, all remaining articles were read in full and assessed for relevance. Here, we defined an article to be relevant if its primary focus is OBPM or an intersection of BPM and OBPM. Also, due to funding constraints, the article had to be publically available. Based on these review phases, we identified 47 works as relevant. For the works selected to be relevant, we performed a backward- and forward-search (by references), as suggested in [18]. This resulted in 4 additional identified works. To summarize, we identified 51 (47 keyword-based + 4 f/b) relevant works. In the following, we assess these works in regard to our proposed requirements.

3.2 Literature Analysis

Table 1 shows which of the raised requirements R1–R7 is satisfied (x), resp. partially satisfied (o), by the identified relevant works[2].

Table 1. Support of the considered works w.r.t. the identified requirements for implementing OBPM (x = satisfied; o = partially satisfied; m = manual).

Work	R1	R2	R3	R4	R5	R6	R7
Lin et al. (2005)			o		o		
Thomas et al. (2005)			o		o		
Lautenbacher et al. (2006)			o		o		
Ma et al. (2006)			o		o		
Barjis et al. (2007)					x		
Born et al. (2007)		x	x				
Ehrig et al. (2007)			o				
Höfferer et al. (2007)			x				
Sujanto et al. (2008)					x		
Cabral et al. (2009)			o		o		
Di Franc. et al. (2009)			x				
Fengel et al. (2009)	x		x				
Hinge et al. (2009)			o				
Markovic et al. (2009)					x		
Norton et al. (2009)			o				
Thomas et al. (2009)			o/m		x		
Barnickel et al. (2010)			m		x		
Hua et al. (2010)					o	o	
Tan et al. (2010)			o		o	o	
Benaben et al. (2011)					x		
Fellmann et al. (2011)			o/m		x		
Fellmann et al. (2011)					x	x	
Kim et al. (2011)			o		o		
Gong et al. (2012)				x			
Stolfa et al. (2012)			o				
Fill et al. (2013)			o				

Work	R1	R2	R3	R4	R5	R6	R7
Kherbouche et al. (2013)					o	o	
De Cesare et al. (2014)	x						
Maalouf et al. (2014)			o		o	o	
Rospocher et al. (2014)			o			o	
Wang et al. (2014)			o			o	
Di Martino et al. (2015)						x	
Kalogeraki et al. (2015)						x	
Leopold et al. (2015)			x	o			
Ngo et al. (2015)			o		o	o	
Fan et al. (2016)		x	o	x		o	x
Pham et al. (2016)						x	
Corea et al. (2017)						x	
Effendi et al. (2017)						x	
Elstermann et al. (2017)			o			o	
Fauzan et al. (2017)			x			x	
Gailly et al. (2017)					x		
Hassen et al. (2017)			m			x	
Pawelozek et al. (2017)			m			x	
Riehle et al. (2017)		x	x				
Soltysik et al. (2017)			m			x	
Sungoko et al. (2017)				x	x		
Bartolini et al. (2019)			o			x	
Wang et al. (2019)			o/m			o	
Yanuarifiani et al. (2019)			o			o	
Cao et al. (2021)	x						

---

[2] Due to space limitations, the references from Table 1 can be found in the supplementary material: https://arxiv.org/abs/2107.06146.

For the identified works, the level of research in regard to 5 out of the 7 raised requirements is alarmingly low (R1, R2, R4, R5, R7). Also, regarding R3, many of the works only partially satisfy this requirement due to different limitations (cf. the below discussion). In result, we see the following research gaps:

- **Insufficient ontology support.** Virtually all approaches assume "ready-to-go" ontologies, placing a heavy burden on companies. Here, novel approaches are needed that integrate ontology creation in the OBPM-lifecycle.
- **Limitations in annotation support.** For creating semantic annotations, we can identify three main approaches from the identified literature, namely *manual annotation (m), transformation (o)*, and *matching*. For manual annotation, while we agree that this could be used for revision or fine-tuning, a completely manual annotation of process models must be considered as unfeasible, as this forces modelers to compare thousands of elements and map their relations manually [13]. For annotation through transformation, a major limitation of this approach is that the annotations are on a pure syntactical level, i.e., process model elements are instantiated as an instance of their type, however, the "real-life" semantics of the process activities cannot be captured. Therefore, approaches are needed that match semantically equivalent model and ontology elements. Regarding this line of approaches, while see some results based on terminological matching, we see a strong lack of works integrating other matching techniques, e.g., constraint-based matching, graph-based matching, instance (data) based matching, model based matching or incorporating context information in matching (cf. e.g. the classification of matching techniques in [12]). Here, more comparative studies are needed to facilitate better automated annotation. Also, machine-learning approaches are needed that can mimic human annotations.
- **Missing verification support.** As motivated in Sect. 2, a terminological matching between process model elements and ontology elements without considering their contexts can lead to the resulting ontology-based process model being inconsistent or implausible. Yet, the majority of annotation approaches via matching implement such an annotation based on linguistic mapping. While this raises strong demand for annotation verification, we see from Table 1 that there is currently no sufficient support for verifying consistency process model and the ontology. Here, novel approaches are needed for analyzing and resolving inconsistencies in ontology-based process models.
- **Missing evolution support.** Current works for annotations are mainly geared towards an *initialization* of an ontology-based process model. However, as ontologies or the process models may need to be evolved over time, the other corresponding artifact also needs to be altered in a synchronized manner. Here, new methods are needed that can support companies in model evolution. Otherwise, there is no sufficient support for sustainable OBPM.
- **Missing studies with human participants.** As a major warning-sign, we found almost no studies investigating the use of OBPM with human participants. Therefore, the effects for workers of introducing OBPM are unclear, e.g., do ontology-based process modelling really improve understanding and

efficiency, or are they too complicated to use? Such experimental research should urgently be conducted.

4 Research Agenda

Based on our literature analysis, it seems that much research is still needed to implement the requirements R1–R7 identified in this work. Based on the identified research gaps, we therefore propose the following research agenda to guide future research and leverage the implementation of OBPM, shown in Table 2.

Table 2. Proposed research agenda

Research gap	Research needed
Ontology support	• Integrating ontology creation in the OBPM-lifecycle • Ontology mining (e.g. from data, textual descriptions) • Recommendations during ontology-modelling
Annotation support	• Improving mapping approaches, e.g., with novel matching techniques (cf. the classification in [12]) and novel similarity measures • Combining matching techniques to leverage matching • In case of repositories of ontology-based process models: Identify similarities of models in order to recommend annotations, e.g. via collaborative filtering, cf. [1] • Creating AI systems that can learn/mimic human annotations • Consideration of context information for annotation suggestions (e.g. preceding and succeeding elements, granularity of surrounding model contents, general topic of the model, industry-specific process knowledge) • For evaluating matching techniques: Evaluation based on probabilistic gold standards [10] (i.e. averaged over multiple users), to avoid bias of the creator of the gold standard
Annotation verification	• Identifying incoherent or implausible mappings between process models and ontologies • Analyzing inconsistencies or pin-pointing highly problematic elements, e.g. by means of element-based inconsistency measures • Means for resolving inconsistencies, e.g. in the scope of systems for semi-automated/guided inconsistency resolution
Evolution support	• Support of change propagation during modelling, e.g., automatedly synchronizing process model and ontology if an element is deleted in one of the two artifacts • Using ontology-based reasoning and insights from process monitoring to recommend changes needed in the process models or ontologies • Leveraging insights from process monitoring to recommend changes needed for the company ontology • Means for long-term model management, e.g. versioning
Contextual fit/people	• Evaluation of approaches and tools for OBPM with human participants, i.e., do all the studied results really offer competitive advantages, for example in the form of increased efficiency, understanding accuracy or reduced cognitive load • Guidelines for the design of OBPM tools and interfaces • More research on how OBPM affects people and company culture
Other	• Maturity models and procedure models for guiding companies in adopting OBPM • Success stories/case studies to share knowledge and leverage OBPM adoption • OBPM lifecycle models, e.g., how to integrate insights from process monitoring and ontology-based reasoning to improve process models and ontologies • Monitoring process execution for ontology-based process execution

The distilled agenda identifies technical challenges that need to be addressed in regard to implementing OBPM, e.g., in the areas of *ontology-support, annotation support, annotation verification* and *evolution support*. Furthermore, research investigating the *contextual fit* of OBPM is much needed, e.g., how can OBPM results be aligned with the skill sets of the involved stakeholders and does OBPM really offer positive cognitive effects for humans, such as better understanding efficiency?

5   Conclusion

So, OBPM: will we live to see it? As a main takeaway, while the primary focus in research has been on R6 (ontology-based reasoning, cf. Sect. 3), the proposed requirements show that there are many more components still needed for implementing OBPM, especially in regard to initializing and evolving models. To this aim, our distilled research agenda provides a guideline for developing these needed results, and – on a positive note – shows that the field of OBPM offers many opportunities for future research. If we would have to propose one "paradigm change", we would opt for less works such as "yet another approach for using ontology-based process models" and more awareness for the initial creation and long-term management of ontology-based process models themselves. Also, the number of works that investigate the actual cognitive effects and usability of process models is alarmingly low, which urgently has to be addressed to ensure that academic results and company use cases are aligned. Should these requirements be met, OBPM can and will be successfully implemented.

We identify the following limitations. First, this review was limited to ontologies formalized with description logics. While this is an important fragment of OBPM, further works could also investigate the role of foundational ontologies in regard to OBPM. Second, the requirements identified in this work were derived from a design science perspective, i.e., they are requirements needed for an initial implementation. While we could already use these initial requirements to show limitations in the state of the art, these requirements were not further evaluated. In future works, we will therefore evaluate these requirements with domain experts. Last, this work investigates the state of the art of scientific contributions. In future work, we will further investigate industrial applications and solutions and consolidate them with the findings of this work.

Acknowledgements. We thank Hagen Kerber for his preliminary research for this report. We also thank Tosatto and colleagues for letting us borrow their title idea [16].

References

1. Chan, N.N., Gaaloul, W., Tata, S.: Assisting business process design by activity neighborhood context matching. In: Liu, C., Ludwig, H., Toumani, F., Yu, Q. (eds.) ICSOC 2012. LNCS, vol. 7636, pp. 541–549. Springer, Heidelberg (2012). https://doi.org/10.1007/978-3-642-34321-6_38

2. Colquhoun, H.L., et al.: Scoping reviews: time for clarity in definition, methods, and reporting. J. Clin. Epidemiol. **67**(12), 1291–1294 (2014)
3. Corea, C., Delfmann, P.: Detecting compliance with business rules in ontology based process modeling. In: Proceedings of the WI 2017. University of St. Gallen (2017)
4. Di Francescomarino, C., Tonella, P.: Supporting ontology-based semantic annotation of business processes with automated suggestions. In: Halpin, T., et al. (eds.) BPMDS/EMMSAD -2009. LNBIP, vol. 29, pp. 211–223. Springer, Heidelberg (2009). https://doi.org/10.1007/978-3-642-01862-6_18
5. Fellmann, M., Delfmann, P., Koschmider, A., Laue, R., Leopold, H., Schoknecht, A.: Semantic technology in business process modeling and analysis. Part 1: Matching, modeling support, correctness and compliance. In: EMISA Forum 2015 (2015)
6. Fellmann, M., Hogrebe, F., Thomas, O., Nüttgens, M.: Checking the semantic correctness of process models-an ontology-driven approach using domain knowledge and rules. Enterp. Model. Inf. Syst. Archit **6**(3), 25–35 (2011)
7. Gailly, F., Alkhaldi, N., Casteleyn, S., Verbeke, W.: Recommendation-based conceptual modeling and ontology evolution framework. Bus. Inf. Syst. Eng. **59**(4), 235–250 (2017). https://doi.org/10.1007/s12599-017-0488-y
8. Hassen, M.B., Turki, M., Gargouri, F.: Using core ontologies for extending sensitive BPM with the knowledge perspective. In: Proceedings of the ECBS. ACM (2017)
9. Leopold, H., Meilicke, C., Fellmann, M., Pittke, F., Stuckenschmidt, H., Mendling, J.: Towards the automated annotation of process models. In: Zdravkovic, J., Kirikova, M., Johannesson, P. (eds.) CAiSE 2015. LNCS, vol. 9097, pp. 401–416. Springer, Cham (2015). https://doi.org/10.1007/978-3-319-19069-3_25
10. Leopold, H., Niepert, M., Weidlich, M., Mendling, J., Dijkman, R., Stuckenschmidt, H.: Probabilistic optimization of semantic process model matching. In: Barros, A., Gal, A., Kindler, E. (eds.) BPM 2012. LNCS, vol. 7481, pp. 319–334. Springer, Heidelberg (2012). https://doi.org/10.1007/978-3-642-32885-5_25
11. Meilicke, C., Stuckenschmidt, H.: Incoherence as a basis for measuring the quality of ontology mappings. In: Proceedings of the International Workshop on Ontology Matching (OM) Collocated with ISWC (2008)
12. Otero-Cerdeira, L., Rodríguez-Martínez, F.J., Gómez-Rodríguez, A.: Ontology matching: a literature review. Expert Syst. Appl. **42**(2), 949–971 (2015)
13. Riehle, D.M., Jannaber, S., Delfmann, P., Thomas, O., Becker, J.: Automatically annotating business process models with ontology concepts at design-time. In: de Cesare, S., Frank, U. (eds.) ER 2017. LNCS, vol. 10651, pp. 177–186. Springer, Cham (2017). https://doi.org/10.1007/978-3-319-70625-2_17
14. Rowley, J., Slack, F.: Conducting a literature review. Management Research (2004)
15. Thomas, O., Fellmann, M.: Design and implementation of an ontology-based representation of business processes. Bus. IS Eng. **1**(6), 438–451 (2009)
16. Colombo Tosatto, S., Governatori, G., van Beest, N.: Checking regulatory compliance: will we live to see it? In: Hildebrandt, T., van Dongen, B.F., Röglinger, M., Mendling, J. (eds.) BPM 2019. LNCS, vol. 11675, pp. 119–138. Springer, Cham (2019). https://doi.org/10.1007/978-3-030-26619-6_10
17. Vom Brocke, J., Simons, A., Riemer, K., Niehaves, B., Plattfaut, R., Cleven, A.: Standing on the shoulders of giants: challenges and recommendations of literature search in information systems research. Commun. Assoc. Inf. Syst. **37**(1), 9 (2015)
18. Webster, J., Watson, R.: Analyzing the past to prepare for the future: writing a literature review. MIS Q. **26**, xiii–xxiii (2002)

19. Weske, M.: Business process management architectures. In: Business Process Management. Springer, Heidelberg (2007). https://doi.org/10.1007/978-3-540-73522-9_7
20. Wetzstein, B., et al.: Semantic business process management: a lifecycle based requirements analysis. In: Proceedings of the SBPM 2017. Citeseer (2007)

Process Model Forecasting Using Time Series Analysis of Event Sequence Data

Johannes De Smedt[1]([✉])[iD], Anton Yeshchenko[2][iD], Artem Polyvyanyy[3][iD],
Jochen De Weerdt[1][iD], and Jan Mendling[4][iD]

[1] KU Leuven, Leuven, Belgium
{johannes.desmedt,jochen.deweerdt}@kuleuven.be
[2] Vienna University of Economics and Business, Vienna, Austria
anton.yeshchenko@wu.ac.at
[3] The University of Melbourne, Melbourne, Australia
artem.polyvyanyy@unimelb.edu.au
[4] Humboldt-Universität zu Berlin, Berlin, Germany
jan.mendling@wu.ac.at, jan.mendling@hu-berlin.de

Abstract. Process analytics is an umbrella of data-driven techniques which includes making predictions for individual process instances or overall process models. At the instance level, various novel techniques have been recently devised, tackling next activity, remaining time, and outcome prediction. At the model level, there is a notable void. It is the ambition of this paper to fill this gap. To this end, we develop a technique to forecast the entire process model from historical event data. A forecasted model is a will-be process model representing a probable future state of the overall process. Such a forecast helps to investigate the consequences of drift and emerging bottlenecks. Our technique builds on a representation of event data as multiple time series, each capturing the evolution of a behavioural aspect of the process model, such that corresponding forecasting techniques can be applied. Our implementation demonstrates the accuracy of our technique on real-world event log data.

Keywords: Process model forecasting · Predictive process modelling · Process mining · Time series analysis

1 Introduction

Process analytics is an area of process mining [1] which encompasses Predictive Process Monitoring (PPM) aimed at making predictions for individual process instances or overall process models. At the instance level, various novel PPM techniques have been recently devised, tackling problems such as next activity, remaining cycle time, or other outcome predictions [6]. These techniques make use of neural networks [26], stochastic Petri nets [23], and general classification techniques [27].

© Springer Nature Switzerland AG 2021
A. Ghose et al. (Eds.): ER 2021, LNCS 13011, pp. 47–61, 2021.
https://doi.org/10.1007/978-3-030-89022-3_5

At the model level, there is a notable void. Many analytical tasks require not only an understanding of the current as-is, but also the anticipated will-be process model. A key challenge in this context is the consideration of evolution as processes are known to be subject to drift [15,20,31,32]. A forecast can then inform the process analyst how the will-be process model might differ from the current as-is if no measures are taken, e.g., against emerging bottlenecks.

This paper presents the first technique to forecast whole process models. To this end, we develop a technique that builds on a representation of event data as multiple time series. Each of these time series captures the evolution of a behavioural aspect of the process model in the form of directly-follows relations (DFs), such that corresponding forecasting techniques can be applied for directly-follows graphs (DFGs). Our implementation on six real-life event logs demonstrates that forecasted models with medium-sized alphabets (10–30 activities) obtain below 15% mean average percentage error in terms of conformance. Furthermore, we introduce the Process Change Exploration (PCE) system which allows to visualise past and present models from event logs and compare them with forecasted models.

This paper is structured as follows. Section 2 discusses related work and motivates our work. Section 3 specifies our process model forecasting technique together with the PCE visualisation environment. Section 4 describes our evaluation, before Sect. 5 concludes the paper.

2   Related Work and Motivation

Within the field of process mining, research on and use of predictive modelling techniques has attracted plenty of attention in the last five years. PPM techniques are usually developed with a specific purpose in mind, ranging from next activity prediction [5,26], over remaining time prediction [29], to outcome prediction [11]. For a systematic literature review of the field, we refer to [18]. Beyond the PPM field, this work is related to previous research on stage-based process mining [19], in which a technique is presented to decompose an event log into stages, and work on the detection of time granularity in event logs [22].

The shift from fine-granular PPM techniques, including next activity, remaining time, and outcome prediction, to model-based prediction, allows to obtain new insights into the global development of the process. Consider the example in Fig. 1 where the road fine traffic management event log is partitioned into 100 intervals in which an equal number of DF relations occur. The DFs in the first 50 intervals are used to predict the next 25 intervals. The DFGs show how process model forecasting and change exploration can provide multiple unique insights at a glance:

1. Compared to the initial 50 intervals the proportion of fines sent decreases in the later intervals;
2. The proportion of penalties remains comparable between the first 50 and next 25 time intervals;

3. The number of occurrences and arc weights between *Create Fine* and *Send Fine* are forecasted with reasonable error (±15%);
4. The arc weights of the ending activities are predicted with reasonable error (±15%).

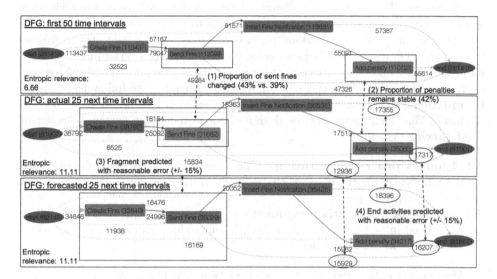

Fig. 1. Directly-follows graphs of the 50 first intervals of the event log, as well as a forecasted and actual DFG of the 25 next intervals.

These results provide insight both in terms of the past and present model, see items (1)–(2), and the quality of forecasts between the actual and forecasted model, (3)–(4). Being able to construct such forecasts allows stakeholders to make estimates regarding how the overall fine system will evolve and allows to answer questions such as "How many more fines will be received?", "Will the backlog of fines be reduced?", "Will all fines be paid", and "Will the ratio of unpaid fines stay the same?" This motivating example shows that, where process mining focuses on learning the as-is model to reason about trajectories of future cases and suggest potential repairs and improvements, process model forecasting allows to grasp the future stage of the overall process model in terms of a will-be model.

A suitable means to evaluate the forecasts quantitatively is entropic relevance [21]. This measure captures the quality of the discovered and forecasted DFGs with respect to the event logs they represent. Entropic relevance penalises the discrepancies in the relative frequencies of traces recorded in the log and described by the DFG as it stands for the average number of bits used to encode a log trace using the DFG, with small values being preferable to large ones. If the entropic relevance of the forecasted DFG and the actual future DFG with respect to the test log is the same, then both DFGs represent the future behaviour similarly well. The entropic relevance of the historical DFG derived from the training log with respect to the testing log is 6.66 as indicated in Fig. 1, suggesting that the future behaviour shifts and the historical DFG still represents the behaviour in the log better than both the actual and forecasted DFGs which sit at an entropic relevance of 11.11.

Measurement values are not enough to fully reveal the change of behaviour to the analyst. To this end, we complement the model-level prediction technique with a visualisation system to enable analysts to understand the forthcoming changes to the processes. Various process analysis tasks benefit from process forecasting [20]; most notably process forecasting helps understanding the incremental changes and adaptations that happen to the process model and to project them into the future. In terms of visualisation principles, we follow the "Visual Information-Seeking Mantra": *overview first, zoom and filter, then details-on-demand* [25]. Thus, we expect the design of our visualisation system to assist in the following tasks:

T1. Identify process adaptations: The visualisation system should assist the user in identifying the changes that happen in the process model of the future in respect to the past;

T2. Allow for interactive exploration: The user should be able to follow the visual information-seeking principles, including overview first, filtering, zooming, and details-on-demand.

Forecasting entire process models provides a new perspective on predictive process monitoring. The forecast horizon is substantially longer as compared to what existing next-activity prediction models can achieve. Moreover, where next activity and related PPM techniques have a strong case-level focus, a forecast at the model level provides a more comprehensive picture of the future development of the process.

3   Process Model Forecasting

This section outlines how time series of directly-follows relationships are extracted from event logs as well as how they are used to obtain process model forecasts with a range of widely-used forecasting techniques. Finally, the visualisation of such forecasts is introduced.

3.1   From Event Log to Directly-Follows Time Series

An event log L contains the recording of traces $\sigma \in L$ which are sequences of events produced by an information system during its execution. A trace $\sigma = \langle e_1, ..., e_{|\sigma|} \rangle \in \Sigma^*$ is a finite sequence over the alphabet of activities Σ which serves as the set of event types. Directly-follows relations between activities in an event log can be expressed as counting functions over activity pairs $>_L: \Sigma \times \Sigma \to \mathbb{N}$ so $>_L (a_1, a_2)$ counts the number of times activity a_1 is immediately followed by activity a_2 in the event log L. Directly-follows relations can be calculated over all traces or a subset of subtraces of the log. Finally, a Directly-Follows Graph (DFG) of the process then is the weighted directed graph with the activities as nodes and DF relations as weighted edges, i.e., $DFG = (\Sigma, >_L)$.

In order to obtain forecasts regarding the evolution of the DFG we construct DFGs for subsets of the log. Many aggregations and bucketing techniques exist for next-step, performance, and goal-oriented outcome prediction [19,26,27], e.g., predictions at a point in the process rely on prefixes of a certain length, or particular state aggregations [3]. In the forecasting approach proposed here, we integrate concepts from time-series analysis. Hence, the evolution of the DFGs is monitored over intervals of the log where multiple aggregations are possible:

- **Equitemporal aggregation:** each sublog $L_s \in L$ of interval s contains a part of the event log of some fixed time duration. This can lead to sparsely populated sublogs when the events' occurrences are not uniformly spread over time; however, it is easy to apply on new traces.
- **Equisized aggregation:** each sublog $L_s \in L$ of interval s contains a part of the event log where an equal amount of DF pairs occurred which leads to well-populated sublogs when enough events are available.

Tables 1 and 2 exemplify the aggregations. These aggregations are useful for the following reasons. First, an equisized aggregation, in general, has a higher likelihood of the underlying DFs approaching a white noise time series which is required for a wide range of time series forecasting techniques [9]. Second, both offer different thresholds at which forecasting can be applied. In the case of the equisized aggregation, it is easier to quickly construct a desired number of intervals by simply dividing an event log into the equisized intervals. However, most time series forecasting techniques rely on the time intervals being of equal duration which is embodied into the equitemporal aggregation [10]. Time series for the DFs $>_{T_{a_1,a_2}} = \langle >_{L_1} (a_1, a_2), \ldots, >_{L_s} (a_1, a_2) \rangle, \forall a_1, a_2 \in \Sigma \times \Sigma$ can be obtained for all activity pairs where $\bigcup_{L_1}^{L_s} = L$ by applying the aforementioned aggregations to obtain the sublogs for the intervals.

3.2 From DF Time Series to Process Model Forecasts

The goal of process model forecasting is to obtain a forecast for future DFGs by combining the forecasts of all the DF time series. To this purpose, we propose to use time series techniques to forecast the DFG at time $T + h$ given time series up until T $\widehat{DFG}_{T+h} = (\Sigma, \{\hat{>}_{T+h|T_{a_1,a_2}} | a_1, a_2 \in \Sigma \times \Sigma\})$ for which various algorithms can be used. In time series modelling, the main objective is to obtain a forecast $\hat{y}_{T+h|T}$ for a horizon $h \in \mathbb{N}$ based on previous T values in the series $(y_1, \ldots, y_T)$ [9]. For example, the naive forecast simply uses the last value of the time series T as its forecast $\hat{y}_{T+h|T} = y_T$. An alternative naive forecast uses the average value of the time series T as its forecast $\hat{y}_{T+h|T} = \frac{1}{T}\Sigma_i^T y_i$.

A trade-off exists between approaching DFGs as a multivariate collection of DF time series, or treating each DF separately. Traditional time series techniques use univariate data in contrast with multivariate approaches such as Vector AutoRegression (VAR) models, and machine learning-based methods such as neural networks or random forest regressors. Despite their simple setup, it is debated whether machine learning methods necessarily outperform traditional statistical approaches. The study in [16] found that this is not the case on a large number of datasets and the authors note that machine learning algorithms require significantly more computational power. This result was later reaffirmed, although it is noted that hybrid solutions are effective [17]. For longer horizons, traditional time series approaches still outperform machine learning-based models. Given the potentially high number of DF pairs in a DFG, the proposed approach uses a time series algorithm for each DF series separately. VAR models would require a high number of intervals (at least as many as there are DFs times the lag coefficient) to estimate all parameters of all the time series despite their potentially strong performance [28]. Machine learning models could potentially leverage interrelations between the different DFs but again would require training set way larger than typically available for process mining to account for dimensionality issues due to the potentially high number of DFs. Therefore, in this paper, traditional time series approaches are chosen and applied to the univariate DF time series, with at least one observation per sublog/time interval present.

Autoregressive, moving averages, ARIMA, and varying variance models make up the main families of traditional time series forecasting techniques [9]. In addition, a wide array of other forecasting techniques exist, ranging from simple models such as naive forecasts over to more advanced approaches such as exponential smoothing and auto-regressive models. Many also exist in a seasonal variant due to their application in contexts such as sales forecasting.

The Simple Exponential Smoothing (SES) model uses a weighted average of past values whose importance exponentially decays as they are further into the past, where the Holt's models introduce a trend in the forecast, meaning the forecast is not 'flat'. Exponential smoothing models often perform very well despite their simple setup [16]. AutoRegressive Integrating Moving Average (ARIMA) models are based on auto-correlations within time series. They com-

Table 1. Example event log with 3 traces and 2 activities.

Case ID	Activity	Timestamp
1	a_1	11:30
1	a_2	11:45
1	a_1	12:10
1	a_2	12:15
2	a_1	11:40
2	a_1	11:55
3	a_1	12:20
3	a_2	12:40
3	a_2	12:45

Table 2. An example of using an interval of 3 used for equitemporal aggregation (75 min in 3 intervals of 25 min) and equisized intervals of size 2 (6 DFs over 3 intervals)).

DF	Equitemporal	Equisized
$<_{Ls} (a_1, a_1)$	(0,1,0)	(1,0,0)
$<_{Ls} (a_1, a_2)$	(1,1,1)	(1,1,1)
$<_{Ls} (a_2, a_1)$	(0,1,0)	(0,1,0)
$<_{Ls} (a_2, a_2)$	(0,0,1)	(0,0,1)

bine auto-regressions with a moving average over error terms. It is established by a combination of an AutoRegressive (AR) model of order p to use the past p values in the time series and to apply a regression over them and a Moving Average (MA) model of order q to create a moving average of the past forecast errors. Given the necessity of using a white noise series for AR and MA models, data is often differenced to obtain such series [9]. ARIMA models then combine both AR and MA models where the integration occurs after modelling, as these models are fitted over differenced time series. ARIMA models are considered to be one of the strongest time series modelling techniques [9]. An extension to ARIMA, which is widely used in econometrics, are the (Generalized) AutoRegressive Conditional Heteroskedasticity ((G)ARCH) models [7]. These models relax the assumption that the variance of the error term has to be constant over time, and rather model this variance as a function of the previous error term. For AR-models, this leads to the use of ARCH-models, while for ARMA models GARCH-models are used as follows. An ARCH(q) model captures the change in variance by allowing it to gradually increase over time or to allow for short bursts of increased variance. A GARCH(p,q) model combines both the past values of observations and the past values of variance. (G)ARCH models often outperform ARIMA models in contexts such as the forecast of financial indicators, in which the variance often changes over time [7].

In general, we can regard linear SES models as a subset of ARIMA models, where (G)ARCH models are specializations of ARIMA models that can be regarded as increasingly complex and better capable of modelling particular intricacies in the time series. However, the success of different models for forecasting purposes does not depend on their complexity, and the most suitable technique is mainly determined by performance on training and test sets.

3.3 Process Change Exploration

In Sects. 3.1 and 3.2 we described the approach for forecasting process models. To that end, gaining actual insights from such forecasted values remains a difficult task for the analyst. This section sets off to present the design of a novel visualisation system to aid analysts in the exploration of the event logs and their corresponding (forecasted) discovered process models.

Following the user tasks T1 and T2 from Sect. 2, we designed a Process Change Exploration (PCE) system to support the interpretation of the process model forecasts. PCE is an interactive visualisation system that consists of three connected views.

Adaptation Directly-Follows Graph (aDFG) View. This is the main view of the visualisation that will show the model of the process. In order to accomplish task T1, we modify the DFG syntax. To display the process model adaptation from time range $T_{i_0} - T_{j_0}, i_0 < j_0$, to $T_{i_1} - T_{j_1}, i_1 < j_1$, we display the union of the process models of these regions, annotating the nodes and edges with the numbers of both ranges. We colour the aDFG as follows: we use colour saturation to show the nodes with higher values. We colour edges with a diverging saturation (red-black-green) schema. This colouring applies red colour to edges that are dominant in the $T_{i_0} - T_{j_0}$ range, and green if edges are dominant in the $T_{i_1} - T_{j_1}$ range, otherwise the edge colour is close to black. For coloring edges, we reused the idea of the three colour schema from [12].

Timeline View with Brushed Regions. This view represents the area chart graph that shows how the number of activity executions changes with time. The colour of the area chart is split into two parts, one for the actual data and the other to show the time range of forecasted values. Analysts can brush one region in order to zoom in, creating one region of interest $T_{i_0}, - T_{j_0}, i_0 < j_0$ that is displayed on the DFG. Analysts can also brush two regions of the area chart to select two time ranges, updating the DFG to the aDFG representation. The brushed regions are coloured accordingly to the schema for colouring aDFG transitions. The earlier brushed region is coloured in red, while the second one is coloured green.

Activity and Path Sliders. We adopt two sliders to simplify the DFG [13] and the aDFG for detailed exploration of the models.

Based on the described views, we conjecture that the analyst can accomplish tasks T1 and T2 with ease.

4   Implementation and Evaluation

In this section, an experimental evaluation over six real-life event logs is reported. The aim of the evaluation is to measure to what extent the forecasted DFG process models are capable of correctly reproducing actual future DFGs in terms of allowing for the same process model behaviour. To this end, we benchmark the actual against the forecasted entropic relevance, as discussed in Sect. 2. This is done for various parts of the log, i.e. forecasts for the middle time spans of the event logs up to the later parts of the event log to capture the robustness of the forecasting techniques in terms of the amount of data required to obtain good results for both the equisized and equitemporal aggregation.

4.1   Re-sampling and Test Setup

To obtain training data, time series are constructed by specifying the number of intervals (i.e., time steps in the DF time series) using either equitemporal or equisized aggregation, as described in Sect. 3.1. Time series algorithms are parametric and sensitive to sample size requirements [8]. Depending on the number of parameters a model uses, a minimum size of at least 50 steps is not uncommon. However, typically, model performance should be monitored at a varying number of steps. In the experimental evaluation, the event logs are divided into 100 time intervals with a varying share of training and test intervals. A constant and long horizon $h = 25$ is used meaning all test sets contain 25 intervals, but the training sets are varied from $ts = 25$ to $ts = 75$ intervals; the forecasts progressively target the forecast of intervals 25–50 (the second quarter of intervals) over to 75–100 (the last quarter of intervals). This allows us to inspect the difference in results when only a few data points are used, or data points in the middle or towards the end of the available event data are used.

Resampling is applied based on 10-fold cross-validation constructed following a rolling window approach for all horizon values $h \in [1, 25]$ where a recursive strategy is used to iteratively obtain $\hat{y}_{t+h|T_{t+h-1}}$ with $(y_1, \ldots, y_T, \ldots, \hat{y}_{t+h-1})$ [30]. Ten training sets are hence constructed for each training set length ts and range from $(y_1, \ldots, y_{T-h-f})$ and the test sets from $(y_{T-h-f+1}, \ldots, y_{T-f})$ with $f \in [0, 9]$ the fold index [4]. While direct strategies with a separate model for every value of h can be used as well and avoid the accumulation of error, they do not take into account statistical dependencies for subsequent forecasts.

Six often-used, publicly available event logs are used: the BPI challenge of 2012 log, 2017, and 2018, the Sepsis cases event, an Italian help desk, and the Road Traffic Fine Management Process log (RTFMP) event log. Each of these logs has a diverse set of characteristics in terms of case and activity volume and average trace length, as shown in Table 3.

Table 3. Overview of the characteristics of the event logs used in the evaluation.

Event log	# cases	# activities	Average trace length
BPI 12	13,087	36	20.02
BPI 17	31,509	26	36.83
BPI 18	43,809	170	57.39
Sepsis	1,050	16	14.49
RTFMP	150,370	11	3.73
Italian	4,580	14	4.66

There are a few considerations concerning the DF time series in these event logs. Firstly, DFs of activity pairs containing endpoint activities (i.e. at the start/end of a trace) often only contain meaningful numbers at very particular parts of the series and are hard to process by longitudinal algorithms which require a more extended pattern to extract a meaningful pattern for foresting. Secondly, the equitemporal aggregation can suffer from event logs in which events do not occur frequently throughout the complete log's timespan. For instance, the Sepsis log's number of event occurrences tails off towards the end which can be alleviated by pre-processing (not done here to remain consistent over the event logs). Finally, suppose the level of occurrences of the DF pairs is low and close to zero. In that case, the series might be too unsuitable for analysis using white noise series analysis techniques that assume stationarity. Ideally, every time series should be evaluated using a stationarity test such as the Dickey-Fuller unit root test [14], and an appropriate lag order established for differencing to ensure a white noise process is used for training. Furthermore, for each algorithm, especially for ARIMA-based models, (partial) auto-correlation has to be established to obtain the ideal p and q parameters. However, for the sake of simplicity and to avoid solutions where each activity pair has to have different parameters, various values are used for p, d, and q and applied to all DF pairs where only the best-performing are reported below for comparison with the other time series techniques. The results contain the best-performing representative of each forecasting family.

4.2   Results

All pre-processing was done in Python with a combination of $pm4py^1$ and the *statsmodels* package [24]. The code is publicly available.[2]

To get a grasp of the forecasting performance in combination with the actual use of DFGs (which are rarely used in their non-aggregated form [2]) we present the mean absolute percentage error (MAPE) between the entropic relevance of the actual and forecasted DFGs at both full size, at 50%, and 75% reduction which is node-based (i.e. only the Q2/Q3 percentile of nodes in terms of frequency is retained). Hence, we obtain a measure of accuracy in terms of the discrepancy of the actual and forecasted model behaviour. Using different levels of aggregation also balances recall and precision, as aggregated DFGs are less precise but possibly less overfitting. The results can be found in Tables 4, 5 and 6. NAs are reported when the algorithms did not converge, no data was available (e.g. Sepsis for the 75–100 equitemporal intervals), or extremely high values were forecasted.

When no reduction is applied, Table 4 shows that for the BPI12 and BPI17 logs, a below 10% error can be achieved, primarily for equisized aggregation. For the Italian help desk log, results are in the 10–37% bracket, while for the other logs, results are often well above a 100% deviation (with the entropic relevance of the actual DFGs being lower, hence better, than the entropic relevance of the forecasted DFGs). However, for the RTFMP and BPI18 log, results are better when more training points are used (e.g., 50 or 75 to obtain forecasts for the 50–75 and 75–100 intervals). There is no significant difference between equisized and equitemporal aggregation except for the occasional outliers. Overall, the percentage error is lower in Table 5 when a reduction of 50% is applied with sub-10% results for the BPI12, Sepsis, and BPI17 logs. The results for the RTFMP log are occasionally better but mostly worse, similar to BPI18. Finally, the results in Table 6 show a further reduction of errors for the BPI12, Sepsis, BPI17, and Italian logs and a drastic decrease to close to 0% for RTFMP. The results for the BPI18 log remain bad at over 100% error rates.

These results are commensurate with the findings in [21], which contains entropic relevance results for the BPI12, Sepsis, and RTFMP logs, indicating that entropic relevance of larger DFGs is lower (better) for RTFMP/Sespsis, and the entropic relevance goes up strongly for small models of RTFMP meaning the drastically improved error rates reported here are for models performing worse in terms of recall and precision. The entropic relevance for the BPI12 log is stable for the full spectrum of DFG sizes as per [21], which is reflected in the consistently

---

[1] https://pm4py.fit.fraunhofer.de.
[2] https://github.com/JohannesDeSmedt/pmf.

good error rates presented here. This means that the low error rates reported are produced by the reduced DFGs, which still score strongly in terms of recall and precision. Matching all results to the event log characteristics, we notice that the event logs with longer traces with medium-sized alphabets (>20) such as BPI12 and BPI17 consistently report good results. The BPI18 log's high number of activities seems to inflate error rates quickly, which is further aggravated when DFGs are reduced. Given that DFGs are based on activity pairs, this result is not surprising. For Sepsis and the Italian event logs, good error rates are obtained once DFGs are reduced, indicating that forecasting the low-frequent edges and activities might lead to high error rates when the alphabet is smaller and traces are shorter, which is potentially also caused by the lack of precision as witnessed with the RTFMP log.

Overall, there exist many scenarios in which process model forecasting is delivering solid results. For the BPI12, BPI17, Italian, and Sepsis event logs, sub-10% error rates can be achieved both for equisized and equitemporal aggregation combined with model reductions which readers of DFGs typically apply. In some cases, even a naive forecast is enough to obtain a low error rate. However, the AR and ARIMA models report the best error rates in most cases. Nevertheless, results are often close except when fewer training points are used. Then, results are often varying widely. In future work, the robustness of the forecast algorithms will be further investigated, e.g., via scrutinising the confidence intervals of the forecasted DF outcomes.

Table 4. Overview of the mean percentage error in terms of entropic relevance for the full DFGs.

		BPI 12			Sepsis			RTFMP			BPI17			Italian			BPI18		
		50	75	100	50	75	100	50	75	100	50	75	100	50	75	100	50	75	100
Equisize	nav	9.74	8.56	9.82	97.09	97.40	100.76	437.14	105.81	115.34	6.86	8.80	7.00	25.93	16.52	37.71	82.10	99.90	38.41
	arima212	12.41	9.75	10.80	NA	83.31	100.58	398.66	NA	NA	10.03	8.54	13.23	24.60	9.17	39.01	82.81	NA	30.12
	ar2	NA	8.45	9.62	97.04	97.40	100.76	NA	NA	110.14	6.83	14.84	13.83	23.81	13.98	36.89	78.82	NA	NA
	hw	8.61	8.96	10.14	97.09	97.40	100.76	402.83	110.17	130.10	6.81	8.68	186.94	22.54	9.14	43.31	81.04	NA	NA
	garch	11.47	8.60	10.17	97.09	97.40	100.76	426.71	109.79	117.15	6.89	8.82	186.94	25.48	31.29	65.54	72.89	NA	28.59
Equitemp	nav	15.57	10.14	12.63	98.51	100.75	NA	199.69	29.70	36.15	7.12	8.63	13.41	27.12	26.86	39.94	NA	NA	54.57
	arima212	NA	11.67	12.00	89.07	100.39	NA	122.63	28.55	33.82	8.13	158.70	18.74	26.59	24.26	38.03	NA	42.83	NA
	ar2	NA	9.97	12.43	98.37	100.75	NA	NA	29.74	NA	7.09	NA	19.60	26.33	30.02	38.68	NA	NA	NA
	hw	13.09	10.46	12.08	98.40	100.75	NA	162.94	29.34	36.15	7.07	8.35	186.91	26.90	23.57	36.20	NA	43.02	NA
	garch	17.80	10.29	12.71	95.75	100.75	NA	199.13	30.44	36.00	7.37	187.45	186.91	27.11	45.58	55.67	NA	46.69	42.97

Table 5. Overview of the mean percentage error in terms of entropic relevance for the DFGs with a 50% reduction.

		BPI 12			Sepsis			RTFMP			BPI17			Italian			BPI18		
		50	75	100	50	75	100	50	75	100	50	75	100	50	75	100	50	75	100
Equisize	nav	4.65	5.83	11.50	8.35	8.80	6.29	234.18	295.99	203.68	7.82	9.22	11.04	23.05	14.18	21.66	252.76	231.44	160.66
	arima212	7.96	22.89	13.43	8.55	8.81	6.14	234.14	288.27	198.86	4.49	5.98	10.67	22.31	7.32	23.17	369.47	252.24	218.93
	ar2	24.53	27.58	30.81	8.54	8.72	6.30	234.57	293.10	201.21	4.27	6.08	10.22	21.26	11.91	20.56	NA	230.02	NA
	hw	45.80	38.02	13.13	8.73	8.65	6.17	233.05	151.19	111.89	4.51	5.37	11.06	20.33	7.28	26.12	391.38	280.59	226.27
	garch	26.30	23.77	48.86	8.63	8.87	7.06	231.70	295.93	203.45	4.50	9.41	11.09	23.18	29.07	45.31	315.99	234.79	217.62
Equitemp	nav	7.15	6.86	17.86	6.41	7.73	NA	75.48	36.18	86.46	5.93	7.23	30.98	24.35	18.64	26.48	NA	219.13	410.13
	arima212	49.87	10.59	19.59	4.91	8.13	NA	135.97	40.22	86.74	5.64	5.13	30.30	23.48	16.32	20.45	205.21	261.81	253.38
	ar2	21.06	7.49	18.85	7.17	8.08	NA	95.44	36.30	86.60	5.70	NA	30.97	23.67	21.71	25.44	NA	NA	443.76
	hw	7.41	7.02	17.54	6.72	10.34	NA	77.93	36.62	86.76	5.95	7.39	30.86	23.55	15.66	22.91	NA	236.37	439.04
	garch	57.44	32.85	37.98	6.76	7.85	NA	75.48	36.20	86.52	5.93	7.33	31.12	24.24	36.51	40.40	NA	283.40	492.85

4.3 Visualising Process Model Forecasts

In Sect. 4.2, we evaluated forecasting results, ensuring the conformance and inter-pretability of the predicted process models. To that end, gaining insights from such predicted data remains a difficult task for the analyst. This section sets off to present a novel visualisation system to aid analysts in exploring the event logs. The process of designing and implementing the system started by design-ing several prototypes that undergone rounds of discussions to mature into the implemented visualisation system.

Table 6. Overview of the mean percentage error in terms of entropic relevance for the DFGs with a 75% reduction.

		BPI 12			Sepsis			RTFMP			BPI17			Italian			BPI18		
		50	75	100	50	75	100	50	75	100	50	75	100	50	75	100	50	75	100
Equisize	nav	0.96	0.87	1.37	2.40	2.91	**3.47**	0.00	0.00	0.01	0.12	**0.29**	**0.14**	13.11	15.11	27.02	**247.32**	223.34	**146.27**
	arima212	0.98	**0.84**	**1.33**	**2.38**	2.85	3.65	0.00	0.00	0.01	**0.06**	0.30	0.16	13.08	14.94	26.97	346.94	236.73	211.17
	ar2	**0.86**	0.85	1.35	2.42	2.58	**3.47**	0.00	0.00	0.01	0.12	0.30	**0.14**	13.10	15.02	26.97	NA	**222.06**	NA
	hw	1.00	0.85	1.35	2.73	2.90	**3.47**	0.00	0.00	0.01	0.11	0.31	0.15	**12.98**	**14.79**	27.08	333.80	255.83	207.86
	garch	0.89	0.86	1.35	2.51	**2.49**	**3.47**	0.00	0.00	0.01	0.12	**0.29**	**0.14**	13.13	15.00	**26.89**	299.59	248.75	182.07
Equitemp	nav	4.92	3.55	4.05	**2.31**	**1.65**	NA	0.03	0.02	0.11	**0.05**	**0.11**	5.92	8.18	30.10	20.61	NA	**203.92**	562.09
	arima212	4.93	3.59	3.86	2.77	2.62	NA	0.03	0.02	0.11	0.11	0.14	**5.82**	8.39	30.20	20.54	**180.36**	245.18	**191.25**
	ar2	4.85	**3.52**	4.04	2.35	2.93	NA	0.03	0.02	0.11	0.06	NA	5.91	8.19	30.17	20.58	NA	NA	559.14
	hw	**4.82**	**3.52**	3.84	2.47	1.67	NA	0.03	0.02	0.11	0.06	0.13	5.85	8.45	**20.00**	**15.90**	NA	228.78	384.37
	garch	7.97	3.54	4.02	2.34	2.92	NA	0.03	0.02	0.11	**0.05**	0.12	5.93	**8.17**	30.03	20.52	NA	226.58	606.03

The design of the PCE system is shown in Fig. 2. It offers an interactive visualisation system with several connected views. The system is implemented using the D3.js JavaScript library and is available as an open-source project.

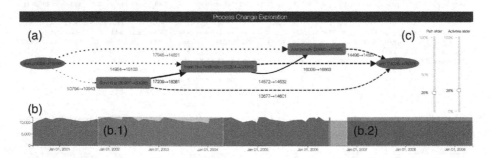

Fig. 2. Process Change Exploration (PCE) system. *(a)* shows *Adaptation Directly-Follows Graph (aDFG)* view. *(b)* shows the *Timeline view with brushed regions* view. Users can brush one or more regions on this graph in order to filter the scope of the analysis *(b.1*, and *b.2)*. Two additional controls in *(c)* show the *activity and path sliders*.

5   Conclusion

In this paper, we presented the first genuine approach to forecast a process model as a whole. To this end, we developed a technique based on time series analysis of DF relations to forecast entire DFGs from historical event data. In this way, we are able to make promising forecasts regarding the future development of the process, including whether process drifts or major changes might occur in particular parts of the process. The presented forecasting approach is supported by the Process Change Exploration system, which allows analysts to compare various parts of the past, present, and forecasted future behaviour of the process. Our empirical evaluation demonstrates that, most notably for reduced process models with medium-sized alphabets, we can obtain below 15% MAPE in terms of conformance to the true models.

In future research, we plan to evaluate the use of machine learning techniques for process model forecasting. More specifically, we aim at using recurrent neural networks or their extension in long short-term memory networks (LSTMs) and transformer-based architectures, as well as hybrid methods or ensemble forecasts with the traditional time series approaches presented here. Furthermore, we want to explore opportunities for enriching our forecasted process models with confidence intervals by calculating the entropic relevance at different confidence levels and reporting the confidence intervals in the PCE system. Finally, we will conduct design studies with process analysts to evaluate the usability of different visualisation techniques.

References

1. Aalst, W.: Data science in action. In: Process Mining, pp. 3–23. Springer, Heidelberg (2016). https://doi.org/10.1007/978-3-662-49851-4_1
2. van der Aalst, W.M.P.: A practitioner's guide to process mining: limitations of the directly-follows graph. Procedia Comput. Sci. **164**, 321–328 (2019)
3. van der Aalst, W.M.P., Rubin, V.A., Verbeek, H.M.W., van Dongen, B.F., Kindler, E., Günther, C.W.: Process mining: a two-step approach to balance between underfitting and overfitting. Softw. Syst. Model. **9**(1), 87–111 (2010)
4. Bergmeir, C., Benítez, J.M.: On the use of cross-validation for time series predictor evaluation. Inf. Sci. **191**, 192–213 (2012)
5. Evermann, J., Rehse, J.R., Fettke, P.: Predicting process behaviour using deep learning. Decis. Support Syst. **100**, 129–140 (2017)
6. Di Francescomarino, C., Ghidini, C., Maggi, F.M., Milani, F.: Predictive process monitoring methods: which one suits me best? In: Weske, M., Montali, M., Weber, I., vom Brocke, J. (eds.) BPM 2018. LNCS, vol. 11080, pp. 462–479. Springer, Cham (2018). https://doi.org/10.1007/978-3-319-98648-7_27
7. Francq, C., Zakoian, J.M.: GARCH Models: Structure, Statistical Inference and Financial Applications. Wiley, Hoboken (2019)
8. Hanke, J.E., Reitsch, A.G., Wichern, D.W.: Business Forecasting, vol. 9. Prentice Hall, Hoboken (2001)
9. Hyndman, R.J., Athanasopoulos, G.: Forecasting: Principles and Practice. OTexts, Melbourne (2018)

10. Kil, R.M., Park, S.H., Kim, S.: Optimum window size for time series prediction. In: 19th Annual International Conference on IEEE Engineering in Medicine and Biology Society, vol. 4, pp. 1421–1424. IEEE (1997)
11. Kratsch, W., Manderscheid, J., Röglinger, M., Seyfried, J.: Machine learning in business process monitoring: a comparison of deep learning and classical approaches used for outcome prediction. Bus. Inf. Syst. Eng. **63**(3), 261–276 (2020). https://doi.org/10.1007/s12599-020-00645-0
12. Kriglstein, S., Rinderle-Ma, S.: Change visualizations in business processes - requirements analysis. In: GRAPP/IVAPP, pp. 584–593. SciTePress (2012)
13. Leemans, S., Poppe, E., Wynn, M.: Directly follows-based process mining: a tool. In: Proceedings of the ICPM Demo Track 2019, pp. 9–12 (2019)
14. Leybourne, S.J., et al.: Testing for unit roots using forward and reverse dickey-fuller regressions. Oxford Bull. Econ. Stat. **57**(4), 559–571 (1995)
15. Maaradji, A., Dumas, M., La Rosa, M., Ostovar, A.: Detecting sudden and gradual drifts in business processes from execution traces. IEEE Trans. Knowl. Data Eng. **29**(10), 2140–2154 (2017)
16. Makridakis, S., Spiliotis, E., Assimakopoulos, V.: Statistical and machine learning forecasting methods: concerns and ways forward. PLoS One **13**(3), e0194889 (2018)
17. Makridakis, S., Spiliotis, E., Assimakopoulos, V.: The m4 competition: 100,000 time series and 61 forecasting methods. Int. J. Forecast. **36**(1), 54–74 (2020)
18. Neu, D.A., Lahann, J., Fettke, P.: A systematic literature review on state-of-the-art deep learning methods for process prediction. Artif. Intell. Rev., 1–27 (2021). https://doi.org/10.1007/s10462-021-09960-8
19. Nguyen, H., Dumas, M., ter Hofstede, A.H.M., La Rosa, M., Maggi, F.M.: Business process performance mining with staged process flows. In: Nurcan, S., Soffer, P., Bajec, M., Eder, J. (eds.) CAiSE 2016. LNCS, vol. 9694, pp. 167–185. Springer, Cham (2016). https://doi.org/10.1007/978-3-319-39696-5_11
20. Poll, R., Polyvyanyy, A., Rosemann, M., Röglinger, M., Rupprecht, L.: Process forecasting: towards proactive business process management. In: Weske, M., Montali, M., Weber, I., vom Brocke, J. (eds.) BPM 2018. LNCS, vol. 11080, pp. 496–512. Springer, Cham (2018). https://doi.org/10.1007/978-3-319-98648-7_29
21. Polyvyanyy, A., Moffat, A., García-Bañuelos, L.: An entropic relevance measure for stochastic conformance checking in process mining. In: ICPM, pp. 97–104 (2020)
22. Pourbafrani, M., van Zelst, S.J., van der Aalst, W.M.P.: Semi-automated time-granularity detection for data-driven simulation using process mining and system dynamics. In: Dobbie, G., Frank, U., Kappel, G., Liddle, S.W., Mayr, H.C. (eds.) ER 2020. LNCS, vol. 12400, pp. 77–91. Springer, Cham (2020). https://doi.org/10.1007/978-3-030-62522-1_6
23. Rogge-Solti, A., Weske, M.: Prediction of remaining service execution time using stochastic petri nets with arbitrary firing delays. In: Basu, S., Pautasso, C., Zhang, L., Fu, X. (eds.) ICSOC 2013. LNCS, vol. 8274, pp. 389–403. Springer, Heidelberg (2013). https://doi.org/10.1007/978-3-642-45005-1_27
24. Seabold, S., Perktold, J.: Statsmodels: econometric and statistical modeling with Python. In: 9th Python in Science Conference, vol. 57, p. 61 (2010)
25. Shneiderman, B.: The eyes have it: a task by data type taxonomy for information visualizations. In: VL, pp. 336–343. IEEE Computer Society (1996)
26. Tax, N., Verenich, I., La Rosa, M., Dumas, M.: Predictive business process monitoring with LSTM neural networks. In: Dubois, E., Pohl, K. (eds.) CAiSE 2017. LNCS, vol. 10253, pp. 477–492. Springer, Cham (2017). https://doi.org/10.1007/978-3-319-59536-8_30

27. Teinemaa, I., Dumas, M., Rosa, M.L., Maggi, F.M.: Outcome-oriented predictive process monitoring: review and benchmark. ACM Trans. Knowl. Discov. Data **13**(2), 17:1-17:57 (2019)
28. Thomakos, D.D., Guerard, J.B., Jr.: Naive, Arima, nonparametric, transfer function and VAR models: a comparison of forecasting performance. Int. J. Forecast. **20**(1), 53–67 (2004)
29. Verenich, I., Dumas, M., Rosa, M.L., Maggi, F.M., Teinemaa, I.: Survey and cross-benchmark comparison of remaining time prediction methods in business process monitoring. ACM TIST **10**(4), 1–34 (2019)
30. Weigend, A.S.: Time Series Prediction: Forecasting the Future and Understanding the Past. Routledge, Abingdon (2018)
31. Yeshchenko, A., Di Ciccio, C., Mendling, J., Polyvyanyy, A.: Comprehensive process drift detection with visual analytics. In: Laender, A.H.F., Pernici, B., Lim, E.-P., de Oliveira, J.P.M. (eds.) ER 2019. LNCS, vol. 11788, pp. 119–135. Springer, Cham (2019). https://doi.org/10.1007/978-3-030-33223-5_11
32. Yeshchenko, A., Di Ciccio, C., Mendling, J., Polyvyanyy, A.: Visual drift detection for sequence data analysis of business processes. IEEE Trans. Vis. Comput. Graph. (2021)

Structural and Behavioral Biases in Process Comparison Using Models and Logs

Anna Kalenkova$^{(\boxtimes)}$ ⓘ, Artem Polyvyanyy ⓘ, and Marcello La Rosa ⓘ

School of Computing and Information Systems, The University of Melbourne, Melbourne, VIC 3010, Australia
{anna.kalenkova,artem.polyvyanyy,marcello.larosa}@unimelb.edu.au

Abstract. Process models automatically discovered from event logs represent business process behavior in a compact graphical way. To compare process variants, e.g., to explore how the system's behavior changes over time or between customer segments, analysts tend to visually compare conceptual process models discovered from different "slices" of the event log, solely relying on the structure of these models. However, the structural distance between two process models does not always reflect the behavioral distance between the underlying event logs and thus structural comparison should be applied with care. This paper aims to investigate relations between structural and behavioral process distances and explain when structural distance between two discovered process models can be used to assess the behavioral distance between the corresponding event logs.

Keywords: Process mining · Variant analysis · Structural distance · BPMN

1 Introduction

Process mining [1] is a branch science at the intersection of data science and process management, focused on the analysis of event logs extracted from enterprise systems. Key process mining capabilities include the *(1) automated discovery* of process models from event logs, *(2) performance mining* to identify friction points in process performance, *(3) conformance checking* to find discrepancies between actual and modeled process behavior, and *(4) variant analysis* to assess different variants of the same business process and identify root causes for their differences.

Automated process discovery algorithms generalize the behavior recorded in event logs by constructing conceptual process models that represent this behavior.

Conformance checking offers a variety of methods for *model-to-log* (M2L) comparison, when the process model corresponds to a prescribed process behavior and the log corresponds to the actual behavior of the process. Most of these

© Springer Nature Switzerland AG 2021
A. Ghose et al. (Eds.): ER 2021, LNCS 13011, pp. 62–73, 2021.
https://doi.org/10.1007/978-3-030-89022-3_6

approaches provide a single number to quantify the model and log similarity and are not supported by visual analytics, i.e., discrepancies of the processes are not explicitly visualized.

Variant analysis techniques [18], on the other hand, focus on *log-to-log* (L2L) and *model-to-model* (M2M) comparison. These techniques are used to compare variants of the same process, e.g., purchasing processes for different customer types. Specialized methods for L2L comparison were proposed in [4] and [5]. The approach [4] provides results in the form of natural language expressions, while technique [5] visualizes discrepancies on transition systems, that are either too abstract to represent real-world data or cannot be properly compared when detailed. Some of the conformance checking techniques [2,9,15,16] can be also used in variant analysis and applied for L2L comparison. However, none of the these techniques provide any visual information highlighting the discrepancies of event logs.

In contrast to the L2L comparison techniques, that lack visual analysis, state-of-the-art model-to-model (M2M) comparison methods are implemented in a variety of tools [8,10,11,13,19] and are primarily intended to visualize differences in conceptual process models. These methods explicitly highlight models' discrepancies.

With state-of-the-art M2M comparison tools and process discovery techniques, process analysts can discover models from event logs and then compare them applying one of the M2M methods, instantly visualizing differences in process variants. Figure 1 presents a prospective schema for variant analysis when an event log L is split into two sub-logs: L_1 and L_2, then from these sub-logs process models M_1 and M_2 are discovered, and after that these models are matched using one of the M2M comparison techniques. Elements that should be deleted from M_1 and added to match it with M_2 are highlighted in red and green, respectively.

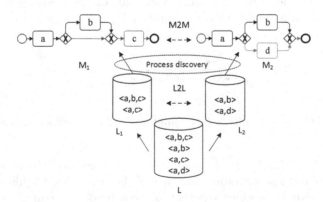

Fig. 1. Using M2M comparison in variant analysis. (Color figure online)

Although this approach seems feasible and readily available, it raises the following research questions:

RQ 1: *Can we use structural M2M comparison as a proxy for the behavioral L2L comparison? In other words, do distances between process models correlate with the distances between the event logs?*
RQ 2: *Does the correlation between L2L and corresponding M2M distances depend on the algorithm used to discover the models from logs?*
RQ 3: *What is the role of representational biases, i.e., process modeling languages and distance metrics, in applying M2M comparison for the L2L analysis?*

To answer these questions we analyzed event logs of real-world systems. In order not to depend on an application domain, we spit the event logs into sub-logs (temporal slices) using time frames. This type of variant analysis is also known as *concept drift* analysis [6]. It assesses how the process changes over time. We discover process models from the sub-logs and then relate structural distances between these process models and behavioral distances between the corresponding sub-logs. We then answer the research questions and make conclusions and recommendations regarding applying the M2M techniques for the L2L analysis.

2 Motivating Example

In this section, we consider simple event logs and process models discovered from these event logs. We then relate the differences of the event logs to the differences of the corresponding process models. Consider event log $L_1 = \{\langle a, b, c, d, e\rangle,$ $\langle a, d, e\rangle\}$. This event log contains two traces, each of the traces is a sequence of events. Figure 2 presents a BPMN model M_1 discovered from L_1 by applying Split miner [3] or Inductive miner [12]. Note that for the event log L_1, these two discovery algorithms produce the same model M_1.

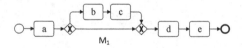

Fig. 2. M_1 discovered from L_1 by Split and Inductive miner algorithms.

Event log $L_2 = \{\langle a, b, c, d, e\rangle, \langle a, d, e\rangle \langle a, b, e\rangle\}$ includes the same set of traces as event log L_1 but also contains trace $\langle a, b, e\rangle$. For event log L_2 different process discovery algorithms produce different process models. Figure 3 presents two process models M_1 and M_{2split} discovered by Split miner from event logs L_1 and L_2, respectively. To transform M_1 to M_{2split}, we remove two red arcs and add two green gateways and five green arcs. In this case, the model is modified by adding an alternative path.

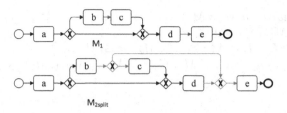

Fig. 3. M_1 and M_{2split} models discovered by Split miner from L_1 and L_2, respectively. (Color figure online)

Two models M_1 and M_{2ind} discovered by Inductive miner from event logs L_1 and L_2 are presented in Fig. 4. The differences between these two models are also highlighted in red and green. In contrast to M_{2split}, model M_{2ind} significantly differs from M_1. One needs to remove four arcs, add four gateways and ten arcs to match model M_1[1]. That means, we need to reorganize the entire structure of the model. However, L_1 and L_2 differ in only one trace. The limitation of Inductive miner is that it cannot construct sequence flows going from one block of constructs to another, allowing only regular hierarchical structures of embedded sub-processes (sequence, choice, loop, parallel executions). This example demonstrates that different process discovery algorithms relate L2L and M2M distances differently.

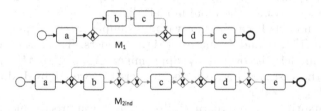

Fig. 4. M_1 and M_{2ind} discovered by Inductive miner from L_1 and L_2, respectively. (Color figure online)

3   Structural and Behavioral Process Distances

In this section, we define process distances that are later used for the analysis of correlations between structural and behavioral characteristics of processes.

Each distance measure is considered together with a set of process models or event logs and forms a *metric space* $(\mathcal{M}, \Delta)$, where $\mathcal{M}$ is the set of models or event logs (represented structurally as graphs or behaviorally as languages, i.e., sets of execution sequences), and $\Delta : \mathcal{M} \times \mathcal{M} \to \mathbb{R}$ is a distance function, such that:

---

[1] Although the model can be simplified (some gateways can be merged), we analyze BPMN models as they are provided by the discovery algorithms.

1. *Identity of indiscernible:* $\forall M \in \mathcal{M} : \Delta(M, M) = 0; \forall M_1, M_2 \in \mathcal{M}$: if $M_1 \neq M_2$, then $\Delta(M_1, M_2) > 0$;
2. *Symmetry:* $\forall M_1, M_2 \in \mathcal{M} : \Delta(M_1, M_2) = \Delta(M_2, M_1)$;
3. *Triangle inequality:* $\forall M_1, M_2, M_3 \in \mathcal{M} : \Delta(M_1, M_2) \leq \Delta(M_1, M_3) + \Delta(M_3, M_2)$.

3.1 Structural Process Distance

The structural distance between two process models can be defined using the *graph edit distance* [7], i.e., the minimum number of atomic operations (insertions and deletions) that transform one process model to another. We will consider BPMN models containing only core elements (tasks, exclusive and parallel gateways, start and end events). The specifics of BPMN process models are that their nodes are typed, and tasks are labeled. Thus, we only match nodes if they are of the same type and their labels coincide.

Once the minimum number of insertion and deletion operations is defined, we calculate the structural distance between two process models M_1 and M_2 as:

$$\Delta_{struct}(M_1, M_2) = 1 - \frac{sim(M_1, M_2)}{sim(M_1, M_2) + diff(M_1, M_2)}, \tag{1}$$

where $sim(M_1, M_2)$ is the number of matching elements and $diff(M_1, M_2)$ is the number of mismatching elements in M_1 and M_2. The structural distance is 0 for perfectly matching models and 1 for completely different models. The higher the distance value, the more models differ.

Recall the models from the motivating example (Sect. 2) that were discovered by Split (Fig. 3) and Inductive (Fig. 4) miners. The structural distance between the models discovered by Split miner $\Delta_{struct}(M_1, M_{2split}) = 0.360$ is less than the distance between the models discovered by Inductive miner $\Delta_{struct}(M_1, M_{2ind}) = 0.563$.

Besides quantifying the structural distance between process models, the proposed distance measure also defines a metric space, i.e., the three properties are satisfied.

3.2 Behavioral Process Distances

The behavior of a process model, as well as an event log, is represented by a language, i.e., a sets of label sequences, it encodes. The distance between two languages L_1 and L_2 can be calculated as:

$$\Delta_{beh}(L_1, L_2) = 1 - \frac{ent\bullet(L_1 \cap L_2)}{ent\bullet(L_1 \cup L_2)}, \tag{2}$$

where $ent\bullet$ is the *short-circuit* entropy measure that estimates the language cardinality (the number of sequences the language contains) [16]. This behavioral distance measure gives a number between 0 and 1, which is 0 for identical languages, when $L_1 \cap L_2 = L_1 \cup L_2$, and 1, when the languages have the empty intersection.

For event logs L_1 and L_2 from the motivating example (Sect. 2), the behavioral distance is estimated as: $\Delta_{beh}(L_1, L_2) = 0.416$. The behavioral distances between the corresponding process models discovered by Split miner and Inductive miner are $\Delta_{beh}(L_{M_1}, L_{M_{2split}}) = 0.416$ and $\Delta_{beh}(L_{M_1}, L_{M_{2ind}}) = 0.708$, respectively, where L_{M_1}, $L_{M_{2split}}$, $L_{M_{2ind}}$ are the languages accepted by these models. Similar to the structural distance, this behavioral distance forms a metric space.

The behavioral distance measure, see Eq. (2), is restrictive and assesses only the share of common sequences of two languages. To also consider common subsequences we use a so-called partial behavioral distance that is calculated for the "diluted" languages (for the details see [15]) that extend the initial languages by allowing any number of label skips. Consider language $L = \{\langle a, b, c \rangle, \langle a, d \rangle\}$. The corresponding "diluted" language $L' = \{\langle a, b, c \rangle, \langle a, b \rangle, \langle a, c \rangle, \langle b, c \rangle, \langle a, d \rangle, \langle a \rangle, \langle b \rangle, \langle c \rangle, \langle d \rangle, \langle \rangle\}$ contains all the subsequences of L that can be obtained by skipping some labels in the words of L. The partial behavioral distance between languages L_1 and L_2 is defined as:

$$\Delta'_{beh}(L_1, L_2) = 1 - \frac{ent \bullet (L'_1 \cap L'_2)}{ent \bullet (L'_1 \cup L'_2)}, \tag{3}$$

where L'_1 and L'_2 are the "diluted" versions of languages L_1 and L_2, respectively. This measure assesses the share of common subsequences in two languages.

Although the behavioral distance, see Eq. (2), forms a metric space, the partial behavioral distance, see eq. (3), does not satisfy the *Identity of indiscernible* rule. Consider two languages: $L_1 = \{\langle a, b \rangle\}$ and $L_2 = \{\langle a, b \rangle, \langle a \rangle\}$. Note that $L_1 \neq L_2$, and at the same time, $L'_1 = L'_2 = \{\langle a, b \rangle, \langle a \rangle, \langle b \rangle, \langle \rangle\}$, and hence, $\Delta'_{beh}(L_1, L_2) = 0$. However, the partial behavioral distance satisfies the other space metric properties, i.e., *Symmetry* and *Triangle inequality*.

4   Evaluation

This section analyzes real-world event logs by relating their behavioral distances to the structural distances between BPMN models discovered from these event logs. The distances between process models were calculated with BPMNDiffViz tool[2] [8] – an open-source tool for structural BPMN model comparison. To overcome the computational costs, we applied the greedy approximation algorithm that, according to [17], gives the minimal edit distance in most of the cases for BPMN models discovered from event logs. Behavioral distances were estimated using Entropia[3] [14] – an open-source and publicly available tool for measuring the quality of discovered process models.

---

[2] https://bitbucket.org/sivanov68/bpmndiffviz/src/master/.
[3] https://github.com/jbpt/codebase/tree/master/jbpt-pm/entropia.

We have analyzed seven real-world publicly available BPI (Business Process Intelligence) Challenge event logs[4]. Table 1 presents characteristics of these event logs, including the numbers of traces, events, and their occurrences. Note that one trace can occur multiple times in a real-life event log. The table also contains event logs' notations that will be used later to denote the corresponding distances.

Table 1. Characteristics of the real-world event logs.

Event log	Name	Notation	# Traces	# Trace Occur.	# Events	# Ev. Occur.
1	Domestic Declarations'20	●	99	10,500	17	56,437
2	International Declarations'20	●	753	6,449	34	72,151
3	Prepaid Travel Cost'20	●	202	2,099	29	18,246
4	Travel Permit Data'20	●	1,478	7,065	51	86,581
5	Request For Payment'20	●	89	6,886	19	36,796
6	Application Receipt Phase	●	116	1,434	27	8,557
7	Road Traffic	●	231	150,370	11	561,470

To not depend on a particular application domain, we have split each of the event logs into six sub-logs that correspond to six equal time frames. Each sub-log includes all the traces that contain events belonging to the corresponding time frame.

We then applied two process discovery algorithms, namely Split miner [3] and Inductive miner [12], to construct BPMN models from the given 42 sub-logs. Eight models produced by Split miner were not sound, i.e., could not be described as finite automata models, so their behavior could not be quantified, and hence, the corresponding sub-logs were excluded from the evaluation.

All possible pairs of the sub-logs of the same event log and corresponding discovered models were compared. Figure 5 relates the behavioral sub-log distances to the structural BPMN model distances. As observed from the two plots for the models discovered by Split miner (Fig. 5a) and Inductive miner (Fig. 5b), the distances between the sub-logs are more correlated with the structural distances between the corresponding models discovered by Split miner.

While the structural distances between the models discovered by Split miner (Fig. 6a) show good correlation with the partial behavioral distances between the corresponding sub-logs ($R^2 = 0.723$), for the models discovered by Inductive miner (Fig. 6b) the correlation is less obvious ($R^2 = 0.371$). However, in both cases the M2M comparison only approximates L2L distances. Especially this can be seen for the sub-logs of the *Road Traffic* event log, i.e., behavioral distances between similar sub-logs cannot be differentiated using the M2M comparison. At the same time, M2M analysis allows distinguishing the cases when event logs are similar or distinct.

---

[4] https://data.4tu.nl/.

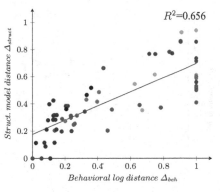
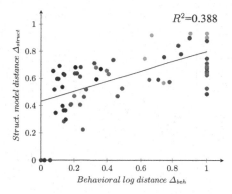

(a) Models discovered by Split miner.   (b) Models discovered by Inductive miner.

Fig. 5. Behavioral distances between the sub-logs and structural distances between the discovered models.

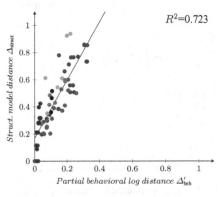
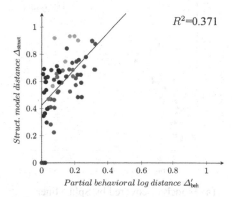

(a) Models discovered by Split miner.   (b) Models discovered by Inductive miner.

Fig. 6. Partial behavioral distances between the sub-logs and structural distances between the corresponding models.

Split miner and Inductive miner produce different types of BPMN models: while models discovered by Inductive miner are hierarchical, models constructed by Split miner represent a wider class of arbitrarily structured BPMN diagrams. To draw more detailed conclusions, we need to understand the role of representational bias.

Figure 7 and Fig. 8 relate distances and partial distances between languages of the analyzed process models to the structural distances between these models. Structural distances between the process models discovered by Split miner (Fig. 7a, Fig. 8a) correlate with the corresponding model behavioral distances, similarly to how they correlate with the distances between the corresponding sub-logs (similar R^2 values). However, structural distances between the models discovered by Inductive miner (Fig. 7b, Fig. 8b) reflect differences in the behavior of these models better than in the behavior of the corresponding sub-logs. In the next section, we discuss and explain this phenomenon.

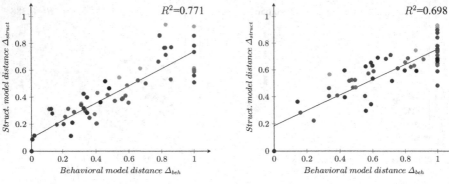

(a) Models discovered by Split miner.   (b) Models discovered by Inductive Miner.

Fig. 7. Behavioral and structural distances between the discovered models.

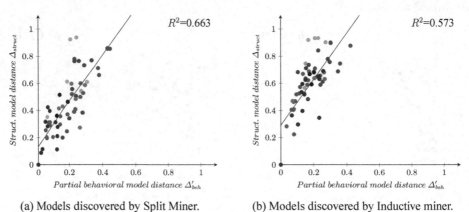

(a) Models discovered by Split Miner.   (b) Models discovered by Inductive miner.

Fig. 8. Partial behavioral and structural distances between the discovered models.

5   Discussion

Although structural distances between process models produced by Inductive miner correlate with the behavioral model distances, there is less correlation with the distances of corresponding event logs. Which means we need to have a closer look at the relations between behavioral M2M distances and corresponding L2L distances.

Figure 9 shows a metric space $(\mathcal{M}, \Delta)$ for languages that represent behaviors of process models and event logs. Consider models M_1 and M_2 discovered from event logs L_1 and L_2, and accepting languages L_{M_1} and L_{M_2}. According to the *Triangle inequality*, $\Delta(L_{M_1}, L_{M_2}) \leq \Delta(L_1, L_2) + \Delta(L_{M_1}, L_1) + \Delta(L_{M_2}, L_2)$ and $\Delta(L_{M_1}, L_{M_2}) \geq \Delta(L_1, L_2) - \Delta(L_{M_1}, L_1) - \Delta(L_{M_2}, L_2)$, i.e., when approximating $\Delta(L_1, L_2)$, distance $\Delta(L_{M_1}, L_{M_2})$, in the worst case, includes $\Delta(L_{M_1}, L_1)$ and $\Delta(L_{M_2}, L_2)$.

The aim of process discovery algorithms is to minimize $\Delta(L_{M_i}, L_i)$, $i \in \{1, 2\}$, distances and construct models that are behaviorally close to the event logs. An ideal discovery algorithm would construct models, such that $\Delta(L_{M_i}, L_i) = 0$, and hence $\Delta(L_{M_1}, L_{M_2}) = \Delta(L_1, L_2)$. However, this is not always possible and, first of all, because of the representational bias. Even if a discovery algorithm makes the best possible attempt to construct a model M that is behaviorally similar to the event log L, the distance $\Delta(L_M, L)$ is bounded by $\Delta_{min}(\mathcal{M}, \Delta)$, i.e., $\Delta(L_M, L) \geq \Delta_{min}(\mathcal{M}, \Delta)$, where $\Delta_{min}(\mathcal{M}, \Delta)$ is the minimal distance between behaviors in the metric space.

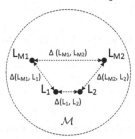

Fig. 9. Behavioral distances between models and logs.

The metric space of block structured BPMN models discovered by Inductive miner is sparser than the space of BPMN models with arbitrary structures constructed by Split miner because it forms a proper subset of the models discovered by Split miner, hence, the value of $\Delta_{min}(\mathcal{M}, \Delta)$ for Split miner is less than for Inductive miner, so, it is easier for Split miner to find a model that is behaviorally closer to a given event log. However, Split miner can produce unsound models that cannot be represented as finite automata models and their behavior cannot be quantified. Apart from the structuredness, there can be other constraints on the sets of models that influence the density of the metric space. For instance, both Split miner and Inductive miner construct process models with uniquely labeled tasks.

These observations provide answers to the research questions: RQ 1. In some cases, M2M comparison can be used as a proxy for L2L comparison. However, M2M analysis only approximates L2L distances; RQ 2. The discovery algorithm plays the pivotal role in relating M2M and L2L distances, because of its two main characteristics: the representational bias and the ability to construct models that behaviorally close to the event logs (this characteristic depends on the representational bias, but also incorporates the quality of the algorithm itself); RQ 3. The role of representational bias is crucial, and together with different metrics it affects correlations between M2M and L2L distances.

These results explain when the M2M comparison can be used for the L2L analysis. Namely, the analyst should consider two characteristics of the discovery algorithm that affect correlations between M2M and L2L distances: (1) *accuracy*, i.e., the distance between an event log and the discovered process model; (2) *representational bias*, i.e., the process modeling language. These results provide a tool for analysing process discovery algorithms, i.e., to assess applicability of a new process discovery algorithm for the comparison of event logs using M2M analysis, one should consider its accuracy and representational bias and then relate to those of other discovery algorithms.

6   Conclusions and Future Work

This paper bridges the gap between behavioral and structural comparison techniques in process mining. It explains the cases when behavioral differences in processes can be learned from the structural differences in the corresponding process models. The results are supported by experiments on real-life event logs. In future work, we plan to conduct large scale experiments and consider further process discovery algorithms and behavioral distance measures. We also plan to run an empirical study that will involve participants assessing structural and behavioral distances between models and logs.

Acknowledgments. This work was partly supported by the Australian Research Council Discovery Project DP180102839.

References

1. van der Aalst, W.: Process Mining: Data Science in Action. Springer, Heidelberg (2016). https://doi.org/10.1007/978-3-662-49851-4
2. Augusto, A., Armas-Cervantes, A., Conforti, R., Dumas, M., La Rosa, M., Reissner, D.: Abstract-and-compare: a family of scalable precision measures for automated process discovery. In: Weske, M., Montali, M., Weber, I., vom Brocke, J. (eds.) BPM 2018. LNCS, vol. 11080, pp. 158–175. Springer, Cham (2018). https://doi.org/10.1007/978-3-319-98648-7_10
3. Augusto, A., Conforti, R., Dumas, M., La Rosa, M., Polyvyanyy, A.: Split miner: automated discovery of accurate and simple business process models from event logs. Knowl. Inf. Syst. **59**(2), 251–284 (2019). https://doi.org/10.1007/s10115-018-1214-x
4. van Beest, N.R.T.P., Dumas, M., García-Bañuelos, L., La Rosa, M.: Log delta analysis: interpretable differencing of business process event logs. In: Motahari-Nezhad, H.R., Recker, J., Weidlich, M. (eds.) BPM 2015. LNCS, vol. 9253, pp. 386–405. Springer, Cham (2015). https://doi.org/10.1007/978-3-319-23063-4_26
5. Bolt, A., de Leoni, M., van der Aalst, W.M.P.: A visual approach to spot statistically-significant differences in event logs based on process metrics. In: Nurcan, S., Soffer, P., Bajec, M., Eder, J. (eds.) CAiSE 2016. LNCS, vol. 9694, pp. 151–166. Springer, Cham (2016). https://doi.org/10.1007/978-3-319-39696-5_10
6. Bose, R., van der Aalst, W., Žliobaitė, I., Pechenizkiy, M.: Dealing with concept drifts in process mining. IEEE Trans. Neural Netw. Learn. Syst. **25**(1), 154–171 (2014)
7. Gao, X., Xiao, B., Tao, D., Li, X.: A survey of graph edit distance. Pattern Anal. Appl. **13**(1), 113–129 (2010). https://doi.org/10.1007/s10044-008-0141-y
8. Ivanov, S., Kalenkova, A., van der Aalst, W.: BPMNDiffViz: a tool for BPMN models comparison. In: BPM Demo Session, BPM. CEUR-WS, vol. 1418, pp. 35–39 (2015)
9. Kalenkova, A., Polyvyanyy, A.: A spectrum of entropy-based precision and recall measurements between partially matching designed and observed processes. In: Kafeza, E., Benatallah, B., Martinelli, F., Hacid, H., Bouguettaya, A., Motahari, H. (eds.) ICSOC 2020. LNCS, vol. 12571, pp. 337–354. Springer, Cham (2020). https://doi.org/10.1007/978-3-030-65310-1_24

10. La Rosa, M., Dumas, M., Uba, R., Dijkman, R.: Business process model merging: an approach to business process consolidation. ACM Trans. Softw. Eng. Methodol. **22**(2), 1–42 (2013)
11. La Rosa, M., et al.: Apromore: an advanced process model repository. Expert Syst. Appl. **38**(6), 7029–7040 (2011)
12. Leemans, S.J.J., Fahland, D., van der Aalst, W.M.P.: Discovering block-structured process models from incomplete event logs. In: Ciardo, G., Kindler, E. (eds.) PETRI NETS 2014. LNCS, vol. 8489, pp. 91–110. Springer, Cham (2014). https://doi.org/10.1007/978-3-319-07734-5_6
13. Pietsch, P., Wenzel, S.: Comparison of BPMN2 diagrams. In: Mendling, J., Weidlich, M. (eds.) BPMN 2012. LNBIP, vol. 125, pp. 83–97. Springer, Heidelberg (2012). https://doi.org/10.1007/978-3-642-33155-8_7
14. Polyvyanyy, A., et al.: Entropia: a family of entropy-based conformance checking measures for process mining. In: ICPM Doctoral Consortium and Tool Demonstration Track. CEUR Workshop Proceedings, vol. 2703, pp. 39–42 (2020)
15. Polyvyanyy, A., Kalenkova, A.A.: Monotone conformance checking for partially matching designed and observed processes. In: ICPM, pp. 81–88. IEEE (2019)
16. Polyvyanyy, A., Solti, A., Weidlich, M., Di Ciccio, C., Mendling, J.: Monotone precision and recall measures for comparing executions and specifications of dynamic systems. ACM Trans. Softw. Eng. Methodol. **29**(3), 1–41 (2020)
17. Skobtsov, A., Kalenkova, A.: Efficient algorithms for finding differences between process models. In: 2019 Ivannikov Ispras Open Conference (ISPRAS), pp. 60–66 (2019)
18. Taymouri, F., La Rosa, M., Dumas, M., Maggi, F.: Business process variant analysis: Survey and classification. Knowl.-Based Syst. **211**, 106557 (2021)
19. Treude, C., Berlik, S., Wenzel, S., Kelter, U.: Difference computation of large models. In: ESEC/FSE, pp. 295–304. ACM, New York (2007)

Top-Down Versus Operational-Only Business Process Modeling: An Experimental Evaluation of the Approach Leading to Higher Quality Representations

Pavani Vemuri[1]([⊠])[iD], Yves Wautelet[1][iD], Stephan Poelmans[1], Simon Verwimp[1], and Samedi Heng[2][iD]

[1] KU Leuven, Leuven, Belgium
{pavani.vemuri,yves.wautelet,stephan.poelmans}@kuleuven.be
[2] HEC Liège, Université de Liège, Liège, Belgium
samedi.heng@uliege.be

Abstract. Business process modeling (BPMo) is of primary importance for assessing the current state of an organizations' practices to discover inefficiencies, redesign business processes, and build software solutions. High-quality representations best capture the true nature of the organization. This paper investigates the hypothesis of whether Business Process Modeling Notation (BPMN), Business Process Diagrams (BPDs) created through a Top-Down Modeling Approach (TDMA) are of higher quality than those made from an operational perspective only. An experiment was conducted where novice modelers were to model a case based on a textual description. The test group used the TDMA by first modeling strategic, tactical aspects using a Business Use-Case Model (BUCM) before the operational realization with BPMN BPDs. In contrast, the control group did not use the BUCM. Representations were then evaluated for overall semantic and syntactic quality by extracting metrics from known literature. Both groups have similar syntactic quality at a granular level. Nevertheless, BPMN BPDs created using TDMA are more complete: required tasks in process execution are significantly more present. An increase in completeness can be beneficial in understanding complex organizations and facilitate modular software development. Alternatively, the diagrams were significantly more complex with more linearly independent paths within workflows than needed.

Keywords: Business process modeling · Use case modeling · Operational processes · Top-down business modeling · Traceability · Experiment

1 Introduction

Business Process Modeling (BPMo) is a collection of techniques used by businesses both in the context of (1) process re-engineering to identify the process' inefficiencies/flaws and modify them for better performance or (2) developing a new software solution to support further or automate existing processes. Visual diagrams representing the processes in a business are drawn using these collective techniques. Having

© Springer Nature Switzerland AG 2021
A. Ghose et al. (Eds.): ER 2021, LNCS 13011, pp. 74–84, 2021.
https://doi.org/10.1007/978-3-030-89022-3_7

an unclear, incorrect, or inconsistent picture of the business processes under scrutiny may increase the inefficiencies or lead to the development of a misaligned information system implying potentially substantial financial losses. Despite the importance of BPMo, research has shown that it is still prone to errors in many cases [9,11,17]. As it is difficult to arrive at standardized criteria to assess process quality, frameworks are necessary. They are developed to determine the quality of a workflow representation (or specific aspects of it) in specific cases. Especially when modeling the processes of a complex organization, multi-modular process models are necessary, and traceability needs to be established across multi-representational levels. In order to furnish support for modeling at the strategic, tactical, and operational representational levels, a formal framework could prove to be of high value.

Wautelet & Poelmans, in [22,23] proposed to use the *Business Use-Case Model (BUCM)* – initially defined in the *Rational Unified Process (RUP)* as an extension of the UML Use Case Model – for strategic and tactical representation and the *BPMN Business Process Diagrams (BPDs)* for the operational ones. (Note: In line with [21–23], when we refer to BPMN BPDs instead of process models, as we focus on an instance of a process model specific to a given case). For the conjunct use of these two models, the authors defined a specific traceability ruleset between the elements found in each layer. The traceability is established by modeling a BPD. Its realizations are initiated by corresponding BUC elements triggered by the Business Worker or Actor elements. *One BUC Realization will initiate one BPMN BPD*, which describes the process realization scenarios on the operational level. We name this the Top-Down Modeling Approach *(TDMA)* in which, first the strategic and tactical levels are modeled with a BUCM and the operational level with BPDs. Hence by using TDMA, when modeling complex multi-modular processes, the modeler is driven onto a specific path - giving him/her a first mental structure to follow or allow him/her to more clearly understand what problem needs to be solved and how to split it into manageable parts. For a complete description of the framework, the added value and need for an integrated framework, and using the TDMA on a real case, we invite the reader to refer to [21–23].

Building the abstract representations first and foremost could impact the quality of the operational workflows, which could be of higher or lower quality. To our knowledge, this question has not been addressed in the literature. A recent structured study of 87 articles on process modeling conveys that only 31 studies provide empirical evidence for their guidelines [3]. This current study seeks to empirically validate the benefits of conjointly using RUP/UML and BPMN with the TDMA framework. We do not intend to overview the ability to produce qualitative design models or code out of a pure software engineering approach, nor do we focus on the process of process modeling [15]. TDMA is evaluated as it offers a fully integrated framework for a structured global business analysis approach to facilitate primary documentation out of a process description.

An experiment was designed and conducted with novice modelers who model a multi-modular case based on a textual description. Consisting of a test and control group, this experiment was aimed to evaluate the usefulness of TDMA in identifying different processes and perceptions in the usability of the framework. Furthermore, this study seeks to identify possible benefits and/or drawbacks from using TDMA by comparing the quality of operational workflow representations between the two groups.

Hence in this experiment, BPMN BPDs were built using TDMA with the traceability ruleset on one side and an immediate operational representation on the other.

2   Related Background on Measuring Model Quality

BPMo is prone to errors, and several studies conclude the importance of high-quality in process models. Reijers et al. [16] noted that the BPMo field suffers from a lack of interest or effort to assess quality models. Error rates of process models are high resulting in poor model quality [11]. Larger extent modeling projects require an increase in qualified process modelers [17]. Poor quality models in the early stages of design have harmful effects on the use and application of these models in later stages of design [16] and can prove to be very expensive. Schmidt [19] confirms correcting errors during integration is much more costly than during the requirements/implementation phases.

A large body of knowledge proposes guidelines to reduce errors and possible metrics to assess Process Modeling Quality (PMQ). Frequently referred to frameworks like Guidelines of Modeling (GoM), seven process modeling guidelines (7PMG), and 3QM propose guidelines to be applied when developing process models and possible metrics to evaluate models. GoM's six generic guidelines include syntactical correctness of models [4] but lack concrete metrics as to how the indicators are measured, making it too abstract for non-experts in practice [12, 14]. 7PMG [12] proposes seven guidelines with easy-to-use indicators for novice modelers but are limited in scope. 3QM incorporates several indicators and dimensions from earlier frameworks such as SEQUAL, GoM, and 7PMG, identifying fundamental PMQ characteristics for evaluation [14] and provides metrics and measurement procedures to quantify quality. Despite the extant literature, a recent comprehensive systematic literature review concluded that "there is a lack of an encompassing and generally accepted definition of PMQ" [13], while another aimed to structure existing knowledge into a framework designed to "raise the transparency of the ... . domain. And facilitate future research" [7].

Metrics were gathered from a recent overview of PMQ literature [7] and other more widely used frameworks. The SIQ framework is among the most simple to use (among many SEQUAL extensions), with semantic, syntactic, and pragmatic metrics considered for overall quality. These three types of metrics are repeated across several frameworks and are used in several empirical studies. Other guidelines and metrics exist focusing on complexity of models [20], understandability [5] and process model comprehension [8]. [7] discusses several frameworks and proposes a comprehensive PMQ framework and quotes from [10] that syntactic quality is the only metric that can be directly observed and objectively measured. Understandability metrics are not considered separately but as syntactic quality.

As we do not have any stakeholders available for formal inspection, pragmatic quality is only measured through semantic metrics (activity and actor) and granularity. The literature identifies syntactic correctness comprising deadlocks, execution of tasks, and if every execution of workflows does not leave any branches active. More about the metrics used is further mentioned in Sect. 3. Finally, it is interesting to note that most frameworks offer guidelines and metrics suitable for measuring PMQ, but do not present procedural guidelines to model BPDs, nor consider modularity (except one) or several abstraction levels required in complex businesses.

Table 1. Process quality metrics: case-specific quality metrics

	Outcomes, 1 = positive; 0 = negative	Control group (operational only)	Test group (TDMA)	Chi-Square significance	Fisher's exact test
Workflow_split	1	5	5	Ns	
	0	15	14	Ns	
Customer_pool	1	9	7	Ns	
	0	11	12	Ns	
Connections	1	14	6	**	
	0	6	13	**	
Delivery_subprocess	1	2	6	Ns	Ns
	0	18	13	Ns	Ns

3   Research Method: Designing the Modeling Experiment

Null Hypothesis H_0: BPMN BPDs created using a TDMA framework are of higher quality than those created from an operational perspective only. The goals of the study are then: (a) To design an experiment with an appropriate case to assess the hypothesis; (b) Provide metrics to assess the quality of BPDs modeled for multi-modular case; (c) Analyze participant perceptions of using the TDMA framework; (d) Analyze results and formulate conclusions about which quality metrics capture significant differences between the two groups.

Subjects: In our experiment, subjects were 40 graduate students of a Master of Business Administration (MBA) program and were novice modelers. These students were familiar with BPMN and the TDMA with traceability ruleset as studied in the Business Information Management course in the MBA program. Participation in the study was voluntary. To motivate students to attend and perform to their best, students could earn a bonus grade for the course specified above.

Objects: The object to be modeled was inspired by a real-life case of a chocolate company (real name withheld due to confidentiality reasons) which includes two separate processes that are related to each other. Subjects of both groups were asked to imagine that they were a business analyst working individually on requirements.

Representation Levels: The respondents were asked to model one Use Case Diagram combining the BUCM and the BGM, i.e., the strategic and tactical level in one model. For the traceability, quite simply - *One BUCM realization will initiate one BPMN BPD*. Hence, one could expect the test subjects to design two use cases, leading to two collaborating BPDs; and the control group would only model two BPDs.

Measured Variables and Metrics: For both groups, the data collected are categorized as profile, pre-test, quality metrics and perceived difficulty variables. An elongated list of variables and their definitions are presented in the Appendix B. (Note: All appendices are available at doi.org/10.17632/w35gp4pmgz)

- Profile: Educational Background; experience in software modeling; familiarity (likert scales) with modeling languages or diagrams (UML, RUP, BUCM, BPMN) and traceability in software design.
- Pre-test: Score on the pre-test consisting of 5 BPMN BPD questions (correct answer = 1, no answer = 0, wrong answer = 0.5), four multiple-choice (with guess correction applied) and one open question.
- Process Quality Metrics: General quality metrics include three global (*Complexity, Process_Interdependence* and *Granularity*), two semantic (*Semantic_activity/Completeness* and *Semantic_Actor*) and one (aggregate of 5 indicators) Syntactic (*Syntactic_Quality*) variable. In the latter metrics, only complexity is a dummy while others are categorical (1 = perfect, 0.4 = solution not significant but not entirely wrong, 0 = worst score possible) variables. From the traceability ruleset, four quality metrics were derived specific to the case (*Workflow_Split, Customer_pool, Connections* and *Deliver_subprocess*) are dummy variables (1 = yes, 0 = no). These variables capture ability to identify modularity and sub_processes, and connect the ruleset correctly.
- Perceived difficulty: Several measures were initially derived from the Technology Acceptance literature [6] using items on a 5-point Likert scale. Further, factor (PCA) and reliability analyses were applied, arriving at four metrics capture perceived difficulty - Ease of use and usefulness of the framework for the test group; and Ease of use of BPMN and the case for both groups.

Response Variables: The general quality metrics, case-specific metrics and an aggregate quality score (combining all the metrics) are considered as the response variables in this study. The scores are to be estimated by comparing each of the participants' models to a reference model of the process for both treatment groups.

4 Performing the Experiment

4.1 Preparation

Pre-experiment: As a part of the preparation for the set-up of the intended experiment, a test experiment was conducted with several PhD researchers in Software Engineering from UCLouvain in Belgium. The feedback gathered about the case and its feasibility was used to optimize the overall presentation of the case, and the modeling task descriptions were adapted and refined.

Experimental Variables: For the set-up to meet the conditions of a true experiment [18], only one experimental variable is to be manipulated while all others held constant. To control all other variables of the experiment, both groups were given the exact same assignment and questions. A profile questionnaire and pre-test were used to take background knowledge of BPMN and possible group effects into account.

Execution: The experiment was conducted as a single event at KULeuven, Brussels. The students were to be split into two treatment groups; a test and a control group; by randomly assigning a number corresponding to a particular treatment group. The test group used the TDMA framework by first modeling strategic, tactical aspects using BUCM before representing the operational realization with BPMN BPDs. The control group does not use BUCM and only the operational aspect with BPMN BPDs. The experiment entailed multiple parts and corresponding artifacts: (1) consent form, (2) profile questionnaire, (3) a pre-test; (4) an overview of the theory that needed to be applied and that could be used as a reference, (5) a case that needed to be solved (6) a final questionnaire; were applied in a sequence.

The participants first received the consent form, profile questionnaire, and the pre-test and next received the case and the theory for reference. Upon completion, they were given a final questionnaire. All artifacts (see Appendix C) were the same for both groups except in Artifact 4: the test group was given the TDMA framework additionally, and in Artifact 6: the test group was asked questions about using the framework. Although the respondents were familiar with a CASE tool (i.e., Visual Paradigm), it was opted to model the required diagrams using pen and paper. This was done in order to prevent the software from influencing their responses. The case (Artifact 5) and a reference solution (constructed, corrected, and agreed upon by the senior members of the research team) are made available in Appendices C and D.

Data Validation: Once the experiment was carried out, the models produced by the participants were first checked for outliers to prevent results from being skewed. One model was discarded as the participant noted that the case was too difficult and did not solve the case. As this observation is incomplete, the data is left out. Two participants indicated on their profile that they do not have any knowledge about UCM, BUCM, or BPMN. Although these participants indicated that they had differing background knowledge from the rest of the participants, their observations were considered in the analysis. The results of their pre-test, diagrams, and questionnaire were similar to those of respondents who indicated better background knowledge. It was assumed that they either misunderstood the profile question or "played-it-safe" by not owning up to background knowledge if they did not perform well on the experiment. Thus, leaving us with 39 observations, 20 from the control group and 19 from the test group.

4.2 Results

Profiles and Pre-test Results: The educational background and the experience with software modeling in that both cohorts have similar profiles (see Appendix A). Using the Independent samples t-Test, no significant differences could be detected in experience, familiarity, and the pre-test scores. The average score on the pre-test was low, with a mean of 1.28 (on 5), confirming that all participants are inexperienced/novice modelers. There was a small cohort of 9 students who already had a bachelor's degree in information management or computer science. Overall, the students had/have been following several software-modeling courses (in previous and current semesters).

Process Quality Metrics: The BPDs were checked for process quality metrics and have been recorded. The Chi-square test of independence was used predominantly to compare the scores of both groups. However, when the expected value was less than five, Fisher's exact test was used additionally. Syntactic quality represents an aggregate score (reflecting five indicators), an Independent Samples t-Test was appropriate.

Table 2. Process quality metrics: general quality metrics

	Outcomes, 1 = positive; 0 = negative	Control group (operational only)	Test group (TDMA)	Chi-Square significance	Fisher's exact test
Process_inter dependence	1	4	0	*	Ns
	0.4	0	0	*	Ns
	0	16	19	*	Ns
Complexity	1	7	1	*	*
	0	13	18	*	*
Granularity	1: (Correct level) 0.4: (2 activities combined in 1) 0: (>2 act. in 1 or act. comb. sev. x)	6	8	Ns	
		1	3	Ns	
		13	8	Ns	
Semantic_Activity/ Completeness Semantic_Actor	1	2	4	**	*
	0.4	0	5	**	*
	0	18	10	**	*
	1	19	18	Ns	Ns
	0.4	0	1	Ns	Ns
	0	1	0	Ns	Ns
Syntactic_Quality	Aggreg. of 5 indicators, scale 0–10	Mean: 5.00	Mean: 6.21	Ns[1]	

*: $p < 0.05$, **: $p < 0.01$
[1]: Independent Samples Test

Table 1 gives an overview of the number of participants who achieved indicated scores per metric in the control and test groups; and the appropriate significance tests.

For case-specific quality metrics, (see Table 1) a significant difference is observed in the variable *Connections*. The significant difference ($p < 0.05$) indicates that respondents in the test group are more likely to have only one connection between the two workflows (to send the invoice), or to have no connection at all. Hence, the control group made significantly fewer mistakes against this metric. In general quality metrics, (see Table 2) significant differences are observed in *Complexity* and *Semantic_Activity/Completeness* variables. The control group is more likely to have simpler models, with only one split resulting in two linearly independent paths (when the Board of Directors decides on the request), compared to the test group. Whereas the test group is significantly more likely to have all, or all but one of the required tasks present in the BPMN BPDs, compared to those who are not using the framework ($p < 0.05$). Hence, the test group performed significantly better on the *Completeness* of the BPDs capture all the activities in the textual description.

Table 3. Total scores description

	Mean	SD	Min 2	Max
All respondants	4.61	1.82	1	8
Group 1	4.52	1.88	1	8
Group 2	4.72	1.8	2.2	7.4
Group IT bachelor (N = 9)	4.34	1.82	2.2	7.8

Table 4. Usability of the approaches

Perceptions/means on a scale 1 to 5	Total (N = 39)	SD	Control grp	Test grp
Ease of use of the framework	/	/	/	3.26
Usefulness of the framework	/	/	/	3.63
Ease of use of BPMN	2.88	0.58	2.73	3.03
Ease of use of the case	3.00	0.56	2.95	3.05

Aggregate Quality Score: The aggregate quality score of all the quality metrics results in a score of 10. To enable this, the syntactic quality was re-scaled into a 0–1 continuous scale. No respondent achieved the maximum score, and only 17 (8 control and 9 test) subjects received a passing score (of 50%). See Table 3. An independent sample t-Test revealed no significant differences between both groups hence the H_0 can be rejected. A Chi-square test of independence confirmed that respondents in one group are not more likely to receive a passing grade than respondents in the other.

The group of students with a bachelor's degree in IS, IM, or Computer Science was also examined as they could be expected to obtain a better score. To further explore potential determinants of the quality scores, besides the differences between the two groups, a correlation analysis was applied. The Kendall's tau correlation coefficients were preferred over Pearson and Spearman correlations because they are more 'conservative' and possess more desirable properties [1, 2]. In particular, experience, familiarity, and pre-test scores were checked with the individual and the total quality scores. No significant coefficients could nevertheless be detected.

Usability: The questions on the final questionnaire were aimed at determining the ease of use and usefulness of the TDMA framework and BPMN. Table 4 presents the means of three ease-of-use and one usefulness measure. The distribution of the four measures approximates a Gaussian curve. Applying Kendal tau did not result in any significant correlations with quality metrics. Overall, the TDMA framework was perceived as useful (M = 3.63) and relatively easy to use (M = 3.26); whereas BPMN was perceived slightly more difficult (M = 2.88) but with comparable scores for both groups.

5   Discussion, Strengths, Limitation and Future Work

It is observed that using the TDMA framework, the BPDs are more complete with more required tasks being captured (reflected by *Semantic_Activity* score). Even the H_0

is rejected, this increase in *Completeness* quality is an important difference indicating the use of TDMA. It could be the result of the modelers evaluating the problem in its entirety. Strategic and tactical requirements, translated into business objectives, goals, and BUC, give a global view and lay the foundation of all operational workflow diagrams produced, and the traceability ruleset ensures the guidance throughout all diagrams created. In large companies with complex processes, this can be a strong advantage.

The strength of the underlying research is applying a randomized experimental set-up, combined with strict objective multiple quality measures and perceptions. Several potentially confounding factors, such as previous experience, knowledge of the subject, or the previous educational background, have been taken into account but did not impact the quality metrics. As both groups are quite similar, we attribute the differences in the quality scores to the treatment, i.e., using the TDMA framework. The observed increase in complexity of the diagrams could be considered the downside of working in this fashion. During the modeling process, actions like refactoring BPDs could be taken to prevent the diagrams from becoming too complex during set intervals. However, attention should be paid to the completeness of the models, as refactoring should not counteract the benefits of working in a top-down fashion. Additionally, the framework was perceived to be rather easy to use and useful to model the case. This study also helps extend knowledge on quality metrics related to traceability.

6   Threats to Validity

The validity of our experiment's results is studied at the light of the categories defined by Wohlin et al. [24].

Construct Validity: We evaluated workflow quality metrics extracted from literature. Other metrics could perhaps be used covering essential aspects that were not taken into account in this study. Further research could be conducted to determine what elements practitioners highlight as particularly relevant and important in the workflows they daily use; to precisely determine what factors they implicitly take into account. With such an evaluation framework, we could reexamine the scores and results. Nevertheless, this threat to validity has been mitigated by evaluating with our quality metrics workflows made by academic specialists; these performed very high to perfectly within the quality metrics so that we can point to some reliability of our evaluation criteria.

Internal Validity: The experiment consisted only of one case and had only two main processes (size). We could also envisage experiment(s) with larger multi-modular complex cases. The mental structure given through the top-down approach on a more complex case is expected to lead to more convincing results. Practically a larger case would be very constraining in terms of time and could lead modelers to discouragement.

External Validity: The group of 39 respondents was homogeneous consisting of only novice modellers and the findings of the study will hold true for students in this particular field. Their findings may be found to differ for individuals with higher expertise with a different occupation, such as researchers or professionals active in the field of BPMo. But the might hold true, as a professional that is active in the BPMo field may have expertise in BPMN but not be familiar with specific fields portrayed in the case like RUP/UML BUCM, and traceability; and be used to handling a case in a certain way different from the procedure in the framework.

7 Conclusion

The quality of the diagrams produced in BPMo is essential when re-engineering or automating processes. Traceability between representation levels allows to ensure continuity in the mental modeling process and ensures consistency between representations. In order to measure the performance of a TDMA versus an operational only one we proceeded to the evaluation of BPDs. To this end, several quality frameworks and quality metrics were studied; relevant metrics were selected and applied. Some quality metrics were explicitly derived from the case used in the experiment with no background in the literature as they capture the traceability ruleset. A total of 10 (9 categorically defined with clear cut-off points while one was an aggregation of 5 underlying syntactic quality criteria) metrics were used to assess and analyze the BPDs provided as a solution by subjects. The total aggregate score on the BPDs are not significantly different between both groups, thus rejecting the null hypothesis. On the other hand the *Completeness* of the BPDs and the perceived ease in using the technique is encouraging to further investigate the usability of the TDMA framework in making qualitative process models for complex projects. BPMN BPDs created using TDMA are more complete but complex. Completeness can be beneficial for modelers in understanding complex organizations and facilitate modular software development. Participants also perceived that the framework was easy to use.

References

1. Amoako-Gyampah, K., Salam, A.F.: An extension of the technology acceptance model in an ERP implementation environment. Inf. Manag. **41**(6), 731–745 (2004)
2. Arndt, S., Magnotta, V.: Generating random series with known values of Kendall's tau. Comput. Methods Programs Biomed. **65**(1), 17–23 (2001)
3. Avila, D.T., dos Santos, R.I., Mendling, J., Thom, L.H.: A systematic literature review of process modeling guidelines and their empirical support. BPM J. (2020)
4. Becker, J., Rosemann, M., von Uthmann, C.: Guidelines of business process modeling. In: van der Aalst, W., Desel, J., Oberweis, A. (eds.) Business Process Management. LNCS, vol. 1806, pp. 30–49. Springer, Heidelberg (2000). https://doi.org/10.1007/3-540-45594-9_3
5. Corradini, F., et al.: A guidelines framework for understandable BPMN models. Data Knowl. Eng. **113**, 129–154 (2018)
6. Davis, F.D.: Perceived usefulness, perceived ease of use, and user acceptance of information technology. MIS Q. **13**, 319–340 (1989)
7. De Meyer, P., Claes, J.: An overview of process model quality literature-the comprehensive process model quality framework. arXiv preprint arXiv:1808.07930 (2018)
8. Dikici, A., Turetken, O., Demirors, O.: Factors influencing the understandability of process models: a systematic literature review. Inf. Softw. Technol. **93**, 112–129 (2018)
9. Gassen, J.B., Mendling, J., Thom, L.H., de Oliveira, J.P.M.: Business process modeling: vocabulary problem and requirements specification. In: SIGDOC 2014, pp. 1–10 (2014)

10. Krogstie, J., et al.: Process models representing knowledge for action: a revised quality framework. Eur. J. Inf. Syst. **15**(1), 91–102 (2006)
11. Mendling, J.: Metrics for Process Models: Empirical Foundations of Verification, Error Prediction, and Guidelines for Correctness, vol. 6. Springer, Heidelberg (2008). https://doi.org/10.1007/978-3-540-89224-3
12. Mendling, J., Reijers, H.A., van der Aalst, W.M.: Seven process modeling guidelines (7PMG). Inf. Softw. Technol. **52**(2), 127–136 (2010)
13. de Oca, I.M.M., Snoeck, M., Reijers, H.A., Rodríguez-Morffi, A.: A systematic literature review of studies on business process modeling quality. Inf. Soft. Technol. **58**, 187–205 (2015)
14. Overhage, S., Birkmeier, D.Q., Schlauderer, S.: Qualitätsmerkmale,-metriken und-messverfahren für geschäftsprozessmodelle. Wirtschaftsinformatik **54**(5), 217–235 (2012)
15. Pinggera, J., et al.: Modeling styles in business process modeling. In: Bider, I., et al. (eds.) BPMDS/EMMSAD -2012. LNBIP, vol. 113, pp. 151–166. Springer, Heidelberg (2012). https://doi.org/10.1007/978-3-642-31072-0_11
16. Reijers, H.A., Mendling, J., Recker, J.: Business process quality management. In: Brocke, J., Rosemann, M. (eds.) Handbook on Business Process Management 1. International Handbooks on Information Systems, pp. 167–185. Springer, Heidelberg (2010). https://doi.org/10.1007/978-3-642-00416-2_8
17. Rosemann, M.: Potential pitfalls of process modeling: part A. BPM J. **12**, 249–254 (2006)
18. Saunders, M., Lewis, P., Thornhill, A.: Research Methods for Business Students. Pearson, Harlow (2009)
19. Schmidt, D.: Guest editor's introduction: model-driven engineering. Computer **39**(2), 25–31 (2006)
20. Vanderfeesten, I., Cardoso, J., Mendling, J., Reijers, H.A., Van der Aalst, W.: Quality metrics for business process models. BPM Workflow Handb. **144**, 179–190 (2007)
21. Wautelet, Y.: Using the RUP/UML business use case model for service development governance: a business and it alignment based approach. In: CBI2020, vol. 2, pp. 121–130 (2020)
22. Wautelet, Y., Poelmans, S.: Aligning the elements of the RUP/UML business use-case model and the BPMN business process diagram. In: Grünbacher, P., Perini, A. (eds.) REFSQ 2017. LNCS, vol. 10153, pp. 22–30. Springer, Cham (2017). https://doi.org/10.1007/978-3-319-54045-0_2
23. Wautelet, Y., Poelmans, S.: An integrated enterprise modeling framework using the RUP/UML business use-case model and BPMN. In: Poels, G., Gailly, F., Serral Asensio, E., Snoeck, M. (eds.) PoEM 2017. LNBIP, vol. 305, pp. 299–315. Springer, Cham (2017). https://doi.org/10.1007/978-3-319-70241-4_20
24. Wohlin, C., Runeson, P., Höst, M., Ohlsson, M.C., Regnell, B., Wesslén, A.: Experimentation in Software Engineering. Springer, Heidelberg (2012). https://doi.org/10.1007/978-3-642-29044-2

Data Modeling

An Empirical Study of (Multi-) Database Models in Open-Source Projects

Pol Benats[1]($\boxtimes$), Maxime Gobert[1], Loup Meurice[1], Csaba Nagy[2],
and Anthony Cleve[1]

[1] Namur Digital Institute, University of Namur, Namur, Belgium
{pol.benats,maxime.gobert,loup.meurice,anthony.cleve}@unamur.be
[2] Software Institute, Università della Svizzera italiana, Lugano, Switzerland
csaba.nagy@usi.ch

Abstract. Managing data-intensive systems has long been recognized as an expensive and error-prone process. This is mainly due to the often implicit consistency relationships that hold between applications and their database. As new technologies emerged for specialized purposes (e.g., graph databases, document stores), the joint use of database models has also become popular. There are undeniable benefits of such multi-database models where developers combine various technologies. However, the side effects on design, querying, and maintenance are not well-known yet. In this paper, we study multi-database models in software systems by mining major open-source repositories. We consider four years of history, from 2017 to 2020, of a total number of 40,609 projects with databases. Our results confirm the emergence of hybrid data-intensive systems as we found (multi-) database models (e.g., relational and non-relational) used together in 16% of all database-dependent projects. One percent of the systems added, deleted, or changed a database during the four years. The majority (62%) of these systems had a single database before becoming hybrid, and another significant part (19%) became "mono-database" after initially using multiple databases. We examine the evolution of these systems to understand the rationale of the design choices of the developers. Our study aims to guide future research towards new challenges posed by those emerging data management architectures.

Keywords: Data models · Open-source projects · Empirical study

1 Introduction

Modeling, querying, and evolving database-centered systems are known as time-consuming, risky, and error-prone. The main challenges related to those processes originate from the possibly complex interdependencies between the application programs and their underlying databases. This is especially true in the absence of a fully explicit database schema, which partly moves the responsibility of data integrity constraints from the database management system to the client programs. This situation may become even more complex with the increasing popularity of NoSQL database technologies. Such scalable technologies are attractive

A. Ghose et al. (Eds.): ER 2021, LNCS 13011, pp. 87–101, 2021.
https://doi.org/10.1007/978-3-030-89022-3_8

due to the flexibility offered by the absence of strict data schema. But the long-term impact of their use on data management still has to be assessed.

Furthermore, as their full name suggests, *Not Only SQL* technologies were not initially intended to *replace* relational database management systems but rather *complement* them. Hence there is a recent emergence of *hybrid* data-intensive systems that rely on both relational and NoSQL technologies. Such heterogeneous systems request that developers master several modeling and query languages, and bring new challenges for research and practice.

This paper presents an empirical study of the use of (multi-)database models in open-source database-dependent projects. We mined four years of development history (2017–2020) of a total number of 33 million projects by leveraging Libraries.io. We identified projects with databases and written in popular programming languages (1.3 million), then applied filters to eliminate "low-quality" repositories and remove project duplicates. We gathered a final dataset of 40,609 projects. We analyzed the dependencies of those projects to assess (1) the popularity of the different database models, (2) the extent that they are combined within the same systems, and (3) how their usage evolved.

Our results confirm the emergence of hybrid data-intensive systems as we found that 16% of all database-dependent projects use (multi-)database models (e.g., relational and non-relational).[1] We also observe that one percent of the systems added, deleted, or changed a database during the four years. The majority (62%) of them became hybrid after using a single database technology. On the other hand, a significant number of systems (19%) became "mono-database" after initially using multiple databases. We examined the evolution of these systems to understand the rationale of the design choices of the developers.

This study has several implications for the research community. It provides empirical evidence for the need for novel solutions supporting the design, querying, and evolution of hybrid database systems. It advances the identification of the most representative data-intensive systems for further empirical studies or evaluation purposes. It aims to guide future research towards new challenges posed by those emerging data management architectures.

The remainder of the paper is structured as follows. Section 2 expresses our research objectives through three research questions and presents the research method we followed in conducting our study. Section 3 presents our main findings. Section 4 proposes a discussion about the contribution of this paper to scientific research. Section 5 lists threats to validity, and Sect. 6 discusses related work. Concluding remarks are given in Sect. 7.

2   Study Method

Research Questions. We seek answers to the following research questions:

RQ1: How Prevalent Are Different Data Models and Their Related Database Technologies?. Based on the database dependencies of the collected open-source projects, we assess the usage of each database technology (*e.g.,* PostgreSQL,

---

[1] The detailed results are publicly available in a replication package [3].

MongoDB, Redis, Neo4J, Cassandra) and, transitively, each data model (*i.e.,* relational, document, key-value, graph, and wide-column).

RQ2: Are Multi-database Models Frequently Used in Software Systems?. We identify projects corresponding to *hybrid* systems, *i.e.,* systems using at least two data models. We analyze which data models are combined in those systems. We call those combined models *multi-database models.*

RQ3: How Does Data Model Usage Evolve?. We analyze the evolution of the database models used in repositories. We track the additions, deletions, or replacements of database models. We then classify the projects based on the evolution of their data models.

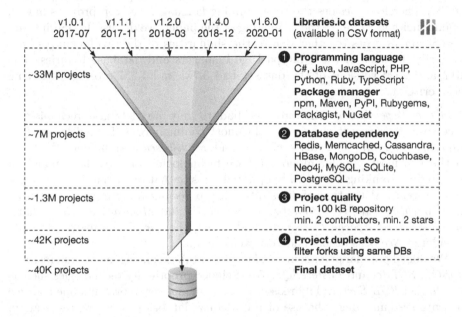

Fig. 1. Overview of project filtering

Preliminaries. Our study took as input the dataset of *Libraries.io,*[2] an open-source web service that lists software development projects and their dependencies. The primary aim of this service is to help developers keeping track of libraries, modules, and frameworks they depend upon. However, its extensive and up-to-date dataset is also representative, thus valuable for empirical software engineering studies [10,29,30]. Libraries.io monitors projects of major source code repositories (*i.e., Bitbucket, GitHub,* and *GitLab*). It lists 33 million repositories with dependencies to 235 million packages in 37 package managers (*e.g., npm, Maven, PyPI*). Libraries.io has five major versions of its dataset at the time of writing, covering four years of evolution from 2017 to 2020. We

---

[2] Libraries.io - https://libraries.io/.

imported each dataset into a database. Then, as shown in Fig. 1, we filtered the projects according to the selection criteria described in the following subsections.

Programming Language. We study projects written in popular programming languages according to *Octoverse*,[3] namely *C#, Java, JavaScript, PHP, Python, Ruby,* and *TypeScript*. We determine the programming language of a project based on the package manager it relies on. Hence, from the complete list of Octoverse, we excluded *C* and *C++* because their usage of package managers is not as common as in the selected languages. Package managers are important for us also when determining the database dependency in the subsequent filtering step. Libraries.io tracks the most popular managers for the selected programming languages, namely, *npm, Maven, PyPI, Rubygems, Packagist,* and *NuGet*. Therefore, besides the programming language, we keep projects having dependencies in these. In the remaining of the paper, we discuss JavaScript and TypeScript projects together due to the similarities of the two languages and, primarily, because of the same package managers and database libraries. The 2017 and 2020 versions of the dataset had 3.7M and 7.2M projects satisfying these criteria.

Database Dependency. The projects had to rely on database technologies. According to a recent survey [8], the most common NoSQL models are *key-value, wide-column, document-oriented,* and *graph-based* data models. We focus on the two most popular mono-database technologies for each data model on DB-Engines Ranking,[4] a monthly updated website that ranks database management systems. At the time of our study, the top *document* stores were *MongoDB* and *Couchbase*; *key-value* databases were *Redis* and *Memcached*; *wide-column* databases were *Apache Cassandra* and *HBase*. For *graph* databases, we only considered *Neo4j* as others had very weak rankings.

We added popular open-source *relational* database management systems, *i.e.,* *MySQL, SQLite,* and *PostgreSQL*. We excluded proprietary technologies such as *Oracle* and *SQL Server*. The reason is that our dataset represents open-source software systems where the use of proprietary databases is not representative. Consequently, we limit our study to open-source technologies. We established a list of search expressions combining database technologies and access types to identify a list of database access drivers. For direct access drivers (*e.g.,* JDBC connectors), we used *client* and *driver* keywords. For object-relational mapping (ORM) and object NoSQL mapping (ONM) [28] technologies, we used *orm, onm, odm, ogm* and *mapper* keywords. We searched for these expressions in the search engines of the package managers to find libraries. We also queried Google for additional libraries missed by the package managers. Each driver's relevance was manually checked based on its description and provided source code samples.

This collection process led to 707 direct database-access drivers, including 220 object mapping libraries. The complete list of selected drivers is available in our **replication package** [3]. Overall, 18% of the projects (710K in 2017 and 1.3M in 2020) depended on database-access libraries.

---

[3] Octoverse - https://octoverse.github.com/.
[4] DB-Engines Ranking - https://db-engines.com/en/ranking.

Project Quality. GitHub is known to host many private and inactive projects [16]. To ensure a representative sample, we filter "low-quality" projects from the list of repositories. In particular, we keep a project if it meets the following selection criteria: (1) a repository with a minimum size of 100 kB, (2) at least two contributors, and (3) having been starred at least twice.

Stars and contributors reflect a level of popularity [6] and collaborative activity [5]; thus, we set minimum thresholds for them. However, for us, a popular Python project with a single file of a few code lines is as important as a less popular Java project with thousands of lines of code, given that they use databases. The database dependency filter already ensures the latter one. So the purpose with the additional minimum size of 100 kB is merely to expect a minimum content in repositories. A total number of 42,176 repositories (∼3%) remained in the dataset after this filtering step.

Project Duplicates. We filter duplicated projects (*i.e.,* exact copies of projects or projects with minor differences like bug fixes) by identifying fork projects. We keep only the source project of forks having the same database dependencies if the source is in the dataset. Otherwise, we keep the project with the longest history, *i.e.,* the project in more dataset versions of Libraries.io. More details of this filtering can be found in our replication package [3]. We identified and removed 1,567 duplicated repositories and finally gathered 40,609 projects (26,745 in 2017 and 38,248 in 2020).

Table 1. Projects by programming language and data model 2020

Data model	Ruby		JavaScript		Python		Java		C#		PHP	
Relational	11,049	44.66%	4,164	16.83%	4,863	19.66%	3,707	14.98%	956	3.86%	2	0.01%
Document	953	9.76%	6,126	62.73%	1,435	14.70%	782	8.01%	273	2.80%	196	2.01%
KeyValue	2,548	28.11%	2,831	31.23%	2,522	27.82%	927	10.23%	228	2.52%	8	0.09%
Column	34	3.26%	79	7.57%	549	52.64%	350	33.56%	27	2.59%	4	0.38%
Graph	49	12.04%	91	22.36%	65	15.97%	176	43.24%	13	3.19%	13	3.19%
Total	12,370	32.28%	11,747	30.66%	7,558	19.72%	5,062	13.21%	1,362	3.55%	221	0.58%

Final Dataset. Table 1 presents an overview of the programming languages and different data models used in the projects of the 2020 dataset. The most common programming languages in the dataset are Ruby (32.28%), JavaScript/-TypeScript (30.66%), Python (19.72%) and Java (13.21%). Interestingly, Ruby, Python, Java and C# are mainly used in systems with relational databases, while document-oriented data stores are frequently used in JavaScript and PHP.

3   Study Results

3.1   RQ1: How Prevalent Are Different Data Models and Their Related Database Technologies?

Table 2 presents the number of projects relying on different data models. Overall, more than half of the projects declare a relational driver dependency. Thus, the relational data model is the most used in the dataset. However, an interesting observation is that the percentage of relational databases is constantly decreasing among the database-dependent projects. It goes down to 54.72% from 57.40% over the four years. In contrast, the ratio of projects relying on NoSQL data models is increasing. Except for graph data models, an increase in the usage ratio can be observed for document-oriented (21.30% to 21.97%), key-value (18.97% to 19.98%), and wide-column (1.40% to 2.44%) data models.

Table 2. Evolution of database-dependent projects by data model

Data model	Relational		Document		Key-Value		Wide-Column		Graph	
2017–07	17,816	57.40%	6,610	21.30%	5,886	18.97%	436	1.40%	288	0.93%
2017–11	19,112	57.27%	7,173	21.49%	6,284	18.83%	487	1.46%	317	0.95%
2018–03	19,622	57.16%	7,372	21.47%	6,524	19.00%	490	1.43%	323	0.94%
2018–11	21,037	56.12%	8,082	21.56%	7,349	19.60%	677	1.81%	344	0.92%
2020–01	24,620	54.72%	9,884	21.97%	8,989	19.98%	1,096	2.44%	402	0.89%

Figure 2 presents the database management systems used in the 2020 snapshot. MongoDB appears as the most used NoSQL database management system competing with relational technologies. It represents the majority of document-oriented database-dependent projects. Both Redis and Memcached are popular technologies for key-value data stores. Redis is almost as popular as SQLite and MySQL among the subject systems. Cassandra is the most used technology for wide-column stores. It is followed by Neo4j, the only graph-based technology on the list, then by HBase and Couchbase.

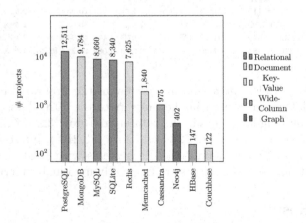

Fig. 2. Usage of database management systems (2020)

Overall, relational models lead the ranking as they are used in over half of the database-dependent projects. Document and key-values stores are the most used NoSQL technologies with approximately 21% and 19% of projects, respectively. Wide-column (1–3%) and graph-based (<1%) database families are much less represented. Interestingly, the proportion of relational database-dependent projects has decreased in the last four years, in contrast to NoSQL datastores.

3.2 RQ2: Are Multi-database Models Frequently Used in Software Systems?

This research question focuses on the heterogeneity of database-dependent projects, $i.e.$, projects having multiple dependencies to different data models.

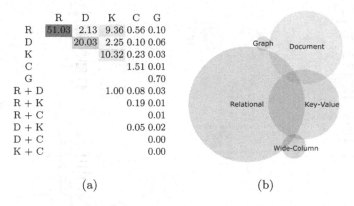

	R	D	K	C	G
R	51.03	2.13	9.36	0.56	0.10
D		20.03	2.25	0.10	0.06
K			10.32	0.23	0.03
C				1.51	0.01
G					0.70
R + D				1.00	0.08	0.03
R + K				0.19	0.01
R + C				0.01
D + K				0.05	0.02
D + C				0.00
K + C				0.00

(a)   (b)

Fig. 3. (a) Percentage of database-dependent projects with one, two and three data models (2020) (b) Distribution of hybrid database-dependent projects

Figure 3a gives the distribution of hybrid database-dependent projects in the 2020 dataset. We only present the percentage of projects relying on one, two or three different data models. The projects with more data models (four or five) represent only 0.19% of all filtered projects. Figure 3b depicts the most common combinations of data models in hybrid projects.

Answering this research question, we make the following observations. More than 16% of our database-dependent projects are hybrid, $i.e.$, define dependencies to access more than one database family. Most systems relying on a relational, document, or graph data model correspond to single-database projects. In contrast, more than 56% of the key-value projects are paired with another data model, typically with a relational or a document database. Another noticeable combination of hybrid projects groups about 45% of the total number of wide-column dependent projects with another technology, such as a relational database or a key-value database. The proportion of hybrid systems increased for almost all models in the last four years, except for key-value models

3.3   RQ3: How Does Data Model Usage Evolve?

We follow the evolution of the repositories in our dataset and keep track of changes (*i.e.,* replacement, addition, or deletion) in their data models. For example, when developers change from a relational model to a document store, we record it as a *replacement* event. Similarly, when they add a new database technology to the existing one, we record it as an *addition* of a new data model. When we see they do not use a data model anymore, we consider it as a *deletion*.

We identified a total number of 471 repositories with changes in their data models throughout the time period of our dataset. We answer this research question considering only these systems.

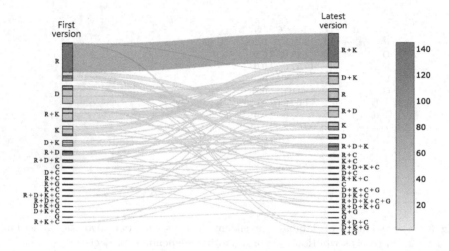

Fig. 4. Changes in projects' database families. Data models: R - relational, D - document, K - key-value, C - column and G - graph

Figure 4 presents how systems changed their data models between their first and latest known versions in our dataset. The first known version can be in 2017 or after it for projects appearing in our dataset later. The latest known version can be 2020 or before if the project became unavailable. For example, if a system had initially used a document store, then changed to a relational model, the system is counted as 'D' on the left side and 'R' on the right side of the diagram. The sizes and colors of the boxes represent the number of systems using the actual data model or the combination of multiple models.

We can make the following interesting observations by looking at the diagram. First, the most common change in the database family is adding a key-value database to an existing relational one. We identified 29.5% of the 471 repositories with such a design decision. This is in line with the findings of RQ2, where we found the combination of key-value and relational data models as the most common in hybrid systems. Second, we found a significant number of projects (7.6%) with the addition of a key-value database to an existing document database. The deletion of a key-value family from a relational and a key-value combination was also common (7.4%), and the addition of a relational database to an existing document database (6.8%), or the addition of a relational database to a key-value database system (5.3%) were also significant.

We also classify the repositories according to their database usage. *Becoming hybrid* indicates that a system starts using more than one database technology, and *staying hybrid* means that it keeps using multiple data models. Similarly, we classify systems as *becoming/staying mono-database* when they start/keep using a single database.

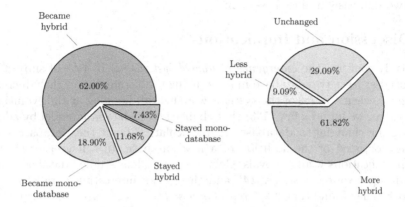

Fig. 5. Changes in data models

Figure 5 presents a summary of the classification of the changes in the database families. In 62% of the repositories which evolved their data model, we observed that the systems became hybrid. They had used a single database model before and added a new model later. On the contrary, 18.9% of the repositories had used a multi-database model before and became mono-database. The right side of Fig. 5 elaborates on the systems that stayed hybrid. Here we observe a general trend of adding more data models to the existing ones as 61.82% of these systems become more hybrid.

To better understand developers in applying such changes to the systems, we contacted the developers of five systems where we found interesting changes in the evolution. We got a response from the developers of the ORCID project.[5] We observed the addition of MongoDB to an existing PostgreSQL database in this system in 2018. The developers used the two databases for a while, but then abandoned MongoDB. The dependency is still there, but it is not used anymore.

Manual inspection revealed that both databases used a table column as a dynamic flag updated when a MongoDB message was received in a queue managing that column. This interaction tracked the transfer of data from the PostgreSQL to the MongoDB database. As the developers explained, the team

---

[5] ORCID Source - https://github.com/ORCID/ORCID-Source.

experimented with the benefits of querying the data from a document data store compared to a relational database. For their purpose, the migration had more disadvantages. Hence, they abandoned the document store later.

Overall, the results of this research question indicate the following. Evolving database-dependent projects tend to add more data models to their existing ones, turning mono-database systems into hybrid or already hybrid systems to even "more hybrid." The most common change in the combination of database families is adding a key-value database to an existing relational or document model. Adding a relational database backend to a current key-value/document database-based system is also a frequent combination. Whereas moving to more than two database families is seldom.

4   Discussion and Implications

Our study confirms the *emergence of hybrid systems*, as 16.41% of subject systems used at least two database models in 2020. This number slightly increased from 2017, when 15.77% of the systems were hybrid. Looking at the evolution of the systems, we found a few (1%) that changed their database model by adding, deleting, or changing a database. In particular, 62% of the database model changes consisted of the addition of a new database. In a few cases (18.9%), these modifications were removals. Goeminne and Mens studied database frameworks in open-source systems [14], and there is an interesting parallelism with our work. They found that *"different database frameworks used in a project tend to co-occur"* and *"all database frameworks remain present in more than 45% of the projects."* Similar findings were confirmed by Decan et al. [9].

Such observations make us assume that *developers rarely change database models* in the lifecycle of the project. However, *when modifications are needed, developers tend to add new database models* to the system. As previous research has shown, the database schema evolves continuously [7,24,26]. Keeping up with the changes is an expensive and error-prone task [27], especially when the database schema is not explicitly provided. Hybrid systems make this evolution process even more complex. The state-of-the-art approaches on data-intensive systems evolution [1,9,11,17,19,21,22,25] mostly consider software systems relying on a relational database and typically written in Java [9,17–19,21] or PHP [1,22,25] (see Sect. 6). Our results show that more complex data architectures and other programming languages are emerging, bringing their own maintainability challenges.

Unfortunately, only a few authors have started investigating the challenges of evolving NoSQL applications [23,24,28] or supporting schema evolution in hybrid systems [12]. In this direction, promising ideas are the use of unified platforms to integrate multiple data sources [15] or provide support in managing multiple schemas [4]. Another approach is to manipulate a unified data schema [2] or query and migrate the data across different databases relying on relational or NoSQL technologies [13]. Developers could greatly benefit from more tools helping them maintain and evolve multi-database systems or recommend useful changes in their data models.

5   Threats to Validity

Construct validity concerns mostly the preparation of the dataset of our study. We rely on the dataset of Libraries.io that monitors Bitbucket, GitHub, and GitLab. While these are the largest open-source repositories, they might not fully represent all open-source projects using databases.

We excluded "low-quality" projects with a quality filter. To balance the quality and the size of the dataset, we chose filtering criteria according to quartiles. Similar, even more strict, values for contributors and stars are used in the literature [5,20]. Filtering only based on popularity is prone to include projects with non-software artifacts (*e.g.,* experimental or teaching purposes) [20]. To mitigate this risk, we use a combined filter and the requirement of database dependency. We also filtered project duplicates through the identification of fork projects with the same database dependencies. This filter could consider individual projects as duplicates and miss "non-forked" copies in rare cases. Overall, the filters resulted in less than 5% of all database-dependent projects. The number of projects remains sufficient to obtain representative results; however, the filters can affect our findings. A more in-depth analysis of the projects could still improve the dataset, particularly by classifying the projects and identifying false positive projects that define database dependencies without using them. Our **replication package** [3] provides all the necessary resources (datasets, extraction scripts) to replicate our study by selecting projects based on different quality criteria. Additionally, we performed control analyses on the whole dataset (*e.g.,* by filtering all fork projects) and did not find contradicting results.

The selection of database access libraries was based on keywords and included manual validation. We identified an exhaustive list of 707 drivers. This step can be biased; however, establishing a complete list of drivers is probably an unreachable goal. The actual list of drivers is also available in our replication package to alleviate this threat. It can be reused and extended in future studies.

Internal validity does not affect this study, being an exploratory study, we did not claim any causation. On the other hand, *external validity* concerns the extent to which our results can be generalized. We present observations concerning the use of seven programming languages of subject systems. Although these languages are popular today, the results might not be generalized to other programming languages. Similarly, databases not considered in our study might affect generalizability. In particular, we aim at open-source technologies, and proprietary systems remained outside of our study. Further research might be needed to investigate whether our findings hold on other technologies.

Conclusion validity concerns relationships in our observations. We do not investigate relationships; consequently, we do not perform statistical tests. However, relationships might exist that we did not observe in our study.

6   Related Work

In this section, we discuss the novelty of our work with respect to previous research literature. The most related study by Decan et al. [9] investigates the introduction and the co-existence of *relational* database *access* technologies. The authors analyzed the evolution of 2,457 Java projects on GitHub and focused on JDBC, Hibernate and JPA as database access technologies. They observed a significant technology migration from Hibernate to JPA but did not find evidence of the massive replacement of JDBC.

Several authors identified database accesses in source code to identify smells, inconsistencies or antipatterns. Muse et al. [21] performed an empirical study on GitHub projects and analyzed the prevalence of SQL code smells in Java applications. Dimolikas et al. [11] studied the evolution of tables in a relational schema over time concerning the structure of the foreign keys to which tables are related. Meurice et al. [19] investigated the co-evolution of source code and database schemas with the ultimate goal to assist developers in preventing inconsistencies. Their study considered three Java systems. Qiu et al. [22] analyzed the co-evolution of SQL database schemas and code in ten open-source PHP applications. Anderson et al. [1] analyzed SQL queries embedded in PHP applications to support their understanding, evolution and security. Shao et al. [25] identified a list of database-access performance antipatterns, mainly in PHP web applications. Integrity violation was addressed by Li et al. [17], who identified constraints from source code and related them to database attributes.

Several previous studies exclusively focus on NoSQL applications. Störl et al. [28] investigated the advantages of using object mapper libraries when accessing NoSQL data stores. They overview Object-NoSQL Mappers (ONMs) and Object-Relational Mappers with NoSQL support. As they say, building applications against the native interfaces of NoSQL data stores create technical lock-in due to the lack of standardized query languages. Therefore, developers often turn to object mapper libraries as an extra level of abstraction. Scherzinger et al. [24] studied how software engineers design and evolve their domain model when building NoSQL applications, by analyzing the denormalized character of ten open-source Java applications relying on object mappers. They observed the growth in complexity of the NoSQL schemas and common evolution operations between the projects. Ringlstetter et al. [23] looked at how NoSQL object-mappers evolution annotations were used. They found that only 5.6% of 900 open-source Java projects using Morphia or Objectify used such annotations to evolve the data model or migrate the data.

The related approaches and studies described above primarily focus on the analysis, maintenance, and evolution of *either* relational *or* NoSQL systems. They mainly consider Java or PHP systems. The number of systems studied varies between 2.5 and 3 thousand projects. In contrast, our study investigates the use of *database models* in 40,609 open-source projects relying on relational *and/or* NoSQL database technologies. Therefore, our work does not restrict to single-database systems but specifically considers *hybrid* systems by covering five different database models (relational, document, key-value, column, and graph) possibly used in combination. Furthermore, we do not focus on a single programming language; we consider seven different languages (C#, Java, JavaScript, PHP, Python, Ruby, and TypeScript) among the most popular languages today.

7 Conclusion

This paper investigates the (joint) use of SQL and NoSQL database models in open-source projects. We started from several million projects, keeping those defining at least one database dependency based on a list of database drivers for the most common programming languages. We then selected only the projects meeting specific quality requirements.

We found that the majority of current database-dependent projects (54.72%) rely on a relational database model, while NoSQL-dependent systems represent 45.28% of the projects. However, the popularity of SQL technologies has recently decreased with respect to NoSQL datastores. As far as programming languages are concerned, we noticed that Ruby and Python systems are often paired with a PostgreSQL database. At the same time, Java and C# projects typically rely on a MySQL database. Data-intensive systems written in JavaScript/TypeScript are essentially paired with document-oriented or key-value databases.

Our results confirm the emergence of hybrid data-intensive systems where (multi-) database models (*e.g.,* relational and NoSQL) are used together (16% of all database-dependent projects). In particular, we found that more than 56% of systems relying on a key-value database also use another database technology, typically relational or document-oriented. Wide-column dependent systems follow the same pattern, with over 47% of them being hybrid. This demonstrates the complimentary usage of SQL and NoSQL database technologies in practice. We also observe that one percent of the database-dependent projects evolved their data model. The majority (62%) were not born hybrid but once relied on a single database model. In contrast, 19% became "mono-database" after initially using multiple database models.

Future work could benefit from analyzing the popularity of business domains in which combinations of database technologies are used together. An investigation of the rationale for adopting or giving up hybrid architectures could also reveal practical implications or lessons that would help the developers. Our findings provide a clear motivation to further understand and address those challenges and constitute an important step towards supporting developers to design and evolve hybrid data-intensive systems.

Acknowledgments. This research is supported by the F.R.S.-FNRS and FWO EOS project 30446992 SECO-ASSIST and the SNF-FNRS project INSTINCT.

References

1. Anderson, D., Hills, M.: Supporting analysis of SQL queries in PHP AiR. In: SCAM 2017, pp. 153–158. IEEE (2017)
2. Basciani, F., Rocco, J.D., Ruscio, D.D., Pierantonio, A., Iovino, L.: TyphonML: a modeling environment to develop hybrid polystores. In: MODELS 2020, pp. 2:1–2:5 (2020)
3. Benats, P.: Repl. pkg. https://github.com/benatspo/Multi-database_Models

4. Bernstein, P.A., Melnik, S.: Model management 2.0: manipulating richer mappings. In: SIGMOD 2007, pp. 1–12. ACM (2007)
5. Bird, C., Nagappan, N., Murphy, B., Gall, H., Devanbu, P.: Don't touch my code! examining the effects of ownership on software quality. In: ESEC/FSE 2011, pp. 4–14. ACM (2011)
6. Borges, H., Tulio Valente, M.: What's in a GitHub star? Understanding repository starring practices in a social coding platform. JSS **146**, 112–129 (2018)
7. Cleve, A., Gobert, M., Meurice, L., Maes, J., Weber, J.: Understanding database schema evolution: a case study. Sci. Comput. Program. **97**, 113–121 (2015)
8. Davoudian, A., Chen, L., Liu, M.: A survey on NoSQL stores. ACM Comput. Surv. **51**, 1–43 (2018)
9. Decan, A., Goeminne, M., Mens, T.: On the interaction of relational database access technologies in open source Java projects. In: SATTOSE 2015, pp. 26–35 (2015)
10. Decan, A., Mens, T., Grosjean, P.: An empirical comparison of dependency network evolution in seven software packaging ecosystems. Empir. Softw. Eng. **24**(1), 381–416 (2018). https://doi.org/10.1007/s10664-017-9589-y
11. Dimolikas, K., Zarras, A.V., Vassiliadis, P.: A study on the effect of a table's involvement in foreign keys to its schema evolution. In: Dobbie, G., Frank, U., Kappel, G., Liddle, S.W., Mayr, H.C. (eds.) ER 2020. LNCS, vol. 12400, pp. 456–470. Springer, Cham (2020). https://doi.org/10.1007/978-3-030-62522-1_34
12. Fink, J., Gobert, M., Cleve, A.: Adapting queries to database schema changes in hybrid polystores. In: SCAM 2020, pp. 127–131 (2020)
13. Gobert, M.: Schema evolution in hybrid databases systems. In: VLDB 2020 (2020)
14. Goeminne, M., Mens, T.: Towards a survival analysis of database framework usage in Java projects. In: ICSME 2015, pp. 551–555 (2015)
15. Jovanovic, P., Nadal, S., Romero, O., Abelló, A., Bilalli, B.: Quarry: a user-centered big data integration platform. Inf. Syst. Front. **23**, 9–33 (2021)
16. Kalliamvakou, E., Gousios, G., Blincoe, K., Singer, L., German, D.M., Damian, D.: The promises and perils of mining GitHub. In: MSR 2014, pp. 92–101. ACM (2014)
17. Li, B., Poshyvanyk, D., Grechanik, M.: Automatically detecting integrity violations in database-centric applications. In: ICPC 2017, pp. 251–262. IEEE (2017)
18. Linares-Vásquez, M., Li, B., Vendome, C., Poshyvanyk, D.: Documenting database usages and schema constraints in database-centric applications. In: ISSTA 2016, pp. 270–281 (2016)
19. Meurice, L., Nagy, C., Cleve, A.: Detecting and preventing program inconsistencies under database schema evolution. In: QRS 2016, pp. 262–273. IEEE (2016)
20. Munaiah, N., Kroh, S., Cabrey, C., Nagappan, M.: Curating GitHub for engineered software projects. Empir. Softw. Eng. **22**(6), 3219–3253 (2017). https://doi.org/10.1007/s10664-017-9512-6
21. Muse, B.A., Rahman, M.M., Nagy, C., Cleve, A., Khomh, F., Antoniol, G.: On the prevalence, impact, and evolution of SQL code smells in data-intensive systems. In: MSR 2020, pp. 327–338 (2020)
22. Qiu, D., Li, B., Su, Z.: An empirical analysis of the co-evolution of schema and code in database applications. In: ESEC/FSE 2013, pp. 125–135 (2013)
23. Ringlstetter, A., Scherzinger, S., Bissyandé, T.F.: Data model evolution using object-NoSQL mappers: folklore or state-of-the-art? In: 2nd International Workshop on BIG Data Software Engineering, pp. 33–36 (2016)

24. Scherzinger, S., Sidortschuck, S.: An empirical study on the design and evolution of NoSQL database schemas. In: Dobbie, G., Frank, U., Kappel, G., Liddle, S.W., Mayr, H.C. (eds.) ER 2020. LNCS, vol. 12400, pp. 441–455. Springer, Cham (2020). https://doi.org/10.1007/978-3-030-62522-1_33
25. Shao, S., et al.: Database-access performance antipatterns in database-backed web applications. In: ICSME 2020, pp. 58–69. IEEE (2020)
26. Sjøberg, D.: Quantifying schema evolution. Inf. Softw. Technol. **35**(1), 35–44 (1993)
27. Stonebraker, M., Deng, D., Brodie, M.L.: Database decay and how to avoid it. In: Proceedings of Big Data (2016)
28. Störl, U., Hauf, T., Klettke, M., Scherzinger, S.: Schemaless NoSQL data stores-Object-NoSQL Mappers to the rescue? In: BTW 2015 (2015)
29. Sun, Z., Liu, Y., Cheng, Z., Yang, C., Che, P.: Req2Lib: a semantic neural model for software library recommendation. In: SANER 2020, pp. 542–546 (2020)
30. Yamamoto, K., Kondo, M., Nishiura, K., Mizuno, O.: Which metrics should researchers use to collect repositories: an empirical study. In: QRS 2020, pp. 458–466 (2020)

An Empirical Study on the "Usage of Not" in Real-World JSON Schema Documents

Mohamed-Amine Baazizi[1], Dario Colazzo[2], Giorgio Ghelli[3], Carlo Sartiani[4], and Stefanie Scherzinger[5(✉)]

[1] Sorbonne Université, LIP6 UMR, 7606 Paris, France
baazizi@ia.lip6.fr
[2] Université Paris-Dauphine, PSL Research University, Paris, France
dario.colazzo@dauphine.fr
[3] Dipartimento di Informatica, Università di Pisa, Pisa, Italy
ghelli@di.unipi.it
[4] DIMIE, Università della Basilicata, Potenza, Italy
carlo.sartiani@unibas.it
[5] University of Passau, Passau, Germany
stefanie.scherzinger@uni-passau.de

Abstract. We study the usage of negation in JSON Schema data modeling. Negation is a logical operator rarely present in type systems and schema description languages, since it complicates decision problems: many software tools, but also formal frameworks for working with JSON Schema, do not fully support negation. This motivates us to study whether negation is actually used in practice, for which aims, and whether it could—in principle—be replaced by simpler operators. We have collected a large corpus of 80k open source JSON Schema documents from GitHub. We perform a systematic analysis, quantify usage patterns of negation, and also qualitatively analyze schemas. We show that negation is indeed used, albeit infrequently, following a stable set of patterns.

Keywords: Empirical study · Conceptual modeling · JSON Schema

1 Introduction

JavaScript Object Notation (JSON) has become one of the most popular formats for data exchange. While many schema languages for JSON been proposed [3], JSON Schema [16] is receiving considerable attention. The theoretical properties of this language have been recently studied [4,7,17]. In this language, a schema is a logical combination of assertions, describing classes of constraints on objects, arrays, and base values. JSON Schema is constantly evolving and new drafts always introduce new features. The language is increasingly used for defining *domain-specific* data exchange formats [13] and as a meta-language for

© Springer Nature Switzerland AG 2021
A. Ghose et al. (Eds.): ER 2021, LNCS 13011, pp. 102–112, 2021.
https://doi.org/10.1007/978-3-030-89022-3_9

```
(a)  1 { "not":
     2    { "required": ["DisplaceModules"] }
     3 }
```

```
(b)  1 { "description": "...",
     2    "@errorMessages":
     3       { "not": "Invalid target: ..." },
     4    "not": { "pattern": "..." } ... }
```

```
(c)  1 { "title" : "Object w/ required foo.",
     2    "type": "object",
     3    "properties": {
     4       "foo": { "type": "integer" },
     5       "bar": { "type": "string" } },
     6    "patternProperties": {
     7       "f.*o": { "type": "integer" } },
     8    "required": ["foo"]
     9 }
```

Fig. 1. Snippets of JSON Schema documents.

defining other languages; a subset of JSON Schema serves as the schema language inside MongoDB [15]. As a consequence, an active and quite broad development community is releasing JSON Schema tools (validators [1], in particular).

JSON Schema is powerful but complex, and its semantics is based on an intricate interplay among logical assertions. A distinctive feature is the not operator, whereby negation can be applied to any assertion. Negation is quite rare in type and schema languages, as it poses severe challenges.

Example 1. One usage of not that startles novices (as discussed on StackOverflow [18]) is in combination with the keyword required, as shown in Fig. 1(a). While "not required" may sound like "optional", it enforces that the object must violate the assertion, so member "DisplaceModules" must be *absent*.

Indeed, the not-operator is often not fully supported, whether in academic prototype tools [10], commercial tools (e.g., [15]), or even formal frameworks [11]. This inspired us to investigate the usage of this operator in real-world schemas, in a principled analysis of 80k JSON Schema documents crawled from GitHub. We formulate these research questions: (1) *how frequent* is negation in practice, (2) *how* is negation used, and (3) *what* are common usage patterns?

Contributions. We summarize the highlights of our systematic empirical study on the usage of not, which we describe in full detail in our extended technical report [5]. Along our journey towards understanding not, we gained a general understanding of JSON Schema modeling in practice. In particular:

- We establish a method for the collection and preparation of JSON Schema documents, and we make our corpus of schemas available (https://doi.org/10.5281/zenodo.5141199), as well as a docker container populated with data and pre-defined pattern queries for interactive, ad-hoc analysis in follow-up studies (https://doi.org/10.5281/zenodo.5141378).
- We measure the frequency of use of JSON Schema operators and of paths that include not, and quantify main patterns of use.
- We identify well-supported *jargons*, i.e., common uses of not that have the potential to mature into JSON Schema *design patterns*.

2   Preliminaries

JSON Data Model. The grammar below captures the syntax of JSON values, which are basic values, objects, or arrays. Basic values B include the null value, booleans, numbers n, and strings s. Objects O represent sets of members, each member being a name-value pair, and arrays A represent sequences of values.

$$
\begin{array}{llll}
J ::= B \mid O \mid A & & \textbf{JSON expressions} \\
B ::= \text{null} \mid \text{true} \mid \text{false} \mid n \mid s & n \in \mathsf{Num}, s \in \mathsf{Str} & \textbf{Basic values} \\
O ::= \{l_1 : J_1, \ldots, l_n : J_n\} & n \geq 0, \;\; i \neq j \Rightarrow l_i \neq l_j & \textbf{Objects} \\
A ::= [J_1, \ldots, J_n] & n \geq 0 & \textbf{Arrays}
\end{array}
$$

JSON Schema. JSON Schema is a language for defining the structure of JSON documents. JSON Schema uses JSON syntax, its semantics has been formalized in [17] (following Draft-04). We limit ourselves to discussing the main keywords, and continue with two illustrative examples:

Assertions include `required`, `enum`, `const`, `pattern` and `type`, and indicate a test that is performed on the corresponding instance.

Applicators include the boolean operators `anyOf`, `allOf`, `oneOf`, `not`, the object operators `properties`, `patternProperties`, `additionalProperties`, the array operator `items`, and the reference operators `$ref`. Applicators indicate a request to apply a different operator to the same instance or to a component of the current instance.

Annotations include `title`, `description`, and `$comment`, they do not affect validation, but they indicate an annotation that should be associated with the instance. Since we are mostly interested in validation, and since, moreover, annotations are removed by the `not` operator, we will ignore them.

Example 2. In the schema in Fig. 1(c), inspired from [1], line 1 carries an annotation. In defining an object (line 2), applicators define constraints on properties (lines 3), and the type of the properties matching a pattern (see line 6). Using an assertion, it is possible to indicate `required` properties (line 8).

Example 3. JSON Schema is an open standard: In Fig. 1(b), `@errorMessages` is a user-defined keyword whose value is an object that describes the error, and not a JSON Schema assertion (link to schema 32451 in our schema corpus, available in the PDF). Hence, `not` in line 3 is just a member name, whereas negation does occur in line 4. The same string token has different semantics, depending on its context, which complicates parsing.

2.1   Pattern Queries

To study which keywords occur below an instance of the `not` operator, we introduce a simple path language. A path such as `.**.not.required` matches any path that ends with an object field named `required` found inside an object field whose name is `not`. Paths are expressed using the following language. Path matching is defined as in JSONPath [9].

$$p ::= step \mid step\ p \qquad step ::= .key \mid .* \mid [*] \mid .**$$

The step $.*$ retrieves all member values of an object, $[*]$ retrieves all items of an array, and $.**$ is the reflexive and transitive closure of the union of $.*$ and $[*]$, navigating to all nodes of the JSON tree to which it is applied.

Complex Sub-schemas. We say that `not` has a *complex* sub-schema, when its object argument contains more than one keyword. In this case, we say these keywords *co-occur* in the negated schema; otherwise, a sub-schema is *simple*. As an example, consider the schema of Fig. 3(b) (link to schema 3460): the argument of `not` is complex, and we match the paths `.not.enum` and `.not.type`.

3 Methodology

Context. We used the cloud service Google BigQuery to search for open source JSON Schema documents (excluding the schemas defining the JSON Schema drafts) on GitHub. We identified 91,6k URLs in July 2020, of which 85,6k could be retrieved (using `wget`). Discarding files with invalid syntax yields 82k files.

For each retrieved file, we analyzed the `$schema` declarations to identify the version of JSON Schema. Draft 2019-09 (also known as Draft-08) is still quite new, and not really represented. Draft-04 is declared in the vast majority of the files (79%), while Draft-07, Draft-06, and the old Draft-03 are each below 5%. An analysis of the file contents showed that the actual version that a schema follows is often different from the version declared.

Data Preparation. As a first data preparation step, we renamed all references (`$ref`) by a new keyword `$eref`, with the target of the reference as its child. Note that we did not expand references recursively. We expanded references to external documents, provided that we were able to locate the referenced document (e.g., either contained within our corpus, or by downloading the document). References were renamed to `$fref` when expansion failed. We observed that by expanding references we lose the conceptual information encoded in the reference path itself. Thus, `$ref` is often more than just a syntactic macro.

The schema corpus contains a large share of near-duplicate schemas, with small variations in syntax. We performed duplicate elimination by comparing compact *schema signatures*, defined as a function that maps each JSON Schema keyword to the number of its occurrences in the schema (encoded as a vector of keyword counts); we assumed that two schemas with the same *signature* are, with high probability, versions of the same schema, and we retained just one.

As illustrated in Example 3, correctly recognizing keywords can be a challenge. For this reason, we renamed all property names to avoid confusion when searching for patterns that involve the keyword `not`. As schema authors can define their own keywords, we have no way to know whether their value should

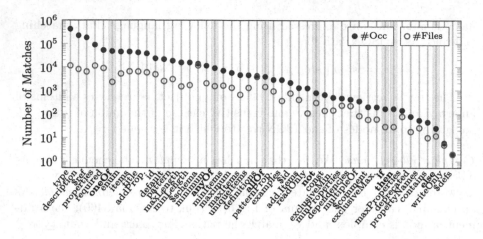

Fig. 2. Number of total occurrences (#Occ), and number of files (#Files), where a JSON Schema keyword appears. Boolean operators are highlighted. (Color figure online)

be interpreted as an assertion. We experimented with two approaches: a "strict" approach in which we renamed everything that was inside a user-defined keyword, hence making it inaccessible by the analysis, and a "lax" approach in which we kept the content of any user-defined keyword, so that all instances of not in Fig. 1(b) would be counted as keywords. With the strict approach, some interesting usage patterns are lost, and keyword usage is under-estimated. With the lax approach, we risk "false positives", and hence over-estimation. We decided that the over-estimation of the lax approach was preferable.

Analysis Process. The bulk of our effort is actually invested in data preparation. After experimenting with different data analysis platforms, we resorted to a relational encoding of the JSON Schema documents in PostgreSQL. This setup met our performance expectations, and allowed us to write queries in plain SQL.

Artifact Availability. Our schema corpus, as well as a docker image with our data analysis setup, are available on Zenodo (see the DOIs linked in the Introduction).

4   Results of the Study

4.1   RQ1: How Frequent Is Negation in Practice?

We study the frequency of JSON Schema keywords within our corpus, and the Boolean operators (among them, negation). The reported absolute values are mainly interesting as indicators as to the relative occurrences of operators. Figure 2 visualizes the results. From left-to-right, we sort keywords by their number of occurrence (note the log-scaled vertical axes). We also show the number of files in which keywords occur, as a further indicator of keyword relevance.

The operator **not** appears in approx. 3% of all schemas, and occupies the 30th position, out of 46 keywords analyzed. Thus, it is a comparatively rare operator. The most common Boolean operator is **oneOf**, more frequent than **anyOf**. **allOf** is even less common. The Boolean operator **if-then-else** is even less common than **not**, but was only been introduced in Draft-07.

Results. We found the dissemination of **oneOf** surprising, since the exclusive-disjunctive semantics of **oneOf** is more complicated than the purely disjunctive **anyOf**: **oneOf** takes as argument a collection of subschemas $S_1, \ldots, S_n$, and a value J satisfies **oneOf** only if it matches exactly one subschema; **anyOf** is satisfied by any value J that matches at least one of the subschemas. Our hypothesis is that the description of a class as a **oneOf**-combination of a set of "subclasses" is familiar from the exclusive-subclassing mechanism of object-oriented languages.

The operator **not** appears 787 times in 298 different files out of 11,500. While not very frequent, its usage nevertheless merits a systematic study.

4.2   RQ2: How is Negation Used in Practice?

We evaluated pattern queries to identify keywords below **not**. Table 1 summarizes the results. Consider the left half. We match the path .**.not.* 840 times (#Occ) in 289 files (#Files). Below the top summary row, we list the individual keywords, breaking down shares of matches in percent (visualized by progress bars). The right half of the table provides statistics for sub-schemas that are negated and referenced, and therefore reachable via a path .**.not.$eref.*.

In the following, we will omit the prefix ".**" from path queries, assuming the context is clear to our readers. We sorted the table on the total number of **not**.k+**not**.$eref.k$ occurrences (see [5] for the absolute values), and it is interesting to compare the weight of different keywords in both parts.

A **not** may not correspond to any **not**.* pattern, when followed by { }. We found 16 such occurrences, expressing the schema **false**, which is not satisfied by any instance. This use of **not** is a consequence of the fact that **false** has only been introduced with Draft-06.

Complex Arguments. Table 1 indicates a total of 840 occurrences of **not**.*, Fig. 2 reported 787 occurrences of **not**. The values differ since the negated sub-schema can be complex. Most instances of **not** have a simple sub-schema. Most negated complex schemas have two keywords, but some have three or four.

The situation is very different with $eref, i.e., references expanded in preprocessing. Here, 93 occurrences of **not**.$eref correspond to 338 occurrences of **not**.$eref.*. Thanks to the mediation of $eref, the schema designer implicitly applies negation to a complex argument, with an average of 3–4 members.

Results. The most common argument of negation is **required**. The pattern **not.items** is second-most common, followed by **not.type** and **not.properties**.

While **not.required** dominates the **not**.* case, the two most common cases of the **not**.$eref group are **not**.$eref.type, whose value is **object** in 80% of the

Table 1. Occurrences of **not.**k paths (overall #Occ, and counting #Files).

Path	#Occ	#Files	Path	#Occ	#Files
not.*	840	289	**not.$eref.***	338	28
required	28.6 %	29.1 %	required	10.7 %	53.6 %
items	15.0 %	9.3 %	items	0.0 %	0.0 %
type	7.4 %	17.7 %	type	15.1 %	71.4 %
properties	8.5 %	16.3 %	properties	11.8 %	64.3 %
$eref	11.1 %	9.7 %	$eref	0.0 %	0.0 %
enum	7.3 %	18.0 %	enum	3.6 %	28.6 %
allOf	2.7 %	8.0 %	allOf	11.2 %	17.9 %
pattern	5.6 %	9.7 %	pattern	0.0 %	0.0 %
anyOf	5.4 %	12.5 %	anyOf	0.6 %	7.1 %
description	0.5 %	1.4 %	description	12.1 %	25.0 %
title	0.2 %	0.7 %	title	11.5 %	25.0 %
$schema	0.0 %	0.0 %	$schema	12.1 %	32.1 %
$fref	3.2 %	4.8 %	$fref	0.0 %	0.0 %
oneOf	0.7 %	1.4 %	oneOf	5.3 %	10.7 %
additionalProperties	1.3 %	3.8 %	additionalProperties	2.7 %	25.0 %
patternProperties	1.8 %	5.2 %	patternProperties	0.0 %	0.0 %
const	0.7 %	0.4 %	const	0.0 %	0.0 %
definitions	0.0 %	0.0 %	definitions	0.9 %	10.7 %
id	0.0 %	0.0 %	id	0.6 %	7.1 %
dependencies	0.0 %	0.0 %	dependencies	0.6 %	7.1 %
not	0.0 %	0.0 %	not	0.6 %	7.1 %
$ref	0.0 %	0.0 %	$ref	0.6 %	7.1 %
$comment	0.1 %	0.4 %	$comment	0.0 %	0.0 %

cases, and **not.$eref.properties**, which indicates that **not.$eref** is mostly used to negate complex object definitions. This explains the much higher occurrence of descriptive keywords inside the referenced argument.

4.3   RQ3: What Are Common Real-World Usage Patterns?

Field and Value Exclusion. Field exclusion via **not.required** is the most frequent path, and this usage was already discussed in Example 1.

We discuss the paths **not.enum** and **not.const** together, as both are used to exclude values. Snippets of example schemas are shown in Figs. 3(a) and (b). Such schemas have an obvious interpretation: the instance may have any type and must be different from the string or strings listed. In the majority of cases, the sub-schema is simple, as in Fig. 3(a) (link to schema 89480). In the complex cases, **enum** is always paired with a "type" : "string" assertion, as in Fig. 3(b) (link to schema 3458). This assertion is redundant, since all values listed by **enum**

```
     "not": {
(a)    "enum": ["markdown",
                "code",
                "raw"] }
```

```
     "not": {
(b)    "enum": ["generic-linux"],
       "type": "string" }
```

```
     "not": {
       "items": {
         "not": {
(c)        "type": "string",
           "enum": [
             "Dataset", "Image",
             "Video", "Sound",
             "Text" ] } }
```

```
     { "type" : "object",
       "oneOf": [
         { "properties":
             { "when": {"enum": ["delayed"]}},
           "required": ["when","start_in"] },
(d)      { "properties":
             { "when": { "not": {"enum": ["delayed"]}
       }}} ] }
```

```
     { "type": "object",
       "if": {
         "required": ["when"],
         "properties":
           { "when": {"enum": ["delayed"]} }},
(e)    "then": {
         "properties":
           { "when": {"enum": ["delayed"] }},
         "required": ["when", "start_in"] }}
```

Fig. 3. JSON Schema snippets exemplifying real-world usage patterns.

are strings. This co-occurrence is not specific to negation, since also in positive schemas, enum is paired with a type assertion in the vast majority of cases.

Paraphrasing contains. The pattern not.items is among the most common not-paths. All such schemas have either the structure not.items.not (as in Fig. 3(c), link to schema 88916) or not.items.enum.

The items assertion is verified by any instance that is not an array, or that is an empty array, or that is an array where every element satisfies the schema associated with items. Hence, it is only violated by instances that are arrays, and which contain at least one element that violates the schema. While items specifies a universally quantified property, not.items can be used to specify an existentially quantified property, as does the **contains** keyword (as we will discuss shortly). The jargon not.items.enum specifies that the array must contain at least one value that is not listed in the argument of enum. The jargon not.items.not specifies that the instance is an array that contains at least one value that satisfies S, according to the following equivalence:

$$\texttt{"not": \{ "items": \{ "not": } S \texttt{ \} \}} \Leftrightarrow \texttt{\{"type": "array", "contains": } S \texttt{ \}}$$

These two cases cover, with minimal variations, all occurrences of not.items. (In fact, all these schemas originate from just two groups of schema designers.)

To sum up, not.items can be used to express **contains**. This is an instance of a pattern that may be replaced by a single (and thus simpler) operator.

Paraphrasing Discriminated Unions. The schema snippet in Fig. 3(d) (link to schema 90970) allows interesting observations about the use of oneOf. JSON Schema specifications do not prescribe that the branches of oneOf are mutually exclusive, but they state that a value must match a single branch only. However, the two branches of oneOf happen to be mutually exclusive: if "when" is absent, then only the second branch holds. If it is present, then it is associated to complementary types in the two branches, so here, oneOf is actually anyOf. Applying equivalent rewritings (from $\neg a \lor b$ to $a \Rightarrow b$, and pushing down negation), the schema can be rewritten as shown in Fig. 3(e). Now the specification is more clear: if `"when"` has the value `"delayed"`, then `"start_in"` is required.

This suggests that `oneOf` is used to express a form of *discriminated unions*. In discriminated unions, also known as *tagged unions* or *labeled unions*, each branch is labeled with a unique label (or tag), and any value matching the union must be prefixed by the label of the only branch it matches.

Results. Certain usage patterns are quite common: field exclusion, value exclusion from sets of strings, and field mutual exclusion. Field exclusion is so common that one may imagine to add an ad-hoc operator to the JSON Schema language.

5   Discussion

In our analysis, we learned that negation is used in many different ways, some of which are extremely creative. In the following, we discuss our key observations.

Redundancy. Schema designers tend to overspecify by adding redundant assertions. A quantitative follow-up study, based on structured interviews, would help to understand their motivation. For instance, redundancy might be introduced to improve schema readability.

Comprehensibility. A general lesson learned is that JSON Schema semantics can be subtle, and the JSON notation can create readability problems. Educational tools for analyzing JSON Schema semantics, such as rewriting schemas to eliminate negation or even generate witnesses to schemas [2,4], may help.

Language Extensions. We observed that negation is often used in order to express, in a cumbersome way, the *discriminated unions* pattern, where the value of one field determines the presence/absence and the type of the others. This may trigger reflections about schema design.

`not.required` is heavily used to forbid the presence of properties. One may imagine adding a `"forbidden"`: [`"k1"`, ..., `"kn"`] operator as a simpler way to specify that properties `"k1"`, ..., `"kn"` cannot be present.

Benchmarks. Some of the most popular jargons found in our study are not reflected in the JSON Schema Test Suite [1], a collection of synthetic schemas for benchmarking JSON Schema validators. At the time of this writing (commit hash #09fd353 of the test suite), the test schemas only include the paths `not.type`, `not.properties`, `not` followed by { }, `not.true`, as well as `not.false`. We hope that our study may help extend such test suites by popular usage patterns.

6 Related Work

We provide more details on the usage of not in our extended technical report [5].

We can safely claim that our collection of real-world JSON Schema documents is so far the most diverse: In an earlier empirical study [13], we analyzed schemas from SchemaStore,[1] a curated collection of real-world JSON Schema documents (150 at that time). This study targeted a comparatively coarse-grained classification of the occurrences of language operators, e.g., all Boolean operators were treated as a single group.

There is an established tradition of empirical studies on schema languages for semi-structured data (e.g., [6,8,12,14]). In hindsight, these studies have guided researchers towards addressing the relevant language features. Understanding how negation is used is also relevant for building practical tools, e.g., for validation [7], containment checking [2,11], or witness generation [2].

7 Summary

In our study on the usage of **not** in JSON Schema, we identified three cases: (a) We found that one reason for using **not** is that schema designers are missing certain negative dual operators, such as a `forbidden` would be the missing dual to `required`. (b) Another case that we encountered is that **not** is used to encode implication (so $a \Rightarrow b$ may be encoded as $\neg a \vee b$). (c) Finally, negation is used for subtraction, e.g., to specify integers that are not multiples of 2.

In case (c), we regard negation as useful, whereas for the other cases, we would prefer to see suitable extensions to the language.

Acknowledgments. This contribution was partly funded by *Deutsche Forschungsgemeinschaft* (DFG, German Research Foundation) grant #385808805. The schemas were retrieved using Google BigQuery, supported by Google Cloud. We thank Thomas Pilz (OTH Regensburg) for his help in making the research artifacts available. We thank Michael Fruth (University of Passau) for feedback on an earlier draft.

References

1. JSON Schema Test Suite (2021). https://github.com/json-schema-org/JSON-Schema-Test-Suite. version of commit hash #09fd353
2. Attouche, L., et al.: A tool for JSON schema witness generation. In: Proceedings of EDBT 2021, pp. 694–697 (2021)
3. Baazizi, M.A., Colazzo, D., Ghelli, G., Sartiani, C.: Schemas and types for JSON data: from theory to practice. In: Proceedings of SIGMOD 2019, pp. 2060–2063 (2019)
4. Baazizi, M.A., Colazzo, D., Ghelli, G., Sartiani, C., Scherzinger, S.: Not elimination and witness generation for JSON schema. In: Proceedings of BDA 2020 (2020)

---

[1] SchemaStore, at https://www.schemastore.org/json/, last accessed 21-Apr-2021.

5. Baazizi, M.A., Colazzo, D., Ghelli, G., Sartiani, C., Scherzinger, S.: An empirical study on the "usage of not" in real-world JSON schema documents (long version). CoRR (2021). https://arxiv.org/abs/2107.08677
6. Bex, G.J., Neven, F., den Bussche, J.V.: DTDs versus XML schema: a practical study. In: Proceedings of WebDB 2004 (2004)
7. Bourhis, P., Reutter, J.L., Suárez, F., Vrgoc, D.: JSON: data model, query languages and schema specification. In: Proceedings of PODS 2017, pp. 123–135 (2017)
8. Choi, B.: What are real DTDs like? In: Proceedings of WebDB 2002, pp. 43–48 (2002)
9. Friesen, J.: Extracting JSON values with JsonPath. In: Java XML and JSON: Document Processing for Java SE, pp. 299–322. Apress (2019)
10. Fruth, M., Baazizi, M.A., Colazzo, D., Ghelli, G., Sartiani, C., Scherzinger, S.: Challenges in checking JSON schema containment over evolving real-world schemas. In: Grossmann, G., Ram, S. (eds.) ER 2020. LNCS, vol. 12584, pp. 220–230. Springer, Cham (2020). https://doi.org/10.1007/978-3-030-65847-2_20
11. Habib, A., Shinnar, A., Hirzel, M., Pradel, M.: Finding data compatibility bugs with JSON subschema checking. In: Proceedings of ISSTA 2021, pp. 620–632 (2021)
12. Laender, A.H., Moro, M.M., Nascimento, C., Martins, P.: An X-ray on web-available XML schemas. SIGMOD Rec. **38**(1), 37–42 (2009)
13. Maiwald, B., Riedle, B., Scherzinger, S.: What are real JSON schemas like? In: Guizzardi, G., Gailly, F., Suzana Pitangueira Maciel, R. (eds.) ER 2019. LNCS, vol. 11787, pp. 95–105. Springer, Cham (2019). https://doi.org/10.1007/978-3-030-34146-6_9
14. Martens, W., Neven, F., Schwentick, T., Bex, G.J.: Expressiveness and complexity of XML schema. ACM Trans. Database Syst. **31**(3), 770–813 (2006)
15. MongoDB Inc.: MongoDB Manual: $jsonSchema (Version 4.4) (2021). https://docs.mongodb.com/manual/reference/operator/query/jsonSchema/
16. json-schema org: JSON Schema (2021). https://json-schema.org
17. Pezoa, F., Reutter, J.L., Suarez, F., Ugarte, M., Vrgoč, D.: Foundations of JSON schema. In: Proceedings of WWW 2016, pp. 263–273 (2016)
18. StackOverflow: JSON Schema - valid if object does *not* contain a particular property. https://stackoverflow.com/questions/30515253/json-schema-valid-if-object-does-not-contain-a-particular-property

Conceptual Modeling of Hybrid Polystores

Maxime Gobert[(✉)], Loup Meurice, and Anthony Cleve

Namur Digital Institute, University of Namur, Namur, Belgium
{maxime.gobert,loup.meurice,anthony.cleve}@unamur.be

Abstract. An increasing number of organisations rely on NoSQL technologies to manage their mission-critical data. However, those technologies were not intended to *replace* relational database management systems, but rather to *complement* them. Hence the recent emergence of heterogeneous database architectures, commonly called *hybrid polystores*, that rely on a *combination* of several, possibly overlapping relational and NoSQL databases. Unfortunately, there is still a lack of models, methods and tools for data modeling and manipulation in such architectures. With the aim to fill this gap, we introduce HyDRa, a conceptual framework to design and manipulate hybrid polystores. We present the HyDRa textual modeling language allowing one to specify (1) the conceptual schema of a polystore, (2) the physical schemas of each of its databases, and (3) a set of mapping rules to express possibly complex correspondences between the conceptual schema elements and the physical databases.

Keywords: Hybrid polystores · Conceptual modeling · Framework

1 Introduction

NoSQL technologies have been around for more than a decade, and a large number of organisations are currently using them to store and manipulate mission-critical data. Despite their increasing popularity it becomes clear that NoSQL backends will not *replace* traditional relational technologies. Each data model has its own benefits and drawbacks, and is most suitable for specific use cases. This may encourage developers to build *hybrid* data-intensive systems, also called *polystores* [8,23,24]. Such systems rely on a combination of multiple databases of different models, relational or NoSQL, each one chosen for its best features.

However, NoSQL database modeling is not yet as stable and mature as standard relational database design. In particular, NoSQL data representation does not often rely on a unique explicit schema. Even within the same paradigm, translating conceptual schema elements into physical data structures can be done in various different ways, depending on the anticipated usage of the data. Existing design techniques are either based on best practices [1–4] or target single data models [18,21]. Some authors proposed to unify the NoSQL data models into a generic modeling framework [6]. However, since NoSQL design choices

© Springer Nature Switzerland AG 2021
A. Ghose et al. (Eds.): ER 2021, LNCS 13011, pp. 113–122, 2021.
https://doi.org/10.1007/978-3-030-89022-3_10

may greatly impact performance [9], it is important that the designer keeps full control on how data is stored physically, which is not always possible with a generic data model. Furthermore, there is still a lack of models, methods, and tools supporting the design and querying of hybrid polystores, where relational and NoSQL databases are used in combination.

As a step to fill this gap, we introduce HyDRa (Hybrid Data Representation and Access), an integrated framework for conceptual modeling and manipulation of hybrid polystores. We focus on the HyDRa modeling language, as depicted in Fig. 1, allowing one to specify the conceptual schema of a polystore, according to the *Entity-Relationship* model, as well as the physical schema of each of its underlying databases. HyDRa currently supports the relational model and the four most popular NoSQL data models, i.e., document, key-value, graph and column-based representations. The language enables the definition of mapping rules, to express correspondences between the conceptual schema elements and their physical database counterparts. Those rules enable possibly complex physical design choices, such as *data structure split*, *data instance partitioning*, *data heterogeneity* and *data duplication*.

The remaining of the paper is structured as follows. Section 2 summarizes the state-of-the-art approaches for NoSQL and hybrid polystore design. Section 3 presents and illustrates the HyDRa modeling language. Section 4 gives concluding remarks and anticipates future work.

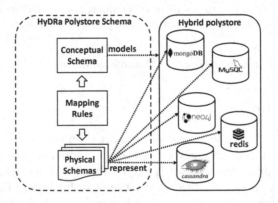

Fig. 1. Overview of the HyDRa modeling languages

2   Related Work

Database design for NoSQL applications is still an emerging research area. Current state-of-the-art approaches mainly consist of technology, data model-specific [18,20,21] design recommendations or best practices [1–4]. Roy-Hubara et al. [22] made a systematic literature review on NoSQL database design. The SOS platform [6] provides a common interface to multiple NoSQL systems. It relies on a generic data model and provides automatic translations towards native backend implementations. BigDAWG [12] is a polystore implementation focusing on query optimization and data placement. NoAM [9] proposes a uniform way to design NoSQL systems by abstracting the common features of each data model and by designing an aggregate identification step. Cabibbo [10] develops a JPA-based object mapper for multiple NoSQL backends, that enables the different data representation strategies presented in [9]. Herrero et al. [17] define a 3-step top-down design method from a conceptual model to physical structures. The logical schema is based on the data types specified in the conceptual schema, or on the build graph of dependent entities. The logical schemas are automatically proposed with optimizing performance as main objective. Bjeladinovic [8] presents an approach to design hybrid SQL/NoSQL databases. Based on database measures and requirements, the user is directed towards either a relational database design or to the NoAM approach.

The TyphonML model [7], which partly inspired HyDRa, also supports conceptual modeling of hybrid polystores, but imposes implicit restrictions on the way conceptual elements are physically translated in each different native backend. In other words, TyphonML does not leave developers the freedom to explicitly define the mappings between conceptual and physical schema elements of the polystore, which is at the core of HyDRa.

The approaches discussed above are either (1) design methods for particular data models, (2) abstraction-based approaches to conceptual modeling of NoSQL systems, or (3) polystore modeling approaches with limited control over the conceptual-to-physical mappings and no support to express cross-database overlapping within the polystore. In this paper, we propose an approach to hybrid polystore modeling that (1) provides users with a full and fine-grained control over the mapping between the conceptual schema and the underlying physical data structures, and (2) supports overlapping between the polystore databases.

3   The HyDRa Polystore Modeling Language

HyDRa polystore model language is composed of five main parts, each having its specific purpose. Figure 2 provides an abstract syntax of those main parts. *Conceptual schema* specifies the domain-specific data model of the complete system. *Physical schema* describes the data structures in the underlying physical databases. *Mapping rules* is where the mapping rules between conceptual schema elements and physical schema elements are expressed. *Databases* declares the physical databases and their respective configurations.

$$\langle \text{Schema} \rangle \models \langle \text{ConceptualSchema} \rangle \langle \text{PhysicalSchema*} \rangle$$
$$\langle \text{Mapping Rules} \rangle \langle \text{Databases} \rangle$$
$$\langle \text{PhysicalSchema} \rangle \models \langle \text{RelationalSchema} \rangle \mid \langle \text{DocumentSchema} \rangle \mid$$
$$\langle \text{KeyValueSchema} \rangle \mid \langle \text{GraphSchema} \rangle \mid \langle \text{ColumnSchema} \rangle$$

Fig. 2. Abstract syntax of HyDRa language main components

The remaining of this section illustrates the HyDRa language, based on the example polystore schema of Fig. 3. This schema, based on the *IMDB* dataset[1], involves three database back-ends: a key-value, a document and a relational database.

3.1   Conceptual Schema

The *conceptual schema* represents the entities the polystore manipulates. As in standard database engineering methods, during conceptual design, the user specifies the domain model [11] based on *Entity-Relationship* model constructions. The domain is described by means of *entity types, attributes, binary relationship types, conceptual identifiers, n-ary relationship types* or *relationship types with attributes*. The conceptual schema of our *IMDB* example is declared in lines 1–36 in Fig. 3. Entity types have attributes and declare one of several identifier(s) in their *identifier* section. Next we specify the relationship types and the roles played by the entity types within them. Relationship types can be *binary* or *n-ary*, and can also have attributes.

3.2   Physical Schemas

The *physical schema* section of our model lets the designer specify how data is actually persisted in native databases. We support the relational data model as well as the four most popular NoSQL data models [16], namely document, key-value, column wide and graph-based representations. One of the key advantage of the physical section is the ability to represent each design technique of each data model, by providing the designer with full control on physical data structures. In our running example, this section spreads from line 38 to line 98. Below, we illustrate the physical data models supported by HyDRa, and how common design strategies fit in this language.

As *Physical Schemas* may represent five different types of data models, we had to define common terms across them to refer to data structures. Below we define the chosen terms of *Physical Structures, Physical Fields* as well as *References* allowing cross-database referencing.

A *Physical Field* is the term we use for data units in the corresponding technology-specific databases: *Columns* in relational, *Fields* in document, *Properties* in graph, *Columns* in column-oriented and *Value Properties* in key-value data models. For NoSQL complex data types such as arrays or objects fields, we use a different word by calling them *ComplexFields*.

A *Physical Structure* is an abstraction of technology-specific structures able to receive multiple data units. They contain multiple *Physical Fields*. Figure 4 describes the specification of this structure in our language. Typical structures include *Table* in a relational database, *Collection* in document database, and *Tablecolumn* in column oriented databases. For graph databases *Nodes* as well as *Edges* are considered physical structures. For key-value databases, we introduce

---

[1] https://www.imdb.com/interfaces/.

```
1   conceptual schema cs{
2     entity type Actor {
3       id : string,
4       fullName : string,
5       yearOfBirth : int,
6       yearOfDeath : int
7       identifier { id }
8     }
9     entity type Director {
10      id : string,
11      firstName : string,
12      lastName : string,
13      yearOfBirth : int,
14      yearOfDeath : int
15      identifier { id }
16    }
17    entity type Movie {
18      id : string,
19      primaryTitle : string,
20      originalTitle : string,
21      isAdult : bool,
22      startYear : int,
23      runtimeMinutes: int,
24      averageRating : string,
25      numVotes : int
26      identifier { id }
27    }
28    relationship type movieDirector{
29      directed_movie[0-N]: Movie,
30      director[0-N] : Director
31    }
32    relationship type movieActor{
33      character[0-N]: Actor,
34      movie[0-N] : Movie
35    }
36  }
37
38  physical schemas {
39
40    key value schema movieRedis :
         myredis {
41      kvpairs movieKV {
42        key : "movie:"[id],
43        value : attr hash{
44          title,
45          originalTitle,
46          isAdult,
47          startYear,
48          runtimeMinutes
49        }
50      }
51    }
```

```
52
53  document schema IMDB_Mongo : mymongo
       , mymongo2{
54
55    collection actorCollection {
56      fields {
57        id,
58        name:[fullname],
59        birthyear,
60        deathyear,
61        movies[0-N]{
62          id,
63          title,
64          rating[1]{
65            rate: [rate] "/10" ,
66            numberofvotes
67          }
68        }
69      }
70    }
71  }
72
73  relational schema myRelSchema {
74
75    table directorTable{
76      columns{
77        id,
78        fullname:
79          [firstname]" "[lastname],
80        birth,
81        death
82      }
83    }
84
85    table directed {
86      columns{
87        director_id,
88        movie_id
89      }
90
91      references {
92        directed_by : director_id ->
         directorTable.id
93        has_directed : movie_id ->
         movieRedis.movieKV.id
94        movie_info : movie_id ->
         IMDB_Mongo.actorCollection.movies.
         id
95      }
96    }
97  }
98  }
```

```
99
100  mapping rules{
101  cs.Actor(id,fullName,yearOfBirth,yearOfDeath) -> IMDB_Mongo.actorCollection
        (id,fullname,birthyear,deathyear) ,
102  cs.movieActor.character-> IMDB_Mongo.actorCollection.movies() ,
103  cs.Director(id,firstName,lastName, yearOfBirth,yearOfDeath) -> myRelSchema.
        directorTable(id,firstname,lastname,birth,death),
104  cs.movieDirector.director  -> myRelSchema.directed.directed_by ,
105  cs.movieDirector.directed_movie -> myRelSchema.directed.has_directed  ,
106  cs.movieDirector.directed_movie -> myRelSchema.directed.movie_info ,
107  cs.Movie(id, primaryTitle) -> IMDB_Mongo.actorCollection.movies(id,title) ,
108  cs.Movie(averageRating,numVotes) -> IMDB_Mongo.actorCollection.movies.
        rating(rate,numberofvotes) ,
109  cs.Movie(id) -> movieRedis.movieKV(id) ,
110  cs.Movie(primaryTitle,originalTitle,isAdult,startYear,runtimeMinutes) ->
        movieRedis.movieKV.attr(title,originalTitle,isAdult,startYear,
        runtimeMinutes)
111  }
```

Fig. 3. Example of a HyDRa schema, conceptual, physical and mapping rules section.

the *KeyValuePair* concept. It reflects a set of key-value pairs sharing the same pattern of keys and values (see lines 40–51 of Fig. 3).

A *Reference* block expresses a link between two physical fields of physical structures. In a polystore, a source field could reference a target field declared in a different database, and relying on a different data model. Therefore HyDRa offers the possibility to express cross-references between heterogeneous databases.

For instance, lines 91–95 in Fig. 3 declare three references. Reference *directed_by* indicates that physical field *director_id* values are also stored in the *id* field of *directedTable*. This reference is the expression of a foreign key of the many-to-many table *directed*. The other column of this join table, *movie_id*, is a multiple hybrid reference, as *has_directed* targets *id* in the *movieRedis* key-value database and *movie_info* targets document database *IMDB_Mongo*.

Relational Schemas. Relational schemas are composed of tables and columns. Columns may only contain simple values. Lines 73–97 show the declaration of a relational schema structures. Following tables declaration are the references declaration. Source fields of the declared references are part of the current relational schema, however target fields may be in a different structure.

Document Schemas. Document schemas follow a JSON-like data model. It consists of key-value pairs organized by documents, each document field may in turn be a document, allowing embedded structures at certain levels of depth. Available design methods for document databases are described by MongoDB [1], the leading technology for this data model. Embedding data structures is referred to as *one to few*. Lines 53–71 show a document database schema declaration. Lines 61–68 show how we can declare such a nested structure, using complex field *movies* as an array. If, for design purposes or for technical reasons, embedding documents is not possible, the user can choose to use referencing values across collections of documents, this is referred to *one to many* design. Our model allows such constructions using reference blocks, as described above.

Key-Value Schemas. Key-value schemas simply consist of key-value pairs, with no constructs allowing references between data instances. Querying data in this model is done only using *put* and *get* operations on the key part. This apparent simplicity may lead to possibly complex schema design problems when deciding how to organize the data. One needs to carefully design and manage the chosen key patterns. Design methods [5,21] and best practices [4] identified two main patterns. The first one, called *Key value per field*, creates a key-value pair for each atomic field. The key is composed of different elements identifying a particular atomic instance. Examples of key patterns for this design includes *ENTITY:[identifier]:FIELD*. It results in data such as *MOVIE:tt0118715:TITLE* as key, and a binary object *The Big Lebowski* as value. The second design type, *Key Value per object*, uses complex data types instead of simple atomic value, the value contains now multiple fields. This allows the grouping of multiple fields under the same key. Lines 40–51 illustrate this pattern.

Column-Oriented Schemas. Column-oriented schemas rely on row identifiers (*rowkey*), and each row is composed of groups of key-value pairs (*column families*). Design methods identified in [2,3], such as *Row per object representation* or *Single cell per object* are also supported in the HyDRa language. We refer to the HyDRa companion website [15] for an illustrative example of a column-based schema.

Graph Schemas. Graph schemas represent data as *Property graphs*. The data model is composed of *Nodes* and *Edges* that may contain *Properties*. The common way to design graph databases is described by the leading technology of graph databases, Neo4j [19]. *Nodes* usually represent entities and relationships between data are expressed using *edges*. Again we refer to our companion website [15] for an illustrative example.

3.3   Mapping Rules

The mapping rules section of an HyDRa polystore schema specifies links between the conceptual schema elements and the physical structures. Exploiting the possibly hybrid nature of those mapping rules, the designer can specify complex constructions such as *data structure split, data instance partitioning, data heterogeneity* and *data duplication* (see Sect. 3.5).

Figure 4 exposes the abstract syntax of mapping rules types and of their components. The left-hand side of the rule (before the arrow) is the *conceptual* component and the right-hand side corresponds to the *physical* component. Two types of mapping rules are supported: *Entity mapping rules* and *Role mapping rules*. Mapping rules are in lines 100–111 in the polystore schema of Fig. 3.

$$\langle \text{PhysicalStructure} \rangle \models \langle \text{Table} \rangle \mid \langle \text{Collection} \rangle \mid \langle \text{TableColumn} \rangle \mid$$
$$\langle \text{Node} \rangle \mid \langle \text{Edge} \rangle \mid \langle \text{KeyValuePair} \rangle$$
$$\langle \text{EntityMappingRule} \rangle \models \langle \text{EntityType} \rangle (\langle \text{Attribute+} \rangle) \rightarrow$$
$$\langle \text{PhysicalStructure} \rangle (\langle \text{PhysicalField+} \rangle)$$
$$\langle \text{RoleMappingRule} \rangle \models \langle \text{Role} \rangle \rightarrow \langle \text{Reference} \rangle \mid \langle \text{ComplexField} \rangle$$

Fig. 4. Abstract syntax of HyDRa structures and mapping rules

EntityMappingRule is a type of rule used to map *Conceptual Entity types* to *Physical Structures*. A conceptual entity type can be mapped to one or more heterogeneous structures. We provide some examples of mapping rules in Fig. 3. First, at line 101, entity type *Actor* and its attributes are mapped to collection *actorCollection* in document database schema *IMDB_Mongo* (schema at lines 53–71). Second, at line 103, entity type *Director* is mapped to table *directorTable*, belonging to relational database schema *myRelSchema* (lines 73–97). Last, entity type *Movie* is mapped to three physical structures and one complex field (lines

107, 108, 109, 110). Line 108 maps attributes *averageRating* and *numVotes* to physical fields contained into a third-level embedded structure *rating* in the *movies* array of *actorCollection*.

RoleMappingRule is another mapping rule type that maps *Roles* of *Relationship types* to *Reference* blocks or to *ComplexFields*. Lines 102, 105 and 106 are examples of such mapping rules for relationship types *movieDirector* and *movieActor*.

3.4   Physical Databases

The physical database section is used to declare the actual databases linked to the physical schemas, and provide their connection information. Each physical schema can be linked to one or several declared database(s). Figure 5 shows the databases declared for the physical schemas of Fig. 3.

```
1   databases {                        11   mongodb mymongo{
2      mariadb mydb {                  12      host : "localhost"
3         host: "localhost"            13      port: 27100
4         port: 3307                   14   }
5         dbname : "mydb"              15   mongodb mymongo2{
6      }                               16      host : "localhost"
7      redis myredis {                 17      port: 27000
8         host:"localhost"             18   }
9         port:6379                    19  }
10     }
```

Fig. 5. Databases declaration section

3.5   Benefits of HyDRa

Data Duplication and Heterogeneity. HyDRa allows data duplication at the level of conceptual objects as well as at the physical schema level. Data duplication at the level of entity types can be expressed through multiple entity mapping rules, with the same entity type as left-hand side, but mapping it to several different physical structures. An example was given above with the mappings of attribute *primaryTitle* of *Movie* entity type (lines 107 and 110) which is mapped to both a document database and a key-value database. HyDRa also allows one to duplicate an entire physical schema into several databases. For instance, line 53 in Fig. 3 declares that physical schema *IMDB_Mongo* is stored in both databases *mymongo* and *mymongo2*.

Composed Fields. The physical fields of an HyDRa schema can have complex values. This is made possible by means of complex physical field declarations and related mapping rules. For instance, line 79 of Fig. 3 specifies that the value of column *fullname* in relational table *directorTable* results from the concatenation of conceptual attributes *firstname* and *lastname*. This is expressed using the entity mapping rule at line 103. As another example, physical field *rate* at line 65 concatenates the *rate* conceptual attribute value with the "/10" string constant.

Data Structure Split. Conceptual entity types can be split and stored in multiple and heterogeneous databases. Multiple entity mapping rules can be expressed for distinct fragments of a single entity type, e.g., by splitting its attributes into multiple and possibly heterogeneous databases. For instance, conceptual entity type *Movie* is composed of eight attributes, but those attributes are stored either in the *IMDB_Mongo* schema or in *movieRedis* schema, or in both physical schemas. As expressed by the mapping rules of lines 107, 108, 109 and 110, some of the movie attributes are subject to data duplication across several physical schemas, while attributes *isAdult, startYear, runtimeMinutes* are only present in the *movieRedis* schema.

Data Instance Partitioning. Using data instance partitioning, an HyDRa poly-store schema can map only a *subset* of the data instances of a given entity type to a particular physical structure. The data instances are discriminated based on user-defined conditions on the value of a particular entity type attribute. For instance, in Listing 1.1, a mapping rule expresses that the instances of entity type *Movie* that have an *averageRating* value greater than 9 must be stored in the *topMovies* physical structure.

```
1    cs.Movie(id,primaryTitle,averageRating,numVotes) -(averageRating > 9)
     -> IMDB_Mongo.topMovies(id,title,rate,numberofvotes),
```

Listing 1.1. Mapping rule data instance partitioning

4 Conclusion

This paper introduces HyDRa, a conceptual framework for hybrid polystore modeling and manipulation. It focuses on the HyDRa modeling language, able to *conceptually design hybrid polystores* while preserving the possibility to design data at physical level and exploit the strengths of each native data model. The conceptual and physical abstraction levels are linked together through a set of *mapping rules*, allowing complex features such as *data structure and instance overlapping* across heterogenous databases. The use of HyDRa is supported by an Eclipse plugin, publicly available on GitHub [15]. This plugin includes a textual editor as well as a conceptual data access API generator.

The HyDRa framework can be used, among others, to build mediated architecture from pre-existing inter-related databases, to assist in a database reverse engineering context or to express explicit schema for schemaless databases. Polystore data management still faces various open challenges for the research community. In particular, specifying polystore schemas and mapping rules still remains a manual task. As future work, we aim at developing automated schema inference and mapping rules recommendation approaches. Our current research agenda also includes extension of generation of conceptual data manipulation APIs, the automation of schema evolution, data migration, and query adaptation in hybrid polystores [13,14].

Acknowledgements. This research is supported by the F.R.S.-FNRS and FWO via the EOS project 30446992 SECO-ASSIST.

References

1. 6 rules of thumb for MongoDB schema design. https://bit.ly/3gYTh8y
2. Cassandra data modeling best practices. https://bit.ly/3eeYGGY
3. Hbase schema case study. https://bit.ly/3nX52y5
4. Spring data Redis - Retwis-J. https://bit.ly/33hEFcg
5. Atzeni, P., Bugiotti, F., Cabibbo, L., Torlone, R.: Data modeling in the NoSQL world. Comput. Stand. Interfaces **67**, 103149 (2020)
6. Atzeni, P., Bugiotti, F., Rossi, L.: Uniform access to non-relational database systems: the SOS platform. In: Ralyté, J., Franch, X., Brinkkemper, S., Wrycza, S. (eds.) CAiSE 2012. LNCS, vol. 7328, pp. 160–174. Springer, Heidelberg (2012). https://doi.org/10.1007/978-3-642-31095-9_11
7. Basciani, F., Di Rocco, J., Di Ruscio, D., Pierantonio, A., Iovino, L.: TyphonML: a modeling environment to develop hybrid polystores. In: MoDELS (2020)
8. Bjeladinovic, S.: A fresh approach for hybrid SQL/NoSQL database design based on data structuredness. Enterp. Inf. Syst. **12**(8–9), 1202–1220 (2018)
9. Bugiotti, F., Cabibbo, L., Atzeni, P., Torlone, R.: Database design for NoSQL systems. In: Yu, E., Dobbie, G., Jarke, M., Purao, S. (eds.) ER 2014. LNCS, vol. 8824, pp. 223–231. Springer, Cham (2014). https://doi.org/10.1007/978-3-319-12206-9_18
10. Cabibbo, L.: ONDM: an object-NoSQL datastore mapper. Faculty of Engineering, Roma Tre University (2013)
11. Carlo, B., Ceri, S., Sham, N.: Conceptual Database Design: An Entity-Relationship Approach. Benjamin/Cummings, Redwood City (1992)
12. Duggan, J., et al.: The BigDAWG polystore system. ACM SIGMOD Rec. **44**(2), 11–16 (2015)
13. Fink, J., Gobert, M., Cleve, A.: Adapting queries to database schema changes in hybrid polystores. In: IEEE SCAM, pp. 127–131 (2020)
14. Gobert, M.: Schema evolution in hybrid database systems. In: VLDB PhD Workshop (2020)
15. Gobert, M.: HyDRa repository (2021). https://github.com/gobertm/HyDRa
16. Hecht, R., Jablonski, S.: NoSQL evaluation: a use case oriented survey. In: 2011 International Conference on Cloud and Service Computing, pp. 336–341 (2011)
17. Herrero, V., Abelló, A., Romero, O.: NOSQL design for analytical workloads: variability matters. In: Comyn-Wattiau, I., Tanaka, K., Song, I.-Y., Yamamoto, S., Saeki, M. (eds.) ER 2016. LNCS, vol. 9974, pp. 50–64. Springer, Cham (2016). https://doi.org/10.1007/978-3-319-46397-1_4
18. de Lima, C., dos Santos Mello, R.: A workload-driven logical design approach for NoSQL document databases. In: iiWAS, pp. 1–10 (2015)
19. Neo4j: Modeling designs. https://neo4j.com/developer/modeling-designs/
20. Pokornỳ, J.: Conceptual and database modelling of graph databases. In: IDEAS 2016 (2016)
21. Rossel, G., Manna, A., et al.: A modeling methodology for NoSQL key-value databases. Database Syst. J. **8**(2), 12–18 (2017)
22. Roy-Hubara, N., Sturm, A.: Design methods for the new database era: a systematic literature review. Softw. Syst. Model. **19**(2), 297–312 (2019). https://doi.org/10.1007/s10270-019-00739-8
23. Sadalage, P.J., Fowler, M.: NoSQL Distilled: A Brief Guide to the Emerging World of Polyglot Persistence. Pearson Education, Upper Saddle River (2013)
24. Schaarschmidt, M., Gessert, F., Ritter, N.: Towards automated polyglot persistence. Datenbanksysteme für Business, Technologie und Web (BTW 2015) (2015)

Dependency Rule Modeling for Multiple Aspects Trajectories

Ronaldo dos Santos Mello[1]($\boxtimes$) (iD), Geomar André Schreiner[1] (iD),
Cristian Alexandre Alchini[2], Gustavo Gonçalves dos Santos[2],
Vania Bogorny[1] (iD), and Chiara Renso[3] (iD)

[1] UFSC, PPGCC, Florianópolis, Brazil
{r.mello,vania.bogorny}@ufsc.br, schreiner.geomar@posgrad.ufsc.br
[2] UFSC, INE, Florianópolis, Brazil
{cristian.alchini,gustavo.gs}@grad.ufsc.br
[3] ISTI-CNR, Pisa, Italy
chiara.renso@isti.cnr.it

Abstract. Trajectories of moving objects are usually modeled as
sequences of space-time points or, in case of semantic trajectories, as
labelled stops and moves. Data analytics methods on these kinds of trajectories tend to discover geometrical and temporal patterns, or simple
semantic patterns based on the labels of stops and moves. A recent extension of semantic trajectories is called *multiple aspects trajectory, i.e.*,
a trajectory associated to different semantic dimensions called *aspects*.
This kind of trajectory increases in a large scale the number of discovered patterns. This paper introduces the concept of *dependency rule* to
represent patterns discovered from the analysis of trajectories with multiple aspects. They include patterns related to a trajectory, trajectory
points, or the moving object. These rules are conceptually represented
as an extension of a conceptual model for multiple aspects trajectories. A
case study shows that our proposal is relevant as it represents the discovered rules with a concise but expressive conceptual model. Additionally,
a performance evaluation shows the feasibility of our conceptual model
designed over relational-based database management technologies.

Keywords: Multiple aspect trajectory · Conceptual model · Data
analytics · Dependency rule

1 Introduction

Mobility data modeling is receiving more and more attention in the recent years
due to the increasing easiness to collect data from mobile applications. In the
beginning of the 2000 decade, trajectories of moving objects were modeled as
sequences of points with space and time information (the so-called *raw trajectories*) [9]. From 2007, a new view over trajectory data called *semantic trajectory*
was proposed. It is represented not only in terms of space and time dimensions,

© Springer Nature Switzerland AG 2021
A. Ghose et al. (Eds.): ER 2021, LNCS 13011, pp. 123–132, 2021.
https://doi.org/10.1007/978-3-030-89022-3_11

but also *stops* and *moves*, to denote parts of trajectories where the object stayed for a certain amount of time or changed its position, respectively [15].

More recently, new data models were conceived to represent semantic trajectories not only as stops and moves, but with other predefined semantic dimensions, like the goal of the trip, the purpose of a visit, or the transportation mode [5,8]. This concept further evolved to the general notion of *multiple aspects trajectory (MAT)*, where the semantic dimensions are not predefined, *i.e.*, it is possible to associate any kind of enrichment information to a trajectory. The pioneer work of Mello et al. [11] introduced a conceptual model for MATs, called *MASTER*, where the semantic dimensions are called *aspects*.

As an example of a MAT, imagine the movement of a person during a weekend day. He/she leaves home, goes to a park and then to a restaurant. The person has a smart watch that constantly collects *blood pressure rate* and *body temperature*. The park, in turn, have *open and close hours*. The weather condition may change during his/her movement (*e.g.*, from *sunny* to *rainy*), as well as the used transportation modes (*e.g.*, *train* and *taxi*). This example highlights how several heterogeneous aspects may coexist in a MAT.

On going to the analysis of MAT data, we may see several challenges related to knowledge discovery as the behaviour of a moving object may involve several aspects and, additionally, some aspects may be strongly correlated (or dependent) and may not be analyzed separately. For instance, suppose the restaurant visited by the person aforementioned has a *spatial location*, a *category*, some *reviews*, *average price*, and *rating*. These last three attributes may hold a *dependency* stating that ratings equal to *10* have average price higher than *US$ 100* and *excellent* or *good* reviews. We call these dependency relationships between attributes as a *dependency rule (DR)*. A DR may be learned through data mining or machine learning methods, or it may be predefined by the user [12].

Finding, representing and storing these dependencies is therefore an essential step when analysing MATs. Although there are advances in trajectory data modeling and mining, there is no consensus among approaches for modeling discovered patterns from trajectory data, and the existing ones have limitations. One example is the work of Bogorny et al. [4], which models patterns for trajectories only in terms of stops and moves, and considers a few/fixed aspects.

This paper conceptually define *DRs* over MATs. For doing that, we extend the MASTER model [11]. Our main contributions are:

- we define the concept of DR as a pattern related to MAT data;
- we introduce a notation for expressing DRs with a power expression higher than the traditional association rules [1];
- we propose an extension of MASTER called *MASTER DR*. With MASTER DR it is possible to query the entities on which the DR holds or vice-versa;
- we provide an evaluation of our model that comprises a case study over real MAT data, as well as a performance experiment over relational-based Database (DB) technologies.

The rest of this paper is organized as follows. Section 2 provides a background about MAT as well as the MASTER model. Section 3 presents the related work and Sect. 4 introduces the concept of DR and its representation. Section 5 describes MASTER DR, Sect. 6 presents some evaluations and Sect. 7 is dedicated to the conclusion.

2 Multiple Aspect Trajectory and the MASTER Model

A *MAT* is a trajectory that may be enriched with an unlimited number of semantic information called *aspects* [11]. An *aspect* is a real-world fact that is relevant for trajectory data analysis, and it is characterized by an *aspect type*. For instance, the aspect *subway* belongs to an aspect type *transportation*, and an aspect *rainy* belongs to an aspect type *weather*. An aspect type act as a metadata definition for an aspect. It holds a set of *attributes* and it may also be a subtype of a more general aspect type, allowing an aspect type *subtypeOf* hierarchy, like *POI ← accommodation ← hotel*. We consider *time* and *space* as possible aspects. So, an aspect can be specialized into *Spatial Aspect* or *Temporal Aspect*. The first one holds *position* attributes (x,y), and the second one a *timestamp* attribute.

A MAT, in turn, is represented by a set of *points* that denotes the movement of a *moving object, i.e.,* a real-world entity that moves along space and time. This object is always associated to a *type*, which can be a person, a drone, an animal, a car, or even a natural phenomenon, like a hurricane.

The MASTER conceptual model combine simplicity and expressive power for representing aspects. The intention is to represent any semantic dimension, independent of the application domain. Figure 1 shows the last version of the MASTER model (the yellow entities inside the MASTER package).

An aspect is associated to a point when it changes frequently during the object movement. One example is a *visited place (a POI)*. When an aspect does not vary during an entire MAT, it is associated to the MAT as a whole. An example could be the *weather* condition. When an aspect holds during the entire life or a long period of a moving object, it is associated to the moving object.

Finally, MASTER introduces the *moving object relationship*. A moving object may maintain any type of relationship with other moving objects, and these relationships may also be characterized by different aspects such as the type of relationship (*e.g., friendship, professional, family*).

3 Related Work

Previous approaches in the literature introduced the notion of semantically enriched trajectories, as the pioneer work of Spaccapietra et al. [15], as well as the *CONSTANT* [5] and *MASTER* [11] data models. It is worth also mentioning works that represent semantic trajectories and associated patterns. Some of them base their novelty in exploiting ontologies to represent both (semantic) trajectories and patterns [8,14]. However, none of them consider dependencies among semantic data and how to represent them.

Some other works propose conceptual models for data mining patterns [2, 4,7,13,15,16]. On compared to our proposal, these works do not necessarily focus on trajectories, or represent trajectories as only spatio-temporal points or sequences of stops and moves, not including complex aspects, or considering a single semantic point of view. Due to it, the modeled patterns are limited.

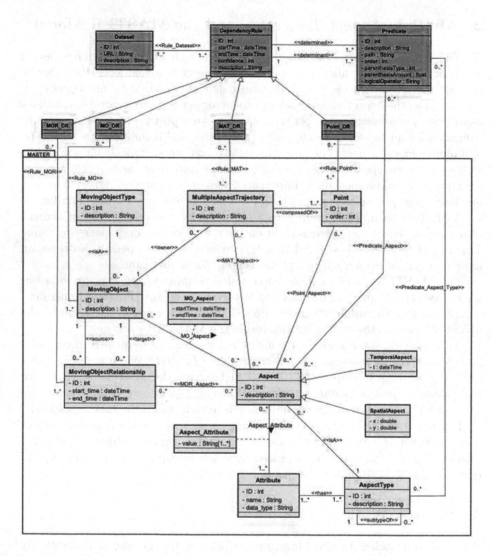

Fig. 1. The MASTER conceptual model and the dependency rule extension

This paper introduces DR as a pattern that is able to represent complex dependencies among trajectory aspects. DRs for MATs has not been considered in the literature so far as MATs is a relatively new trajectory concept, and in previous definitions of semantic trajectories the enrichment component is just a label, being not suitable to discovery dependencies among aspects.

4   Dependency Rule

A *DR* is a pattern[1] that specifies complex dependencies among values of attributes belonging to one or more real-world entities. Our reasoning for a DR is based on the concepts of *rule* [1] and *functional dependency* [3]. A rule is a common formalism for representing knowledge discovered through the application of data mining methods, like frequent itemset or association rule algorithms. A functional dependency is considered in the design of a relational DB schema in order to avoid redundancy and update anomalies. Both of them allow the definition of a set of attributes whose values determine the values of another set of attributes, and are usually specified as follows: $\{att_i, ..., att_k\} \Rightarrow \{att_m, ..., att_p\}$.

A DR also allows the specification of *determinant* and *determined* attribute sets, complex predicates involving these attribute sets, and the real-world entity type on which the DR holds (*target entity type*). Our contribution with the DR modeling on MASTER is to represent discovered patterns for the main real-world entities based mainly on the analysis of the aspects that surround them, as the aspects represent the relevant features of the trajectories, including spatial and temporal information. Suppose we had discovered a pattern in a MATs dataset stating that retired people in a small city usually move on foot when it is not raining. This pattern involves three aspects (*occupation, transportation* and *weather*) and could be specified by the following DR:

DR_x: MAT | owner.is-a[description ='Person'] AND MAT_Aspect
[description ='retired'].is-a[description ='occupation'] AND
MAT_Aspect[NOT(description ='rainy')].is-a[description ='weather']
$\Rightarrow$ MAT_Aspect[description = 'foot'].is-a[description =
'transportation']

It shows that the DR is a pattern for a MAT (the target entity type). It also holds a pre-condition (before the implication) and a discovered data behaviour based on this pre-condition (after the implication).

We define a simple notation for a DR. It represents the DR three components (*target entity type, determinant* and *determined*), being similar to an association rule and a functional dependency. Therefore, this formalism tends to be easy to understand. In fact, we could adopted a rule specification language, like SWRL [10] and RIF [6]. However, they are verbose languages and would generate complex rule definitions. We now formally define a DR as well as its components.

Definition 1 *(Filter). A filter is a data restriction with the form att operator operand, where att is a required entity type attribute name that may be followed by an operator and an operand, with operator $\in \{=, \neq, >, >=, <, <=, IS$ NULL, IS NOT NULL\}, and operand is a required constant value, or another entity type attribute name if operator $\notin \{IS NULL, IS NOT NULL\}$.*

Definition 2 *(Predicate). A predicate is a boolean expression with the form of a path expression $pr_k = e_1.e_2...e_{n-1}.e_n$, $n > 0$, where each element $e_i \in pr_k$ is a MASTER relationship type that may be restricted by a filter optionally enclosed*

---
[1] By pattern we mean an implicit (or hidden) regularity in the data.

by a NOT logical operator and defined between brackets ('[', ']'), and e_1 is a relationship type connected to the MASTER target entity type.

When a predicate has a filter with only the *att* part, we have an *existence* constraint w.r.t. the attribute. For example, the predicate MO_Aspect[endTime] states that the relationship *MO_Aspect* must hold the *endTime* attribute.

Definition 3 *(Condition)*. *A condition is a boolean expression with the form pr_1 AND/OR pr_2 AND/OR ... AND/OR pr_m, $m > 0$, i.e., a non-empty set of predicates $\{pr_1, pr_2, ..., pr_m\}$ connected by the logical operators AND and OR.*

Definition 4 *(Dependency Rule)*. *A DR dr_f is an expression with the form te_x / c_i => c_j, where te_x is a MASTER target entity type, with $te_x \in \{MO, MAT, POINT, MOR\}$, c_i is the pre-condition (or determinant), and c_j is the condition regarding the discovered data regularity (or determined), and a dr_f specification means that if c_i is TRUE for a te_x instance i_x, then c_j is also TRUE for i_x.*

The aforementioned DR_x is an example of DR specified according to Definition 4. We focus on semantic behaviours discovered for the aspects related to the main entity types (*target entity types*) of the MASTER model: moving objects (MO), multiple aspects trajectory (MAT), trajectory point (POINT), and moving object relationship (MOR). Because of this, a predicate must start with a relationship type connected to one of these entities.

A DR may also hold an existence constraint w.r.t. relationship types if their predicates have no filters. One example is DR_y : MO | source OR target => MO_Aspect. It states that when a moving object participates in a moving object relationship, it must be related to an aspect.

5   MASTER DR

This paper regards DRs for MAT data. As several patterns can be found over MATs, they can be valuable or not depending on their accuracy and temporal lifetime. Thus, we associate a *confidence* [1] and a *validity time* to each DR.

Figure 1 shows our MASTER extension to provide the representation of DRs and related concepts (the blue entities): the *MASTER DR*. The DR entity includes the aforementioned attributes. In the following, we define the DR entity.

Definition 5 *(DR Entity)*. *A DR Entity dre = (desc, startTime, endTime, confidence, EXT, PRE, POST, DS) is a discovered data pattern in a set of MAT datasets DS, with a description desc, a confidence and a validity time (startTime and endTime), as well as sets of predicates PRE = $\{pr_1, ..., pr_n\}$ and POST = $\{pr_1, ..., pr_m\}$ that specifies, respectively, its determinant and determined parts, and the set of sets EXT = $\{MOR \mid MO \mid MAT \mid POINT\}$, which are the sets of occurrences of MASTER entities on which the DR holds, being MOR = $\{mor_1, ..., mor_i\}$ the set of moving object relationships, MO = $\{mo_1, ..., mor_j\}$ the set of moving objects, and so on.*

The *dre.EXT* sets are represented in MASTER DR as specialized entities (see Fig. 1) that hold specific relationships with original MASTER entities te_j that are the target of the DR. They are modeled as *many-to-many* relationships because the DR may be valid for several te_j occurrences. The DR entity specializations are not exclusive as a same DR may serve, for example, as a pattern for a whole MAT in one context and a pattern for some MAT points in another context. A same pattern related to *weather*, for example, may occur during all the trajectory long or only for some of its points.

A DR may raise in several MAT datasets. We define a dataset as follows.

Definition 6 (Dataset Entity). *A Dataset Entity dse = (desc, URL, DR) is a source of MAT data with a description desc, an URL with its location, and a set of discovered DR over it.*

As shown in Fig. 1, a DR is composed of the *determinant* and *determined* conditions, which are sets of predicates. Thus, we also define a predicate entity.

Definition 7 (Predicate Entity). *A Predicate Entity pe = (desc, owner, condition type, path, order, ASP, ASPT, parenthesisType, parenthesisAmount, logicalOperator) is part of a DR determinant or determined condition with a description desc, the DR the owns it (owner), the type of DR condition where it is inserted (determinant - 0; determined - 1) (condition type), the path expression that defines it, its order inside the condition, the optional sets of aspects (ASP) and aspect types (ASPT) occurrences on which the predicate holds, and optional attributes denoting whether the predicate is preceded or not by an open parenthesis (0) or succeeded by a close parenthesis (1) (parenthesis type), the amount of this parenthesis type (parenthesis amount), and whether the predicate is preceded by a logical operator: OR (0) or AND (1).*

For sake of understanding of the *Predicate Entity* definition suppose the following predicates that could be part of a determinant of a DR named DR_z:

$$\ldots((\texttt{a.b.c[x = 1]}\ \texttt{OR}\ \texttt{d.e[y = 'q']})\ \texttt{AND}\ \ldots)\ \ldots$$

This condition fragment has two predicates (`a.b.c[x = 1]` and `d.e[y = 'q']`), where the first one is preceded by two open parenthesis, and the second one is preceded by the OR logical operator and succeeded by one close parenthesis. In order to keep track of all the condition structure, we represent the first predicate as $pr_1 = ('predicate'_1, 'DR'_z, 0, 'a.b.c[x = 1]', 1, NULL, \{'aspectType'_i\}, 0, 2, NULL)$, and the second predicate as $pr_2 = ('predicate'_2, 'DR'_z, 0, 'd.e[y = 'q']', 1, \{'aspect'_j, 'aspect'_k\}, \{'aspectType'_l\}, 1, 1, 0)$. We are also supposing that pr_1 is valid to an aspect type $'aspectType_i'$, and pr_2 holds to the aspects $'aspect_j'$ and $'aspect_k'$, which belong to the aspect type $'aspectType_l'$.

This strategy to model predicates allows the representation of a DR condition composed of an arbitrary number of logical operators and parenthesis levels. We also associate a predicate with an aspect and/or an aspect type in order to allow queries like *"what MATs have patterns that enclose the aspect X?"* and *"what aspect types are more frequent in patterns for the moving object Y?"*.

6   Evaluation

We first present a case study with real trajectory data from the *SoBigData Consortium*, an European Union funding project related to Big Data social mining. We got a grant to access a repository with 8392 trajectories describing the movement of 129 users into Tuscany, Italy[2]. We analyzed two datasets of this repository as they provide more *aspects* associated to the trajectories:

- *Diaries* dataset: distance, average speed, day of the week, duration, day period and trajectory purpose (goal).
- *MP* dataset: goal, mean of transportation and duration.

The first dataset comprises people moving by car. In the second one, people had moved using different means of transportation. As both of them are stored into relational databases, we defined SQL grouping queries (queries with the GROUP BY $a_1, ..., a_n$ clause) to group data by sets of attributes' values $(a_1, ..., a_n)$ and verify whether a DR raises when they are viewed together (*e.g.*, to group trajectory data by *duration* and *goal*). We defined a group query for each incremental combination of the attributes' values that correspond to aspects, like *(goal, mean of transportation)*, *(goal, duration)*, ... , *(goal, mean of transportation, duration)* for the *MP* dataset. The result sets were analyzed manually.

Table 1 shows some discovered DRs on both datasets with high confidence, highlighting relevant patterns to be stored. All of these DRs can be represented by MASTER DR, demonstrating its usefulness in real data scenarios.

We also analyze query performance over MASTER DR when designed over open-source relational-based DB technologies: a *traditional DB management systems (DBMSs) (PostgreSQL)*, and a *NewSQL DB (VoltDB)*. We chose them because relational DBs is a dominant technology, and NewSQL is a emerging one. We run the experiments on a host of $Intel^R$ $Core^{TM}$ i5-8200 processor with 8 GB RAM (DDR4 1333 Mhz), 240 GB SSD and Xubuntu 20.04 Server LTS OS 64 bits. The generated relational schema for MASTER DR is shown in Fig. 2.

We define five queries over the DBMSs covering the main MASTER DR entities and relationships, with different levels of complexity (from 3 to 10 table joins). We emulate 20 users randomly run each one of the queries over synthetic data in a DB with three sizes for each table: $10K$, $50K$ and $100K$ rows.

For the smallest DB size, PostgreSQL got a throughput of $3,613.88$ TPS (transactions per second), and VoltDB reached $6,146.41$ TPS. VoltDB has almost 100% more throughput than PostgreSQL for the smallest DB size. For the largest one, the difference falls to 14%. In short, the performance for querying the MASTER DR relational schema sounds good for both DBMSs, as they were able to consume hundreds of requests even for the largest DB size, with a light advantage of VoltDB. Despite the dataset sizes are not large, they were sufficient to evaluate the behavior of relational DBMSs in order to suggest appropriated DB technologies to support MASTER DR, as is the case of NewSQL DBs.

---

[2] https://sobigdata.d4science.org/web/cityofcitizens/catalogue.

Table 1. Some discovered dependency rules.

Dataset	Dependency Rule	Confidence
Diaries	goal = 'Supermarket' ⇒ day period = '6-12' OR day period = '12-18'	99 %
Diaries	goal = 'Work' OR goal = 'Service' OR goal = 'Study' ⇒ NOT(day of the week = 'Sunday')	87 %
Diaries	average speed > 80 AND (day of the week = 'Saturday' OR day of the week = 'Sunday') AND (day period = '0-6' OR day period = '18-24') ⇒ goal = 'Leisure'	72 %
MP	goal = 'Leisure' OR goal = 'Carburator Fixing' ⇒ mean of transportation = 'Motorcycle' OR mean of transportation = 'Automobile'	100 %
MP	goal = 'Pick up or drop out' ⇒ mean of transportation = 'Automobile'	100 %
MP	goal = 'Shopping' ⇒ mean of transportation = 'Automobile'	80 %

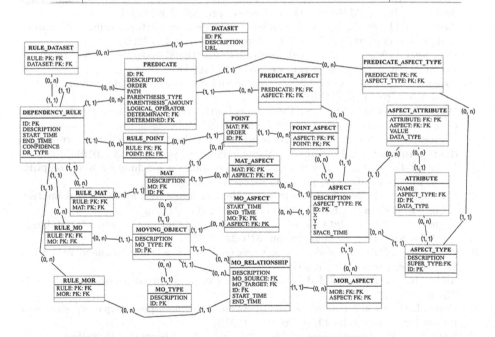

Fig. 2. A relational schema for MASTER DR

7 Conclusion

Proposals regarding trajectory pattern modeling are able to find out a limited set of (and simple) patterns as they consider only spatio-temporal attributes or limited semantic dimensions. This paper novels by proposing a conceptual model for DRs and a formalism to specify data patterns in the context of mobility data that are very rich in terms of semantics (MATs). We represent DRs as an extension of a conceptual model for MATs, thus enabling queries on trajectories and DRs in a joint way. This extended conceptual model combines simplicity by adding few entities to the original model, as well as the capability to represent patterns with different levels of complexity. A case study and a query performance analysis show that our conceptual model is useful and practicable. Future works include the analysis of other MAT datasets to better evaluate performance, expressiveness and limitations of MASTER DR. We also intend to simulate data insertions and updates over several DB technologies.

Acknowledgments. This work has been co-funded by the Brazilian agencies CNPQ and FAPESC (Project Match - Grant 2018TR 1266), and the European Union's Horizon 2020 research and innovation programme under GA N. 777695 (MASTER).

References

1. Agrawal, R., et al.: Mining association rules between sets of items in large databases. In: ACM SIGMOD Conference, pp. 207–216 (1993)
2. Alvares, L.O., et al.: Dynamic modeling of trajectory patterns using data mining and reverse engineering. In: ER Conference, pp. 149–154 (2007)
3. Bernstein, P.A., et al.: A unified approach to functional dependencies and relations. In: ACM SIGMOD Conference, pp. 237–245 (1975)
4. Bogorny, V., et al.: A conceptual data model for trajectory data mining. In: GIS Conference, pp. 1–15 (2010)
5. Bogorny, V., et al.: CONSTAnT - a conceptual data model for semantic trajectories of moving objects. Trans. GIS **18**(1), 66–88 (2014)
6. Damásio, C.V., et al.: Declarative semantics for the rule interchange format production rule dialect. In: Semantic Web Conference, pp. 798–813 (2010)
7. Damiani, E., Frati, F.: Towards conceptual models for machine learning computations. In: ER Conference, pp. 3–9 (2018)
8. Fileto, R., et al.: Baquara: a holistic ontological framework for movement analysis using linked data. In: ER Conference, pp. 342–355 (2013)
9. Forlizzi, L., et al.: A data model and data structures for moving objects databases. In: ACM SIGMOD Conference, pp. 319–330 (2000)
10. Horrocks, I., Patel-Schneider, P.F.: A proposal for an owl rules language. In: WWW Conference, pp. 723–731 (2004)
11. Mello, R., et al.: MASTER: a multiple aspect view on trajectories. Trans. GIS **23**(4), 805–822 (2019)
12. Petry, L.M., et al.: Towards semantic-aware multiple-aspect trajectory similarity measuring. Trans. GIS **23**(5), 960–975 (2019)
13. Rizzi, S.: UML-based conceptual modeling of pattern-bases. In: Workshop on Pattern Representation and Management - EDBT Conference (2004)
14. Ruback, L., et al.: Enriching mobility data with linked open data. In: IDEAS Symposium, pp. 173–182 (2016)
15. Spaccapietra, S., et al.: A conceptual view on trajectories. Data Knowl. Eng. **65**(1), 126–146 (2008)
16. Zubcoff, J., et al.: Integrating clustering data mining into the multidimensional modeling of data warehouses with UML profiles. In: DaWaK Conference, pp. 199–208 (2007)

Forward Engineering Relational Schemas and High-Level Data Access from Conceptual Models

Gustavo L. Guidoni[1,2], João Paulo A. Almeida[1(✉)], and Giancarlo Guizzardi[1,3]

[1] Ontology & Conceptual Modeling Research Group (NEMO), Federal University of Espírito Santo, Vitória, Brazil
jpalmeida@ieee.org
[2] Federal Institute of Espírito Santo, Colatina, Brazil
gustavo.guidoni@ifes.edu.br
[3] Free University of Bozen-Bolzano, Bolzano, Italy
gguizzardi@unibz.it

Abstract. Forward engineering relational schemas based on conceptual models is an established practice, with a number of commercial tools available and widely used in production settings. These tools employ automated transformation strategies to address the gap between the primitives offered by conceptual modeling languages (such as ER and UML) and the relational model. Despite the various benefits of automated transformation, once a database schema is obtained, data access is usually undertaken by relying on the resulting schema, at a level of abstraction lower than that of the source conceptual model. Data access then requires both domain knowledge and comprehension of the (non-trivial) technical choices embodied in the resulting schema. We address this problem by forward engineering not only a relational schema, but also creating an ontology-based data access mapping for the resulting schema. This mapping is used to expose data in terms of the original conceptual model, and hence queries can be written at a high level of abstraction, independently of the transformation strategy selected.

Keywords: Forward engineering · Model-driven approach · Ontology-based data access · Model transformation

1 Introduction

Forward engineering relational schemas based on conceptual models (such as ER or UML class diagrams) is an established practice, with a number of commercial tools available and widely used in production settings. The approaches employed establish correspondences between the patterns in the source models and in the target relational schemas. For example, in the *one table per class* approach [11,16], a table is produced for each class in the source model; in the *one table per leaf class* approach [21], a table is produced for each leaf class in the

© Springer Nature Switzerland AG 2021
A. Ghose et al. (Eds.): ER 2021, LNCS 13011, pp. 133–148, 2021.
https://doi.org/10.1007/978-3-030-89022-3_12

specialization hierarchy, with properties of superclasses accommodated at the tables corresponding to their leaf subclasses. An important benefit of all these approaches is the automation of an otherwise manual and error-prone schema design process. Automated transformations capture tried-and-tested design decisions, improving productivity and the quality of the resulting schemas.

Despite the various benefits of automated transformation, once a database schema is obtained, data access is usually undertaken by relying on the resulting schema, at a level of abstraction lower than that of the source conceptual model. As a consequence, data access requires both domain knowledge and comprehension of the (non-trivial) technical choices embodied in the resulting schema. For example, in the *one table per class* approach, joint access to attributes of an entity may require a query that joins several tables corresponding to the various classes instantiated by the entity. In the *one table per leaf class* approach, queries concerning instances of a superclass involve a union of the tables corresponding to each of its subclasses. Further, some of the information that was embodied in the conceptual model—in this case the taxonomic hierarchy—is no longer directly available for the data user.

In addition to the difficulties in accessing data at a lower level of abstraction, there is also the issue of the suitability of the resulting schema when considering its quality characteristics (such as usability, performance). This is because a transformation embodies design decisions that navigate various trade-offs in the design space. These design decisions may not satisfy requirements in different scenarios. Because of this, there is the need to offer the user more than one transformation to choose from or to offer some control over the design decisions in the transformation.

This paper addresses these challenges. We identify the primitive refactoring operations that are performed in the transformation of conceptual models to relational schemas, independently of the various transformation strategies. As the transformation advances, at each application of an operation, we maintain a set of traces from source to target model, ultimately producing not only the relational schema, but also a high-level data access mapping for the resulting schema using the set of traces. This mapping exposes data in terms of the original conceptual model, and hence queries can be written at a high level of abstraction, independently of the transformation strategy selected.

This paper is further structured as follows: Sect. 2 discusses extant approaches to the transformation of a structural conceptual model into a target relational schema, including the definition of the primitive "flattening" and "lifting" operations that are executed in the various transformation strategies; Sect. 3 presents our approach to generating a high-level data access mapping in tandem with the transformation of the conceptual model; Sect. 4 compares the performance of high-level data access queries with their counterparts as handwritten SQL queries; Sect. 5 discusses related work, and, finally, Sect. 6 presents concluding remarks.

2   Transformation of Conceptual Models into Relational Schemas

2.1   Extant Approaches

The relational model does not directly support the concept of inheritance, and, hence, realization strategies are required to preserve the semantics of a source conceptual model in a target relational schema [13]. Such strategies are described by several authors [2,11,16,18,21] under various names. We include here some of these strategies solely for the purpose of exemplification (other approaches are discussed in [13]).

One common approach is the *one table per class* strategy, in which each class gives rise to a separate table, with columns corresponding to the class's features. Specialization between classes in the conceptual model gives rise to a foreign key in the table that corresponds to the subclass. This foreign key references the primary key of the table corresponding to the superclass. This strategy is also called "class-table" [11], "vertical inheritance" [21] or "one class one table" [16]. In order to manipulate a single instance of a class, e.g., to read all its attributes or to insert a new instance with its attributes, one needs to traverse a number of tables corresponding to the depth of the whole specialization hierarchy. A common variant of this approach is the *one table per concrete class* strategy. In this case, an operation of "flattening" is applied for the abstract superclasses. In a nutshell, "flattening" removes a class from the hierarchy by transferring its attributes and relations to its subclasses. This reduces the number of tables required to read or to insert all attributes of an instance, but introduces the need for unions in polymorphic queries involving abstract classes.

The extreme application of "flattening" to remove all non-leaf classes of a taxonomy yields a strategy called *one table per leaf class*. In this strategy, also termed "horizontal inheritance" [21], each of the leaf classes in the hierarchy gives rise to a corresponding table. Features of all (non-leaf) superclasses of a leaf class are realized as columns in the leaf class table. No foreign keys emulating inheritance are employed in this approach.

A radically different approach is the *one table per hierarchy* strategy, also called "single-table" [11] or "one inheritance tree one table" [16]. It can be understood as the opposite of *one table per leaf class*, applying a "lifting" operation to subclasses instead of the "flattening" of superclasses. Attributes of each subclass become optional columns in the superclass table. This strategy usually requires the creation of an additional column to distinguish which subclass is (or which subclasses are) instantiated by the entity represented in the row (a so-called "discriminator" column). The "lifting" operation is reiterated until the top-level class of each hierarchy is reached.

Other approaches propose the combined and selective use of both "lifting" and "flattening". For example, the approach we have proposed called *one table per kind* [13] uses ontological meta-properties of classes to guide the "flattening" of the so-called *non-sortals* in the conceptual model and the "lifting" of all (non-kind) sortals.

2.2 Flattening and Lifting Operations

In order to support the transformation strategies discussed in the previous section and their variations, we define our approach in this paper in terms of the "flattening" and "lifting" operations. Here we present these operations in detail, including their consequences to the existing attributes and associations in the model.

In the flattening operation, shown in the first row of Table 1, every attribute of the class that is to be removed from the model (in gray) is migrated to each of its direct subclasses. Association ends attached to the flattened superclass are also migrated to the subclasses. The lower bound cardinality of the migrated association end is relaxed to zero, as the original lower bound may no longer be satisfied for each of the subclasses.

In the lifting operation, shown in the last row of Table 1, every attribute of the class that is lifted (in gray) is migrated to each direct superclass, with lower bound cardinality relaxed to zero. Association ends attached to the lifted class are migrated to each direct superclass. The lower bound cardinality constraints of the association ends attached to classes other than the lifted class ($RelatedType_i$) are relaxed to zero.

Table 1. Transformation patterns.

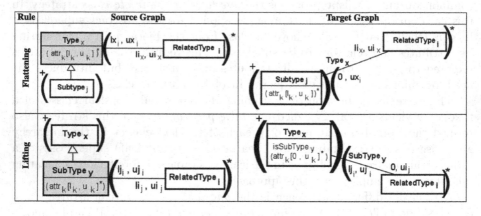

When no generalization set is present, a Boolean attribute is added to each superclass, to indicate whether the instance of the superclass instantiates the lifted class ($isSubType_j$). If a generalization set is used, a discriminator enumeration is created with labels corresponding to each $SubType_j$ of the generalization set. An attribute with that discriminator type is added to each superclass. Its cardinality follows the generalization set: it is optional for incomplete generalization sets (and mandatory otherwise); and multivalued for overlapping generalization sets (and monovalued otherwise).

2.3 Example Transformation

In order to illustrate the consequences of the transformation strategy selected on the resulting relational schema and on the production of queries, we apply here

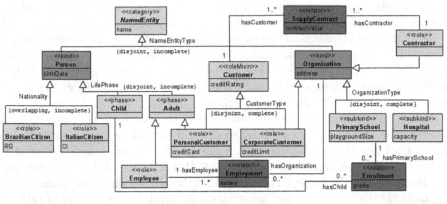

(a) Running Example

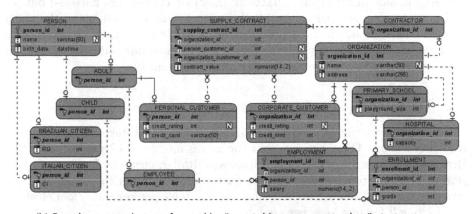

(b) Running example transformed by *"one table per concrete class"* strategy

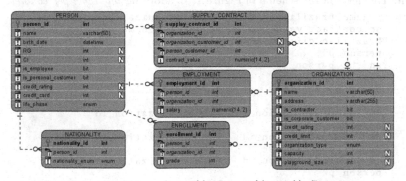

(c) Running example transformed by *"one table per kind"* strategy

Fig. 1. Transformations.

two different transformations to the model shown in Fig. 1(a). The transformation approaches selected for illustration are *one table per concrete class* and *one table per kind*, and are used throughout the paper. The former relies on the flattening of abstract classes, and the latter makes use of OntoUML stereotypes [14] to guide the application of flattening and lifting. Flattening is applied to non-sortals (in this example, the classes stereotyped «category» and «roleMixin») and lifting is applied to sortals other than kinds (in this example, the classes stereotyped «subkind», «phase» and «role»).

Figure 1(b) presents the resulting schema in the *one table per concrete class* strategy. The abstract classes NamedEntity and Customer have been flattened out, and a table is included for each concrete class. Foreign keys are used to emulate inheritance (e.g., the table HOSPITAL corresponding to the concrete class Hospital has a foreign key organization_id which is the primary key of ORGANIZATION). The strategy generates a relatively large number of tables.

Figure 1(c) presents the result of applying the *one table per kind* strategy. Again, NamedEntity and Customer (abstract classes) are flattened out. In addition, all concrete classes are lifted until only one concrete class (the kind) remains. There is no emulation of inheritance with foreign keys; discriminators are used instead to identify the subclasses that are instantiated by an entity. No joins are required to access jointly attributes of an entity.

2.4   Data Access

Once a database schema is obtained, data access needs to take into account the resulting schema. Consider, e.g., that the user is interested in a report with "the Brazilian citizens who work in hospitals with Italian customers". This information need would require two different queries depending on the transformation strategy. Listing 1 shows the query for the *one table per concrete class* strategy and Listing 2 for *one table per kind*.

Listing 1. Query on the schema of Figure 1(b), adopting *one table per concrete class*

```
select   p.name brazilian_name, o.name organization_name,
         sc.contract_value, p2.name italian_name
from     brazilian_citizen bc
join     person p
         on  bc.person_id      = p.person_id
join     employment em
         on  p.person_id       = em.person_id
join     organization o
         on  om.organization_id = o.organization_id
join     hospital h
         on  o.organization_id = h.organization_id
join     supply_contract sc
         on  o.organization_id = sc.organization_id
join     person p2
         on  sc.person_id      = p2.person_id
join     italian_citizen ic
         on  p2.person_id      = ic.person_id
```

Listing 2. Query on the schema of Figure 1(c), adopting *one table per kind*

```
select   p.name brazilian_name, o.name organization_name,
         sc.contract_value, p2.name italian_name
from     person p
join     nationality n
         on  p.person_id             = n.person_id
         and n.nationality_enum      = 'BRAZILIANCITIZEN'
join     employment em
         on  p.person_id             = em.person_id
join     organization o
         on  em.organization_id      = o.organization_id
         and o.organization_type_enum = 'HOSPITAL'
join     supply_contract sc
         on  o.organization_id       = sc.organization_id
join     person p2
         on  sc.person_id            = p2.person_id
join     nationality n2
         on  p2.person_id            = n2.person_id
         and n2.nationality_enum     = 'ITALIANCITIZEN'
```

Note that the second query trades some joins for filters. In the *one table per concrete class* strategy, many of the joins are used to reconstruct an entity whose attributes are spread throughout the emulated taxonomy. In the *one table per kind* strategy, filters are applied using the discriminators that are added to identify the (lifted) classes that are instantiated by an entity. The different approaches certainly have performance implications (which will be discussed later in this paper). Regardless of those implications, we can observe that the database is used at a relatively low level of abstraction, which is dependent on the particular realization solution imposed by the transformation strategy. This motivates us to investigate a high-level data access mechanism.

3   Synthesizing High-Level Data Access

We reuse a mature Ontology-Based Data Access (OBDA) technique [19] to realize data access in terms of the conceptual model. OBDA works with the translation of high-level queries into SQL queries. Users of an OBDA solution are required to write a mapping specification that establishes how entities represented in the relational database should be mapped to instances of classes in a computational (RDF- or OWL-based) ontology. The OBDA solution then enables the expression of queries in terms of the ontology, e.g., using SPARQL. Each query is automatically rewritten by the OBDA solution into SQL queries that are executed at the database. Results of the query are then mapped back to triples and consumed by the user using the vocabulary established at the ontology.

In our approach, instead of having the OBDA mapping specification written manually, we incorporate the automatic generation of this mapping specification into the transformation. Therefore, our transformation not only generates a target relational schema, but also generates an OBDA mapping specification to accompany that schema. Although the source models we consider are specified here with UML (or OntoUML), a transformation to OWL is used as part of the overall solution; this transformation preserves the structure of the source conceptual model, and hence SPARQL queries refer to classes in that model. The overall solution is implemented as a plugin to Visual Paradigm[1] (also implementing the *one table per kind* transformation from [13]).

3.1   Tracing Flattening and Lifting

In order to generate the OBDA mapping specification, we keep a set of *traces* at each application of the operations of flattening and lifting. In sum, a trace establishes the class that is flattened or lifted and the target class to which its attributes are migrated. With the final set of traces, we are able to synthesize the OBDA mapping for Ontop [5], the OBDA solution we adopt.

As discussed in Sect. 2.2, the flattening operation consists of removing a superclass and migrating its attributes to each subclass, with association ends attached to the flattened superclass also migrated to each subclass. Each time the flattening operation is executed, one trace is produced for each pair of flattened superclass and subclass. For example, the flattening of NamedEntity, depicted by the green dashed arrows in Fig. 2, creates one trace from this class to Person and another to Organization. Likewise, the flattening of Customer, creates one trace from this class to PersonalCustomer and another to CorporateCustomer.

Naturally, tracing for lifting occurs in the opposite direction in the hierarchy. For every class lifted, traces are created from the lifted subclass to its superclasses. Differently from flattening, the traces for lifting require the specification of a "filter" determining the value of the discriminator. This filter is used later to preserve information on the instantiation of the lifted subclass. For example, the lifting of Child creates a trace from that class to Person (represented in blue arrows in Fig. 2). However, not every Person instance is a Child instance. The added filter thus requires the discriminator lifePhase='Child'.

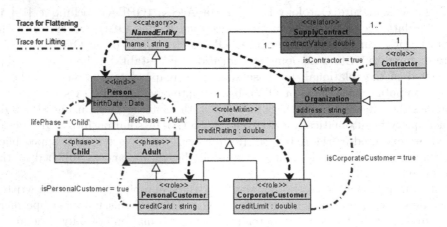

Fig. 2. Tracing example for each execution of flattening and lifting.

---

[1] http://purl.org/guidoni/ontouml2db.

3.2 Generating the Data Mapping

For each tracing path from a class in the source model to a 'sink' class (one with no outgoing traces), a mapping is generated by composing all the traces along the path. Any discriminator filters in a path are placed in a conjunction. For example, there are two end-to-end traces for Customer, mapping it to (i) the PERSON table (through PersonalCustomer and Adult), provided isPersonalCustomer=true and lifePhase='Adult' and also to (ii) the ORGANIZATION table, provided isCorporateCustomer=true. Table 2 shows all composed traces in the application of the *one table per kind* strategy in the running example.

For each end-to-end trace and for each class that is neither flattened nor lifted, an Ontop mapping is produced. Mappings are specified in Ontop as *target* Turtle templates for the creation of an instance of the ontology corresponding to *source* tuples that are obtained by simple SQL queries in the relational database. In the following, we present examples of these mappings generated for three classes of the running example in the *one table per kind* strategy: (i) a class that is neither flattened nor lifted (Person); (ii) a class that is flattened (NamedEntity) and (iii) a class that is lifted (ItalianCitizen).

Listing 3 shows the Ontop mapping generated for the kind Person. Given the absence of flattening and lifting, the mapping establishes the straightforward correspondence of a source entry in the PERSON table and a target instance of Person; the primary key of the PERSON table is used to derive the URI of the instance of Person corresponding to each entry of that table. Labels between brackets in the target template of the mapping ({person_id} and {birth_date}) are references to values in the source pattern select clause. Corresponding attributes (birthDate) are mapped one-to-one.

Listing 3. OBDA mapping for the Person class in Ontop.

```
mappingId RunExample-Person
target    :RunExample/person/{person_id} a :Person ;
          :birthDate {birth_date}^^xsd:dateTime .
source    SELECT person.person_id, person.birth_date
          FROM person
```

Table 2. End-to-end traces involving flattened or lifted classes.

Trace	Source Class	Target Table	Discriminator Conditions
1	NamedEntity	PERSON	–
2	NamedEntity	ORGANIZATION	–
3	Customer	ORGANIZATION	is_corporate_customer = true
4	Customer	PERSON	is_personal_customer = true
			life_phase_enum = 'ADULT'
5	BrazilianCitizen	PERSON	nationality_enum = 'BRAZILIANCITIZEN'
6	ItalianCitizen	PERSON	nationality_enum = 'ITALIANCITIZEN'
7	Child	PERSON	life_phase_enum = 'CHILD'
8	Adult	PERSON	life_phase_enum = 'ADULT'
9	Employee	PERSON	is_employee = true
			life_phase_enum = 'ADULT'
10	PersonalCustomer	PERSON	is_personal_customer = true
			life_phase_enum = 'ADULT'
11	PrimarySchool	ORGANIZATION	organization_type_enum = 'PRIMARYSCHOOL'
12	Hospital	ORGANIZATION	organization_type_enum = 'HOSPITAL'
13	CorporateCustomer	ORGANIZATION	is_corporate_customer = true
14	Contractor	ORGANIZATION	is_contractor = true

Listing 4 shows the mappings generated for a class that is flattened: **NamedEntity**. Because the class is flattened to two subclasses, two mappings are produced, one for each table corresponding to a subclass (**PERSON** and **ORGANIZATION**). Since attributes of the flattened superclass are present in each table, one-to-one mappings of these attributes are produced.

Listing 4. OBDA mapping for the flattened **NamedEntity** class in Ontop.

```
mappingId  RunExample-NamedEntity
target     :RunExample/person/{person_id} a :NamedEntity ;
           :name {name}^^xsd:string .
source     SELECT person.person_id, person.name
           FROM person

mappingId  RunExample-NamedEntity2
target     :RunExample/organization/{organization_id} a :NamedEntity;
           :name {name}^^xsd:string .
source     SELECT organization.organization_id, organization.name
           FROM organization
```

Listing 5 shows the mapping generated for a class that is lifted (**ItalianCitizen**) to the **Person** class, again in the *one table per kind* strategy. Here, the filter captured during tracing are included in the SQL query to ensure that only instances of the lifted superclass are included. Because of the multivalued discriminator employed to capture the overlapping generalization set **Nationality**, a join with a discriminator table is required (otherwise, a simple filter would suffice). For performance reasons, an index is created in the transformation for enumerations corresponding to generalization sets. The complete specification with resulting mappings for this example can be obtained in https://github.com/nemo-ufes/forward-engineering-db.

Listing 5. OBDA mapping for the lifted class `ItalianCitizen` in Ontop.

```
mappingId  RunExample-ItalianCitizen
target     :RunExample/person/{person_id} a
           :ItalianCitizen ; :CI {ci}^^xsd:string .
source     SELECT person.person_id, person.ci
           FROM person
           JOIN nationality
             ON person.person_id = nationality.person_id
           AND nationality.nationality_enum = 'ITALIANCITIZEN'
```

4 Performance of Data Access

In order to evaluate the performance of data access in our approach, we have created a randomly populated database using the models in Fig. 1. We have employed the two transformation strategies as discussed before. Our main objective was to consider the overhead of the high-level data access approach. Because of that, we have contrasted the time performance of handwritten SQL queries with those automatically rewritten from SPARQL. A secondary objective was to validate our motivating assumption that the different transformation strategies lead to different time performance characteristics.

The database was populated with synthetic instances, including: 50k organizations (30.6k hospitals and 19.4k primary schools); 200k persons (about 45% Brazilian citizens, 45% Italian citizens and 10% with double nationality, over 161k adults, 38k children, 129k employees); about 252k supply contracts; 170k employments (30% of the employees with more than one employment) and 61k enrollments (40% of the children with more than one employment). The database size was 91.34 MB for the *one table per concrete class* strategy and 77.22 MB for the *one table per kind* strategy, in MySql 8.0.23. Measurements were obtained in a Windows 10 notebook with an i3 1.8 GHz processor, 250 GB SSD and 8 GB RAM.

The following queries were written to retrieve: (1) the credit rating of each customer; (2) the name of each child, along with the playground size of the schools in which the child is enrolled; (3) the names of Brazilian citizens working in hospitals with Italian customers; this query reveals also the names of these customers and the contract values with the hospital; (4) all data of organizations regardless of whether it is registered as a Hospital or Primary School; (5) given the CI of an Italian citizen, the name of the Hospital with which he/she has a contract and the value of that contract.

The queries were designed to capture different query characteristics. Query 1 represents an example of polymorphic query with reference to the abstract class `Customer` and retrieves an attribute defined at that abstract class. Queries 2 and 3 involve navigation through associations in the conceptual model. Query 3 is the most complex one and corresponds to the realizations we have shown earlier in Listings 1 and 2. Its representation in SPARQL is shown in Listing 6. Query 4 is polymorphic with reference to **Organization** and, differently from query 1, retrieves all attributes of organizations, including those defined in subclasses. Query 5 retrieves data of a specific person.

Listing 6. SPARQL query

```
PREFIX : <https://example.com#>
SELECT ?brazilianName ?organizationName ?value ?italianName {
    ?brazilianPerson    a               :BrazilianCitizen ;
                        :name           ?brazilianName .
    ?employment         a               :Employment ;
                        :hasEmployee    ?brazilianPerson;
                        :hasOrganization ?hospital .
    ?hospital           a               :Hospital .
    ?hospital           a               :Contractor ;
                        :name           ?organizationName .
    ?contract           a               :SupplyContract ;
                        :hasContractor  ?hospital ;
                        :hasCustomer    ?personalCustomer ;
                        :contractValue  ?value.
    ?personalCustomer   a               :PersonalCustomer .
    ?personalCustomer   a               :ItalianCitizen ;
                        :name           ?italianName .}
```

Table 3 shows the results obtained, comparing the performance of manually written queries with those rewritten from SPARQL by Ontop (version 2.0.3 plugin for Protégé 5.5.0). In order to exclude I/O from the response time, which could mask the difference between the approaches, we have performed a row count for each query effectively "packaging" it into a "select count (1) from (query)". Further, in order to remove any influence from caching and other transient effects, each query was executed in a freshly instantiated instance of the database three times; the values presented are averages of these three measurements. Values in bold represent the best performing alternative.

The results indicate the performance varies as expected for the two transformation strategies, depending on the characteristics of the queries. In the *one table per concrete class* strategy, the performance of the automatically transformed queries is roughly equal to the manual queries (2, 3 and 5), and some overhead is imposed for queries 1 and 4. This overhead is imposed whenever unions are

Table 3. Performance comparison of relational schemas (in seconds).

Query	One Table per Concrete Class		One Table per Kind	
	Manual Query	Ontop Query	Manual Query	Ontop Query
1	**0.286**	0.333 (+16.4%)	0.385	1.906 (+394.63%)
2	7.436	7.523 (+1.3%)	**1.906**	2.245 (+17.8%)
3	121.797	122.943 (+0.9%)	**102.646**	134.318 (+30.9%)
4	0.610	0.625 (+2.5%)	**0.078**	0.094 (+19.6%)
5	**0.166**	0.167 (+0.4%)	0.271	1.526 (+463.8%)

required in polymorphic queries, as Ontop needs to add columns to the select to be able to translate the retrieved data back to instances of classes in the high-level model. In the *one table per kind* strategy, significant overhead is imposed for queries 1, 4 and 5. Upon close inspection of the generated queries, we were able to observe that the automatically rewritten queries include filters which are not strictly necessary and that were not present in the manual queries. For example, in query 1, we assume in the manual query that only adults enter into supply contracts, as imposed in the conceptual model. However, Ontop adds that check to the query, in addition to several IS NOT NULL checks. As a result, the Ontop queries are 'safer' than the manual ones. Removing the additional check from the rewritten queries significantly reduces the overhead: query 1 reduces to 0.463s (now +20.2% in comparison to the manual query), query 2 to 1.942s (+1.9%), query 3 to 106.573s (+3.8%), query 4 to 0.078s (0.0%) and query 5 to 0.338s (+25.0%). This makes the imposed overhead always lower than 25% of the response time.

5   Related Work

There is a wide variety of proposals for carrying out data access at a high level of abstraction. Some of these rely on *native graph-based representations*, instead of relational databases. These include triplestores such as Stardog, GraphDB, AllegroGraph, ArangoDB, InfiniteGraph, Neo4J, 4Store and OrientDB. A native graph-based solution has the advantage of requiring no mappings for data access. However, they depart from established relational technologies which are key in many production environments and on which we aim to leverage with our approach.

Some other OBDA approaches such as Ultrawrap [20] and D2RQ [3], facilitate the *reverse engineering* of a high-level representation model from relational schemas. Ultrawrap[20] works as a wrapper of a relational database using a SPARQL terminal as an access point. Similarly to Ontop it uses the technique of rewriting SPARQL queries into their SQL equivalent. It includes a tool with heuristic rules to provide a starting point for creating a conceptual model through the reverse engineering of a relational schema. D2RQ [3] also allows access to relational databases through SPARQL queries. It supports automatic and user-assisted modes of operation for the ontology production. Virtuoso [10] also supports the automatic conversion of a relational schema into an ontology through a basic approach. It allows complex manual mappings which can be specified with a specialized syntax. There are also a range of bootstrappers like [6,15] that perform automatic or semi-automatic mapping between the relational schema and the ontology. However, these bootstrappers assume that the relational schema exists and provide ways to map it into an existing ontology or help to create an ontology.

Differently from these technologies, we have proposed a forward engineering transformation, in which all mapping is automated. Combining both reverse and forward engineering is an interesting theme for further investigation, which could serve to support a conceptual model based reengineering effort.

Calvanese et al. propose in [4] a two-level framework for ontology-based data access. First, data access from a relational schema to a domain ontology is facilitated with a manually written OBDA mapping. A second ontology-to-ontology mapping—also manually specified—further raises the level of data access to a more abstract reference ontology. An interesting feature of this approach is that, based on the two mappings, a direct mapping from the abstract reference ontology to the relational schema is produced. Such a two-level schema could be combined with our approach to further raise the level of abstraction of data access.

There are also different approaches that aim at supporting forward engineering of relational databases from logical languages typically used for conceptual modeling. These include approach that propose mappings from OCL to SQL, but also approaches that propose mappings from OWL to relational schemas. In the former group, some of these approaches, e.g., OCL2SQL [7], Incremental OCL constraints checking [17] and OCL_{FO} [12] are restricted to just mapping Boolean expressions, while others such as SQL-PL4OCL [8] and MySQL4OCL [9] are not limited in this way; in the latter group, we have approaches such as [1] and [23], which implement a *one table per class* strategy, thus, mapping each OWL class to a relational table.

Our proposal differs from these approaches as it is applicable to different transformation strategies. In particular, by leveraging on the ontological semantics of OntoUML, it is unique in implementing the *one table per kind* strategy. Moreover, as empirically shown in [22], this language favors the construction of higher-quality conceptual models—quality attributes that can then be transferred *by design* to the produced relational schemas. Finally, unlike [1,23], our proposal also generates an ontology-based data access mapping for the transformed database schema.

6 Conclusions and Future Work

We propose an approach to automatically forward engineer a data access mapping to accompany a relational schema generated from a source conceptual model. The objective is to allow data representation in relational databases and its access in terms of the conceptual model. Since the approach is defined in terms of the operations of flattening and lifting, it can be applied to various transformation strategies described in the literature. The approach is based on the tracing of the transformation operations applied to classes in the source model. It is implemented as a plugin to Visual Paradigm; it generates a DDL script for relational schemas and corresponding mappings for the Ontop OBDA platform. Ontop uses the generated mappings to translate SPARQL queries to SQL, execute them and translate the results back. Although we adopt OBDA technology, it is only part of our solution. This is because by using solely OBDA, the user would have to produce an ontology and data access mappings manually. Instead, these mappings are generated automatically in our approach, and are a further result of the transformation of the conceptual model.

We present a pilot study of the performance aspects of the approach. We show that the overhead imposed by the generated mappings and Ontop's translation varies for a number of queries, but should be acceptable considering the benefits of high-level data access. Further performance studies contrasting various transformation strategies should be conducted to guide the selection of a strategy for a particular application. In any case, the writing of queries in terms of the conceptual model can be done independently of the selection of a transformation strategy.

We also intend to support operations other than reads (creation, update and deletion of entities), which are currently not supported by Ontop. Our plan is to generate SQL templates that can be used for these operations. We expect performance of update operations to reveal interesting differences between transformation strategies, in particular, as dynamic classification comes into play.

Acknowledgments. This research is partly funded by Brazilian funding agencies CNPq (grants numbers 313687/2020-0, 407235/2017-5) and CAPES (grant number 23038.028816/2016-41).

References

1. Afzal, H., Waqas, M., Naz, T.: OWLMap: fully automatic mapping of ontology into relational database schema. Int. J. Adv. Comput. Sci. Appl. **7**(11), 7–15 (2016)
2. Ambler, S.W.: Agile Database Techniques: Effective Strategies for the Agile Software Developer. Wiley, Hoboken (2003)
3. Bizer, C., Seaborne, A.: D2RQ-treating non-RDF databases as virtual RDF graphs. In: ISWC 2004 (posters) (2004)
4. Calvanese, D., Kalayci, T.E., Montali, M., Santoso, A., van der Aalst, W.: Conceptual schema transformation in ontology-based data access. In: Faron Zucker, C., Ghidini, C., Napoli, A., Toussaint, Y. (eds.) EKAW 2018. LNCS (LNAI), vol. 11313, pp. 50–67. Springer, Cham (2018). https://doi.org/10.1007/978-3-030-03667-6_4
5. Calvanese, D., et al.: Ontop: answering SPARQL queries over relational databases. Semant. Web **8**(3), 471–487 (2017). https://doi.org/10.3233/SW-160217
6. de Medeiros, L.F., Priyatna, F., Corcho, O.: MIRROR: automatic R2RML mapping generation from relational databases. In: Cimiano, P., Frasincar, F., Houben, G.-J., Schwabe, D. (eds.) ICWE 2015. LNCS, vol. 9114, pp. 326–343. Springer, Cham (2015). https://doi.org/10.1007/978-3-319-19890-3_21
7. Demuth, B., Hussmann, H.: Using UML/OCL constraints for relational database design. In: France, R., Rumpe, B. (eds.) UML 1999. LNCS, vol. 1723, pp. 598–613. Springer, Heidelberg (1999). https://doi.org/10.1007/3-540-46852-8_42
8. Egea, M., Dania, C.: SQL-PL4OCL: an automatic code generator from OCL to SQL procedural language. In: Proceedings of the MODELS 2017, Austin, TX, USA, 17–22 September 2017, p. 54 (2017)
9. Egea, M., Dania, C., Clavel, M.: Mysql4ocl: a stored procedure-based MySQL code generator for OCL. Electron. Commun. Eur. Assoc. Softw. Sci. Technol. **36** (2010)
10. Erling, O., Mikhailov, I.: RDF support in the virtuoso DBMS. In: Auer, S., Bizer, C., Müller, C., Zhdanova, A.V. (eds.) Proceedings of the CSSW 2007, Leipzig, Germany. LNI, vol. P-113. GI (2007)

11. Fowler, M.: Patterns of Enterprise Application Architecture. Addison-Wesley Longman Publishing Co., Inc., Boston (2002)
12. Franconi, E., Mosca, A., Oriol, X., Rull, G., Teniente, E.: Logic foundations of the OCL modelling language. In: Fermé, E., Leite, J. (eds.) JELIA 2014. LNCS (LNAI), vol. 8761, pp. 657–664. Springer, Cham (2014). https://doi.org/10.1007/978-3-319-11558-0_49
13. Guidoni, G.L., Almeida, J.P.A., Guizzardi, G.: Transformation of ontology-based conceptual models into relational schemas. In: Dobbie, G., Frank, U., Kappel, G., Liddle, S.W., Mayr, H.C. (eds.) ER 2020. LNCS, vol. 12400, pp. 315–330. Springer, Cham (2020). https://doi.org/10.1007/978-3-030-62522-1_23
14. Guizzardi, G., Fonseca, C.M., Benevides, A.B., Almeida, J.P.A., Porello, D., Sales, T.P.: Endurant types in ontology-driven conceptual modeling: towards OntoUML 2.0. In: Trujillo, J.C., et al. (eds.) ER 2018. LNCS, vol. 11157, pp. 136–150. Springer, Cham (2018). https://doi.org/10.1007/978-3-030-00847-5_12
15. Jiménez-Ruiz, E., et al.: BootOX: practical mapping of RDBs to OWL 2. In: Arenas, M., et al. (eds.) ISWC 2015. LNCS, vol. 9367, pp. 113–132. Springer, Cham (2015). https://doi.org/10.1007/978-3-319-25010-6_7
16. Keller, W.: Mapping objects to tables: a pattern language. In: EuroPLoP 1997: Proceedings of the 2nd European Conference Pattern Languages of Programs. Siemens Technical report 120/SW1/FB (1997)
17. Oriol, X., Teniente, E.: Incremental checking of OCL constraints through SQL queries. In: Proceedings of the MODELS 2014). CEUR Workshop Proceedings, vol. 1285 (2014)
18. Philippi, S.: Model driven generation and testing of object-relational mappings. J. Syst. Softw. **77**, 193–207 (2005)
19. Poggi, A., Lembo, D., Calvanese, D., Giacomo, G.D., Lenzerini, M., Rosati, R.: Linking data to ontologies. J. Data Semant. **10**, 133–173 (2008)
20. Sequeda, J.F., Miranker, D.P.: Ultrawrap: SPARQL execution on relational data. J. Web Semant. **22**, 19–39 (2013)
21. Torres, A., et al.: Twenty years of object-relational mapping: a survey on patterns, solutions, and their implications on application design. Inf. Softw. Technol. **82**, 1–18 (2017)
22. Verdonck, M., et al.: Comparing traditional conceptual modeling with ontology-driven conceptual modeling: an empirical study. Inf. Syst. **81**, 92–103 (2019)
23. Vyšniauskas, E., et al.: Reversible lossless transformation from owl 2 ontologies into relational databases. Inf. Technol. Control **40**(4), 293–306 (2011)

Remaining in Control of the Impact of Schema Evolution in NoSQL Databases

Andrea Hillenbrand[1](✉) ⓘ, Stefanie Scherzinger[2], and Uta Störl[3] ⓘ

[1] Darmstadt University of Applied Sciences, Darmstadt, Germany
andrea.hillenbrand@h-da.de
[2] University of Passau, Passau, Germany
stefanie.scherzinger@uni-passau.de
[3] University of Hagen, Hagen, Germany
uta.stoerl@fernuni-hagen.de

Abstract. During the development of NoSQL-backed software, the database schema evolves naturally alongside the application code. Especially in agile development, new application releases are deployed frequently. Eventually, decisions have to be made regarding the migration of versioned legacy data which is persisted in the cloud-hosted production database. We address this schema evolution problem and present results by means of which software project stakeholders can manage the operative costs for schema evolution and adapt their software release strategy accordingly in order to comply with service-level agreements regarding the competing metrics of migration costs and latency. We clarify conclusively how schema evolution in NoSQL databases impacts these metrics while taking all relevant characteristics of migration scenarios into account. As calculating all combinatorics in the search space of migration scenarios by far exceeds computational means, we use a probabilistic Monte Carlo method of repeated sampling, serving as a well-established method to bring the complexity of schema evolution under control.

Keywords: NoSQL · Schema evolution · Migration cost · Latency

1 Introduction

Developing a software-as-a-service application requires the management of ever-growing amounts of data and their co-evolution with the software code [14, 26]. Schema-flexible NoSQL databases are especially popular backends in agile development, as they allow developers to write code assuming a new schema that is different from the current database schema. Furthermore, new software releases can be deployed without migration-related application downtime. In fact, a very recent empirical study on the evolution of NoSQL database schemas

---

This work has been funded by the German Research Foundation (DFG, grant #385808805). An extended version of this paper is available as a preprint [20].

A. Ghose et al. (Eds.): ER 2021, LNCS 13011, pp. 149–159, 2021.
https://doi.org/10.1007/978-3-030-89022-3_13

has shown that releases include considerably more schema-relevant changes [28]. Furthermore, schemas grow in complexity over time and take longer to stabilize.

Eventually, stakeholders have to address the handling of variational data in the database. A decision has to be made when to migrate which legacy data that is structured according to earlier schema versions. If all of the legacy data is curated according to the latest schema at the release of schema changes, i.e., with an *eager* migration strategy, then maximal charges are produced with the cloud provider. This significantly drives up the operational costs, especially in case of frequent software releases. For instance, for 10M persisted entities on *Google Cloud* and 100 monthly schema changes throughout a year, charges of approx. USD 13,000 are incurred just for database writes[1], not even considering reads or storage costs. The benefit of this investment is that the application then accesses a structurally homogeneous database instance. Then, reads and writes against the database come at no migration-induced overhead accounting for structural variety and hence, the time that it takes for requested data to be retrieved, the *data access latency*, is minimal. Short latencies are indeed crucial to application performance, especially in cloud-hosted applications [4,6,8,11].

If latency is the sole criterion, then an *eager* strategy is clearly most suitable. However, if saving costs is most important, then a *lazy* strategy should be applied which minimizes *migration costs*, as data remains unchanged in the event of a schema changes. In this case, if a legacy entity is accessed, it is migrated individually and on-the-fly, then being in congruence with the latest schema version, yet introducing a considerable runtime overhead [22,27]. These two metrics, *migration costs* and *latency*, are in fact competitors in a tradeoff. They cannot be optimized independently from each other and thus, a choice of a migration strategy is also a choice on the tradeoff between these metrics at different opportunity costs for alternative migration strategies. Stakeholders should be aware that this decision can only be realized as a cost-aware compromise that complies with latency-related SLAs if the relationship between these metrics is clarified and opportunity costs are transparent, which we contribute in this paper. In fact, the data management community has identified schema evolution as one of the hardest problems that is currently being ignored [29]. Especially when a database is considered to be run in a cloud-hosted environment, concerns about high costs are most often cited in surveys, high latencies being an issue as well [1].

Solving the schema evolution problem is not trivial, because data migration scenarios are highly complex as they rely on many factors that influence the impact on the metrics and potentially obscure correlations. Completely searching the solution space by far exceeds computational means. We use a probabilistic *Monte Carlo* method of repeated sampling to investigate the scenario characteristics while bringing the complexity of the problem under control [13,24]. We

---

[1] Writing an entity currently costs USD 0.108 per 100,000 documents for regional location pricing in North America as of July 21, 2021 (see https://cloud.google.com/datastore/pricing). Not all schema changes add properties to the entities, yet we assume this rough estimate, as there are both cheaper schema changes (deletes) and more expensive schema changes (reorganizing properties affecting multiple types).

parameterize each scenario and calculate the metrics for each migration strategy by means of the tool-based migration advisor *MigCast*, which we presented in earlier work [18,19]. By repeatedly sampling all relevant migration scenarios and randomizing some algorithm parameters—the Monte Carlo method—we uncover the correlations of the scenario characteristics and their impact on the metrics.

Contributions. Our paper makes the following contributions:

- We clarify conclusively how schema evolution impacts the competing metrics migration costs and latency. We investigated all relevant migration scenario characteristics with an underlying cost model that takes into account i.) intensity and distribution of data entity accesses, ii.) different kinds of schema changes, and iii.) cardinality of the entity relationships.
- We present the results and discuss the implications so that software project stakeholders can control the impact of schema evolution and adapt the pace of their software release strategy accordingly in order to ascertain compliance with cost- and latency-related service-level agreements.

2 Architecture of the Monte Carlo Experiment

When schema changes are implied through new software code, a migration strategy can handle the migration of legacy data. Different strategies can be applied, each of which settling on another compromise regarding the tradeoff between the competing metrics of migration costs and latency.

The *eager* and *lazy* migration strategies are complemented by two more *proactive* strategies, which act in advance of situations when migrating legacy entities could cause latency overhead, the *incremental* and the *predictive* migration. The *incremental* strategy migrates all legacy entities at certain points in time. Lazy periods are then interrupted by regular bouts of tidying up the structurally heterogeneous database instance in order to get rid of the runtime overhead intermittently. In order to keep a steady balance on the tradeoff between migration costs and latency, we devised a *predictive* strategy [18]. It allows improving latency at moderate costs in case that data entity accesses are *Pareto*-distributed, i.e., concentrate on *hot* entities. Then, the prediction is based on the assumption that the oftener entities were accessed in the past, the more likely it is that they be accessed again in the future. The *predictive* strategy keeps track of past accesses and orders the entities accordingly via *exponential smoothing* [23].

Uncovering the correlation of migration scenario characteristics and their impact on the investigated metrics necessitates searching a huge problem space. The *Monte Carlo* approach [13,24], i.e., an approach using the *Monte Carlo method*, is suitable to our use case and a well-established probabilistic approach in data management [2,21,30]. *MigCast in Monte Carlo* runs *MigCast* repeatedly, a tool-based advisor that we published in earlier work [18,19]. By means of *MigCast in Monte Carlo*, we now realize a systematic exploration of the search space and conclusively investigate the impact of schema evolution for SLA compliance.

Category	Input Parameter	Default Value	Investigated Variations
Workload	Distribution of data accesses	Pareto 80/20	Pareto 80/20, Uniform
	Percentage accessed data	10% (constant)	
	Intensity, in measures of 10%	Low (2x 10%)	Low (2x 10%), Medium (4x 10%), High (8x 10%)
Schema Changes	Releases of schema changes	12	12
	Multi-type SMO complexity	25%	0%, 25%, 50%, 75%, 100%
Data Set	Initial number of entities	1,000	
	Data growth per release	10%	
	Cardinality of 1:n-relationships	1:1	1:1, 1:10, 1:25

Fig. 1. Parameter instantiations of the *MigCast in Monte Carlo* experiment.

MigCast calculates the metrics for migration scenarios based on a cost model that takes characteristics of the data set instance, database management system, and cloud provider pricing models into account, as well as workload of served data entity accesses and schema changes. In order to calculate the costs, database reads, writes, and deletes are counted in *MigCast* and multiplied by parameterizable charges per I/O-requests, like cloud providers commonly charge in their cost models. Yet, in this paper, we discuss relative, not absolute costs. Although single results varied easily by factor 100, we could calculate expected sample means and possible ranges of the metrics and bring the complexity under control.

Figure 1 summarizes the scenario parameters. We refer to the entity accesses in between two releases of schema changes as *workload*. We distinguish between different *workload distributions* and between amounts of served workload of data entity accesses (*workload intensity*), implemented as executions of a certain amount of entity accesses relative to the existing number of entities. The workload is then randomized within the parameterized bounds. With the *uniform* distribution, the probability of a single entity being accessed is the same for all entities, whereas under *Pareto* it is greater for *hot* data entities. We used a Pareto distribution common in OLTP database applications [23], where 80% of the workload concentrates on 20% of *hot* data and 20% is spread over 80% of *cold* data. We used MongoDB, but other *DBMS* are also integrated in *MigCast*.

As regards schema changes, we differentiate between *single-type* and *multi-type schema modification operations* (SMOs). *Single-type* SMOs affect exactly one entity type, specifically, these are add, delete, and rename. *Multi-type* SMOs affect two entity types at once, the most common are copy and move. By means of *multi-type SMO complexity*, the percentage of those operations can be parameterized that involve more than one entity type. The concrete sequence of SMOs is then randomized within the bounds of this ratio. Last but not least, we investigate the *cardinalities of the entity relationships* of the application data.

The sampling size is determined by its *initial number of entities*, which can be upscaled to a certain number of entities. With each release of new software, events take place in the following order: The workload of entity accesses is served, which can cause on-read migration costs with migration strategies that delay migrating legacy entities. Then an SMO is applied, which causes on-release migration costs in case of the *eager*, *incremental*, and *predictive* strategies. Lastly, new data entities are added to the existing data set according to the specified *data growth rate* and the cardinalities of the entity relationships.[2]

---

[2] More details and illustrations can be found in the long version of this paper [20].

3   Results of the *MigCast in Monte Carlo* Experiments

In the following, we present the results structured corresponding to Fig. 1: *Workload, schema changes*, and *cardinality of the entity relationships of the data set*.

Workload. The impacts of different distributions of the workload on the metrics of migration costs and latency is shown in Fig. 2. The charts show how the metrics develop for 12 releases of schema changes with each strategy. The relative differences between the strategies are annotated next to the charts.

The distribution of entity accesses influences the metrics due to the varying number and age of the legacy entities. With the *eager* strategy, all legacy entities are migrated to the current schema version, so that no runtime overhead exists, however, migration costs are then maximal. With the *lazy* strategy, legacy data remains unchanged in the event of schema changes. Savings in terms of on-release migration costs are paid for in form of on-read migration costs and a higher latency, once a legacy entity needs to be accessed. Yet, the *lazy* strategy performs better under the Pareto than under the uniform distribution: migration costs drop by 58% and latency by 50%.

Located in between is the *incremental* migration, which migrates all legacy entities at certain points in time, here at releases 5 and 10. Characteristic for *incremental* strategy is that it fluctuates between the graphs of the *eager* and *lazy* strategy both in terms of migration costs and latency[3]. This can be utilized when the workload is known to vary in a certain pattern, to which the migration of legacy entities can be adapted. The *predictive* strategy shows its full potential under the Pareto distribution, benefiting from the presence of hot data in similar measure like the *lazy* strategy: While latency decreases by 41%, 44% of migration costs can be saved. It convinces with more stable and thus more predictable metrics, especially important for SLA-compliance and when migration increments cannot be matched to intervals of low workload.

Thus, a concentration of accesses amplifies the differences of the strategies in terms of migration costs and levels them in terms of latency, i.e., the strategy graphs diverge more or less, when accesses concentrate on hot entities. Within this range of divergence, any shifts of the hot data set itself can drive up migration costs and latency to measures taken for the uniform distribution.

With increasing workload, the percentage of legacy entities declines for the *lazy, incremental*, and *predictive* strategies and thus, it can be observed that, while the cumulated costs continuously increase with each release, the advantage over other strategies diminishes, and the graphs diverge less. Regarding the latency it can be observed that an increase of the workloads corresponds to a decrease of the latency for strategies that delay migration. Specifically, with four times as much workload (low to high) the migration costs for *lazy* increase by 130% (cp. to Fig. 5, mind the rounding differences) and for *predictive* by 149%. Latency then drops for *lazy* from 7.09 ms to 6.15 ms (13%), and for *predictive* from 5.72 ms to 5.11 ms (11%). Hence, the graphs are less divergent with higher

---

[3] In case of the *incremental* strategy, the snapshots of latency after 12 releases do not fully represent all releases. Thus, we projected the values in Fig. 5 accordingly.

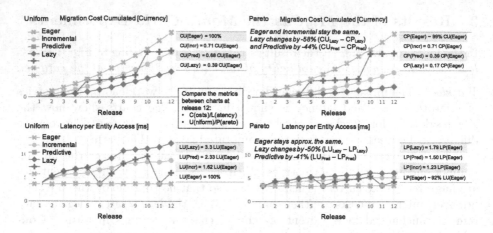

Fig. 2. Comparing uniform and Pareto distribution: The migration strategies diverge more or less; Medium workload, 25% multi-type SMO complexity, 1:1-relationships.

workload, because more entity accesses result in higher costs, except for *eager* which stays invariant under workload. Latency also becomes less divergent as more legacy entities are migrated with strategies that delay migration.

Schema Changes. The higher multi-type complexity is, the higher the migration costs become across all migration strategies (see Fig. 3). Although, the absolute difference between *lazy* and *eager* more than doubles (+128%), the relative differences decrease from factor 8.1 in case of 0% multi-type complexity (100% single-type SMOs) to factor 4.7 in case of 100%. Their increase corresponds with the number of affected types and the amount of legacy entities that are being migrated. The increases in latency consistently reflects the investments of migration costs with each of the different strategies. Thus, high multi-type complexity can be considered the most important cost driver for both metrics.

Cardinality of the Entity Relationships. In order to clarify how the cardinality of the relationships of the persisted entities influences the resulting metrics, we have run *MigCast in Monte Carlo* with varying cardinalities. In case of 1:1-relationships, we assume the entities to be evenly distributed over the types, whereas at higher cardinalities there exist more entities on the n-sides of the 1:n-relationships: With 1:25-relationships there are 0.2% *Player*, 3.8% entities *Mission*, and 96% *Place* entities. Although the number of affected entities per type changes drastically with higher cardinality, the average of affected entities does not change as single-type SMOs affect types uniformly. However, counter-intuitively, in case of multi-type SMOs higher cardinality means less affected entities on average by a schema change, as the evolution affects *Player:Mission:Place* in a 1:2:1-ratio, slanted towards the *Mission* type with less entities. Thus, in case of 25% multi-type complexity, the migration costs for *eager* amount to relative values of 93% for 1:10 and 92% for 1:25 compared to 1:1 (cp. with Fig. 5).

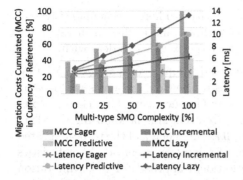

Fig. 3. The metrics increase proportionally with multi-type SMO complexity (Pareto-distr. medium workload, 1:1-relationships).

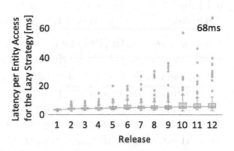

Fig. 4. With higher cardinality of relationships, the variance of latencies increases, particularly for the *lazy* migration strategy (Pareto-distributed medium workload, 25% multi-type SMO complexity).

The migration costs for the *predictive* and the *lazy* strategy tend to increase slightly for higher cardinality. This is because with higher cardinality the workload concentrates on *Place* entities as these are prevalent in number, the SMOs affect the types evenly by a third in case of single-type operations and in a 1:2:1-relationship in case of multi-type operations. The measured latency corresponds quite consistently to the invested migration costs, though in case of the *lazy* strategy, it stands out that latency increases considerably with higher cardinality because of rather frequent tail latencies. This shows the difficulty to comply with latency-related SLAs with regard to this scenario characteristic. Although the median is at 5.8ms and the 75th percentile is at 7.9ms, we have measured tail latencies up to 68ms per one entity (see Fig. 4). The high variance in case of higher cardinalities can also be observed for migration costs, where individual values can vary by as much as 600% for the *eager* strategy after 12 releases.

4 Related Work

Schema Evolution. There are several empirical studies on schema evolution in real-world applications backed by relational databases [10, 26, 31]. Various frameworks for managing schema changes in relational database management systems have been proposed [3, 7, 9, 17]. Schema evolution has also been investigated in the context of XML [5, 15] and object-oriented databases [32].

In the context of application development with schema-flexible NoSQL database systems, new challenges arise, such as the lack of a global schema. As the schema is implicitly declared within the application code, evidence of schema changes can be observed by analyzing the change history of the application code [25, 28], rather than an explicitly declared database schema. Moreover, there is evidence that suggests that the application-inherent schema evolves at a higher frequency than what is observed with schema evolution in relational databases [28]. This makes the problem ever more pressing to deal with.

Data Migration. In [12], the costs, duration, and running costs are estimated for migrating entire relational database instances to the cloud, whereas we focus on the impact of legacy data on migration costs and latency caused by schema evolution. The estimates of [12] are based on discrete-event simulation using workload and structure models taken from logs, as well as the schema of the to-be-migrated database, whereas we investigate a range of migration scenario characteristics in a Monte Carlo approach. Since the traditional approach of *eager* migration can become very expensive—especially in a cloud environment [12,18]—other approaches to data migration such as *lazy* [22,27] and proactive [18] approaches have been proposed. To our knowledge, there is no related study on the effects of the various migration strategies, comparable to ours in its systematics. In [18], we have demoed the tool-based advisor *MigCast*, which serves as a basis for the Monte Carlo approach presented here.

Monte Carlo Methods in Data Management. In terms of probabilistic methods in the context of database research, surveying uncertain data algorithms and applications, and uncertain data management has been proposed [2]. In particular, Monte Carlo methods for uncertain data have been studied in detail [16,21].

5   Discussion and Conclusion

We presented the results of near-exhaustive calculations of *MigCast in Monte Carlo* by means of which software project stakeholders can remain in control of the consequences of schema evolution. We can equip them with information so that they can base their decisions during software development on transparency regarding the impact on the metrics by selecting a migration strategy to suit the production settings. Figure 5 summarizes the impacts of the scenario characteristics after 12 releases of schema changes. Although the results are scenario-specific, they are representative and constitute a heuristic that allows making predictions about a scenario by multiplying the factors accordingly. With this transparency, compromises in accordance with service-level agreements can be reached in terms of opportunity costs caused by the tradeoff between migration costs and latency.

	WL Distribution				WL Intensity						Multi-type SMO Complexity										Cardinality of Relationships					
	CU	CP	LU	LP	CL	CM	CH	LL	LM	LH	C0	C25	C50	C75	C100	L0	L25	L50	L75	L100	C1	C10	C25	L1	L10	L25
Eager	1	1	1	1	1	1	1	1	1	1	0.7	1	1.3	1.6	1.8	1	1	1.1	1.1	1.1	1	0.9	0.9	1	1	1
Incr.	0.7	0.7	2.3	1.5	0.7	0.7	0.7	1.6	1.5	1.5	0.5	0.7	0.9	1.1	1.4	1.2	1.5	1.6	1.8	2.1	0.7	0.7	0.7	1.5	1.6	1.6
Pred.	0.7	0.4	2.3	1.5	0.2	0.4	0.6	1.6	1.5	1.5	0.2	0.4	0.5	0.7	0.8	1.2	1.5	2	2.3	2.8	0.4	0.4	0.4	1.5	1.8	1.8
Lazy	0.4	0.2	3.3	1.8	0.1	0.2	0.3	2	1.8	1.7	0.1	0.2	0.2	0.3	0.4	1.2	1.8	2.4	3	3.8	0.2	0.2	0.2	1.8	2.4	2.8

Fig. 5. Impact of 12 releases on costs (C, orange) and latency (L, blue); Latency of *incremental* projected to release 13; reference values of the default parameters in green. (Color figure online)

The characteristics of the migration scenario are beyond a direct control, certainly in case of workload distribution and intensity. In case of multi-type SMO complexity and the cardinalities of the relationships a direct influence is conceivable, yet certainly not recommendable. By means of selecting a migration strategy that most likely suits the given SLAs regarding migration costs and latency, stakeholders can now make a decision that is a cost-aware compromise. However, neither the scenario characteristics nor their impact can be predicted exactly, thus SLA compliance can still be in jeopardy. In this case, the impact can be mitigated by changing how often a new release is rolled out productively, because the release frequency indirectly moderates the impact.

A good compromise can be achieved by *predictive* migration, especially if data accesses are Pareto-distributed. For giving up on a certain amount of latency, the migration costs are reduced considerably, much more so than under the uniform distribution. Depending on the preferences regarding the tradeoff, maximally saving of costs with the *lazy* migration seems as too good of a bargain, because if the entity relationships have a high cardinality, then individual costs and latency vary considerably. Depending what the consequences of a non-compliance of SLAs would entail, a confidence interval regarding the metrics can be specified to be on the safe side. In comparison to the *incremental* strategy, the *predictive* strategy achieves more stable and predictable metrics under both workload distributions. The metrics though increase with higher multi-type complexity like with no other characteristic and can thus be considered the most important cost driver of schema evolution. This is often the case during major changes in agile development when attributes of entity types are restructured.

Acknowledgments. We thank Tobias Kreiter, Shamil Nabiyev, Maksym Levchenko, and Jan-Christopher Mair for their contributions to *MigCast*.

References

1. 3T Software Labs Ltd.: MongoDB Trends Report. Cambridge, U.K. (2020)
2. Aggarwal, C.C., Yu, P.S.: A survey of uncertain data algorithms and applications. IEEE Trans. Knowl. Data Eng. **21**(5), 609–623 (2009)
3. Aulbach, S., Jacobs, D., Kemper, A., Seibold, M.: A comparison of flexible schemas for software as a service. In: Proceedings of the SIGMOD 2009. ACM (2009)
4. Barker, S., Chi, Y., Moon, H.J., Hacigümüş, H., Shenoy, P.: "Cut me some slack" latency-aware live migration for databases. In: Proceedings of the EDBT 2012 (2012)
5. Bertino, E., Guerrini, G., Mesiti, M., Tosetto, L.: Evolving a set of DTDs according to a dynamic set of XML documents. In: Proceedings of the EDBT 2002 Workshops (2002)
6. Chen, J., Jindel, S., Walzer, R., Sen, R., Jimsheleishvilli, N., Andrews, M.: The MemSQL query optimizer: a modern optimizer for real-time analytics in a distributed database. Proc. VLDB Endow. **9**(13), 1401–1412 (2016)
7. Cleve, A., Gobert, M., Meurice, L., Maes, J., Weber, J.: Understanding database schema evolution. Sci. Comput. Program. **97**(P1), 113–121 (2015)

8. Curino, C., et al.: Relational cloud: a database-as-a-service for the cloud. In: Proceedings of the CIDR 2011 (2011)
9. Curino, C., Moon, H.J., Deutsch, A., Zaniolo, C.: Automating the database schema evolution process. VLDB J. **22**(1), 73–98 (2013)
10. Curino, C., Moon, H.J., Tanca, L., Zaniolo, C.: Schema evolution in wikipedia - toward a web information system benchmark. In: Proceedings of the ICEIS 2008 (2008)
11. Dean, J., Barroso, L.A.: The tail at scale. Commun. ACM **56**(2), 74–80 (2013)
12. Ellison, M., Calinescu, R., Paige, R.F.: Evaluating cloud database migration options using workload models. J. Cloud Comput. **7**(1), 1–18 (2018). https://doi.org/10.1186/s13677-018-0108-5
13. Fishman, G.: Monte Carlo: Concepts, Algorithms, and Applications. Springer Series in Operations Research and Financial Engineering, Springer, Heidelberg (2013)
14. Goeminne, M., Decan, A., Mens, T.: Co-evolving code-related and database-related changes in a data-intensive software system. In: 2014 Software Evolution Week - IEEE Conference on Software Maintenance, Reengineering, and Reverse Engineering (CSMR-WCRE) (2014)
15. Guerrini, G., Mesiti, M., Rossi, D.: Impact of XML schema evolution on valid documents. In: Proceedings of the WIDM 2005 Workshop. ACM (2005)
16. Haas, P.J.: Monte Carlo methods for uncertain data. In: Liu, L., Özsu, M.T. (eds.) Encyclopedia of Database Systems. Springer, New York (2018). https://doi.org/10.1007/978-1-4899-7993-3_80692-2
17. Herrmann, K., Voigt, H., Behrend, A., Rausch, J., Lehner, W.: Living in parallel realities: co-existing schema versions with a bidirectional database evolution language. In: Proceedings of the SIGMOD 2017. ACM (2017)
18. Hillenbrand, A., Levchenko, M., Störl, U., Scherzinger, S., Klettke, M.: MigCast: Putting a price tag on data model evolution in NoSQL data stores. In: Proceedings of the SIGMOD 2019. ACM (2019)
19. Hillenbrand, A., Störl, U., Levchenko, M., Nabiyev, S., Klettke, M.: Towards self-adapting data migration in the context of schema evolution in NoSQL databases. In: Proceedings of the ICDE 2020 Workshops. IEEE (2020)
20. Hillenbrand, A., Störl, U., Nabiyev, S., Scherzinger, S.: MigCast in Monte Carlo: The Impact of Data Model Evolution in NoSQL Databases. CoRR abs/2104.11787 (2021)
21. Jampani, R., Xu, F., Wu, M., Perez, L., Jermaine, C., Haas, P.J.: The Monte Carlo database system: stochastic analysis close to the data. ACM TODS **36**(3), 1–41 (2011)
22. Klettke, M., Störl, U., Shenavai, M., Scherzinger, S.: NoSQL schema evolution and big data migration at scale. In: Proceedings of the SCDM 2016. IEEE (2016)
23. Levandoski, J.J., Larson, P., Stoica, R.: Identifying hot and cold data in main-memory databases. In: Proceedings of the ICDE 2013. IEEE (2013)
24. MacKay, D.J.C.: Information Theory, Inference and Learning Algorithms. Cambridge University Press, Cambridge, USA (2003)
25. Meurice, L., Cleve, A.: Supporting schema evolution in schema-less NoSQL data stores. In: Proceedings of the SANER 2017 (2017)
26. Qiu, D., Li, B., Su, Z.: An empirical analysis of the co-evolution of schema and code in database applications. In: Proceedings of the SIGSOFT 2013. ACM (2013)
27. Saur, K., Dumitras, T., Hicks, M.W.: Evolving NoSQL databases without downtime. In: Proceedings of the ICSME 2016. IEEE (2016)

28. Scherzinger, S., Sidortschuck, S.: An empirical study on the design and evolution of NoSQL database schemas. In: Dobbie, G., Frank, U., Kappel, G., Liddle, S.W., Mayr, H.C. (eds.) ER 2020. LNCS, vol. 12400, pp. 441–455. Springer, Cham (2020). https://doi.org/10.1007/978-3-030-62522-1_33

29. Stonebraker, M.: My top ten fears about the DBMS field. In: Proceedings of the ICDE 2018. IEEE (2018)

30. Suciu, D., Olteanu, D., Ré, C., Koch, C.: Probabilistic databases. Synth. Lect. Data Manag. **3**(2), 1–180 (2011)

31. Vassiliadis, P., Zarras, A., Skoulis, I.: Gravitating to rigidity: patterns of schema evolution -and its absence- in the lives of tables. Inf. Syst. **63**, 24–46 (2016)

32. Li, X.: A survey of schema evolution in object-oriented databases. In: Proceedings of the TOOLS 1999. IEEE (1999)

Temporal Keyword Search
with Aggregates and Group-By

Qiao Gao$^{(\boxtimes)}$, Mong Li Lee, and Tok Wang Ling

National University of Singapore, Singapore, Singapore
{gaoqiao,leeml,lingtw}@comp.nus.edu.sg

Abstract. Temporal keyword search enables non-expert users to query temporal relational databases with time conditions. However, aggregates and group-by are currently not supported in temporal keyword search, which hinders querying of statistical information in temporal databases. This work proposes a framework to support aggregate, group-by and time condition in temporal keyword search. We observe that simply combining non-temporal keyword search with aggregates, group-by, and temporal aggregate operators may lead to incorrect and meaningless results as a result of data duplication over time periods. As such, our framework utilizes Object-Relationship-Attribute semantics to identify a unique attribute set in the join sequence relation and remove data duplicates from this attribute set to ensure the correctness of aggregate and group-by computation. We also consider the time period in which temporal attributes occur when computing aggregate to return meaningful results. Experiment results demonstrate the importance of these steps to retrieve correct results for keyword queries over temporal databases.

Keywords: Temporal keyword search · Aggregates and group-by · Semantic approach

1 Introduction

Keyword query over relational databases has become a popular query paradigm by freeing users from writing complicated SQL queries when retrieving data [20]. Recent works in this area are focusing on efficiency of query execution [21], quality of query results [12], and expressiveness of keyword query [10,24].

Temporal keyword search enriches the query expressiveness by supporting time conditions in keyword query and makes data retrieval on temporal databases easier. The corresponding SQL query will be automatically generated by the keyword search engine where temporal joins as well as time conditions are associated with the correct relations [10]. However, the aggregate and group-by haven't been supported in current temporal keyword search, which hinders users from querying the statistical information over time. We observe that simply combining non-temporal keyword search with aggregates, group-by, and temporal aggregate operators may lead to incorrect aggregate results. The reason is that when multiple relations are involved in a keyword query, there might be

© Springer Nature Switzerland AG 2021
A. Ghose et al. (Eds.): ER 2021, LNCS 13011, pp. 160–175, 2021.
https://doi.org/10.1007/978-3-030-89022-3_14

Employee

Eid	Ename	DOB	Employee_Start	Employee_End
E01	Alice	1985-03-12	2017-01-01	now
E02	Bob	1978-05-20	2017-05-01	now
E03	John	1990-10-15	2018-01-01	2018-10-31

Project

Pid	Pname	Budget	Did	Project_Start	Project_End
P01	Healthcare with AI	300k	D01	2017-07-01	2018-12-31
P02	KWS	250k	D01	2017-07-01	2018-06-30
P03	Smart City with AI	400k	D02	2018-01-01	now

Department

Did	Dname
D01	CS
D02	IS

EmployeeSalary

Eid	Salary(per month)	Salary_Start	Salary_End
E01	3k	2017-06-01	2018-03-31
E01	3.5k	2018-04-01	2018-09-30
E01	4k	2018-10-01	now
E02	4k	2017-05-01	2018-12-31
E02	4.5k	2019-01-01	now
E03	3k	2018-01-01	2018-10-31

WorkFor

Eid	Did	WorkFor_Start	WorkFor_End
E01	D01	2017-01-01	2017-08-31
E01	D02	2017-09-01	now
E02	D01	2017-05-01	2018-02-28
E02	D02	2018-03-01	2018-04-30
E02	D01	2018-05-01	now
E03	D01	2018-01-01	2018-10-31

Participatein

Eid	Pid	Participatein_Start	Participatein_End
E01	P01	2017-07-01	2018-12-31
E02	P01	2018-01-01	2018-12-31
E02	P02	2017-07-01	2018-06-30
E03	P02	2018-01-01	2018-06-30
E01	P03	2018-01-01	2018-06-30
E02	P03	2018-10-01	now
E03	P03	2018-07-01	2018-09-30

Fig. 1. Example company temporal database.

some data duplication involved in the intermediate relations of temporal joins and leading to incorrect results of accumulative aggregates, such as SUM and COUNT.

Example 1 (Incorrect aggregate results). Consider the temporal database in Fig. 1. Suppose we issue a query $Q_1 = \{$Employee SUM Salary Project AI DURING [2018]$\}$ to compute the total salary of employees participating in AI projects in 2018. Multiple projects match the keyword "AI" ($P01$ and $P03$), and two employees $E01$ and $E02$ participated in these projects in 2018. As such, the salary of $E01$ and $E02$ will be duplicated in the join sequence relation, and simply applying existing temporal aggregate operators, e.g., those proposed in [3,6,7,14], on the intermediate relation of joins will give incorrect total salaries for the employees.

The work in [23] first highlights the problem of incorrect query results in non-temporal keyword search with aggregates and group-by, and uses Object-Relationship-Attribute (ORA) semantics [22] to remove the duplicate data when relations capturing n-ary (n > 2) relationships are joined. However, this work cannot handle all the data duplication occurred in temporal keyword search, since they are more prevalent due to the repeating attribute values and relationships over time, and the join between temporal and non-temporal relations.

In this work, we propose a framework to process temporal keyword queries involving aggregate functions, group-by and time conditions. Our framework utilizes ORA semantics to identify object/relationship type and attributes, and remove data duplication in the intermediate relation. Further, frequent data updates over time may lead to fine-grained temporal aggregate results that are not meaningful to users. Hence, we support aggregates over user-specified time units such as year or month in the keyword query. Finally, a temporal attribute may have an inherent time unit, e.g., monthly salary or daily room rate. Our framework provides an option to compute meaningful accumulative sum over such attributes by weighting its value with its duration. Experiment results indicate the importance of these steps to return correct and meaningful results for keyword queries over temporal databases.

2   Preliminaries

Temporal Keyword Query. We extend the temporal keyword query defined in [10] to allow aggregate functions and group-by as follows:

$$<Q> ::= <basic\_query>[<groupby\_cond>][<time\_cond>]$$

where $<basic\_query>$ is a set of keywords $\{k_1\ k_2...k_i\}$, and each keyword can match a tuple value, a relation or attribute name, or an aggregate MIN, MAX, AVG, SUM or COUNT; $<groupby\_cond>$ is a set of keywords $\{k_{i+1}\ k_{i+2}...k_j\}$ such that k_{i+1} is the reserved word GROUPBY, and the remaining keywords match either a relation or attribute name; $<time\_cond>$ contains two keywords $\{k_{j+1}\ k_{j+2}\}$ such that k_{j+1} is a temporal predicate like AFTER or DURING [2], and k_{j+2} is a closed time period $[s,e]$[1].

Temporal ORM Schema Graph. [22] proposes an Object-Relationship-Mixed (ORM) schema graph to capture the ORA semantics in a relational database. Each node in the graph is an object/relationship/mixed node comprising an object/relationship/mixed relation and its component relations. An object (or relationship) relation stores all the single-valued attributes of an object (or relationship) type. A mixed relation stores an object type and its many-to-one relationship type(s). A component relation stores a multivalued attribute of an object/relationship type. Two nodes u and v are connected by an undirected edge if there is a foreign key-key constraint from the relations in u to those in v.

In temporal databases, an object type or relationship type becomes temporal when it is associated with a time period indicating its lifespan [8]. An attribute of some object/relationship type becomes temporal when its value changes over time and the database keeps track of the changes. We extend the ORM schema graph to a temporal ORA schema graph for temporal databases.

A node with superscript T in a temporal ORA schema graph denotes it contains some temporal relations. A temporal relation R^T is essentially a relation R with a closed time period $R^T.period$ consisting of a start attribute and an end attribute. The temporal ORA semantics of a temporal relation could be identified via the relation type. A temporal object/relationship relation stores a temporal object/relationship type, while a temporal mixed relation stores a temporal object type with its non-temporal many-to-one relationship type(s), and a temporal component relation stores a temporal attribute.

Figure 2 shows the temporal ORM schema graph for the database in Fig. 1. The object node Employee contains the temporal object relation $Employee$ and its temporal component relation $EmployeeSalary$, depicting the temporal object Employee and the temporal attribute Salary respectively.

---

[1] We use the format YYYY-MM-DD for start and end times, and allow shortened forms with just YYYY or YYYY-MM. We will convert the short form, by setting the start/end time to the earliest/latest date of given year or month, e.g., [2017,2018] to [2017-01-01, 2018-12-31].

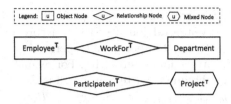

Fig. 2. Temporal ORM schema graph of the temporal database in Fig. 1.

Fig. 3. Annotated query pattern generated for query Q_1.

Annotated Query Pattern. We adopt the approach in [23] to generate a set of annotated query patterns to depict the different interpretations of a keyword query. Keywords are matched to relations in a temporal ORM schema graph. Aggregates and GROUPBY are reserved keywords and are used to annotate the query pattern according to the matches of the keywords that follow them. Note that the time condition in keyword query is not considered in this process.

Figure 3 shows one of query patterns generated from the query without time condition {Employee SUM Salary Project AI} of Q_1 in Example 1. The keywords Employee and Salary match the node *Employee* in the temporal ORM graph in Fig. 2, while keywords Project and AI match the node *Project*. Since there is a cycle in the temporal ORM graph, we have two ways to connect these two nodes: via the node *ParticipateIn* or the nodes *WorkFor − Department*, giving us two possible query interpretations. Since the keyword Salary follows the aggregate SUM, the attribute *Salary* in the node *Employee* is annotated with SUM, depicting the user's search intention to find the sum of the salaries of employees who participated in AI projects.

3   Proposed Framework

Our framework to process a temporal keyword query consists of 3 key steps:

> **Step 1.** Generate a temporal join sequence from an annotated query pattern, and use it to compute a join sequence relation.
>
> **Step 2.** Identify a subset of attributes (called *unique attribute set*) from join sequence relation and remove data duplicates on this attribute set.
>
> **Step 3.** Compute temporal aggregate and group-by over the relation obtained from step 2.

3.1   Generate Temporal Join Sequence

We generate one temporal join sequence from each annotated query pattern to compute a join sequence relation[2]. The sequence contains relations in the query pattern augmented with selections (σ) and projections (Π), if any. The selection is used to apply the time condition in query to each relevant temporal relation,

---

[2] The detailed algorithm is given in the technical report [9].

while the projection is used to drop attributes irrelevant to this query. These relations are joined with natural join ($\bowtie$) or temporal join ($\bowtie^T$) [11] according to the edge connections in the query pattern. Temporal join operator is used between temporal relations to avoid incorrect join results [10]. For example, the temporal join sequence generated for the query pattern in Fig. 3 is $J = R_1 \bowtie^T R_2 \bowtie^T R_3 \bowtie^T R_4$ where $R_1 = \Pi_{Eid \cup Salary \cup period}(\sigma_\varphi(Salary^T))$, $R_2 = \Pi_{Eid \cup period}(\sigma_\varphi(Employee^T))$, $R_3 = \Pi_{Eid \cup Pid \cup period}(\sigma_\varphi(ParticipateIn^T))$, $R_4 = \Pi_{Pid \cup period}(\sigma_{Pname\ contains\ "AI" \cup \varphi}(Project^T))$. The select condition "$\varphi = R^T.period\ TP\ [s, e]$" denotes to apply time condition "$TP\ [s, e]$" to time period $R^T.period$, where TP denotes a temporal predicate.

We have 3 types of attributes in the join sequence relation R_J obtained from the temporal join sequence: (1) all the key attributes of the relations in the query pattern, (2) attributes involved in the aggregate function and the group-by, and (3) time period attributes (*start* and *end*), if any. Note that attributes that are involved only in the select conditions are not included in the join sequence relation, since they are not used subsequently.

3.2   Remove Duplicate Data

Generating the join sequence relation may introduce data duplicates on the attributes related to aggregates and group-by, which may lead to incorrect aggregate results. This is so because relations in the temporal join sequence have many-to-one or many-to-many relationships, multivalued and time period attributes. Note that a join sequence relation R_J has no duplicate tuples, but it may have data duplicates with respect to a *unique attribute set* $\mathcal{U} \subset R_J$ depicting the ORA semantics the aggregate function and group-by applied to.

We determine the attributes in $\mathcal{U}$ as follows. Let X and Y be the sets of attributes that the aggregate function and group-by are applied to respectively. Note that $Y = \emptyset$ if the keyword query does not have GROUPBY reserved word.

Case 1. X only contains the identifier attribute(s) of some object/relationship. Unique objects or relationships are identified via the values of their identifiers. From the temporal ORM schema graph, we know whether X is the identifier of a non-temporal or temporal object/relationship type. For non-temporal object/relationship type, $\mathcal{U} = (X, Y)$. Otherwise, the time period attributes *start* and *end* in R_J are included to remove duplicates, i.e., $\mathcal{U} = (X, Y, R_J.start, R_J.end)$.

Case 2. X only contains a non-prime attribute A.
Let *oid* be the identifier attribute(s) of the object/relationship type for A. If A is non-temporal, $\mathcal{U} = (oid, A, Y)$. Otherwise, A is temporal and $\mathcal{U} = (oid, A, Y, R_J.start, R_J.end)$. The reason why *oid* is added to $\mathcal{U}$ is that we need to distinguish the same attribute value of different objects/relationships.

If $\mathcal{U}$ does not contain time period attributes *start* and *end*, then two tuples in R_J are duplicates iff their $\mathcal{U}$ values are the same. Otherwise, we say that two tuples are duplicates over time iff their $\mathcal{U} - \{R_J.start, R_J.end\}$ values are the same and time periods of those two tuples intersect. Note that the duplication

---

Algorithm 1: Remove Duplicate Data

Input: join sequence relation R_J, unique attribute set $\mathcal{U}$
Output: Relation $R_{\mathcal{U}}$ with no duplicate data

1   **if** $\{start, end\} \not\subseteq R_J$ **then**
2     $R_{\mathcal{U}} = \Pi_{\mathcal{U}}(R_J)$;
3   **else**
4     $R_{\mathcal{U}} = \emptyset$; $prev = null$;
5     $\mathcal{U}' = \mathcal{U} - \{start, end\}$;
6     $R_{\Pi} = \Pi_{\mathcal{U}}(R)$;
7     $R_{sorted} = R_{\Pi}.sort(key = \mathcal{U}' \cup \{start\})$;
8   **foreach** $tuple\ t \in R_{sorted}$ **do**
9   **if** $prev$ is $null$ **then**
10        $prev = t$;
11   **else if** $prev.\mathcal{U}' == t.\mathcal{U}'$ and $prev.end >= t.start$ **then**
12        $prev.end = max(prev.end, t.end)$;
13   **else**
14         $R_{\mathcal{U}}.append(prev)$;
15         $prev = t$;
16   **if** $prev \neq null$ **then**
17       $R_{\mathcal{U}}.append(prev)$;
18 **return** $R_{\mathcal{U}}$

---

occurs in the intersected time period. We use the functional dependency (FD) theory to determine if there are data duplicates over $\mathcal{U}$. Let K be the key of R_J. If $K \to \mathcal{U}$ is a full FD, and not a transitive FD, then there is no data duplicate on $\mathcal{U}$. Note that when both K and $\mathcal{U}$ contain time period attributes, the FD should hold for the same time points in the corresponding time periods.

Algorithm 1 gives the details to remove data duplicates from R_J over $\mathcal{U}$. Line 2 uses projection to remove data duplicates if $\mathcal{U}$ does not contain time period attributes. Otherwise, let $\mathcal{U}' = \mathcal{U} - \{start, end\}$ be the non-period attributes set in $\mathcal{U}$. We first sort the tuples based on $\mathcal{U}' \cup \{start\}$ (lines 4–7). Then, we perform a linear scan to remove data duplication over time by merging the overlapped time periods for tuples with same values on $\mathcal{U}'$ (Lines 8–17). The time complexity of this step is $O(n * log(n))$[3], where n is the number of tuples in R_J.

Example 2 (Case 1: Temporal object). Consider query {COUNT Employee GROUPBY Project DURING [2017,2018]} to count employees who participated in each project between 2017 to 2018. We generate a join sequence relation R_J from relations *Employee, ParticipateIn, Project*. Since COUNT is applied on *Eid* of temporal object relation *Employee*, and GROUPBY on *Pid* of temporal object relation *Project*, we have $\mathcal{U} = (Eid, Pid, R_J.start, R_J.end)$.

Example 3 (Case 2: Temporal attribute). Recall query $Q_1 = $ {Employee SUM Salary Project AI DURING [2018]} in Example 1, and its join sequence relation with duplicated data highlighted in Fig. 4. From the temporal ORM schema graph, we know that *Salary* is a temporal attribute of the object Employee whose identifier is *Eid*. Hence, $\mathcal{U} = \{Eid, Salary, Join\_Start, Join\_End\}$. Algorithm 1 is used to remove the data duplicates on $\mathcal{U}$.

---

[3] Projection over R_J requires $O(n)$ time, sorting the tuples requires $O(n*log(n))$ time, and linear scan to remove duplicates over time takes $O(n)$ time.

JoinSequenceRelation_1

Eid	Salary(per month)	Pid	Join_Start	Join_End
E01	3k	P01	2018-01-01	2018-03-31
E01	3.5k	P01	2018-04-01	2018-09-30
E01	4k	P01	2018-10-01	2018-12-31
E02	4k	P01	2018-01-01	2018-12-31
E01	3k	P03	2018-01-01	2018-03-31
E01	3.5k	P03	2018-04-01	2018-06-30
E02	4k	P03	2018-10-01	2018-12-31
E03	3k	P03	2018-07-01	2018-09-30

Fig. 4. Join sequence relation for Q_1.

3.3   Compute Temporal Aggregates

Let $R_{\mathcal{U}}$ be the join sequence relation with no data duplicates over unique attribute set $\mathcal{U}$. If $R_{\mathcal{U}}$ does not contain time period attributes, a traditional aggregate is computed over it. Otherwise, a temporal aggregate is computed. Our framework supports two types of temporal aggregate computation: (1) aggregate at each time point, and (2) aggregate over user-specified time unit. Moreover, for attributes with inherent time unit, such as monthly salary, we provide the option of computing a time-weighted sum to generate meaningful results.

Aggregate at Each Time Point. This captures the aggregate result at each time point along a timeline. A new aggregate value is computed using temporal aggregate operators [6,7] when the data is updated, and each aggregate value is associated with a non-overlapped time period indicating when the value is computed. Figure 5(a) visualizes the non-duplicated data in $R_{\mathcal{U}}$ of query Q_1, and how the temporal aggregates at each time point are computed. The salary of employees $E01$, $E02$ and $E03$ change over time, and each change leads to a new aggregate result. The timeline in Fig. 5(a) is segmented by each salary change, and a sum is computed over the monthly salaries in each segment. Figure 5(b) gives the aggregate results, capturing the changes in the sum of the monthly salary for employees participating in AI projects in 2018.

Aggregate over User-Specified Time Unit. Computing aggregate at each time point may lead to overly detailed results when updates are frequent, e.g., bank account balances. Thus, we provide users the option of specifying the granularity of the time unit with a reserved word YEAR, MONTH or DAY in the group-by condition. This will return one aggregate tuple per year or month or day respectively. For example, the query Q_3 = {COUNT Employee Department CS GROUPBY YEAR DURING [2017,2018]} counts employees who have worked for the CS department each year from 2017 to 2018. Two results will be returned for the COUNT aggregate: one for 2017, and another for 2018.

Figure 6(a) gives the visualization of data used to compute the results for query Q_3. If we simply utilize the operator in [3] which applies the traditional aggregate function to tuples whose time periods overlap with the specified time unit, we will get incorrect results for 2018 because the same employee E02

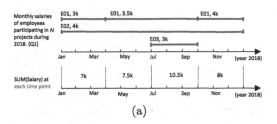

SUM (Salary)	Aggr_Start	Aggr_End
7k	2018-01-01	2018-03-31
7.5k	2018-04-01	2018-06-30
10.5k	2018-07-01	2018-09-30
8k	2018-10-01	2018-12-31

(a)   (b)

Fig. 5. (a) Sum of salaries and (b) Aggregate results at each time point for Q_1.

is counted twice, and the different work periods of employees are not taken into account (see Fig. 7(a)). Instead, we compute a summary on top of the aggregate results at each time point based on the user-specified time unit (per year/month/day). The idea is to determine the min, max and time-weighted average for tuples whose time periods overlap with the time unit. The min and max reflect the extreme aggregate values over each time unit, while the time-weighted average captures the time period of the aggregate result at each time point.

Let $\mathcal{R}_{aggr}$ be the relation of aggregate results obtained at each time point. We use the user-specified time unit to segment the timeline in $\mathcal{R}_{aggr}$ into a set of consecutive non-overlap time periods W. Then we find the tuples in each time period $[s,e] \in W$, and compute the max, min, time-weighted average over these tuples, as a summary of aggregate results over this $[s,e]$. The max and min values can be computed directly, while the average is obtained as follows:

$$AVG^T(\mathcal{R}_{aggr},[s,e]) = \frac{\sum_{t \in (\mathcal{R}_{aggr} \bowtie^T [s,e])} t.value \times |t.period|}{|[s,e]|} \tag{1}$$

where $R_{aggr} \bowtie^T [s,e]$ are the tuples in $\mathcal{R}_{aggr}$ that overlap with time period $[s,e]$, each tuple value $t.value$ is weighted by the length of its time period $|t.period|$ to compute a time-weighted sum, and the weighted sum is divided by the length of period $[s,e]$ to compute the time-weighted average. Note that the time unit used to compute the length of $t.period$ and $[s,e]$ are the same[4].

Figure 7(b) shows the results for Q_3 after computing the max, min and time-weighted average over each year based on the aggregate results at each time period in Fig. 6(b). For 2017, the min and max count of employees in the CS department is 1 and 2 respectively. The time-weighted average in 2017 is given by $\frac{1 \times 4(months) + 2 \times 4(months) + 1 \times 4(months)}{12(months)} = 1.33$ indicating that there are 1.33 full-time equivalent employees in the CS department in 2017. In the same way, we compute that there are 1.67 full-time equivalent employees in 2018.

Aggregate over Attributes with Inherent Time Unit. Some attributes have inherent time units, e.g., monthly salary or daily room rate, and it is often useful to compute the sum of these attributes over their time unit. Such inherent

---

[4] The detailed algorithm is given in the technical report [9].

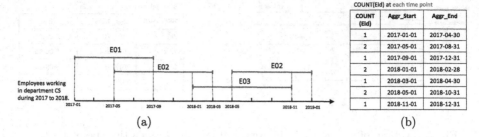

Fig. 6. (a) Data visualization (b) Aggregate results at each time point for Q_3.

COUNT (*)	Aggr_Start	Aggr_End
2	2017-01-01	2017-12-31
3	2018-01-01	2018-12-31

COUNT(Eid) per year

MIN	MAX	AVG^T	Aggr_Start	Aggr_End
1	2	1.33	2017-01-01	2017-12-31
1	2	1.67	2018-01-01	2018-12-31

(a) Incorrect results using [3]   (b) Correct results using our approach

Fig. 7. Results of count of employees per year in Q_3.

time unit is obtained from the metadata of database. For instance, Fig. 1 has an attribute *Salary* which captures the monthly salary of employees, i.e., the time unit of *Salary* is per month.

Similar to the time-weighted average in Eq. (1), we also weight the attribute values to compute the sum of a temporal attribute with an inherent time unit over a time period. Here, the weight is the ratio of the length of the attribute's time period over the inherent time unit. Given a join sequence relation with duplicates removed $R_\mathcal{U}$, let A_z be a temporal attribute with an inherent time unit z. The accumulated sum SUM^T over $[s, e]$ of A_z is given by

$$SUM^T(R_\mathcal{U}, A_z, [s, e]) = \sum_{t \in (R_\mathcal{U} \bowtie^T [s,e])} t.A_z \times \frac{|t.period|}{z} \tag{2}$$

Note that if we compute both SUM^T and AVG^T over the same time period $[s, e]$, then we can derive AVG^T directly as $SUM^T \times \frac{z}{|[s,e]|}$.

Consider query Q'_1 = {Employee SUM Salary Project AI GROUPBY YEAR DURING [2018]} which is similar to Q_1 but has a group-by condition with user-specified time unit YEAR. Figure 8(a) shows the aggregate results for Q'_1 computed based on the aggregate results in Fig. 5(b). Since *Salary* has an inherent time unit "month" ($z = 1$(month)), we compute an accumulated SUM in 2018 based on the unique salaries in Fig. 5(a): $3k \times \frac{3(months)}{1(month)} + 3.5k \times \frac{6(months)}{1(month)} + ... + 3k \times \frac{3(months)}{1(month)} = 99k$. The result is shown in Fig. 8(b), which reflects the actual sum of salary paid to employees participating in AI projects in 2018.

MIN	MAX	AVG$^\mathsf{T}$	Start	End
7k	10.5k	8.25k	2018-01-01	2018-12-31

(a) Results using our approach

SUM(Salary)	Aggr_Start	Aggr_End
99k	2018-01-01	2018-12-31

(b) Accumulated SUM

Fig. 8. Results of aggregate per year for Q'_1.

4   Experimental Evaluation

We implemented our algorithms in Python and evaluated the effectiveness of our proposed approach to process temporal keyword queries correctly. We use the temporal operators in [7] to compute the temporal join in temporal join sequence and the temporal aggregate at each time point.

We synthesized a database with temporal ORA semantics, including temporal many-to-one relationship type, temporal many-to-many relationship type, and temporal attribute, which often lead to data duplicates in the join sequence relation. Table 1 shows the schema. We have 10,000 employees, 121 departments and 5,000 projects. The average number of salaries per employee is 3.86, average number of departments per employee is 1.23, average number of projects per employee is 11.26, and the average number of projects per department is 333.3.

Correctness of Query Results. For each temporal keyword query in Table 2, we examine the correctness of the temporal aggregate results before and after removing duplicate data in the join sequence relation. The correct results are obtained from data that has no duplicates. Table 3 shows the results, as well as the size of the join sequence relation in terms of the number of tuples and attributes, and the percentage of duplicate tuples. We observe that the percentage of duplicate tuples in the join sequence relations for different keyword queries ranges from 1.3% to 99.5%. The data duplication arises from repeats of the same temporal relationship (C1), join between temporal and non-temporal semantics (C2), keyword matching multiple tuples (C3), and join between multiple many-to-many and/or many-to-one relationships (C4), as we will elaborate.

Queries C1 and C2 have aggregate functions over *non-temporal* semantics. The aggregate in C1 is applied to a predefined function AGE() which computes the age of employees based on the difference between the start time in the query and the non-temporal attribute *DOB* in relation *Employee*. Since one employee could leave a department and return to the same department in 2019, so his age would occur multiple times for this department, leading to an incorrect average employee age. By removing the data duplication on unique attribute set $\mathcal{U} = $ (Eid,DOB,Did) from join sequence relation $R_J = $ (Eid,DOB,Did,Join_Start,Join_End), we are able to obtain correct average age.

The aggregate in C2 is applied to the non-temporal object Department, and the cause of duplicate data in the join sequence relation is due to the join between the non-temporal relation *Department* and the temporal relations *WorkFor*, *Employee* and *EmployeeSalary*. A department is duplicated many times in this process, since it can have many employees with salaries more than 10000, and an

Table 1. Schema of company database

Employee(Eid, Employee_Start, Employee_End, Ename, DOB)
Department(Did, Dname)
Project(Pid, Project_Start, Project_End, Pname, Budget, Did)
EmployeeSalary(Eid, Salary_Start, Salary_End, Salary(per month))
WorkFor(Eid, WorkFor_Start, WorkFor_End, Did)
ParticipateIn(Eid, Pid, ParticipateIn_Start,ParticipateIn_End)

Table 2. Temporal keyword queries and their search intentions.

Keyword query		Search intention
C1	Employee AVG AGE() GROUPBY Department DURING [2019]	Compute the average age of employees in each department in 2019
C2	COUNT Department Employee Salary > 10000 DURING [2010, 2019]	Count the departments which had employee salary larger than 10,000 during 2010 to 2019
C3	Employee SUM salary Project AI DURING [2015, 2019]	Sum the monthly salaries of employee working in AI project during 2015 to 2019
C4	COUNT Employee Project Department CS DURING [2019]	Count the employees who participated in projects belonging to department CS in year 2019
C5	Employee MAX Salary GROUPBY Department DURING [2010, 2019]	Compute the maximum salary for employees working in each department during 2010 to 2019
C6	COUNT Project Budget ≥ 2000000 GROUPBY Department DURING [2018, 2019]	Count projects whose budget is larger or equal to 2,000,000 in each department during 2018 to 2019

Table 3. Correctness of results before and after removing duplicates.

Query	Size of join sequence relation		% Duplicate tuples	Correct before duplicate removed	Correct after duplicate removed
	#tuple	#attribute			
C1	12295	6	1.3	N	Y
C2	23739	5	99.5	N	Y
C3	15489	10	17.9	N	Y
C4	302	6	81.8	N	Y
C5	40917	5	0	Y	Y
C6	1922	4	0	Y	Y

employee can have many salary records. By removing data duplication on $\mathcal{U} = $ (Did) from $R_J = $ (Did,Join_Start,Join_End), we get the correct result 121, while the incorrect result is 23739 without the duplicates removed.

Table 4. Sample results for temporal *aggregate at each time point.*

Q#	#Tuples	Sample aggregate results			Q#	#Tuples	Sample aggregate results		
		Aggr_Start	Aggr_End	SUM(Salary)			Aggr_Start	Aggr_End	COUNT(Eid)
C3	1807	2015-01-01	2015-01-01	14657665	C4	27	2019-01-01	2019-02-01	36
		2015-01-02	2015-01-02	14668065			2019-02-02	2019-02-20	36
		2015-01-03	2015-01-03	14668938			2019-02-21	2019-02-23	36
		2015-01-04	2015-01-04	14652725			2019-02-24	2019-02-26	37

Q#	#Tuples	Did	Aggr_Start	Aggr_End	MAX(Salary)	Q#	#Tuples	Did	Aggr_Start	Aggr_End	COUNT(Pid)
C5	427,101	D1	2010-03-16	2010-03-16	3300	C6	9,690	D1	2018-01-01	2018-01-01	78
		D1	2010-03-17	2010-03-17	3300			D1	2018-01-02	2018-01-02	79
		D1	2010-03-18	2010-03-18	3300			D1	2018-01-03	2018-01-03	79
		D1	2010-03-19	2010-03-19	3300			D1	2018-01-04	2018-01-04	79

Queries C3 to C6 have aggregates over *temporal* semantics. Temporal aggregate operators are used to compute aggregate at each time point, and the data duplicates over time periods would lead to incorrect results in the corresponding time periods. The reason for duplicate data in C3 is query keyword matching multiple tuples, i.e., multiple projects match the keyword "AI" with common employees, leading to 17.9% of salary values are duplicated over time. We remove the data duplication on $\mathcal{U}$ = (Eid,Salary,Join_Start,Join_End) from R_J = (Eid,Salary,Pid,Did,Join_Start,Join_End) and obtain the correct sum of salaries over time.

For query C4, the reason for its data duplicates is due to the join between many-to-many relationship type in relation *ParticipateIn* and the many-to-one relationship type in relation *Project*. Specifically, the department CS could have multiple projects involving the participation of same employees, and such employees are duplicated in the join sequence relation. By identifying $\mathcal{U}$ = (Eid,Join_Start,Join_End) from join sequence relation R_J = (Eid,Pid,Did, Join_Start, Join_End), we are able to remove then 81.8% duplicate employees over time and get the correct employee count.

Queries C5 to C6 do not have data duplicates in the join sequence relation. For query C5, the aggregate MAX is not an accumulative function, hence the results are not affected by data duplicates, even if they exist. The reason that C5 and C6 do not have data duplication is that they have identical unique attribute set $\mathcal{U}$ and temporal join sequence relation R_J. For C5, $\mathcal{U}$ = R_J = (Eid,Salary,Did,Join_Start,Join_End). For C6, $\mathcal{U}$ = R_J = (Pid,Did,Join_Start,Join_End). Therefore, there is no duplicates on $\mathcal{U}$ to be removed.

Usefulness of Aggregate over User-Specified Time Unit. When an aggregate function is applied to some temporal semantics, a temporal aggregate operator is required to compute the aggregate at each time point (recall Sect. 3.3). Table 4 shows the number of tuples in the result table for queries C3 to C6, and a sample of the aggregate results. The average length of the time period for the aggregate results of C3 to C6 are 1.01, 13.51, 19.65, 1.13 days, respectively. These results are rather fine-grained due to the frequent updates to the temporal database. We see that some of the results have the same aggregate values in the

Table 5. Statistics and sample results for keyword queries involving temporal *aggregates over user-specified time unit.*

	Keyword Query	#Tuple	Sample aggregate results					
C3'	Employee SUM salary Project AI **GROUPBY YEAR** DURING [2015,2019]	5	Aggr_Start	Aggr_End	Min (SUM(Salary))	Max (SUM(Salary))	AVG^T (SUM(Salary))	
			2015-01-01	2015-12-31	14115375	16122708	15360017.46	
			2016-01-01	2016-12-31	15357130	16005648	15651395.31	
			2017-01-01	2017-12-31	15136870	15897157	15538076.16	
			2018-01-01	2018-12-31	15408131	16535220	16106415.25	
C4'	COUNT Employees Project Department CS **GROUPBY MONTH** DURING [2019]	12	Aggr_Start	Aggr_End	Min (COUNT(EId))	Max (COUNT(EId))	AVG^T (COUNT(EId))	
			2019-01-01	2019-01-31	36	36	36.00	
			2019-02-01	2019-02-28	36	38	36.25	
			2019-03-01	2019-03-31	37	38	37.58	
			2019-04-01	2019-04-30	37	39	37.93	
C5'	Employee MAX salary **GROUPBY** Department **YEAR** DURING [2010,2019]	22,990	Did	Aggr_Start	Aggr_End	Min (MAX(Salary))	Max (MAX(Salary))	AVG^T (MAX(Salary))
			D1	2010-03-16	2010-12-31	3300	20000	13303.44
			D1	2011-01-01	2011-12-31	20000	20000	20000.00
			D1	2012-01-01	2012-12-31	20000	21600	20935.52
			D1	2013-01-01	2013-12-31	21600	21600	21600.00
C6'	COUNT Project Budget >= 2000000 **GROUPBY** Department **YEAR** DURING [2018,2019]	30	Did	Aggr_Start	Aggr_End	Min (COUNT(PId))	Max (COUNT(PId))	AVG^T (COUNT(PId))
			D1	2018-01-01	2018-12-31	78	90	82.70
			D1	2019-01-01	2019-12-31	86	91	87.92
			D10	2018-01-01	2018-12-31	66	87	74.15
			D10	2019-01-01	2019-12-31	66	73	69.85

consecutive time periods, e.g., query C5. This is because the temporal aggregate computation follows the change preservation property [4], which implies that a new tuple will be generated in the result table based on the update even though it does not lead to a new aggregate value. Hence, we provide an option that allows users to specify the time unit, e.g., year or month, in the keyword query's group-by condition. Then we will compute one aggregate tuple for each time unit based on the previous aggregate results at each time point.

We extend queries C3 to C6 in Table 2 with time units in the group-by condition such that the results of C3, C5 and C6 are grouped by year, and that of C4 by the month. Table 5 shows the new queries C3' to C6', as well as their statistics and sample aggregate results. We observe that the results of C3' to C6' are more meaningful and easier to understand compared to the results in Table 4. This is because the time period in the results are computed based on user-specified time unit and they are significantly longer than the time periods in the original queries C3 to C6.

Consider query C5' in Table 5. By including a GROUPBY YEAR in the keyword query, we have one tuple generated for each combination of department and year. The first tuple in results indicates that for department D1 and year 2010, the minimum of the employees' maximum monthly salary is 3300, while the maximum is 20,000. Given an employee's maximum monthly salary over time, the AVG^T gives an average by considering the duration of each maximum salary, so users will know that the time-weighted average maximum salary is 13303.44. Similarly, the first tuple in results of query C6' indicates that for department D1 and year 2018, the minimum number of projects with a budget larger than or equal to two million is 78, while the maximum is 90. By considering the duration of such projects, there are 82.7 equivalent projects with a duration of one year.

5   Related Work

Existing works on keyword search over temporal databases have focused on improving query efficiency [13,16] and identifying query interpretations [10]. The work in [13] annotates parent nodes in a data graph with time boundaries computed from its child nodes, while the work in [16] extends the traditional keyword search approach BANKS[1] with time dimension. The work in [10] uses ORA semantics to apply the time condition in a query. These works do not support aggregate functions and group-by in their temporal keyword query.

SQAK [19] is the first work that supports keyword search with aggregate functions and group-by over non-temporal relational databases. However, it does not handle the data duplication in the join sequence relation and may return incorrect aggregate results. PowerQ [23] addresses the data duplication caused by n-ary (n > 2) non-temporal relationships and utilizes projection to remove duplicate data. However, PowerQ does not consider the data duplication caused by many-to-many, many-to-one relationships and time periods. Since PowerQ is the latest work supporting aggregate in non-temporal relational keyword search, our work is built on top of it to handle data duplication caused by more reasons, e.g., many-to-many relationships, many-to-one relationships and the join between temporal and non-temporal relations.

Except for querying temporal databases via keyword search as this work, a more commonly used approach is to query the database utilizing extended SQL query with the support of temporal operators, e.g., temporal join and temporal aggregate operators [14,15]. These works in this field are mainly focusing on improving the efficiency of temporal operators, which can be achieved by specially designed indices [3,14,17,25], time period partition algorithms [6,7] or parallel computation [5,18]. On the one hand, our framework could take advantage of these works to improve the efficiency of computing the temporal join sequence as well as temporal aggregate. On the other hand, our framework removes data duplication automatically and correctly, therefore avoids returning incorrect results of temporal aggregate, while querying with extended SQL requires the users noticing and manually removing the possible data duplicates, which is error-prone.

6   Conclusion

In this work, we have extended temporal keyword queries with aggregates and group-by, and described a framework to process these queries over temporal databases. Our framework addresses the problem of incorrect aggregate results due to data duplication in the join sequence relation, and meaningless aggregate results due to updates. We use a temporal ORM schema graph to capture temporal objects/relationships and temporal attributes, and use these semantics to identify an unique attribute set required by the aggregate in the join sequence relation. We also support aggregation over user-specified time units and attributes with inherent time units to return meaningful results.

Limitations of this approach include not considering recursive relationships in database and the extraction of ORA semantics is not fully automatic. Since one keyword query may have multiple query interpretations, the future work includes to design a mechanism to rank these interpretations, and propose algorithms to share some intermediate relations when computing results for different query interpretations of the same keyword query.

References

1. Aditya, B., Bhalotia, G., Chakrabarti, S., et al. BANKS: browsing and keyword searching in relational databases. In: VLDB (2002)
2. Allen, J.F.: Maintaining knowledge about temporal intervals. Commun. ACM **26**, 832–843 (1983)
3. Böhlen, M., Gamper, J., Jensen, C.S.: Multi-dimensional aggregation for temporal data. In: Ioannidis, Y., et al. (eds.) EDBT 2006. LNCS, vol. 3896, pp. 257–275. Springer, Heidelberg (2006). https://doi.org/10.1007/11687238_18
4. Böhlen, M.H., Jensen, C.S.: Sequenced semantics. In: Liu, L., Özsu, M.T. (eds.) Encyclopedia of Database Systems, 2nd edn. Springer, New York (2018). https://doi.org/10.1007/978-1-4614-8265-9_1053
5. Bouros, P., Mamoulis, N.: A forward scan based plane sweep algorithm for parallel interval joins. Proc. VLDB Endow. **10**, 1346–1357 (2017)
6. Cafagna, F., Böhlen, M.H.: Disjoint interval partitioning. VLDB J. **26**(3), 447–466 (2017). https://doi.org/10.1007/s00778-017-0456-7
7. Dignös, A., Böhlen, M.H., Gamper, J., Jensen, C.S.: Extending the kernel of a relational DBMS with comprehensive support for sequenced temporal queries. ACM TODS **41**, 1–46 (2016)
8. Gao, Q., Lee, M.L., Dobbie, G., Zeng, Z.: A semantic framework for designing temporal SQL databases. In: Trujillo, J.C., et al. (eds.) ER 2018. LNCS, vol. 11157, pp. 382–396. Springer, Cham (2018). https://doi.org/10.1007/978-3-030-00847-5_27
9. Gao, Q., Lee, M.L., Ling, T.W.: Temporal keyword search with aggregates and group-by. Technical report TRA7/21, NUS (2021). https://dl.comp.nus.edu.sg/handle/1900.100/10184
10. Gao, Q., Lee, M.L., Ling, T.W., Dobbie, G., Zeng, Z.: Analyzing temporal keyword queries for interactive search over temporal databases. In: Hartmann, S., Ma, H., Hameurlain, A., Pernul, G., Wagner, R.R. (eds.) DEXA 2018. LNCS, vol. 11029, pp. 355–371. Springer, Cham (2018). https://doi.org/10.1007/978-3-319-98809-2_22
11. Gunadhi, H., Segev, A.: Query processing algorithms for temporal intersection joins. In: IEEE ICDE (1991)
12. Hormozi, N.: Disambiguation and result expansion in keyword search over relational databases. In: ICDE. IEEE (2019)
13. Jia, X., Hsu, W., Lee, M.L.: Target-oriented keyword search over temporal databases. In: Hartmann, S., Ma, H. (eds.) DEXA 2016. LNCS, vol. 9827, pp. 3–19. Springer, Cham (2016). https://doi.org/10.1007/978-3-319-44403-1_1
14. Kaufmann, M., Manjili, A., Vagenas, P., et al.: Timeline index: unified data structure for processing queries on temporal data in SAP HANA. In: SIGMOD (2013)
15. Kulkarni, K.G., Michels, J.: Temporal features in SQL: 2011. SIGMOD Rec. **41**, 34–43 (2012)

16. Liu, Z., Wang, C., Chen, Y.: Keyword search on temporal graphs. TKDE **29**, 1667–1680 (2017)
17. Piatov, D., Helmer, S.: Sweeping-based temporal aggregation. In: Gertz, M., et al. (eds.) SSTD 2017. LNCS, vol. 10411, pp. 125–144. Springer, Cham (2017). https://doi.org/10.1007/978-3-319-64367-0_7
18. Pilman, M., Kaufmann, M., Köhl, F., Kossmann, D., Profeta, D.: Partime: parallel temporal aggregation. In: ACM SIGMOD (2016)
19. Tata, S., Lohman, G.: SQAK: doing more with keywords. In SIGMOD (2008)
20. Yu, J.X., Qin, L., Chang, L.: Keyword search in relational databases: a survey. IEEE Data Eng. Bull. **33**, 67–78 (2010)
21. Yu, Z., Abraham, A., Yu, X., Liu, Y., Zhou, J., Ma, K.: Improving the effectiveness of keyword search in databases using query logs. Eng. Appl. Artif. Intell. **81**, 169–179 (2019)
22. Zeng, Z., Bao, Z., Le, T.N., Lee, M.L., Ling, T.W.: ExpressQ: identifying keyword context and search target in relational keyword queries. In: CIKM (2014)
23. Zeng, Z., Lee, M.L., Ling, T.W.: Answering keyword queries involving aggregates and GROUP-BYS on relational databases. In: EDBT (2016)
24. Zhang, D., Li, Y., Cao, X., Shao, J., Shen, H.T.: Augmented keyword search on spatial entity databases. VLDB J. **27**(2), 225–244 (2018). https://doi.org/10.1007/s00778-018-0497-6
25. Zhang, D., Markowetz, A., Tsotras, V.J., Gunopulos, D., Seeger, B.: On computing temporal aggregates with range predicates. ACM TODS **33**, 1–39 (2008)

Towards a Taxonomy of Schema Changes for NoSQL Databases: The Orion Language

Alberto Hernández Chillón[✉][ID], Diego Sevilla Ruiz[ID], and Jesús García Molina[ID]

Faculty of Computer Science, University of Murcia, Murcia, Spain
{alberto.hernandez1,dsevilla,jmolina}@um.es

Abstract. The emergence of NoSQL databases and polyglot persistence demands to address classical research topics in the context of new data models and database systems. Schema evolution is a crucial aspect in database management to which limited attention has been paid for NoSQL systems. The definition of a taxonomy of changes is a central issue in the design of any schema evolution approach. Proposed taxonomies of changes for NoSQL databases have considered simple data models, which significantly reduce the set of considered schema change operations. In this paper, we present a unified logical data model that includes aggregation and reference relationships, and takes into account the structural variations that can occur in schemaless NoSQL stores. For this data model, we introduce a new taxonomy of changes with operations not considered in the existing proposed taxonomies for NoSQL. A schema definition language will be used to create schemas that conform to the generic data model, and a database-independent language, created to implement this taxonomy of changes, will be shown. We will show how this language can be used to automatically generate evolution scripts for a set of NoSQL stores, and validated on a case study for a real dataset.

Keywords: NoSQL databases · Schema evolution · Taxonomy of changes · Schema change operations · Domain specific language

1 Introduction

NoSQL (Not only SQL) systems and polyglot persistence emerged to tackle the limitations of relational databases to satisfy requirements of modern, data-intensive applications (e.g., social media or IoT). The predominance of relational systems will probably continue, but they will coexist with NoSQL systems in heterogeneous database architectures. In this scenario, new database tools are needed to offer for NoSQL systems the functionality already available for relational systems. Moreover, these tools should support several data models, as four

This work has been funded by the Spanish Ministry of Science, Innovation and Universities (project grant TIN2017-86853-P).

kinds of NoSQL systems are widely used: columnar, document, key-value, and graphs, with interest in polyglot persistence continuously growing.

Among those aforementioned tools are schema evolution tools. Schema evolution is the ability to make changes on a database schema and adapting the existing data to the new schema. This topic has been extensively studied in relational [1,6] and object-oriented databases [10]. So far, the attention paid to NoSQL schema evolution has been limited, and building robust solutions is still an open research challenge.

Most NoSQL systems are "schema-on-read", that is, the declaration of schemas is not required prior to store data. Therefore, schemas are implicit in data and code. In addition, no standard or specification of NoSQL data model exists. This means that schema evolution approaches for the same type of NoSQL store could be based on different definitions of data models. The proposals published are limited in three aspects: (i) The data models considered do not cover all the possible elements to be subject to evolution; (ii) This leads to taxonomies of changes that do not include some schema change operations potentially useful; (iii) Except for [3,7], the proposals do not embrace the NoSQL paradigm heterogeneity. Two features not considered in these proposals are structural variations and the existence of aggregation and reference relationships. Taking into account these modeling concepts, new operations can be included into the taxonomy of changes.

In this paper, we present a NoSQL schema evolution proposal based on a unified data model that includes aggregation and reference relationships, and structural variations [2]. This paper contributes in the following: (i) A taxonomy of changes that includes valuable operations not included in previous proposals; (ii) A *domain-specific language* (DSL), *Orion*, was developed to implement the set of *schema change operations* (SCOs) defined in the taxonomy; (iii) Our approach is based on a unified data model with more expressive power than other proposals [3,7]; and (iv) A non-trivial refactoring case study for a real dataset used to improve query performance. Given an Orion script, the operations that adapt databases to the schema changes are automatically generated. Also, the inferred or declared schema is automatically updated from Orion scripts.

This paper is organized as follows. First, we present the unified data model for the four NoSQL paradigms considered. Then, we will define the taxonomy of changes and present the Orion language. Next, the validation process will be described, finally ending with the discussion of the related work and drawing some conclusions and future work.

2   Defining Schemas for a Unified Data Model

U-Schema is a unified metamodel that integrates the relational model and data models for the four most common NoSQL paradigms [2]. The taxonomy presented here is based on U-Schema. We will describe the elements of *U-Schema* through the *Athena* language. Figure 1 shows an Athena schema for a gamification application. We will use this schema as a running example.

```
 1 Schema Gamification_athena:1        24 Root entity User {
 2                                     25   Common {
 3 FSet timeData                       26    +id:         Identifier,
 4 {                                   27    email:       String /^.+@.+\.com$/,
 5   createdAt:      Timestamp,        28    personalInfo: Aggr<PersonalInfo>&
 6   updatedAt:      Timestamp         29   }
 7 }                                   30   Variation 1
 8                                     31   Variation 2 {
 9 Root entity Stage                   32    games:       Aggr<MinigameSummary>+,
10 {                                   33    points:      Integer (0..9999)
11   +id:            Identifier,       34   }
12   description:    String,           35 }
13   name:           String            36 Entity PersonalInfo {
14 } + timeData                        37   name:         String /^[A-Z][a-z]*$/,
15                                     38   street:       String,
16 Root entity Minigame                39   city:         String,
17 {                                   40   ?postcode:    Integer
18   +id:            Identifier,       41 }
19   isActive:       Boolean,          42 Entity MinigameSummary {
20   name:           String,           43   gameId:       Ref<Minigame>&,
21   points:         Integer (0..99),  44   ?completedAt: Timestamp,
22   stageIds: Ref<Stage as Identifier>+ 45   ?points:      Integer
23 } + timeData                        46 }
```

Fig. 1. The Gamification schema defined using Athena.

An Athena schema is formed by a set of *schemas types* that can be *entity types* to represent domain entities or *relationship types* to represent relationships between nodes in graph stores. In the Gamification example, there are five entity types: User, PersonalInfo, Stage, Minigame, and MinigameSummary. User, Stage, and Minigame are root entity types, that is, their objects are not embedded in any other object, while PersonalInfo and MinigameSummary are non-root as their instances are embedded into User objects. Each entity type can have a set of structural variations that include a set of features or properties. The features that are *common* to all the variations are separately declared. User has three common features: id, email, and personalInfo. Each variation may add optional features: the second User variation has games and points.

A feature declaration specifies its name and type. There are three kinds of features: *attributes*, *aggregates*, and *references*. For example, the User.personalInfo feature specifies that PersonalInfo objects are embedded in User objects, and the Minigame.stageIds feature specifies that Minigame objects reference Stage objects by holding values of their key attributes. A cardinality needs to be specified for references and aggregations, such as *one to one* or *one to many*. The features may have modifiers as *key* ("+") or *optional* ("?").

Attributes have a scalar type as Number or String, e.g., email and points. The Identifier scalar type is used to declare unique identifiers, e.g., id for users. Certain scalar types allow to add restrictions to their possible values, such as numeric ranges, value enumeration or using regular expressions. The most frequently used collection types are offered: such as Maps, Lists or Tuples.

Athena provides mechanism to favor reuse: schema import and inheritance. Also, composition of schemas is possible through a set of operators. In addition to types, the notion of *set of features* is used to group any set of features, that can be later combined to create more complex schemas.

3   A Taxonomy of Changes for NoSQL Databases

A taxonomy determines the possible changes to be applied on elements of the database schema that conforms to a particular data model. Different categories are established according to the kind of schema element affected by the changes. A taxonomy also specifies the change semantics. Here, we present a taxonomy for U-Schema, which includes novel operations related to the abstractions proper to U-Schema, such as aggregates, references, and structural variation. Our taxonomy also incorporates the operations of previous proposals for NoSQL evolution.

As shown in Table 1, our taxonomy has categories for the following U-Schema elements: *schema types, features, attributes, aggregates* and *references. Schema type* category groups change operations on *entity* and *relationship types*. The *Feature* category groups the operations with the same semantics for the three kinds of features. Three operations for variations have been included in the *schema type* category: create a union schema, adapt a variation to other, and delete a variation. The former is useful to squash variations into a single variation for a schema type, and the other two with several uses, such as removing outliers [8].

Next, the terminology used to define the semantics in the taxonomy is introduced. Let $S = E \cup R$ be the set of schema types formed by the union of the set of entity types $E = \{E_i\}, i = 1 \ldots n$, (and the set of relationship types $R = \{R_i\}, i = 1 \ldots m$, if the schema corresponds to a graph database.) Each schema type t includes a set of structural variations $V^t = \{v_1^t, v_2^t, \ldots, v_n^t\}$, and $v_i^t.features$ denotes the set of features of a variation v_i^t. Then, the set of features of a schema type t is $F^t = \bigcup_{i=1}^{n} v_n^t \cup C^t$, where C^t denotes the set of common features of t. The set F^t will include attributes, aggregates, and references. We will use *dot notation* to refer to parts of a schema element, e.g., given an entity type e, $e.name$ and $e.features$ refer to the name and set of features (F^e), respectively, of the entity type. Finally, the symbol "←" will be used to express the change of state of a schema element by means of an assignment statement.

For the *Schema type* category, in addition to the atomic operations: add, delete, and rename, three complex SCOs are added to create new schemas types: The *extract, split* and *merge* operations. Also three operations to manipulate variations are introduced: The *delvar, adapt* and *union* operations. Due to space restrictions, the semantics of these operations is only formally given in Table 1.

The *Feature* category includes complex SCOs to copy a feature from a schema type to another one, either maintaining (*copy*) or not (*move*) the feature copied in the original schema type. Also, it includes SCOs to move a feature from/to an aggregate: *nest* and *unnest*. The *Attribute* category includes operations to *add* a new attribute, change its type (*cast*), and add/remove an attribute to/from a key: *promote* and *demote*. Finally, the *Reference* and *Aggregate* categories include the *morph* operations to transform aggregates into references and vice versa, *card* to change the cardinality, as well as *add* and *cast* commented for attributes.

The operations in Table 1 have attached information regarding the gaining or loss of information they cause. C^+ is used for an *additive change*, C^- for a *subtractive change*, $C^{+,-}$ when there is a loss and gain of information (e.g., *move*

Table 1. Schema change operations of the taxonomy.

Schema Type Operations

Add (C^+) Let t be a new schema type, $S \leftarrow S \cup \{t\}$.

Delete (C^-) Given a schema type t, $S \leftarrow S \setminus \{t\}$.

Rename $(C^=)$ Given a schema type t and a string value n, $t.name \leftarrow n$.

Extract $(C^{+,=})$ Given a schema type t, a set of features f of t, $f \subset F^t$, and a string value n, then a new type t_1 is created such that $t_1.name \leftarrow n \wedge t_1.features \leftarrow f$ and $S \leftarrow S \cup \{t_1\}$.

Split $(C^=)$ Given a schema type t and two sets of features $f_1 \subset t.features$ and $f_2 \subset t.features$, and two string values n_1 and n_2, then two new types t_1 and t_2 are created such that $t_1.name \leftarrow n_1 \wedge t_1.features \leftarrow f_1$ and $t_2.name \leftarrow n_2 \wedge t_2.features \leftarrow f_2$, and $S \leftarrow S \setminus \{t\}$ and $S \leftarrow S \cup \{t_1, t_2\}$.

Merge $(C^=)$ Given two schema types t_1 and t_2 and a a string value n, a new schema type t is created such that $t.name \leftarrow n \wedge t.features \leftarrow t_1.features \cup t_2.features$ and $S \leftarrow S \setminus \{t_1, t_2\}$ and $S \leftarrow S \cup \{t\}$.

DelVar (C^-) Given a variation v^t of a schema type t, then $t.variations \leftarrow t.variations \setminus \{v^t\}$.

Adapt $(C^{+/-})$ Given two variations v_1^t and v_2^t of a schema type t, then $v_1^t.features \leftarrow v_2^t.features$, and $t.variations \leftarrow t.variations \setminus \{v_1^t\}$.

Union (C^+) Given a schema type t that has m variations, $t.features \leftarrow t.features \cup_{i=1}^m v_i^t$.

Feature Operations

Delete (C^-) Given a schema type t and a feature $f \in t.features$, then $t.features \leftarrow t.features \setminus \{f\}$.

Rename $(C^=)$ Given a schema type t, a feature $f \in t.features$, and a string value n, then $f.name \leftarrow n$.

Copy (C^+) Given two schema types t_1 and t_2 and a feature $f \in t_1.features$, then $t_2.features \leftarrow t_2.features \cup \{f\}$.

Move $(C^{+,-})$ Given two schema types t_1 and t_2 and a feature $f \in t_1.features$, then $t_2.features \leftarrow t_2.features \cup \{f\} \wedge t_1.features \leftarrow t_1.features \setminus \{f\}$.

Nest $(C^{+,-})$ Given an entity type e_1, a feature $f \in e_1.features$, and an aggregate $ag \in e_1.aggregates \wedge ag.type = e_2$, then $e_2.features \cup \{f\} \wedge e_1.features \setminus \{f\}$.

Unnest $(C^{-,+})$ Given an entity type e_1, an aggregate $ag \in e_1.aggregates \wedge ag.type = e_2$, and a feature $f \in e_2.features$, then $e_1.features \cup \{f\} \wedge e_2.features \setminus \{f\}$.

Attribute Operations

Add (C^+) Given a schema type t and an attribute at (name and type), then $t.attributes \leftarrow t.attributes \cup \{at\}$.

Cast $(C^{+/-})$ Given a schema type t, an attribute $at \in t.attributes$, and a scalar type st, then $at.type \leftarrow st$.

Promote $(C^=)$ Given an entity type t and an attribute at, then $at.key \leftarrow True$.

Demote $(C^=)$ Given an entity type t and an attribute at, then $at.key \leftarrow False$.

Reference Operations

Add (C^+) Given a schema type t and a reference rf (name and entity type), then $t.references \leftarrow t.references \cup \{rf\}$.

Cast $(C^{+/-})$ Given a schema type t, a reference $rf \in t.references$, and a scalar type st, then $rf.type \leftarrow st$.

Card $(C^{+/-})$ Given a schema type t, a reference $rf \in t.references$, and two numbers $l, u \in [-1, 0, 1] \wedge l \leq u$, then $rf.lowerBound \leftarrow l \wedge rf.upperBound \leftarrow u$.

Morph $(C^=)$ Given a schema type t and a reference $rf \in t.references$, then $t.aggregations \leftarrow t.aggregations \cup \{ag\}$, where $ag.name \leftarrow rf.name \wedge ag.type \leftarrow rf.type$ and $t.references \leftarrow t.references \setminus \{rf\}$.

Aggregate Operations

Add (C^+) Given an entity type e and an aggregation ag (name an entity type), then $e.aggregations \leftarrow t.aggregations \cup \{ag\}$.

Card $(C^{+/-})$ Given an entity type e, and an aggregation $ag \in e.aggregations$ and two numbers $l, u \in [-1, 0, 1] \wedge l \leq u$, then $ag.lower \leftarrow l \wedge ag.upper \leftarrow u$.

Morph $(C^=)$ Given an entity type e and an aggregation $ag \in e.aggregations$, then $e.references \leftarrow e.references \cup \{rf\}$, where $rf.name \leftarrow ag.name \wedge rf.type \leftarrow ag.type$ and $e.aggregations \leftarrow e.aggregations \setminus \{rf\}$.

feature), $C^=$ means no change in information, and $C^{+/-}$ adds or subtracts, depending on the operation parameters (e.g., *casting* a feature to boolean).

4   Implementing the Taxonomy: The Orion Language

Once the taxonomy was defined, we created the Orion language to allow developers to write and execute their schema change operations. Orion keeps the system-independence feature of the taxonomy by providing the same abstract and concrete syntax for any database system, although the semantics of each operation must be implemented in a different way depending on each system.

Figure 2 shows a Orion script to refactor the running example schema. Using specifies the schema to apply changes, which allows checking the feasibility of all the change operations. This checking requires sequentially executing the operations, and updating the schema before launching the execution of the following operation.

```
1  Gamification_refactoring operations   24  CAST ATTR MinigameSummary::isCompleted
2  Using Gamification_athena:1           25    TO Boolean
3                                        26
4  // Minigame operations               27  //Adding a new entity type
5  CAST ATTR *::points TO Double         28  ADD ENTITY Company
6  DELETE Minigame::isActive             29  {
7                                        30    +id: Identifier,
8  // User operations                    31    code: String,
9  ADAPT ENTITY User::v1 TO v2           32    name: String,
10 NEST User::email TO personalInfo      33    numOfEmployees: Number
11 MORPH AGGR User::personalInfo         34  }
12     TO privateData                    35
13 RENAME ENTITY User TO Employee        36  //Adding new features
14                                       37  PROMOTE ATTR Company::code
15 // PersonalInfoData operations        38  ADD REF Company::staff+ TO Employee
16 CAST ATTR PersonalInfo::postcode      39  ADD AGGR Company::media:
17     TO String                         40  {
18 NEST PersonalInfo::city,postcode,     41    twitterProf: String,
19     street TO Address                 42    fbProf: String,
20                                        43    webUrl: String,
21 // MinigameSummary operations         44    ytProf: String
22 RENAME MinigameSummary::completedAt   45  }&
23     TO isCompleted
```

Fig. 2. Refactoring of the Gamification schema using Orion.

Figure 2 shows changes on entity types of the *Gamification* schema: casting on attributes (lines 5, 16, and 24), deleting attributes (line 6), nesting attributes to an aggregate (lines 10 and 18), morphing an aggregate to a reference (11), renaming entity types (line 13) and attributes (22), and adapting a variation (line 9). Entity types and features are also created (lines 28–45).

Implementing a taxonomy of schema changes entails tackling the update of both the schema and the data. The Orion engine generates the updated schema as well as the code scripts to produce the changes required in the database. So far, MongoDB and Cassandra are supported. Orion can also provide an estimation of the time required to perform the change operations.

Table 2 gives insights on the implementation of some operations for each database, as well as a time estimation. The ○ symbol is used for constant-time operations; ◐ when traversing all the instances of an entity type is required; ◑ is used when traversing one or two entity types and creating a new entity type, and ● is used if all the instances of an entity type have to be serialized and then imported back into the database. ●● is used for operations with very high cost.

Not all operations can be applied to all database systems. For example variation-related operations cannot be applied in Cassandra, since it requires the definition of a schema prior to store data.

Table 2. Excerpt of operation costs in Orion for each database system considered.

	MongoDB operations	Cost	Cassandra operations	Cost
Add schema type	createCollection(),$addFields	○	CREATE Tab	○
Split schema type	2x($project,$out),drop()	◑	(4xCOPY,2xCREATE,DROP) Tab	●●
Rename feature	$rename	◐	2xCOPY Tab,DROP Col,ADD Col	●
Copy feature	$set	◐	2xCOPY Tab,ADD Col	●
Add attribute	$addFields	◐	ADD Col	○
Cast attribute	$set,$convert	◐	(2xCOPY,DROP,CREATE) Tab	●
Card reference	$set	◐	(2xCOPY,DROP,CREATE) Tab	●
Morph reference	$lookup,$out,$unset,drop()	◑	CREATE Type,ADD Col,DROP Tab*	—
Add aggregate	$addFields	◐	CREATE Type,ADD Col	○
Card aggregate	$set	◐	(2xCOPY,DROP,CREATE) Tab	●

Although the main purpose of the Orion language is to support schema changes in a platform-independent way, it may have other uses: (i) An Orion script can bootstrap a schema by itself if no initial schema is given; (ii) Differences between Athena schemas may be expressed as Orion specifications; and (iii) Orion specifications may be obtained from existing tools such as PRISM/PRISM++ [1].

5   The Validation Process

A refactoring was applied on the StackOverflow dataset[1] in order to validate Orion. We injected this dataset into MongoDB, and its schema was inferred by applying the strategy from [2]. Figure 3 shows an excerpt of four of the seven entity types discovered, visualized with the notation introduced in [5].

Analyzing the schema, we realized that this dataset did not take advantage of constructs typical for document databases such as aggregations (nested documents), and that some features could be casted to specific MongoDB types. By slightly changing the schema we might improve query performance in MongoDB. We designed a scenario to measure the query performance by introducing changes in the schema. We aggregated `Badges` into `Users`, `PostLinks` into `Posts`, and created two new aggregates for the metadata information for `Posts` and `Users`.

---

[1] https://archive.org/details/stackexchange.

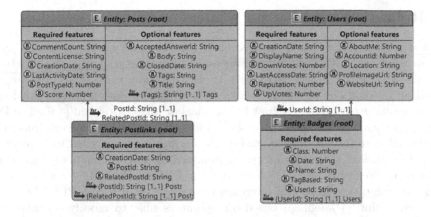

Fig. 3. Excerpt of the StackOverflow inferred schema.

The Orion script that specifies the StackOverflow schema changes is shown in Fig. 4. The first operations (lines 4–6) are CASTs of attributes to types more suitable for MongoDB. Then some NEST operations on Posts and Users are applied to create aggregated objects (PostMetadata and UserMetadata, lines 8–9). We also embedded Postlinks into Posts (lines 13–14) and Badges into Users. These two last operations are not trivial, as Postlinks and Badges are the entity types referencing Posts and Users, and therefore it is needed to first copy certain features and then morph them (lines 16–18).

```
1  StackOverflow_ops operations
2  Using stackoverflow
3
4  CAST ATTR *::CreationDate TO Timestamp
5  CAST ATTR *::LastAccessDate TO Timestamp
6  CAST ATTR Posts::LastActivityDate TO Timestamp
7
8  NEST Posts::CreationDate,LastActivityDate TO PostMetadata
9  NEST Users::CreationDate,LastAccessDate,DownVotes,UpVotes TO UserMetadata
10
11 CARD REF Posts::Tags TO *
12
13 COPY Postlinks::_id TO Posts::postlinkId WHERE Postlinks.PostId = Posts._id
14 MORPH REF Posts::postlinkId ( rmId rmEntity ) TO Postlinks
15
16 COPY Badges::_id TO Users::badgeId WHERE Badges.UserId = Users._id
17 MORPH REF Users::badgeId ( rmId rmEntity ) TO Badges
18 RENAME Users::badgeId TO badges
```

Fig. 4. Orion operations to be applied to the StackOverflow schema and data.

Given the Athena schema shown in Fig. 3 and the Orion script of Fig. 4, the Orion engine generates the updated schema and the MongoDB API code script to execute the changes on the data. Queries can then be adapted, and performance can be measured and compared. MongoDB code is implemented using aggregation pipelines and bulk writes to improve the performance.

6   Related Work

A great research effort has been devoted to the database schema evolution problem for relational databases. Some of the most significant contributions have been the DB-Main and PRISM/PRISM++ tools. DB-Main was a long-term project aimed at tackling the problems related to database evolution on relational systems and other paradigms such as hierarchical or object-oriented [4,6]. The DB-Main approach was based on two main elements: The GER unified metamodel to achieve platform-independence, and a transformational approach to implement operations such as reverse and forward engineering, and schema mappings; More recently, Carlo Curino et al. [1] developed the PRISM/PRISM++ tool aimed to automate migration tasks and rewriting legacy queries. PRISM/PRISM++ provides an evolution language based on operators able to modify schemas and integrity constraints. Although much more mature and evolved than our work, neither of these two approaches address the NoSQL database evolution.

A proposal of schema evolution for NoSQL document stores was presented by Stefanie Scherzinger et al. in [9]. The work defines a 5-operation taxonomy for a very simple data model: schemas are a set of entities that have properties (attributes and embedded objects), but relationships or variations are not considered. The operations are add/remove/rename properties, and copy or move a set of properties from an entity type to another. In our proposal, the generic data model is more complex, which results in a richer change taxonomy.

Vavrek et al. explored schema evolution for multi-model database systems [7,11]. They suppose a layered architecture in which a database engine interacts with individual engines for each data model, instead of defining a unified metamodel. A taxonomy of 10 operations is defined: 5 for entity types (*kinds*) and 5 for properties. These latter correspond to those defined in [9], and the first 5 are *add*, *drop*, *rename*, *split*, and *merge*, with the same meaning as in our taxonomy. We propose a complex engine architecture for a unified model, instead of a layered one, as most databases share a common set of features which can be included in a single core model, which will act as a pivot model to support schema mappings. Our goal is to provide native and broader support for the most popular databases. Also, our taxonomy includes new operations such as transforming aggregations into references and vice versa, joining all the variations, removing a variation, or add/remove/rename references and aggregates.

In [3], a taxonomy is proposed as part of an approach to rewrite queries for polystore evolution. The taxonomy includes six operations applicable to *entity types*, four to *attributes* and four to *relations*. A generic language, TyphonML, is used to define relational and NoSQL schemas. The language also includes physical mapping and schema evolution operations. Our richer data model allowed us to define operations that separately affect aggregates and references, and variations and relationship types are considered, among other differences.

7   Conclusions and Future Work

In this paper, we have taken advantage of the U-Schema unified data model to present a schema changes taxonomy for NoSQL systems, which includes more complex operations than previous proposals. Evolution scripts for this taxonomy are expressed by means of the Orion language.[2] Currently, Orion works for two popular NoSQL stores: MongoDB (document and schemaless) and Cassandra (columnar that requires a schema declaration). Orion has been validated by applying a refactoring on the StackOverflow dataset.

Our future work includes (i) The implementation of generators for different database paradigms, such as Neo4j for graphs and Redis for key-value; (ii) Investigating optimizations of the generated code to evolve databases; (iii) Query analysis and query rewriting; and (iv) Integrating Orion into a tool for agile migration.

References

1. Curino, C., Moon, H.J., Deutsch, A., Zaniolo, C.: Automating the database schema evolution process. VLDB J. **22**, 73–98 (2013)
2. Fernández Candel, C., Sevilla Ruiz, D., García Molina, J.: A Unified Metamodel for NoSQL and Relational Databases. CoRR abs/2105.06494 (2021)
3. Fink, J., Gobert, M., Cleve, A.: Adapting queries to database schema changes in hybrid polystores. In: IEEE 20th International Working Conference on Source Code Analysis and Manipulation (SCAM), pp. 127–131 (2020)
4. Hainaut, J.-L., Englebert, V., Henrard, J., Hick, J.-M., Roland, D.: Database evolution: the DB-MAIN approach. In: Loucopoulos, P. (ed.) ER 1994. LNCS, vol. 881, pp. 112–131. Springer, Heidelberg (1994). https://doi.org/10.1007/3-540-58786-1_76
5. Hernández, A., Feliciano, S., Sevilla Ruiz, D., García Molina, J.: Exploring the visualization of schemas for aggregate-oriented NoSQL databases. In: 36th International Conference on Conceptual Modeling (ER), ER Forum 2017, pp. 72–85 (2017)
6. Hick, J.-M., Hainaut, J.-L.: Strategy for database application evolution: the DB-MAIN approach. In: Song, I.-Y., Liddle, S.W., Ling, T.-W., Scheuermann, P. (eds.) ER 2003. LNCS, vol. 2813, pp. 291–306. Springer, Heidelberg (2003). https://doi.org/10.1007/978-3-540-39648-2_24
7. Holubová, I., Klettke, M., Störl, U.: Evolution management of multi-model data. In: Gadepally, V., et al. (eds.) DMAH/Poly 2019. LNCS, vol. 11721, pp. 139–153. Springer, Cham (2019). https://doi.org/10.1007/978-3-030-33752-0_10
8. Klettke, M., Störl, U., Scherzinger, S.: Schema extraction and structural outlier detection for JSON-based NoSQL data stores. In: BTW Conference, pp. 425–444 (2015)
9. Klettke, M., Störl, U., Shenavai, M., Scherzinger, S.: NoSQL schema evolution and big data migration at scale. In: IEEE International Conference on Big Data (2016)
10. Li, X.: A survey of schema evolution in object-oriented databases. In: TOOLS: 31st International Conference on Technology of OO Languages and Systems, pp. 362–371 (1999)
11. Vavrek, M., Holubová, I., Scherzinger, S.: MM-evolver: a multi-model evolution management tool. In: EDBT (2019)

---

[2] The implementation of Orion and its specification may be found at https://catedrasaes-umu.github.io/NoSQLDataEngineering/tools.html.

Enterprise Modeling

Quantitative Alignment of Enterprise Architectures with the Business Model

Wilco Engelsman[1,3]([✉]) [iD], Jaap Gordijn[2,4] [iD], Timber Haaker[1] [iD],
Marten van Sinderen[3] [iD], and Roel Wieringa[2,3] [iD]

[1] Saxion, University of Applied Sciences, Enschede, The Netherlands
w.engelsman@saxion.nl
[2] The Value Engineers, Soest, The Netherlands
[3] University of Twente, Enschede, The Netherlands
[4] Vrije Universiteit Amsterdam, Amsterdam, The Netherlands

Abstract. For many companies, information and communication technology (ICT) is an essential part of the value proposition. Netflix and Spotify would not have been possible without internet technology.

Business model up-scaling often requires a different ICT architecture, because an up-scaled business model imposes different performance requirements. This new architecture needs investments and has different operational expenses than the old architecture and requires recalculation of the business model. Investment decisions, in turn are guided by performance requirements.

There are currently no methods to align a quantified business value model of a company with performance requirements on the enterprise architecture. In this paper, we show how to derive performance requirements on an enterprise architecture (EA) specified in ArchiMate from a quantification of a business model specified in e^3value. Second, we show how we can aggregate investments and expenses from an ArchiMate model and insert these into an e^3value model.

Keywords: e^3value · ArchiMate · Traceability · Business value model · Enterprise architecture · Quantitative alignment

1 Introduction

Commercial services and physical products rely heavily on ICT. For example, Netflix and Spotify would not have been possible without the large scale deployment of content servers and networks. Physical products often have digital twins, which complement the product with additional features, allowing for simulation, training, etc. Since ICT is an intrinsic part of the value proposition of these organizations, it can no longer be considered as a cost-only factor. ICT should be part of value proposition design.

In an ecosystem products and services are exchanged between at least two, but often more enterprises. Each enterprise focuses on its core competences and jointly they satisfy a complex customer need. Following Moore [10], we define an

© Springer Nature Switzerland AG 2021
A. Ghose et al. (Eds.): ER 2021, LNCS 13011, pp. 189–198, 2021.
https://doi.org/10.1007/978-3-030-89022-3_16

ecosystem as a collection of companies that work cooperatively and competitively to satisfy customer needs.

To assess financial sustainability of an ecosystem, we need a *business value model* of the ecosystem (henceforth called "business model"), which we define as a conceptual model that represents the creation, distribution, and capture of value in a *network* of participants [4]. Valuable objects are services and products that satisfy customer needs, as well as payment for these. We use e^3value as a business modeling language, because it allows quantification of ecosystem business models [4,5].

A *quantified* business model of an ecosystem contains estimations of revenues and expenses of the ecosystem members. Revenues result from sales. Expenses are made to obtain e.g. raw materials, services or goods from others.

In ICT-intensive value propositions, expenses often relate to ICT components, both hard- and software. Therefore, in case of ICT-intensive services and products, the design of the provisioning *Enterprise Architecture* (EA) should be coordinated with business model design.

An EA is a high-level conceptual model of an enterprise designed to put the business strategy of an organization into operation [16]. In accordance with our networked view, EAs too should be extended to an ecosystem of enterprises [15].

In previous work we created, validated and refined guidelines by which to design the business layer of an Archimate EA from an e^3value business model [3]. In this paper we extend this with (1) guidelines to quantify workload requirements in an EA based on quantificiation of an e^3value model, (2) a technique by which to specify investments in and expenses on ICT in ArchiMate, and (3) a mechanism to import the specification of investments and expenses in e^3value models.

This paper is structured as follows. Section 2 describes related work, Sect. 3 introduces our research methodology. In Sect. 4 we introduce the design of our approach. In Sect. 5 we discuss some lessons learned and introduce future work.

2   Related Work

In previous work we have created guidelines between e^3value and ArchiMate to create a bridge between e^3value and ArchiMate [3]. We use ArchiMate as the EA modeling language [12], where we focus on its capability to model business services and collaborations. ArchiMate is the defacto standard for EA modeling. This is the main reason why we use ArchiMate. We use e^3value because it captures the value network in a conceptual model and contains formal quantifications. This paper extends on this, the guidelines are required to realize the desired traceability. We build on this traceability to propagate economic transactions as workload requirements over the architecture and we aggregate investments and expenses of an IT architecture into an e^3value model.

Derzi et al. [1] realize traceability between UML deployment diagrams and e^3value. They annotate UML diagrams with investments and expenses and create traceability between UML and e^3value to be able analyze the profitability of an organization with the proposed IT. Deployment diagrams are used because they indicate ownership of ICT components, and ownership comes with an investment and operational expenses. These financials are important for the e^3value business model. Our work shares some similarities, we take the basic idea, but extend on this. We realize bi-directional traceability. We import economic transactions into ArchiMate for scalability reasoning in conjunction with aggregating investments and expenses from ArchiMate into e^3value. Our solution also has more semantics, which can be used to create tool support.

Iacob et al. [7] propose a mapping from the Business Model Canvas (BMC) [11] to ArchiMate. Since the BMC is oriented towards the *single* enterprise, this work misses the networked ecosystem point of view that is crucial to most ecosystems. We claim that exploration of the ecosystem, e.g. all participating actors and the ICT systems, need to be included in business model analysis, rather than just a single enterprise and its direct customers and supplier. Moreover, the BMC does not have the capability to quantify the business model and simulate market scenarios, as e^3value has, nor does the BMC have the capability to quantify ArchiMate and bring this quantification to a business model expressed in e^3value.

Iacob and Jonkers introduce a generic quantification approach for ArchiMate [6]. They describe a generic approach of how to perform performance analysis using workload and response times on an ArchiMate model. Our work is based on the same principles, we derive our performance requirements from e^3value and we quantify ArchiMate with investments and expenses. Obviously, the work of Iacob and Jonkers is restricted to ArchiMate only and therefore does not include a networked business model point of view.

Miguens [9] proposes to introduce an additional viewpoint for ArchiMate where investment information can be assigned and calculated. We do not want to perform actual investment calculations in ArchiMate beyond aggregating the information. We do all the calculations in e^3value because they are part of business model analysis. Miguens also does not take the business ecosystem perspective as we do, nor do they have a way to identify performance requirements based on economic transactions.

De Kinderen, Gaaloul and Proper [8] propose to link ArchiMate to e^3value using an intermediary language. They do not propose a direct mapping between ArchiMate and e^3value. They wish to introduce transactionality in ArchiMate by using the DEMO language as an intermediary language, since ArchiMate cannot represent economic transactions. [2]. Introducing a third language adds an additional complexity we wish to avoid. Second, we do not believe it is necessary to use a third language, since we can calculate the economic transactions in e^3value and import it into ArchiMate using the profiling language. They do not use the realized traceability for quantitative alignment. We use the economic transactions from e^3value as workload requirements for IT systems and quantify the ArchiMate model with investments and expenses to identify the investments and expenses and insert them into the e^3value model for Net Present Value (NPV) calculations.

Overall, the unique element of our approach is that we take a network approach, separate business model analysis from enterprise architecture design, define links between the business model and EA to synchronize the two models. We also provide an initial evaluation of this link.

3   Design Goals, Research Questions and Methodology

Our design goal is to design techniques by which to determine if a business model is feasible in terms of financial sustainability and technological feasibility.

e^3value models contain a *transaction table* that identifies and counts all commercial transactions among ecosystem actors. The transaction table contains crucial information to assess long-term financial sustainability of the ecosystem because it determines revenues and expenses of each actor. Our first sub-goal is now to include information from the transaction table in an ArchiMate model. Our second sub-goal is to find a way to use this information to identify workload requirements on the components of an EA. Our third sub-goal is to find a way to specify investments and expenses on ICT in ArchiMate that will meet these workload requirements, and export these to the corresponding e^3value model. This gives us the following research questions.

- Q1: How can ArchiMate represent the economic transactions of e^3value?
- Q2: How can performance requirements in ArchiMate be identified from the transaction table?
- Q3: How can ArchiMate be quantified with investments and expenses?
- Q4: How can expenses and investments in an ArchiMate model be fed back into an e^3value model?

We present our answers to Q1–Q4 in Sect. 4 by means of a toy example. We follow a design science methodology [14]. In our previous work we created guidelines for designing an ArchiMate business layer model from an e^3value model, based on a conceptual analysis of the two language, combined with field tests and real world validations [3]. The current paper is a further extension of the guidelines with quantification.

4   Design of Quantitative Alignment

Figure 1 contains the value network and transaction table of an e^3value model on the left and bottom, and an ArchiMate model on the right. We will explain all parts of the figure in what follows.

4.1 e^3value

Relevant definitions of e^3value and ArchiMate concepts are given in Table 1. The e^3value model of Fig. 1 shows an *actor* train company exchanging *value objects* (tickets and money) with a *market segment* travelers. This is done through a

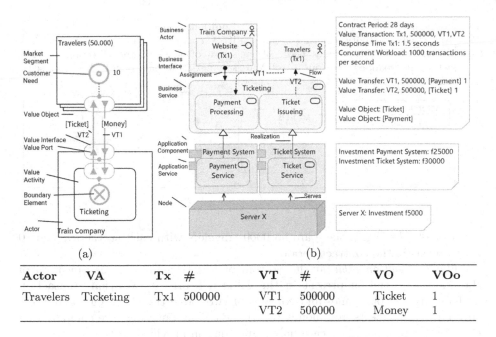

Actor	VA	Tx	#	VT	#	VO	VOo
Travelers	Ticketing	Tx1	500000	VT1	500000	Ticket	1
				VT2	500000	Money	1

Fig. 1. e^3value model and ArchiMate model of a toy example.

Table 1. Definitions of e^3value and ArchiMate concepts. The first parts lists corresponding concepts. Using a business interface to represent a port is optional. Using a Serves relation to represent a value transfer is optional too.

e^3value	Definition	ArchiMate	Definition
Actor	An entity that is economically independent	Business Actor	Business entity capable of performing behavior
Value Activity	Profitable task performed by an actor	Business Service	Defined behavior that is exposed to the environment
Value Port	Willingness to provide or request value objects	Business Interface	Channel that exposes behavior
Value Transfer	Willingness to transfer value objects between actors	Flow	Transfer from one element to another
		Serves	Provide functionality to other element

value activity Ticketing. To quantify an e^3value model, we use a so-called *contract period*, which is the period in which actors perform the transactions represented in the e^3value value network. A quantification says how large a market segment is, how often consumer needs occur, what the monetary value of money

Table 2. Transformation guideline G9 [3].

No	Guideline	Additional advice
G9	An e^3value activity connected through a value exchange to a need of an actor is mapped to an ArchiMate business service serving the actor.	If B contains a boundary element instead of a need, the direction of the serving relation would be reversed.

flows is, etc. In Fig. 1, there are 50 0000 travelers with each on the average 10 ticket needs in the contract period.

The *transaction table* at the bottom of Fig. 1 contains a quantification of the single transaction present in the value network. It says that transaction Tx1 occurs 500 000 times and consists of two value transfers, VT1 and VT2, through which tickets and money pass hands. These numbers are computed by the e^3value tool based on cardinality information provided by the tool user.

4.2   ArchiMate

The right part of Fig. 1 contains an ArchiMate model. The yellow layer is the business layer, blue layer is the application layer and the green layer is the infrastructure layer. The *business layer* of this model has been designed following the guidelines of our previous work [3]. This business layer now represents the relevant parts of the value network and can serve as a bridge between ArchiMate and e^3value. The crucial guideline G9 is shown in Table 2. Figure 1 shows two ArchiMate actors, *Train Company* and *Travelers*, and a *Ticketing* service decomposed into two sub-services, *Payment Processing* and *Ticket Issuing*. In general, we define one (sub)service for each value transfer entering or leaving a business actor.

In this EA, these services are implemented in two applications that run on the same server.

We explain the remaining parts of Fig. 1 in the section that follows.

4.3   Representing the Contract Period in ArchiMate

To quantify an ArchiMate model, we need a contract period in ArchiMate too, because the ArchiMate model exists in the same time-frame was the e^3value model. Workloads, investments and expenses will refer to this contract period. We add the contract period to an ArchiMate model simply as a comment.

Just as in e^3value, we can define a sequence of consecutive contract periods, called a *time series*. This is useful for investment analysis, as we will see below. In Fig. 1 the duration of the contract period is 28 days.

4.4 Representing Economic Transactions in ArchiMate

In e^3value an economic transaction is created using *value ports*, *value interfaces* and *value transfers*. Except for value transfers, ArchiMate does not contain equivalent concepts. Therefore it is impossible to represent economic transactions in ArchiMate without extensions.

To solve this, we add the information in an e^3value transaction table to ArchiMate models. In ArchiMate 3.1 one can define attributes for model components [12]. The collection of attributes defined for a component is called a *profile*.

- For each *value object*, we define an attribute of the ArchiMate model. The name of the attribute is the name of the value object. The EA in Fig. 1 has two value objects, *Ticket* and *Payment*.
- Each e^3value transfer corresponds to a flow in the ArchiMate model. For this flow we define a profile consisting of the attributes name, number of occurrences, and a reference to the value object. The two flows in the EA of Fig. 1 have value transfer profiles with attributes VT1, 500 000 occurrences, and value objects *Payment* and *Tickets*.
- Each transaction in e^3value consists of two or more value transfers, where each value transfer is part of a value interface of the two e^3value actors connected by the transfer. The connection points are *ports* in e^3value. In the corresponding EA, ports may be explicitly represented by *business interfaces* or implicitly by the incidence of a flow relation on an actor. This is a design choice of the ArchiMate model designer.
  We define a transaction profile for these business interfaces and actors, consisting of the transaction name, the number of occurrences, and references to the participating transfers. In Fig. 1 transaction Tx1 is defined for the business interface *Web Site* and for the business actor *Travelers*.

Figure 2 illustrates how value objects, value transfers and value transactions are mapped to the ArchiMate model.

4.5 Identification of Additional Performance Requirements

In our approach we identify *performance requirements* derived from the transaction profiles assigned to the business layer elements of the ArchiMate model and the *duration* of the contract period. The transaction profiles imply workload requirements.

The number of transactions in e^3value indicate the number of transactions that happen in a stated contract period, say one year. However, an e^3value model has no notion of time (except the contract period), so it does not model

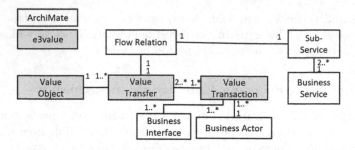

Fig. 2. Relations among e^3value concepts (grey) and ArchiMate concepts (white).

the distribution of transactions over the contract period. However, for technical scalability it is important to know this distribution, and more specifically the maximum number of transactions per second that can happen in the contract period. Therefore we define *peak economic transactions* requirements to represent this. These are additional to the requirements derived from the transaction table. Figure 1 contains a Concurrent Workload requirement as illustration.

In certain cases economic transactions needs to be completed within a time frame where the exchange of value objects is useful for the customer. Therefore, we also define *response time requirements*. This is based on work from IT performance metrics. Service performance is measured with the time it takes to execute a single instance of the service [13]. These are additional too. In Fig. 1 we see that Tx1 has a Response Time requirement.

The workload requirements are propagated from the business layer of ArchiMate over the actors that are needed to realize the business services. The response time requirements are propagated down to the business processes, application services and technology services.

4.6   Introducing Investments and Expenses in ArchiMate

e^3value has three types of quantifications for investment analysis [4]. First, *investments*. Investments are often needed when a new business idea is implemented. They are done in the first contract period of a time series and are subtracted from the revenue generate in that period.

Second, *fixed expenses*. These are the expenses that do not change from period to period, for example maintenance costs of IT systems. Fixed expenses can be specified for value activities, market segments and actors.

Finally *variable expenses*. These are the expenses associated with the execution of a single economic transaction, for example power consumption of IT systems or utilization of cloud services. The more economic transactions there are, the higher the total variable expenses are. Variable expenses are associated with value transfers, through the value ports in e^3value.

ArchiMate [12] has so-called *internal active structure* elements, which are actors that can be hired, bought or built. For these, we define a profile consisting of the attributes *investment* and *fixed expenses*.

For *behavioral* elements (e.g. business processes and application services), we define the attribute *variable expenses*. The amount of these expenses depends on the number of executions of the behavior.

Finally, we define a profile consisting of the attributes *aggregated investments*, *aggregated fixed expenses*, and *aggregated variable expenses* for the ArchiMate business actors and services that correspond to e^3value actors and value activities. The investments in and expenses of the application and technology layers can be aggregated in these profiles and then transferred to the e^3value model. Our main strategy is to collect investments and expenses from an ArchiMate model and insert these into the e^3value model. This strategy is based on the work of Iacob en Jonkers [6]. We will collect investments and expenses in a bottom-up manner and will insert these into an e^3value model through our constructed bridge between the two languages. This approach has been applied on a realistic example in practice and can be found on researchgate[1].

5   Discussion and Future Work

We *have learned* that creating direct traceability between ArchiMate and e^3value is not possible. The economic transactions and their occurrences need to be calculated in e^3value and exported to ArchiMate, but can be accurately mapped to an ArchiMate model. Realizing complete equivalence between ArchiMate and e^3value is not possible. Nor is it desirable. Combining all this information in one model would result in unmanageable models that are hard to understand.

Answering the Research Questions. ArchiMate can represent the economic transactions of e^3value (Q1) by exporting the transaction table into ArchiMate. The transactions are stored in custom profiles and assigned to ArchiMate elements. Performance requirements are identified (Q2) from the economic transactions and propagated down the ArchiMate model. Additionally peak concurrent transactions and response time requirements are identified as well. ArchiMate model elements can be extended (Q3) with a custom profile for investments and expenses and fed back into e^3value (Q4) because we have a custom profile aggregated expenses at the business services. These are mapped to the value activities and value transfers. Since our results are derived from an analysis of the meta-models of e^3value and ArchiMate and refined in experiments and case studies using these languages, we do not expect generalizability beyond these languages.

In order to further test the internal and external validity of our conclusions, we must first implement these techniques in the e^3value tool[2] and an ArchiMate tool. The tools should allow export of quantified transactions from e^3value to ArchiMate, and export of investments and expenses from ArchiMate to e^3value. Using this, we can test our ideas in more cases with different stakeholders and tool users.

---

[1] https://tinyurl.com/4zyvycj3.
[2] https://e3web.thevalueengineers.nl/.

References

1. Derzsi, Z., Gordijn, J., Kok, K., Akkermans, H., Tan, Y.-H.: Assessing feasibility of IT-enabled networked value constellations: a case study in the electricity sector. In: Krogstie, J., Opdahl, A., Sindre, G. (eds.) CAiSE 2007. LNCS, vol. 4495, pp. 66–80. Springer, Heidelberg (2007). https://doi.org/10.1007/978-3-540-72988-4_6
2. Dietz, J.L.G.: Understanding and modelling business processes with DEMO. In: Akoka, J., Bouzeghoub, M., Comyn-Wattiau, I., Métais, E. (eds.) ER 1999. LNCS, vol. 1728, pp. 188–202. Springer, Heidelberg (1999). https://doi.org/10.1007/3-540-47866-3_13
3. Engelsman, W., Gordijn, J., Haaker, T., van Sinderen, M., Wieringa, R.: Traceability from the business value model to the enterprise architecture: a case study. In: Augusto, A., Gill, A., Nurcan, S., Reinhartz-Berger, I., Schmidt, R., Zdravkovic, J. (eds.) BPMDS/EMMSAD -2021. LNBIP, vol. 421, pp. 212–227. Springer, Cham (2021). https://doi.org/10.1007/978-3-030-79186-5_14
4. Gordijn, J., Wieringa, R.: e3valueUser guide. The Value Engineers (2021). https://e3value-user-manual.thevalueengineers.nl/
5. Gordijn, J., Akkermans, J.M.: Value Webs: Understanding E-business Innovation. The Value Engineers (2018). www.thevalueengineers.nl
6. Iacob, M.E., Jonkers, H.: Quantitative analysis of enterprise architectures. In: Konstantas, D., Bourrières, J.P., Léonard, M., Boudjlida, N. (eds.) Interoperability of Enterprise Software and Applications, pp. 239–252. Springer, London (2006). https://doi.org/10.1007/1-84628-152-0_22
7. Iacob, M.E., Meertens, L.O., Jonkers, H., Quartel, D.A.C., Nieuwenhuis, L.J.M., van Sinderen, M.J.: From enterprise architecture to business models and back. Softw. Syst. Model. **13**(3), 1059–1083 (2012). https://doi.org/10.1007/s10270-012-0304-6
8. de Kinderen, S., et al.: Bridging value modelling to ArchiMate via transaction modelling. Softw. Syst. Model. **13**(3), 1043–1057 (2014)
9. Miguens, J., da Silva, M.M., Guerreiro, S.: A viewpoint for integrating costs in enterprise architecture. In: Panetto, H., Debruyne, C., Proper, H.A., Ardagna, C.A., Roman, D., Meersman, R. (eds.) OTM 2018. LNCS, vol. 11229, pp. 481–497. Springer, Cham (2018). https://doi.org/10.1007/978-3-030-02610-3_27
10. Moore, J.F.: The Death of Competition: Leadership and Strategy in the Age of Business Ecosystems. Harper (1996)
11. Osterwalder, A., Pigneur, Y.: Business Model Generation: A Handbook for Visionaries, Game Changers, and Challengers. Wiley, Hoboken (2010)
12. The Open Group. ArchiMate 3.01 Specification. Van Haren Publishing (2017)
13. Traore, I., et al.: Software performance modeling using the UML: a case study. J. Netw. **7**(1), 4 (2012)
14. Wieringa, R.J.: Design Science Methodology for Information Systems and Software Engineering. Springer, Heidelberg (2014)
15. Wieringa, R., et al.: A business ecosystem architecture modeling framework. In: 2019 IEEE 21st Conference on Business Informatics (CBI), vol. 1, pp. 147–156. IEEE (2019)
16. Zachman, J.A.: The concise definition of the Zachman framework (2017). https://www.zachman.com/about-the-zachman-framework

Towards Graph-Based Analysis
of Enterprise Architecture Models

Muhamed Smajevic and Dominik Bork$^{(\boxtimes)}$ (iD)

Business Informatics Group, TU Wien, Vienna, Austria
e11742556@student.tuwien.ac.at, dominik.bork@tuwien.ac.at

Abstract. A core strength of enterprise architecture (EA) models is
their holistic and integrative nature. With ArchiMate, a de-facto industry standard for modeling EAs is available and widely adopted. However,
with the growing complexity of enterprise operations and IT infrastructures, EA models grow in complexity. Research showed that ArchiMate
as a language and the supporting EA tools lack advanced visualization
and analysis functionality. This paper proposes a generic and extensible
framework for transforming EA models into graph structures to enable
the automated analysis of even huge EA models. We show how enterprise architects can benefit from the vast number of graph metrics during decision-making. We also describe the implementation of the Graph-
based Enterprise Architecture Analysis (eGEAA) Cloud platform that
supports the framework. The evaluation of our approach and platform
confirms feasibility and interoperability with third-party tools.

Keywords: Enterprise architecture · Model transformation ·
ArchiMate · Graph theory · Analysis

1 Introduction

Enterprises are complex systems composed of different domains that affect each
other. Describing enterprises holistically is helpful in many aspects like business
and IT alignment. Enterprise Architecture (EA)s represent the high-level view of
different enterprise domains and the connections between them. However, holistic EA models grow in size, thereby hampering manual analysis by enterprise
architects [11]. To mitigate this problem ArchiMate, the de-facto industry standard for EA modeling defines a viewing mechanism where only selected aspects
are considered in one model (i.e., view) and most EA tools provide a repository of EA entities to ease reuse. Still, more advanced support in addressing
the inherent complexity of EA models is required. Although EA modeling is
widely adopted, the analysis of EA models is surprisingly underrepresented in
research so far [3,14]. Only recently, the first proposals emerged aiming to equip
EA modeling by advanced visualization and analysis techniques [4,12,16,20,25].

Automated EA model analysis can mitigate some of the discussed problems
by scaling well and by providing interactive analysis means that extend static

© Springer Nature Switzerland AG 2021
A. Ghose et al. (Eds.): ER 2021, LNCS 13011, pp. 199–209, 2021.
https://doi.org/10.1007/978-3-030-89022-3_17

ones [17]. In this exploratory and applied research, we present a *generic* and *extensible* framework for the transformation of EA models into graph structures that addresses the challenges mentioned at the outset. Thus, we aim to *"extract valuable information from the EA component's relationships to support the analytic process."* [27, p. 1] Once the EA model is transformed into a graph, enterprise architects can apply the plethora of existing algorithms/metrics (e.g., centrality and community detection) and tools to assist in decision making [15]. Our approach is generic in the sense of being realized on the meta-metamodel level (i.e., independent of a particular modeling tool platform) and extensible to ease its adoption for other conceptual modeling languages. We report on the prototypical implementation of our approach and its evaluation in a case study.

With the paper at hand, we aim to address the following research objectives:

RO-1: Development of a generic and extensible framework for the transformation of conceptual models into graph structures.

RO-2: Investigate the benefits of supporting enterprise architects by graph-based analysis.

RO-3: Implementation of an EA graph analysis platform.

This paper unfolds as follows. Foundations of Enterprise Architecture Modeling (EAM) and graph analysis are defined in Sect. 2. Section 3 then introduces our generic framework for transforming conceptual models into graphs. The prototypical implementation of our framework is presented in Sect. 4 and evaluated in Sect. 5. Eventually, concluding remarks are given in Sect. 6.

2 Foundations

2.1 Enterprise Architecture Management

Enterprise Architecture Management (EAM) is broadly defined as *"management practice that establishes, maintains and uses a coherent set of guidelines, architecture principles and governance regimes that provide direction for and practical help with the design and the development of an enterprise's architecture in order to achieve its vision and strategy"* [1]. ArchiMate [18,21] is nowadays one of the most used EA languages in practice. ArchiMate depicts an enterprise in the ArchiMate Framework where the core entities of an enterprise are categorized along two dimensions (layers and aspects). A strength of ArchiMate is its possibility to cover relevant aspects of an enterprise in a holistic, multi-layered, and integrated manner. A shortcoming of ArchiMate is though its limited semantic specificity [23] and the limited processing of the information specified in the models [7]. Consequently, proprietary EAM tools often come with additional functionality realized on top of ArchiMate models to enable model value.

2.2 Graph Analysis

A graph connects two or more entities where entities can be anything like human beings, machines, animals, and variables in literature [22]. In Graph Theory, these entities are considered as *Nodes* while the relationships are considered as *Edges* and their connections form a graph. Graphs can be classified into *directed*, *undirected*, and *mixed* graphs [22]. Analysis of such graphs is a wide research area with many applications in different domains. In the following, we will briefly introduce the two analysis techniques relevant for this paper: *quantitative graph analysis* and *visual analysis*.

Quantitative Graph Theory is defined as a measurement approach to quantify structural information of graphs [10]. In Graph Theory, quantitative measures describe the structural characteristics of graphs instead of characterizing graphs only descriptively [9]. Two well known examples of such measures are *PageRank* and *Betweeness* (cf. [9]). The former algorithm applies the well-known PageRank algorithm for websites to graphs, whereas the latter treats graphs as social networks, aiming to, e.g., identify communities and clans. Many tools exist for graph visualization, all of them providing a rich set of powerful graph layout algorithms (see [13] for an overview). The power of the tools comes with the customizability of the algorithms, e.g., different sizes and colors of nodes and edges based on graph properties or quantitative metrics.

Different formats for storing a graph structure exist. One such format is GraphML. It is XML-based and supports attributes, nodes, edges, and hierarchical ordering of graphs by means of sub-graphs [19].

3   Transforming Enterprise Architectures into Graphs

In order to analyze the EA in a graph-based manner we propose the framework visualized in Fig. 1. In contrast to the related works, this framework is generic and extensible in two ways: First, it builds upon the conceptual models produced by state-of-the-art metamodeling platforms (Ecore and ADOxx), which enables the transformation of any conceptual model created with these platforms into a graph. Second, we transform the conceptual model into GraphML that enables the use of any graph analysis tool provided that it supports the standardized GraphML format. Consequently, our framework bridges powerful modeling (and metamodeling platforms) on the one side with graph analysis tools on the other instead of implementing a solution for an individual modeling language or tool.

As highlighted in Fig. 1, our framework starts on the meta^2-level. The reason behind this is the idea to define a generic transformation on the meta-meta level which can then be further customized at the modeling language level to the specifics of a modeling language. Eventually, the produced GraphML output forms the input for analysis by powerful tools like Neo4j and Gephi. The thick border around some aspects of Fig. 1 highlights the subset of the framework we will discuss in the following. Consequently, we will describe the transformation of Ecore models into GraphML graphs. This focus is a consequence of the limited space available, however, we realized, implemented, and tested the transformation also for ADOxx-based models which further increases the applicability of our generic framework. We evaluated our platform with both, Ecore- and ADOxx-based EA models (see Sect. 5).

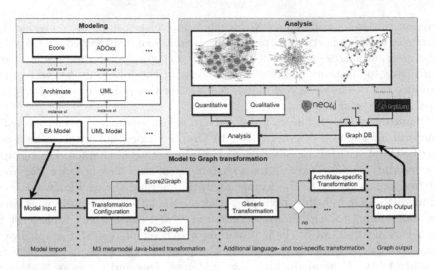

Fig. 1. Generic framework for enterprise architecture models into graphs.

3.1 Generic Model to Graph Transformation

The transformation of EA models created with the Archi modeling tool is decomposed into two parts. First, the generic transformation from Ecore to GraphML is discussed (as Archi is based on Ecore). Thereafter, the specific rules for transforming Archi-based ArchiMate models into GraphML are presented.

The generic rules for transforming Ecore models into GraphML are visualized in Fig. 2 by means of mapping the concepts of the Ecore metamodel to the concepts of the GraphML metamodel. The initial *EPackage* is mapped to *GraphML* while the others are then mapped to *Graph*. Each *EClass* is mapped to *Node* while each *EReference* is mapped to an *Edge* with the *source* and *target* values. All additional information defined by an *EClass* and *EReference* by means of *EAttributes* are transformed to *Data*.

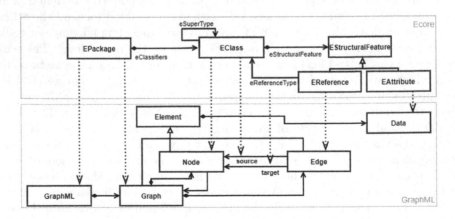

Fig. 2. Generic transformation from Ecore to GraphML.

In the following, some generic Ecore2GraphML transformation rules are overridden to address the specifics of the modeling tool (i.e., Archi) and the modeling language (i.e., ArchiMate (ArchiMate)). The first rule transforms a *Grouping*, *Folder*, or *View* element into a nested *Graph* (instead of creating a Node). All *nested elements* of the Grouping in the ArchiMate model will be added as *Nodes* in the nested graph. Secondly, since Archi stores the ArchiMate relationships as entities (i.e., *IArchimateRelationshipEntitys*), instances of that entity need to be transformed into an *Edge* with additional edge data to store the relationship endpoints.

3.2 Graph-Based Analysis of ArchiMate Models

Once the transformation from ArchiMate models into GraphML is achieved, enterprise architects can analyze the resulting graph structure. Table 1 lists several graph metrics and maps them to exemplary Competency Questions (CQ) an enterprise architect might have, and that can be responded to by that metric. Noteworthy to say is that the GraphML specification opens the door to manifold graph analysis algorithms already implemented in openly available tools.

Table 1. Interpretation of sample graph metrics for ArchiMate models

Graph metric	EA interpretation and exemplary competency question (CQ)
Centralities	
Degree	The higher the value the more edges a node has
	CQ: How many business services are used by one business role?
Closeness	How close is a Node to the other graph components
	CQ: What is the closest switch that can be used to connect two servers?
Betweenness	How important is a Node in connecting different parts of a graph?
	CQ: What is the impact of removing a web server?
Community detection	
Connected Components	For one community there exists a path from each node to another one without considering the direction of the relationship
	CQ: Which connections exist between two network components?
Strongly Connected Components	For one community every node is reachable from every other node when considering the direction of the relationship
	CQ: Can each device in a group exchange information with another one?

4 Implementation

In this section, we report on the prototypical implementation of our framework (see Fig. 1) called extensible Graph-based Enterprise Architecture Analysis (eGEAA). eGEAA is cloud-based, thereby offering the transformation and analysis functionality without the need to install any software. The implementation and the example models can be found in the accompanying repository [5].

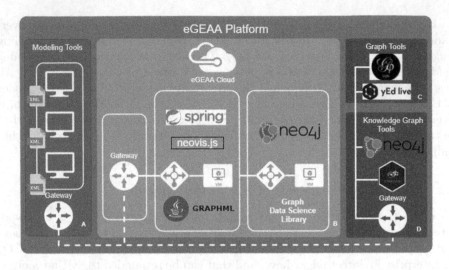

Fig. 3. eGEAA Cloud platform architecture.

The architecture of the eGEAA platform consists of three components (cf. Fig. 3): *Modeling, eGEAA Cloud,* and *Third Party Tools.* In the modeling component, users export the created enterprise architecture models created with any EMF- or ADOxx-based modeling tool in XML format, which serves as the input for the *eGEAA Cloud* component. eGEAA Cloud consists of two virtual machines running the web server and the database, respectively. The web server serves the web application and the model transformation service, while the Neo4j database stores the graph and offers additional functionality. The front-end is realized with the neovis.js [8] library, which provides a rich set of graph visualizations. If further analysis is required, eGEAA Cloud enables the export of the GraphML files, which can then be used as an input for any dedicated graph analysis or Knowledge Graph tools like Gephi, yEd, Neo4j, and Stardog [6]. Due to limited space, in the following, we focus on the core functionality provided by the eGEAA Cloud platform.

Model Transformation & Inspection. The eGEAA Cloud platform offers the functionality to upload an EA model in XML format, transform it into a GraphML-conforming XML format, and inspect both source and transformed model in the browser. Moreover, the created GraphML file can be directly downloaded or accessed via the database reference.

Graph Visualisation & Analysis. The eGEAA Cloud platform enables the customization of the graph visualization in the browser (e.g., size, color, and labels of the graph elements) by providing visualization parameters or executing graph algorithms. eGEAA Cloud provides pre-defined graph centrality and community detection algorithms. When an algorithm is selected, the corresponding Neo4j command is shown, enabling the user to either directly execute or customize it. Eventually, users can define powerful Neo4j queries, directly execute them on the Neo4j database, and investigate the query results in the browser.

Interoperability. eGEAA Cloud provides the reference to the graph in the Neo4j database. This enables a direct connection via the Neo4j Desktop Browser or any third-party graph analysis software for further analysis.

5   Evaluation

In the following, we will report the extent to which the individual research objectives specified in the introduction have been achieved.

RO-1: Generic Transformation Framework. The first research objective is further decomposed into three research objectives, formulated as requirements for the generic transformation: 1. applicability for arbitrary conceptual modeling languages, 2. applicability for models created with different meta-modeling platforms, and 3. enabling the use of third-party tools. In contrast to existing approaches, we thus aim to develop a generic transformation that can be widely applied and that is open for future extensions.

To evaluate to what extent our approach meets RO-1, we used two different EA modeling tools: *Archi*[1] which is based on Ecore and *TEAM* [4] which is ADOxx-based; and three third-party graph analysis tools: Neo4j, Gephi, and yEd. Due to the limited space, we will show selected results for the ArchiMate models. The supplementary material in the Github repository [5] features all evaluation experiments (also comprising different modeling languages).

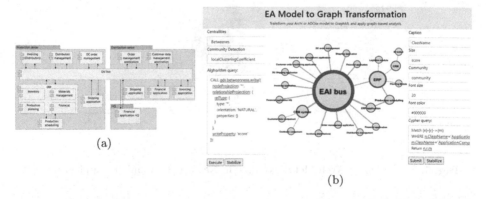

(a)

(b)

Fig. 4. ArchiMetal Application Architecture [2] (left) and User Interface of the eGEAA Cloud platform (right)

As a running example throughout the evaluation we use the publicly available ArchiMetal [2] case (see Fig. 4a). Figure 5 shows the result of importing the

---

[1] Archi modeling tool [online]: https://www.archimatetool.com/.

transformed GraphML specification of the ArchiMetal case in the three third-party tools, thereby providing evidence on the validity of the transformation output. Consequently, we can state that we achieved a generic transformation.

RO-2: Benefits of Graph-based Analysis for EAs. We evaluated the possibility of responding to the previously introduced competency questions (cf. Table 1) using the ArchiMetal example. We exemplify how graph centrality and community detection metrics can be used in the analysis process. Figure 5c exemplary shows the result of applying the Betweenness centrality metric to the ArchiMetal example in the yEd tool. The higher the Betweenness value, the more intense the color and the larger the square. The importance of the *EAI bus* for the application layer can be easily detected when looking at the resulting graph. From a business perspective, this graph-based analysis indicates the severity with which individual components of the application architecture threaten the continuation of business operations.

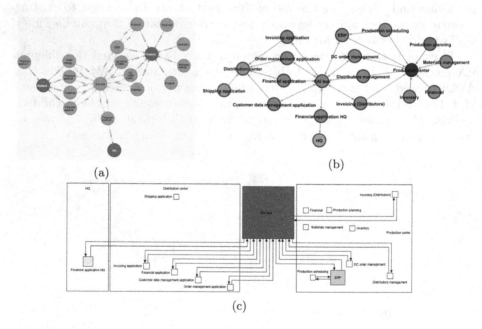

Fig. 5. Transformed ArchiMetal example in Neo4j (a), Gephi (b), and yEd (c)

Exemplary for the community detection metrics, we applied the *Strongly Connected Components* metric on the ArchiMetal example. Figure 5b shows the resulting graph in the Gephi tool. Identified communities are color-coded. Consequently, one can visually grasp that all purple application components belong to the same community, i.e., can communicate with each other. The previous examples showcase the potential of supporting enterprise architects by the application of graph metrics. Much more can be done obviously. However, we believe that eGEAA Cloud can support the community in developing a taxonomy of graph-based analysis of EAs in the future.

RO-3: EA Graph-Based Analysis Platform. Figure 4b shows an overview of the user interface of the eGEAA Cloud platform realizing the architecture defined in Fig. 3. On the top left side, users can select the graph metric they want to apply. The corresponding query is then presented in the text area on the lower left side. Here is where users can customize the pre-defined query before validating and eventually executing it. On the right side, different customization possibilities for graph rendering are provided. On the lower right side, a text field allows the user to easily directly define Cypher queries that will be executed on the corresponding Neo4j database. Eventually, the central area uses the neovis.js package to render the graph. Consequently, we can state that we achieved RO-3.

6   Concluding Remarks

With this paper, we introduced a generic and extensible framework and an open source implementation of the eGEAA Cloud platform [5] for transforming conceptual models into graphs. We instantiated the approach to show, how graph analysis can support enterprise architects in decision making. We used several existing EA models and tools, realized with the two widely used meta-modeling platforms EMF and ADOxx, to evaluate the feasibility of transforming and analyzing EA models.

We hope that this generic contribution raises interest in this promising research field of conceptual model analysis. We don't see this proposal as a means to replace enterprise architects but rather to complement their domain expertise with a more scalable approach [24]. In our future research, we aim to define a taxonomy of graph-based EA analysis metrics and extend our approach to support EA mergers. Transforming two EAs into graphs and applying, e.g., euclidean distance or overlap graph metrics might be handy, especially for large EAs. Future work will also concentrate on qualitative analysis. e.g., by proposing complex queries that span multiple ArchiMate layers like impact analysis or the use of the graph structure to detect EA Smells [26].

References

1. Ahlemann, F., Stettiner, E., Messerschmidt, M., Legner, C.: Strategic Enterprise Architecture Management. Springer, Heidelberg (2012)
2. Archi: Archimetal (2016). https://github.com/archimatetool/ArchiModels/tree/master/ArchiMetal
3. Barbosa, A., Santana, A., Hacks, S., von Stein, N.: A taxonomy for enterprise architecture analysis research. In: 21st International Conference on Enterprise Information Systems, vol. 2, pp. 493–504. SciTePress (2019)
4. Bork, D., et al.: Requirements engineering for model-based enterprise architecture management with ArchiMate. In: Pergl, R., Babkin, E., Lock, R., Malyzhenkov, P., Merunka, V. (eds.) EOMAS 2018. LNBIP, vol. 332, pp. 16–30. Springer, Cham (2018). https://doi.org/10.1007/978-3-030-00787-4_2

5. Bork, D., Smajevic, M.: Companion source code repository of the eGEAA platform (2021). https://github.com/borkdominik/eGEAA
6. Brandes, U., Eiglsperger, M., Lerner, J., Pich, C.: Graph markup language (GraphML). In: Tamassia, R. (ed.) Handbook of Graph Drawing Visualization. Discrete Mathematics and its Applications, pp. 517–541. CRC Press (2013)
7. Buschle, M., Johnson, P., Shahzad, K.: The enterprise architecture analysis tool - support for the predictive, probabilistic architecture modeling framework, pp. 3350–3364 (2013)
8. Contrib, N.: neovis.js (2021). https://github.com/neo4j-contrib/neovis.js
9. Dehmer, M., Emmert-Streib, F., Shi, Y.: Quantitative graph theory: a new branch of graph theory and network science. Inf. Sci. **418–419**, 575–580 (2017)
10. Dehmer, M., Kraus, V., Emmert-Streib, F., Pickl, S.: What is quantitative graph theory?, pp. 1–33, November 2014
11. Florez, H., Sánchez, M., Villalobos, J.: A catalog of automated analysis methods for enterprise models. Springerplus **5**(1), 1–24 (2016). https://doi.org/10.1186/s40064-016-2032-9
12. Gampfer, F., Jürgens, A., Müller, M., Buchkremer, R.: Past, current and future trends in enterprise architecture-a view beyond the horizon. Comput. Ind. **100**, 70–84 (2018)
13. Herman, I., Melancon, G., Marshall, M.S.: Graph visualization and navigation in information visualization: a survey. IEEE Trans. Vis. Comput. Graph. **6**(1), 24–43 (2000). https://doi.org/10.1109/2945.841119
14. Iacob, M.E., Jonkers, H.: Quantitative analysis of enterprise architectures. In: Konstantas, D., Bourrières, J.P., Léonard, M., Boudjlida, N. (eds.) Interoperability of Enterprise Software and Applications, pp. 239–252. Springer, London (2006). https://doi.org/10.1007/1-84628-152-0_22
15. Johnson, P., Ekstedt, M.: Enterprise architecture: models and analyses for information systems decision making. Studentlitteratur (2007)
16. Jugel, D.: An integrative method for decision-making in EA management. In: Zimmermann, A., Schmidt, R., Jain, L.C. (eds.) Architecting the Digital Transformation. ISRL, vol. 188, pp. 289–307. Springer, Cham (2021). https://doi.org/10.1007/978-3-030-49640-1_15
17. Jugel, D., Kehrer, S., Schweda, C.M., Zimmermann, A.: Providing EA decision support for stakeholders by automated analyses. In: Digital Enterprise Computing (DEC 2015), pp. 151–162. GI (2015)
18. Lankhorst, M., et al.: Enterprise Architecture at Work, vol. 352. Springer, Heidelberg (2009)
19. Messina, A.: Overview of standard graph file formats. Technical report, RT-ICAR-PA-2018-06 (2018). http://dx.doi.org/10.13140/RG.2.2.11144.88324
20. Naranjo, D., Sánchez, M., Villalobos, J.: PRIMROSe: a graph-based approach for enterprise architecture analysis. In: Cordeiro, J., Hammoudi, S., Maciaszek, L., Camp, O., Filipe, J. (eds.) ICEIS 2014. LNBIP, vol. 227, pp. 434–452. Springer, Cham (2015). https://doi.org/10.1007/978-3-319-22348-3_24
21. OMG: ArchiMate® 3.1 Specification. The Open Group (2019). http://pubs.opengroup.org/architecture/archimate3-doc/
22. Pachayappan, M., Venkatesakumar, R.: A graph theory based systematic literature network analysis. Theor. Econ. Lett. **8**(05), 960–980 (2018)
23. Pittl, B., Bork, D.: Modeling digital enterprise ecosystems with ArchiMate: a mobility provision case study. In: ICServ 2017. LNCS, vol. 10371, pp. 178–189. Springer, Cham (2017). https://doi.org/10.1007/978-3-319-61240-9_17

24. Potts, M.W., Sartor, P., Johnson, A., Bullock, S.: A network perspective on assessing system architectures: foundations and challenges. Syst. Eng. **22**(6), 485–501 (2019)
25. Roelens, B., Steenacker, W., Poels, G.: Realizing strategic fit within the business architecture: the design of a process-goal alignment modeling and analysis technique. Softw. Syst. Model. **18**(1), 631–662 (2019)
26. Salentin, J., Hacks, S.: Towards a catalog of enterprise architecture smells. In: Gronau, N., Heine, M., Krasnova, H., Poustcchi, K. (eds.) 15. Internationalen Tagung Wirtschaftsinformatik, WI 2020, pp. 276–290. GITO Verlag (2020)
27. Santana, A., Fischbach, K., Moura, H.: Enterprise architecture analysis and network thinking: a literature review. In: 2016 49th Hawaii International Conference on System Sciences (HICSS), pp. 4566–4575. IEEE (2016)

Towards Improvement of IT Service Adoption in Multi-Business Organizations

Fathi Jabarin[1]([⊠])(iD), Alan Hartman[1](iD), Iris Reinhartz-Berger[1]([⊠])(iD), and Doron Kliger[2](iD)

[1] Information Systems Department, University of Haifa, Haifa, Israel
fjabarin@campus.haifa.ac.il, {ahartman,iris}@is.haifa.ac.il
[2] Economics Department, University of Haifa, Haifa, Israel
kliger@econ.haifa.ac.il

Abstract. IT departments in Multi-Business Organizations (MBOs) face challenges when providing services to satisfy business needs. In many cases, the services provided by an IT department do not address all the requirements of the relevant business units and hence are only partially adopted by a subset of units. While existing research on enterprise architecture and service provision focuses on business-IT alignment and optimization of quality or efficiency, our objective is to maximize the number of stakeholders and business units fully adopting the services provided by the IT department. In this paper, we introduce a conceptual model which comprises organizational and IT service-related concepts. With this underlying model, we propose a method for improving the cooperation among IT departments and business units in order to increase the adoption of the most appropriate services taking into account the variation in business unit characteristics and performance indicators. We describe how the analysis and presentation of the information gathered from the stakeholders can support decision makers and advance the adoption goals of the IT department and the whole MBO. We present the results of a case study whose aim is to determine the feasibility of the approach. The case study deals with a business need for scheduling meetings between customers and bankers in a large bank.

Keywords: Service adoption · Multi-business organizations · Service value · Multi-criteria decision making

1 Introduction

Multi-Business Organizations (MBOs) are defined as organizations that consist of several business units providing services, either to external customers, or to other business units. The business units work collaboratively to provide those services.

The type of MBO we focus on has a central IT department which provides services for a variety of business needs. Some of the needs of different units may have common elements, thus the IT department may choose to provide

A. Ghose et al. (Eds.): ER 2021, LNCS 13011, pp. 210–223, 2021.
https://doi.org/10.1007/978-3-030-89022-3_18

a service incorporating some variants, which satisfies the requirements of each of the business units to the greatest extent possible. A major challenge is to develop and maintain such services and their variants, subject to resource or other constraints, and ensuring that most - if not all - relevant business units adopt them.

As an example, consider a bank. Different units of the bank need to set up meetings with existing and potential customers. While the detailed requirements of each unit may differ, the basic functionality and core features of the meeting-setup service share commonalities among the units. As the bank faces resource constraints, the service development inevitably requires compromises by some of the business units, which eventually might choose not to adopt the proposed service. Avoiding adoption of the service may have local effects, negatively affecting the performance of an individual business unit; it may also have global effects, influencing the performance of other business units or even the whole MBO through indicators such as the customer satisfaction index.

To address this challenge, we propose a hybrid conceptual model containing organizational elements (such as business units and performance indicators) as well as IT-related terms (e.g., services and features). We further introduce a decision-support method to assist IT departments in deciding (and convincing business units) which services to adopt. Our approach is value-based, assuming that participation in a service yields some (positive) value to the participants. The adoption of a service is defined as the acceptance of the value proposition by the participants [19].

We evaluated the feasibility of the approach through a case study in a bank. The data for the case study was obtained through in-depth interviews with nine stakeholders interested and/or involved in the operation or use of a meeting scheduling service: the retail division, the financial division, the IT department, upper level management and customers (a potential customer and an actual customer).

The rest of the paper is structured as follows. Section 2 contains a brief review of the relevant literature, while Sects. 3 and 4 present the conceptual model and the decision-support method, respectively. Section 5 presents preliminary results from our case study and discusses threats to validity. Finally, Sect. 6 summarizes and highlights some future research directions.

2   Related Work

Previous studies conceptualize a multi-business organization (MBO) as a complex adaptive system of unique, partially connected agents (the business units) [5,10,13]. Many MBOs do not operate on strictly authoritarian lines, but are actually composed of loosely coupled business units, each of which has a large measure of independence in decision making. Examples are university departments, merged conglomerates, or the totality of public services provided by government departments.

The units in an MBO provide services, both externally to customers and internally to other business units. We adopt the widely accepted definition of a service system [15] - a configuration of people, technologies and other resources that interact with other service systems to create mutual value. The value created by a service system has been widely researched from the earliest monetary definition of value as income minus expenses to the more nuanced notions found in [4,6] or [7]. In [18], the value delivered is modified by less tangible constructs including service quality, service equity (also referred to as service image or service brand equity), confidence benefits, and perceived sacrifice. A framework for ranking of cloud computing services is suggested in [9]. It refers to service response time, sustainability, suitability, accuracy, transparency, interoperability, availability, reliability, stability, cost, adaptability, elasticity, usability, throughput & efficiency, and scalability.

Value creation is also extensively studied in the area of Enterprise Architecture (EA) which aims to offer a high-level overview of an enterprise's business and IT systems and their interrelationships [21]. The use of EA is assumed to result in value for organizations. The systematic literature review in [11] found that the value of EA is related to various aspects of the organization - inter-organizational, internal, strategic, operational, communicational, transformational and more. Supported by a resource-based theory and dynamic capabilities, the authors in [20] argue that EA services lead to benefits through business-driven and IT-driven change opportunities. We aim to contribute to this area of research by explicitly referring to the business units that compose the MBOs and their preferences and performance indicators.

MBOs that have central IT departments face challenges related to the management of conflicting requirements and overcoming IT adoption barriers. The literature suggests different solutions to these challenges, including requirements prioritization [1] and conflict resolution through negotiation [22]. Even when applying such solutions, there are many barriers to the adoption of IT services [2]. These include technological barriers (problems of security, insufficient infrastructure), organizational factors (management style, shortage of financial sources), barriers arising from the surrounding environment (insufficient knowledge of the market), and individual barriers (insufficient knowledge, personal relations in organisation). A recent systematic review [8] suggests guidelines for the adoption of IT and overcoming the barriers to adoption in Small and Medium Enterprises. One of their suggestions is that "decision makers should adopt IT in a formalized way; making IT planning and strategy necessary before implementing IT." Our approach follows this guideline. Moreover, to the best of our knowledge, there is no prior research whose objective is to maximize IT adoption by a group of distinct entities, and this is the focus of our method.

3   The Conceptual Model

Returning to the concept of a service system [6], it can be represented as a graph or hypergraph whose nodes represent business units and (hyper) edges represent service interactions between business units. An edge in such a representation indicates a binary service (between a provider and a consumer). More generally, a hyperedge of cardinality k represents a service with k mutually dependent participants [14]. Our model refines this by separating between concepts related to the external organization view (the service system) and those related to the internal IT view while exposing the concepts that bridge between these views (see Fig. 1).

The organization view includes two main concepts: business unit (*BU*) and performance indicator (*PI*). We define a *business unit* in its widest form: any group of stakeholders with similar or mutual goals and expectations from a given point of view. Customers, bankers, management, and the IT department. Business units may be further refined into sub-business units (e.g., VIP customers, old customers, Board of Directors, unit managers, and so on). Each business unit may be evaluated using different *performance indicators* - measures for evaluating the success of an organization or of a particular business unit [3]. We assume that each performance indicator is a scalar and, without loss of generality, may be presented such that higher values/levels are better than lower ones. The performance indicators may be prioritized differently by the business units (e.g., ranging from irrelevant to very high priority, represented in the model by *PriPI*).

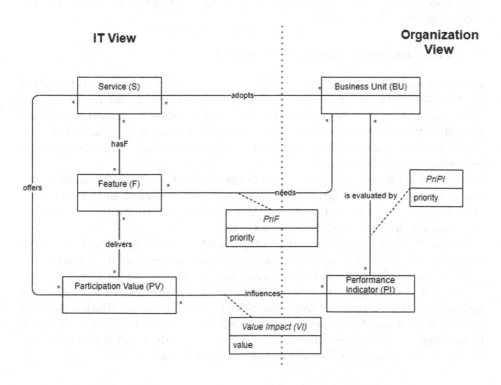

Fig. 1. The suggested conceptual, value-based model

Focusing on a specific business need, we discuss two IT-related concepts: services and features. A *service*, defined as the application of resources for the benefit of another [15], has different *features* - prominent or distinctive user-visible aspects, qualities, or characteristics (adapted from [12]). A service may or may not implement a particular feature (represented in the model by the relation *HasF*). Furthermore, a service offers a range of *participation values* (*PV*), namely values which the participants may gain from using the service. Those participation values are delivered by the service features.

The organization and IT views connect to each other through different relations. Primarily, business units adopt services with certain features in order to satisfy their business needs while improving their performance based on the values delivered by the features. Features are needed by the business units at varying levels of priority (represented in the model as *PriF*). Participation values (e.g., economic value or less tangible but equally important values like service quality, service equity, confidence benefits, and perceived sacrifice [18]) influence the performance indicators by a value impact factor represented in the model by the relation *VI*.

The next section describes the use of this conceptual model in supporting the IT department and other business units to make decisions that maximize service adoption in the MBO.

4   The Decision-Support Method

Based on the above model, we propose a three-phase decision-support method for formulating the value offered by adopting IT services. In the first phase, the IT department gathers information concerning the desired features of the service, the values that they offer and their expected influence on the performance of each of the business units. This can be done through a holistic co-creation process involving all stakeholders [17].

The second phase involves analysis of the information obtained and the computation of a set of summaries to be presented to the business units, in the form of radial diagrams that compare the feasible alternatives with respect to their expected impact on each of the business units.

In the third and final phase, the business units receive the method outcomes, including the different factors that lead to the recommended solution and discuss adoption strategies of the selected service to solve their business need.

We now elaborate on the two first phases, using a meeting scheduling service in a bank as the running example. The third phase requires negotiation and may require utilization of external interfering techniques and tools. Hence, it is out of the scope of this paper and future research in this direction is planned (e.g., exploring solutions from the field of behavioral economics).

4.1   The Value-Based IT Service Adoption Model

Following the conceptualization so far, we define a *value-based IT service adoption model* as follows.

Definition 1. *A value-based IT service adoption model of an MBO is a tuple (BU, PI, PriPI, S, F, HasF, PriF, PV, Dlv, VI), where:*

- *BU is the set of relevant business units in the MBO.*
- *PI is the set of performance indicators used to evaluate the different business units.*
- *PriPI : $BU \times PI \to [0, 1]$ is a mapping with a range of 0 to 100%, indicating how business units prioritize their performance indicators; we will represent the mapping as a matrix of dimensions $|BU| \times |PI|$ indexed by members of the sets BU and PI with $PriPI[b, p] = PriPI(b, p)$ for each business unit $b \in BU$ and performance indicator $p \in PI$.*
- *S is the set of services proposed by the IT department.*
- *F is the set of relevant features of the set of services S.*
- *HasF : $S \times F \to \{0, 1\}$ is the incidence function of services and the features they implement; the notation HasF will also be used for the $|S| \times |F|$ matrix representation of the mapping.*
- *PriF : $BU \times F \to [0, 1]$ is a mapping with a range of 0 to 100%, indicating how business units prioritize the features in F; the notation PriF will also be used for the $|BU| \times |F|$ matrix representation of the mapping.*
- *PV is the set of participation values delivered by the features in F.*
- *Dlv : $F \times PV \to \{0, 1\}$ is the incidence function of features and the participation values that they deliver; Dlv will also refer to the matrix representation of the mapping.*
- *VI : $PV \times PI \to \mathbb{R}^+$ is a mapping indicating how participation values impact the performance indicators; VI will also refer to the matrix representation of the mapping.*

In our running example, we assume five business units and eleven performance indicators for their evaluation:

$$BU = \{Cst, Mng, IT, Ret, Fin\}$$

where Cst, Mng, IT, Ret, Fin represent the Customers, Management, IT, Retail Division and Financial Division, respectively.

$$PI = \{CSAT, FCC, CRR, DIFOT, SS, QI, ROI, MGR, CONV, ESI, CPROF\}$$

where CSAT is the customer satisfaction index, FCC is the frequency of customer complaints, CRR is the customer retention rate, DIFOT is the full delivery on time rate, SS is the six sigma level, QI is the quality index, ROI is the return on investment, MGR is the market growth rate, CONV is the conversion rate of potential customers into actual customers, ESI is the employee satisfaction index and CPROF is the customer profitability [16]. Explanations on the selection of these performance indicators for the chosen business units in the context of our case study are provided in Sect. 5.

Some performance indicators may be more relevant to a particular business units and some are less important. For example, $PriPI(IT, MGR)$ should be low (close to 0), since market growth rate is of little relevance to the IT department, whereas $PriPI(IT, DIFOT)$ is expected to be high (close to 1), since this is a key measurement of the IT department, imposed by the need to supply quality solutions on time.

The services alternatives in our running example may have five features relevant to the given business need:

$$F = \{Rem, Team, Rep, Self, TFS\}$$

where Rem stands for appointment reminders, Team - for team scheduling, Rep - for automated reporting, Self - for online self-scheduling and TFS - for 24/7 Access. Discussion of these features and their relevance to the MBO and its units is provided in Sect. 5, in the context of the case study.

The features are prioritized differently by the different business units, according to their needs and goals. For example, $PriF(Mng, Rem)$ should be low, since the management is less concerned with the details of daily operations. However, $PriF(Mng, Rep)$ is expected to be high since the reporting capability directly enables management to monitor and control the employees.

Those services, and particularly the features we focus on, may deliver different participation values relevant to the bank and its stakeholders. We concentrate here on eight participation values inspired from [9]: Efficiency, Reliability, Usability, Elasticity, Interoperability, Availability, Accessibility, and Service Response Time. These are abbreviated as follows.

$$PV = \{Eff, Rel, Use, Ela, IOP, Avl, Acc, SRT\}$$

The contents of the Dlv matrix are exemplified by the observation that the feature online self scheduling $Self$ delivers the following values $\{Eff, Use, Ela, IOP, Avl, Acc, SRT\}$ whereas it fails to deliver reliability due to the nature of human fallibility.

Examples of the impact of participation value on performance indicators are: $VI(SRT, CSI)$ is assessed as high, since the service response time is a key contributor to customer satisfaction, whereas $VI(IOP, ROI)$ is assessed as low since the cost of interoperability does not justify its impact on the organization.

4.2 Transformation and Analysis

Since we aim to maximize service adoption by the business units, the model can be used to generate the impact of the various service alternatives (different combinations of features). Accordingly, we define two types of outcomes: IT-driven and BU-driven.

Definition 2. *An IT-driven outcome represents the impact of the participation values of the proposed services on the MBO performance indicators. It is computed as:*

$$HasF \otimes Dlv \otimes VI$$

where $\otimes$ indicates matrix multiplication.

Definition 3. *A BU-driven outcome represents the values offered by the proposed services to each business unit, taking into account the priorities of the BU for specific features and performance indicators. This is computed by*

$$HasF \otimes PriF^T \otimes PriPI$$

where $PriF^T$ is the transpose of the matrix $PriF$.

These outputs are presented to the stakeholders as radial axis plots. The radial axes represent the different performance indicators and each proposed service is represented as a polygon. An example of a possible IT-driven outcome for our running example is shown in Fig. 2. As can be seen, the differences between services may be negligible, but there is slight tendency to prefer Services $S1$ and $S3$ over the others.

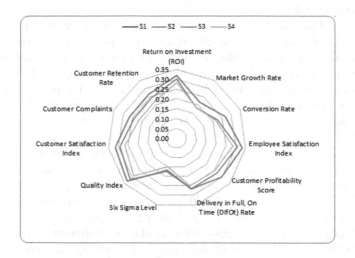

Fig. 2. An example of an IT-driven outcome

The BU-driven outcome is intended to predict the motivation to adopt the services by each of the business units and will serve as a tool for the IT department and top-level management to balance between the features and incentives offered to each business unit in order to maximize the number of business units adopting a particular service. We next evaluate these claims in a case study.

5   Preliminary Results on a Case Study

Our case study was performed in a large Israeli commercial bank. The bank serves about one million customers with over 100 branches and contact points. It offers a range of banking and financial services for private, business and institutional customers, including investment, financing and consulting.

The bank is interested in improving the efficiency and effectiveness of its relations with customers and minimizing the frustration of bankers and loss of productivity due to last-minute cancellation of meetings. The IT department was tasked with proposing a solution to this issue using a meeting scheduling application. Below we exemplify how our approach supports decision making in this context, with the aim of maximal adoption by the involved stakeholders. We also refer to potential threats to validity.

5.1 The Organization View

The meeting scheduling application mainly involves stakeholders from four internal business units: Retail Division, Financial Division, IT Department and Management; it also directly involves the bank's customers. These business units are evaluated through the eleven aforementioned performance indicators (listed in [16]) as detailed below.

The Retail Division serves most of the bank's customers and employs most of its bankers. Its activities are directed at private customers and small and medium-sized businesses. It offers them credit solutions, mortgages and small-scale investments. As a main touch-point with customers, the Retail Division is expected to use the meeting scheduling application to improve its services to customers, increase bankers' time efficiency and address performance indicators including the customer satisfaction index and the frequency of customer complaints.

The Financial Division provides service to institutional customers and offers solutions in the form of financing large projects, large investments and brokerage. The meeting scheduling application is intended to improve the availability of service to large customers and address performance indicators including the customer satisfaction index and the customer retention rate.

The IT Department is responsible for developing, delivering and maintaining IT services for all units. It is fully responsible for the meeting scheduling application as a developer, providing long term maintenance and internal support for users. Among the main performance indicators of the IT Department we consider full delivery on time (DIfOt) rate, six sigma level (namely, the process capability of delivering error-free work) and quality index (i.e., an aggregated measure relating performance indicators to fitness for purpose).

The Management is the central actor making strategic and policy decisions that may impact the development of a meeting scheduling application. The management sets performance indicators for the subordinate units in some cases, especially when it comes to a strategic issue like improving the customer experience. It also has performance indicators itself such as return on investment (ROI), market growth rate, conversion rate of potential customers into actual customers, employee satisfaction index and customer profitability.

Finally, in our case study, the customers are the only stakeholder group which is external to the bank, and do not actively make decisions about the service before its implementation. However, the meeting scheduling application is designed for customers to use, so they should be a key factor in the decision making process and in determining the required features of the application. Although customers do not have their own performance indicators from an organizational point of view, there are performance indicators that measure the customers and their interactions with the bank, such as the customer satisfaction index and the frequency of customer complaints.

5.2   The IT View

Possible features of the meeting scheduling application are appointment reminders, team scheduling, automated reporting, online self-scheduling and 24/7 Access. These features are common in meeting scheduling applications and are prioritized differently by each of the business units. The source of these preferences are related to the value that each feature delivers when using the service [9], and the influence that this value has on the performance indicators relevant to the business unit.

Appointment reminders are important to the Retail Division and Financial Division and also for Customers. These reminders can improve the ratio of meetings held to meetings scheduled, improving time utilization and facilitating timely schedule changes when needed. This feature is expected to deliver participation value in the form of efficiency and reliability.

The Team Scheduling feature is important to the Retail Division, as most of the bankers who schedule a meeting work in teams. The feature enables backup between team members and vacations without compromising service levels. Team scheduling delivers value in the form of usability and elasticity.

The Automated Reporting feature is important to Management giving tools and reports to decision makers, optimizing the data collection and analysis process, and indicating points of failure and possible improvements. Automated Reporting delivers values of interoperability and accuracy.

The Online Self-Scheduling feature is important to the Retail Division, the Financial Division and also for Customers. It allows resource saving and increase of customer satisfaction (for many customer segments) by providing a remote service independent of other service participants. The main participation values of this feature are availability, usability and accessibility.

The last feature, 24/7 Access, is important to Customers, allowing them flexibility in service. This feature delivers participation values and availability and service response time.

We considered four possible service configurations, whose features are presented in Table 1. The columns of the table represent the features.

5.3   Decision Making Support

As already noted, nine stakeholders from the different business units were interviewed regarding their needs and preferences. Based on the interview outcomes, values were assigned for the different parameters of the model, ranging from 1 (completely disagree) to 5 (completely agree).

Table 1. Examined Services

Service	Rem	Team	Rep	Self	24/7	Comments
Service 1	0	0	0	1	1	Focuses on online support and partially neglects organizational needs
Service 2	0	1	1	0	0	Focuses on the organizational needs, does not offer online support
Service 3	0	1	0	0	1	Focuses on team work and accessibility
Service 4	1	0	0	0	1	Focuses on reminders and accessibility

The BU-driven results are shown in Fig. 3. It presents the influence on performance indicators for each service, taking into consideration the prioritization of both PIs and features by the individual business units. As shown, and in contrast with the IT-driven view depicted in Fig. 2, there is no service that dominates all others with respect to all performance indicators. However, it is clear that there are services which dominate others across the board (Service 2 and Service 3). Service 1 highlights the Customer Complaints and the Customer Satisfaction PIs, supporting the fact that it is a customer-centric service that focuses on online services and ignores organizational needs as noted in Table 1. Service 2, on the other hand, focuses on organizational needs, highlighting the Return on Investment (ROI) and Customer Profitability PIs.

Both Service 2 and Service 3 provide salient advantages, and the choice between them will be made based on strategy and organizational needs. At the same time, it is not inconceivable that the organization will choose another alternative to balance its various needs or choose a path that will not prefer a certain PI over another PI.

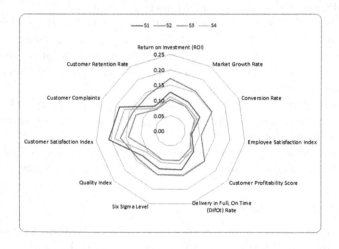

Fig. 3. An example of a BU-driven outcome

The approach can be further extended to show additional outcomes from different perspectives. Figure 4, for example, presents an outcome which relates services to business units, according to feature preferences ($PriF$). Service 1 and Service 4 are the best solutions for Customers, while Service 2 is better for Management and the Retail Division. In our holistic value-based approach, the selection of a service is not exclusively the province of Management or IT. In many cases, the most appropriate service for Management is the one that brings the greatest financial benefit and the most appropriate service for IT is the service that is easy to develop and maintain. Our approach formally introduces additional considerations into the organizational decision making process such as the preferences of customers, employees and other stakeholders.

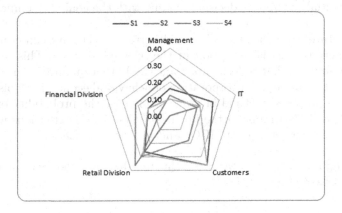

Fig. 4. An additional BU-driven outcome, highlighting the individual business units

5.4   Threats to Validity

The evaluation of our approach was performed using a case study based on in-depth interviews of the bank's stakeholders in a meeting scheduling application. One of the main threats to validity is the fact that the bank employees representing different stakeholders all work in the same bank, and may share similar views because of a particular organizational culture or because of a particular recruitment profile. Moreover, the case study took place in a specific MBO and referred to a specific IT service. There are many types of MBOs, some are conservative and some are technology-minded, and hence we intend to extend the evaluation of the approach in further case studies performed in MBOs with different characteristics and with respect to different kinds of services.

Another threat to validity is the size of the model: we interviewed a small number of stakeholders and considered small numbers of characteristics (features, PIs, participation values and so on). To create some uniformity of the interviewees' responses, we mapped them to a 5 point Likert scale. Evaluating our approach in larger settings with direct inputs from a larger number of stakeholders is planned, especially to assess the scalability of the approach.

6   Summary and Future Research

We have developed a value-based approach for improving IT service adoption in Multi-Business Organizations (MBOs). The approach relies on a model that brings together organizational and IT concepts and bridges between them through the concepts of *participation value (PV)* and *value impact (VI)*. The approach generates two types of outcomes: IT-driven and BU-driven. The IT-driven outcome juxtaposes the service's features with the participation values they generate and their impact on the performance of the organization. The BU-driven outcome factors in both the business units' preferences for service features and also the BU-specific performance indicators (PI).

A case study in a large Israeli bank indicates that the approach is feasible and has the potential to support decision making with the goal of maximal adoption of services.

In the future we intend to utilize multi-criteria decision making methods to better support the actual adoption of the selected services. This may require introducing weights that reflect importance and other qualitative measures. We further plan to explore the incorporation of behavioral economics tools and techniques to the proposed method in order to increase the probability of adoption of a consensus decision among the business units. These extensions will require evaluation in larger settings of MBOs and variety of services.

Acknowledgments. This research is supported by the Israel Science Foundation under grant agreements 1065/19.

References

1. Achimugu, P., Selamat, A., Ibrahim, R., Mahrin, M.N.R.: A systematic literature review of software requirements prioritization research. Inf. Softw. Technol. **56**(6), 568–585 (2014)
2. Antlová, K.: Motivation and barriers of ICT adaptation in small and medium-size enterprises (2009)
3. Antony, J.: Six sigma for service processes. Bus. Process. Manag. J. **12**(2), 234–248 (2006)
4. Banavar, G., Hartman, A., Ramaswamy, L., Zherebtsov, A.: A formal model of service delivery. In: Maglio, P., Kieliszewski, C., Spohrer, J. (eds.) Handbook of Service Science. SSRI, pp. 481–507. Springer, Boston (2010). https://doi.org/10.1007/978-1-4419-1628-0_21
5. Brown, S.L., Eisenhardt, K.M.: Competing on the Edge: Strategy as Structured Chaos. Harvard Business School Press, Boston (1998)
6. Caswell, N.S., Nikolaou, C., Sairamesh, J., Bitsaki, M., Koutras, G.D., Iacovidis, G.: Estimating value in service systems: a case study of a repair service system. IBM Syst. J. **47**(1), 87–100 (2008)
7. Chen, C.F., Wang, J.P.: Customer participation, value co-creation and customer loyalty-a case of airline online check-in system. Comput. Hum. Behav. **62**, 346–352 (2016)

8. Chouki, M., Talea, M., Okar, C., Chroqui, R.: Barriers to information technology adoption within small and medium enterprises: a systematic literature review. Int. J. Innov. Technol. Manag. **17**(01), 2050007 (2020)

9. Garg, S.K., Versteeg, S., Buyya, R.: A framework for ranking of cloud computing services. Futur. Gener. Comput. Syst. **29**(4), 1012–1023 (2013)

10. Gilbert, C.G.: Unbundling the structure of inertia: resource versus routine rigidity. Acad. Manag. J. **48**, 741–763 (2005)

11. Gong, Y., Janssen, M.: The value of and myths about enterprise architecture. Int. J. Inf. Manag. **46**, 1–9 (2019)

12. Kang, K.C., Cohen, S.G., Hess, J.A., Novak, W.E., Peterson, A.S.: Feature-oriented domain analysis (FODA) feasibility study. Carnegie-Mellon University Pittsburgh, PA, Software Engineering Institute (1990)

13. Karim, S.: Modularity in organizational structure: the reconfiguration of internally developed and acquired business units. Strateg. Manag. J. **27**, 799–823 (2006)

14. Kowalkowski, C., Kindström, D., Carlborg, P.: Triadic value propositions: when it takes more than two to tango. Serv. Sci. **8**(3), 282–299 (2016)

15. Maglio, P.P., Vargo, S.L., Caswell, N., Spohrer, J.: The service system is the basic abstraction of service science. IseB **7**(4), 395–406 (2009)

16. Marr, B.: Key Performance Indicators (KPI): The 75 Measures Every Manager Needs to Know. Pearson (2012)

17. Payne, A.F., Storbacka, K., Frow, P.: Managing the co-creation of value. J. Acad. Mark. Sci. **36**(1), 83–96 (2008)

18. Ruiz, D.M., Gremler, D.D., Washburn, J.H., Carrión, G.C.: Service value revisited: specifying a higher-order, formative measure. J. Bus. Res. **61**(12), 1278–1291 (2008)

19. Sales, T.P., Guarino, N., Guizzardi, G., Mylopoulos, J.: An ontological analysis of value propositions. In: 2017 IEEE 21st International Enterprise Distributed Object Computing Conference (EDOC), pp. 184–193. IEEE, October 2017

20. Shanks, G., Gloet, M., Someh, I.A., Frampton, K., Tamm, T.: Achieving benefits with enterprise architecture. J. Strateg. Inf. Syst. **27**(2), 139–156 (2018)

21. Tamm, T., Seddon, P.B., Shanks, G., Reynolds, P.: How does enterprise architecture add value to organisations? Commun. Assoc. Inf. Syst. **28**(1), 10 (2011)

22. Tito, L., Estebanez, A., Magdaleno, A.M., de Oliveira, D., Kalinowski, M.: A systematic mapping of software requirements negotiation techniques. In: ICEIS (2), pp. 518–525 (2017)

Goals and Requirements

Goal-Oriented Models for Teaching and Understanding Data Structures

Xavier Franch[1] and Marcela Ruiz[2](✉)

[1] Universitat Politècnica de Catalunya, Barcelona, Spain
franch@essi.upc.edu
[2] Zürich University of Applied Sciences, Winterthur, Switzerland
marcela.ruiz@zhaw.ch

Abstract. Most computer science curricula include a compulsory course on data structures. Students are prone to memorise facts about data structures instead of understanding the essence of underlying concepts. This can be explained by the fact that learning the basics of each data structure, the difference with each other, and the adequacy of each of them to the most appropriate context of use, is far from trivial. This paper explores the idea of providing adequate levels of abstractions to describe data structures from an intentional point of view. Our hypothesis is that adopting a goal-oriented perspective could emphasise the main goals of each data structure, its qualities, and its relationships with the potential context of use. Following this hypothesis, in this paper we present the use of iStar2.0 to teach and understand data structures. We conducted a comparative quasi-experiment with undergraduate students to evaluate the effectiveness of the approach. Significant results show the great potential of goal modeling for teaching technical courses like data structures. We conclude this paper by reflecting on further teaching and conceptual modeling research to be conducted in this field.

Keywords: Goal-oriented models · iStar2.0 · *i** · Data structures · Software selection · Comparative quasi-experiment

1 Introduction

Data structures (DS for short) are a programming concept that emerged in the early 70s as standardized solutions to the need of storing and manipulating data elements according to some particular requirements [19]. In spite of the profound changes that the computing discipline has experienced since then, DS still play a crucial role in programming. Fundamental DS such as lists and hash tables are in use in a myriad of contexts, from classical problems such as compiler construction or networking [21], to emerging domains such as blockchain [17]. In addition, new DS emerge to respond to specific challenges, e.g., compact DS [31] for storing large quantities of data, or concurrent DS [25] used in programs running on server machines with hundreds of cores.

As a result, most (if not all) computer science curricula include a compulsory course on DS to ensure that students acquire the necessary knowledge and skills on the topic.

© Springer Nature Switzerland AG 2021
A. Ghose et al. (Eds.): ER 2021, LNCS 13011, pp. 227–241, 2021.
https://doi.org/10.1007/978-3-030-89022-3_19

However, teaching DS and conversely, from the students' point of view, learning the basics of each DS, the difference with each other, and the adequacy of a DS to a context of use, is far from trivial. On the one hand, student difficulties with DS span over comprehension of recursive programs, analysis, identification, and implementation of basic DS [29, 38]. On the other hand, students are prone to memorize facts about DS instead of understanding the essence of the underlying concepts [38].

One possible solution to provide an adequate level of abstraction to the description of DS is to adopt an intentional viewpoint [37] for their teaching and study. This way, the emphasis is shifted towards understanding the main goals of every DS, what are their qualities, and relationships with their context of use.

Aligning with this vision, we explore in this paper the use of goal-oriented models [7] for describing DS. To this end, we propose an extension of the iStar2.0 language [6] as the basis for building these models and we evaluate the effectiveness of the approach through a quasi-experiment with students. We show that a group of students who studied DS specified with the iStar2.0 language is significantly more effective when analysing DS in contrast to a control group that studied DS without iStar2.0.

The rest of the paper is organized as follows. Section 2 describes the background of this research and related work. Section 3 states the problem context and the main research question of our research. Section 4 introduces iStarDust, an extension to iStar2.0 for DS. Section 5 describes the design and results from a controlled quasi-experiment conducted with a group of 2nd year computer science students of an algorithms and DS course. Finally, in Sect. 6 we summarise the main conclusions and future work.

2   Background and Related Work

2.1   DS as Implementations of Abstract Data Types

As commented above, DS emerged at the early 70s, at the same time as the related concept of abstract data type (ADT) [13]. ADTs provide a high-level specification of a DS, declaring its operations and the properties that they fulfil. ADTs are implemented using DS which remain hidden to the client of the ADT. In the context of programming with ADTs [24], two questions arise:

1) Which is the most appropriate ADT according to some functional characteristics? Typical ADTs are lists, mappings, graphs and trees.
2) What is the DS that best implements the chosen ADT according to some quality requirements? DS differ mainly in efficiency both in time (of their operations) and space (to store its elements).

Along time, there were a number of proposals either defining new languages with specific constructs for manipulating ADTs and DS, like CLU [23] and SETL [33], or annotation systems like NoFun [3]. Both types of proposals supported the declaration of main characteristics of DS (like their efficiency) and requirements from the program looking for the most appropriate implementation. While they provided some support to the problem of DS selection, their constructs were at the programming level and made their use cumbersome when a more lightweight approach suffices, e.g. to summarize the main characteristics of the DS in a teaching context. This motivates the use of a higher-level notation as $i*$.

2.2 $i*$ as a Conceptual Tool for Software Analysis

The $i*$ language has been primarily used for strategic reasoning in the context of socio-technical systems that include human-related actors (people, organizations, etc.) [37]. However, a line of research has focused on using $i*$ as a conceptual tool for software analysis. The common characteristic of these works is the predominant role that software elements, represented as actors, play in the model, in contrast to human-related actors, which are less significant (or even are not represented in the models).

There are several proposals using $i*$ for software analysis. Some researchers propose $i*$ models as a representation of software architectures [14, 35]: software components are modelled as actors and their connections represent expectations from one component to another (e.g., a goal to be fulfilled, a file to be delivered, an API to be provided). In a similar vein, other works use $i*$ to model or reason about product lines [1], service-oriented systems [8] and systems in domains like IoT [1] or business intelligence [20]. These proposals made use of $i*$ constructs in a particular way (e.g., importance of $i*$ positions to represent components that cover different roles), and relied on softgoals to represent software quality (inside actors) or quality requirements (as dependencies).

In our paper, we are primarily interested in the use of $i*$ to support software package selection [11], considering DS as the software to be selected. We explored this objective in a short paper presented at the iStar'20 workshop [12]. The current paper extends this preliminary contribution in several directions. On the one hand, the proposal is formulated following a well-defined methodology for extending $i*$ that includes a systematic analysis of requirements and needs for the extension, and the inclusion of the new proposed constructs in the $i*$ metamodel. On the other hand, it includes a preliminary evaluation of the proposal by means of a controlled quasi-experiment.

2.3 Teaching DS

Students suffer from misconceptions during their learning process [4], whose existence needs to be identified and mitigated to continuously improve a subject matter. In the computing science discipline, several works have focused on misconceptions related to introductory programming [27], while for more specialized topics like DS, contributions are scarce, but indeed still exist, as enumerated below.

Some researchers have focused on particular DS, e.g., misconceptions on heaps [34] or in binary search trees and hash tables [18]. In our paper, we take a more general viewpoint and target DS in general, looking for a framework that can be customized or extended to any set of DS.

In 2018, Zingaro et al. [38] reported a multi-method empirical study about the difficulties that students have on understanding DS. After a round of think-aloud interviews to gather a series of questions to elicit barriers to understanding, the authors ran a final exam study session containing 7 questions for a Java-based CS2 course on DS. While the results of this paper are highly interesting, the study was explorative in nature and focuses on highlight students difficulties; in contrast, our paper seeks for a constructive solution proposing a concrete framework to improve students' DS understanding and effectiveness, and provides empirical data to elucidate potential benefits in helping students to achieve intended learning goals.

3   Problem Scope

The goal of this paper can be stated as: to **analyse** $i*$ **for the purpose of** *teaching and learning DS* **with respect to** *functional and non-functional requirements* **from the point of view of** *educators and students* **in the context of** *software development.* In order to make this goal more concrete, we have taken the following decisions:

- We select iStar2.0 [6] as the language used to formulate $i*$ models. The reason is that iStar2.0 has been proposed as a standard di facto in the $i*$ community with the purpose of having an agreed definition of the language core constructs.
- We follow the PRISE method [15] to extend iStar2.0 with constructs that fit the goal. For space reasons, in this paper the reporting of the method application is kept at the level of main steps (sub-processes) and focusing on the essential tasks and artifacts.
- We select as DS a typical subset that is taught in a DS introductory course in a computer science syllabus, namely sequences and tables, well-documented in a number of classical textbooks [5, 10].

From this goal and these decisions, we derive the following research questions:

RQ1: What extensions can be applied over iStar 2.0 to make it suitable to describe DS? Following PRISE [15], we will identify the constructs needed to make iStar2.0 suitable to the DS domain. We will identify the needs, conceptualize the solution, and extend the iStar2.0 metamodel [6].

RQ2: When the subjects study DS specified with iStar2.0, is their performance in describing DS affected? To answer this question, we compare completeness and validity of described DS by subjects that have studied DS specified with iStar; to a control group that has studied DS specified in the traditional way (without iStar2.0).

4   iStarDust: iStar2.0 for DS

In this section, we show the application of PRISE to the domain of DS in order to answer RQ1. We call iStarDust (arguably, quasi-acronym of *iStar2.0 for DS*) the resulting language extension. We focus on the first three PRISE steps, because: Step 4 is evaluation of the extension, which deserves a full section in this paper (Sect. 5); Step 5 provides a sense of iteration which is in fact embedded in our way of working; Step 6 consists of reporting and publicizing the results, which turns out to be this very paper.

4.1 Analyse the Need for an Extension

PRISE first step checks whether an extension of iStar2.0 is really needed. It may certainly happen that the iStar2.0 constructs suffice to represent the concepts that we need. We list below the requirements that make iStar2.0 fall short to support DS description:

- **Req1.** *The language should allow relating specification and implementation of DS.* As explained in Sect. 2, we distinguish among the specification of a DS (i.e., the ADT it represents) and the implementation of a DS (i.e., the code used to implement the operations). We need to keep this relation explicit in order to accurately describe the DS. The current actors, and association among actors, that iStar2.0 includes, do not allow representing this concept.
- **Req2.** *The language should allow to encapsulate intentional descriptions.* DS are modular in nature. They become integrated into software programs as building blocks. In fact, they are normally reused from some existing software library. The original iStar2.0 does not provide such encapsulation mechanisms, beyond the notion of actor, which is not enough for our purposes.
- **Req3.** *The language should allow representing similarities among DS.* Typical DS are organized following a hierarchical structure to keep similarities among them. For instance, sequences are a category of DS, including stacks, queues and lists. At their turn, lists can be sub-categorized (at least) in one-direction lists and bi-directional lists (depending on the type of traversals they support). Likewise, there are several variations of hash tables that share a number of commonalities. iStar2.0 does not include a concept for representing such hierarchies.

These requirements yield to the concepts to be included in iStarDust extending iStar2.0:

- **Conc1.** Specification and implementation of a DS
- **Conc2.** Relationship among specification and implementation of a DS
- **Conc3.** Encapsulation of specifications and implementations of DS
- **Conc4.** Hierarchical organization of specifications & implementations of similar DS.

4.2 Describe Concepts of the iStar2.0 Extension

Following PRISE recommendations, we first searched in the available *i** literature for constructs already proposed, and found **Const1** and **Const3** (see below). In addition, we proposed an additional construct (**Const2**) to cover a missing concept. Figure 1 shows the mapping between concepts and constructs.

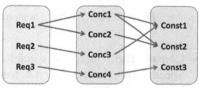

Fig. 1. From requirements to constructs

- **Const1.** The concept of *module* for representing encapsulation. Modules have been proposed as a means to encapsulate a set of actors and dependencies [28]. With respect to this proposal [28], we restrict modules to contain only one actor that will represent either the specification or the implementation of a DS. We prefer not to distinguish explicitly the two types of modules to keep the number of new constructs as low as possible. Every module will have open incoming or outcoming dependencies to/from its enclosed actors, representing the intentions that the DS specification or implementation offers/requires. These open dependencies become complete when the DS is inserted in a particular context. Figure 2 shows three examples: two modules encapsulating a specification (*Stack*, *Mapping*) and one module encapsulating an implementation (*Hash Table*). While *Stack* does not require anything from its context of use, *Mapping* requires that the stored elements have the concept of *Key* (to provide individual element look-up). The *Hash Table* implementation offers fast look-up and requires to know the approximate number of elements to store (to size the table) plus a hashing function.

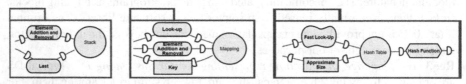

Fig. 2. Modules for the *Stack* and *Mapping* specifications, and *Hash Table* implementation[1,2]

- **Const2.** A type of actor link, *implements*, to connect an implementation to the corresponding specification. A specification may (and usually, will) have several implementations, while the opposite is false. As a side effect, the link allows to clearly identify when a module defines an implementation or a specification, considering whether it is the source or the target of an *implements* link. Figure 3 shows the link from the *Hash Table* implementation to the *Mapping* specification presented above.

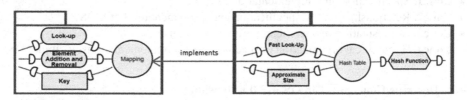

Fig. 3. The *Hash Table* implementation *implements* the *Mapping* specification

- **Const3.** The concept of specialization for representing the requested hierarchies. Specialization makes a good fit to represent commonalities and differences. We adopt López et al.'s framework to make precise the effects of the iStar2.0 *is-a* actor link at the level of intentional elements [26], distinguishing three types of specializations:

---

[1] All diagrams have been drawn with the piStar tool, https://www.cin.ufpe.br/~jhcp/pistar/, and manually modified to add constructs not included in iStar 2.0.

[2] For clarity of the paper, the examples already present the concrete syntax proposed for the constructs, which PRISE considers as part of the next step (developing an iStar2.0 extension).

extension, reinforcement and cancellation. Figure 4 shows an example that puts the *Mapping* specification presented above into context. As root of the hierarchy, the *Function* specification represents the family of DS that support individual operations (addition, removal and access). *Mapping* and *Set* are two particular DS belonging to this family. They only specialize through reinforcement the access operation to better reflect the differences: while sets provide membership only, mapping allows looking up elements. These specifications can be further specialized, as we show with *Mathematical Set*, which extends *Set* with *Union* and *Intersection*.

4.3 Develop iStar2.0 Extension

In this step, the original iStar2.0 metamodel [6] is enriched with the new constructs, also including integrity constraints needed to ensure the correctness of the models.

Figure 5 shows the excerpt of the iStarDust metamodel which contains changes with respect to the iStar2.0 metamodel. Table 1 lists the corresponding integrity constraints and one derivation rule. We observe:

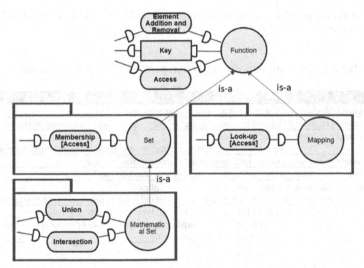

Fig. 4. Specialization for functions[3]

- The new *Module* class contains one actor and a number of open dependencies in and out. For clarity, we add a derived attribute stating whether the module corresponds to a specification or an implementation (**DR**). An intentional element cannot participate in more than one association (**IC1**), and specifications cannot have qualities as dependencies (**IC2**) (qualities should appear only at the level of implementations).
- The new *implements* association among actors is required to bind one implementation to one specification (**IC3, IC4**).

---

[3] We fill with yellow colour the elements affected by the specialization.

- Last, we add the notion of *reinforcement* at the intentional element level. **IC5** ensures that, given a reinforcement at the level of intentional elements, there is a corresponding *is-a* relationship at the level of actors, while **IC6** states that the types of intentional elements match according to [26] (e.g., we cannot reinforce a task into a goal).

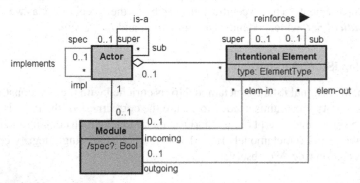

Fig. 5. iStarDust metamodel (elements added to the iStar2.0 metamodel appear in blue colour) (Color figure online)

Table 1. iStarDust integrity constraints required by the added constructs

ID	Derivation Rules and Integrity Constraints
DR	**context** Module **def**: spec? = not actor.implements <> null
IC1	**context** IntentionalElement **inv**: actor->size() + incoming->size() + outgoing->size() = 1
IC2	**context** Module **inv**: spec? **implies** (not elem-in->exists(type=quality) and not elem-out->exists(type=quality))
IC3	**context** Actor **inv**: spec <> null **implies** actor.module.spec? = false
IC4	**context** Actor **inv**: impl->notEmpty() **implies** actor.module.spec? = true
IC5	**context** IntentionalElement **inv**: super <> null **implies** (incoming.actor.super = super.incoming.actor or outgoing.actor.super = super.outgoing.actor)
IC6	**context** IntentionalElement **inv**: super <> null and type <> super.type **implies** ((type = task **or** type = resource) **implies** (super.type = goal **or** super.type = quality) **and** (type = goal **implies** super.type = quality))

5   Validation by Means of a Comparative Quasi-experiment

We have performed a comparative quasi-experiment to measure undergraduate students' performance in describing DS, after being exposed to DS described with the iStar2.0 language. This quasi-experiment has been designed according to Wohlin et al. [36], and it is reported according to Jedlitschka and Pfahl [16].

5.1   Experimental Design

The experimental goal, according to the Goal/Question/Metric template [2] is to **analyse** DS descriptions **for the purpose of** *understanding whether iStar2.0 could help to* *describe DS in a more structured form,* **with respect to** *its effectiveness* **from the point of view of** *computer science students and teachers* **in the context of** *a bachelor course on algorithms and DS at the Zürich University of Applied Sciences in Switzerland.* The main research question of this experiment is formulated as RQ2 presented in Sect. 3.

Experimental Subjects. The experiment was conducted in the academic year 2020–2021 (from September 2020 until January 2021) within the bachelor-level course of Algorithms and DS (ADS) offered at the Zürich University of Applied Sciences[4]. The subjects were 61 s year students of the computer science curriculum enrolled in two different groups with distinct schedules. Both groups have students with experience in industry. In general, some students are currently working in industry (79%), and none of them had been in contact with the *i** framework or used iStar2.0 for describing DS. The course planning was not updated to incorporate the experimental set-up, still maintaining the original course objectives. However, the content presented to one of the two groups was updated adding an iStar2.0 description to some of the DS taught. The group who received materials of DS with iStar was considered as experimental group. The subjects executed the experimental task as part of the course's end-of-semester exam. Properly speaking, we have performed a quasi-experiment because the subjects were not sampled randomly across the population; however, this is typical in software engineering experiments [32].

Variables. We consider one independent variable:

- **DS Specification.** The way DS are described by the subjects. This variable has two values:

  - DS specified with iStar2.0, as defined in Sect. 4.
  - DS specified without iStar2.0, serving the purpose of a control group.

We consider the following dependent variables, which are expected to be influenced to some extent by the independent variable. We have adapted the Method Evaluation Model (MEM) to structure the dependent variables of this experiment [30]. In this way, the effectiveness of iStar2.0 to describe DS is measured by evaluating subjects' performance regarding completeness and validity of subjects' described DS [22] (see Fig. 6).

- **DS completeness.** The degree to which all the intrinsic characteristics that should be described regarding a certain DS (because they explain the meaning of a DS or its differences with another DS) are actually mentioned by the subjects. To facilitate this calculation, the researchers consider a reference solution containing the minimum indispensable description.
- **DS validity.** The degree to which the characteristics of a certain DS are described by the subjects in the right way. Acting as reviewers, the researchers identify properly or wrongly described characteristics based on a reference solution, and then discuss them until they agree on the verdict.

---

[4] Course description available at https://tinyurl.com/3pdnb3xa.

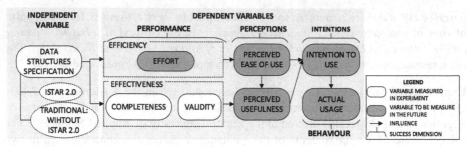

Fig. 6. Variables structure according to [30], and envisioned variables to be measured in future empirical evaluations.

For this experiment we consider two types of possible analysis of DS: **type A)**, description of differences between two given DS; **type B)**, description of the most important requirements or operations of a given DS. We consider these two possibilities to formulate below the hypotheses of our study and experimental objects.

Hypotheses. We define null hypotheses (represented by a 0 in the subscript) that correspond to the absence of an impact of the independent variables on the dependent variables. Alternative hypotheses (represented by a 1 in the subscript, e.g., $H1_1$ is the alternative hypothesis to $H1_0$) suppose the existence of such an impact. Alternative hypotheses correspond to our expectations: DS specified with iStar2.0 will have a positive impact on the dependent variables (For the sake of brevity, alternative hypotheses are omitted) (Table 2).

Table 2. Hypothesis description

Null Hypothesis id	Statement: DS specified with iStar2.0 does not influence the...
H10	...completeness of identified differences between two given DS
H20	...completeness of described requirements of a given DS
H30	... validity of stated characteristics of a given DS when subjects intent to draw differences
H40	... validity of described characteristics of a given DS

5.2   Procedure and Data Analysis[5]

As part of the experimental task, we provided to the subjects with three different types of input questions to increase the external validity of the experiment based on questions' objective (see Table 3).

Table 3. Description of the experimental objects

Question type	Objective of the question	Example
A	Description of the main differences and similarities between two DS	Which are the differences and similarities between stacks and lists in ADS?
B	Description of the main requirements (i.e., operations) of a given DS	What is a stack, and which are the basic operations?
C	Control question about DS without associated iStar 2.0 language description	What is the main difference between a singly and doubly linked list?

We created four equivalent versions for each question type, changing the type of DS (e.g., queues, lists, etc.) but maintaining the overall objective of the question so that resulting answers are isomorphic. The design, according to [36] is a "one factor with two treatments", where the factor is the DS specification and treatments are the DS specified with iStar2.0 or in the traditional way (without iStar 2.0). The experimental procedure is presented in Fig. 7. The control group received the ADS content as it was designed for the course. In contrast, the experimental group received slides with the prescribed ADS content including DS exemplified by means of iStar2.0. Before the exam, the students answered some learning questions, and the experimental group provided qualitative feedback regarding the use of iStar2.0. The experimental task was executed in the context of the oral end-of-semester exam. During the exam, each subject randomly selected a set of questions and received the experimental objects as presented in Table 3. Two teachers assessed the subjects' performance, gave a grade, and took notes of the answers.

Data Analysis. For this type of experimental design, the most common analysis is to compare the means of the dependent variable for each treatment [36].

DS Completeness. The results of descriptive statistics for the control group show completeness average of 12% for question type A, 96% for question type B, and 89% for

---

[5] To facilitate further replication of this controlled experiment, the material describing the experimental objects, sample slides of DS in iStar provided to experimental subjects, set of questions used during the execution of the experimental task, experimental design, and output from statistical analysis can be found at https://drive.switch.ch/index.php/s/6IuFjG tONSWV2bB.

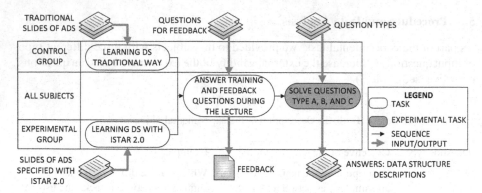

Fig. 7. Experimental procedure

question type C; vs 72% for question type A, 91% for type B, and 84% for type C of the experimental group. The ANOVA Test was applied, and we verified a **significant difference** ($p < 0,05$) between the two groups for $H1_0$. Thus, the alternative hypothesis $H1_1$ is corroborated, demonstrating that <u>iStar2.0 does influence the completeness of described DS when subjects are comparing them.</u> On the other hand, no significant difference was observed for question type B. As a result, our hypothesis $H2_1$ is not corroborated and we conclude that iStar2.0 does not influence the completeness of described DS.

DS Validity. The results of descriptive statistics show an average of 48% of valid answers for question type A, 84% for questions type B, and 90% for our control question type C for the control group, versus 91% for questions type A, 88% for type B, and 81% for type C for the experimental group. By applying the ANOVA test, we observe there is **significant difference** for question type A ($p < 0,05$) between the two groups. Therefore, the null hypothesis $H3_0$ is rejected and the alternative hypothesis $H3_1$ is corroborated demonstrating that <u>iStar2.0 does influence the validity of described DS when the subjects are analysing differences.</u> Nevertheless, no significant difference is observed for questions type B. As a result, our hypothesis $H4_1$ is not corroborated and we conclude that iStar2.0 does not influence the validity of described DS.

Results to the control question type C did not show any significant difference between the two groups when answering questions without associated iStar2.0 DS. This minimises the internal validity threat regarding the maturity and experience of the subjects. Further research needs to be conducted for question type B.

5.3 Analysis of the Threats to the Validity of the Results

Internal Validity. The subjects *matured* their competence in DS through the semester, which can have had a positive impact in their performance. To minimise this threat, we conceived an experimental design involving both control and experimental groups. The *selection-maturation* threat could indicate that the experimental group could have learnt DS skills faster and better than the control group. To minimise this threat, we have included a control question in our experiment that is not related to a DS we had introduced with iStar2.0. *Social threats* are unlikely to happen because control and experimental groups are totally independent from each other through their course of studies. Our experimental design assures that both control and experimental groups do not suffer disadvantages by keeping the original course's plan and objectives for both groups.

External Validity. Since this experiment is conceived to be conducted in an educational context, the subjects have been properly selected. However, we acknowledge limits in the *generalisation of the experiment results*. We have performed a quasi-experiment since our subjects were not randomly selected from the target population. Yet the experiment was conducted in a real educational setting. We acknowledge that we need to conduct further experiments involving groups of students from different countries and take into consideration variations in the computer science curricula. The results from this study just apply to the set of DS selected for this quasi-experiment. As explained below in the construct validity analysis, we plan to perform deep analysis on the impact of iStarDust for each data type. Moreover, we plan to investigate the extent iStarDust affects overall subjects' performance.

Construct Validity. We minimised the *threat of inadequate preoperational explication of constructs* by means of using a widely accepted model for method evaluation. On other matters, the fact that we compare a new method for describing DS with traditional approaches may seem an inadequate comparison of treatments. Nevertheless, our objective is to advance current DS teaching practices by involving conceptual modeling methods and techniques. A potential threat regarding the equivalence of questions' sets given to the subjects' groups could pose a *mono-method bias threat*. The questions' sets evaluate the extent a subject can identify similarities, differences, and requirements for given DS, which are wide-known difficulties when understanding DS. Since our subjects did not answer the questions at the same time, we opted for not giving the same questions to both groups. We plan to perform further experiments where each data type is analysed in a controlled experiment. This experiment presents valuable results towards a new generation of teaching content for traditional computer science courses.

6 Conclusions and Future Work

This paper presents our research efforts in effectively implementing goal-oriented perspectives for the teaching and understanding of DS concepts. Our research is motivated by the need to augment how DS are taught to mitigate students' difficulties when using DS, and their need to simply memorise DS characteristics to excel in their studies [38]. Our hypothesis is that by teaching DS with a goal-oriented perspective, students will be able to experience a better understanding of the main goals of every DS, what their qualities are, and relationships with their context of use. To test this hypothesis, we follow the PRISE method [15] to extend iStar2.0 with constructs that facilitate teaching and learning DS with respect to functional and non-functional requirements. In this paper we present iStarDust: iStar 2.0 for DS, and report on an initial validation regarding students' effectiveness by means of a controlled experiment. The results from the controlled experiment have shown that iStar 2.0 can improve students' effectiveness in terms of completeness and validity of described DS. However, further experiments must be conducted to be able to generalise the results to a wider population.

As part of our future endeavours, we plan to conduct further controlled experiments to observe students' effectiveness, efficiency, perceptions, and intentions when using iStarDust for learning DS (see Fig. 6). Despite having students as a target population to validate iStarDust is considered a valid approach in software engineering [9], we also envision to investigate to what extent iStarDust can also be adopted by professionals. We also envision to perform a focused analysis on the impact of using iStarDust for each data type concerning wide-known learning difficulties. This would allow us to observe the benefits of teaching each data type and the impact in students' effectiveness when learning DS. Last, to facilitate the adoption of iStarDust by both instructors and students, we plan to develop a plug-in for the piStar tool to support the specification of iStar models with the extensions provided by iStarDust.

Acknowledgements. This work has been partially supported by the by the DOGO4ML Spanish research project (ref. PID2020-117191RB-I00), the Digitalization Initiative of the Canton of Zürich (DIZH), and ZHAW Digital.

References

1. Ayala, I., Amor, M., Horcas, J.M., Fuentes, L.: A goal-driven software product line approach for evolving multi-agent systems in the Internet of Things. Knowl.-Based Syst. **184**, 104883 (2019)
2. Basili, V., Caldiera, C., Rombach, H.D.: Goal question metric paradigm. In: Marciniak, J.J. (ed.) Encyclopedia of Software Engineering, vol. 1, pp. 528–532. Wiley (1994)
3. Botella, P., Burgués, X., et al.: Modeling non-functional requirements. JIRA (2001)
4. Confrey, J.: A review of the research on student conceptions in mathematics, science, and programming. Rev. Res. Educ. **16**(1), 3–56 (1990)
5. Cormen, T.H., Leiserson, C.E., Rivest, R.L.: Introduction to Algorithms. The MIT Press (1990)
6. Dalpiaz, F., Franch, X., Horkoff, J.: iStar 2.0 Language Guide. arXiv preprint arXiv:1605.07767 (2016)
7. Dardenne, A., van Lamsweerde, A., Fickas, S.: Goal-directed requirements acquisition. Sci. Comput. Program. **20**(1–2), 3–50 (1993)
8. Estrada, H., Rebollar, A.M., Pastor, O., Mylopoulos, J.: An empirical evaluation of the *i** framework in a model-based software generation environment. In: Dubois, E., Pohl, K. (eds.) CAiSE 2006. LNCS, vol. 4001, pp. 513–527. Springer, Heidelberg (2006). https://doi.org/10.1007/11767138_34
9. Falessi, D., et al.: Empirical software engineering experts on the use of students and professionals in experiments. Empir. Softw. Eng. **23**(1), 452–489 (2017). https://doi.org/10.1007/s10664-017-9523-3
10. Franch, X.: Estructuras de Datos: Especificación, Diseño e Implementación. Ed. UPC (1993)
11. Carvallo, J.P., Franch, X., Quer, C.: Determining criteria for selecting software components: lessons learned. IEEE Softw. **24**(3), 84–94 (2007)
12. Franch, X.: Using *i** to describe data structures. In: iStar Workshop 2020, pp. 59–64 (2020)
13. Goguen, J.A., Thatcher, J.W., Wagner, E.G.: An initial algebra approach to the specification, correctness and implementation of abstract data types. In: Current Trends in Programming Methodology, vol. IV. Prentice-Hall (1978)

14. Grau, G., Franch, X.: On the adequacy of $i*$ models for representing and analyzing software architectures. In: Hainaut, J.-L., et al. (eds.) Advances in Conceptual Modeling – Foundations and Applications, pp. 296–305. Springer, Heidelberg (2007). https://doi.org/10.1007/978-3-540-76292-8_35
15. Gonçalves, G., Araujo, J., Castro, J.: PRISE: a process to support iStar extensions. J. Syst. Softw. **168**, 110649 (2020)
16. Jedlitschka, A., Pfahl, D.: Reporting guidelines for controlled experiments in software engineering. In: ESEM 2005 (2005)
17. Junhui, W., Tuolei, W., Yusheng, W., Jie, C., Kaiyan, L., Huiping, S.: Improved blockchain commodity traceability system using distributed hash table. In: CAC 2020, pp. 1419–1424 (2020)
18. Karpierz, K., Wolfman, S.A.: Misconceptions and concept inventory questions for binary search trees and hash tables. In: SIGCSE 2014, pp. 109–114 (2014)
19. Knuth, D.E.: The Art of Computer Programming, vol. 3. Addison-Wesley (1973)
20. Lavalle, A., Maté, A., Trujillo, J., Rizzi, S.: Visualization requirements for business intelligence analytics: a goal-based, iterative framework. In: RE 2019, pp. 109–119 (2019)
21. Le Scouarnec, N.: Cuckoo++ hash tables: high-performance hash tables for networking applications. In: ANCS 2018, pp. 41–54 (2018)
22. Lindland, O.I., Sindre, G., Sølvberg, A.: Understanding quality in conceptual modeling. IEEE Softw. **11**(2), 42–49 (1994)
23. Liskov, B.H., Guttag, J.V.: Abstraction and Specification in Program Development. MIT (1986)
24. Liskov, B., Zilles, S.: Programming with abstract data types. ACM SIGPLAN Not. **9**(4), 50–59 (1974)
25. Liu, Z., Calciu, I., Herlihy, M., Mutlu, O.: Concurrent data structures for near-memory computing. In: SPAA 2017, pp. 235–245 (2017)
26. López, L., Franch, X., Marco, J.: Specialization in the iStar2.0 language. IEEE Access **7**, 146005–146023 (2019)
27. Ma, L., Ferguson, J., Roper, M., Wood, M.: Investigating and improving the models of programming concepts held by novice programmers. Comput. Sci. Educ. **21**(1), 57–80 (2011)
28. Maté, A., Trujillo, J., Franch, X.: Adding semantic modules to improve goal-oriented analysis of data warehouses using I-star. J. Syst. Softw. **88**, 102–111 (2014)
29. McAuley, R., Hanks, B., et al. Recursion vs. iteration: an empirical study of comprehension revisited. In: SIGSE 2015, pp. 350–355 (2015)
30. Moody, D.: The method evaluation model: a theoretical model for validating information systems design methods. In: ECIS 2003, pp. 1327–1336 (2003)
31. Navarro, G.: Compact Data Structures. Cambridge University Press (2016)
32. Robson, C.: Real World Research: A Resource for Social Scientists and Practitioner-Researchers. Wiley-Blackwell (2002)
33. Schwartz, J.T., Dewar, R.B.K., Schonberg, E., Dubinsky, E.: Programming with Sets: An Introduction. Springer, New York (1986). https://doi.org/10.1007/978-1-4613-9575-1
34. Seppälä, O., Malmi, L., Korhonen, A.: Observations on student misconceptions—a case study of the build-heap algorithm. Comput. Sci. Educ. **16**(3), 241–255 (2006)
35. Soares, M., Pimentel, J., et al.: Automatic generation of architectural models from goal models. In: SEKE 2012, pp. 444–447 (2012)
36. Wohlin, C., Runeson, P., et al.: Experimentation in Software Engineering. Springer, Heidelberg (2012). https://doi.org/10.1007/978-3-642-29044-2
37. Yu, E.: Modeling organisations for information systems requirements engineering. In: ISRE 1993, pp. 34–41 (1993)
38. Zingaro, D., Taylor, C., et al.: Identifying student difficulties with basic data structures. In: ICER 2018, pp. 169–177 (2018)

Model-Based Knowledge Searching

Maxim Bragilovski$^{(\boxtimes)}$ (ID), Yifat Makias, Moran Shamshila, Roni Stern(ID),
and Arnon Sturm(ID)

Ben-Gurion University of the Negev, Beer Sheva, Israel
{maximbr,makias,moranshi}@post.bgu.ac.il, {sternron,sturm}@bgu.ac.il

Abstract. As knowledge increases tremendously each and every day,
there is a need for means to manage and organize it, so as to utilize it
when needed. For example, for finding solutions to technical/engineering
problems. An alternative for achieving this goal is through knowledge
mapping that aims at indexing the knowledge. Nevertheless, searching
for knowledge in such maps is still a challenge. In this paper, we propose
an algorithm for knowledge searching over maps created by ME-MAP, a
mapping approach we developed. The algorithm is a greedy one that aims
at maximizing the similarity between a query and existing knowledge
encapsulated in ME-maps. We evaluate the efficiency of the algorithm
in comparison to an expert judgment. The evaluation indicates that the
algorithm achieved high performance within a bounded time. Though
additional examination is required, the sought algorithm can be easily
adapted to other modeling languages for searching models.

Keywords: Conceptual modeling · Matching · Searching

1 Introduction

Knowledge, especially in technology and engineering domains, is developing at
a tremendous pace [5]. In such domains, we are especially concerned with know-
how, the kind of knowledge that guides action towards practical objectives, pre-
scribing solutions to technical problems, and evaluating alternative solutions
[4,15]. Know-how management can provide various benefits such as: domain
review, trade-off analysis, and support for decision making. While there is almost
instant access to published know-how online, to the best of our knowledge, there
has been little advance in how a body of know-how is organized for easier access,
in particular, for searching the knowledge. Nowadays, searching for knowledge
is mostly done textually using search engines. Yet, the outcomes of such search
results are of limited accuracy, that is, many non-relevant answers are being
retrieved leading to low efficiency of the search. To address this limitation, we
suggest taking advantage of the underlying structure of the knowledge under
examination. In the case of know-how, the underlying structure resembles the
means-end relationship. For that purpose, we devised a knowledge scheme called
ME-MAP [17] that uses the means-end relationship to map out know-how. Using

© Springer Nature Switzerland AG 2021
A. Ghose et al. (Eds.): ER 2021, LNCS 13011, pp. 242–256, 2021.
https://doi.org/10.1007/978-3-030-89022-3_20

that scheme, we are structuring and organizing the knowledge and are able to query it more precisely. The population of the scheme can be regarded as a graph that can now be searched using various techniques. In this paper, we adapt an algorithm for searching ME-maps and explore its effectiveness [2]. We also evaluated the performance of the algorithm by various information retrieval metrics and found the result promising.

The paper is structured as follows. Section 2 provides a background of the ME-MAP approach. Section 3 refers to search problems in graphs. Section 4 introduces the sought algorithm and Sect. 5 presents its evaluation. Finally, Sect. 6 concludes and sets plans for future research.

2   ME-MAP in a Nutshell

The ME-MAP approach draws its core concepts from the goal-oriented requirement engineering (GORE) paradigm [20]. It further leverages on concept maps [11] and specializes its nodes and link types. A main objective of the ME-MAP is to take advantage of the inherent means-ends relationship that characterizes know-how, where the identification of problems and development of feasible solutions is a key concern. The approach aims at presenting problems identified in a domain, properties of problems that are particularly relevant in the domain, and offer a systematic review of proposed solutions. In the following, we briefly introduce the ME-MAP language elements.

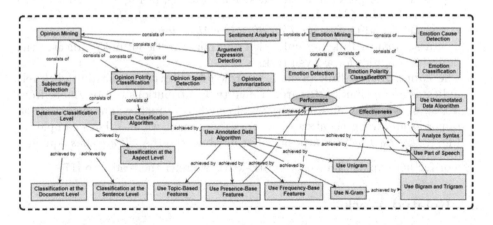

Fig. 1. A partial ME-MAP of the Sentiment Analysis domain

– A **Task** is a key element in the means-ends hierarchy. A Task can be interpreted either as a problem or as a solution depending on its location within the hierarchy. Tasks are graphically depicted as rectangular shapes. In Fig. 1, the task *Execute Classification Algorithm* is a problem that should be addressed, whereas the task *Use Annotated Data Algorithm* is one alternative solution for that problem. When referring to the latter it is now a problem to be addressed. One alternative solution is the *Use Topic-Based Features*. Tasks are usually named as an action (verbal sentence), other alternatives exist such as placing a known technique (i.e., noun) with its name, implying the usage of the technique.

- A **Quality** expresses an attribute or a property that is desired for a task. In the ME-MAP a quality is depicted as an ellipse. For example, in Fig. 1, *Performance* and *Effectiveness* are qualities, which further characterize how a solution that supports the *Execute Classification Algorithm* task should be designed. A quality is therefore associated with a task. A quality can also be linked to another quality independently of a task.

Link elements connect tasks and qualities. In the following we elaborate on the link types included in ME-MAP:

- The **achieved by** link (a line arrow labeled by "achieved by") represents the means-ends relationship. The arrow points from the "end" to the "means". For example, in Fig. 1, *Use Topic-based Feature* is a means to accomplish Use *Annotated Data Algorithm*. The link indicates an alternative for achieving an end.
- The **consists of** link (a line arrow labeled by "consists of") indicates that a task has several sub-parts, all of which should be accomplished for the parent task to be accomplished. Note that this link does not refer to the ordering or dependencies of performing the task. For example, in Fig. 1, in order to use *Opinion Polarity Classification*, there is a need for both *Determine Classification Level* and to *Execute Classification Algorithm*.
- The **association link** (an unlabeled and non-directional link) indicates the desirable qualities for a given task.
- The **contribution link** (a curved arrow labeled with a contribution level) indicates a contribution towards a quality. Contributions can originate from a task or a quality and are always directed to a quality. The contribution ranges from strong negative ($--$) to strong positive ($++$). For example, in Fig. 1, *Use Part of Speech* positively contributes to the *Effectiveness* quality.

For further explanations on the ME-MAP we refer the reader to [17].

3   Related Work

One of the challenges in searching knowledge refers to how to store the mined knowledge. Different studies suggest various structural databases that store knowledge from natural language text that might be ambiguous, contextual, and implicit [3]. In our research we use knowledge graph structure, yet, the structure also refers to the actual knowledge semantics. As we explicitly refer to know-how, we use the means-ends notion to store the knowledge [17].

Query knowledge graphs can be classified into four main categories: (1) graph-based query [18], (2) keyword-based query [6], (3) natural-language-based query

[7,23], and (4) path query language queries [13]. Most of these methods (2–4) transform the query to graph and then perform graph searching [18]. Searching the graph is based on checking the alignment between the query and the graph based on the node similarity and structure similarity.

Three different main path query languages described in [1] that are SPARQL, Cypher, and Gremlin for querying a graph. SPARQL standard structural query language to access Resource Description Framework (RDF) data and Cypher a declarative language for querying property graphs are based on SQL language while Gremlin, a query language of the Apache TinkerPop3 graph Framework, is more similar to functional language. These query languages are based on the assumption that users have prior knowledge about the graph that they search in. However, it is impractical for users to write statements in these languages due to the complexity of syntax and the lack of prior knowledge [6]. In contrast to these languages, keywords search [6] and natural language questions provide users with an interface for querying RDF data. However, they are still facing problems. Keyword-based search lack due to the ambiguity presented either by the keywords or their orders. Natural languages based search lacks due to the challenge of transforming these into formal queries (which is an NP-hard problem) [23].

The similarity flooding algorithm [9] also helps to find pairs of elements that are similar in two data schemes or two data instances. Yet, in this work we are interested in paths considering also the labels of the vertices and edges.

Similar to our work, Wang et al. [18] present an algorithm that finds subgraphs in knowledge graphs given a query graph. They divided the task into several phases: knowledge graph embedding, semantic graph generation, and A* semantic search that is based on a defined path semantic similarity. They further attempt to optimize response time. They experiment with the effectiveness and efficiency and got a recall of 0.69 and the answering time took 136.81 ms for top 200 answers in DPpedia[1]. In our work, the proposed algorithm is inspired by their semantic search algorithm. What differentiates it, is our use of a semantic search that also includes graph semantics in addition to using words semantics, and that we adopted the greedy approach.

4   The Search Algorithm

The problem we are aiming to address is the search within ME-maps. For that purpose, we devised a Greedy Search in Means-End Maps (GSME) algorithm that addresses the concerns of complexity and semantics. GSME adopts the similarity considerations appears in [14] and refers to label matching (exact match among labels), structure matching (in terms of links), semantic matching (in terms of labels semantic similarity and links' semantics, e.g., synonyms and related concepts), and type matching. In the following, we first set the ground for the algorithm and then elaborate on its design and execution.

---

[1] https://wiki.dbpedia.org/.

Definition 1. *A **ME-MAP** is a graph (G) consists of vertices (V) and edges (E). G = (V, E).*

> **V = Task ∪ Quality,**
> **E = AchievedBy ∪ ConsistsOf ∪ Association ∪ Contribution**

Definition 2. sim_w *refers to the similarity of two words. This can be calculated using for example WordNet [10], or Sematch [22].*

Definition 3. sim_l *refers to the similarity of two vertices labels. We suggest achieving this task by two alternatives:*

1. Using words similarity:

$$sim_l(list_1, list_2) = \frac{\Sigma_{w_1 \epsilon list_1}(\arg max_{w_2 \epsilon list_2}(sim_w(\mathbf{w_1}, \mathbf{w_2})))}{\arg max(length(list_1), length(list_2))} \quad (1)$$

   Where the lists order the words from the vertex's label.
2. Using sentence similarity: *We transform the labels into vectors and measure the similarity using sbert[2].*

Definition 4. sim_t *refers to a predefined similarity among vertex types. In the case of the ME-MAP, based on our exploration we set sim_t(Task, Quality) = 0.5.*

Definition 5. sim_v *refers to the similarity of two vertices.*

$$sim_v(v_1, v_2) = \frac{sim_l(v_1, v_2) + sim_t(v_1, v_2)}{2} \quad (2)$$

sim_l *can be either defined by Definition 3(1) or by Definition 3(2).*

Definition 6. sim_e *refers to a predefined similarity among edge types. Table 1 presents the similarity among ME-MAP edges. These similarities were determined by ME-MAP experts and represent the semantic similarity between types of edges.*

Table 1. Edge similarity

	Achieved by	Consists of	Association	Contribution
Achieved by	1	0.5	0.25	0.25
Consists of	0.5	1	0.25	0.25
Association	0.25	0.25	1	0.25
Contribution	0.25	0.25	0.25	1

Definition 7. *Node-edge similarity is calculated as follow:*

$$sim_{ne}(v_1, e_1, v_2, e_2) = \frac{2 * sim_v(v_1, v_2) + sim_e(e_1, e_2)}{3} \quad (3)$$

---

[2] https://www.sbert.net/.

This definition captures the similarity of a vertex along with its incoming edge. We considered the vertex similarity of double importance as it is used as the basis for the similarity.

Definition 8. *A query Q is represented as a ME-map.* **Single path** *query has a single path of vertices and edges (see Fig. 2a).* **Multi paths** *query has multiple paths (see Fig. 2b).*

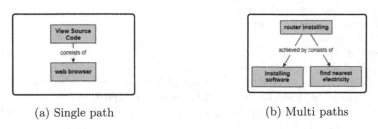

(a) Single path   (b) Multi paths

Fig. 2. Multi paths and Single path queries

Definition 9. *To answer a query, we actually compare the similarity of the paths of the query with those of the map. The following formula is used for that purpose (NodeEdgeSim is a set of sim_{ne}).*

$$Path\ Sim\left(G^1, G^2, NodeEdgeSim\right) =$$

$$sim_v\left(v_1^{G^1}, v_1^{G^2}\right) + \sum_{i=1}^{|NodeEdgeSim|} NodeEdgeSim_i$$

This formula actually sums all the node-edge similarities between paths and therefore we used it as an estimator for path similarity measurement.

In the following, we elaborate the algorithm for single path queries. We differentiate between two types of node similarity. The first relies solely on the node information, we call this Node-based similarity. The second also refers to the edge connecting the node from the previous one, we call this node-edge based similarity.

- The function of **Node-based similarity** returns the most similar node in the ME-map to a node within the query as calculated by Definition 5.
  Input: $G = (V, E)$, query node, similarity function. The similarity function is the one appears in Definition 3.
  Output: a node from G.
- The function of **Node-edge based similarity** is responsible for retrieving up to K most similar neighbors' nodes that exceed a predefined threshold as determined by Definition 7. If there is no single node that its similarity exceeds the threshold, the function returns all the neighbor's nodes with similarity of the threshold.
  Input: G, query node, parent node, similarity function, threshold, K
  Output: node list and their similarities from G.

Algorithm 1. GSME

Input $similarNodes, knowledgeGraph, queryGraph, K, threshold,$
$queryID, isVisited$
Output Set of sub graphs with their similarities

1: $results \leftarrow \{\theta\}$
2: **if** $similarNodes \equiv \{\theta\}$ $\|$ $v_{queryID} \notin V_{queryGraph}$ **then**
3:     $return\ results$
4: **end if**
5: **for** $node$ in $similarNodes$ **do**
6:     **if** $node \in isVisited$ **then**
7:         $continue$
8:     **end if**
9:     $isVisited \leftarrow isVisited \cup node$
10:     $similarNodes \leftarrow Node - edge\_based\_function($
    $knowledgeGraph, queryGraph[queryID], node, K, threshold)$
11:     **if** $similarNodes \equiv \{\theta\}$ $\|$ $arg\ max_{sim \in similarNodes}(sim) \leq threshold$ **then**
    $results' \leftarrow GSME($
    $similarNodes, knowledgeGraph, queryGraph, K, th, queryID, isVisite)$
12:     **else**
13:         $results' \leftarrow GSME(similarNodes, knowledgeGraph, queryGraph, K,$
    $threshold, queryID + +, isVisite)$
14:     **end if**
15:     $results \leftarrow results' \cup results$
16: **end for**
17: $return\ results$

To start the execution of the GSME, the number of nodes (K) the algorithm handles in each round (that refers to the next step of the query) and the threshold for the similarity need to be determined. The algorithm uses the Node-edge based similarity function to find the appropriate list of nodes for its execution in each iteration. We also have to determine the knowledge graph(s) in which the search should take place and $similarNodes$ where the search should start (this task can be achieved by the Node-based similarity function). For the query, we have the $queryGraph$ that needs to be found in the (set of) $knowledgeGraph$. Additional required parameters include the $queryID$ that refers to the id of the node in a $queryGraph$ and is initialized with '-1' that represents the first node of the query where we want to start the search from. $isVisited$ is a list that contains all the nodes that GSME already iterates over in the $knowledgeGraph$ to allow GSME to handle graphs with cycles. The output of the algorithm is a set of subgraphs from the $knowledgeGraph$ that are the most similar to the $queryGraph$. The algorithm is described in Algorithm 1.

The GSME algorithm steps are as following: (line 1) Initialize results with an empty set; (lines 2–4) Stop GSME if there are no nodes in the $similarNodes$ or there are no nodes with a given ID in the $queryGraph$; (lines 6–8) skip already visited nodes; (line 9) For each node in $similarNodes$ we add it to $isVisited$ list; (line 10) Get up to K most $similarNodes$ by the Next-edge based function described above; (lines 11–12) If there are no nodes in *similarNodes* or the similarity of the nodes in the *similarNodes* is below the threshold the algorithm will run recursively for the selected *similarNodes* and *queryID*, without moving on the next node; (lines 12–14) If there are nodes in *similarNodes* and the similarity of the nodes in the *similarNodes* are above the threshold - the algorithm will run recursively for the selected *similarNodes* (up to K nodes) and *queryID*, each time moving on to the next node – in other words, in order to allow the return of results that are transitive, the node in the query is promoted only when the similarity obtained for the node is higher than the threshold; (line 15) Merge the results that the algorithm retrieved with the results within the function arguments. The algorithm continues until it passes all the nodes and edges of the query. At the end of the algorithm, sub-graphs from the ME-maps that answer the query will be obtained. The sub-graphs will be sorted by their similarity ranking, as determined by Definition 9 and normalized by the length. The ranking is a weighing of the similarity of the edges and nodes and is represented by a number 0-1.

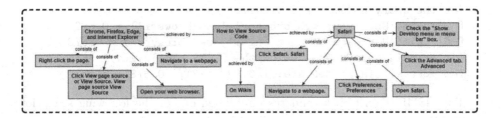

Fig. 3. GSME execution example

In the following, we demonstrate the execution of GSME over the ME-map shown in Fig. 3 whereas the expected output is marked in green with the requested query shown in Fig. 2a. We set the threshold to 0.65 and the number of lookup nodes (K) to 2. These parameters were determined based on a pre-execution evaluation. We also did a sensitivity analysis on the threshold ('th') and found that the value of 0.65 leads to the most accurate results.

1. In the first stage, the Node-based similarity function is executed. The following results demonstrate the output for the node "View Source Code" in the query graph:

   ```
   For the query node: 'View Source Code'
   [-1]: sim('How to View Source Code','View Source Code') = 0.526
   [-3]: sim('Open your web browser.','View Source Code') = 0.513
   ```

   (For all other nodes in the graph, the similarity was below 0.513)
2. Following the highest similarity of 0.526, GSME starts from the node 'How to View Source Code' (id: '−1'). In this stage, the algorithm keeps trying to

find the K (K = 2 in our case) most similar adjacent nodes to the selected node in the knowledge graph to the next node of the query graph, that is, 'web browser'. The results were the following:

```
For the query node: ['web browser']
[-2]: sim('Chrome, Firefox, Edge, and Internet Explorer',
'web browser') = 0.512
[-7]: sim('Safari','web browser') = 0.513
[-14]: sim('On Wikis','web browser') = 0.511
The most similar node is: [(0.6, -2), (0.6, -7), (0.6, -14)]
```

3. Since all the nodes sim_{ne} value (Definition 7) is below the threshold, all the nodes advance recursively to the next step without advancing to the next query node. We will only demonstrate the iteration over the node with id '−2' in this step, and the iteration over node '−14' in step number 4(b), despite the fact that the algorithm does a similar iteration also over the node with id '−7'.

```
For the query node: ['web browser']
[-3]: sim('Open your web browser','web browser') = 0.682
[-4]: sim('Navigate to a webpage.','web browser') = 0.678
(other neighbors nodes  below the 0.678 similarity)
The most similar nodes are: [(0.682, -3), (0.678, -4)]
```

4. The GSME algorithm terminates only when one of the following scenarios occur:
   (a) GSME finishes iterating over the nodes in the *queryGraph* therefore, GSME finds at least one sub-graph among all the potential sub-graphs like in step 3.
   (b) There are no more nodes to iterate in the *knowledgeGraph*. For example, in one of the steps of the GSME, it reaches node '−14':

   ```
   For the query node: ['web browser']
   The neighbors of vertex: -14 are: []
   The most similar node is: []
   ```

   therefore, all the sub-graphs that end with node '-14' are irrelevant answers.
5. Finally, the results paths are calculated for their similarity based on Definition 9 and are sorted accordingly.

```
1 : (path: '-1,-2,-3', Path-Sim: 0.603, map id: 4796)
2 : (path: '-1,-7,-4', Path-Sim: 0.601, map id: 4796)
```

Indeed, the first row in the results appears in Fig. 3. Its path similarity is calculated by Definition 9 as follow: $\frac{0.526+0.6+0.682}{3} = 0.603$.

5   Evaluation

To evaluate GSME, we conducted three experiments to check the algorithm performance in various settings. This section will be focusing on the technical aspects of GSME rather than the benefits of using GSME.

5.1   Settings

We considered several maps from the Human Know-How Dataset [12] for the first experiment. For the second experiment, we considered three domains for which we developed ME-maps: (1) a simple map referring to the search domain. (2) a DPSL map that (partially) maps out [8]. (3) a Sentiment Analysis map that (partially) maps out [19]. For the domains from the Human Know-How Dataset, we performed transformations from their graph format to the ME-MAP representation. These maps contain only tasks and two link types: 'Achieved By' and 'Consists of' unlike the maps in the second experiment that have all the types of edges and vertices. The transformations rules were the following rules:

1. 'MainTask', 'Steps', 'Methods' and 'Parts' nodes were transformed to a 'Task' node.
2. The label of the nodes was set according to the name of the attribute of the JSON object.
3. An edge from 'MainTask' to 'Methods' is labeled with 'Achieved By' label.
4. All the other edges were labeled with 'Consists of' label.

The purpose of the first experiment was to examine the algorithm's ability to handle maps with long labels and to check its accuracy, in terms of finding the relevant map. The goal of the second experiment is to examine how well GSME performs against maps that have short labels, especially in finding the relevant sub-graphs. The third experiment was executed on a synthetic map to examine GSME's performance on a large map.

We set several queries for each experiment that were classified into three categories of complexity. The complexity of the categories was determined based on two parameters: (1) **Length** the number of vertices in the graph; and (2) **N-hop** supporting *hop* edge in the map according to the expected result. In other words, the difference between the length of the query graph and the expected graph. That is, the number of skips on the graph edges required to get to the desired result.

The categories were as following: (1) **Simple** the query length is less then 3 and n-*hop* equals to 0. (2) **Medium** the query length is more then 2 and n-*hop* equals to 0. (3) **Complex** the query has more then 1 n-*hop*.

Examples of simple, medium, and complex queries are shown in Fig. 4. The labels for each node of the queries are matched to the node labels in Fig. 3 to simplify the demonstration of how the complexity parameters influence the difficulty level of each category. Figure 4a is a simple query because the expected result is *'How to View Source Code'* $\rightarrow$ *'On Wikis'* therefore, N-hop $= 0$

and *Length* = 2. Figure 4b is a medium query because the expected output is *'How to View Source Code'* → *'Safari'* → *'Open Safari'* and as a result N-hop = 0 and *Length* = 3. Finally Fig. 4c is a complex query seeing as *'How to View SourceCode'* → *'Safari'* → *'Open Safari'* results in N-hop = 1.

Table 2. Graph statistics

Experiment	Nodes	Edges	Number of neighbors	Label length	Number of queries	Number of maps
1	12.452(4.17)	11.452(4.17)	5.359(2.33)	6.169(2.37)	15	200
2	21.333(2.35)	37.333(11.26)	2.770(0.12)	2.355(0.68)	18 each map (56)	3
3	65,599	131,951	3.964	1	9	1

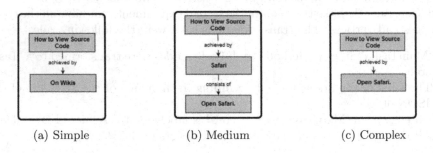

(a) Simple   (b) Medium   (c) Complex

Fig. 4. Three complexity query levels

Table 2 shows the statistical information of the maps and queries in each experiment. The numbers indicate the average and the standard deviation in brackets. The experiment material and results can be found in[3].

To evaluate the performance of the GMSE algorithm we used the following metrics. (1) **Exact and Domain Mean Reciprocal rank (MRR)** indicates whether the right path and map were retrieved, respectively; (2) **Graph Similarity (G-sim)** measures the similarity between a query graph and a sub-graph from the knowledge graph as defined in Definition 9. The G-sim takes into the account the highest G-sim score of each query and ignores cases in which no answer was found; (3) **Recall@5** that determines whether the expected result appears within the top five results in term of domain match; (4) The **time** it took the algorithm to return a result;

We executed GSME with K = 2, threshold = 0.65, and with two different label similarity (sim_l) functions. The first is Definition 3(1) and the second is Definition 3(2). We also checked whether sim_e and sim_t contributed to improving the search results by running the algorithm using sim_l as the only semantic

---

[3] https://tinyurl.com/y4ar8bhb.

similarity (LSO) using both Definition 3(1) and Definition 3(2) and comparing the results to a GSME that uses all similarity functions (sim_l, sim_e, sim_t) as defined in Definition 9. We measured the execution time on an Intel® Core™ i-7 6700HQ CPU @ 2.600 GHz processor with 16 GM of RAM.

5.2 Results

Table 3 presents the results of the first two experiments. The complexity column refers to the query complexity. The similarity column refers to the label similarity function used in the experiment: word2vec is used for sim_l as defined in Definition 3(1), sent2vec is used for sim_l as described in Definition 3(2), and LSO as defined above. Next, the various metrics are presented. Each metric column was split into two sub-columns. In the first experiment, it appears that using sent2vec leads to better results in terms of E-MRR, D-MRR and Recall@5. In the second experiment, it appears that the mean results achieved by executing GSME on the three different maps using 18 queries using sim_l as defined in Definition 3(1), led to more accurate results in terms of E-MRR.

With respect to performance, executing the queries on small maps takes a fraction of a second. In the third experiment, in which we checked the performance of GSME on large maps, we found out that the time it took to get the response was on average 2.23 s with a standard deviation of 0.104 s. The measured runtime of GSME was achieved without the use of sim_l. The decision not to use sim_l is due to the fact that the use of the said function increases the runtime during the initialization of GSME due to a lack of indexing.

In addition, we checked which value of the threshold yields a better result in certain groups of complexity. We found a positive correlation between the complexity and threshold values.

Table 3. Experiments Results

Comp.	Sim.	E-MRR		D-MRR	Recall@5	Time		G-sim	
		FE	SE	FE	FE	FE	SE	FE	SE
Simp.	word2vec	0.222	**0.944(0.471)**	0.49	0.6	12.39s(3.41)	0.047s(0.028)	0.803	0.897(0.012)
	sen2vec	0.8	0.388(0.360)	**0.802**	0.8	0.430s(0.07)	0.005s(0.024)	0.6	0.664(0.153)
	LSO	0.002	0.665(0.209)	0.602	0.6	0.003s(0.0)	0.064s(0.031)	0.561	0.913(0.043)
Med.	word2vec	0.3	**0.638(0.274)**	0.47	0.6	8.049s(2.74)	0.041s(0.017)	0.732	0.861(0.076)
	sen2vec	0.4	0.333(0.272)	**0.801**	0.8	0.450s(0.06)	0.021s(0.019)	0.6	0.446(0.377)
	LSO	0.281	0.221(0.314)	0.610	0.4	0.394s(0.04)	0.055s(0.016)	0.57	0.935(0.068)
Complex	word2vec	0.072	**0.666(0.360)**	0.487	0.6	9.74s(3.47)	0.064s(0.028)	0.6	0.8(0.103)
	sen2vec	0.25	0.611(0.437)	**0.850**	1	0.401s(0.04)	0.064s(0.028)	0.601	0.412(0.352)
	LSO	0.281	0.666(0.417)	0.803	0.4	0.369s(0.06)	0.059s(0.016)	0.575	0.792(0.072)

E-MRR = Exact-MRR;LSO_{se} = LSO using sematch; FE = First experiment; SE = Second experiment; Comp. = Complexity; Sim = Similarity; Simp. = Simple; Med. = Medium

5.3 Discussion

In this section, we discuss the results with respect to the parameters of GSME and the input characteristics.

In the experiment, we set the number of neighbors (K) to 2. It might be beneficial to increase K in correlation to the number of neighbors of each node. This might increase the accuracy of the search and allow the exploration of additional paths. On the other hand, it might increase the execution time.

The threshold parameter also affects the results by determining the relevant nodes from which the algorithm moves forward. It's possible that the threshold should be determined based on the domain and the sim_l function. The semantic of two nodes (sim_l) depends on two parameters: the similarity of two labels (Definition 3(1) or Definition 3(2)) and the length of a node's label in terms of how many words the vertex contains. In the case of long labels, the similarity that is defined in Definition 3(2) leads to better accuracy. For short labels, using the similarity in Definition 3(1) achieves better results.

Recent path algorithms showed similar results in terms of recall, and in the second experiment also in terms of time [18,21]. Still, there are differences between recent works to ours. The results of [21] are dependent on the quality of prior knowledge while queries in our experiments are constructed by the assumption that the user does not has this knowledge. [18] assumes that each edge in the target path needs to be similar to at least one edge in the query graph. We speculate that this assumption leads to better performances in terms of time than ours in the third experiment. In addition, these path algorithms are focused only on the similarity between paths rather than the similarity of the path to the domain that the path comes from. This domain similarity is expressed in our experiment by the D-MRR metric.

Alternatives path algorithms appear in [16]. These algorithms look for a specific pattern in an unknown graph. Therefore they search for isomorphic graph. In our problem, isomorphic graph may not be the optimal result for a query graph because we also consider the semantic similarities of the labels. Using such algorithms, for complex queries will not retrieve relevant result.

5.4   Threats to Validity

The initial evaluation we performed should be taken with caution and should consider the following threats to validity:

- **Small maps**: The maps in the experiment are of limited size. Wang et al. [18] used DBPedia, Freebase, Yago, and a synthetic set for experimental validation. These knowledge graphs are more convincing but they are not based on know-how mapping. We should explore the algorithm with much larger know-how maps.
- **Self-authoring**: We as the authors of the paper, developed the queries and the domain maps in the second experiment, so some biases might exist. Nevertheless, our aim in this evaluation was to challenge the algorithm, so the queries we devised accordingly.
- **Simple queries**: As the domain maps are small, so are the queries. There is a need to incorporate more complex queries and multi-paths ones as well.

– **Comparing to other works**: Indeed, the results should be compared to other alternatives. Yet, such alternatives need to be adjusted for searching Know-How maps.

6 Summary

In this paper, we propose GSME, an algorithm for searching ME-maps. The algorithm is a greedy one that takes into account structure, semantic, and type similarity. The initial evaluation we performed shows promising results.

Nevertheless, we want to test how well the algorithm performs with other domains and examine alternatives for calculating the similarity of the vertices and edges. This includes the tuning of the algorithm's parameters, either a-priory or during its execution. We also plan to test the GSME performance with respect to other adjusted alternatives (i.e., datasets and algorithms).

Acknowledgment. This research was partially supported by the Data Science Research Center at Ben-Gurion University of the Negev (DSRC@BGU).

References

1. Angles, R., Arenas, M., Barceló, P., Hogan, A., Reutter, J., Vrgoč, D.: Foundations of modern query languages for graph databases. ACM Comput. Surv. (CSUR) **50**(5), 1–40 (2017)
2. Bragilovski, M., Makias, Y., Shamshila, M., Stern, R., Sturm, A.: Searching for class models. In: Augusto, A., Gill, A., Nurcan, S., Reinhartz-Berger, I., Schmidt, R., Zdravkovic, J. (eds.) BPMDS/EMMSAD -2021. LNBIP, vol. 421, pp. 277–292. Springer, Cham (2021). https://doi.org/10.1007/978-3-030-79186-5_18
3. Ferrucci, D., et al.: Building Watson: an overview of the DeepQA project. AI Mag. **31**(3), 59–79 (2010)
4. Garud, R.: On the distinction between know-how, know-why, and know-what. Adv. Strateg. Manag. **14**, 81–101 (1997)
5. Greenstein, L.: Assessing 21st Century Skills: A Guide to Evaluating Mastery and Authentic Learning. SAGE Publications, Thousand Oaks (2012)
6. Han, S., Zou, L., Yu, J.X., Zhao, D.: Keyword search on RDF graphs-a query graph assembly approach. In: Proceedings of the 2017 ACM on Conference on Information and Knowledge Management, pp. 227–236 (2017)
7. Hu, S., Zou, L., Zhang, X.: A state-transition framework to answer complex questions over knowledge base. In: Proceedings of the 2018 Conference on Empirical Methods in Natural Language Processing, pp. 2098–2108 (2018)
8. Khwaja, S., Alshayeb, M.: Survey on software design-pattern specification languages. ACM Comput. Surv. **49**(1), 1–35 (2016)
9. Melnik, S., Garcia-Molina, H., Rahm, E.: Similarity flooding: a versatile graph matching algorithm and its application to schema matching. In: Proceedings 18th International Conference on Data Engineering, pp. 117–128. IEEE (2002)
10. Miller, G.A.: Wordnet: a lexical database for English. Commun. ACM **38**(11), 39–41 (1995)

11. Novak, J., Cañas, A.: The theory underlying concept maps and how to construct them (2006)
12. Pareti, E.H., Klein, P.: The human know-how dataset (2014). https://doi.org/10.7488/ds/1394
13. Pérez, J., Arenas, M., Gutierrez, C.: Semantics and complexity of SPARQL. ACM Trans. Database Syst. (TODS) **34**(3), 1–45 (2009)
14. Reinhartz-Berger, I.: Towards automatization of domain modeling. Data Knowl. Eng. **69**(5), 491–515 (2010)
15. Sarewitz, D., Nelson, R.R.: Progress in know-how: its origins and limits. Innov. Technol. Gov. Global. **3**(1), 101–117 (2008)
16. Stern, R., Kalech, M., Felner, A.: Finding patterns in an unknown graph. AI Commun. **25**(3), 229–256 (2012)
17. Sturm, A., Gross, D., Wang, J., Yu, E.: Means-ends based know-how mapping. J. Knowl. Manag. **21**, 454–473 (2017)
18. Wang, Y., Khan, A., Wu, T., Jin, J., Yan, H.: Semantic guided and response times bounded top-k similarity search over knowledge graphs. In: 36th International Conference on Data Engineering (ICDE), pp. 445–456. IEEE (2020)
19. Yadollahi, A., Shahraki, A.G., Zaiane, O.R.: Current state of text sentiment analysis from opinion to emotion mining. ACM Comput. Surv. **50**(2), 1–33 (2017)
20. Yu, E., Giorgini, P., Maiden, N., Mylopoulos, J.: Social Modeling for Requirements Engineering. The MIT Press, Cambridge (2011)
21. Zheng, W., Zou, L., Peng, W., Yan, X., Song, S., Zhao, D.: Semantic SPARQL similarity search over RDF knowledge graphs. Proc. VLDB Endow. **9**(11), 840–851 (2016)
22. Zhu, G., Iglesias, C.A.: Sematch: semantic similarity framework for knowledge graphs. Knowl.-Based Syst. **130**, 30–32 (2017)
23. Zou, L., Huang, R., Wang, H., Yu, J.X., He, W., Zhao, D.: Natural language question answering over RDF: a graph data driven approach. In: Proceedings of the ACM SIGMOD International Conference on Management of Data, pp 313–324 (2014)

Trustworthiness Requirements: The Pix Case Study

Glenda Amaral[1(✉)], Renata Guizzardi[2], Giancarlo Guizzardi[1,2],
and John Mylopoulos[3]

[1] CORE/KRDB, Free University of Bozen-Bolzano, Bolzano, Italy
{gmouraamaral,giancarlo.guizzardi}@unibz.it
[2] University of Twente, Enschede, The Netherlands
r.guizzardi@utwente.nl
[3] University of Toronto, Toronto, Canada
jm@cs.toronto.edu

Abstract. The advent of socio-technical, cyber-physical and artificial intelligence systems has broadened the scope of requirements engineering, which must now deal with new classes of requirements, concerning ethics, privacy and trust. This brings new challenges to Requirements Engineering, in particular regarding the understanding of the non-functional requirements behind these new types of systems. To address this issue, we propose the Ontology-based Requirements Engineering (ObRE) method, which aims to systematize the elicitation and analysis of requirements, by using an ontology to conceptually clarify the meaning of a class of requirements, such as privacy, ethicality and trustworthiness. We illustrate the working of ObRE by applying it to a real case study concerning trustworthiness requirements.

Keywords: Trustworthiness requirements · Requirements elicitation and analysis · Unified Foundational Ontology

1 Introduction

Requirements Engineering (RE) is a critical system development activity that makes or breaks many software development projects [12]. A myriad of RE methods, following different paradigms, have been around for at least four decades. Early methods focused on 'what' stakeholders need, resulting in a list of system functionalities directly indicated by stakeholders or inferred by requirements analysts. In the early nineties, goal-oriented RE (GORE) inaugurated a new paradigm that focused on 'why' a system was needed and 'how' needs of stakeholders can be addressed [14]. Also around this time, the realization that not only functionalities but also *qualities* are important to shape the system-to-be led to newfound attention on non-functional requirements (e.g., privacy, security, etc.) [6]. In the 2000s, the agile software engineering paradigm emerged, leading to new RE methods focusing on incremental software delivery and teamwork

© Springer Nature Switzerland AG 2021
A. Ghose et al. (Eds.): ER 2021, LNCS 13011, pp. 257–267, 2021.
https://doi.org/10.1007/978-3-030-89022-3_21

(e.g., capturing requirements via user stories [7])[1]. Generally, RE has evolved in response to an ever-increasing system complexity that today spans not only system concerns, but also social (e.g., security, privacy), physical (as in cyber-physical systems), and personal (e.g., ethical concerns for artificial intelligence systems) ones. A major challenge for RE today is to propose concepts, tools and techniques that support requirements engineering activities for incorporating high-level societal concerns and goals, such as privacy, fairness ands trustworthiness, into the software development processes as explicit requirements.

This paper is intended to address this challenge with a novel method named Ontology-based Requirements Engineering (ObRE). The method aims to systematize the elicitation and analysis of requirements, by using an ontological account for a class of requirements, such as privacy, fairness and trustworthiness. ObRE is intended to help by "semantically unpacking" concepts such as trustworthiness or fairness where the analysts may struggle in understanding, for example, which requirements can make the system under development trustworthy or fair. Ontological analysis provides a foundation for ObRE as it enables a deep account of the meaning of a particular domain. The notions of *ontology* and *ontological analysis* adopted here are akin to their interpretations in philosophy [4]. In this view, the goals of *ontological analysis* are: (i) characterize what kinds of entities are assumed to exist by a given conceptualization of a domain; (ii) the metaphysical nature of these kinds of entities. An *ontology*, in turn, is a collection of concepts and relationships that together address questions (i) and (ii).

The paper presents in detail the ObRE and illustrates its use with a case study, focused on a recently released real system, named Pix. Pix is an instant payment solution, created and managed by the Central Bank of Brazil (BCB), which enables its users to send or receive payment transfers in few seconds at any time. The success achieved by Pix has led us to consider it an appropriate case study for our approach.

The remainder of the paper is structured as follows. First, in Sect. 2 we explain the ontological account of trustworthiness requirements adopted in this work. Then, in Sect. 3 we present the ObRE method. In Sect. 4 we present the Pix case study and in Sect. 5 we use ObRE to analyse the trustworthiness requirements of Pix. In Sect. 6 we make some final remarks on the implications of our proposal to the requirements engineering practice, and we describe our future research agenda.

2   The Reference Ontology of Trustworthiness Requirements

Trustworthiness requirements are a class of requirements where the objective is to get user stakeholders to adopt an attitude of trust towards the system-to-be. We

---

[1] This is a brief historical account intended to highlight the evolution of ideas and methods in RE. This account is not meant to be exhaustive; we acknowledge the existence of many other high impact RE methods, such as feature-based RE, recent methods based on CANVAS.

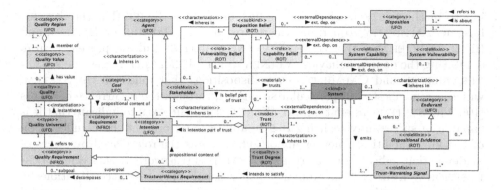

Fig. 1. The reference ontology of trustworthiness requirements

propose to first unpack the concept of trust. This is done here with a fragment of the Reference Ontology of Trustworthiness Requirements[2] (ROTwR) [1], which is a reference ontology grounded on UFO [9], and based on the trust-related concepts defined in the Reference Ontology of Trust[3] (ROT) [2,3] and on the ontological interpretation of non-functional requirements presented in [11]. Some of the main ontological commitments of ROTwR on the nature of trust and trustworthiness requirements are: (i) trust is relative to intentions [5]; (ii) trust is grounded on beliefs [5]; (iii) trustworthiness requirement is related to an intention that is part of a trust relation between a stakeholder and the system-to-be [1]; (iv) trustworthiness requirements are quality requirements [11]; and (v) the system can emit trust-warranting signals to ensure trustworthy behavior [13].

Figure 1 presents an excerpt of ROTwR, represented in OntoUML (an ontology-driven conceptual modeling language based on UFO [9]). In ROTwR, REQUIREMENT is modeled as a GOAL, which is the propositional content of a STAKEHOLDER's INTENTION. QUALITY REQUIREMENT is a type of REQUIRE-MENT, and TRUSTWORTHY REQUIREMENT is a type of QUALITY REQUIRE-MENT. All QUALITY REQUIREMENTS are such that they restrict the value of the qualities at hand to a particular set of values of the corresponding QUALITY REGION. For example, "being trustworthy" is a constraint on the mental state of the trustor to be in the trustworthiness region of a space that also includes an untrustworthiness region. STAKEHOLDERS are represented as AGENTS that play the role of trustor, while the SYSTEM is an existentially independent object that plays the role of trustee. The SYSTEM intends to satisfy the TRUSTWOR-THINESS REQUIREMENTS. As for TRUST, it is represented as a complex mode composed of a STAKEHOLDER's INTENTION and a set of BELIEFS that inhere in the STAKEHOLDER and are externally dependent on the dispositions [10] that

---

[2] The complete version of ROTwR in OntoUML and its implementation in OWL is available at https://purl.org/krdb-core/trustworthiness-requirements-ontology.

[3] The complete version of ROT in OntoUML and its implementation in OWL are available at http://purl.org/krdb-core/trust-ontology.

inhere in the SYSTEM. These beliefs include: (i) the BELIEF that the SYSTEM has the CAPABILITY to perform the desired action (CAPABILITY BELIEF); and (ii) the BELIEF that the SYSTEM's VULNERABILITIES will not prevent it from exhibiting the desired behavior (VULNERABILITY BELIEF). The SYSTEM's VULNERABILITIES and CAPABILITIES are dispositions that inhere in the SYSTEM, which are manifested in particular situations, through the occurrence of events [10]. The SYSTEM can emit TRUST-WARRANTING SIGNALS to indicate that it is capable of successfully realizing the capabilities and prevent the manifestation of the vulnerabilities. Another important aspect is the role played by pieces of evidence that indicate that a trustee (SYSTEM) is trustworthy, named here DISPOSITIONAL EVIDENCE. Examples of dispositional evidences are certifications by trusted third parties, history of performance, recommendations, past successful experiences, among others. Ontologically speaking, DISPOSITIONAL EVIDENCES are social entities, typically social relators (e.g., a relator binding the certifying entity, the certified entity and referring to a capability, vulnerability, etc.), but also documents (social objects themselves) that represent these social entities (e.g., in the way a marriage certificate documents a marriage as a social relator). They are modeled as roles played by endurants (objects, relators, etc.) related to a DISPOSITION of the SYSTEM.

3   Ontology-Based Requirements Engineering

In ObRE, we address the challenge of dealing with non-functional requirements, such as trustworthiness, by relying on ontological analysis. Ontological analysis provides a foundation for our proposal as it enables a deep account of the meaning of a particular domain, thus allowing to "semantically unpack" the requirements concepts at-hand, thereby facilitating requirements activities. Figure 2 illustrates the process of the ObRE method, showing the three activities that compose it, which are described below.

1. Adopt or develop an ontology for conceptualizing a class of requirements: In this step, requirements analysts and ontology engineers can choose between reusing an existing ontology or performing ontological analysis for the particular class of requirement. Having the requirements explicitly defined and understood, the analyst may proceed to the next step.

2. Instantiate the ontology for a system-to-be, resulting in a domain model: In this step, key concepts of the ontology can be used as a guide to define the right questions to be asked to the stakeholders during requirements elicitation (e.g., Table 1). The answers can be used as input to instantiate elements of the ontology. This is intended to serve as a domain model for conducting requirements analysis.

3. Analyze requirements based on the domain model: In this step, the analyst uses the domain model to define and analyze system requirements. For instance, she may simply define a requirements table, listing the requirements instantiated with the help of the ontology. Or if she prefers a more sophisticated analysis methodology, she may use goal modeling, defining the contribution of different choices to accomplish a particular goal (i.e., requirement), and specifying how goals relate to each other, as well as to relevant stakeholders' resources and tasks. Or yet, she may create user stories based on the identified ontological instances. From this point on, the requirements analysis may progress as the chosen method prescribes, however, with the benefit of having the ontology and ontological instances as guides.

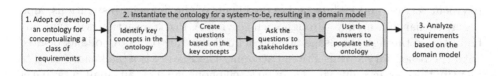

Fig. 2. Ontology-based requirements engineering method

4 Case Study

4.1 Research Method

To evaluate and demonstrate the contribution of our ontology-based method for the analysis of trustworthiness requirements, we conducted a case study in the Central Bank of Brazil (BCB), in the context of the Brazilian Instant Payments Ecosystem.

The research procedure was adapted from [15]. The initial stage involved the planning and designing of the case study. We defined the purpose of the case study - *evaluate the feasibility of the application of ObRE for the analysis and elicitation of Pix's trustworthiness requirements* - and held a planning meeting to identify different areas of interest and select the interviewees.

In the collect stage, we gathered information from documentation and interviews. Firstly, documents describing and documenting the project were collected from the BCB's website[4] to deepen the knowledge about Pix. Then, we conducted interviews with the stakeholders responsible for the areas of interest, namely communication, instant payment systems, communication interfaces, transaction accounts identifier directory, security and infrastructure. The questions in the interviews were based on the notions of trust and trustworthiness requirements described in the adopted ontology (Sect. 2) (step 1 of ObRE method, in Fig. 2). The interviews were recorded and transcribed to facilitate and improve the analysis. In the analyze stage, the interviewers examined the transcripts and searched for the elements to instantiate the ontology of trustworthiness requirements (step 2 of ObRE method, in Fig. 2). Then, we used the ontology instantiation as a domain model to define and analyze trustworthiness requirements (step 3 of ObRE method, in Fig. 2).

---

[4] https://www.bcb.gov.br/en/financialstability/pix_en.

4.2   The Brazilian Instant Payments Ecosystem (Pix)

The Central Bank of Brazil is a special nature agency, characterized by the absence of ties or hierarchical subordination to any Ministry. Among the main tasks of the BCB are the regulation and supervision of the National Financial System and the administration of the payments system.

Pix is the instant payment solution, created and managed by the BCB, having two kinds of stakeholders: *financial institutions* that want to offer this instant payment service, and *end users*, i.e. the clients of the financial institutions, aiming at exchanging money through such service. A Pix transaction will typically be initiated through the usage of a predefined Pix Key or a QR code associated with the beneficiary's transactional account. The Pix key is a 'nickname' used to identify the user account, which can be a cell phone number, an email, a taxpayer number or a random key. The key links one of these basic items of information to the complete information that identifies the customer's transactional account. Once started, Pix transactions are irrevocable and processed individually in a few seconds. Pix can be processed between: Person-to-Person (P2P), Person-to-Business (P2B), Business-to-Business (B2B), Person-to-Government (P2G), or Business-to-Government (B2G).

Pix operates through a centralized framework comprising messaging communication among the various participants and BCB. All transactions take place through digitally signed messages exchanged, in encrypted form, through a private network apart from the Internet. In order to promote public awareness, BCB created the Pix's brand, whose principles—Design, Sonority, Governance—aim at promoting an easily identifiable brand that should be displayed by all participating financial institutions.

5   Using ObRE to Analyze Pix's Requirements

This section presents the results of the case study. As aforementioned, our findings are based in the analysis of the documentation and the interviews conducted with stakeholders responsible for Pix key areas. Our analysis took into account the whole ecosystem in which the system is included, whose main stakeholders are the *Pix ecosystem participants* (financial and payment institutions that offer transaction accounts) and *end users* (individuals and organizations).

5.1   Domain Ontology Development or Adoption

We reused our previous Reference Ontology on Trustworthiness Requirements [1] (Sect. 2) to unpack the notions of trust and trustworthiness requirements (step 1 of ObRE method, in Fig. 2). Then, we defined the initial questions that would guide the interviews with the stakeholders (Table 1). The ontology served as guidance for our work from the beginning of the case study, helping us focus on the domain being investigated and supporting the creation of the interview questions. As can be seen on Table 1, these questions are actually formulated based on the concepts from ROTwR (see column 2).

Table 1. Questions related to key ontology concepts

Question	ROTwR concept
Stakeholders trust the system to...	Intention
Stakeholders trust the system because they believe that it is capable of...	Capability Belief System Capability
Stakeholders trust the system because they believe that it has mechanisms to prevent...	Vulnerability Belief System Vulnerability
How can the system indicate that it is trustworthy?	Trust-warranting Signal
What pieces of evidence show that the system is trustworthy?	Dispositional Evidence

5.2 Domain Ontology Instantiation

We adopt the following coding to refer to instances of key ROTwR concepts hereafter: (i) INT for intentions; (ii) BEL for disposition beliefs; (iii) TS for trust-warranting signals; (iv) DE for dispositional evidences; and (v) TR for trustworthiness requirements.

The interviews showed that, in general, *end users trust Pix to send or receive payment transfers safely and easily, in few seconds on a 24/7 basis* (INT1). According to an interviewee, "users want to be sure that the system will access their money only when they want, and in the way they want". In other words, users who trust the system believe that *it is safe* (BEL1) and that *it will be available when they need* (BEL2). Interviewees also expressed that it is important that Pix participants feel safe to perform transactions in the ecosystem. It was a consensus among the interviewees that *security* (TR1), *availability* (TR2) and *instantaneity* (TR3) are essential to build sustainable trust in the system.

As stated by the Pix project team and explained in the documentation, *security* has been a part of Pix design since its inception, and it is prioritized in all aspects of the ecosystem, including transactions, personal information and the fight against fraud and money laundering. The requirements for the *availability*, *confidentiality* (TR4), *integrity* (TR5) and *authenticity* (TR6) of the information were carefully studied and several controls were implemented to ensure a high level of security. All transactions take place through digitally signed messages that travel in encrypted form, over a protected network, apart from the Internet. In addition, user information is also encrypted and protected by mechanisms that prevent scans of personal information in the sole and centralized proxy database, an addressing database that will store Pix keys information. There are also *indicators that assist the ecosystem participants in the process of prevention against fraud and money laundering* (TS1). Another important aspect related to security is *traceability* (TR7). All Pix operations are fully traceable, which means that the Central Bank and the institutions involved can, at the request of the competent authorities, identify the origin and destination account holders of any and all payment transactions in Pix. Thus, in a situation of kidnapping or other means of unlawful coercion, the recipient of a financial transfer is fully identified.

In addition, *all participants must comply with basic regulation on operational and liquidity risk management framework* (DE1); *cybersecurity policy* (DE2); a *service level agreement that establishes high availability parameters and processing time limits* (DE3); among others.

Another aspect that emerged from the interviews is the importance of providing a simple experience for end users. Interviewees mentioned that "people are more likely to trust in something they understand" and "simplicity leads to trust". Simply put, users who trust the system believe that *it is simple and easy to use* (BEL3). The general consensus is that *usability* (TR8) is of paramount importance for effectively promoting trust in the system. *Visual identity* (TS2) was mentioned by interviewees as an important attribute to facilitate the understanding and adoption of the functionality. According to them, the establishment of a universal brand was essential for users to identify the new way of making/receiving payments and transfers, in a clear and unambiguous way. Equally important was the definition of a *manual with minimum usability requirements* (DE4), which must be followed by all participants of the Pix ecosystem.

Still in this direction, actions focusing on *explainability* (TR9) have been taken since the beginning of the project. Some examples mentioned during the interviews are: *advertising campaigns in the media and social networks using everyday examples* (TS3); *documentation available on the BCB website* (See footnote 4) (TS4); *dissemination events* (held in virtual mode, due to the COVID-19 pandemic) *for different market sectors* (TS5); (iv) partnership with the press and digital influencers for advertising, as well as for monitoring and preventing the spread of fake news about the system.

Finally, *transparency* (TR10) was another attribute mentioned by a number of interviewees. One of the reasons for the prioritization of *transparency*, as explained by several interviewees, is that "if the participants are involved in the discussions from the beginning, *they believe that their needs will be considered and that they will not be taken by surprise, consequently, they feel safe and trust the system*" (BEL4). Interviewees also mentioned that "participants' trust in the Pix ecosystem contributed to foster end users' trust". In this direction, the Pix operational framework development has been an open and transparent process, with intense participation from market agents and potential users. In order to foster a collaborative implementation process, BCB created a specific forum, named *'Pix Forum'* (DE5), which has about 200 participating institutions. Lastly, as previously mentioned, an extensive documentation about the Pix project and the Pix ecosystem is available at the BCB website (See footnote 4), providing information such as a Pix regulations, Frequently Asked Questions, and Pix statistics[5], which contribute to *transparency* at different levels. Pix statistics include indicators, such as number of registered Pix keys, number of Pix transactions, number of users transacting Pix, among others. We identified that, in general, *these indicators* positively exceeded the initial expectations, thus demonstrating the success of the project. In this case, they can be seen as pieces of evidence (DE6) that indicate that the Pix ecosystem is trustworthy.

---

[5] https://www.bcb.gov.br/en/financialstability/pixstatistics.

5.3   Requirements Analysis Method Execution

We exemplify the step 3 of ObRE method (Fig. 2) by analyzing the requirements of Pix. In particular, we present both a requirements table and a goal model for this case.

We start by presenting Table 2, showing how a requirements table may be enriched with the inclusion of columns representing some of ROTwR concepts. All words highlighted in boldface in Table 2 refer to ontological concepts analyzed in Sect. 2, while the ontological instances are written as non-emphasized text. Due to space limitations, we focused only on security. To build a requirements table such as Table 2, we first capture the elements that compose the trust of stakeholders in Pix, namely their intentions and beliefs about Pix dispositions, and then we come up with particular requirements for the system-to-be to fulfill these goals and beliefs. In particular, these are requirements for the developing capabilities (i.e. system's functionalities) needed to accomplish the desired requirements.

Table 2. Requirements table of the Pix Ecosystem focusing on security

Stakeholder	Intention	Capability belief	Trustworthiness requirement	Capability
End Users, Participants	Send and receive payment transfers safely	Pix is Safe (BEL1)	Security (TR1)	Has security mechanisms
			Confidentiality (TR4)	Make info traffic in protected network
				Encrypt info and messages
			Integrity (TR5)	Encrypt info and messages
			Authenticity (TR6)	Digitally sign messages
			Traceability (TR7)	Use traceability mechanisms

As an alternative, consider a requirements analysis for the Pix case using goal modeling. Given the limited space available, we only present, in Fig. 3, a fragment of goal model for this case using the i^* framework [8]. The model shows the goals that the stakeholders referred to in Table 2 delegate to the Pix Ecosystem (through the i^* dependency relation). Besides dependencies, the goal model depicts the internal perspective of Pix, assisting in the analysis of the system's requirements. Note that security (TR1), availability (TR2), instantaneity (TR3), confidentiality (TR4), integrity (TR5), authenticity (TR6), traceability (TR7), usability (TR8), explainability (TR9), transparency (TR10) were represented as qualities and goals that contribute to (help) the ultimate goal of being trustworthy. Then, for each of them, more specific goals and qualities were identified and related to them by contribution links. For instance, the *protecting information confidentiality* goal helps the achievement of *being secure*.

The goal model also allows the requirements analyst to progressively identify more concrete requirements and solutions and the resources needed to accomplish them. For example, *making the information traffic in a protected network* contributes to the *protecting information confidentiality* goal, and the *protected*

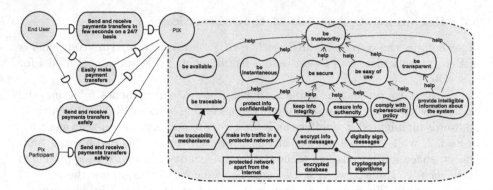

Fig. 3. A fragment of the goal model of the pix ecosystem focusing on security

network itself is a resource needed in this task. To accomplish the higher level of *being secure*, other tasks, qualities and goals are involved. The complete diagrams presenting the case study can be found at https://purl.org/krdb-core/obre. We emphasize that ObRE does not subscribe to a specific RE method, leaving this choice for the requirements analyst, based on their particular preference or skill.

6 Final Remarks

In this paper, we proposed the ObRE method to support requirements elicitation and analysis for challenging requirements, such as trustworthiness, fairness and privacy. The ObRE method has important implications for RE research and practice. For RE research, it suggests first and foremost that for a host of requirements families, including security, privacy, ethicality, trustworthiness and fairness, we need ontologies that capture relevant concepts. Many such ontologies have been proposed for security and privacy. For other families that only recently became prominent because of advent of AI systems, such ontologies are currently being developed. Secondly, we need tools for domain building by instantiating relevant ontologies for a particular system-to-be. Thirdly, for RE practice such tools need to be made available to practitioners who can't be expected to be knowledgeable in these fancy requirements in order to conduct requirements analysis for their next project.

The case study experience confirmed that the ontology-based method proposed here can have a positive impact in the requirements engineering activities of requirements related to high-level societal concerns and goals, such as trustworthiness, and suggests that this approach could be used to systematize the elicitation of other abstract requirements, such as privacy, fairness and ethical requirements. We acknowledge that our case study has some limitations in terms of evaluating the use of ObRE. First, the interviews and analysis were made by the developers of the method. Moreover, only members of the Pix project team were interviewed, and not Pix's stakeholders. However, for the latter, the results shown by the Pix statistics confirm the team's perception regarding Pix's trustworthiness and indicate that they are going in the right direction.

Our research agenda for the future includes a full-fledged evaluation of the method, including surveys and other empirical studies. Moreover, we aim at applying ObRE for other classes of requirements, such as fairness, privacy, and ethical requirements.

Acknowledgments. This work is partially supported by CAPES (PhD grant# 88881.173022/2018-01) and NeXON project (UNIBZ). The authors would like to thank the Central Bank of Brazil for sharing their experience with the Pix project.

References

1. Amaral, G., Guizzardi, R., Guizzardi, G., Mylopoulos, J.: Ontology-based modeling and analysis of trustworthiness requirements: preliminary results. In: Dobbie, G., Frank, U., Kappel, G., Liddle, S.W., Mayr, H.C. (eds.) ER 2020. LNCS, vol. 12400, pp. 342–352. Springer, Cham (2020). https://doi.org/10.1007/978-3-030-62522-1_25
2. Amaral, G., Sales, T.P., Guizzardi, G., Porello, D.: Towards a reference ontology of trust. In: Panetto, H., Debruyne, C., Hepp, M., Lewis, D., Ardagna, C.A., Meersman, R. (eds.) OTM 2019. LNCS, vol. 11877, pp. 3–21. Springer, Cham (2019). https://doi.org/10.1007/978-3-030-33246-4_1
3. Amaral, G., Sales, T.P., Guizzardi, G., Porello, D.: Ontological foundations for trust management: extending the reference ontology of trust. In: 15th International Workshop on Value Modelling and Business Ontologies (2021)
4. Berto, F., Plebani, M.: Ontology and Metaontology: A Contemporary Guide. Bloomsbury Publishing, London (2015)
5. Castelfranchi, C., Falcone, R.: Trust Theory: A Socio-cognitive and Computational Model, vol. 18. Wiley, Hoboken (2010)
6. Chung, L., Nixon, B., Yu, E., Mylopoulos, J.: Non-Functional Requirements in Software Engineering. International Series in Software Engineering, vol. 5. Springer, Heidelberg (2000). https://doi.org/10.1007/978-1-4615-5269-7
7. Cohn, M.: User Stories Applied: For Agile Software Development. Addison Wesley Longman Publishing Co., Inc., Boston (2004)
8. Dalpiaz, F., Franch, X., Horkoff, J.: iStar 2.0 language guide. arXiv:1605.07767 [cs.SE] (2016). dalp-fran-hork-16-istar.pdf
9. Guizzardi, G.: Ontological foundations for structural conceptual models. Telematica Instituut/CTIT (2005)
10. Guizzardi, G., Wagner, G., de Almeida Falbo, R., Guizzardi, R.S.S., Almeida, J.P.A.: Towards ontological foundations for the conceptual modeling of events. In: Ng, W., Storey, V.C., Trujillo, J.C. (eds.) ER 2013. LNCS, vol. 8217, pp. 327–341. Springer, Heidelberg (2013). https://doi.org/10.1007/978-3-642-41924-9_27
11. Guizzardi, R., et al.: An ontological interpretation of non-functional requirements. In: 8th International Conference on Formal Ontology in Information Systems, vol. 14, pp. 344–357 (2014)
12. Hussain, A., Mkpojiogu, E., Kamal, F.: The role of requirements in the success or failure of software projects. EJ Econjournals **6**, 6–7 (2016)
13. Riegelsberger, J., et al.: The mechanics of trust: a framework for research and design. Int. J. Human-Comput. Stud. **62**(3), 381–422 (2005)
14. Van Lamsweerde, A.: Requirements Engineering - From System Goals to UML Models to Software Specifications. Wiley, Chichester (2009)
15. Yin, R.K.: Case Study Research: Design and Methods (Applied Social Research Methods). Sage Publications, Thousand Oaks (2008)

Modeling the Internet of Things

A Conceptual Model for Digital Shadows in Industry and Its Application

Fabian Becker[1], Pascal Bibow[1], Manuela Dalibor[2], Aymen Gannouni[3],
Viviane Hahn[4], Christian Hopmann[1], Matthias Jarke[5,6], István Koren[7],
Moritz Kröger[8], Johannes Lipp[5,6], Judith Maibaum[4], Judith Michael[2]([✉]),
Bernhard Rumpe[2], Patrick Sapel[1], Niklas Schäfer[4], Georg J. Schmitz[9],
Günther Schuh[4], and Andreas Wortmann[10]

[1] IKV - Institute for Plastics Processing, RWTH Aachen University,
Aachen, Germany
{fabian.becker.sg,pascal.bibow,patrick.sapel}@ikv.rwth-aachen.de
[2] Software Engineering, RWTH Aachen University, Aachen, Germany
{dalibor,michael,rumpe}@se-rwth.de
[3] Chair of Information Management in Mechanical Engineering,
RWTH Aachen University, Aachen, Germany
aymen.gannouni@ima.rwth-aachen.de
[4] Laboratory for Machine Tools and Production Engineering (WZL),
RWTH Aachen University, Aachen, Germany
{v.hahn,j.maibaum,n.schaefer}@wzl.rwth-aachen.de
[5] Chair of Information Systems and Databases, RWTH Aachen University,
Aachen, Germany
{jarke,lipp}@dbis.rwth-aachen.de
[6] Fraunhofer Institute for Applied Information Technology FIT,
Sankt Augustin, Germany
[7] Chair of Process and Data Science, RWTH Aachen University, Aachen, Germany
koren@pads.rwth-aachen.de
[8] Chair for Laser Technology, RWTH Aachen University, Aachen, Germany
moritz.kroeger@llt.rwth-aachen.de
[9] ACCESS e.V. at the RWTH Aachen, Aachen, Germany
g.j.schmitz@access-technology.de
[10] Institute for Control Engineering of Machine Tools and Manufacturing Units
(ISW), University of Stuttgart, Stuttgart, Germany
wortmann@isw.uni-stuttgart.de

Abstract. Smart manufacturing demands to process data in domain-specific real-time. Engineering models created for constructing, commissioning, planning, or simulating manufacturing systems can facilitate aggregating and abstracting the wealth of manufacturing data to faster processable data structures for more timely decision making. Current research lacks conceptual foundations for how data and engineering models can be exploited in an integrated way to achieve this. Such research demands expertise from different smart manufacturing domains to harmonize the notion space. We propose a conceptual model to describe digital shadows, data structures tailored to exploit models and data in smart manufacturing, through a metamodel and its notion space. This conceptual model was established through interdisciplinary research in

© Springer Nature Switzerland AG 2021
A. Ghose et al. (Eds.): ER 2021, LNCS 13011, pp. 271–281, 2021.
https://doi.org/10.1007/978-3-030-89022-3_22

the German excellence cluster "Internet of Production" and evaluated
in various real-world manufacturing scenarios. This foundation for an
understanding helps to manage complexity, automated analyses, and syn-
theses, and, ultimately, facilitates cross-domain collaboration.

Keywords: Digital shadow · Conceptual model · Smart
manufacturing · Internet of production

1   Introduction

Digital transformation shapes our world: from communication, to transportation, to medicine, to manufacturing, documents and processes become digital
to enable smarter data analyses, better integration of stakeholders, and more
efficient automated information processing. In manufacturing, long-living cyber-
physical production systems produce tremendous data that can be exploited
to reduce downtime, consumption of resources, and increase manufacturing
agility towards lot-size one [29]. Analyzing and processing this data fast enough
demands its appropriate abstraction and meaningful aggregation. Current manufacturing environments leverages different and redundant IT-system silos comprising domain-specific data and models [23]. Therefore, access, and analysis of
production data is difficult [21]. Often, models of the involved systems and processes (*e.g.,* structure, behavior, knowledge) can be exploited to give meaning
to that data and provide a foundation for adaptive Digital Twins (DTs), the
digital representations of a cyber-physical system.

Research has produced a vast number of publications on DTs in manufacturing [9,25,30]. These DTs are conceived ad-hoc, for specific real-world applications and related data structures, *e.g.,* for CNC machining [15], injection molding [12], monitoring [6], or fatigue testing [7]. There is *no conceptual foundation*
for describing, abstracting, aggregating, and relating the data shared between
DTs. To mitigate this, we have conceived a conceptual model [16] of Digital
Shadows (DSs), describing data structures capturing the quintessential concepts
of manufacturing processes: data-traces including data-points and metadata, different kinds of engineering models, data-sources, and related assets as well as
purposes for creating DSs. This model has been defined and refined through a
series of interdisciplinary workshops in the Internet of Production (IoP)[1] cluster
of excellence and evaluated in various manufacturing scenarios, *e.g.,* injection
molding [3], pressure die casting, factory planning, ultra-short pulse ablation.

Overall, the contributions of this paper are (1) a novel conceptual model
of DSs in manufacturing including its metamodel and notion space and (2) its
practical application on a manufacturing scenario and its impact.

Outline. Section 2 introduces preliminaries before Sect. 3 presents our conceptual model. Afterwards, Sect. 4 shows its practical application on a real-world
manufacturing scenario. Sect. 5 discusses related research. Sect. 6 concludes.

---

[1] Funded by the Deutsche Forschungsgemeinschaft (DFG, German Research Foundation) under Germany's Excellence Strategy – EXC 2023 Internet of Production -
390621612. Website: https://www.iop.rwth-aachen.de/.

2   Background

One major difficulty when speaking of models, DS and DT is that these terms are often not clearly distinguished and even used interchangeably. We differentiate these terms based on the information flow between the digital and the physical object [10]. While a model and the physical object it represents are synchronized only through manual updates, a DS follows the physical object based on an automatic data flow. Accordingly, a DS is defined as *a set of contextual data-traces and their aggregation and abstraction collected concerning a system for a specific purpose with respect to the original system* [3]. A DT extends the definition of the DS by automatically influencing the physical object as well.

DSs do not fully represent, but provide a purposeful view of the observed object or process, which is referred to as its asset. Accordingly, they are created with a specific focus and by selection and aggregation of data that may originate from heterogeneous sources. The context for the respective data-traces is given by the metadata. The combination of the metadata with referenced models enables data structuring required for subsequent semantic processing. DSs must therefore contain domain-specific knowledge in suitable form. This allows for task-specific analysis and enrichment of underlying models with relevant data, which thereby enables knowledge- and real-time-based decision making in production.

The DS concept is investigated by means of a conceptual model for DSs. The conceptual model consolidates a set of concepts, which are presented as elements in linguistic format. The notion space [16] clarifies the meaning of all elements of DSs and their relationship on its basis.

3   Digital Shadow Metamodel and Notion Space

To achieve the benefits of a standardized information architecture of relevant data in production such as knowledge-based decision making across domains, a metamodel for DSs is proposed. The corresponding metamodel and its elements are presented in Fig. 1. The concepts of the DS are further detailed in the following descriptions, which define the notion space for the metamodel.

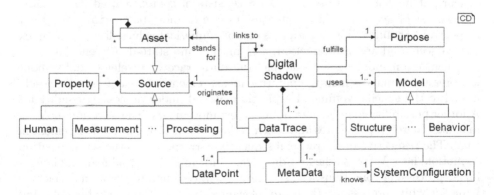

Fig. 1. The metamodel of the DS in UML class diagram (CD) notation.

Asset. According to DIN SPEC 91345 [2] and DIN ISO 55000, "an asset is an item, thing or entity that has potential or actual value to an organization" [1]. An `Asset` can be physical as well as virtual and always fulfills a specific role within a system. Becoming an asset is always concomitant with development, engineering, measurement, construction, or a manufacturing process, regarding the asset's type and role [26]. Physical assets are, *e.g.,* machines, components, and tools. Virtual assets are, *e.g.,* plans, mechanical drawings, standards, or metamodels. A combination of several assets results in a new asset, *e.g.,* by connecting multiple machines to a production cell and vice versa [20]. By characterizing the asset with suitable attributes that reflect its properties, the organization and stakeholders establish the asset in the virtual world so it is applicable as a source [2]. Each DS is associated with exactly one asset which represents the described system. This asset (system) can comprise subsystems of the type `Asset`.

Sources. As the DS is always considered within a context, all data that is regarded as part of it must be connected with its primary source. Therefore, each `DataTrace` must be associated with one distinct `Source`. A `Source` is composed of any number of defined properties, that specify at least the name, the data type, and the unit of the source's data. Sources can be of manifold kinds, which peculiarities shall not be limited in the context of the metamodel. In our metamodel, the `Asset` is a `Source`. While being the considered system within the DS, an asset can serve as a source (*e.g.,* for process limits due to machine specifications) for its own and also other DSs. Other source types could be human inputs via human-machine interfaces, sensors delivering measurement data, or any type of algorithms and simulations delivering specific information. A simple example is the error-acknowledgment by a machine operator. The source is a human and the property a Boolean. A more complex one is an injection molding machine as a source of type asset with diverse properties. Those could vary being specifications like a screw diameter as a float with the metric unit 'mm", actual values like the current clamping force as a float with the unit "kN", or simply the machine name as a string. Those are just a few examples to demonstrate the variety of possible sources and thus the cross-domain applicability of this model.

DataTrace. The core element of the DS is data that describes the matter of concern about the given asset. The DS consists of contextualized `DataTraces` as a subset of accessible data consisting of one or more `DataPoints` and their respective `MetaData`. These data-sets can be numerical values, lists, or complex data objects and are in production, *e.g.,* motion and state-dependent data.

In injection molding, for example, the data-trace may refer to data about the pressure signals or melt temperature measurements of a cavity sensor closely linked to the specific volume of a plastic material under processing conditions. Another possibility may be data about screw movements. The injection molding machine, therefore, measures and controls the screw position at each increment in time. The respective data-trace subsequently corresponds to the screw position as motion data. Whereas the first data-trace indicates the actual material behavior at processing conditions, the second data-trace refers to the actual machine behavior while processing. Both are relevant subsets of the accessible data and can be analyzed independently in direct comparison to underlying models of an ideal system. However, they can also be correlated with each other and thereby generate information about the correlation of temperature and pressure rising at specific screw movements.

DataPoint. As elaborated above, the DS may consist of multiple `DataTraces` and subsequently, a multitude of `DataPoints` that originate from several `Sources`. The data-points refer to the data a DS needs to describe the system's behavior following the targeted `Purpose`. It may be accessible by value in case of only small amounts of data or by reference to a database.

MetaData. To enable contextualizing and interpreting the actual data of concern that describe a system's behavior, the DS itself as well as the `DataTraces` hold `MetaData`. The metadata of the DS, therefore, lists on the one-hand side the complete system configuration (system setup) with all relevant master data about system components and subcomponents. Some of those subcomponents may serve as sources for individual data-traces and some might just act as supporting assets to the process of concern. Whereas the `SystemConfiguration` itself is integrated as a `Model`. Further structural, physical, or otherwise relevant models are also integrated to achieve the targeted `Purpose` of the DS.

The metadata of the individual sub data-traces on the other hand only need a reference to the overall system configuration as well as a reference to the process model and the respective asset that serves as the source for the data-points. Furthermore, it lists the settings of the data-source and the parameters that can be found in the data-points. The point identifier finally indicates the one parameter inside the point header that serves for unique identification.

Figure 2 presents an exemplary shadow object about actual process data of an injection unit during injection. The overall system is referenced by an 'uid' as well as the general process model and the injection unit as the `Source` of this `DataTrace`. To keep the trace and thereby also the DS lean, the data specification is separated from the final values accessible as `DataPoints`. To access the respective data, a point identifier from the list of actual values is determined, which might be the actual machine cycle or a timestamp. The `MetaData` finally enables the recombination of several `DataTraces` that, *e.g.,* originate from other processes and DS, to generate new `DigitalShadows` with new `Purposes`.

Models. `Models` are a central constituent of `DigitalShadows`. According to Stachowiak [24], models (1) consist of a mapping to an original object, that the model represents, (2) are reduced to the relevant aspects and abstract from details of the original, and (3) have a pragmatism that lets them replace the original in certain scenarios. Models may map to the DS's `Asset` (the physical thing that it represents). In this scenario, the `Model` adds information about the `Asset` to the `DigitalShadow` and helps evaluate/understand the data that this asset provides. For instance, a SysML Block Definition Diagram (BDD) [27] can represent the asset's structure, a BPMN model [28] describes an established process, or a simulation model [8,17] provides information about the expected system behavior at a specific time. Models may also represent the context in

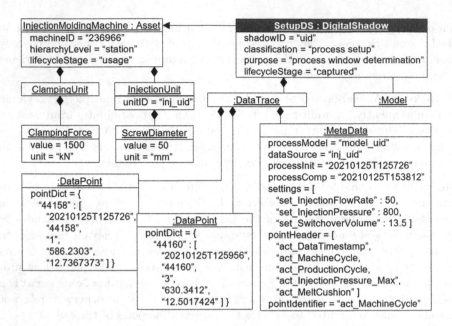

Fig. 2. Structure of an instantiated DS object in injection molding

which the DS is created or in which its asset operates. Models about the context help to understand why `DataPoints` change and relate these changes to events that happen in the operating context. Models also specify the Digital Shadow itself. They define which elements should be part of it, *i.e.*, it is beneficial for the intended purpose. A model's purpose also varies. Models describe the DS itself, thus, serve as the construction plan. They specify its asset and hint how the data-traces are interrelated. Further, when describing the context, models qualify specific values or value changes in the DS, *e.g.*, models can help to decide whether a sensed value can be considered as good or bad.

Purpose. Purpose in a general understanding is "what the DS is supposed to do". DSs must be tailored to a specific `Purpose`, because they neither act on their own nor do they interact directly with the regarded system (see Sect. 2). The purpose definition is a basis for correct cross-domain interoperability as well as a precise understanding of the DS in future use. A DS is designed for its exact purpose. Regarding complex purposes, it is possible to associate several thematically connected DS more comprehensively. To achieve said `Purpose` the functionalities are defined within the `Models` or can be realized through `DataTraces` from sophisticated simulation or processing sources. These functionalities can vary from simply monitoring a heartbeat of a referred system to very complex data analyses, *e.g.*, AI-based predictions. The format of the `Purpose` has no further specifications but the requirement to define it clearly and understandable.

4   Application Example

In the following section, we demonstrate the usability of the introduced meta-model with one real-world application example by adding application-specific instances to the generic classes. We will illustrate a production planning process in injection molding domain to outline the metamodel's usability.

Figure 3 shows the metamodel enhanced with instances for the production planning process of an injection molding production. In this application example, the objective for a production controller is to set an optimal schedule. Finding the injection molding machine (IMM) where the expected rejection rate for part X is minimal is the **purpose** the controller aims for. Because production planning processes are often highly complex, we assume that the shopfloor comprises only two injection molding machines (A and B) that only differ in the rejection rate for part X. Further, no other constraints are given. To support the controller in the decision, the DS must provide the machine ID (IMM-ID) of the injection molding machine, where the expected rejection rate for part X is the lowest. This necessary information comes from multiple **assets**, namely the Manufacturing Execution System (MES) containing multiple data sources, and the machines.

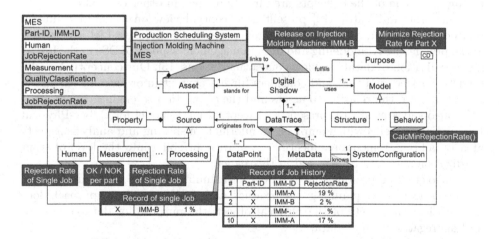

Fig. 3. Metamodel enhanced with specific instances for the planning process.

Relevant *attributes* are Part-ID, IMM-ID, and the current rejection rate of machine A and machine B for part X. The MES as **Source** provides the Part-ID and IMM-ID. The gathering of the rejection rates was made, on the one hand, manually by a human operator via plant data acquisition for a single, finished job on machine A. The relating attribute in the **Property** class for the human **Source** calls JobRejectionRate. On the other hand, sensors at machine B inspect every single part and automatically classifies the approved part as OK, while rejected parts are classified as NOK (not OK). After the job on machine B is terminated, it directly proceeds the JobRejectionRate and forwards the information to the MES. The MES enhances the corresponding job record with the received rejection rate. Hence, a record of a single job represents one single DataPoint. After combining all single data points to a DataTrace, a mathematical model (CalcMinRejectionRate) first computes the mean rejection rate for machines A and B. Subsequently, the model selects the machine ID concerning the minimum rejection rate and provides the result to the controller. The controller finally sets the optimal schedule that presumably minimizes the number of rejects of part X. One benefit is a possible faster termination of the job when producing on IMM-B instead of IMM-A. That leads to a reduction of the waiting time for the following jobs. Besides, in comparison to IMM-A, less input of resin on IMM-B is necessary to manufacture the desired quantity of part X. Consequently, material costs are saveable.

5   Related Work

By now, there exists no conceptual model for DSs from the computer science perspective and following the conceptual model definition from Mayr and Thalheim [16]. However, Digital Shadows play an important role in smart manufacturing and some of the concepts are already defined in other contexts.

Quix, Hai and Vatov [19] present a conceptual view on a metadata-model related to metadata extraction and management in data lakes. Liebenberg and Jarke present the AI modeling and data management aspects of DSs in the IoP as a generalization of database view conceptualizations [13]. Our conceptual model for DSs goes beyond that and considers further context information such as the source of data, the relation to assets and the connection to engineering models.

Loucopoulos et al. [14] present a conceptual meta model for Cyber-Physical Production Systems which emphasizes information sharing and analysis aspects at a broad requirements engineering level, without going into the level of standardization and detail presented in this paper.

Bravo et al. [4] present a meta model for manufacturing which focuses on the resources, execution, planning, the product, and the client. Their approach does not consider the assets of the physical object, the purpose for data collection, and aggregation or metadata.

Ladj et al. [11] propose a framework for a knowledge-based DS including a physical and a virtual system. Their DS is a data and knowledge management system. Data analytics are applied to the database to generate the knowledge base of the DS. The analysis of the physical system by the DS supports the decision process. The proposed DS is self-learning and therefore improves continuously. Their approach describes elements of DSs for the specific purpose of a machine as physical object but it lacks a generic description of DS elements.

Schuh et al. [22] develop a data structure for DSs. The database consists of the organization's knowledge that can be utilized to solve its tasks. The data structure model is based on a generic order fulfillment process. An entity-relationship model describes the relationships between the data, resources, and elements of the order fulfillment. To complete the data structure, information requirements are modeled and linked with the data. Within [22], no conceptual model is given and concepts such as purpose or engineering models are not considered.

Parri et al. [18] create an architecture for a DT-based knowledge base. They present a metamodel as UML CD describing the knowledge base including the concepts DTs and Meta-DTs. Their metamodel has a focus on digital systems of a company, further elements of DSs like data or models are not considered.

6 Conclusion and Outlook

In this paper, we proposed a conceptual model for DSs and successfully evaluated it in real-world scenarios. Researchers in the smart manufacturing domain process and analyze data from various sources with heterogeneous formats and interfaces. They create models during all lifecycle stages of products, machines, and other entities. One major issue is the insufficient integration between data and models. Our conceptual model tackles that issue.

The impact of the proposed conceptual model of the DS in the production domain is multifaceted. Besides general model-driven benefits such as complexity management and code generation [5], it facilitates cross-domain collaboration by providing a base to define instances, as our real-life application in Sect. 4 showed. Its adequate and compact core enables interoperability on multiple levels, while it allows flexible extensions as well as domain-specific additions based on future requirements. Our application example in the manufacturing domain proof that this DS conceptual model can be a foundation to enable benefits in real-world applications in the short and long term.

References

1. DIN ISO 55000:2017–05, Asset Management - Übersicht, Leitlinien und Begriffe
2. DIN SPEC 91345:2016–04, Reference Architecture Model Industrie 4.0 (RAMI4.0)
3. Bibow, P., et al.: Model-driven development of a digital twin for injection molding. In: Dustdar, S., Yu, E., Salinesi, C., Rieu, D., Pant, V. (eds.) CAiSE 2020. LNCS, vol. 12127, pp. 85–100. Springer, Cham (2020). https://doi.org/10.1007/978-3-030-49435-3_6
4. Bravo, C., Aguilar, J., Ríos, A., Aguilar-Martin, J., Rivas, F.: A generalized data meta-model for production companies ontology definition. Int. J. Syst. Appl. Eng. Dev. **2**, 191–202 (2008)
5. Dalibor, M., Michael, J., Rumpe, B., Varga, S., Wortmann, A.: Towards a model-driven architecture for interactive digital twin cockpits. In: Dobbie, G., Frank, U., Kappel, G., Liddle, S.W., Mayr, H.C. (eds.) ER 2020. LNCS, vol. 12400, pp. 377–387. Springer, Cham (2020). https://doi.org/10.1007/978-3-030-62522-1_28
6. Desai, N., Ananya, S.K., Bajaj, L., Periwal, A., Desai, S.R.: Process parameter monitoring and control using digital twin. In: Auer, M.E., Ram B., K. (eds.) REV2019 2019. LNNS, vol. 80, pp. 74–80. Springer, Cham (2020). https://doi.org/10.1007/978-3-030-23162-0_8
7. Gomez-Escalonilla, J., Garijo, D., Valencia, O., Rivero, I.: Development of efficient high-fidelity solutions for virtual fatigue testing. In: Niepokolczycki, A., Komorowski, J. (eds.) ICAF 2019. LNME, pp. 187–200. Springer, Cham (2020). https://doi.org/10.1007/978-3-030-21503-3_15

8. Gosavi, A., et al.: Simulation-Based Optimization. Springer, Heidelberg (2015). https://doi.org/10.1007/978-1-4899-7491-4
9. Hu, L., et al.: Modeling of cloud-based digital twins for smart manufacturing with MT connect. Proc. Manuf. **26**, 1193–1203 (2018)
10. Kritzinger, W., Karner, M., Traar, G., Henjes, J., Sihn, W.: Digital twin in manufacturing: a categorical literature review and classification. IFAC-PapersOnLine **51**(11), 1016–1022 (2018)
11. Ladj, A., Wang, Z., Meski, O., Belkadi, F., Ritou, M., Da Cunha, C.: A knowledge-based digital shadow for machining industry in a digital twin perspective. J. Manuf. Syst. **58**, 168–179 (2021)
12. Liau, Y., Lee, H., Ryu, K.: Digital twin concept for smart injection molding. In: IOP Conference Series: Materials Science and Engineering, vol. 324, p. 012077 (2018)
13. Liebenberg, M., Jarke, M.: Information systems engineering with digital shadows: concept and case studies. In: Dustdar, S., Yu, E., Salinesi, C., Rieu, D., Pant, V. (eds.) CAiSE 2020. LNCS, vol. 12127, pp. 70–84. Springer, Cham (2020). https://doi.org/10.1007/978-3-030-49435-3_5
14. Loucopoulos, P., Kavakli, E., Chechina, N.: Requirements engineering for cyber physical production systems. In: Giorgini, P., Weber, B. (eds.) CAiSE 2019. LNCS, vol. 11483, pp. 276–291. Springer, Cham (2019). https://doi.org/10.1007/978-3-030-21290-2_18
15. Luo, W., Hu, T., Zhang, C., Wei, Y.: Digital twin for CNC machine tool: modeling and using strategy. J. Ambient Intell. Humaniz. Comput. **10**(3), 1129–1140 (2019)
16. Mayr, H.C., Thalheim, B.: The triptych of conceptual modeling. Softw. Syst. Model. **20**(1), 7–24 (2020). https://doi.org/10.1007/s10270-020-00836-z
17. Mujber, T., Szecsi, T., Hashmi, M.: Virtual reality applications in manufacturing process simulation. J. Mater. Process. Technol. **155-156**, 1834–1838 (2004)
18. Parri, J., Patara, F., Sampietro, S., Vicario, E.: A framework for model-driven engineering of resilient software-controlled systems. Computing **103**(4), 589–612 (2021)
19. Quix, C., Hai, R., Vatov, I.: Metadata extraction and management in data lakes with GEMMS. Complex Syst. Inf. Model. Q. **9**, 67–83 (2016)
20. Schmertosch, T., Krabbes, M.: Automatisierung 4.0: Objektorientierte Entwicklung modularer Maschinen für die digitale Produktion. Carl Hanser Verlag (2018)
21. Schuh, G., Gützlaff, A., Sauermann, F., Maibaum, J.: Digital shadows as an enabler for the internet of production. In: Lalic, B., Majstorovic, V., Marjanovic, U., von Cieminski, G., Romero, D. (eds.) APMS 2020. IAICT, vol. 591, pp. 179–186. Springer, Cham (2020). https://doi.org/10.1007/978-3-030-57993-7_21
22. Schuh, G., Kelzenberg, C., Wiese, J., Ochel, T.: Data structure of the digital shadow for systematic knowledge management systems in single and small batch production. Proc. CIRP **84**, 1094–1100 (2019)
23. Schuh, G., Prote, J.-P., Gützlaff, A., Thomas, K., Sauermann, F., Rodemann, N.: Internet of production: rethinking production management. In: Wulfsberg, J.P., Hintze, W., Behrens, B.-A. (eds.) Production at the Leading Edge of Technology, pp. 533–542. Springer, Heidelberg (2019). https://doi.org/10.1007/978-3-662-60417-5_53
24. Stachowiak, H.: Allgemeine Modelltheorie. Springer, Heidelberg (1973)
25. Urbina Coronado, P.D., Lynn, R., Louhichi, W., Parto, M., Wescoat, E., Kurfess, T.: Part data integration in the shop floor digital twin: mobile and cloud technologies to enable a manufacturing execution system. J. Manuf. Syst. **48**, 25–33 (2018). Special Issue on Smart Manufacturing

26. VDI: Industrie 4.0 - Technical Assets - Basic terminology concepts, life cycles and administration models (2016)
27. Weilkiens, T.: Systems Engineering with SysML/UML: Modeling, Analysis, Design. Elsevier (2011)
28. White, S.A.: Introduction to BPMN. IBM Cooper. **2**, 1–26 (2004)
29. Wortmann, A., Barais, O., Combemale, B., Wimmer, M.: Modeling languages in industry 4.0: an extended systematic mapping study. Softw. Syst. Model. **19**(1), 67–94 (2020)
30. Zambal, S., Eitzinger, C., Clarke, M., Klintworth, J., Mechin, P.: A digital twin for composite parts manufacturing: effects of defects analysis based on manufacturing data. In: International Conference on Industrial Informatics (INDIN 2018), pp. 803–808. IEEE (2018)

A Conceptual Modelling Approach for the Discovery and Management of Platoon Routes

Dietrich Steinmetz[1], Sven Hartmann[1(✉)], and Hui Ma[2]

[1] Clausthal University of Technology, Clausthal-Zellerfeld, Germany
{dietrich.steinmetz,sven.hartmann}@tu-clausthal.de
[2] Victoria University of Wellington, Wellington, New Zealand
hui.ma@vuw.ac.nz

Abstract. The rapid advancements in autonomous driving enable the formation of vehicle groups with small distances between vehicles, known as platooning. This technology has attracted research interest as it offers great benefits for future transportation, e.g., fuel economy, reduced CO_2 emissions, increased road capacity and improved road safety. Previous works lack unified concepts and are therefore incompatible with each other. This work provides a conceptual model and operations for unified planning of platooning routes. Specifically, this work provides concepts for routing, scheduling, and platoon lifecycles.

Keywords: Geographic information · Data modelling · Graph database

1 Introduction

Platooning is the linking of two or more vehicles with small inter-vehicle distances with automatic control. This innovative technology optimizes the safety of road transportation [5,12], increases the capacity of road networks [5], and reduces the CO_2 emissions [2,4]. In the European Union, 23% of the total CO_2 emissions in 2017 were caused by road transportation [7]. According to the ITF [11], the total freight transport will grow by a factor of 1.6 between 2017 and 2050.

Vehicle platooning is an important technology to reduce the CO_2 emissions in road transportation. This is essentially achieved by reducing the vehicle aerodynamic drag when vehicles drive very closely one after another [26].

Platooning has many advantages that make it beneficial for various stakeholders. Through platooning, road users can reduce CO_2 emissions considerably. For drivers, driving smoothness and safety are improved enormously. For transportation companies, revenue is increased and costs are reduced. Due to all these advantages, platooning is highly relevant for policy makers to counteract the ever-growing traffic volumes.

Platooning is usually a part of a large supply chain with multi-layered tasks. Companies can organize their own vehicle fleets or use the services of logistic

A. Ghose et al. (Eds.): ER 2021, LNCS 13011, pp. 282–296, 2021.
https://doi.org/10.1007/978-3-030-89022-3_23

service providers to deliver the goods in a certain time. The planning of the platoons and vehicle routes is a major challenge. Numerous diverse stakeholders and the consideration of different objectives significantly complicates the planning. The lack of standards for platooning concepts makes cross-company and cross-fleet cooperation difficult. Numerous requirements have to be checked such as compatibility of vehicle types, deadlines of orders, verification of vehicle routes, different platoon requirements and others. Using platooning for transportation requires planning and adapting the process to different levels of abstraction. Figure 1 shows a layered transport model with the integration of platooning, inspired by [10]. The first layer is devoted to *Service/Fleet Management*. It has as input flows of goods that are assigned to the vehicles and drivers, depending on delivery conditions, legal restrictions and company policies. This layer is the most abstract one and largely decoupled from platooning tasks. Here, only the framework for transport with platooning is described.

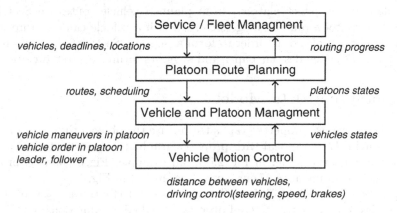

Fig. 1. Platooning Layer Model, inspired by [10].

The second layer is devoted to *Platoon Route Planning*. It is responsible for planning vehicle routes, platoon formation, assigning vehicles to platoons, scheduling incl. travel times and waiting times determination. Operations such as forming a platoon, adding and removing vehicles from a platoon, dissolving a platoon and adjusting speeds are performed on the underlying road network. There are numerous approaches to planning routes and platoons, with similar semantic concepts and own terms. However, the standardization of platooning concepts in this layer is missing. This paper is motivated by this gap and presents a conceptual model for platoon route planning.

The third layer is devoted to *Vehicle and Platoon Management*. It manages the tactical aspects of the vehicles and platoons. This includes vehicle maneuvering operations such as changing the order of vehicles, adding new vehicles, changing the lanes of vehicles and others. These operations are performed in accordance with previously determined platoon plans.

The fourth layer is devoted to *Vehicle Motion Control*. It takes care of speed and distance compliance in accordance with maneuvering operations. In particular, this layer controls the engine actuators, brakes and steering.

It should be emphasized that the huge majority of works deal with technical aspects of the formation and the behavior of platoons. There are only very few papers are targeted towards a conceptualization of platooning. A recent example is [16] where a preliminary ontology for ad hoc platooning proposed, i.e., where platoons are formed spontaneously. In particular, a conceptualization of the local operations is given that are needed for spontaneous platooning.

Research articles as well as practical implementation of platooning in industry often use similar term when thy talk about platooning, but the descriptions of terms are often not compatible with each other.

Organization. This paper is organized as follows. In Sect. 2, we present basic definitions and basic concepts that are central in the vehicle routing domain. In Sect. 3, we propose more specialized concepts that are crucial for platoon route management, and introduce the corresponding semantic constraints. In Sect. 4, we present a our platoon discovery algorithm, which can be used by platoon route planners to detect platoons from planned vehicle routes. In Sect. 5, we discuss how platoon route managers can check if a vehicle can catch up with a vehicle or platoon ahead, in order to form a platoon. Section 6 discusses related work. Section 7 concludes our paper and suggests future research directions.

2   Conceptual Data Model

In this paper, we use property graphs to capture the objects that are of interest in our domain. Here we deal with property graphs that constitute instances of the conceptual data model in Fig. 2. As an example, Fig. 3 shows a property graph which is an instance of our conceptual model in Fig. 2.

A property graph $G = (N, E, \alpha, \beta, \lambda, \nu)$ consists of a finite set $N \subseteq O$ of objects, called nodes, a finite set $E \subseteq O$ of objects, called edges, functions $\alpha : E \to N$ and $\alpha : E \to N$ that assign to each edge e its source and its sink, a function $\lambda : N \cup E \to P(L)$ that assigns to each object $o \in N \cup E$ a finite set $\lambda(o)$ of labels, and a partial function $\nu : (N \cup E) \times K \to V$ that assigns domain values for properties to objects, such that the set of domain values where ν is defined is finite, cf. [1].

To begin with, we focus on the underlying road network. Road points are used to model junctions, terminal nodes and other points of interest on the road network. Road segments are used to model roads or parts of roads. A road point $j \in N_J$ is represented by a node with label :Road_Point. For each road point we store the properties *latitude, longitude*. A road segment $s \in E_S$ is represented by an edge with label :road_segment. The source $\alpha(s)$ and sink $\beta(s)$ of a road segment s are road points. For each road segment we store the properties *distance, state, lanes, speed_limits*.

A vehicle $v \in N_V$ is represented by a node with label :Vehicle. For a vehicle we store the properties *earliest_departure, latest_arrival, speed_min, speed_opt, speed_max, capacity, technical_requirements, legal_requirements*. For each vehicle v we assume that there is a planned route from its origin j_o^v to it destination j_d^v. A route node $r \in N_R$ is represented by a node with label :Route_Node. For each route node we store the property *departure_time*. The location of a route node is captured by an edge with label :is_at that connects the route node to a road point.

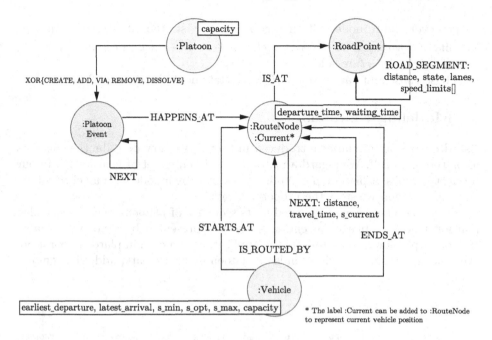

Fig. 2. Our conceptual data model.

A *vehicle route* $\mathcal{R}^v$ for vehicle v is given by a finite sequence of route nodes $r_1^v, r_2^v, \ldots, r_l^v$, where any two consecutive ones are connected by an edge with label :next and properties *speed_current, travel_time, waiting_time*. The first route node is located at the vehicle's origin, the last one at the vehicle's destination. There is an edge with label :is_routed_by connecting the vehicle v to each route node on its route $\mathcal{R}^v$, an edge with label :starts_at to its first and an edge with label :ends_at to its last route node. We call a vehicle route $\mathcal{R}^v$ *valid* when these constraints are satisfied (Table 1).

Table 1. Relevant parameters

T_e^v	Earliest time that vehicle v can leave its origin j_o^v
T_{max}^v	Latest time by which vehicle v must arrive at its destination j_d^v
MD^v	Maximum allowable detour of vehicle v over its shortest path distance
SD_{ij}	Shortest path distance from road point i to road point j
t_j^v	Departure time of vehicle v from road point j to go to the next road point on its route (if it exists)
$\mathcal{R}^v$	Planned route of vehicle v from its origin j_o^v to its destination j_d^v
s_{opt}^v	Fuel-optimal speed of vehicle v between its minimum speed s_{min}^v and its maximum speed s_{max}^v

To check the validity of vehicle routes, one can use regular path queries in the property graph, cf. [1]. For every vehicle v, to meet the earliest departure time, the edges $v. \xrightarrow{\text{:starts\_at}}$ and $v. \xrightarrow{\text{:origin}}$ exist and are unique, and the inequality $v. \xrightarrow{\text{:starts\_at}} .departure \geq v. \xrightarrow{\text{:origin}} .earliest\_departure$ holds.

For every route node r, if an edge $r. \xrightarrow{\text{:next}}$ exists then it is unique, and the equality $r.departure + r. \xrightarrow{\text{:next}} .travel\_time + r. \xrightarrow{\text{:next}} .waiting\_time = r. \xrightarrow{\text{:next}}$ $..:Route\_Node.departure$ holds.

These constraints are listed as *Cypher* statements in Listing 1.2 and 1.3.

3   Modeling Platoons

Based on the preliminaries introduced in Sect. 2, we now describe the concepts of platooning itself. We regard a platoon as a dynamic set of vehicles $\mathcal{V}^p$. In our property graphs, a platoon $p \in N_P$ is represented by a node with label *:Platoon*. For each platoon we store the property *length*.

For a platoon, we are interested in its sequence of *platoon events* (also called platoon trace). A platoon events $e \in N_E$ is represented by a node with label *:Event*. A platoon event e reflects the application of a certain platoon operation. We distinguish the following kinds of platoon events: create, add, via, remove, dissolve.

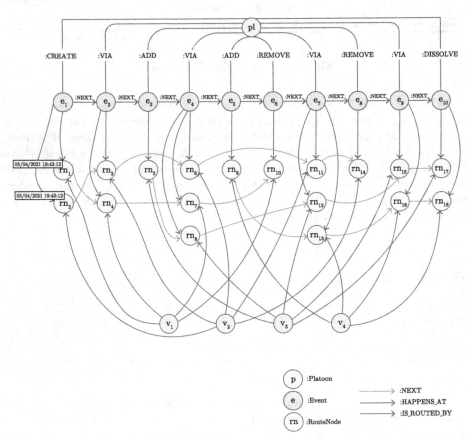

Fig. 3. An (artificially small) example of a property graph that is an instance of our conceptual model in Fig. 2.

A *platoon trace* T^p of a platoon p is a finite sequence of events $e_1^p, e_2^p, \ldots, e_k^p$ that happen during the lifetime of the platoon. Initially a platoon is created, and eventually it is dissolved. There is an edge with label :create connecting the platoon p to its first event node e_1^p, and an edge with label :dissolve to is last event node e_k^p. During the life time of a platoon, vehicles can be added and removed from it. Whenever a vehicle is added or removed, this is reflected by an event node e_i^p in the platoon trace.

When a platoon p passes a road point j, then this is reflected by an edge with label :via that connects the platoon node p to an event node e_i^p, which again is connected by an edges with label :happens_at to the route nodes located at j.

Figure 3 shows a property graph which is instance of our conceptual model in Fig. 4. The platoon is linked to a sequence of event nodes that represent the life cycle, i.e., the platoon trace. Simpler queries can be used to retrieve important information. The event sequence can be queried as follows: $MATCH(e1{:}Event) \xleftarrow{\ :CREATE\ } (p) \xrightarrow{\ :DISSOLVE\ } (e2{:}Event), event\_sequence = (e1) \xrightarrow{\ :NEXT\ } (e2)$. From this, the platoon route can be derived by extending the query. The other way round, the individual vehicle routes of the platoon can as well be queried.

3.1 Platoon Event Precedence Constraints

A platoon must be created before it can be dissolved. A vehicle must be added to a platoon before it can be removed. A platoon must be created before any vehicle can be added to it. A platoon can only be dissolved when all vehicles have been removed. When a vehicle is added to a platoon then it will stay for at least one road segment.

3.2 Vehicle Compatibility Constraints

Two vehicles are *compatible* if they fulfil the same technical (i.e., on-board control system) and legal requirements that permit them to platoon together. Now the notion of compatibility must be extended to the cover also the spatio-temporal dimension.

Two route nodes are *compatible* if their vehicles are *compatible*, they are located at the same road point and their departure times from this road point coincide.

A new platoon can only be created if there are at least two compatible route nodes. For platoon route management, Algorithm 1 can be used to effectively check the compatibility of two route nodes. In this case a new platoon node and a new platoon event node are inserted, both connected by an edge with label :Create.

Once compatible route nodes have been found, the platoon route planner can examine them their next route nodes exist and are located at the same road point, they travel on this road segment with the same speed, and their arrival time in the next route node is before the latest arrival time (if this is the destination) or before the departure time (if this is not yet the destination).

Algorithm 1. Compatible

Input: two route nodes r_1, r_2
Output: true if compatible, false otherwise

1: $v_1 = r_1. \xleftarrow{\text{:is\_routed\_by}} .:Vehicle$
2: $v_2 = r_2. \xleftarrow{\text{:is\_routed\_by}} .:Vehicle$
3:     % check for compatible vehicles
4: **if** $v_1.technical\_regulations = v_2.technical\_regulations$ **and**
5:      $v_1.legal\_regulations = v_2.legal\_regulations$ **and**
6:        % check for same road point
7:      $r_1. \xleftarrow{\text{:is\_at}} .:Road\_Point = r_2. \xleftarrow{\text{:is\_at}} .:Road\_Point$ **and**
8:        % check for same departure time
9:      $r_1.departure\_time = r_2.departure\_time$ **then**
10:     **return** true
11: **else**
12:     **return** false
13: **end if**

3.3 Platoon Consistency Constraints

There are further semantic constraints that must hold throughout the life time of a platoon. At any time, a platoon consists of at least two vehicles. At any time, the platoon size is bounded by the maximum platoon size. At any time, any two vehicles in a platoon are compatible. At any time, a vehicle can only belong to one platoon.

We call a platoon p *valid* when the platoon consistency constraints and the platoon event precedence constraints are satisfied.

4 Platoon Discovery from a Set of Planned Vehicle Routes

In this section, we discuss an application to illustrate how our proposed conceptual model can be helpful in platoon route planning. We describe how to analyze planned routes of vehicles to discover platooning opportunities. Our approach is outlined in Algorithm 2. The core idea of our algorithm is to examine the vehicles (and the associated vehicle routes) in pairs, and to gradually identify platoons and generate the associated platoon events. Recall that for platoon management, route nodes r_1, r_2 are relevant which are located at the same road point and whose the departure_time matches. This is verified by calling Algorithm 1 in line 3.

The algorithm works in two phases. In the first phase, the platoons are created and expanded, and in the second phase, the platoons are dismantled and dissolved. In the first phase, the considered vehicle pair are traveling in same direction, at the same time and place. In the first phase, the considered pairs of vehicles travel together in the same direction. The pair can be combined into a platoon, single vehicle can be added to a platoon or intermediate node of the route is created, depending on whether the vehicles are in platoon at the considered moment.

If the considered vehicles are not in any platoon and there are no *available platoons* at road point $r_1.j$, then a new platoon node with label *:Platoon* is created. Whether a platoon is available for a certain vehicle depends on the requirements (i.e., technical and legal regulations) and whether the platoon has free capacity. The compatibility ensures that a vehicle meets all the necessary requirements of a platoon and can be added. Birth of a new platoon is represented by new event *:Event*. The relationship between platoon and event defines the type of event, in this case it is :CREATE. Event is also associated with respective route nodes of v_1 and v_2. Lines 7–9 show the realization using *Cypher*.

Algorithm 2. Platoon Discovery

Input: a set of vehicles N_V with their vehicle routes
Output: a set of platoons N_P with their platoon event sequences

1: **for all** $v_1, v_2 \in N_V : v_1 \neq v_2$ **do**
2:     **for all** $r_1 \in v_1. \xrightarrow{\text{:is\_routed\_by}} .{:}Route\_Node, r_2 \in v_2. \xrightarrow{\text{:is\_routed\_by}}$
    $.{:}Route\_Node$ **do**
3:         **if** Compatible (r_1, r_2) **then**
4:             **if** $r_1. \xrightarrow{\text{:next}} .{:}road\_Point = r_2. \xrightarrow{\text{:next}} .{:}Road\_Point$ **then**   % phase 1
5:                 **if** v_1, v_2 *are not in platoon and no available platoons at* $r_1.j$ **then**
6:                     % *create new platoon with* v_1 *and* v_2
7:                     CREATE $(:Platoon) \xrightarrow{\text{:create}} (e{:}Event)$
8:                     CREATE $(e) \xrightarrow{\text{:HAPPENS\_AT}} (r_1)$
9:                     CREATE $(e) \xrightarrow{\text{:HAPPENS\_AT}} (r_2)$
10:                 **else if** v_1 *in platoon and* v_2 *not in platoon* **then**
11:                     % *add* v_2 *to the same platoon that* v_1 *is in*
12:                     MATCH$(p{:}Platoon) \xrightarrow{\text{:CREATE—ADD—VIA}} (:Event) \xrightarrow{\text{:HAPPENS\_AT}} (r_1)$
13:                     CREATE $(p) \xrightarrow{\text{:ADD}} (:Event) \xrightarrow{\text{:HAPPENS\_AT}} (r_2)$
14:                 **else if** v_1, v_2 *are in same platoon* p *at* $r_1.j$ **then**
15:                     % *create or update via node*
16:                     MERGE $(p) \xrightarrow{\text{:VIA}} (e{:}Event) \xrightarrow{\text{:HAPPENS\_AT}} (r_1)$
17:                 **end if**
18:             **else**   % phase 2
19:                 **if** v_1, v_2 *are in same platoon* p *at* $r_1.j$ *and platoon size* > 2 **then**
20:                     % *remove* v_1 *from platoon at* $r_1.j$
21:                     CREATE $(p) \xrightarrow{\text{:REMOVE}} (:Event) \xrightarrow{\text{:HAPPENS\_AT}} (r_1)$
22:                 **else if** v_1, v_2 *are in same platoon* p *at* $r_1.j$ & *platoon size* $= 2$ **then**
23:                     % *dissolve current platoon*
24:
25:                     CREATE $(p) \xrightarrow{\text{:DISSOLVE}} (e{:}Event)$
26:                     CREATE $(e) \xrightarrow{\text{:HAPPENS\_AT}} (r_1)$
27:                     CREATE $(e) \xrightarrow{\text{:HAPPENS\_AT}} (r_2)$
28:                 **end if**
29:             **end if**
30:         **end if**
31:     **end for**
32: **end for**

If v_1 is already in the platoon and v_2 is not, then v_2 will be added to the same platoon (In addition, other compatibility conditions can be checked, among others legal aspect, company strategy, etc.). On insertion, the platoon in which v_1 is travelling is queried, see line 12. So that a new node with label *:Event* is created and vehicle and platoon are linked with relationship :ADD in next line. If both vehicles are in a platoon, only the node *:VIA* need to be updated or created. *:VIA* node links all route nodes of vehicles in platoon at a time. With via nodes, platoon chronology can be explicitly traced.

Figure 4 illustrates the application of Algorithm 2 by an example. It shows the life time of an example platoon from its creation till its dissolution, including the generation of all the associated events during the platoon discovery. We consider vehicles $v_1, \ldots, v_4$. In the lower part of the figure, the route nodes of the vehicles under consideration are depicted as gray solid circles. For each vehicle, the associated vehicle route is displayed by a sequence of route nodes in a row. Let us imagine the example platoon p moves from left to right on the road network.

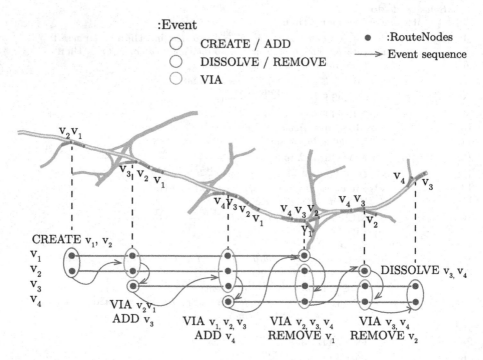

Fig. 4. An example of a platoon that has been generated by Algorithm 2 together with the associated events).

The first platoon event node (of kind :create) is generated when vehicles v_1 and v_1 meet at the leftmost road point, where they are combined into a new platoon p. The route nodes involved in this event are outlined in green. The first platoon event node is connected to the route nodes that are outlined. In red line in the lower part of the figure connects subsequent platoon events, and thus illustrates the entire sequence of event nodes, i.e., the platoon trace. At the second road point, another vehicle v_3 is added to the existing platoon p, thus generating event nodes (of kind :add and :via). At the third road point, a further vehicle v_4 is added to the platoon p. Now the platoon consists of four vehicles. Afterwards, at the next road points vehicles are removed from it. At the fourth road point, vehicle v_1 is removed from the platoon. For that a platoon event node (of kind :remove) is generated. At the fifth road point, vehicle v_2 leaves the platoon, for which again an event node (of kind :remove) is generated. Eventually, at the sixth road point, vehicles v_3 and v_4 leave the platoon p, which is then dissolved. For that the final event node (of kind :dissolve) is generated.

5   Platoon Facilitation by Catching-Up

In this section, we discuss a further application where our proposed conceptual model can assist platoon route planning. A vehicle v can deviate from its fuel-optimal speed s^v_{opt} to catch up with another vehicle or platoon. For platoon route planners, it is crucial to know if a vehicle can catch up with another vehicle or platoon just by increasing its speed. The vehicle ahead can also reduce its speed to allow catching up. The minimum and maximum speeds of a vehicle v are given by an interval $[s^v_{min}, s^v_{max}]$, taking into account the speed limits.

Let v_1 and v_2 denote the vehicle behind and the vehicle ahead, respectively. The vehicle behind v_1 can accelerate to $s^{v_1}_{max}$, while the vehicle ahead v_2 reduces its speed to $s^{v_2}_{min}$ in order to reduce the distance between the two vehicles as fast as possible. If the distance between the vehicles is too large compared to the remaining distance of the respective vehicles, then it is not possible to form a platoon.

Let $dist^{v_1,v_2}$ be the distance between the current location of vehicle v_1 and the current location of vehicle v_2. To check this condition, the distance between the vehicles and the remaining travel distance of each of the vehicles are examined. The following *Cypher* query retrieve remaining distance d^v of vehicle v to its destination j^v_d.

```
MATCH (c:Current)<-[:IS_ROUTED_BY]-(v:Vehicle)-[:ENDS_AT]->(e:RouteNode),
    route = (c)-[:NEXT]->(e)
RETURN apoc.coll.sum([edge IN relationships(route) | edge.distance])
```

Listing 1.1. Retrieve remaining distance of vehicle v.

Now we are ready to check whether vehicle v_1 can catch up with vehicle v_2, thus enabling them to form a platoon. This condition checks constraint 1. The left side of the inequality calculates the speed at which vehicle 2 must travel in order to catch up with vehicle 1 and to be able to platoon at least 10% of the remaining distance $\min(d^{v_1}, d^{v_2})$. The calculated speed must not exceed the maximum allowed speed of vehicle 2. This constraint is shown in Listing 1.4 as a *Cypher* statement.

$$dist^{v_1,v_2} \cdot \frac{s^{v_1}_{min}}{\min(d_{v_1}, d_{v_2}) - \frac{\min(d_{v_1}, d_{v_2})}{10}} + s^{v_2}_{opt} \leq s^{v_2}_{max} \tag{1}$$

The vehicle ahead must not drive too slowly, as it may miss its *v.latest_arrival* deadline. To check this, the current location of the vehicle is queried $(v) \xrightarrow{\text{:IS\_ROUTED\_BY}} (c : Current)$ then it can be checked if the slower travel speed is sufficient $v.latest\_arrival \leq \frac{d_v}{s^v_{min}} + c.departure\_time$.

6   Related Work

We give a brief overview of recent work on platoon routing as far as related to this paper. First we outline state-of-the-art approaches in the literature and identify the research gap that we will address in this paper. While fuel-optimal vehicle platooning is a special class of vehicle routing problems, existing algorithms [14,20,27] of often not directly adaptable to this problem. [9] computed fuel-optimal schedules on shortest paths and investigated whether vehicles can adjust their speed to catch up with other vehicles and form platoons. [13] proposed two approaches to determine fuel-optimal platooning routes. First heuristic compares pairwise all vehicle routes to find a best vehicle pair and determines on this basis the platoon routes. In the second approach, vehicles are routed via selected hub in road network, thus new platooning opportunity is then created. [21] proposed a variation of the integer linear program with waiting times. [23] proposed a spatial grouping approach for forming platoons. [17] discussed realistic assumptions of time constraints for the departure and arrival of vehicles in platoons, with waiting and detour options. These works are mostly concerned with strategic planning of platoons and route optimization. Basic concepts are often modeled in different ways. Road networks are modeled as uni or bidirectional graphs. The road segments are annotated with different types such as cost, weights, travel time, distance although it is meant the same.

Some works deal with conceptual modeling of special routing and scheduling problems. [8] concepts for dial-a-ride vehicle routing and scheduling system. Customer-specific constraints check seating requirements, pickup and drop-off times, and maximum travel time. In addition, capacities, operating times and number of vehicles are checked. [18] conceptual modeling of route planning and scheduling of waste collection. Here the vehicles, waste sites, stop points, working hours and the routes are modeled. The road nodes are used as a basis and a distance matrix is used to store the distance between nodes. [22] developed a conceptual model for an agricultural fleet management system. [24] presented a conceptual model for road networks to guide the transformation of OSM road data to a graph database. [25] developed a intuitive graph data model for dynamic taxi ride sharing. [28] presented semantic graph model for flexible job shop scheduling problem. Besides, some semantic constraints are presented there. Thereby order of the jobs, operations, filling level of the warehouses and temporal aspects are checked. The jobs, processes and operation are implemented as linked-list, so that convenient traveling is possible. The concepts are represented with ontology and the concrete instances are stored in the Neo4j database. The constraints are implemented in graph query language *Cypher*. [3, 6, 19] proposed ontologies for vehicle routing but without any attention to platooning.

So far, only a few works exist that deal with conceptual aspects of platooning. [15, 16] conceptualizes the platooning problem on the tactical level, i.e. lane changes, sequence of vehicles, roles of vehicles in the platoon. An ontology for platooning was also proposed with platooning objects, platoon properties, and platoon operations. Basically, tactical abstraction level is considered here. Basically, tactical abstraction level is considered here. The routes and scheduling of the vehicles and platoons are not represented. These concepts can be used for ad-hoc platooning, where the vehicles that are in the vicinity spontaneously form a platoon. At the strategic level the conceptual aspect was not addressed.

This article closes this research gap and deals with the conceptual modeling of strategic platoon planning. The focus is on the management of vehicles and platoons and their routes.

7 Conclusion and Outlook

In this paper we have proposed a conceptual model for platoon route management that covers core concepts such as vehicles, vehicle routes, platoons, and platoon events. One purpose of this model is to provide a common conceptualization for different stakeholders in the transportation domain, who aim to integrate platooning as an emerging technology. Another purpose is that it offers immediate assistance for platoon route planers in their everyday work. We use property graphs to capture the instances of our proposed conceptual model.

On this basis, we have presented two applications for the discovery of platoons and for the facilitation of platoons by catch-up. The first application is more devoted to centralized platoon route planning, a task which is usually done beforehand. The second application is an addition to this which allows platoon route managers to take dynamic changes into account and to react to them while the vehicles are already on their way. Both applications make use of our proposed conceptual model. Our proposed algorithm for platoon discovery generates the event sequence of a potential platoon, i.e., the platoon trace. The platoon events allow easy management of the involved vehicles, platoons and the routes. We have implemented our approach using the Neo4j graph database system which is a popular for managing and querying graph data. The two described applications are also implemented on top of Neo4j, and they demonstrate the potential of our proposed conceptual model.

In future we plan to extend our approach to support a wider range of tasks that are important for platoon route managers. For example, we also explore how the conceptual model can help platoon route managers in finding an optimized balance between centralized ahead planning and on-the-fly detection of opportunities for spontaneous platooning.

We plan to enhance our model to incorporate further semantic constraints that reflect business rules of the target domain and could be effectively monitored by the database management system to relieve platoon route managers and other decision makers. Furthermore, we want to add more and more specialized concepts into our conceptual model to make it interesting for additional stakeholders beyond platoon route planners.

A   Appendix

```
MATCH (platoon:Platoon)<-[:PLATOON_AT]-(v:Vehicle),(new_vehicle:Vehicle)
WHERE id(platoon) = 10 AND id(new_vehicle)=93489 AND
v.latest_arrival <= new_vehicle.earliest_departure
RETURN id(v), id(new_vehicle)
```

Listing 1.2. Validity of vehicle routes 1.

```
MATCH (n:RouteNode)-[r:NEXT]->(m:RouteNode)
WHERE n.departure_time<=m.departure_time + r.travel_time
RETURN id(n),id(m)
```

Listing 1.3. Validity of vehicle routes 2.

```
MATCH (cr1:RoadPoint)<-[:IS_AT]-(c1:Current)<-[:IS_ROUTED_BY]-(v1:Vehicle
    )-[:ENDS_AT]->(e1:RouteNode), r1 = (c1)-[:NEXT]->(e1)
WHERE id(v1)=323 WITH r1
MATCH (cr2:RoadPoint)<-[:IS_AT]-(c2:Current)<-[:IS_ROUTED_BY]-(v2:Vehicle
    )-[:ENDS_AT]->(e2:RouteNode), r2 = (c2)-[:NEXT]->(e2),
dif_r = (cr2)-[:ROAD_SEGMENT]->(cr1)
WHERE id(v2)=34223 WITH r1, r2
WITH apoc.coll.sum([x IN relationships(r1) | x.distance]) as d2, apoc.
    coll.sum([x IN relationships(r2) | x.distance]) as d1, apoc.coll.sum
    ([x IN relationships(dif_r) | x.distance]) as vehicle_distance
RETURN vehicle_distance*(90/(min(d1,d2)-(min(d1,d2)/10)))+100 as speed
```

Listing 1.4. Catching-up vehicle constraint.

References

1. Angles, R., Arenas, M., Barceló, P., Hogan, A., Reutter, J., Vrgoč, D.: Foundations of modern query languages for graph databases. ACM Comput. Surv. **50** (2017)
2. Bonnet, C., Fritz, H.: Fuel consumption reduction in a platoon: experimental results with two electronically coupled trucks at close spacing. SAE Technical Paper (2000)
3. Boudra, M., Hina, M.D., Ramdane-Cherif, A., Tadj, C.: Architecture and ontological modelling for assisted driving and interaction. Int. J. Adv. Comput. Res. **5**(20), 270 (2015)
4. Browand, F., McArthur, J., Radovich, C.: Fuel saving achieved in the field test of two tandem trucks. UC Berkeley Research Reports (2004)
5. Carbaugh, J., Godbole, D.N., Sengupta, R.: Safety and capacity analysis of automated and manual highway systems. Transport. Res. Part C: Emerg. Technol. **6**(1–2), 69–99 (1998)

6. Choi, S.K.: An ontological model to support communications of situation-aware vehicles. Transport. Res. Part C: Emerg. Technol. **53**, 112–133 (2015)
7. Directorate-General for Mobility and Transport (European Commission): Eu transport in figures: Statistical pocketbook (2019)
8. Fu, L., Teply, S.: On-line and off-line routing and scheduling of dial-a-ride paratransit vehicles. Comput.-Aided Civil Infrastr. Eng. **14**(5), 309–319 (1999)
9. van de Hoef, S., Johansson, K.H., Dimarogonas, D.V.: Fuel-efficient EN route formation of truck platoons. IEEE Trans. Intell. Transport. Syst. **19**(1), 102–112 (2017)
10. van de Hoef, S., Mårtensson, J., Dimarogonas, D.V., Johansson, K.H.: A predictive framework for dynamic heavy-duty vehicle platoon coordination. ACM Trans. Cyber-Phys. Syst. **4**(1), 1–25 (2019)
11. International Transport Forum: ITF transport outlook (2017). https://www.oecd-ilibrary.org/content/publication/9789282108000-en
12. Jamson, A.H., Merat, N., Carsten, O.M., Lai, F.C.: Behavioural changes in drivers experiencing highly-automated vehicle control in varying traffic conditions. Transport. Res. Part C: Emerg. Technol. **30**, 116–125 (2013)
13. Larsson, E., Sennton, G., Larson, J.: The vehicle platooning problem: computational complexity and heuristics. Transport. Res. Part C: Emerg. Technol. **60**, 258–277 (2015)
14. Ma, H., Tovey, C.A., Sharon, G., Kumar, T.K.S., Koenig, S.: Multi-agent path finding with payload transfers and the package-exchange robot-routing problem. In: AAAI, pp. 3166–3173 (2016)
15. Maiti, S.: A study on the behavior of vehicle platoons and platoon formation and dissolution strategies. Ph.D. thesis, University of Melbourne (2019)
16. Maiti, S., Winter, S., Kulik, L.: A conceptualization of vehicle platoons and platoon operations. Transport. Res. Part C: Emerg. Technol. **80**, 1–19 (2017)
17. Nourmohammadzadeh, A., Hartmann, S.: Fuel-efficient truck platooning by a novel meta-heuristic inspired from ant colony optimisation. Soft. Comput. **23**(5), 1439–1452 (2018). https://doi.org/10.1007/s00500-018-3518-x
18. Nuortio, T., Kytöjoki, J., Niska, H., Bräysy, O.: Improved route planning and scheduling of waste collection and transport. Expert Syst. Appl. **30**(2), 223–232 (2006)
19. Pollard, E., Morignot, P., Nashashibi, F.: An ontology-based model to determine the automation level of an automated vehicle for co-driving. In: International Conference Information Fusion, pp. 596–603. IEEE (2013)
20. Sachenbacher, M., Leucker, M., Artmeier, A., Haselmayr, J.: Efficient energy-optimal routing for electric vehicles. In: AAAI (2011)
21. Sokolov, V., Larson, J., Munson, T., Auld, J., Karbowski, D.: Maximization of platoon formation through centralized routing and departure time coordination. Transp. Res. Rec. **2667**(1), 10–16 (2017)
22. Sørensen, C.G., Bochtis, D.D.: Conceptual model of fleet management in agriculture. Biosys. Eng. **105**(1), 41–50 (2010)
23. Steinmetz, D., Burmester, G., Hartmann, S.: A fast heuristic for finding near-optimal groups for vehicle platooning in road networks. In: Benslimane, D., Damiani, E., Grosky, W.I., Hameurlain, A., Sheth, A., Wagner, R.R. (eds.) DEXA 2017. LNCS, vol. 10439, pp. 395–405. Springer, Cham (2017). https://doi.org/10.1007/978-3-319-64471-4_32

24. Steinmetz, D., Dyballa, D., Ma, H., Hartmann, S.: Using a conceptual model to transform road networks from OpenStreetMap to a graph database. In: Trujillo, J.C., et al. (eds.) ER 2018. LNCS, vol. 11157, pp. 301–315. Springer, Cham (2018). https://doi.org/10.1007/978-3-030-00847-5_22
25. Steinmetz, D., Merz, F., Ma, H., Hartmann, S.: A graph model for taxi ride sharing supported by graph databases. In: Laender, A.H.F., Pernici, B., Lim, E.-P., de Oliveira, J.P.M. (eds.) ER 2019. LNCS, vol. 11788, pp. 108–116. Springer, Cham (2019). https://doi.org/10.1007/978-3-030-33223-5_10
26. Vegendla, P., Sofu, T., Saha, R., Kumar, M.M., Hwang, L.K.: Investigation of aerodynamic influence on truck platooning. SAE Technical Paper (2015)
27. Zhang, Z., He, H., Luo, Z., Qin, H., Guo, S.: An efficient forest-based tabu search algorithm for the split-delivery vehicle routing problem. In: AAAI, pp. 3432–3438 (2015)
28. Zhu, Z., Zhou, X., Shao, K.: A novel approach based on Neo4j for multi-constrained flexible job shop scheduling problem. Comput. Ind. Eng. **130**, 671–686 (2019)

Semantics for Connectivity Management in IoT Sensing

Marc Vila[1,2](✉) (iD), Maria-Ribera Sancho[1,3] (iD), Ernest Teniente[1] (iD),
and Xavier Vilajosana[2,4] (iD)

[1] Universitat Politècnica de Catalunya, Barcelona, Spain
{marc.vila.gomez,maria.ribera.sancho,ernest.teniente}@upc.edu
[2] Worldsensing, Barcelona, Spain
{mvila,xvilajosana}@worldsensing.com
[3] Barcelona Supercomputing Center, Barcelona, Spain
maria.ribera@bsc.es
[4] Universitat Oberta de Catalunya, Barcelona, Spain
xvilajosana@uoc.edu

Abstract. There are a large number of Internet of Things (IoT) devices
that transmit information over the Internet, each with a different data
format to denote the same semantic concept. This often leads to data
incompatibilities and makes it difficult to extract the knowledge underlying that data. The only way to close this gap is to establish a common
vocabulary in order to achieve interoperability between different sources
and semantic data integration. This is the main goal of our proposal:
to specify a general semantics for IoT sensing that allows the management of data between gateways, nodes, and sensors in a homogeneous
way. Our proposal builds upon the joint Semantic Sensor Network and
Sensor-Observation-Sample-Actuator (SSN/SOSA) ontology.

Keywords: IoT · Interoperability · Sensors · Ontologies · Semantics

1 Introduction

Kevin Ashton coined the term Internet of Things (IoT) about twenty years ago
when he spoke of Radio Frequency IDentification (RFID) [11]. A *Thing*, in this
context, is a physical object that aims to connect and exchange information
with other devices over the Internet. Currently, there are more than 8 billion
IoT devices communicating data periodically, heterogeneously, and globally.

The IoT world has evolved drastically since then, due to the need for comprehensive monitoring of different devices to provide real-time information about
the status of a given domain.

Today, all IoT devices have the ability to communicate, at least, with their
own ecosystems. What happens, though, when you need to include different
devices from different manufacturers in the same system? All devices have their
own properties, data format, and communication technologies. This makes it
difficult to share information with each other.

© Springer Nature Switzerland AG 2021
A. Ghose et al. (Eds.): ER 2021, LNCS 13011, pp. 297–311, 2021.
https://doi.org/10.1007/978-3-030-89022-3_24

To be able to provide generic solutions that apply to different monitoring environments and domains, we need to abstract from the particular syntax and data formats of the different devices and provide common semantics to all the data managed. We achieve it through the definition of an *ontology* for connectivity management in the IoT sensing domain. Ontologies provide several benefits: (1) share a common understanding of the structure of information among software agents; (2) enable the reuse of domain knowledge; (3) domain assumptions are made explicit; (4) domain and operational knowledge are kept separated [14].

In our understanding, an ontology is an abstract interpretation of the concepts and properties of the domain and of the data stored in the information base, in the same way as a data model is. Therefore, both ontology and data model can be understood as synonyms.

Our work is related to industrial research at Worldsensing[1], a company focused on providing services through the monitoring of industrial environments from IoT devices. The development of a platform able to control and act on its own and third-party industrial IoT devices has become a critical goal for the success of the company, and the need to consider different types of devices can only be successfully addressed through this common vocabulary.

The ontology we propose aims to interact and manage a custom platform based on ThingsBoard[2], an open source IoT platform for device management, data collection, processing and visualization. Our project will extend the management and interaction capabilities of ThingsBoard, not only to IoT devices but also to its network elements; sensors, nodes and gateways needed to communicate information over the Internet. Our ontology is specified as an instantiation of common sensing ontologies such as Semantic Sensor Network Ontology (SOSA/SSN) and the information gathered from their surrounding standards.

LoRa[3] is the main technology used to communicate nodes and gateways. In [13], the authors compare three standards for transmitting low-power messages over a long distance; NB-IoT, Sigfox, and LoRa; and concludes that LoRa is currently the best option for smart monitoring applications. This technology makes it possible to operate low-cost devices with very long range, infrequent communication rates, and high battery longevity. However, it is beyond the scope of this paper to decide which technology will be used. Data packets have a maximum size of 243 bytes, sent over a configured schedule in a given installation. The advertised commercial maximum range is currently between 5 and 15 km [1].

Summarizing, we propose in this paper the *Connectivity Management Tool Semantics (CMTS)* ontology; an extension of the World Wide Web (W3C) and the Open Geospatial Consortium (OGC) joint Semantic Sensor Network and Sensor-Observation-Sample-Actuator (SSN/SOSA) ontology [10,12]. Our proposal makes use of two auxiliary ontologies for location (GeoSPARQL - Geographic Query Language for RDF Data) and temporal properties (OWL-Time Ontology). Our main contribution is to provide such a system, with the set of language elements needed to achieve semantics interoperability.

---

[1] Worldsensing: https://www.worldsensing.com.

[2] ThingsBoard: https://thingsboard.io.

[3] Long Range - LoRa Alliance Standardisation Committee: https://lora-alliance.org.

We build upon and extend our previous work in [15] where we proposed a prototype to monitor IoT devices to automatically react and notify through alarms when data surpasses a certain threshold.

2   Related Work

2.1   Semantic Web Background

The World Wide Web uses the term "Semantic Web" to refer to the representation of the world data and vocabularies, with the objective of making it readable for humans and machines. In the Semantic Web, the information is written in the form of Triples, three entities with which to refer to a concept.

Consider the example *geo:Barcelona geo:partOf geo:Catalonia*, which follows the subject-predicate-object format. In this example; *geo:partOf* means that the *geo*[4] "Barcelona", is a location which is part of "Catalonia". Where the non-literal values are URIs[5]; like "Barcelona" or "Catalonia".

As mentioned in [3]; "the Resource Description Framework (RDF) is the basis of the Semantic Web. Things in the world are referred to as *resources* and they can be anything that someone might want to talk about. *i.e.* '*the value of X*' *or* '*all the cows in Texas*'". RDF is intended to be used for representing information about those resources in a graphical form.

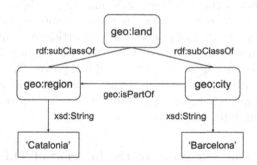

Fig. 1. Sample RDF in graphical notation

As shown in Fig. 1; classes are rounded rectangles while literal values are represented in rectangles. The text linking classes refers to properties of an object, while the text linking classes and literal values refers to the property of the data to be displayed. The property *rdf:subClassOf* makes one class a subclass of another. Hence *Region* and *City* are both subclasses of *Land*. Whilst *xsd* stands for *XML Schema Definition* and indicates that the element linked is a String. So to say, *"Catalonia"* is an instance of *Region* but also of *Land*. At the same time, *"Barcelona"* is an instance of *City* but also of *Land*. And also that *"Barcelona"* is part of the *"Catalonia" Region*.

---

[4] Namespace made-up but understood to refer to geography.

[5] URI: Uniform Resource Identifier, a sequence of characters that identifies a resource.

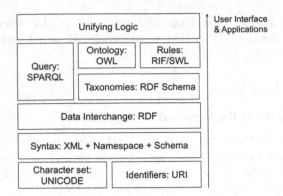

Fig. 2. Simplification of the semantic layer web

Figure 2 represents a simplified view of the technological elements used in the "Semantic Web Architecture". Starting with the character set; UNICODE ensures that the language can be read by humans and computers using a standardized form. The resulting character string forms a URI. In the next layer, there is the Extensible Markup Language (XML), together with its Namespace and Schema, ensuring that the syntax used is common through the Semantic Web. Following this is the RDF we have just seen. Then, the RDF Schema (RDFS) provides guidelines on how to use or combine different RDFs and allows describing taxonomies of classes and properties to be used in lightweight ontologies. Going up, we find the OWL ontology; a language derived from logical descriptions that enable extending vocabulary over RDFS. At this point, RIF/SWL rules can be introduced in order to constrain the ontologies. Finally, the SPARQL -Simple Protocol and RDF Query Language- allow executing queries in RDF and SQL.

2.2   Ontologies and Semantics in the Internet of Things

The first ontology proposed for wireless sensor networks was defined in OWL-Lite[6] and dates back to 2004. In 2007, Eid et al. [7] proposed a universal ontology to solve the data heterogeneity problem in sensor networks.

The Open Geospatial Consortium (OGC) then published a series of standards with the aim of improving the interoperability of sensor and actuator systems. Among those that stand out in the subject treated are: Observations and Measurements (O&M)[7], which defines standard XML Schema and models for observations and features involved in sensor measurements; Sensor Model Language (SensorML)[8], which provides robust and semantic means of defining characteristics and capabilities of sensors, actuators, and computational mecha-

---

[6] OWL-Lite: https://www.w3.org/TR/owl-features/.
[7] Observations and Measurements (O&M): https://www.ogc.org/standards/om.
[8] Sensor Model Language (SensorML): https://www.ogc.org/standards/sensorml.

nisms; and Sensor Observation Service (SOS)[9], which defines a web service for querying and manipulating observations and sensors.

In 2011, the Semantic Sensor Network Incubator Group (SSN-XG) developed an ontology to describe sensors and sensor network resources [17]. They also gave recommendations for using the ontology to semantically enable applications and to provide better support for abstraction, categorization, and reasoning. In 2017, the World Wide Web Consortium (W3C) recommended an updated version of the SSN/SOSA Ontology [16] to be used when Semantic Web and Linked Data technologies are needed.

Work is pursuing to steer the IoT ecosystem towards the homogenization of the data to be transmitted, and tools to facilitate the integration of IoT devices into systems are being developed [8]. A similar problem, interoperability of multiple sensors from different manufacturers, is addressed in [4] by using SOSA/SSN for the development of semantics to manipulate this data. In [9], the M3 ontology was proposed as an extension of the SSN ontology, which allows reasoning on cross-domain M2M sensor data using rules to infer contextual information. IoT-Lite [5] proposes a lightweight instantiation of the SSN ontology where the concepts *Object, Service, Coverage* are defined and where devices are divided into three groups *Sensing Devices, Actuating Devices* and *Tag Devices* but this is a different classification than the one we consider. In [2], a unified ontology (FIESTA-IoT) is presented with the aim of addressing interoperability issues, merging different IoT Ontologies (*SSN, IoT-Lite, M3*, among others).

If we consider domain-specific applications, we find that ontologies such as SAREF (Smart Appliance Reference) [6] that are close to ours. However, they do not manage a multi-level architecture and in this approach, devices are not related to each other.

Summarizing, we can observe that there is a need to develop new solutions to improve the interoperability of IoT devices. Generic solutions exist when there is a need to have a platform based on device observations but where the concern is simply to obtain sensor data, without having a more complex level of detail in the structure of the devices. When a higher granularity is introduced at the device level (by distinguishing, for instance, between gateways, nodes and sensors) no solutions have yet been found. This is the main objective of this work.

3   Knowledge-Engineering Methodology

We have been motivated by [14] to develop semantics that can be correct. As they suggest, there is no single way to develop semantics, and the modeling of a domain depends to some extent on several factors, including the purpose of the system it will support. The process of modeling an ontology is iterative. Below there is a summary of the steps to follow as proposed by [14]:

1. **Determine the domain and scope to be covered**
   We have provided in the Introduction a description of the project domain and its intended use.

---

[9] Sensor Observation Service (SOS): https://www.ogc.org/standards/sos.

2. **Sketch a list of competency questions that should be answered**
   We give in Sect. 3.1 the competency questions that the ontology should be able to answer.
3. **Consider reuse of existing ontologies**
   In Sect. 2 there is an introduction to Semantic Web and ontologies related to the project domain. A detailed explanation is given in Sect. 5.
4. **Enumerate important terms in the ontology**
   This is done in Sect. 4 when explaining our ontology.
5. **Develop the ontology**
   The ontology we propose for connectivity management in IoT sensing is explained in Sect. 4.
6. **Validate the list of competency questions**:
   Competency questions are formulated in Sect. 3.1 and answered in 4.

3.1 Competency Questions

One of the ways to determine the scope of an ontology is to make a list of questions, in order to obtain the baseline knowledge. These questions are called "Competency Questions". The answers of which should define the scope of the ontology. If the ontology is able to provide an answer for each question, it will mean that the described ontology contains enough information to work.

- **Q1**: Which elements or features can be observed by a sensor?
- **Q2**: How can an observation be made?
- **Q3**: How can the embedded sensor of a gateway be observed?
- **Q4**: How can the embedded sensor of a node be observed?
- **Q5**: How can an external sensor connected to a node be observed?
- **Q6**: If there are a batch of devices, is there any way to group them?
- **Q7**: Where is a given sensor located?
- **Q8**: How can we know which is the gateway providing an observation?
- **Q9**: Are there any other devices than gateway, node and sensor?
- **Q10**: How can one know if the device is enabled in a site?

These competency questions arise from the current industrial needs of World-sensing and the IoT domain under consideration and are aimed at providing an abstract interpretation of the different implementations of the kind of IoT devices they handle, in order to be able to provide a uniform treatment of all this information. They are complete in the sense that they correspond to their actual needs, but this does not ensure that they will remain exactly as such forever.

4   CMTS Ontology

The Connectivity Management Tool Semantics (CMTS) Ontology is aimed at allowing tools for monitoring physical infrastructures through the use of three common types of IoT devices: gateways, nodes and sensors. The ontology builds from two key concepts: *Site*, i.e. a physical area being monitored, and the *Devices* installed in the *Site* to allow it. In our sites, three different types of devices co-exist: *Gateways, Nodes*, and *Sensors*. A *Sensor* may be either *Hardware* or *Software* and the structure of *Gateways* and *Nodes* can also be specified through the ontology. Finally, *Observations* are registered as a means to monitor the *ObservableProperty* of each *Sensor*.

The proposed ontology is depicted in Fig. 3 by means of a UML Class Diagram that states the concepts of the domain that have to be specified in order to provide the aimed connectivity management in IoT sensing across different devices and settings of the sites being monitored. "*cmts*" is the default namespace when none is provided. A more detailed explanation of the concepts in the ontology is given in Sect. 4.2.

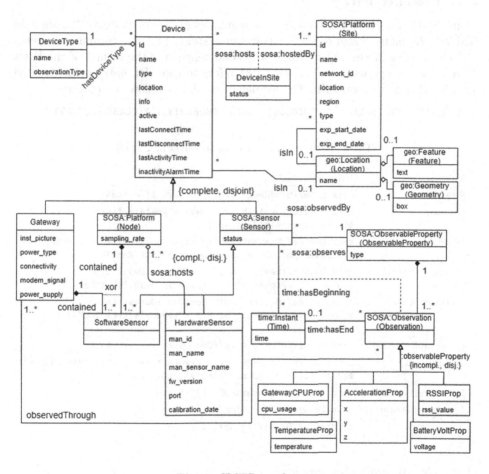

Fig. 3. CMTS ontology

We have also had to specify some integrity constraints (i.e. conditions that any instance of the ontology should satisfy) to properly model the domain:

- C1: Location must have at least one Feature or one Geometry.
- C2: Sensors of a Node must be at the same Site as the Node.

- C3: Sensors of a Gateway must be at the same Site as the Gateway.
- C4: Software Sensors must be at the same Location as the Gateway or Node they are connected to.

This ontology is complete in the sense that it incorporates all concepts and properties required by the IoT domain under consideration. Moreover, as it happens with all the approaches based on ontologies, it is easily extendable since new concepts and properties can be added to the ontology without having to modify the programs running on the current ontology.

4.1 Resource URIs

Using URIs increases the simplicity and manageability of systems. We show in Table 1 the main design of the URIs in our system. The first column represents the class name of the object, and the second represents the format of the URIs that have been generated. The BASE_URI refers to the URL entry point, located in a Worldsensing's domain. The format of the URIs follow the pattern:

{BASE_URI}:{CLASS_NAME}/{CLASS_ID}?{CLASS_PROPERTY_1}&{CLASS_PROPERTY_N}

Table 1. Summary of the main URIs in CMTS

Class	URI Patterns
Site	cmts:Site/{SiteName}?{LocationName}&{Devices}
Gateway	cmts:Device/{DeviceName}?{DeviceType}&{SoftwareSensors}&{LocationName}&{SiteName}
Node	cmts:Device/{DeviceName}?{DeviceType}&{SoftwareSensors}&{HardwareSensors}&{LocationName}&{SiteName}
Hardware Sensor	cmts:Device/{DeviceName}?{NodeName}&{DeviceType}&{ObservablePropertyName}&{LocationName}&{SiteName}
Software Sensor	cmts:Device/{DeviceName}?{NodeName|GatewayName}&{DeviceType}&{ObservablePropertyName}&{LocationName}&{SiteName}
ObservableProperty	cmts:ObservableProperty/{ObservablePropertyName}
Observation	cmts:Observation/{ObservablePropertyName}?{ObservationName}&{Value}&{Time}&{SensorName}&{GatewayName}
Location (Feature)	cmts:Location/{LocationName}?{Feature}
Location (Geometry)	cmts:Location/{LocationName}?{Geometry}
Time	cmts:Time/{Date}T{Time}+{TimeZone}

4.2 Component Description

Site. A *Site* is a physical working area in the project. They are intended to group devices in the system by work areas so as to monitor these devices by granularity levels. It contains location information; the type of work being carried out; and, optionally, the start and end dates. This covers the competency question **Q6**.

Figure 4 provides a visual description of a *Site* having one *Gateway*, one *Node*, and one *Sensor*, whose *Location* is "LocationBCN".

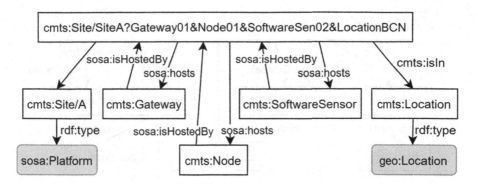

Fig. 4. Example of a site description

Device. *Devices* are the essential elements that carry out the monitoring of the infrastructures. A *Site* can contain multiple *Devices*. A *Device* is categorized by a *DeviceType*, such as the model name. This covers the competency question **Q9**. A *Device* is an element which can report to different *Sites*; the system can discern availability of a *Device* for each *Site*, whether it is active or not. This covers the competency question **Q10**. *Devices* have information about the infrastructure communication in terms of connection status and can handle *Location* information. *Devices* are classified in three types: *Gateways*, *Nodes*, and *Sensors*:

Gateway. It is a physical element that acts as a router, gathering data from incoming wireless transmissions, grouping it and sending it to the data server, thus allowing to receive information sent wirelessly via the *Nodes*. *Gateways* are in charge of receiving the message via *LoRa* and send it to the Internet. *Gateways* contain *Sensors* that capture metrics related to the *Gateway* such as the internal temperature or processor usage. For each *Gateway* we know its location, the way it communicates with the *Sites*, as well as other operational aspects.

Figure 5 provides a visual description of a *Gateway* having "GW_EU" as *DeviceType*; contains a *Software Sensor* "SoftwareSen03" as *Sensor*; its *Location* is "LocationBCN", and it is in the *Site* "Site A".

Node. It is a small physical element with limited processing capabilities, i.e. that of communicating directly to *Sensors* through a wired connection. They are responsible for collecting raw data measurements from the *Sensors*, building a well-formed message and sending it via *LoRa* to the *Gateways* in range, and reporting *Sensor* failures. They also have internal *Sensors* to be monitored. The visual description of *Node* is similar to the one of *Gateway* given in Fig. 5.

Sensor. They are the elements capable of making observations of a given feature. They can be either *Software* or *Hardware*. *Software Sensors* are used to monitor the infrastructure that supports the work, and we are only interested to know their sensor type, whether they work correctly and the values they report. They are the ones embedded into *Gateways* and *Nodes* and are used to

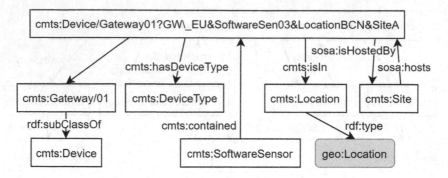

Fig. 5. Example of a gateway description

monitor information like temperature, voltage, etc. This covers the competency questions **Q3** and **Q4**. For *Hardware Sensors* we need to know data related to the manufacturer, the model, and specifics on how are they working and how they communicate. In addition to emphasizing the calibration of the data they report. They are the ones that are directly connected to the *Nodes*. This covers the competency question **Q5**.

Figure 6 provides a visual description about a *Hardware Sensor*. It has "Tiltmeter" as *DeviceType*; the *Sensor* has been named "HardwareSen01"; is connected to the *Node* "Node01"; is measuring *ObservableProperty* "Accelerometer"; its *Location* is "LocationBCN", and it is in the *Site* "Site A".

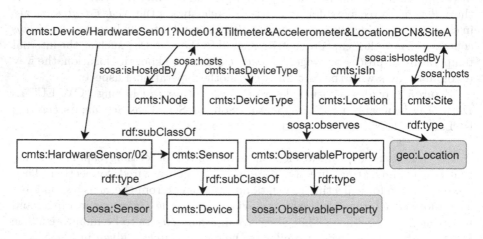

Fig. 6. Example of a hardware sensor description

ObservableProperty. Are the properties to be observed in *Sensors*; for a given characteristic, property or feature. For example, the temperature inside a *Gateway*; the temperature of a sensor in an environment or the inclination of a surface.

This covers the competency question **Q1**. Figure 3 explicitly distinguishes five possible *ObservableProperty*. However, other properties to be observed can be added when necessary as new subclasses of *Observation*.

Observation. When a *Sensor* captures the value of an *ObservableProperty* at a given time it generates an *Observation*. In addition, it is possible to include a time interval to support those *Observations* that cannot obtain the value instantly. This covers the competency question **Q2**.

An *Observation* will always be generated from a *Sensor*. The *Node* is the device that sends it wirelessly as a radio signal. *Gateways* are the devices that will listen to this information, hence the "observedThrough" of an *Observation*, and will transmit it to the data server. This covers the competency question **Q8**.

Figure 7 and Fig. 8 provide a visual description about an *Observation* made by a *Hardware Sensor* "HardwareSen01"; the communication of this *Observation* was made through the *Gateway* named "Gateway01"; is measuring *ObservableProperty* "Accelerometer"; its *Location* is "LocationBCN"; it is in the "Site A"; it also has the value measured "0_0_9.8m/2", and the *Time* has a value of "2021-03-15 at 16:15".

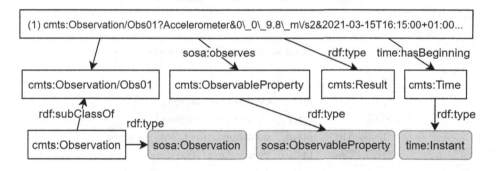

Fig. 7. Example of an observation description - Part 1

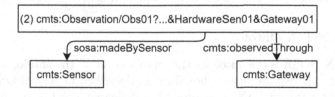

Fig. 8. Example of an observation description - Part 2

Due to the use of *LoRa* communication technology; active communication between a *Gateway* and a *Node* is not possible. The *Node* sends out radio waves with the information, and the *Gateways* independently listen to these transmissions. More than one *Gateway* can receive the information. The server will only consider one packet as valid, and duplicated messages will be discarded.

Location. If desired, the user is given the possibility to indicate the location of the elements in the physical world. With this purpose, the system is provided with the ability of locating elements, as well as *Sites* and *Devices*, which comprise *Gateways*, *Nodes* and *Sensors*. This covers the competency question **Q7**.

5   Matching Existing Ontologies

The Semantic Sensor Network and Sensor Observation Sample Actuator (SSN/-SOSA) ontology [16] is being used as the core ontology for the observation of measurements. Hence, a network of ontologies has been achieved, which is structured as follows (see Table 2 for the URLs):

- SSN/SOSA: Ontology to gather measurements from devices and sensors.
- GeoSPARQL: Ontology to describe geographical locations.
- OWL-Time: Ontology to describe temporal properties.

Table 2. Ontologies used in this project

Prefix	Namespaces
SSN	http://www.w3.org/ns/ssn/
SOSA	http://www.w3.org/ns/sosa/
GeoSPARQL	http://www.opengis.net/ont/geosparql
OWL-Time	http://www.w3.org/2006/time

In the following, we briefly explain how these ontologies have been used, along with the elements that have been newly added in order to define our solution.

5.1   SSN/SOSA Ontology

As said, SSN/SOSA is the ontology that comes closer to the ontology we propose here. This is why we use it as a baseline. As described in [16]: "SOSA provides a lightweight core for SSN and aims at broadening the target audience and application areas that can make use of Semantic Web ontologies. At the same time, SOSA acts as minimal interoperability fall-back level, i.e. it defines those common classes and properties for which data can be safely exchanged across all uses of SSN, its modules, and SOSA."

The SOSA/SSN classes that have been (re)used in our solution are:

- *sosa:Platform*, to describe:
  - *Sites*, the physical working areas, which can contain multiple devices.
  - *Nodes*, the physical elements that gather information from *Sensors* and send it to *Gateways*.
- *sosa:Sensor*, to describe the low-level *Sensors* that are collecting information.
- *sosa:ObservableProperty*, to specify the elements to be observed by a *Sensor*.
- *sosa:Observation*, to provide the value of the measurements of the *ObservableProperty* collected by the *Sensors*.

This is also true for some of the properties in our ontology that allow us giving more clarity to the actions being carried out: *sosa:hostedBy*, *sosa:hosts*, *sosa:observedBy*, *sosa:observes*.

5.2   OGC GeoSPARQL

Several ontologies exist for the management of geospatial elements. However, we decided to use GeoSPARQL; an OGC Standard that has a small but powerful ontology that fits perfectly with the scope of this project. It enables describing data in *Geographic Markup Language* (GML) and also with *Well-Known Text representation of geometry* (WKT).

The GeoSPARQL classes that have been (re)used in our ontology are:

- *geo:Location*, to describe the location of *Sites* and *Devices*.
- *geo:Feature*, to specify points of interest from written language, in other words, as a *String*. For instance, "Barcelona".
- *geo:Geometry*, to define points of interest as coordinates from geometries such as points, lines and polygons, etc.

Moreover, we have used the properties *geo:hasGeometry*, *geo:hasGML* and *geo:hasWKT* to complement the definition of geometries and spatial objects.

5.3   OWL-Time Ontology

The *OWL-Time* allows the Semantic Web to describe concepts and temporal properties. In our use case, this ontology is used to define when there has been an *Observation*, i.e. when a *Sensor* has taken a measurement. Using the properties *time:hasBeginning* and *time:hasEnd*. Also, through the class *time:Instant* we define the moment of time in which it has occurred.

6   Conclusions and Future Work

The interest in facilitating homogeneous information handling in IoT sensor networks has been acknowledged. Homogenization makes it simpler to enable compatibility between devices from different manufacturers. In this work, we proposed a semantics for the data management of gateways, nodes, and sensors, carrying out the theoretical and descriptive part of it. The ontology we used to specify such semantics builds upon recognized ontologies like SSN/SOSA or GeoSPARQL. We have used competency questions, stating what we expected from the semantics, to validate the appropriateness of our ontology.

As further work, we plan to incorporate additional features to our ontology to integrate IoT monitoring with the operational part of the company and we are also focused on the implementation of a system taking advantage of our ontology for IoT sensing of Worldsensing' sites.

As far as further applications, we have in mind the possibility of adding rule inference to the ontology, thus first enabling to develop applications with a context-awareness system and then allowing to incorporate an automatic notification system when a certain declarative condition over the data is met.

Acknowledgements. This work is partially funded by Industrial Doctorates DI-2019 from Generalitat de Catalunya and Grup de Recerca Consolidat IMP, 2017-SGR-1749. Also with the support of inLab FIB at UPC, Worldsensing and the REMEDiAL project (TIN2017-87610-R). Also to the Worldsensing's team (T. Martinez-del-Hoyo and T. Fisher). We also thank the anonymous reviewers for their valuable comments.

References

1. Adelantado, F., Vilajosana, X., et al.: Understanding the limits of LoRaWAN. IEEE Commun. Mag. **55**(9), 34–40 (2017)
2. Agarwal, R., Fernandez, D.G., et al.: Unified IoT ontology to enable interoperability and federation of testbeds. In: IEEE World Forum on Internet of Things (WF-IoT), pp. 70–75 (2016)
3. Allemang, D., Hendler, J.: Semantic Web for the Working Ontologist, 1st edn. Morgan Kaufmann, Burlington (2008)
4. Berges, I., Ramírez-Durán, V.J., Illarramendi, A.: Facilitating data exploration in Industry 4.0. In: Guizzardi, G., Gailly, F., Suzana Pitangueira Maciel, R. (eds.) ER 2019. LNCS, vol. 11787, pp. 125–134. Springer, Cham (2019). https://doi.org/10.1007/978-3-030-34146-6_11
5. Bermúdez-Edo, M., Elsaleh, T., et al.: IoT-Lite ontology (2015). https://www.w3.org/Submission/iot-lite/. Accessed 25 Mar 2021
6. Daniele, L., den Hartog, F., et al.: Study on semantic assets for smart appliances interoperability. Technical report, TNO (2015)
7. Eid, M., Liscano, R., et al.: A universal ontology for sensor networks data. In: IEEE International Conference on Computational Intelligence for Measurement Systems and Applications. CIVEMSA 2007, pp. 59–62 (2007)
8. Frigo, M., Hirmer, P., et al.: A toolbox for the internet of things - easing the setup of IoT applications. In: ER Forum, Demo and Posters. International Conference on Conceptual Modeling. ER 2020, pp. 80–100 (2020)
9. Gyrard, A., Bonnet, C., et al.: Enrich machine-to-machine data with semantic web technologies for cross-domain applications. In: IEEE World Forum on Internet of Things (WF-IoT), pp. 559–564 (2014)
10. Haller, A., Janowicz, K., et al.: The modular SSN ontology: a joint W3C and OGC standard specifying the semantics of sensors, observations, sampling, and actuation. Semant. Web J. **10**, 9–32 (2018)

11. IoT Analytics: Why the Internet of Things is called Internet of Things: Definition, history, disambiguation (2014). https://iot-analytics.com/internet-of-things-definition. Accessed 25 Mar 2021
12. Janowicz, K., Haller, A., et al.: Sosa: a lightweight ontology for sensors, observations, samples, and actuators. J. Web Semant. **56**, 1–10 (2019)
13. Mekki, K., Bajic, E., et al.: A comparative study of LPWAN technologies for large-scale IoT deployment. ICT Exp. **5**, 1–7 (2019)
14. Noy, N.F., McGuiness, D.L.: Ontology development 101: a guide to creating your first ontology. Knowledge Systems - Stanford University, Technical report (2001)
15. Vila, M., Sancho, M.-R., Teniente, E.: XYZ monitor: IoT monitoring of infrastructures using microservices. In: Hacid, H., et al. (eds.) ICSOC 2020. LNCS, vol. 12632, pp. 472–484. Springer, Cham (2021). https://doi.org/10.1007/978-3-030-76352-7_43
16. W3C - OGC: semantic sensor network ontology - W3C recommendation (2017). https://www.w3.org/TR/vocab-ssn/. Accessed 18 Apr 2021
17. W3C Incubator Group: semantic sensor network XG Final report (2011). https://www.w3.org/2005/Incubator/ssn/XGR-ssn/. Accessed 23 Apr 2021

Ontologies

Consolidating Economic Exchange Ontologies for Corporate Reporting Standard Setting

Ivars Blums[1](✉) ⓘ and Hans Weigand[2] ⓘ

[1] SIA ODO, Riga, Latvia
Ivars.Blums@odo.lv
[2] University of Tilburg, Tilburg, The Netherlands

Abstract. In the last decade, several UFO-grounded economic exchange ontologies have been developed, notably COFRIS, OntoREA, REA2, and ATE. It is time to take the next step in the direction of corporate reporting standard setters, for which an ontological approach is of high potential value. In this paper, we first describe the foundational assumptions for exchange conceptualization and consolidate the latest developments in COFRIS - a core ontology for financial reporting information systems, within the most recent versions of the UFO theories and the OntoUML tool. We then confront COFRIS with the conceptual framework and standards for accounting and financial reporting and compare it with other UFO grounded exchange ontologies.

Keywords: IFRS · UFO · OntoUML · COFRIS · OntoREA · REA2 · ATE · Contracts

1 Introduction

Ontology-driven conceptual modeling celebrates its 40th anniversary but much domain ontology development work remains within the realm of academic research without significant practical use. However, in biomedicine, ontologies have made significant inroads as valuable tools for achieving interoperability between data systems whose contents derive from widely heterogeneous sources [1]. Other potential fields for using ontologies, but requiring different approaches, are law, economics, and accounting. In corporate accounting and reporting the primary users of upper core ontologies could be standard setters for whom a core ontology of their frameworks could be used to develop and improve standards, taxonomies, and compliant IS.

Concepts of economic exchanges and their governing contracts play a fundamental role in corporate accounting and reporting. A major part of international and national reporting standards [2, 3] is dedicated to different types of contracts or specifies requirements for capturing exchanges of specific economic resource categories. The conceptual framework for reporting [3, 4] sets forth *principles* of transaction effect recognition, measurement, and presentation, and guides the development of standards, which in turn specify *rules* of transaction and their effect categorization, measurement, and disclosure.

© Springer Nature Switzerland AG 2021
A. Ghose et al. (Eds.): ER 2021, LNCS 13011, pp. 315–329, 2021.
https://doi.org/10.1007/978-3-030-89022-3_25

Despite a high level of rigor in the standard-setting processes, the framework and standards suffer from internal inconsistencies and semantic interoperability problems [5]. The ontological analysis of framework and standards and tools for their ontology-driven conceptual model development and use can help to prevent these issues.

In this paper, we build forth on COFRIS – a core ontology for financial reporting information systems [6–8] to address current shortcomings and bring the ontology work closer to the standards-setting. Our ontology is grounded on Unified Foundational Ontology (UFO) [9]. Using the new edition of UFO theories and tools [10], we extend the social relator pattern that provides a foundation for valued economic resource, performance obligation, and contract patterns. Furthermore, we introduce the contract pattern structured in four multilateral independent-view modules and four corresponding unilateral enterprise dependent-view modules.

Several economic exchange ontologies have been built, grounded on different editions of UFO, that claim to cover the exchange concept in the accounting domain. We attempt to show by comparing our proposal with reporting standards and frameworks that several important elements for standard-setting – of recognition and measurement, and contract formation and execution – are still missing.

The methodology of our ontology research is dialectical. We start with foundational assumptions in accounting theories for economic exchanges and foundational concepts of UFO in Sect. 2. In Sect. 3, we present the extended social relator and contract patterns of our ontology in more detail within the most recent versions of UFO theories and the tool. In Sect. 4, we confront our ontology with the framework and standards, and then in Sect. 5, we review current UFO grounded exchange and contract ontological approaches and their limitations. Section 6 concludes and outlines future work.

2   Background

The foundational assumptions of contract and property law, economics, and accounting principles, used for the ontology, are briefly covered in Subsect. 2.1.

To ground an ontology for standard-setting, a foundational ontology is needed, that covers ultimate categories and ties, contains building blocks in law and economics, and tools for framework and standard ontology-driven conceptual model building, specializing, verification, and validation. An obvious candidate is the Unified Foundational Ontology (UFO) [9], with its sub-ontologies, e.g., [11–16], ontology engineering tool OntoUML 2 [10], and advanced treatment of a *relator* as an ultimate sortal and a disposition of an exchange. The new development of theories and the most recent version of the tool incorporates an extension of OntoUML to address ultimate sortals [10], events, and their relations [11], and allows the verification and conversion of models to be suitable for Semantic Web OWL 2 DL applications. The main constructs of UFO used in this paper are briefly covered in Subsect. 2.2.

2.1   Foundational Assumptions for Corporate Reporting

The preemptive foundational assumption and the objective of corporate reporting is to provide periodic financial and non-financial information about the reporting enterprise that is useful to stakeholders, primarily to existing and potential investors, and creditors in making decisions relating to providing resources to the enterprise [3, 4]. Business transactions, mainly economic exchanges, together with some other metrics are the source of corporate reporting. In this concern, we are interested to conceptualize answers to the following questions. Who is involved in the performance and observation of economic exchanges? What entities relevant for standards are exchanged and affected during the exchange from the independent and enterprise perspective? How are these entities measured in terms of money? What are exchange lifetime events, and when and why they do unfold?

Economic Exchange. Complementing the definition by Ijiri [17], we define the *economic exchange* as a transaction whereby an enterprise *transfers* control [or *assumes* obligations] over some resources in order to obtain control [or settle, transfer, or replace obligations] over other resources.

Standardized Reporting today reflects a unilateral view of an enterprise's position and performance in a complex IS environment where economic agents using markets and multilateral contractual agreements exchange and fulfill reciprocal performance obligations to transfer economic resources (or to assume obligations) in order to achieve individual goals. Economic agents are [communities of] people and enterprises, or society at large, capable to exchange.

Exchange Information is captured by complementarily observing exchange actions and action effects on the situation of an enterprise. The so-called *dependent-view* [18] of unilateral observation by reporting enterprise primarily *recognizes* and *measures* the *effects* of transactions on assets, liabilities, and on periodic income and expenses of the enterprise and is governed by accounting assumptions and standards. The bilateral and multilateral [6] so-called *independent-view* [18] in a centralized, market, or shared ledger system, observes contract formation and execution *events,* their context and economic resources and obligations exchanged, measured at market or transaction price and is governed by legal and economic assumptions and laws.

Transferred and Valued Economic Resources of economic agents, are *rights* (including those that are correlative *obligations* of a converse agent) over resources, such as *ownership* or *use rights* over goods or *immediate consumption rights* (e.g., vaccination) over services or goods, that have the disposition to produce economic benefits [3, 4]. Economic resources have a market value dependent on economic benefit value. Economic resources and obligations to transfer resources (e.g., bonds or stock) and their combinations are participants and characteristics of property transfer actions observed independently. We interpret obligation transfer as an *obligation assumption* by the obligor and will depict it and related items in brackets. We regard economic resources as specializations of *valued performance rights*. This interpretation is wider than in the framework [4] and likewise as in [14], includes an executory contract or even an offering as an "agentive or non-agentive" resource. It is similar to the *input* to a business defined in the Business Combination standard exemplified as "the *ability* to obtain access to necessary materials or rights and employees" [2].

Affected Assets (Liabilities and Equity) are present economic resources (resp., obligations) controlled (owed) by an enterprise as a result of economic exchanges and other events. An enterprise, being in the *going concern* state, performs holder-specific *recognition* and categorization of resources, their value *measurement*, presentation, and *disclosure* according to the standards, resource *use pattern,* and uncertainty. Use can be internal when an enterprise creates value by combining its resources to produce goods and services whereby assets are measured at historical or use-value, or external when assets are categorized for exchange and measured at market value [5]. Note that assets are goods or promises and are categorized and measured additionally to (specializing) underlying resources. For example, assume that some goods (a resource) were transferred together with accompanying services (another resource) to an enterprise. The successfully *transferred ownership rights* and *value* of goods affect the forward-looking asset of raw materials (valued at cost) or merchandise (valued at price) of the enterprise. The transferred *value* and *consumption rights to the effect* of services affect the *same* goods asset or are expensed.

An Economic Exchange Lifecycle governed by contracts [17] comprises the contract *formation* between two parties – an *offer* and *acceptance* of *valued performance obligations* – and *execution* phases. In the execution phase, mutual performance obligations are *fulfilled* by transfers of economic resources. A fulfillment of a particular performance obligation results in a consideration *value right* (*claim* against the other party). A so-called contract *half-execution* [17] is a completion of the exchange by one party which induces a *consideration claim* against the other party in exchange for the accumulated value right. Consideration claims are unconditional obligations to be *settled* by the other party.

2.2 UFO Background

In UFO [9, 11], *Concrete Individuals* comprise *Objects* (John, his car), *Reified Aspects* of concrete individuals (John's height), *Events* (the acquisition of GitHub by Microsoft), and *Situations* (the situation in which John weighs 80 kgs). Together, objects and aspects are called *Endurants*, as they are those concrete individuals that endure in time and may change qualitatively while keeping their identity. A concrete individual has *Begin Point* and *End Point*. Reified aspects are further divided into intrinsic aspects (qualities and intrinsic modes) and extrinsic aspects (relators and extrinsic modes). An *Intrinsic Aspect* depends on a single concrete individual in which it inheres. Intrinsic aspects are divided into *Qualities* in case the aspect is measurable by a certain value space (e.g., John's weight), and *Intrinsic Modes*, which are not given a direct value (e.g., John's capabilities). *Extrinsic Aspects* are reified relationships, e.g., John and Mary's marriage, Mary's employment contract at NASA. A distinction is made between *formal* relations holding between two or more entities "directly without any further intervening individual" [9, p. 236], and *material* relations, which require the existence of an intervening individual – a specific construct, called a relator. A *Relator* mediates the mutual relationships of two or more concrete individuals. Extrinsic aspects can also be reified one-sided relationships, e.g., John's admiration for Obama (which depends on Obama but does not characterize him).

An *Event* is a concrete individual that occurs or happens in time [11]. Events are those things that happen to or are performed by endurants, e.g., actions and processes, such as an offer and negotiation; as well as natural occurrences such as an earthquake. The relations between objects and events are captured with «participation», «creation», and «termination» properties. Part-whole relations between events can be represented with the «component of» and other relations. An event can have a «historicalDependence» on another event. An event can be related to the endurants that are created or terminated in it. For instance, John and Mary's marriage was brought into existence in their wedding ceremony, a marriage as an event is the manifestation of properties of the marriage as a relator. The «manifestation» property can be used to identify specific aspects that manifest themselves in an event. Endurants play *processual* (or *historical*) roles in events in contrast to *relational* roles in relators.

An *Individual Type* is a type whose instances are individuals. *Kinds* are sortals that classify their entities necessarily and provide a uniform principle of identity for their instances. Kinds are decorated with the «kind» stereotype for Substantial kinds, «relator» for Relator kinds, «mode» for Mode kinds, and «quality» for Quality kinds respectively. Instances of a kind can (contingently) instantiate *Roles* in relational contexts or instantiate *Phases* in intrinsic contexts. For instance, a person can move in the extension of the role of Employee by participating in Employment relators. Relators and Qualities are existentially dependent entities. For example, the Employment of Mary in NASA can only exist if both Mary and NASA exist. This particular relation of multiple existential dependency is stereotyped as «mediation». A role-like anti-rigid non-sortal that can be played by individuals of multiple kinds is termed a *roleMixin*. OntoUML diagrams represent types and second-order types by the «type» stereotype.

3 The Economic Exchange Ontology for Standard-Setting

3.1 The Extended Social Relator

Per UFO-C [14], "Social Commitments and Claims always form a pair that refers to a unique propositional content, and a Social Relator is an example of a relator composed of ... associated commitments/claims" (see Fig. 1(a)). The concept has been further employed developing a legal relator in UFO-L [16] that associates different kinds of *correlative* obligations/rights of two agents. However, most relator examples in UFO literature, such as marriage or employment, as well as service agreements are modeling relations of relations, and particularly *reciprocity*. A contract is reciprocal in requiring the exchange of performance of one party in consideration of the counterparty. A valued performance obligation is reciprocal in requiring accrual of value rights in exchange for the transferred resources. An offering and a valued economic resource are reciprocal (but subject to greater uncertainty) in the sense of market response (as a constructive right expected or based on previous experience) of at least one agent. For modeling exchange contracts, economic resources, and obligations, we initially introduce a pattern of reciprocal legal positions and their lifecycle. A reciprocal relator has been used before in UFO literature for modeling service offerings and agreements. Our pattern generalizes its use and introduces a number of additional concepts.

Firstly, we avoid using correlative positions when they are formal, thus a contract can be specified by two obligations without specifying correlative rights. The reciprocal relationship in a social relator is *material* in both observation views. The correlative relationship is *formal* in the independent-view as it is instituted by law, but *material* between the subjective dependent-views.

Secondly, we introduce the concept of reciprocal relator second-order *type* whereby we specify all the relationships and characteristics common to the relator, for contracts it could be the analog of a standard[1]. Such types would be gradually *materialized* by specialization and instantiation of category, mode, and quality types.

Thirdly, we specify resource rights required to fulfill commitments, the ability to commit these resources, their transfer while fulfilling, and affected resource rights of the counterparties. The resource is a concept of the REA Ontology [18]. The distinction in our pattern is that resources are rights, and affected resources are not the same as transferred resources (e.g., services) or are categorized (recognized) and measured differently from enterprise dependent-view perspective.

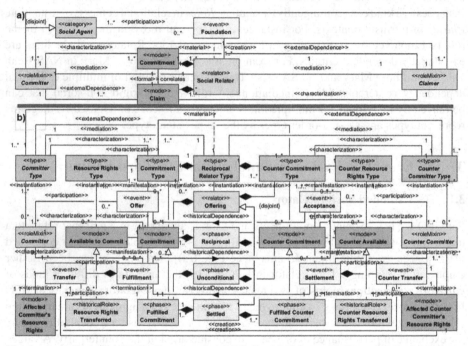

Fig. 1. A verified OntoUML diagram of a) UFO Social Relator, b) Extended Social Relator. Second-order types in violet, agents in pink, events in yellow, relators in green, modes in blue. (Color figure online)

The Extended Social Relator Pattern, is depicted in Fig. 1(b). To simplify Fig. 1 we assume that the committer offers and performs first, and omit its multiple roles and situation types. The creation of the commitment modes as instantiations of the commitment types by committers is represented by the «creation» stereotype [12] with the *Offer* event (which creates a power of acceptance) and historically dependent *Acceptance* event. Social relators with one commitment instantiated are *Offerings*, while with

---

[1] A similar Standard-Intended Process Definition and Execution methodology is used in [19].

both commitments instantiated are in the *Reciprocal Executory* phase. The termination of commitment modes as specializations is represented by the «termination» stereotype [11] which relates historically dependent *Fulfillment* or *Settlement* events to a class stereotyped «phase» which is instantiated by the endurant when it takes on a "historical"[2] nature. Social Relators with one commitment fulfilled are in the *Unconditional* phase and with both commitments fulfilled in the fulfilled or *Settled* phase. In this relator pattern, legal positions (and their correlatives) and thus the economic relator will progress through the «phases» created by events and situations.

3.2 The Economic Exchange Ontology

The ontology consists of four independent-view modules and corresponding four dependent-view modules possibly for each involved economic agent, as depicted in Fig. 2.

1. Standard. The first module represents types of (possibly *related* [2]) *Economic Agents* – persons and enterprises involved in an *Economic Exchange* of a *specified Type*. Exchange Types are represented by exchange contract standards. Exchange contracts are enforceable economic agreements concluded between two exchange parties – economic agents – a *Party* and a *Counterparty* and comprise of valued performance obligations (POBs) of one party in consideration for the other.

A *Valued Performance Obligation* of an *Obligor* to the *Obligee* is a reciprocal relator that comprises *Commitments to Transfer* (*to Assume*) *Economic Resources* (*Obligations*) of specified *Types* and a reciprocal right to the consideration amount measured per specified *Expected Valuation Type* in a single *Contract Currency*.

A valued performance represents a transfer process that produces an economic benefit to the obligee in exchange for consideration. Resource Types often suggest Transfer Types, which indicate Performance Types, which prompt Exchange Types when the consideration consists of money payments. Examples of other obligation types and features are – condition, timing based, or recurring; enforceable or cancelable; simple or complex; transferable; requiring a reservation. Examples of valuation types are – fixed, volume-based, future or spot market pricing, regulated, cost plus, or the counterparty's consideration valuation dependent. *Net Valuation* of the contract is a balance of a party's and counterparty's present amount of the right to consideration and is zero at inception. A party is a *Creditor* to a particular commitment, obligation, or contract if the party's present amount of the right to consideration is larger than the counterparty's (who is a *Debtor*).

Economic agents own economic resources and owe obligations measured at *Present Value* in *Functional Currency*. Obligors have powers to transfer by themselves or mediated or facilitated by *Third Party*. Contracted Third Parties directed by Obligors provide resources for the Obligees and/or to facilitate or mediate Obligors' resource transfers. If an agent – a Debtor – has an obligation to the Creditor it must settle it or contract with some Obligor who assumes this obligation.

The corresponding modules depict *bookings* of the parties' subjective views of *Asset (Liability) Types* affected by resource (obligation) transfers (assumptions), including

---

[2] A different approach is taken in [20], whereby commitments cease to exist after fulfillment.

tracking of contract formation and fulfillment in *Valued Performable or Payable* and *Receivable* accounts that specialize POBs. Enterprises are owned by the *Owner* – claimer of the residual of Changes in *Equity*. Enterprises specify measurement bases of these accounts and *Equity Change Types* related to the exchange type, such as *Income* and *Expenses* classified by *Nature, Function,* and *Accounting Period*. We depict only bookings of Obligors, assuming that the Obligees' actions are opposite (but not correlative).

2. Intended. An Enterprise decides upon the intended exchange types and its performance within such types and counterparty's reciprocal performance types. An enterprise must have or be certain about the rights or license and its capability to perform. That would allow it to offer and take performance obligations. The objects of a transfer are present or available to commit economic resources. Economic resources conform to possible transfers and have exchange value. Assets that represent these resources have carrying value. The second module depicts Intended *Exchange Types* of some *Performer.*

For each performance, the party decides what resources are available to commit and for what pricing. Economic resources in this case represent a *Valued Performance Right and Capability* with an *Availability to Commit*.

The corresponding module depicts the financial position from each agent's subjective view as *Assets* (resources) and *Liabilities* and enterprise owner *Equity Claims* (obligations) under the *control* [17] of the Enterprise and their disposition – *Use Pattern. The Carrying Amount* of assets and claims is measured at historical or present value [17]. In a most detailed form, the dependent-view accounts represent *reciprocal value propositions* [12] of the obligor to target obligee type.

3. Formation. The third module represents the contract formation process, which starts with the instantiation of an intended exchange type into an exchange *Offering* by a party or its agent playing a processual role [11] of the *Offerer* that via an *Offer* event transfers the *Offeror's* instantiated POBs to the *Offerees* of a specified *Type*. Offeror's POBs are conditioned by reciprocal offeree POBs of a specified type *required* in consideration.

In the corresponding module, the Offeror makes its *Assessments* of the recognition and measurement for the Offering. An Offeree playing an *Acceptor* role continues with a lapse or *Acceptance* event, instantiating its POBs, transferring the contract to the Offeror, and making its Assessments. This concludes the *Executory Contract* formation.

4. Execution. In the fourth module, the exchange contract *Execution* process is structurally decomposed into generally concurrent *Obligation Fulfillment* processes of resource (obligation) economic transfers (assumptions) – successful and accepted actions by each party in the processual roles of the *Obligor*, and *Obligee*. These actions affect the accounts in the corresponding module by booking actions of [de-]recognition and measurement.

The Resource (Obligation) *Economic Transfer (Assumption)* fulfills and terminates the *Committed Transfer* and terminates and derecognizes the resource rights or creates and recognizes the obligations of the obligor and the opposites for the obligee. *Affected Asset (Liability)* costs are terminated and recognized into *Expenses* accounts. The *Transferred Resource* is produced from the affected assets (liabilities) and is a «characterization» of the transfer event, the «participation» involves transferred rights and value, that

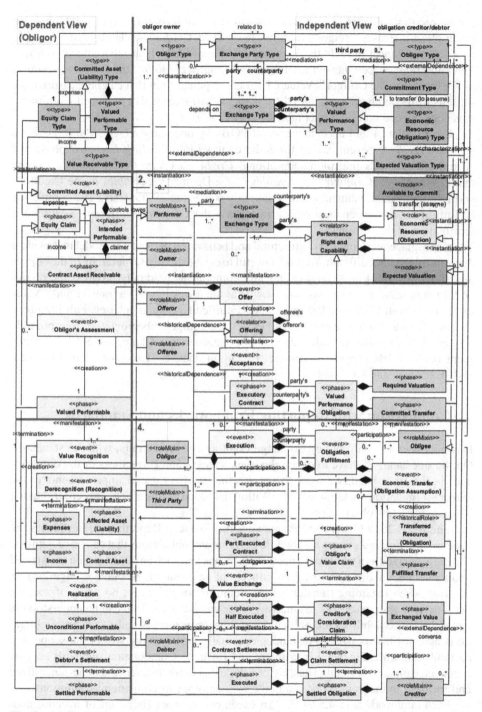

Fig. 2. COFRIS. A verified OntoUML diagram of Basic Economic Exchange Contract Pattern.

can be recognized by the obligee or consumed in production or expensed. Obligation assumption increases Obligor's Liability to Obligee, Creditor, or Third Party.

POB fulfillment turns POB into *Obligor's Value Claim* phase that affects *Contract Asset* and *Income* accounts of the Obligor and *Contract Liability* and *Expenses* accounts of the Obligee. The Obligor's Value Claim is a separate right that can be measured and sold. Its timing is conditional until the contract is half-executed or breached. Fulfillment advances the executory contract into the *Part-Executed*.

The fulfillment and acceptance of all POBs by one party *triggers* the Realization or *Value Exchange* event, which turns the contract into the *Half-Executed* phase and all unfulfilled POBs into the unconditional *Creditor's Claim to Consideration* phase that affects the *Performables* or *Payables* of the Debtor (*Receivables* of the Creditor), and requires extinguishment of the contract's Net Value by transfers. The completion of fulfillment and acceptance by both parties – the *Contract Settlement* – causes the termination of the contract.

A simultaneous depiction of structural and behavioral parts in one model makes clear diagramming rather difficult. We find it useful to establish a phase hierarchy of the objects and show how the lowest level events and components gradually progress the hierarchy. In summary, we have two components at the lowest level – a transfer and a value exchange – with Committed/Required and Fulfilled/Exchanged phases. Fulfilling by a transfer or value exchange event of either of these components progresses four possible phases of POBs – Reciprocal, Value Claim, Consideration Claim, and Settled. Fulfillment of the POBs progresses contract execution phases – Executory, Part-Executed, Half-Executed, and Executed.

4   Comparison with Reporting Frameworks and Standards

It is necessary to confront any exchange ontology, including ours, with the standards. On the one hand, we have to check the completeness and correctness of the ontology, and on the other hand, we want to see whether it offers useful improvements to the current formulations in the standards. Within the scope of this article, this confrontation is limited to a few observations.

The IASB 2018 Conceptual Framework for Financial Reporting [4] introduces the concept of a *Unit of Account* as a bundle of rights and obligations that can be recognized and derecognized as a whole or in parts. This means that such an object can be transferred upon a contract and is similar to our concept of an economic resource (obligation). In contrast, when regarding transfers in the definition of liabilities, not units of account but only economic resources in a narrow sense are included. That can be understood in general because liabilities are obligations to transfer resources and a transfer of obligations assumes the transfer of resources eventually, however not within the scope of a particular contract. Financial Instrument and Business Combination standards support transfers of units of account. Thus, we conclude that these transfers are to be generalized and included in the framework and in the core ontology as obligation assumptions.

Per Framework para 4.57 [4], "An executory contract [is a unit of account and] establishes a combined right and obligation to exchange economic resources. The right and obligation are interdependent and cannot be separated. Hence, the combined right and obligation constitute a single asset or liability. The entity has an asset if the terms of the exchange are currently favorable; it has a liability if the terms of the exchange are currently unfavorable." Similarly, in our model, the contract is represented by the relator of reciprocal obligations and their consideration. Initially, the total valuation is equal to zero and off-balance.

Furthermore, per Framework para 4.58 [4], "To the extent that either party fulfills its obligations under the contract, the contract is no longer executory. If the reporting entity performs first under the contract, that performance is the event that changes the reporting entity's right and obligation to exchange economic resources into a right to receive an economic resource. That right is an asset." The difference with our model is that we distinguish between a conditional and unconditional right to receive respectively a value and a consideration, where the former is before and the latter is after the realization (value exchange) and both are phases of the contract and POB. For example, if a party makes a transfer and fulfills only part of the contract, a *conditional* right to receive consideration value is accrued, but a complete fulfillment by one party raises an *unconditional* right to receive consideration.

We will finish our short analysis by reviewing some aspects of the most comprehensive contract standard – IFRS 15 *Revenue from Contracts with Customers* [2]. In addition to the duplication of concepts in the framework, IFRS 15 states that an enterprise "shall recognize revenue when (or as) the entity satisfies a performance obligation by transferring a promised good or service to a customer." This standard conforms to the Basic Contract Pattern. The main purpose of the standard is to specify more detailed rules of estimating the consideration value (revenue) that the enterprise expects and receives in exchange for transferring its goods and services during the execution of the contract.

Per para 105 of IFRS 15, "When either party to a contract has performed, an entity shall present the contract in the statement of financial position as a contract asset or a contract liability, depending on the relationship between the entity's performance and the customer's payment. An entity shall present any unconditional rights to consideration separately as a receivable." This statement not only proves the first-class concept omnipresence of intermediate consideration value rights (obligations) but also, in contrast with the framework, regards contract asset (liability) as a contract phase and not as a new object. At the same time, it proves that contract assets and receivables are material, but not computable (formal), and can be subject to exchange and impairment, per para 107: "A contract asset is an entity's right to consideration."

5 Comparison with Related Work

The conceptual modeling "in a shared data environment" of economic resources, events, and agents - in fact of economic exchange of causal events of resource flows between participating agents and added later reciprocal commitments in contracts - started in the late 70s with the development of REA Ontology by McCarthy [18, 21].

While our research was largely based on REA initially, some distinctive issues as raised in [7, 22, 23] do not allow REA "to cover essential accounting requirements" [23]. In addition, the issues of claims, of difference in transferred and affected resources are analyzed in this paper. Economic claims in the REA sense are computable [formal] imbalances between currently incomplete promised and transferred resources. We have shown that claims are *material* relationships created at the moment of transfer, i.e., *consideration* or *value claims* and *phases* of *contracts,* and are resources themselves. REA Ontology as an ISO standard [18] introduced the *independent-view* of collaboration space as a business activity space where an economic exchange of valued resources is viewed independently and not from the perspective [the *dependent-view*] of any business partner.

Separate from REA, UFO grounded conceptualizations of service and legal exchanges were developed in [15, 16]. These do not involve resource, right, obligation, complete or partial transfers, and do not regard the measurement and recognition issues (cf. [7]). The claim in [15] that "it is service, not value that is exchanged because the value is subjective" is different as in accounting where the transferred *exchange value* of a service from an independent view is objective.

During the last decade, several attempts were made to ground and improve the REA Ontology in UFO. The first attempts to compare REA conceptualizations in UFO were reviewed and found not to be fully compliant [24].

Laurier et al. formalized part of REA-ISO using OntoUML, called REA2 [25]. The approach was based on an original approach of introducing duality, stock-flow, and participations relators with events as UFO roleMixins. However, the approach of involving events as relata was not supported by the UFO-B model [11], which treats these relationships as formal.

Another issue is that the standards allow or require that exchange parties recognize, measure, and disclose an exchange differently [4], hence "an automated transformation of view-dependent data into view-independent data and vice versa" [25] is not possible in general. However, it is important to recognize the *maximally* consensual and independent recognition, measurement, and disclosure of exchange. That makes the works in [25] important, especially for DLT and auditing [8].

A separate Action Based Core Ontology for economic exchanges - ATE [26] evolved in the UFO Economics project, claiming to cover REA Ontology. Its main contribution and a difference to, e.g., [25] is the introduction of the *preference* concept and *convergence* of agents' preferences during the whole lifecycle. Accounting ignores opportunity costs, and standards do not require capturing the preference options of an enterprise. However, they can be tracked by comparing lapsed and accepted offerings for some exchange type or by comparing the transaction price with the market price. These options are included in our model. Perhaps other UFO developments in economics such as risk, value, trust, decision, game theory could enrich the exchange concept in the future.

ATE includes phases of contract formation, but the economic exchange is portrayed as a set of actions that is not sufficient for economic and accounting models. A depiction of action effects on the situation of each exchange party is necessary as well as explicit resource (obligation) participation, recognition, and measurement.

An effort to improve REA, to achieve accountants' traction, and to provide UFO grounding is OntoREA [23]. OntoREA models recognition of the effects and in some sense could be regarded as an antipode to the ATE. What we lack in OntoREA is the independent-view and the lifecycles of contract formation and execution. The most recent model [23] is in our view generally correct but covers only the final states of future and spot market contracts. From the fundamental accounting concepts, the income and expenses are not covered, at least as different from owner-initiated equity changes. The income and expense accounts are not just formal equity changes, they provide periodic transaction and other event activity categorization and valuation.

Like all reviewed ontologies, OntoREA has goals in addition to standard-setting, such as a deep consideration of derivative instruments and uncertainty representation. The latter underlines the distinction between the old accounting [and the ontologies which do not include recognition and measurement] related backward-looking perspective into the past and the finance-related forward-looking perspective into the future [23]. A forward-looking perspective can include forecasting and planning, and their mathematical modeling as suggested in [17] and [23], although standard-setting today does not require it [4].

An ontological issue raised in [23] is the anti-eternalist view of events, which is different than in other regarded exchange ontologies and in UFO-B, where the events are the past events and future events are specified by second-order event types.

Table 1 shows how the current version of COFRIS compares with the related work described in 2.2 in terms of contract phases and contract information processing. Our claim is that COFRIS addresses all required concerns. However, the development of Measurement and Disclosure is still in the initial stage.

Table 1. Comparison of economic exchange ontologies.

Exchange ontology	Contract and obligation lifecycle				Affected resource processing	
	Standard	Intended	Formation	Execution	Recognition	Measurement
REA ISO [18]	Basic	Basic	Commitments	Basic	Goods	Historical
REA2 [25]	No	Basic	No	Basic	Goods	Historical
UFO-S [15]	No	No	Commitments	Services	No	No
UFO-L [16]	No	No	Legal positions	Services	No	No
ATE [26]	No	No	Commitments	Services	No	No
OntoREA [23]	No	No	No	Basic	Balance-sheet	Derivatives
COFRIS v 0.5	Detailed	Detailed	Detailed	Detailed	Detailed	Basic

6 Conclusions and Future Work

The research work presented in this paper is motivated by the need to investigate the foundational grounds for economic exchange modeling in corporate reporting standard-setting. Our contribution has been presented in Sect. 3, where the main features for economic activities of the extended relator lifecycle, contract formation and execution, and resource control recognition and measurement are unified in a single framework.

An initial confrontation with the reporting conceptual framework and standards shows compliance, with minor inconsistencies among them, outlining a possibility to generalize some standards' conceptualizations into the framework and core ontology.

We compared COFRIS with other UFO grounded work in exchange conceptualization and indicated their deficiencies for standard-setting. Given that the regarded ontology development is continued, the common grounding in UFO will allow for shared understanding and formulation of economic exchange phenomena for different purposes.

This paper regards the application of the economic exchange ontology in one domain – corporate reporting. Our ongoing work started in [8] involves analysis and design of IFRS [2] contract and resource standard and their illustrative case ontologies as a *specialization* of the presented one. In parallel that should include formal validation, representative example instance generation [10], and standard-setter interviews, including ontology-based commenting of the IFRS projects and discussion papers.

Another promising area of future work is the analysis and redesign of the ISO/IEC 15944-4:2015 Standard [18] and the formalization of its existing ontology based on COFRIS. This formalized ontology can then be specialized to a conceptualization of the environmental, social, and corporate governance (ESG) impact of economic exchanges, as a foundation for required new ESG business and reporting standards.

In the context of enterprise and information systems engineering the ontology and its specializations can be used to base *applications* that are compliant with and realize reporting standards, including receiving information from the blockchain environment for the independent view. One way of incorporating the ontology into widespread systems and their realization is through developing ArchiMate patterns that have been shown as the main bridge of UFO grounded ontologies and enterprise architecture, e.g., in [13, 16].

Acknowledgments. The authors are thankful to Vítor E. Silva Souza for his valuable comments on the topics of this paper.

References

1. Karray, M., et al.: The Industrial Ontologies Foundry (IOF) perspectives. In: International Conference on Interoperability for Enterprise Systems and Applications, Tarbes (2021)
2. IASB (2021). IASB: http://www.ifrs.org/issued-standards/list-of-standards
3. FASB Accounting Standards Codification, FASB (2021). FASB: https://asc.fasb.org/
4. IASB Conceptual Framework for Financial Reporting, IASB (2018)
5. Botosan, C.: Pathway to an integrated conceptual framework for financial reporting. Account. Rev. **94**(4), 421–436 (2019)
6. Blums, I., Weigand, H.: Towards a core ontology of economic exchanges for multilateral accounting information systems. In: EDOC 2020, pp. 227–232 (2020)

7. Blums, I., Weigand, H.: Towards a reference ontology of complex economic exchanges for accounting information systems. In: EDOC 2016, pp. 119–128 (2016)
8. Weigand, H., Blums, I., de Kruijff, J.: Shared ledger accounting—implementing the economic exchange pattern. Inf. Syst. **90**,101437 (2020)
9. Guizzardi, G.: Ontological foundations for structural Conceptual Models. Ph.D. thesis, CTIT, Centre for Telematics and Information Technology, Enschede (2005)
10. Guizzardi, G., Fonseca, C., Almeida, J.P., Sales, T.P., Benevides, A.B., Porello, D.: Types and taxonomic structures in conceptual modeling: a novel ontological theory and engineering support. Data Knowl. Eng. (2021, accepted, forthcoming).
11. Almeida, J.P.A., Falbo, R.A., Guizzardi, G.: Events as entities in ontology-driven conceptual modeling. In: Laender, A.H.F., Pernici, B., Lim, E.-P., de Oliveira, J.P.M. (eds.) ER 2019. LNCS, vol. 11788, pp. 469–483. Springer, Cham (2019). https://doi.org/10.1007/978-3-030-33223-5_39
12. Sales, T.P., Guarino, N., Guizzardi, G., Mylopoulos, J.: An ontological analysis of value propositions. In: EDOC 2017 (2017)
13. Azevedo, C.L.B., et al.: Modeling resources and capabilities in enterprise architecture: a well-founded ontology-based proposal for ArchiMate. Inf. Syst. **54**, 235–262 (2015)
14. Bringuente, A.C., Falbo, R.A., Guizzardi, G.: Using a foundational ontology for reengineering a software process ontology. J. Inf. Data Manag. **2**, 511 (2011)
15. Nardi, J.C., et al.: A commitment-based reference Ontology for services. Inf. Syst. **54**, 263–288 (2015)
16. Griffo, C., Almeida, J.P.A., Guizzardi, G., Nardi, J.C.: Service contract modeling in Enterprise Architecture: an ontology-based approach. Inf. Syst. **101**, 101454 (2021)
17. Ijiri, Y.: Theory of Accounting Measurement. American Accounting Association (1975)
18. ISO/IEC 15944-4:2015. Information Technology—Business Operational View—Part 4: Business Transactions Scenarios—Accounting and Economic Ontology (2015)
19. Borges Ruy, F., de Almeida Falbo, R., Perini Barcellos, M., Dornelas Costa, S., Guizzardi, G.: SEON: a software engineering ontology network. In: Blomqvist, E., Ciancarini, P., Poggi, F., Vitali, F. (eds.) EKAW 2016. LNCS (LNAI), vol. 10024, pp. 527–542. Springer, Cham (2016). https://doi.org/10.1007/978-3-319-49004-5_34
20. Guarino, N., Sanfilippo, E.M.: Characterizing IOF terms with the DOLCE and UFO ontologies. In: JOWO 2019 (2019)
21. McCarthy, W.E.: The REA accounting model: a generalized framework for accounting systems in a shared data environment. Account. Rev. **57**(3), 554–578 (1982)
22. Melse, E.: The Financial Accounting Model from a System Dynamics' Perspective, MPRA Paper, University Library of Munich, Germany (2006)
23. Schwaiger, W.S.A., Nasufi, A., Kryvinska, N., Fischer-Pauzenberger, C., Dural, Ö.F.: The OntoREA© accounting and finance model: inclusion of future uncertainty. In: Gordijn, J., Guédria, W., Proper, H.A. (eds.) PoEM 2019. LNBIP, vol. 369, pp. 53–67. Springer, Cham (2019). https://doi.org/10.1007/978-3-030-35151-9_4
24. Guarino, N., Guizzardi, G., Sales, T.: On the ontological nature of REA core relations. In: 12th VMBO 2018, pp. 89–98 (2018)
25. Laurier, W., Kiehn, J., Polovina, S.: REA 2: a unified formalisation of the Resource-Event-Agent ontology. Appl. Ontol. **13**(3), 201–224 (2018)
26. Porello, D., Guizzardi, G., Sales, T.P., Amaral, G.: A core ontology for economic exchanges. In: Dobbie, G., Frank, U., Kappel, G., Liddle, S.W., Mayr, H.C. (eds.) Conceptual Modeling: 39th International Conference, ER 2020, Vienna, Austria, November 3–6, 2020, Proceedings, pp. 364–374. Springer International Publishing, Cham (2020). https://doi.org/10.1007/978-3-030-62522-1_27

Empirically Evaluating the Semantic Qualities of Language Vocabularies

Sotirios Liaskos[1]([✉]) [iD], John Mylopoulos[2] [iD], and Shakil M. Khan[3] [iD]

[1] School of Information Technology, York University, Toronto, Canada
liaskos@yorku.ca
[2] Department of Computer Science, University of Toronto, Toronto, Canada
jm@cs.toronto.edu
[3] Department of Computer Science, University of Regina, Regina, Canada
shakil.khan@uregina.ca

Abstract. Developing and representing conceptualizations is a critical element of conceptual modeling language design. Designers choose a set of suitable concepts for describing a domain and make them the core of the language using suggestive terms that convey their meaning to language users. Additional documentation and training material, such as examples and guides, aims at ensuring that the chosen terms indeed evoke the concepts designers intended. However, there is no guarantee that language designers and users will eventually understand the correspondence between terms and concepts in the same way. This paper proposes a framework for empirically evaluating the vocabulary appropriateness of modeling languages and characterizing its absence in terms of established language design issues. The framework is based on the definition of a set of abstract empirical constructs that can be operationalized into different concrete measures, depending on study requirements and experimental design choices. We offer examples of such measures and demonstrate how they inform language design through a hypothetical language design scenario using a mix of realistic and simulated data.

Keywords: Conceptual modelling · Conceptualization quality · Empirical conceptual modelling · Goal models

1 Introduction

Designing and representing conceptualizations lies at the very core of conceptual modeling language development. Conceptualizations are sets of concepts selected by designers as suitable for modeling a domain [6,7]. Each concept in a conceptualization is meant to capture intuitively some facet of the domain and is conveyed to users through a term that is familiar to domain users. Guides with definitions and examples are available to further ensure that the meaning of each term is shared between designers and users. However, whether such a vocabulary of terms is properly understood by users is not straightforward to

© Springer Nature Switzerland AG 2021
A. Ghose et al. (Eds.): ER 2021, LNCS 13011, pp. 330–344, 2021.
https://doi.org/10.1007/978-3-030-89022-3_26

determine. The chosen terms may evoke among users a meaning that is different from the one the designers designated it for, or users may be found to be confused or disagreeing among themselves about the meanings of those terms.

For example, consider i^*, a requirements modeling language, proposed in 1995 by E. Yu [23]. The language was intended to model stakeholders and their goals, as well as ternary social dependence relationships among them. Towards this end, the language offered concepts signified through terms such as "*actor*", "*agent*", "*position*" and "*role*". Since its inception, the language has been used extensively for research and teaching purposes by many research groups, largely organized around the iStar workshop series. In 2015, that community decided to conduct an evaluation of the i^* experience, and on the basis of its findings proposed iStar 2.0 [4]. One of the findings was that users, especially students, of i^* were confusing the notions of "*position*" and "*role*" in their models. As a result, "*position*" was dropped from the new concept set and vocabulary. While the i^* community had the benefit of many years of experience to inform such updates, one wonders if there is a quicker and more systematic way to empirically assess the success of a vocabulary selection for any language.

In this paper, we propose a framework for empirically measuring the vocabulary appropriateness of conceptual modeling languages. The framework is based on offering domain descriptions to representative language users and inviting them to categorize domain elements relative to the terms in the vocabulary. The framework includes a set of abstract empirical constructs for analyzing the resulting data, informed by an established model of vocabulary pathologies [7,25]. The constructs can be operationalized into concrete measures, based on the format of the data collection instruments and the needs of the study at hand. An application of the framework on a mix of realistic data from a past experiment and simulated data demonstrates how the constructs can be translated to concrete metrics and how they can indicate the type of corrections needed in the design. The work generalizes and systematizes our earlier work [15] so that it is compatible with established approaches for understanding and analyzing language qualities. It further introduces measures for additional quality issues such as construct deficit, construct excess, and construct redundancy. Moreover, thanks to a new formulation, our framework accounts for conceptual relations of arbitrary arity, rather than just unary arity [15].

The rest of the paper is organized as follows. In Sect. 2 we offer the necessary background on conceptualizations, in Sect. 3 we introduce our empirical framework and in Sect. 4 we describe an application thereof. We review related work and conclude in Sects. 5 and 6.

2   Research Baseline

2.1   Conceptualizations, Languages and Ontological Commitments

Following [6] consider a system S that we are interested in modeling. We first define conceptual relations (aka concepts) and conceptualizations over a domain D of distinguished elements of S, given a set of possible worlds W (states of S).

Definition 1. *A conceptual relation (henceforth:* **concept***) is a total function* $\rho^n : W \mapsto 2^{D^n}$ *from worlds to all possible extensional n-ary relations on D. A* **conceptualization** *is, then, a triple* $\mathbf{C} = (D, W, \Re)$ *in which* $\Re$ *is a set of such concepts on the domain space* $<D, W>$.

Such concepts need to somehow be built into a language that users can use to build models of the domain. Towards this end, language designers select an appropriate *term* (name or expression) for each concept based on its intended meaning and the cultural context where the language is meant to be used. In the goal modeling domain, for example, the concept *goal* can be represented in English using terms such as *"goal"*, *"intention"* or *"objective"*. A language is thus grounded on terms for representing concepts, matching such semantic preconceptions. Thus [6]:

Definition 2. *Let* **L** *be a language with vocabulary V. A model for* **L** *is a tuple* $M = (S, I)$ *where* $I : V \mapsto D \cup \mathbf{R}$, *the* **interpretation***, maps names and terms from V to elements in either D or* **R***, the latter being a set of n-tuples from D. The exact subset of* $D \cup \mathbf{R}$ *to which a vocabulary element* $v \in V$ *maps is called the* **extension** *of v.*

Definition 3. *An* **ontological commitment** *for* **L** *is a tuple* $\mathbf{K} = (\mathbf{C}, \mathfrak{I})$, *where* $\mathfrak{I}$ *is a total function* $\mathfrak{I} : V \mapsto D \cup \Re$, *i.e., where every symbol in V maps to either an element of D or a concept in* $\Re$*. We, further, denote as* V_D *the portion of the vocabulary reserved for mapping to elements of D and* $V_\Re$ *the terms reserved for mapping to concepts. We will henceforth refer to elements in* $V_\Re$ *as* **concept terms** *(or simply* **terms***).*

For example, for a vocabulary $V = V_D \cup V_\Re$ with $V_D = \{$ *"Alice"*, *"pay the bills"*$\}$ and $V_\Re = \{$ *"actor"*, *"goal"*, *"wants"*$\}$, an ontological commitment maps the term *"actor"* to, say, the concept of an individual who can act in a domain, the term *"goal"* to the concept of a desired state of affairs, and the term *"wants"* to the concept that an actor is inclined to pursue a goal. Models of the language can be compatible or incompatible with the commitment. For example, including *"Alice"* in an extension of term *"actor"* in a model M is consistent with the commitment. However, including *"pay the bills"* is inconsistent, as the latter does not satisfy the definition of an actor as per the ontological commitment.

To accomplish clear communication, the language designers must choose a vocabulary V that intuitively conveys the right commitment $\mathbf{K}$ to modelers and model readers. However, achieving such a shared understanding of the commitment is neither guaranteed nor trivial to assess.

2.2   Language Qualities and Their Measurement

To characterize inadequate sharedness of the ontological commitment of a vocabulary we adopt a framework for language quality due to Wand and Weber [25]. The key concern in that framework is the degree of alignment between language terms and concepts, whose absence the authors characterize using four (4) different quality issues. Firstly, when there are concepts in the domain that are not

Table 1. Running example.

Language and empirical set-up:

$V_\Re$ = { "goal", "objective", "argument", "wants", "desires"}
E = {e_1 = "Alice plans to pay her bills.",
  e_2 = "Alice would like to pay her bills but it is not her priority now."}
V_D = { "Alice", "pay bills"}
D = { "Alice", "pay bills", ⟨ "Alice", "pay bills"⟩}

Extensions:

Rater:	p_1		p_2	
Descr.:	e_1	e_2	e_1	e_2
"goal"	"pay bills"	"pay bills"	–	–
"objective"	–	–	"pay bills"	"pay bills"
"argument"	–	–	–	–
"wants"	⟨ "Alice", "pay bills"⟩	–	⟨ "Alice", "pay bills"⟩	⟨ "Alice", "pay bills"⟩
"desires"	⟨ "Alice", "pay bills"⟩	⟨ "Alice", "pay bills"⟩	⟨ "Alice", "pay bills"⟩	–

represented in the vocabulary we have *construct deficit*. Secondly, if there are vocabulary terms that represent multiple concepts, we have *construct overload*. Thirdly, when there are multiple vocabulary terms that represent the same concept, this is a case of *construct redundancy*. Finally, when there are vocabulary terms that do not relate to any concept we have *construct excess*.

Let us explore how the above vocabulary issues can be empirically detected. The proposed measurement process is inspired by processes for measuring *reliability* in the context of qualitative content analysis [12,15]. In content analysis, *units* of content (text, audiovisual segments) representing information about the domain are classified by *raters* into a set of categories (*codes*) that best describe each unit. The exercise is meant to allow the development of theories about the content grounded on codes and is predicated on the presence of agreement among raters on what codes best describe each unit. Lack of inter-rater agreement implies an unreliable coding process, which can be due to a variety of factors, including problems with the appropriateness of the coding language.

To apply these ideas to our measurement problem, we have (a) samples of language users play the role of raters, (b) descriptions of elements from the domain play the role of content units, and (c) the terms in the vocabulary $V_\Re$ play the role of codes. As in content analysis, we ask language users to assign domain elements to one or more vocabulary terms – if applicable. Ideally, they will all agree with their assignments indicating good sharing of the ontological commitment. If not, however, the different ways by which raters disagree are indicative of different categories of issues with the choice of vocabulary, in accordance with Wand and Weber's framework. We offer more details below.

3 Empirically Measuring Semantic Qualities

3.1 Method Overview and Notation

Let us now describe more concretely the method for acquiring and analyzing vocabulary quality data with reference to the example of Table 1:

1. Identify the Language. Consider a language $\mathbf{L}$ with an ontological commitment $\mathbf{K}$ and a set of terms for representing concepts $V_\Re = \{r_1, r_2, \ldots\} \subseteq V$. Let $V_\Re = \{$ *"goal"*, *"objective"*, *"argument"*, *"wants"*, *"desires"*$\}$ of the upper part of Table 1 be the vocabulary of interest for our running example.

2. Sample Raters. Select a set $p \in P$ of human raters. Selected raters are representative users of the vocabulary so to allow generalization of findings to all intended users of the language. They should also have good knowledge of the domain to ensure that their categorizations reflect the features of the language, rather than their own understanding of the domain.

3. Construct Descriptions. Construct a set of descriptions $E = \{e_1, e_2, e_3, \ldots\}$ each partially describing in natural language a world in W. Descriptions present domain phenomena that the language is meant to model. For our example, two such descriptions can be seen in Table 1, though descriptions are meant to be much more extensive in practice – see [16]. Sampling of such descriptions is biased towards descriptions that test all expressive capabilities of the language and are expected to trigger utilization of all language terms.

4. Identify Discourse Elements. Extract from the descriptions a set of discourse element representations V_D and n-tuples from that set that, according to the designers, are relevant to the domain. For our example of Table 1, we identify two elements (*"Alice"*, *"pay bills"*) and one tuple therewith ($\langle$ *"Alice"*, *"pay bills"*$\rangle$). Let $\mathbf{D} \subset 2^{(V_D)^n}$ be the union of V_D with the set of all n-tuples constructed from it.

5. Raters Form Term Extensions. For each description $e \in E$, ask each rater $p \in P$ to form the extension of each concept term $r \in V_\Re$ using elements from $\mathbf{D}$. As described above, the rater goes over the samples $\mathbf{d} \in \mathbf{D}$ and, for each, she decides whether it should be included in the extension of r based on the evoked concept. If yes, we say then that the rater p *classifies* $\mathbf{d}$ under r. We, further call the pair $(\mathbf{d}, e)$, i.e. an element or n-tuple of elements from V_D in a context of a description e, *subject*.

The result of a rating exercise can be seen in the lower part of Table 1. We consider two raters $p_1, p_2 \in P$. Each cell in the table describes the extension that each rater constructed for each term under each description. For example, for both e_1 and e_2, out of all elements in V_D rater p_1 classifies only *"pay bills"* under term *"goal"*. Thus, both subjects (*"pay bills"*, e_1) and (*"pay bills"*, e_2) are classified under *"goal"*. However, only subject ($\langle$ *"Alice"*, *"pay bills"*$\rangle$, e_1) is in the extension of term *"wants"* according to p_1.

6. Analyze Extensions. Extensions developed in the previous step are compared and analyzed to identify and characterize problems with the proposed vocabulary. We define the constructs for such characterizations below.

3.2   Rater-Based Measures of Completeness and Clarity

Denote $I_p(r, e) \subseteq \mathbf{D} \times E$ to be the extension of concept term r finally constructed by rater p given description e in Step #5 above. Consider also the union $X_p(r) = \bigcup_{e \in E} I_p(r, e)$ of all subjects that rater p classified under r. For instance, in our running example: $X_{p_1}(\text{"goal"}) = \{(\text{"pay bills"}, e_1), (\text{"pay bills"}, e_2)\}$ and $X_{p_2}(\text{"desires"}) = \{(\langle\text{"Alice"},\text{"pay the bills"}\rangle, e_1)\}$. Further, let $B = \{s \in \mathbf{D} \times E \mid \exists p \in P, \exists r \in V_{\Re} \text{ s.t. } s \in X_p(r)\}$ all subjects rated and $R_s(r) = \{p \in P \mid s \in X_p(r)\}$ be the subset of raters that classified s under r. For instance $R_{(\text{"pay bills"},e_2)}(\text{"goal"}) = \{p_1\}$ and $R_{(\langle\text{"Alice"},\text{"pay bills"}\rangle,e_1)}(\text{"desires"}) = \{p_1, p_2\}$, $R_{(\text{"Alice"},e_1)}(\text{"argument"}) = \{\}$. We then define the following constructs:

Construct Deficit: Let $B_{\tilde{d}} \subseteq \mathbf{D} \times E$ be the set of subjects that involve $\tilde{d} \in V_D$. The greater the difference $B_{\tilde{d}} \setminus B$ the more the evidence of *construct deficit*, i.e., there are elements $\tilde{d}$ of the domain of discourse that are consistently excluded from extensions.

In our example, consider $\tilde{d} = \text{"Alice"}$. $B_{\tilde{d}} = \{(\text{"Alice"}, e_1), (\text{"Alice"}, e_2),$ $(\langle\text{"Alice"}, \text{"pay bills"}\rangle, e_1), (\langle\text{"Alice"},\text{"pay bills"}\rangle, e_2)\}$ and, thus, $B_{\tilde{d}} \setminus B = \{(\text{"Alice"}, e_1), (\text{"Alice"}, e_2)\}$. That is, unary element *"Alice"* was not classified under any term by any rater, yet was included in V_D as an element that needs to be modeled. Thus, a new term, such as *"actor"*, may need to be introduced in $V_{\Re}$ to describe elements like *"Alice"*.

Construct Excess: Let r be one of the concept terms. If $\forall s \in B$, $|R_s(r)| \leq c$, for some small c, this is evidence of *construct excess*, with r being the excessive vocabulary construct. The smaller the c the stronger the evidence.

In our example, $R_s(\text{"argument"}) = \{\}$ for all $s \in B$, as in neither of the descriptions has any of the raters classified any element of $\mathbf{D}$ under *"argument"*. This is a symptom of *"argument"* being an excessive term, i.e. a term that is not useful for representing something of interest in the domain.

Overlaps: Let subject $s \in \mathbf{D} \times E$ and two terms r_i and r_j such that $r_i \neq r_j$. Assume that for several pairs of raters l, m (possibly the same rater $l = m$), $s \in X_{p_l}(r_i)$ while $s \in X_{p_m}(r_j)$ – so s is classified both under r_i and under r_j by the same or by different raters. We say that this is a *conceptual overlap* between r_i and r_j with respect to s. The more the instances of such classification divergence between r_i and r_j over s, the more the overlap between r_i and r_j over s.

In our example, there is no subject that is classified both under *"goal"* and under *"wants"* by the same or different rater. Hence, there is no overlap between those terms. However, between *"wants"* and *"desires"* there is an overlap with respect to $(\langle\text{"Alice"}, \text{"pay bills"}\rangle, e_2)$ and $(\langle\text{"Alice"}, \text{"pay bills"}\rangle, e_1)$, as both subjects are assigned in the extensions of both two terms.

Construct Redundancy: Let a subject $s \in \mathbf{D} \times E$ be *relevant* to a construct r, if a minimum number of raters have included the subject in the extension of r. Assume that two different constructs r_i, r_j almost always overlap with respect to any subject that is relevant to either of them. This is an indication of *construct redundancy* of r_i or r_j, i.e., according to the raters, whenever any of the two terms is used, the other term could have been used as well.

In our example, (*"pay bills"*, e_1) and (*"pay bills"*, e_2) are the only subjects that are relevant to *"goal"* and *"objective"*. The two terms overlap with

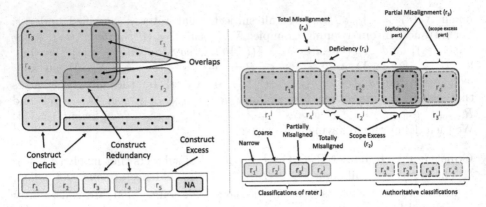

Fig. 1. Rater-based assessments (left) and accuracy (right). Inclusion of dots to solid-lined frames represents frequent inclusion of subjects to the corresponding extensions.

respect to both subjects due to inter-rater disagreements. There is no subject relevant to the terms with respect to which there is no overlap. Thus, we can mark either term *"goal"* and *"objective"* as possibly redundant.

In Fig. 1, left side, an abstract schematic representing the logic of the above is shown. The inclusion of dots to frames represents the frequent inclusion of subjects to the corresponding term extensions.

3.3 Measures in the Presence of Authoritative Ratings

Consider now that one of the raters p_a is the designer of the language, i.e., the agent that develops the vocabulary on the basis of the ontological commitment **K**. Like the other raters, she forms her own authoritative extensions $X_{p_a}(r)$ for each concept term, based on V_D and E. These extensions can be seen as exemplifications of **K**. If most other raters develop extensions that are in agreement with the designer's, it can be empirically argued that the language is conducive to the sharing of **K** between designers and users.

As above, we are interested in indications of imperfect communication of **K**. Considering the sets $X_{p_i}(r)$ of a given rater p_i and the authoritative set $X_{p_a}(r)$:

Perfect Alignment: When $X_{p_i}(r) = X_{p_a}(r)$ the authoritative and the rater's concept are understood to be perfectly aligned.
  In our running example of Table 1, let p_1 be the authoritative judge and p_2 a community rater. There is no term r for which $X_{p_1}(r) = X_{p_2}(r)$. Hence there is no occurrence of perfect alignment.

Construct Coarseness: When $X_{p_i}(r) \supset X_{p_a}(r)$ the choice of term r for the concept is too coarse, i.e. evokes an extension that is broader than the concept it is meant to represent. The difference $X_{p_i}(r) \setminus X_{p_a}(r)$ is the *scope excess* of term r with respect to the concept it represents (not to be confused with construct excess).

In our example $X_{p_2}($ *"wants"*$) \supset X_{p_1}($ *"wants"*$)$, i.e., the term *"wants"* evokes a broader interpretation than what the designer (p_1) expected.

Construct Fineness: When $X_{p_i}(r) \subset X_{p_a}(r)$ the choice of term r for the concept is too narrow, i.e. evokes an extension that excludes elements that the concept it is meant to represent. The difference $X_{p_a}(r) \setminus X_{p_i}(r)$ is the *deficiency* of term r with respect to the concept it is designed to represent.

In our example $X_{p_2}($ *"desires"*$) \subset X_{p_1}($ *"desires"*$)$, i.e., the term *"desires"* evokes a more restricted set of interpretations than what the designers thought.

Partial and Total Misalignment: When both $X_{p_i}(r) \setminus X_{p_a}(r)$ and $X_{p_a}(r) \setminus X_{p_i}(r)$ are non-empty then the term and the concept are misaligned in a less specific sense. Such misalignment is total when $X_{p_a}(r) \cap X_{p_i}(r) = \emptyset$.

In the example, there is a clear misalignment for each of the terms *"goal"* and *"objective"*, due to, in this case, the overlap between the terms.

Figure 1 (right), offers a schematic showing the logic of the above constructs. Note that the constructs compare the authoritative with the output of one rater. Practical operationalizations must appropriately express the measures in terms of statistics from the output of multiple raters, as we demonstrate below.

4   Application

4.1   Overview and Data Collection

We now present a demonstration of how the empirical constructs developed above can be used to analyze a language. We base the application on real data collected in the context of our earlier experimental study [15] which are here updated and augmented with additional simulated values. An extended presentation can be found in our accompanying report [16] including code snippets, instrument templates, and description examples that can be used for studies with the same or different languages.

The real data were collected in an experiment in which a goal modeling language with concept terms $V_{\Re} = \{$ *"goal"*, *"task"*, *"quality"*, *"belief"*$\}$ was evaluated. Twenty (20) Mechanical Turk workers with a North American bachelor's/college degree, were invited as a proxy for a sample of real language users. They first watched videos that presented the language through informal definitions and examples. Then, four different fictional scenarios were presented in textual form ($\sim$250 words each), each corresponding to a description $e \in E$. Beneath each scenario, a set of domain elements V_D mentioned in the scenario were presented – representing a domain of discourse D. Only single elements $d \in V_D$ were presented, hence $\mathbf{D} = V_D$. For each element, the participants were asked to pick one and only one concept term r from $V_{\Re}$ that best describes it. According to what we discussed, the participant response is equivalent to a classification of the subject (d, e) in r, where d is now unary.

To demonstrate the additional empirical constructs we present here, the data was subsequently altered to simulate the following hypothetical conditions.

Firstly, a number of elements representing the concept *actor* were part of the experimental prompts, and a term for such actors with the name *"principal"* is added to the language. We assume that the term largely (prob. = 0.9) does not evoke the concept *actor*. Secondly, a *"None of the Above"* (NA) option was included in the options, mentioned henceforth as r_{NA}. We alter the data assuming that if such an option were presented, it would occasionally randomly appear in place of other ratings (prob. = 0.05) and it would be the predominant (prob. = 0.8) response for *actor* instances given the supposed obscurity of *"principal"*. The third hypothetical condition is that in place of the *"belief"* term two terms *"assumption"* and *"assertion"* were part of the vocabulary. To simulate indistinguishability between the two, all *"belief"* ratings are replaced by a random choice of one of those two new terms. We call this initial language $L2$. Given the above manipulations, the data should be indicative of two language problems: (i) a sub-optimal term is used to represent *actor* and (ii) two constructs are overlapping in a way that one of them is redundant.

4.2   Construct Operationalizations

To perform the analysis we first generate concrete operationalizations according to the above data collection method. Let function $n : P \times (\mathbf{D} \times E) \times V_{\Re} \mapsto \{0, 1\}$, be $n(p, s, r) = 1$ if rater p has classified $s = (d, e)$ under r, and $n(p, s, r) = 0$ otherwise; $p \in P, s \in (\mathbf{D} \times E), r \in V_{\Re}$. Denote the marginal sums as, e.g., $n(\cdot, s, r) = \sum_{p \in P} n(p, s, r)$ and likewise for s, r and combinations. Then:

Construct Deficit. We measure construct deficit by calculating the relative proportion of NA responses per element and then identifying elements where such is maximum. Hence, letting $(d, \cdot)$ be subjects of d, the larger the following value the more the evidence for construct deficit of the vocabulary $V_{\Re}$:

$$\mathbf{inc}(V_{\Re}) = \max_{d \in D}\{\frac{n(\cdot, (d, \cdot), r_{NA})}{n(\cdot, (d, \cdot), \cdot)}\}$$

Construct Excess. Let $U(r) = \{n(\cdot, s_1, r), n(\cdot, s_2, r), \ldots\}$ be the set of total classifications each subject s received under r – each, note, is bounded by $|P|$.
  Values of the metric below that are closer to 1 indicate construct excess:

$$\mathbf{exc}(r) = 1 - \max[U(r)]/|P|$$

Construct Redundancy. We calculate overlap between r_1 and r_2 on the basis of pairwise disagreements involving the two concepts over the maximum such disagreements can possibly be:

$$ov(s, r_1, r_2) = \frac{n(\cdot, s, r_1) \times n(\cdot, s, r_2)}{\lfloor n(\cdot, s, \cdot)/2 \rfloor \times \lceil n(\cdot, s, \cdot)/2 \rceil}$$

Let $O(r, r') = \{ov(s, r, r') \mid s \in \mathbf{D} \times E\}$ be the set of overlap measures between r and r' over all subjects. Construct redundancy for r can then be measured by:

$$\mathbf{rdn}(r) = \max_{r' \in \mathbf{V}_{\Re} \setminus \{r\}} \{\min[O(r, r')]\}$$

i.e., the maximum overlap exhibited in comparison to every other construct, measured as the minimum of the elementary overlaps that occurred between r and the other construct. To exclude outliers, in all above constructs, percentiles can be used instead of min (in redundancy) and max (in deficit, excess).

Alignment to Authoritative. Given the set of authoritative ratings, we can now define three functions:

- $acc(p, s, r) = \{1$ if $n(p_a, s, r) = 1$ and $n(p, s, r) = 1$, 0 otherwise$\}$
- $def(p, s, r) = \{1$ if $n(p_a, s, r) = 1$ and $n(p, s, r) = 0$, 0 otherwise$\}$
- $exc(p, s, r) = \{1$ if $n(p_a, s, r) = 0$ and $n(p, s, r) = 1$, 0 otherwise$\}$

The marginal totals as per the above notation $acc(\cdot, \cdot, r)$, $def(\cdot, \cdot, r)$, and $exc(\cdot, \cdot, r)$ offer a measure of the *accuracy, deficiency* and *scope excess* of a given term vis-à-vis its corresponding concept. The numbers can be used to develop Euler diagrams for visualizing the quality and level of misalignment. An extended discussion on the development of the operationalizations from the empirical constructs introduced earlier is included in our technical report [16].

4.3 Analysis

Let us now explore the output of the metrics given the data we constructed. In the bottom of Fig. 2 some indications are shown for language $L2$. The construct excess indices are 0.7, 0.4, and 0.4, for *"principal"*, *"assumption"* and *"assertion"*, indicating possible excess issues with each construct. Furthermore, redundancy is zero everywhere except for *"assumption"* and *"assertion"*, meaning a possible overlap between the two. A look at the accuracy Euler diagrams shows that accuracy, i.e., the intersection of the rater and authoritative circles, is very low in those constructs. For *"principal"*, the deficiency of the construct, i.e. all the ratings it should attract but it did not, is also notable. On the table on the left, general measures about the language can be seen, including the minimum accuracy observed across all constructs, and the maximum scope excess and deficiency measures observed for the language. The construct deficit index of $L2$ is 0.85, meaning that some elements are not represented in the conceptualization evoked by the language.

After observing the results, assume that we decide to engage in corrective measures, resulting in language $L1$, as follows. What *"principal"* used to represent has now been renamed as *"actor"*. To simulate raters now successfully recognizing the *actor* concept, the corresponding elements are classified to that construct rather than r_{NA} (simulated with prob. = 0.8). Further, the constructs *"assertion"* and *"assumption"* are merged into *"belief"*; the corresponding ratings are reverted to the original. Finally, constructs *"goal"*, *"quality"* and *"task"* are replaced by a new construct *"intention"*. Assuming that raters who classified a subject under one of the three original terms, would have classified the same subject under *"intention"*, the corresponding classifications are replaced accordingly in the data. We can see in Fig. 2 that for $L1$, the excess and redundancy measures are now normal, and the accuracies have improved.

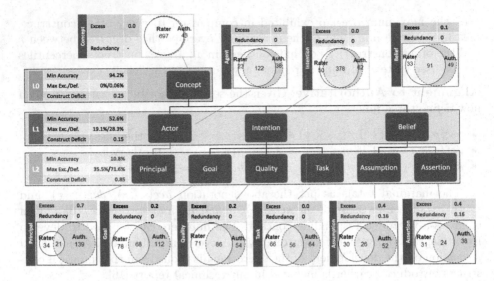

Fig. 2. Analysis of two languages.

Figure 2 also shows how lowering the granularity [9] of the concepts may result in an improvement of the proposed metrics. At the extreme, language $L0$ includes only one concept, called *"concept"* allowing for limited room for disagreement and inaccuracies. However, such language as $L0$ may lack the expressiveness needed, and the construct may suffer from *construct overload* [25]. As opposed to the other quality characteristics, measuring overload by ratings from a given language alone is difficult. Rather, when refinement of the language is attempted and the result is a language that performs well in all other aspects, then we can hypothesize the presence of remediable construct overload in the original language.

4.4   Validity Threats

The above analysis is a demonstration of the metrics based on data that has been simulated to exactly exhibit their merits. In studies with real data, experimenters need to be mindful of some validity threats and limitations.

In terms of *external validity*, that is, the generalizability of an analysis, the metrics are as good indicators as the representativeness of the world descriptions and domain elements. Sampling that consistently leaves out a class of domain phenomena, will result in false construct redundancy or construct excess indications. Inflated construct deficit indications may also emerge when phenomena that are irrelevant to the language are included in the samples. Note, further, that the choice of a Mechanical Turk sample in our study was possible for demonstration purposes due to the familiarity of the broad population with the concepts considered. However, for evaluating a language against a specific group of prospective users, external validity requires the selection of a representative sample from that exact group. Further, while individual differences in terms of linguistic ability and expertise will affect the outcome of a language evaluation, if the rater sample is representative, then whatever variability and issues emerge will still reflect the quality of the language for the given user group. The main concern regarding *internal validity* is the relationship between the metrics and the pathology they indicate. Although the constructs are direct consequences of the pathology definitions, the question of whether they constitute necessary and/or sufficient evidence for the presence of the pathology is a matter for further investigation. One of the enablers of such correspondence is proper operationalization of the metric including both the statistical instantiations of the constructs, to control for, e.g., chance responses, and the data collection instruments.

Overall, empirical evaluation of our framework is largely interpreted into studying the quality of the instruments developed for a specific language in question, including questionnaire format, training material, descriptions, and domain elements. Established techniques for instrument quality assessment can help with this task. These include measuring retest reliability, which establishes if the same rater produces the same rating at different times, and inter-rater reliability, which refers to the agreement between raters. For the latter, however, a benchmark language and instrument with known good quality, as per, e.g., expert opinion, would need to be used. In this way, possible disagreements can be attributed to the instrument or process rather than to the language. Likewise, specific issues (construct redundancies, excesses, etc.) can be introduced to the language by experts, for checking if the instruments accurately detect them – a method we simulated in our study. Finally, languages with large vocabularies imply longer and more complex rater tasks. When this appears to threaten experimental task integrity, evaluation can take place in a piecemeal fashion whereby either different groups of raters are given different domain elements and descriptions or different, possibly semantically related, subsets of terms are evaluated separately – at the expense of not capturing issues that span across subsets. These strategies and when they are necessary are yet to be investigated.

5   Related Work

Several efforts for empirically evaluating modeling languages have been proposed in the literature. One line of work concerns the identification of language quality dimensions that are subject to evaluation [13, 21]. The notions of *comprehensibility appropriateness* and *domain appropriateness* are the most closely relevant to the Wand and Weber framework adopted here. Similar notions include *semantic transparency* and *semiotic clarity*, as discussed by Moody [20].

Empirical efforts for assessing model understandability have also been reported. Houy et al. [11] survey empirical studies that evaluate the particular construct for various kinds of models including entity, class, and process models. Requirements goal models have also been a focus of such investigation [2, 5, 8, 10, 24]. In our past work, we studied the *intuitive* (i.e. without training) evocation of the meaning of a language construct via observing inferences participants perform with the construct [1,14,17,18]. However, most of these empirical efforts focus on diagrammatic constructs (boxes, lines, icons) and their visual efficiency, rather than on the choice of terms.

Work focused on terms and concepts can be found in the area of ontology engineering. Annotation of text as a terminology building and evaluation step has been proposed [3,26]. Measures of inter-rater agreement [12] to attain *semantic agreement* can be applied in such exercises [22]. Ontology learning techniques also have components that are relevant to our proposal [3]. An important process in ontology learning [3,26] is *term extraction*, i.e., the identification of terms that are relevant in the domain – e.g. [19]. Term extraction serves the purpose of supporting domain appropriateness in that terms are grounded on "true" discourse taking place in the domain as documented in the texts being processed. Comparatively, our process is geared towards evaluating an existing terminology and characterizing its appropriateness in a way that informs improvement.

Finally, analytical methods can promote the sharedness of an ontological commitment. Developing ontologies [6] allows explication of the commitment through the formulation of properties of the terms within language, e.g., meaning postulates, that are consequences of the commitment. Upper-level ontologies can, further, be used to identify issues with a language meta-model [7]. Empirical analyses are meant to complement such approaches and to also measure the extent to which a language is learned by the community of practitioners.

6   Conclusions and Future Work

We presented a framework for empirically measuring the appropriateness of vocabulary choices for conceptual modeling languages. The framework is based on the measurement of the degree of sharedness of the ontological commitment of the language via observing how experimental participants map descriptions of possible worlds to extensions of the vocabulary terms. A set of empirical constructs are defined for characterizing the resulting mappings in terms of specific pathologies of the vocabulary choice as per an established model. The constructs allow different concrete operationalizations that fit the needs of specific data collection techniques. We demonstrated the utility of the framework over a hypothetical language design scenario using a mix of real and simulated data.

There are several opportunities for further consolidating and extending our framework, in addition to empirical evaluation suggestions mentioned above. These include analytically and empirically studying possible operationalizations of our proposed constructs with respect to exhibiting statistical properties suitable for generalizations and comparisons. Further, experiments with various languages need to be conducted both for validation and for the establishment of community norms/baselines as is commonly the case with standardized empirical instruments – e.g., what levels of "excess" or "deficit" are common.

References

1. Alothman, N., Zhian, M., Liaskos, S.: User perception of numeric contribution semantics for goal models: an exploratory experiment. In: Mayr, H.C., Guizzardi, G., Ma, H., Pastor, O. (eds.) ER 2017. LNCS, vol. 10650, pp. 451–465. Springer, Cham (2017). https://doi.org/10.1007/978-3-319-69904-2_34
2. Caire, P., Genon, N., Heymans, P., Moody, D.L.: Visual notation design 2.0: towards user comprehensible requirements engineering notations. In: Proceedings of the 21st IEEE International Requirements Engineering Conference (RE 2013), Rio de Janeiro, Brazil, pp. 115–124 (2013)
3. Cimiano, P., Mädche, A., Staab, S., Völker, J.: Ontology learning. In: Staab, S., Studer, R. (eds.) Handbook on Ontologies. IHIS, pp. 245–267. Springer, Heidelberg (2009). https://doi.org/10.1007/978-3-540-92673-3_11
4. Dalpiaz, F., Franch, X., Horkoff, J.: iStar 2.0 language guide. The Computing Research Repository (CoRR) abs/1605.0 (2016). http://arxiv.org/abs/1605.07767
5. Estrada, H., Rebollar, A.M., Pastor, O., Mylopoulos, J.: An empirical evaluation of the i^* framework in a model-based software generation environment. In: Dubois, E., Pohl, K. (eds.) CAiSE 2006. LNCS, vol. 4001, pp. 513–527. Springer, Heidelberg (2006). https://doi.org/10.1007/11767138_34
6. Guarino, N., Oberle, D., Staab, S.: What is an ontology? In: Staab, S., Studer, R. (eds.) Handbook on Ontologies. IHIS, pp. 1–17. Springer, Heidelberg (2009). https://doi.org/10.1007/978-3-540-92673-3_0
7. Guizzardi, G.: Ontological foundations for structural conceptual models. Ph.D. thesis, University of Twente (2005)
8. Hadar, I., Reinhartz-Berger, I., Kuflik, T., Perini, A., Ricca, F., Susi, A.: Comparing the comprehensibility of requirements models expressed in use case and tropos: results from a family of experiments. Inf. Softw. Technol. 55(10), 1823–1843 (2013)
9. Henderson-Sellers, B., Gonzalez-Perez, C.: Granularity in conceptual modelling: application to metamodels. In: Parsons, J., Saeki, M., Shoval, P., Woo, C., Wand, Y. (eds.) ER 2010. LNCS, vol. 6412, pp. 219–232. Springer, Heidelberg (2010). https://doi.org/10.1007/978-3-642-16373-9_16
10. Horkoff, J., Yu, E.: Finding solutions in goal models: an interactive backward reasoning approach. In: Parsons, J., Saeki, M., Shoval, P., Woo, C., Wand, Y. (eds.) ER 2010. LNCS, vol. 6412, pp. 59–75. Springer, Heidelberg (2010). https://doi.org/10.1007/978-3-642-16373-9_5
11. Houy, C., Fettke, P., Loos, P.: Understanding understandability of conceptual models – what are we actually talking about? In: Atzeni, P., Cheung, D., Ram, S. (eds.) ER 2012. LNCS, vol. 7532, pp. 64–77. Springer, Heidelberg (2012). https://doi.org/10.1007/978-3-642-34002-4_5
12. Krippendorff, K.: Content Analysis: An Introduction to it Methodology. SAGE (2004)
13. Krogstie, J.: Model-Based Development and Evolution of Information Systems. Springer, Heidelberg (2012). https://doi.org/10.1007/978-1-4471-2936-3
14. Liaskos, S., Dundjerovic, T., Gabriel, G.: Comparing alternative goal model visualizations for decision making: an exploratory experiment. In: Proceedings of the 33rd ACM Symposium on Applied Computing (SAC 2018), Pau, France, pp. 1272–1281 (2018)
15. Liaskos, S., Jaouhar, I.: Towards a framework for empirical measurement of conceptualization qualities. In: Dobbie, G., Frank, U., Kappel, G., Liddle, S.W., Mayr, H.C. (eds.) ER 2020. LNCS, vol. 12400, pp. 512–522. Springer, Cham (2020). https://doi.org/10.1007/978-3-030-62522-1_38

16. Liaskos, S., Mylopoulos, J., Khan, S.M.: Replication data for: empirically evaluating the semantic qualities of language vocabularies. Scholars Portal Dataverse (2021). https://doi.org/10.5683/SP2/H4BHLT

17. Liaskos, S., Ronse, A., Zhian, M.: Assessing the intuitiveness of qualitative contribution relationships in goal models: an exploratory experiment. In: Proceedings of the 11th ACM/IEEE International Symposium on Empirical Software Engineering and Measurement (ESEM 2017), Toronto, Canada, pp. 466–471 (2017)

18. Liaskos, S., Tambosi, W.: Factors affecting comprehension of contribution links in goal models: an experiment. In: Laender, A.H.F., Pernici, B., Lim, E.-P., de Oliveira, J.P.M. (eds.) ER 2019. LNCS, vol. 11788, pp. 525–539. Springer, Cham (2019). https://doi.org/10.1007/978-3-030-33223-5_43

19. Medelyan, O., Witten, I.H.: Thesaurus-based index term extraction for agricultural documents. In: Proceedings of the 2005 EFITA/WCCA Joint Congress on IT in Agriculture, pp. 1122–1129. EFITA/WICCA, Vila Real (2005)

20. Moody, D.L.: The "physics" of notations: toward a scientific basis for constructing visual notations in software engineering. IEEE Trans. Softw. Eng. (TSE) **35**(6), 756–779 (2009)

21. Nelson, H.J., Poels, G., Genero, M., Piattini, M.: A conceptual modeling quality framework. Softw. Qual. J. **20**, 201–228 (2012)

22. Obrst, L., Ceusters, W., Mani, I., Ray, S., Smith, B.: The evaluation of ontologies. In: Baker, C.J.O., Cheung, K.H. (eds.) Semantic Web: Revolutionizing Knowledge Discovery in the Life Sciences, pp. 139–158. Springer, Boston (2007). https://doi.org/10.1007/978-0-387-48438-9_8

23. Yu, E., Giorgini, P., Maiden, N., Mylopoulos, J. (eds.): Social Modeling for Requirements Engineering. MIT Press, Cambridge (2011)

24. Santos, M., Gralha, C., Goulão, M., Araújo, J.: Increasing the semantic transparency of the KAOS goal model concrete syntax. In: Trujillo, J.C., et al. (eds.) ER 2018. LNCS, vol. 11157, pp. 424–439. Springer, Cham (2018). https://doi.org/10.1007/978-3-030-00847-5_30

25. Wand, Y., Weber, R.: On the ontological expressiveness of information systems analysis and design grammars. Inf. Syst. J. **3**(4), 217–237 (1993)

26. Wong, W., Liu, W., Bennamoun, M.: Ontology learning from text: a look back and into the future. ACM Comput. Surv. **44**(4), 1–36 (2012)

Mining Tag Relationships in CQA Sites

K. Suryamukhi$^{(\boxtimes)}$ ⓘ, P. D. Vivekananda, and Manish Singh

Department of Computer Science and Engineering, IIT Hyderabad, Hyderabad, India
{cs17m19p100001,cs17btech11025}@iith.ac.in, msingh@cse.iith.ac.in

Abstract. Community Question Answer (CQA) sites are very popular means for knowledge transfer in the form of questions and answers. They rely on tags to connect the askers with the answerers. Since each CQA site contains information about a wide range of topics, it is difficult for users to navigate through the set of available tags and select the best ones for their question annotation. At present, CQA sites present the tags to the users using simple orderings, such as order by popularity and lexical order. This paper proposes a novel unsupervised method to mine different types of relationships between tags and then create a forest of ontologies to representing those relationships. Extracting the tag relationships will help users to understand the tags meanings. Representing them in a forest of ontologies will help the users in better tag navigation, thereby providing the users a clear understanding of the tag usage for question annotation. Moreover, our method can also be combined with existing tag recommendation systems to improve them. We evaluate our tag relationship mining algorithms and tag ontology construction algorithm with the state-of-the-art baseline methods and the three popular knowledge bases, namely DBpedia, ConceptNet, and WebIsAGraph.

Keywords: Ontology construction · Relationship extraction · Knowledge graphs

1 Introduction

Community Question Answering (CQA) sites, such as Stack Exchange[1], Stack Overflow[2] and Quora[3], are a few among the famous online platforms for sharing knowledge. They allow users to post questions or answer them. In CQA sites, users can quickly get multiple answers to their questions. Moreover, there may not be a single web page that answers the specific question of the user. These sites are enabled with tagging system that helps the askers to route their questions to the experts. These are the main reasons why CQA sites are thriving. For example, Stack Overflow, a Stack Exchange site, has over 13 million users, 20 million questions, 30 million answers, and 59k tags as of October 2020.

---

[1] https://stackexchange.com/.
[2] https://stackoverflow.com/.
[3] https://www.quora.com/.

A. Ghose et al. (Eds.): ER 2021, LNCS 13011, pp. 345–355, 2021.
https://doi.org/10.1007/978-3-030-89022-3_27

In all the CQA sites of Stack Exchange, users are allowed to annotate their questions with at most 5 tags from the available massive number of tags. Thus, it can be challenging for the users to find the best tags to annotate the questions. To aid them, we construct tag ontology, which can show them the relationships between tags. Since a single ontology for all the tags in a CQA site will be too huge for the users to explore and have many weak relationships, we propose automatic creation of a forest of ontologies, where each ontology will be small and will show only the strong tag relationships.

Identifying semantic relationships between tags can help the users to recognise similar tags. Furthermore, distinguishing a tag as either generic or specific can help them to select broader or narrower tags for annotation. In this work, we call the former relationship between tags as sibling relationship and the latter as parent-child relationship.

Most of the existing works [2,3] have focused only on parent-child relationship for ontology construction using either simple co-occurrence measures or textual relationship extraction. In this paper, we show that for CQA sites, these methods cannot properly capture the directed associations between tags. The key contributions of the paper are:

- Extracting three types of tag relationships using tag co-occurrence and tag related meta data.
- An unsupervised algorithm to create forest of tag ontologies.
- A comprehensive evaluation with state of the art baselines and three knowledge bases, namely DBpedia [1], ConceptNet [9], WebIsAGraph [4].

The rest of the paper is organised as follows: We discuss the related work in Sect. 2. In Sect. 3, we detail the algorithms for mining tag relationships and constructing ontology. Section 4 presents experimental setup, evaluations and results. Finally, Sect. 5 concludes the work.

2   Related Work

Our related work can be grouped into three categories, namely generic relation extraction, specific relation extraction and ontology construction. They are presented as follows:

Generic Relationship Extraction. There are many related works [11,12] that focus on extracting any generic relation between entities from raw text. These works rely on the sentences of the text to extract the relationships between entities. For example, in the sentence, *Joe Biden is the president of the USA*, these methods would extract the entities, namely 'Joe Biden' and 'USA', and then extract the 'president-of' relation between them. Since our data does not have tag relationships in the form of text or sentences, we cannot use them.

Specific Relationship Extraction. In these works, the type of relationships to be extracted is pre-defined. Most of them focus on parent-child relation. There are few related works [2,8] that find out whether two entities are semantically related, but they do not differentiate if they have parent-child, sibling or some other relation. In this paper, we present methods to extract two types of tag relationships, namely parent-child and sibling.

[2,6] infer parent-child relation using co-occurrence based measures such as support, confidence and overlapping scores. However, these co-occurrence based measures do not accurately capture the semantics of parent-child relation. [3] use text of the resource to mine relationship but as mentioned, the question content is not helpful in CQA sites. In our paper, we extract sibling tags using tag information provided by the CQA site and external resources.

Ontology Construction. There are many related works on ontology construction. [5] constructs a large web scale user-centered ontology having relationships like parent-child, sibling from vast number of user-action logs using graph neural networks. [3] constructed a large ontology in a supervised manner by using classifiers to detect parent-child relation between all the tag pairs. This is very expensive due to the combinatorial explosion of all the tag pairs. In our work, we construct a forest of ontologies in an unsupervised manner where each ontology will have only strong relations between tag pairs.

3   Mining Tag Relationships

In this section, we present our approach to mine pairwise tag relationships and create forest of ontologies to represent them. Section 3.1 presents the problem definition, Sect. 3.3 details the tag relationships mining algorithms and in Sect. 3.4, we present the method to construct ontologies.

3.1   Problem Definition

Our proposed tag ontologies and tag relationships will help users to easily locate related tags and also understand their ontological relationships. We divide our problem into the following 3 sub-problems.

Problem 1 Grouping Related Tags. *Given the set of all tags T in a CQA site and various tag statistics, such as tag count, tag co-occurrence, etc., our task is to group the tags into candidate groups. All relationships will be explored between tags only within each group.*

As it is computationally expensive to compute relationships between all possible pairs of tags and tags belong to specific topics, we cluster the tags into small candidate groups, which are easier to comprehend. We then mine tag relationships only between tags within each group and use the groups to form a forest of ontologies.

We perform tag grouping at a coarser level so that we don't miss tags that do have a relationship but end up in different candidate groups. So, we use only various types of count measures to form the candidate groups. In the following problems, we present methods to extract fine-grained relationships For creating groups, we use standard community detection algorithms exploring various similarity scores between tags in the tag graph as detailed in Sect. 3.2.

Problem 2 Mining Pairwise-tag Relationships. *Given a tag pair* (a, b), *where both tags a and b belong to some tag community C, and their descriptions in the CQA site as well as in external knowledge bases, our task is to mine various types of predefined relationships between the tag pair a and b.*

In CQA sites, the user is expected to use a mix of generic and specific tags to annotate their questions. If the user uses only generic tags, many answerers may not be keen on going through the questions text and answering them. While, if the question has only specific tags, the site may not be able to route the question to answerers as only a few of them may have explicitly shown interest in those specific tags. Our parent-child relationship will help users to select the right mix of generic and specific tags. Suggesting similar sibling tags can help the users to understand the better alternative tags.

We use co-occurrence information and along with tag descriptions to extract these tag relationships. In Sect. 3.3, we present the algorithms which scores each tag pair for these relationships.

Problem 3 Forest of Tag Ontology. *Given the tag communities $C_1...C_k$ and the relationship between tags within each community, construct a tag ontology for each tag community.*

Since in a single huge ontology, there can be many weak or wrong relationships, we propose an algorithm to create a forest of ontologies by creating an ontology for each tag community. Our ontologies are directed acyclic graphs that organize the tags in the form of hierarchies using the two tag relationship scores.

The ontology consists of parent-child and sibling relationships as the edge types.

Our ontology construction algorithm is presented in Sect. 3.4.

3.2 Grouping Related Tags

To form tag communities we use a community detection algorithm known as Infomap [7], which is based on MapEquation. We also used Louvain and Walk-Trap, but Infomap performed the best. We build the tag graphs using the following three tag similarity scores as edge weight.

Edge Weight. We use Google Distance to give edge weight between tags. It is a co-occurrence based symmetric measure that can capture the intuitive directed associations between the tags. It is given by:

$$gd(a, b) = \frac{max(logN(a), logN(b)) - logN(a, b)}{logN_{total} - min(logN(a), logN(b))} \tag{1}$$

where, $N(a)$ and $N(b)$ are the number of posts containing tags a and b respectively. $N(a, b)$ is the number of posts containing both the tags. N_{total} is the total number of posts in our dataset. We define edge weight as:

$$EW(a, b) = \frac{1}{exp(gd(a, b))} \tag{2}$$

Edge Weight using only Popular Tags. Since there were many infrequent tags and their relationship with other tags is not so well-defined, including them in the graph resulted in a very low modularity score for all the three community detection algorithms.

We filtered infrequent tags from the graph G and constructed a new tag graph G^{pop} using only the popular tags. Edge weight using only popular tags, $EWP(a, b)$, is then defined same as above.

Edge Weight based on Probabilistic Association. We observed that taking EWP improved modularity score of community detection algorithms. We further improved it by taking into account the probabilistic association between the tags, which quantify the likelihood of their co-occurrence. We model this likelihood using conditional probability. The directed weighted tag graph G^{cp} has edge weight defined as:

$$EWPA(a|b) = \frac{EWP(a, b)}{\sum_c EWP(b, c)} \tag{3}$$

3.3 Mining Pairwise-Tag Relationships

In this section, we present algorithms to mine the two types of tag relationships.

Parent-child Relationship. To detect the parent-child relationship between tags a and b, we use their co-occurrence based probabilistic association score $EWPA(a|b)$, defined in Eq. 3, and their entropy. The $EWPA(a|b)$ tells us how likely the tag a would be mentioned in the post given the tag b. The entropy of a tag is defined as follows:

$$H(a) = -\sum_c EWPA(a|c) log EWPA(a|c) \tag{4}$$

Tags having higher entropy are expected to have a generic meaning. If $EWPA(a|b)$ and H(a) are significantly greater than $EWPA(b|a)$ and H(b), respectively, then tag a is most likely a parent of tag b. Otherwise, they may not have any relationship or may have sibling relationship, which is described in the next subsection.

Sibling Relationship. Sibling tags occur at the same level in the tag ontology. In the ontology, the siblings are kept in the order of decreasing entropy. In other words, the first tag would be the most popular sibling.

To detect siblings we use three knowledge sources, namely the Tag Excerpt and the Tag Wiki Description, which are available as metadata in the CQA site; and the Tag Abstract available from Wikipedia using the DBpedia SPARQL Endpoint[4]. The Tag Excerpt briefly describes the tags and the Tag Wiki contains a more detailed description. These are written by the CQA site topic experts. Tag Abstract includes the abstract of the tag's Wikipedia article.

We create a corpus by combining the information from the above three information sources and use it to train a Glove word embedding model, where we

---

[4] https://wiki.dbpedia.org/.

represent each word using 300-dimensional vector. For two tags a and b, we define their sibling score as:

$$sib(a, b) = 1 - WMD(a, b) \tag{5}$$

We say that the tags a and b are siblings if the value of $sib(a, b)$ is greater than some threshold value. WMD is defined as:

$$WMD(a, b) = min_{T \geq 0} \sum_{i,j} T_{i,j} c(x_i, x_j), \tag{6}$$

where T is the transportation cost to transfer every word i in the description of tag a to every word j in the description of tag b. Finally, the minimum travel or transfer cost is chosen. c is the Euclidean distance between the embedding of word i and word j denoted by x_i and x_j respectively.

Instead of representing the tag embedding vectors with all the words present in the tag descriptions, we can choose only the top-n words that best represent the tag. For this purpose, we use a supervised variant of LDA topic modelling algorithm, Labelled LDA (L-LDA). It defines a one-to-one correspondence between LDA's latent topics and the category links of the tags used as labels. The category links are obtained from Wikipedia tag articles using DBpedia SPARQL Endpoint. We then extract top-n ($n = 10$) words to represent each tag and calculate similarity between them using Eq. 5 defined as $sibLLDA(a, b)$.

3.4 Constructing Tag Ontology

After extracting the relationships between the tag pairs, we propose an hierarchical ontology construction algorithm which, constructs the ontology graph in the form of a DAG. We obtain forest of ontologies for all the tag communities. The ontologies consist of the two relationships. The type of the edge is chosen based on the similarities thresholds in the precedence order of siblings and parent-child. The process of setting these thresholds is detailed in Sect. 4.5.

Given the tag community as input, our algorithm follows a greedy approach to organize the tags in the ontology by ordering them in the decreasing order of their entropies. First, the tag with highest entropy is chosen and then the parent-child scores satisfying the threshold with that tag as the parent are ranked in decreasing order. Next, each tag in those pairs are ranked in the decreasing order of their entropy. Then, each tag pair is checked for the presence of the two relationships. First, the presence of sibling relationship is checked for each tag pair. If it satisfies the sibling threshold, then we add sibling edge to the ontology graph. Otherwise, the parent-child edge is added, as it already satisfies the threshold.

4 Evaluation

In this section, we present the evaluation of our algorithms. We first describe the dataset and then we present the evaluations and results.

4.1 Dataset

We used the SuperUser[5] data from StackExchange site. It contains over 10 million posts and a total of 5500 unique tags. The posts are from a variety of domains like databases, security, web browsers, programming languages, etc.

We used three users to label a part of our dataset for evaluation. Any ambiguity in labelling was resolved through discussion and mutual agreement. We gave 5150 tag pairs to users and asked them to label them individually as parent child or sibling.

Our dataset had 1378 unique tags after removing the infrequent tags. We obtained 18 communities using the Infomap algorithm on the tag graph G^{cp}. We evaluate our ontology generation algorithm on 5 tag communities.

4.2 Evaluation Metric

Tag relationships are evaluated using Precision, Recall and F1-score against the ground truth human labelled dataset. We also compare our results with the state of the art baselines.

Tag ontologies are evaluated by calculating their similarity with ground truth ontologies. The standard metrics are taxonomic precision (TP), taxonomic recall (TR) and taxonomic F-measure (TF). The idea is to find the similarity between the proposed ontology L and the ground truth ontology G for each tag community C, and to generate a characteristic extract from each of them, $ce(C, L)$ and $ce(C, G)$, which is inline with [3, 10]. TP, TR and TF can then be computed by averaging the tp, tr and tf of all the communities. tf is the harmonic mean of tp and tr. For each community, the evaluation metrics tp and tr can be computed as follows:

$$tp(C, L, G) = \frac{|ce(C, L) \cap ce(C, G)|}{|ce(C, L)|} \qquad (7)$$

$$tr(C, L, G) = \frac{|ce(C, L) \cap ce(C, G)|}{|ce(C, G)|} \qquad (8)$$

4.3 Baseline Methods

We compare the performance of each of the proposed tag relationship mining algorithms with state of the art methods. For parent-child relationship, we compared with co-occurrence based methods as used in [2, 6]. For sibling relationship, we followed a evaluation set up as in [3], where we use three similarity metrics, namely Jaccard similarity, Cosine similarity and KL-divergence, on the topics generated using unsupervised LDA as our baseline methods.

We compare the ontology generation algorithm with three popular Knowledge-bases (KBs) namely DBpedia [1], ConceptNet [9] and WebIsA-Graph [4], which has around 65 billion, 34 million and 3 million relationships,

---

[5] https://superuser.com/.

respectively. DBpedia and ConceptNet contain both parent-child and sibling relationship, whereas WebIsAGraph contains only parent-child relationships between entities.

4.4   Tag Grouping Evaluation

Here, we present the the evaluation and results of our tag grouping algorithm. We run Infomap algorithm [7] on three tag graphs, G, G^{pop} and G^{cp} and evaluated them based on the modularity and clustering coefficient measures. G is constructed over all the tags in the dataset. For the communities to be comparable, they should be compared on the same nodes. So, after forming communities in G using all the tags, we removed all the infrequent tags before computing the two evaluation measures.

The modularity values are 0.28, 0.55 and 0.8 and the clustering coefficient values are 0.1, 0.26 and 0.6 for G, G^{pop} and G^{cp}, respectively. The communities from G are of very low quality because of infrequent tags and no edge directionality. Since G^{cp} considers both these factors, it gives very high scores.

4.5   Tag Relationship Mining Evaluation

Here, we present the results of our tag relationship mining algorithms by comparing them with the baselines and KBs listed in Sect. 4.3.

Table 1. Parent-child and Sibling

Classifier	Feature set	Performance (%)					
		Parent-Child			Sibling		
		Precision	Recall	F1-score	Precision	Recall	F1-score
LR	Our Method	97.05	93.8	95.4	78	68	70
	Baseline	77	76	76.5	67	62	64
NB	Our Method	95.66	90.8	93.2	79	72	74
	Baseline	71	65	67.9	55	56	56
RF	Our Method	98.9	93.8	96.28	76	60	62
	Baseline	82	83	82.5	58	53	55

To evaluate the performance of each relationship mining algorithm separately, we use three binary classifiers, namely Logistic Regression (LR), Naive Bayes (NB) and Random Forest (RF) as in [3].

For the parent-child case, we took entropy of both the tags participating in the parent-child relationship and edge weight $EWPA$ as the feature set to train the classifiers. In our labelled data, the ratio of positive to negative instances was 2:1. To overcome class imbalance, we reversed some random tag pairs to create the negative instances. For the baseline, we used the three co-occurrence based features, namely support, confidence and mutual overlap, which was used in [3,6]. Table 1 shows the comparison of our method with the baseline for the three classifiers.

We can observe that all the classifiers achieved higher F1-scores for our method compared to the baseline. Baseline method gave an average F1-scores of 77%, whereas our gave average accuracy of 95%, which demonstrates that our entropy and probabilistic association based feature can capture the parent-child relationship very well.

For the sibling relationship case, we used the two scores, namely sib and $sibLLDA$, as features for our method. sib score is calculated using the similarities of the tag embeddings, and $sibLLA$ score is obtained by calculating the similarities of the tag embeddings of the top-n words from the topics generated using the L-LDA algorithm. For the baseline, we use three similarity metrics given in Sect. 4.3. To maintain consistency with our results, we took the number of topics equal to the number of labels, as in our L-LDA method.

Table 1 shows the comparison of our method with the baseline for the three classifiers. We can observe that NB achieved the best performance on our method with an F1-score of 74%. Classification on the baseline method performed poorly with LR giving the highest F1-score of 64%. On an average, there was 15.63% improvement in prediction accuracy using our method compared to the baseline. One of the main reasons is that assigning the tag documents to the category links as pre-defined topic classes in case of L-LDA is more accurate rather than assigning them to less interpretable latent topics as in case of unsupervised LDA.

4.6   Ontology Construction Evaluation

Most of the previous work [3,10] have evaluated their ontology by comparing it with the ontologies of KBs. But since existing KBs have very low recall for our extracted relations, we compare our and KBs ontology with manually created ground truth ontologies.

Table 2. Comparison of Ontologies

Method	Data	Performance (%)		
		TP	TR	TF
Our Method	All Communities	**49.6**	**74.4**	**57.65**
	Big Communities	49.33	73.66	57.22
	Small Communities	48.8	74.26	56.17
Combined KBs	All Communities	39.35	4.17	7.55
	Big Communities	46.9	2.16	3.9
	Small Communities	35.41	3.37	6.01

Ground truth ontologies were constructed for five tag communities, in which there were three big and two small communities, each having around 200 and 60 relations, respectively. We compared the ontology of our method with ontologies of each KB. Due to space constraint, we omit those results. We observed that WebIsAGraph gives the best result. Since it only contains parent-child relations, we union it with ConceptNet that also had siblings. In Table 2, we present the comparison of our ontology with this combined KBs. The evaluation metrics were detailed in Sect. 4.2. We consider three cases: average of all five communities, average of the three big communities, and average of the two small communities.

For both the cases, our method gives an average TF score of 57%, whereas the combined KBs gave an average TF score of around 6%. As there were many missing relationships in the KBs, the TR values for all the three cases are very low. The precision for big communities for Combined KBs is higher than that of small communities. This is because, as the cluster size grows, the number of highly accurate relations increase. But we can observe that the recall of big communities for KBs is lesser than that of small communities. This is again because as the cluster size grows, the number of missed accurate relations also increase. Our method for all the three cases gives almost the same performance.

5   Conclusion

In this work, we propose algorithms for mining parent-child and sibling relationships between tag pairs, and for constructing an automatic tag ontology. We construct forest of tag ontologies where, each ontology only contains strong relationships between tags. Our evaluation shows that our algorithms can extract accurate tag relations compared to the existing works as well as the standard KBs.

References

1. Auer, S., Bizer, C., Kobilarov, G., Lehmann, J., Cyganiak, R., Ives, Z.: DBpedia: a nucleus for a web of open data. In: Aberer, K., et al. (eds.) ASWC/ISWC -2007. LNCS, vol. 4825, pp. 722–735. Springer, Heidelberg (2007). https://doi.org/10.1007/978-3-540-76298-0_52
2. Chen, K., Dong, X., Zhu, J., Shen, B.: Building a domain knowledge base from Wikipedia: a semi-supervised approach. In: SEKE, pp. 191–196 (2016)
3. Dong, H., Wang, W., Coenen, F., Huang, K.: Knowledge base enrichment by relation learning from social tagging data. Inf. Sci. **526**, 203–220 (2020)
4. Faralli, S., Finocchi, I., Ponzetto, S.P., Velardi, P.: WebIsAGraph: a very large hypernymy graph from a web corpus. In: CLiC-it (2019)
5. Liu, B., et al.: Giant: scalable creation of a web-scale ontology. In: Proceedings of the 2020 ACM SIGMOD International Conference on Management of Data, pp. 393–409 (2020)
6. Rêgo, A.S.C., Marinho, L.B., Pires, C.E.S.: A supervised learning approach to detect subsumption relations between tags in folksonomies. In: SAC (2015)
7. Rosvall, M., Bergstrom, C.T.: Multilevel compression of random walks on networks reveals hierarchical organization in large integrated systems. PloS ONE **6**, e18209 (2011)

8. Saleh, I., El-Tazi, N.: Finding semantic relationships in folksonomies. In: WI, pp. 174–181 (2018)
9. Speer, R., Chin, J., Havasi, C.: ConceptNet 5.5: an open multilingual graph of general knowledge. arXiv preprint arXiv:1612.03975 (2016)
10. Strohmaier, M., Helic, D., Benz, D., Körner, C., Kern, R.: Evaluation of folksonomy induction algorithms. TIST **3**(4), 1–22 (2012)
11. Yu, H., Li, H., Mao, D., Cai, Q.: A relationship extraction method for domain knowledge graph construction. World Wide Web **23**(2), 735–753 (2020). https://doi.org/10.1007/s11280-019-00765-y
12. Zhang, N., Deng, S., Sun, Z., Chen, X., Zhang, W., Chen, H.: Attention-based capsule networks with dynamic routing for relation extraction. In: EMNLP, pp. 986–992 (2018)

Ontological Unpacking as Explanation: The Case of the Viral Conceptual Model

Giancarlo Guizzardi[1,2]([✉]), Anna Bernasconi[3], Oscar Pastor[4],
and Veda C. Storey[5]

[1] Free University of Bozen-Bolzano, Bolzano, Italy
gguizzardi@unibz.it
[2] University of Twente, Twente, The Netherlands
g.guizzardi@utwente.nl
[3] Politecnico di Milano, Milan, Italy
anna.bernasconi@polimi.it
[4] Universitat Politècnica de València, Valencia, Spain
opastor@dsic.upv.es
[5] Georgia State University, Atlanta, GA 30302, USA
VStorey@gsu.edu

Abstract. Inspired by the need to understand the genomic aspects of COVID-19, the Viral Conceptual Model captures and represents the sequencing of viruses. Although the model has already been successfully used, it should have a strong ontological foundation to ensure that it can be consistently applied and expanded. We apply an ontological analysis of the Viral Conceptual Model, using OntoUML, to unpack and identify its core components. The analysis illustrates the feasibility of bringing ontological clarity to complex models. The process of revealing the *ontological semantics* of a data structuring model provides a fundamental type of *explanation* for symbolic models, including conceptual models.

Keywords: Viral Conceptual Model (VCM) · Ontological analysis · OntoUML · Virus genomics · COVID-19

1 Introduction

Since the scientific breakthrough of the sequencing of the human genome, efforts have been made to model this sequencing so it can be effectively used. Efforts to apply conceptual modeling to describe genomics databases began in the early 2000s [15]. Pastor et al. proposed the Conceptual Schema of Human Genome [14, 16]; Bernasconi et al. introduced the Genomic Conceptual Model [5]. The Viral Conceptual Model (VCM) [4] was motivated by interest in representing the genomic aspects of COVID-19 so they can be shared among the scientific and medical communities that are attempting to understand SARS-CoV-2 and similar pathogens. The model is being used for designing: an integrated data warehouse and search system [8]; a linked Phenotype Data Dictionary [3]; a knowledge base of variant impacts [1]; and a visualization engine [6]. To facilitate a further,

© Springer Nature Switzerland AG 2021
A. Ghose et al. (Eds.): ER 2021, LNCS 13011, pp. 356–366, 2021.
https://doi.org/10.1007/978-3-030-89022-3_28

robust, application of VCM to projects with other viruses and pathogens, there needs to be some way to assess the quality of the model.

A conceptual model provides an *information structuring function* for the application domain. VCM focuses on genomic data structuring for the purposes of characterizing genomic sequences. However, a conceptual model should also be able to provide *conceptual clarification* and *unambiguous communication*. We call this the *ontological function* of a conceptual model. The model should reconstruct the exact *intended conceptualization* (set of possible interpretations) and be explicit and transparent with respect to its *ontological semantics*. Revealing the ontological semantics of an information artifact is a fundamental type of *explanation* for symbolic models (including conceptual models). *Ontological unpacking* refers to a process of ontological analysis that reveals the *ontological conceptual model* behind an information structuring conceptual model.

2 The Viral Conceptual Model (VCM)

The Viral Conceptual Model (VCM) [4] is organized into four perspectives and centered around the notion of a virus genome SEQUENCE. A viral sequence can be either DNA or RNA. In both cases, sequences are composed of nucleotides, i.e., guanine (G), adenine (A), cytosine (C), and thymine (T)—replaced by uracil (U) in RNA.

For the **technical perspective**, sequences are derived from one experiment of a given type (EXPERIMENT TYPE entity) in which the biological material is analysed with a given *Sequencing Technology* platform (e.g., Illumina Miseq), which provides a *Coverage* and an *Assembly Method*, collecting algorithms applied to obtain the final sequence.

For the **biological perspective**, each sequence belongs to a specific VIRUS, described by a complex taxonomy, which is, in turn, represented by attributes: *Species Name* (e.g., Severe acute respiratory syndrome coronavirus 2), comparable forms in the *Equivalent List* (e.g., 2019-nCoV, COVID-19, SARS-CoV-2, SARS2), within a *Genus* (e.g., Betacoronavirus), *Sub-family* (e.g., Orthocoronavirinae), and finally *Family* (e.g., Coronaviridae). A virus species corresponds to a specific *Molecule Type* (e.g., genomic RNA, viral cRNA, unassigned DNA), which has either double or single-stranded structure. Each strand is positive or negative. A biological sample (tissue) is extracted from an organism, that hosted the virus for a certain amount of time. This is represented by the HOST SAMPLE entity. The host (of given *Age* and *Gender*) also belongs to a *Species*. The sample is extracted on a specific *Collection Date*, from a specific host tissue (e.g., nasopharyngeal or oropharyngeal swab, lung), at a specific location identified by the quadruple: *Originating Lab, Region, Country, Geo Group* (e.g., continent).

From an **organizational perspective**, SEQUENCING PROJECT is a project in which a particular sequencing activity is carried out. Each sequence is connected to a number of studies, represented by a research publication (with *Authors, Title, Journal, Publication Date*). When a study is not available, only the *Sequencing Lab* and *Submission Date* are provided, along with the *Database Source* where the sequence is deposited.

The **analytical perspective** addresses the secondary analyses of genomic sequences. ANNOTATIONs include subsequences representing segments (characterized by *Start* and *Stop* coordinates) of the original sequence with a particular *Feature Type* (e.g., gene, peptide, coding DNA region, or untranslated region), the recognized *Gene Name* to which it belongs (e.g., gene "E"), and the *Product* it produces (e.g., Spike protein, nsp2 protein, RNA-dependent RNA polymerase, membrane glycoprotein, envelope protein). Annotations whose *Feature Type* is coding region (CDS) also have an associated *Aminoacid Sequence*. The *Nucleotide Variant* entity contains subsequences of the main sequence that differ from the reference sequence of the same virus species. They can be defined with a *Start* position coordinate for an arbitrary *Length*, a specific variant *Type* (insertion, deletion, single-nucleotide polymorphism or others), and an alternative sequence of nucleotides (*Alt Sequence*). A similar role is given to the *Aminoacid Variant* entity, containing subsequences of proteins (i.e., only of a subset of all annotations) that differ from the reference amino acid sequence of the virus species. These also have a start position, a length, a variant type, and an alternative sequence of amino acid residues.

3   OntoUML

OntoUML is a language whose meta-model complies with the ontological distinctions and axiomatization of a theoretically well-grounded foundational ontology, UFO (Unified Foundational Ontology) [12,13]. Stereotypes reflect the correspondence between the OntoUML profile and UFO ontological categories.

We start by focusing on the category of endurants (roughly objects), and to object *Kinds* (the genuine fundamental types of objects that exist according to a particular conceptualization of the given domain). All objects belong necessarily to exactly one kind (e.g., Person, Virus). There can, however, be other static subdivisions (or subtypes) of a kind. These are naturally termed *Subkinds*. For example, the kind 'Organization' can be specialized into the subkinds 'University' and 'Funding Agency'. Object kinds and subkinds represent essential properties of endurants. These include: *Phases* (e.g., 'being a living person' captures a cluster of contingent *intrinsic* properties of a person, or 'being a puppy' captures a cluster of contingent *intrinsic* properties of a dog) and *Roles* (for example, 'being a husband' captures a cluster of contingent *relational* properties of a man participating in a marriage). Kinds, Subkinds, Phases, and Roles are categories of object *Sortals*. A sortal is either a kind (e.g., 'Person') or a specialization of a kind (e.g., 'Student', 'Teenager', 'Woman').

Relators represent clusters of relational properties that "hang together" by a nexus (provided by a relator kind). Relators (e.g., marriages, enrollments, presidential mandates, citizenships) are the truth-makers of relational propositions. Relations (as classes of n-tuples) can be completely derived from relators. Objects typically participate in relators playing certain "roles".

In general, types that represent properties shared by entities of multiple kinds are termed *Non-Sortals*. Besides *RoleMixin*, another type of non-sortal in UFO is

Category. A category represents necessary properties that are shared by entities of multiple kinds (e.g., the category 'Physical Object' represents properties of all kinds of entities that have masses, spatial extensions, etc.). In contrast to rolemixins, categories are static and *Relationally Independent* Non-Sortals.

Objects can be *collectives*, i.e., plural entities that aggregate parts (members), all of which play the same role with respect to the whole, or *functional complexes*, i.e., entities whose parts (called components) play different functional roles w.r.t. the whole. Finally, objects can also be *quantities*, i.e., portions of matter whose parts belong to the same type as the whole. Besides endurants, OntoUML has perdurants (occurrents, events) [2]. Events can bear their own properties, be decomposed, and have their types falling into taxonomies. However, events only exist in the past and, thus, are immutable. There are two categories of events: event kinds (stereotyped as «event») and event subkinds. Between endurants and events, we have a relation of participation, but events can also bring existence (i.e., *create*) objects. Finally, OntoUML embeds a theory of multi-level modeling and higher-order types [10]. Higher-order types (represented by the stereotype «type») are types whose instances are themselves types. A relation of *instantiation* connects individuals to these higher-order types.

4   Unpacking the VCM in OntoUML

We reconstruct the original conceptualization underlying VCM using ontological analysis associated with OntoUML[1]. The result of this analysis is captured in a series of modules comprising an integrated model[2].

Virus Infection. A VIRUS is a BIOLOGICAL ORGANISM that can group, forming VIRUS COLLECTIVES. A VIRAL INFECTION is a bundle of relational dispositions connecting a VIRUS COLLECTIVE and a VIRUS HOST. The latter can be either a LIVING HOST, which is a *role mixin* played by an ANIMAL that could be, e.g., of BAT or PERSON kind, or an IN VITRO HOST, which is a role played by a CELL LINE (itself a complex system of cells). The dispositions composing a VIRAL INFECTION can be manifested as VIRAL DISEASE events in living hosts, whereas cell lines, once infected, clearly show a VIRAL RESPONSE, but this is not considered a disease in full [7]. VIRUSES are instances of VIRUS SPECIES, which are associated with VIRAL DISEASE TYPES. All BIOLOGICAL ORGANISMS are instances of BIOLOGICAL SPECIES, which can be characterized by a *name*, a *genus*, a *sub-family*, and a *family*[3]. If a BIOLOGICAL ORGANISM happens to be

---

[1] The only aspect of the VCM not presented here is the analysis the virus sequence publication. This is due to space constraints.

[2] In OntoUML models, we employ the generally-accepted color coding scheme: light red is used for types whose instances are objects, green when instances are relators, yellow when instances are events, and purple when instances are higher-order types.

[3] By using the multi-modeling support in UFO/OntoUML, one could proceed further and explicitly capture the relations of *subordination* between, for example, species and genus, namely, that a type *is subordinate to* another iff the instances of the former are specializations of instances of the latter [9]. For space reasons, we do not elaborate further.

a VIRUS then it instantiates a particular type of BIOLOGICAL SPECIES called a
VIRUS SPECIES. Likewise, if a BIOLOGICAL ORGANISM happens to be an ANI-
MAL then it instantiates a particular type of BIOLOGICAL SPECIES called an
ANIMAL SPECIES. Therefore, in the model of Fig. 1, we have, for example, the
instantiation relation between ANIMAL and ANIMAL SPECIES that *redefines* the
association ends of the more general relation between BIOLOGICAL ORGANISM
and BIOLOGICAL SPECIES[4].

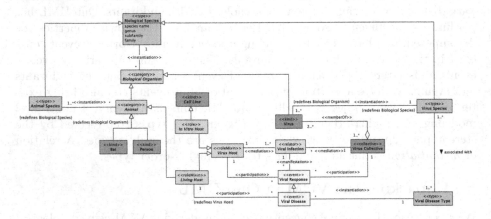

Fig. 1. A virus infection

Tissue Sampling. A TISSUE SAMPLING is an event occurring at a particular
collection date, in which a SAMPLING LABORATORY and an ANIMAL participate,
and in which a BIOLOGICAL TISSUE is extracted. A BIOLOGICAL TISSUE is
a portion of tissue of a given a BIOLOGICAL TISSUE TYPE. If it is a VIRUS
INFECTED TISSUE then that ANIMAL is a LIVING HOST within the scope of a
VIRAL INFECTION. Thus, a VIRUS INFECTED TISSUE is *historically dependent*
on the existence of a (current or previous) VIRAL INFECTION involving that
ANIMAL as a VIRUS HOST[5]. A VIRUS INFECTED TISSUE is then a sample of
viruses of a given VIRUS SPECIES (the type present in that VIRAL INFECTION).
Finally, a SAMPLING LABORATORY is a (processual) role played by a RESEARCH
LABORATORY (a particular type of ORGANIZATION) in a TISSUE SAMPLING
event. A RESEARCH LABORATORY is located in a given *country*, *region*, and
geo-group (e.g., continent) (Fig. 2).

Virus Sequencing. A SAMPLE SEQUENCING is an event characterized by a
SEQUENCING PLATFORM, a SEQUENCING LABORATORY, and a VIRUS INFECTED
TISSUE. A SAMPLE SEQUENCING event creates the collective of VIRUS RAW

---

[4] See [11] for an in depth discussion about the semantics of redefinition.

[5] Since the VIRAL INFECTION is existentially dependent on that particular ANIMAL,
then we can infer that the VIRUS INFECTED TISSUE is also *historically dependent* on
that ANIMAL.

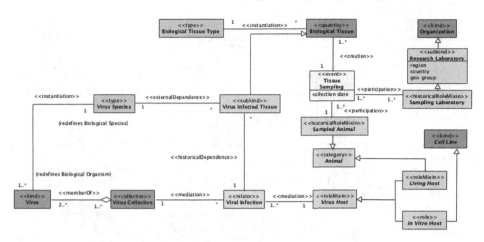

Fig. 2. Tissue sampling

DATA (comprising many thousands of READS) from a sampled VIRUS INFECTED TISSUE. The VIRUS RAW DATA then participates to a GENOME ASSEMBLY event performed by an ASSEMBLING LABORATORY, and instantiating a particular GENOME ASSEMBLY METHOD. This event produces a FULL CONSENSUS SEQUENCEi i.e., a complete data record that represents the real virus sequence[6]. A FULL CONSENSUS SEQUENCE is composed of NUCLEOTIDE SUBSEQUENCES which, in turn, is composed of NUCLEOTIDES. A VIRUS SPECIES is associated with molecules of a given MOLECULE TYPE (see discussion in paragraph 'Virus Sequence Annotation'). So, a VIRUS SEQUENCE (of a virus of that species) instantiates exactly molecules of that type (again, see 'Virus Sequence Annotation'). The events of TISSUE SAMPLING, SAMPLE SEQUENCING, and GENOME ASSEMBLY compose a super-event termed a VIRUS SEQUENCING event. Since a VIRUS INFECTED TISSUE is created by a TISSUE SAMPLING event, we can infer that a SAMPLE SEQUENCING event must always be temporally preceded by a TISSUE SAMPLING event. Analogously, since a VIRUS RAW DATA collective is created by a SAMPLE SEQUENCING event, a GENOME ASSEMBLY event must always be temporally preceded by a SAMPLE SEQUENCING event. Given the transitivity of these temporal precedence relations, we can infer that a VIRUS SEQUENCING event is composed of these sub-events that must occur in this particular temporal order (Fig. 3).

---

[6] FULL CONSENSUS SEQUENCE is a type of complete VIRUS SEQUENCE record. Given the purpose of VCM, these entities are information/representation entities and not the actual chemical structures. In reality, a FULL CONSENSUS SEQUENCE is a representation of a virus sequence type that is instantiated by actual complex chemical structures (actual sequences of nucleotides). Making this distinction explicit is beyond the scope of this paper.

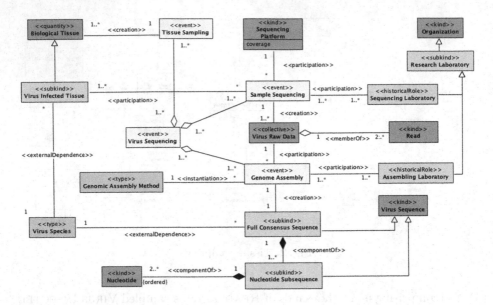

Fig. 3. Virus sequencing

Virus Sequence Annotation. A VIRUS SEQUENCE instantiates a MOLECULE TYPE[7]. A VIRUS SEQUENCE is ultimately a sequence of NUCLEOTIDES. A FULL CONSENSUS SEQUENCE is a VIRUS SEQUENCE composed of a number of NUCLEOTIDE SUBSEQUENCES. A NUCLEOTIDE SUBSEQUENCE, thus, provides further structure to the NUCLEOTIDES composing the FULL CONSENSUS SEQUENCES. NUCLEOTIDES are of certain types. In DNA these are ADENINE (A), CYTOSINE (C), GUANINE (G), and THYMINE (T), whereas in RNA there is URACIL (U) in place of Thymine.

Particularly relevant NUCLEOTIDE SUBSEQUENCES are CODONS (sequences of three NUCLEOTIDES responsible for coding given AMINO ACID TYPES) and CODING REGIONS (aggregations of CODONS responsible for coding particular PROTEIN types). A CODING REGION participates in TRANSLATION events[8], which produce amino acid sequences (i.e., PROTEINS composed of a particular sequence of AMINO ACIDS). There 20 known subtypes of AMINO ACIDS of which we only show four examples: LEUCINE, ARGININE, THREONINE, AND PROLINE. The type of PROTEIN created by a TRANSLATION event can be derived from the involved CODING REGION. This is because a CODING REGION is composed of a

---

[7] MOLECULE TYPES can be double-stranded or single-stranded. These, in turn, can be positive- or negative-stranded. We restrict ourselves to single-stranded molecule types because the VCM focuses on single-stranded RNA viruses.

[8] Once more, VIRUS SEQUENCES and their proper parts are information objects. Therefore, a TRANSLATION event here is not the actual biochemical event involving the real-world counterpart of these entities, but an information processing event that generates PROTEIN representations from CODING REGION representations.

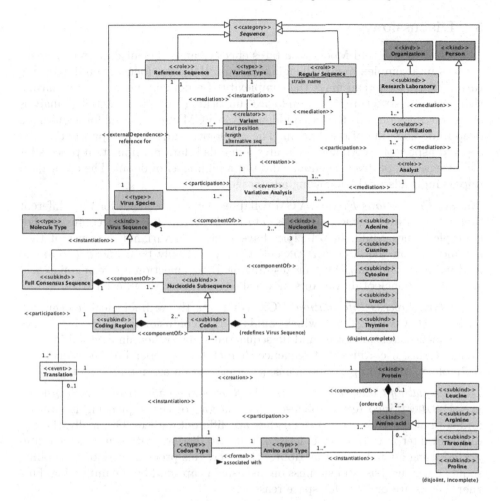

Fig. 4. Virus sequence annotation

particular sequence of CODONS, each of which is of a CODON TYPE, determining
a particular AMINO ACID TYPE. So, the PROTEIN created by that event from
a particular CODING REGION will be composed of a sequence of AMINO ACIDS
instantiating exactly those types determined by the CODONS composing that
CODING REGION (Fig. 4).

VIRUS SEQUENCES and PROTEINS are subkinds of SEQUENCE. A SEQUENCE
has two possible roles: REFERENCE SEQUENCE (unique for a VIRUS SPECIES)
and REGULAR SEQUENCE. These two entities are mediated by the relator VARI-
ANT, which is of a given VARIANT TYPE (e.g., INSERTION, DELETION, etc.).
This relator is created during a VARIATION ANALYSIS event, to which one reference and one regular sequence participate. The event of VARIATION ANALYSIS
is mediated by ANALYSTS, who have an ANALYST AFFILIATION to a RESEARCH
LABORATORY, which is another ORGANIZATION.

5   Discussion

The Viral Conceptual Model facilitates effective and efficient data management process in a complex and challenging domain. However, focusing on data structure features alone can mask the complexity of a domain when concepts have a rich semantic structure. Our ontological unpacking provided a detailed analysis of the complex notions that are hidden within VCM and essential for acquiring a deep understanding of the domain. The ontological unpacking supports the conceptual aspect of VCM, and facilitates a detailed data manipulation process for the integration of diverse genomic data at a high level of detail. The ontological unpacking leads to the following advantages.

Making Connections Explicit. VCM collapses the feature types for very different biological entities (genes, peptides, etc.), which could lead to confusion. For example, genes could, in principle, have nucleotide variants; however, if they are included in the ANNOTATION entity, they can only be connected to amino acid variants. Our unpacking makes tangible the connection between amino acid variants and nucleotide variants, now called a TRANSLATION event.

Unpacking Process Information. VCM compacts the technological information within EXPERIMENT TYPE, which could result in confusion for users who observe the sequence creation event and its sequential steps. When understood in ontological terms, it clarifies that sequence characteristics depend on the sequencing technology, which impacts both a sequencing and an assembling event.

Disambiguating Collapsed Concepts. The *Sequencing Lab* attribute of SEQUENCING PROJECT incorrectly collapses the concepts of the sequencing laboratory and submitting laboratory, even if they are different entities. Originally, the two different interpretations were derived from two distinct data sources, then integrated using a single VCM attribute. However, this process overlooks sampling, sequencing/analysis, and submission, as instead captured by the unpacking. Further details are omitted for space reasons.

Clarifying Underspecified Aspects. VCM includes all the information about the host sample in one single entity, thus generating a denormalized structure that is conceptually incorrect. The event of data sampling which involves actors such as a healthcare worker, an individual being tested, and the testing facility, are underspecified, even though the event occurs at a precise point in time and space. Consider the evolution of SARS-CoV-2 variants: when a claim is made that a specific lineage is becoming prevalent in a geographical area, it is important to correctly interpret the spatial information. Sequences are assigned a "location", which could describe *where*: i) human hosts *live*; ii) phials were *sampled/stored*; iii) sequence information was *extracted* into files; or iv) information was *deposited* to public databases.

6   Conclusion

This research analyzed the Viral Conceptual Model, which was developed for sequencing viruses. Using OntoUML, we conducted an ontological analysis to unpack and identify the core components of the Viral Conceptual Model. The results demonstrate the effectiveness of this conceptual model and the usefulness of unpacking a complicated model to improve its clarity, beyond data structuring. Future research could perform similar unpacking to assesses and explain the clarity of other conceptual models developed for biological and additional complex domains.

Acknowledgements. A. Bernasconi is supported by ERC Advanced Grant 693174 GeCo; V. Storey by J. Mack Robinson College of Business, Georgia State University; G. Guizzardi by the NeXON Project (UNIBZ).

References

1. Al Khalaf, R., Alfonsi, T., Ceri, S., Bernasconi, A.: CoV2K: a knowledge base of SARS-CoV-2 variant impacts. In: Cherfi, S., Perini, A., Nurcan, S. (eds.) RCIS 2021. LNBIP, vol. 415, pp. 274–282. Springer, Cham (2021). https://doi.org/10.1007/978-3-030-75018-3_18
2. Almeida, J.P.A., Falbo, R.A., Guizzardi, G.: Events as entities in ontology-driven conceptual modeling. In: Laender, A.H.F., Pernici, B., Lim, E.-P., de Oliveira, J.P.M. (eds.) ER 2019. LNCS, vol. 11788, pp. 469–483. Springer, Cham (2019). https://doi.org/10.1007/978-3-030-33223-5_39
3. Bernasconi, A., et al.: A review on viral data sources and search systems for perspective mitigation of COVID-19. Brief. Bioinform. **22**, 664–675 (2021)
4. Bernasconi, A., Canakoglu, A., Pinoli, P., Ceri, S.: Empowering virus sequence research through conceptual modeling. In: Dobbie, G., Frank, U., Kappel, G., Liddle, S.W., Mayr, H.C. (eds.) ER 2020. LNCS, vol. 12400, pp. 388–402. Springer, Cham (2020). https://doi.org/10.1007/978-3-030-62522-1_29
5. Bernasconi, A., Ceri, S., Campi, A., Masseroli, M.: Conceptual modeling for genomics: building an integrated repository of open data. In: Mayr, H.C., Guizzardi, G., Ma, H., Pastor, O. (eds.) ER 2017. LNCS, vol. 10650, pp. 325–339. Springer, Cham (2017). https://doi.org/10.1007/978-3-319-69904-2_26
6. Bernasconi, A., et al.: VirusViz: comparative analysis and effective visualization of viral nucleotide and amino acid variants. Nucleic Acids Res. (2021)
7. Boyd, K.M.: Disease, illness, sickness, health, healing and wholeness: exploring some elusive concepts. Med. Humanit. **26**(1), 9–17 (2000)
8. Canakoglu, A., et al.: ViruSurf: an integrated database to investigate viral sequences. Nucleic Acids Res. **49**(D1), D817–D824 (2021)
9. Carvalho, V.A., et al.: Multi-level ontology-based conceptual modeling. Data Knowl. Eng. **109**, 3–24 (2017)
10. Carvalho, V.A., Almeida, J.P.A., Guizzardi, G.: Using a well-founded multi-level theory to support the analysis and representation of the powertype pattern in conceptual modeling. In: Nurcan, S., Soffer, P., Bajec, M., Eder, J. (eds.) CAiSE 2016. LNCS, vol. 9694, pp. 309–324. Springer, Cham (2016). https://doi.org/10.1007/978-3-319-39696-5_19
11. Costal, D., Gómez, C., Guizzardi, G.: Formal semantics and ontological analysis for understanding subsetting, specialization and redefinition of associations in UML. In: Jeusfeld, M., Delcambre, L., Ling, T.-W. (eds.) ER 2011. LNCS, vol. 6998, pp. 189–203. Springer, Heidelberg (2011). https://doi.org/10.1007/978-3-642-24606-7_15

12. Guizzardi, G.: Ontological foundations for structural conceptual models. CTIT, Centre for Telematics and Information Technology (2005)
13. Guizzardi, G., et al.: Towards ontological foundations for conceptual modeling: the unified foundational ontology (UFO) story. Appl. Ontol. **10**(3–4), 259–271 (2015)
14. Pastor, O., et al.: Enforcing conceptual modeling to improve the understanding of human genome. In: Proceedings of (RCIS) 2010, pp. 85–92. IEEE (2010)
15. Paton, N.W., et al.: Conceptual modelling of genomic information. Bioinformatics **16**(6), 548–557 (2000)
16. Reyes Román, J.F., Pastor, Ó., Casamayor, J.C., Valverde, F.: Applying conceptual modeling to better understand the human genome. In: Comyn-Wattiau, I., Tanaka, K., Song, I.-Y., Yamamoto, S., Saeki, M. (eds.) ER 2016. LNCS, vol. 9974, pp. 404–412. Springer, Cham (2016). https://doi.org/10.1007/978-3-319-46397-1_31

Type or Individual? Evidence of Large-Scale Conceptual Disarray in Wikidata

Atílio A. Dadalto[1], João Paulo A. Almeida[1(✉)], Claudenir M. Fonseca[2], and Giancarlo Guizzardi[1,2]

[1] Ontology and Conceptual Modeling Research Group (NEMO),
Federal University of Espírito Santo (UFES), Vitoria, Brazil
atilio.dadalto@aluno.ufes.br, jpalmeida@ieee.org
[2] Conceptual and Cognitive Modeling Research Group (CORE),
Free University of Bozen-Bolzano, Bolzano, Italy
{cmoraisfonseca,giancarlo.guizzardi}@unibz.it

Abstract. The distinction between types and individuals is key to most conceptual modeling techniques. Despite that, there are a number of situations in which modelers navigate this distinction inadequately, leading to problematic models. We show evidence of a large number of modeling mistakes associated with the failure to employ this distinction in the Wikidata knowledge graph, which can be identified with the incorrect use of *instantiation*, which is a relation between an individual and a type, and *specialization* (or *subtyping*), which is a relation between two types.

Keywords: Types and instances · Taxonomies · Wikidata · Multi-level modeling

1 Introduction

Types are predicative entities, whose instances share some general characteristics, i.e., they are said to be repeatable invariances across multiple individuals. Individuals (or tokens), in their turn, are not general sorts of things, they are not repeatable; instead, they are particular entities, like Paul McCartney and John Lennon (instances of "person") or Jupiter and Mars (instances of "planet"). While we seem to be able to grasp this distinction intuitively, the boundaries between types and individuals are not always sharply drawn in everyday discourse. Consider, for instance, the paradigmatic case of "word" [11]. How many words are there in the sentence "the book is on the table"? The answer is *six* if we count the two occurrences of "the" as distinct words (or word tokens), or *five* if we count the word *types* used in the sentence. When we say "they drive the same car", do we mean the same *type of car* of the same *individual car*?

Given its occurrence in natural language, it is not surprising that this kind of ambiguity can arise also in knowledge representation and conceptual modeling.

© Springer Nature Switzerland AG 2021
A. Ghose et al. (Eds.): ER 2021, LNCS 13011, pp. 367–377, 2021.
https://doi.org/10.1007/978-3-030-89022-3_29

For instance, if we are capturing invariants about the domain of cars, what kinds of properties will characterize an entity named "car"? An *individual car* has a license plate and a production date, while a *car model* (a type) can be characterized by the tag sales price, the available colors, etc. Distinguishing between these two interpretations is key to grasp to what notion of "car" we refer to and what relations it can establish with other entities. An instance of *car model* can specialize another type of car, in the way that "Porsche Speedster 23F" specializes "Four-Wheeled Car". An instance of *individual car* can instantiate "Porsche Speedster 23F", in the way that James Dean's Porsche did.

This paper examines the use of this distinction in practice, by employing Wikidata as a source of empirical data. Wikidata is structured as a graph with millions of nodes called *items*, which may represent a type (class) (e.g., the item for planet (Q634)) or an individual (e.g., the item for Earth (Q2)). The edges of this graph represent relations between items including specialization and instantiation. We here uncover a large number of items whose relations to other items indicate that their interpretation as a type or as an individual may be ambiguous. We investigate possible reasons behind these problems and, by using logical, ontological and semantic considerations, we propose some possible interpretation solutions for eliminating them. Finally, we demonstrate how we can leverage on an anti-pattern underlying the problems to build automated procedures that can proactively detect them before they are introduced to Wikidata.

This paper is further organized as follows: Sect. 2 introduces Wikidata's primitives for (multi-level) taxonomies. It shows some problems that occur when instantiation and specialization are combined in the platform. Section 3 identifies these problems at scale, updating some of the statistics collected in 2016 for Wikidata [2]. Section 4 examines these results in an attempt to identify a conceptual basis for explaining the identified problems, as well as proposing possible interpretation solutions for rectifying them. Section 5 presents a web application that can detect occurrences of the anti-pattern before they are introduced in Wikidata. Finally, Sect. 6 presents final considerations, including related work.

2   Taxonomies in Wikidata

Knowledge in Wikidata consists of *statements* that capture relations between *items*, which are *"are used to represent all the things in human knowledge"* [12]. A statement has the form of a "<subject> <property> <object>" triple. Examples of widely-used properties include instance of (P31) and subclass of (P279). The property instance of (P31) represents a relation between an instance and a class (i.e., type), where the latter is predicated of the former. For example, Earth (Q2) is an instance of terrestrial planet (Q128207), therefore exhibiting the properties of that class, in this case, being a planet of mostly rocky and metallic composition. The property subclass of (P279), on the other hand, holds between two classes where the subclass has as instances a subset of the instances of the superclass. For example, terrestrial planet

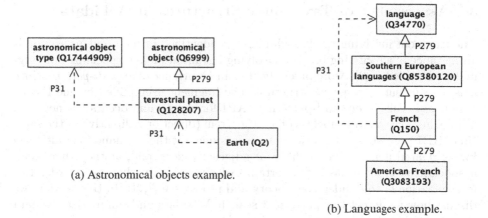

(a) Astronomical objects example.

(b) Languages example.

Fig. 1. Wikidata examples: (a) terrestrial planet as instance of astronomical object type and subclass of astronomical object; (b) French as instance and subclass of language.

(Q128207) is a subclass of planet (Q634) meaning that every instance of the former is also an instance of the latter.

Wikidata also allows the declaration of classes of classes (or meta-classes). For example, terrestrial planet is instance of the class astronomical object type (Q17444909), whose instances are specializations of astronomical object (Q6999). See Fig. 1(a), where boxes represent items; dashed and solid arrows represent instance of (P31) and subclass of (P279) respectively. We retain the capitalization of labels from Wikidata.

The work of [3] clarifies this scheme of classes stratified in meta-levels (i.e., class, meta-class, meta-meta-class), using the concept of order, where individuals (entities that cannot have instances, like Earth (Q2) and Alpha Centauri (Q12176)) instantiate first-order classes (like terrestrial planet (Q128207), star (Q523)), which in turn instantiate second-order classes (like astronomical object type), and so on into orders above (e.g., third-order, fourth-order).

This same clear stratification into orders is not present in other taxonomic structures of Wikidata, however. Consider, for instance, the following fragment concerning the French language, depicted in Fig. 1(b). French (Q150) is both *instance of* and *subclass of* language (Q34770). This opens up multiple interpretations: is French meant to be referring to a type of language or a specific, particular language? Of course, it is known that the French language is a particular language that has a certain number of speakers at a given point in time; however, variants of that language have spawned over the years, which can be considered instances of a class of French languages. The same applies to variants such as American French (Q3083193), which denote the "varieties of the French language that are spoken in North America". The two facets (language as a class and language as a particular) are confounded in Wikidata.

3   Assessment of Taxonomic Structures in Wikidata

The fragment involving the French language identified in the previous section is an instance of a recurring pattern involving instantiation and specialization originally identified in [2]. More precisely, it is an occurrence of an *anti-pattern*, since it is a recurrent error-prone structure. The fragment exemplified by the French language is called here anti-pattern 1 (AP1 for short), and occurs whenever an item is instance of and subclass of another item (direct or indirectly) at the same time. AP1 prevents stratification into orders since, at the one hand, instantiation forces related items to be at different adjacent orders, and, at the other hand, a specialization of a class at a certain order must be in that same order (for formalization of the underlying theory and proofs, see [1,3]). In this section, we discuss how we detect this pattern at scale in Wikidata and summarize the data we collected in the platform.

3.1   Data Collection

In order to deal with the size of Wikidata, we used a filtered dump of the Wikidata database[1]. Because our interest is only on taxonomic structures, only statements with the **subclass of (P279)** property were selected. The dump was created using wdumper[2] and processed using Stardog 7.4 and Jena 4.0.0. It has 2,452,006 entities, 26,264,034 statements and 38,224,283 triples, roughly 2.5% of the now almost 100,000,000 entities present in the complete Wikidata database as of April 2021.

3.2   Anti-Pattern Occurrences

To assess the occurrence of the anti-pattern, we have executed SPARQL queries in the filtered dump. Listing 1.1 shows the SPARQL query used to find AP1 occurrences considering transitiveness for *subclass of* statements. We have found 2,035,434 **?subject ?class** pairs involved in AP1, covering domains such as biology, gastronomy, awards, professions, sports, among others. Transitivity of subclassing is important as it reveals a large number of anti-pattern occurrences, which could indicate that it is harder to identify the specialization paths to indirect superclasses. The AP1 query without transitivity yields 1,279,629 results, while a query considering P279 transitivity returns 2,035,434 results.

Listing 1.1. SPARQL query for AP1.

```
SELECT DISTINCT ?subject ?class WHERE {
  ?subject wdt:P31 ?class .
  ?subject wdt:P279+ ?class .
}
```

---

[1] Wikidata dump generated in 14 September 2020, https://zenodo.org/record/4046102.

[2] Further dump details and mirrors at https://wdumps.toolforge.org/dump/749.

Table 1. Ranking of occurrences of entities involved in AP1.

Place	Wikidata QID	English label	AP1 occurrences
1	Q7187	Gene	971,982
2	Q8054	Protein	757,360
3	Q4164871	Position	103,545
4	Q277338	Pseudogene	49,404
5	Q427087	Non-coding RNA	49,132
6	Q2996394	Biological process	30,315
7	Q12136	Disease	12,293
8	Q14860489	Molecular function	11,204
9	Q34770	Language	6,795
10	Q5058355	Cellular component	4,287

3.3   Entities Most Frequently Involved in Anti-Pattern AP1

We have produced a ranking of the entities most frequently involved in the anti-pattern so that they could be further analyzed. The 10 top-ranked entities involved in AP1 are listed in Table 1 along with the number of times it participates in the anti-pattern. A comprehensive ranking with 200 entities and all scripts used in this paper are available at https://purl.org/nemo/wapa.

There is a clear overlap of subdomains in the ranking, especially but not limited to entities related to biology and biochemistry, e.g., **gene** as a *"basic physical and functional unit of heredity"* and **pseudogene (Q277338)** as a *"functionless relative of a gene"*. For example, gene is a well-known complex concept frequently referring to a particular gene type repeatable in chromosomes of every cell (gene instances, i.e., particular biochemical structures composed of particular nucleotides) but also to the representation of a gene type (a data object) that results from genome sequencing operations. Multiple anti-pattern occurrences involving gene and pseudogene are introduced from batch adding or merging statements from external datasets such as UniProt and NCBI Gene, without proper consideration of imported entities as types or individuals. Hundreds of thousands of genes are directly related to **gene (Q7187)** in immediate instantiation and specialization relations! This pattern repeats for instances of **protein, protein domain, disease, rare disease, development defect during embryogenesis, head and neck disease, non-coding RNA, transfer RNA.** Users and softbots alike leverage databases such as GeneDB (genes), UniProt (proteins) Disease Ontology (diseases), InterPro, PubMed, NCBI Gene (RNAs), Gene Ontology (biological processes, cellular components), thus, introducing these violations. Other domains often present in AP1's top 20 entities are social roles and titles (e.g., **award (Q618779), grade of an order (Q60754876), position (Q4164871)**, and **public office (Q294414)**), language classification (e.g., **language (Q34770)**), and products of controlled origin denomination (e.g., **wine (Q282)**).

We inspected some of these top entities in the ranking to identify in which exact revision in the history of the Wikidata updates a violation was introduced. For example, take language (Q34770). Originally, the item Guarani (Q35876) was simply represented as being an *instance of* language. However, revision 174811757 introduced the statement that Guarani (Q35876) is a *subclass of* indigenous language of the Americas (Q51739)—which is an indirect *subclass of* language (Q34770). Together these statements configure a case of anti-pattern AP1. An anti-pattern checker could play a role in this context by detecting revisions that introduce inconsistencies prior to the inclusion of new statements.

4   Analysis and Discussion

The top-ranking entity involved in the anti-pattern we investigated is gene, which is described in Wikidata as a "basic physical and functional unit of heredity" with instances such as TP53 (Q14818098), a "protein-coding gene in the species Homo sapiens". Inspecting their use in Wikidata, instances of gene like TP53 are most likely not "a particular gene from one cell from one person" but instead a *type* of which "many of us have tokens of—in fact many tokens of in each cell of our bodies" [11]. There is evidence for this in the properties ascribed to TP53, such as "found in taxon Homo Sapiens" and "encodes Tumor protein p53". This is consistent with an interpretation of gene as a second-order class, and its instances (e.g., TP53) as first-order classes. However, TP53, besides being declared as an instance of gene, is declared a subclass of protein-coding gene (Q20747295), which is itself a subclass of gene. Therefore, TP53 (and most of the other instances of gene) is also a subclass of gene. How should instances of TP53 be interpreted then, as they are also instances of gene like TP53 itself? We hypothesize that the subclassing statement is incorrect. TP53 is not a subclass, but an instance of the protein-coding gene subclass of gene. This issue may have never been flagged in Wikidata as instances of instances of gene are never instantiated explicitly in the platform (as it is not tracking "a particular gene from one cell from one person", but types of these). In fact, most gene talk is quantifying over types as discussed by Wetzel [11]. The same observation can be made for the other entities in the ranking related to biology and biochemistry such as: protein, pseudogene, non-coding RNA, and cellular component. These are all second-order types whose instances are first-order types classifying individual entities not recorded in the platform. Hence, there is a mismatch between ontological considerations (TP53 is a class instantiated by structures inside individual cells) and knowledge representation considerations (instances of TP53 are never recorded in Wikidata, suggesting it to be an individual).

Further in the ranking, we have the entity position (Q4164871), carrying the notion of "*social role [...] within an [...] organization*"). An instance of position is mayor (Q30185), "head of municipal government such as a town or city", instantiated by Frank Hilker (Q104772317). Clearly, he is an individual! Hence, mayor is a first-order class, suggesting position is a second-order class.

However, **mayor** is declared as a subclass of **public office (Q294414)** which is a subclass of **position**. As a consequence, we come to the absurd inference that **Frank Hilker** is an instance of **position** (and consequently an instance of its superclasses, like **artificial entity (Q16686448)**)! We hypothesize the declaration of **mayor** as a subclass of **position** is incorrect. The former being a first-order class and the latter a second-order class. As discussed in [3], order-crossing specialization is logically incorrect. Differently from the case of gene, the platform includes instances of instances of **position** (such as **Frank Hilker**); similarly, though, **gene** and **position** are second-order classes (meta-classes). It is important to note here that Wikidata has a specialized property to declare occupation of a position by a person (**position held (P39)**) and this is used instead of instantiation for most declarations of occupation. In any case, one needs to settle whether **mayor** and other entities like this are instances or specializations of **position** irrespective of the use of **position held**.

The case of **biological process (Q2996394)** also reveals confusion regarding the entity's order. It is a subclass of **process (Q3249551)**, which in turn is a subclass of **occurrence (Q1190554)**, the latter described as "occurrence of a fact or object in space-time". An occurrence may be qualified by **point in time (Q186408)**, indicating that its instances are individual occurrences. Hence, **biological process** should be considered a first-order class. However, **biological process** includes among its instances entities such as **birth (Q14819852)** and **death (Q4)**, entities bearing their own instances (e.g., the instance of **death, death of James Dean (Q15213260)**). Hence, death is a class of biological processes, which leads to an interpretation of **biological process** as a second-order class contradicting the earlier conclusion. Although present and declared as an instance of **second-order class (Q24017414)**, the entity **biological process type (Q47989961)** has no **instance of** properties connecting it to any other items, not even the subclasses of **biological process** such as **birth** and **death**.

The case of **language (Q34770)**, which we have raised earlier, involves the representation of extremely rich phenomena with much variation and diversity (a spectrum including macrolanguages, language families, and dialects). In this case, the criteria for individuation for a language is difficult to establish, and, as discussed earlier, items such as **French** can be regarded as a particular language or as a class of similar languages (given that each of its variations may be considered itself a language). We should note that **language** is an instance of **languoid class (Q28923954)**, a *"[...] dialect, language, macrolanguage, language subfamily, family, or superfamily; each instance of these is a subclass of languoid"* according to its English description. Moreover, **languoid class** is explicitly marked as second-order class in Wikidata (it is an instance of **Wikidata metaclass (Q19361238)** which is an instance of **third-order class (Q24017465)**). This makes **language** a first-order class, and its instances individuals. As individuals, instances of language must not be involved in *subclass of* statements. To separate the two facets of a language, we need two items: one representing the language (say **French of France (Q3083196)**) as an instance of language (or dialect), and another as a subclass of language (or dialect) (referring to the class of French variants, whose instances include Quebec French (Q979914), Swiss French (Q1480152), and French of France).

Note that the ranking we have presented in this paper has been filtered to remove entities that are marked as instances of variable-order class (Q23958852), since these are explicitly flagged as not being stratified into a particular order. Variable-order [5] (or orderless [1]) classes have instances at different orders. Thus, being an orderless class can justify its *bona fide* occurrence in the (anti-)pattern, with no error incurred.

5 Automated Support

By leveraging on the type of analysis conducted in the previous section and the anti-pattern that can be identified with it, one can implement automated procedures for proactively identifying occurrences of this anti-pattern before it is introduced in Wikidata. In this section, we illustrate that by implementing such a procedure for the case of AP1 as a web application termed the Wikidata Anti-Pattern Analyzer[3] (WAPA). WAPA allows the user to input any entity from Wikidata to check for existing occurrences of AP1, or input a hypothetical statement to verify whether it would introduce new violations. Since it retrieves data directly from Wikidata's SPARQL endpoint, the results reflect the current state of Wikidata (in the screenshots below, they reflect the state of Wikidata during the writing of this paper, April 2021).

As presented in Fig. 2, one may check for AP1 violations that could be introduced to Wikidata with the addition of a statement "Pulitzer Prize (Q46525) subclass of science award (Q11448906)". Indeed, in this case, Pulitzer

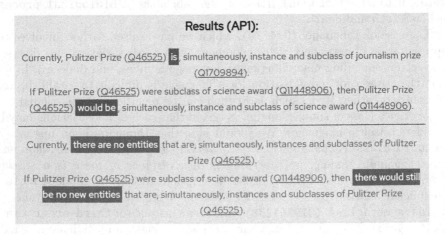

Results (AP1):

Currently, Pulitzer Prize (Q46525) is, simultaneously, instance and subclass of journalism prize (Q1709894).

If Pulitzer Prize (Q46525) were subclass of science award (Q11448906), then Pulitzer Prize (Q46525) would be, simultaneously, instance and subclass of science award (Q11448906).

Currently, there are no entities that are, simultaneously, instances and subclasses of Pulitzer Prize (Q46525).

If Pulitzer Prize (Q46525) were subclass of science award (Q11448906), then there would still be no new entities that are, simultaneously, instances and subclasses of Pulitzer Prize (Q46525).

Fig. 2. WAPA results regarding hypothetical statement about Pulitzer Prize (Q46525), reflecting the state of Wikidata as of April 2021.

---

[3] Available at https://atilioa.github.io/WikidataAntiPatternAnalyzer/.

Prize would be, simultaneously instance and subclass of **science award**. Since WAPA always checks for existing violations before testing the hypothetical scenario, it would also inform that **Pulitzer Prize** is, simultaneously, instance and subclass of **journalism prize (Q1709894)** beyond the results for the hypothetical statement.

6   Final Considerations

In this paper, we conduct an empirical analysis of the Wikidata platform. We do that as a way to demonstrate how recurrent are anti-patterns exemplifying problems related to modeling of types and instances in large multi-level knowledge models. As this empirical data corroborates, this is a widespread problem with thousands and even million of occurrences in Wikidata. We also identify the items in Wikidata appearing in the highest number of occurrences of AP1. By conducting a conceptual analysis of these cases, we manage to venture an explanation for their occurrence, and propose interpretation solutions that would eliminate them. (Due to space limitations, the analysis conducted in Sect. 4 was limited to a subset of the top-ranking notions.) Finally, we show how this anti-pattern can inform the construction of automated procedures that can proactively detect this anti-pattern before it is introduced in such a knowledge model. In an earlier work, some of us explored the role of a multi-level modeling language (ML2) in detecting the occurrence of the anti-patterns discussed here [4]. Differently from that work, here we proposed a web application that can be used by Wikidata users to detect the problems in a language-independent manner.

We should note that the concepts of *order* and the stratification of taxonomies into consistent multi-level structures are concerns present in Wikidata since revisions introduced in mid 2016. Since then, to support stratified taxonomies, the platform includes at the top of its specialization hierarchy a set of classes representing different orders, namely **first-order class (Q104086571)**, **second-order class (Q24017414)**, **third-order class (Q24017465)**, **fourth-order class (Q24027474)**, **fifth-order class (Q24027515)**, and **fixed order metaclass of higher order (Q24027526)**. These classes are declared as equivalent to their counterparts in the OpenCyc ontology [5]. However, they are underused in the platform, and, as we show here and in [4], their mere inclusion in the platform without adequate computational aid has been insufficient to prevent the introduction of anti-patterns in new revisions. This motivated us to provide some automated support as shown here.

The dual facet of entities that are both types and instances is a phenomenon that is well-documented in (multi-level) conceptual modeling [3], in formal ontology [5,8], and in linguistics [10]. In particular, the phenomenon of *systematic polysemy* in language accounts for many cases of this problem. For example, when we say "these ducks in the backyard are common around Europe", we are making a polysemic reference that overloads the term duck with particular duck instances (those in the backyard) with a duck type (that which is repeatable in a population of ducks and, hence, which is common around Europe). This polysemy that is present in natural language, we conjecture, is also manifested in the construction of lightweight representation structures such as Wikidata. This is specially the case when such a structure is collectively constructed in an asynchronous manner by millions of users, many of which are not expert modelers. This is made worse when these naive modeling strategies (oblivious to these problems) are codified in computer programs (e.g., softbots) that automatically transfer knowledge snippets from other existing data sources.

As we show here, by conducting an analysis of the logical and ontological reasons behind the phenomena causing these semantic confusions, we can proactive devise methodological (e.g., anti-patterns) and computational tools that can assist users in avoiding these mistakes. In this sense, the work presented here is in line with a number of successful initiatives of employing ontological principles to evaluate and rectify large-scale knowledge structures. These include, for example: (i) [6] and [7], which respectively use the DOLCE foundational ontology and the OntoClean methodology for analyzing and proposing correction to the Wordnet top-level; (ii) [9], which uses a lightweight version of DOLCE (termed DOLCE-Zero) for detecting anti-patterns in DBPedia. The works in (i) focus on detecting taxonomic problems related to ontological notions such as identity, unity, and dependence. In contrast, in (ii), the most common patterns detected are related to logical conflicts between disjoint types that are expected by and asserted to given properties. These are related to confusions between objects and events, agents and places, physical and social objects, etc. For example, `dbpedia#AlfonsoXIIofSpain` `dbo#birthPlace` `dbpedia#Madrid`, where `dbpedia#Madrid` is erroneously typed as `dbo#Agent`(as a geopolitical entity), which is a confusion between the disjoint types Place and Agent. One of the one of the patterns detected in (ii), however, is what the authors call *metonymy*, which is a conflict arising from disjoint but related interpretations of the same concept. In particular, they make the example of `dbo#family`, which is used to related instances of `dbo#Species` and its property specializing concepts. However, `dbo#Species` are aligned to the type Organism, because "species in DBpedia include species as well as individual exemplars of a species (for example, famous race horses)". Although this case seems to exemplify a type/instance confusion, the authors arrive at it by, once more, detecting disjoint types in the domain/range of properties, as opposed to explicitly identifying anti-patterns related to this problem. Moreover, they seem to have a somewhat lenient approach with respect to these problems: "[t]he metonymy anti-pattern is difficult to resolve, because it is due to ambiguities that seem widespread in human language. Metonymy seems related to human propensity for an economy of means... [we try] to accommodate this 'power of ambiguity"'. We take here a radically different approach in this respect by advocating that these problems can cause logical contradictions and conceptual confusion, and by proposing concrete means to detect and correct them.

Acknowledgments. This research is partly funded by Brazilian funding agencies CNPq (grants 313687/2020-0, 407235/2017-5) and CAPES (grant 23038.028816/2016-41). Claudenir M. Fonseca and Giancarlo Guizzardi are supported by the NeXON Project (Free University of Bozen-Bolzano).

References

1. Almeida, J.P.A., Fonseca, C.M., Carvalho, V.A.: A comprehensive formal theory for multi-level conceptual modeling. In: Mayr, H.C., Guizzardi, G., Ma, H., Pastor, O. (eds.) ER 2017. LNCS, vol. 10650, pp. 280–294. Springer, Cham (2017). https://doi.org/10.1007/978-3-319-69904-2_23
2. Brasileiro, F., Almeida, J.P.A., Carvalho, V.A., Guizzardi, G.: Applying a multi-level modeling theory to assess taxonomic hierarchies in Wikidata. In: Proceedings of 25th International Conference Companion on World Wide Web, pp. 975–980. WWW 2016 Companion (2016)
3. Carvalho, V.A., Almeida, J.P.A.: Toward a well-founded theory for multi-level conceptual modeling. Softw. Syst. Model. **17**(1), 205–231 (2016). https://doi.org/10.1007/s10270-016-0538-9
4. Fonseca, C.M., Almeida, J.P.A., Guizzardi, G., Carvalho, V.A.: Multi-level conceptual modeling: theory, language and application. Data Knowl. Eng. **134**, 101894 (2021). https://doi.org/10.1016/j.datak.2021.101894
5. Foxvog, D.: Instances of instances modeled via higher-order classes. In: Workshop on Foundational Aspects of Ontologies, 28th German Conference on Artificial Intelligence, pp. 46–54 (2005)
6. Gangemi, A., Guarino, N., Masolo, C., Oltramari, A.: Sweetening WORDNET with DOLCE. AI Mag. **24**(3), 13 (2003). https://doi.org/10.1609/aimag.v24i3.1715
7. Gangemi, A., Guarino, N., Oltramari, A.: Conceptual analysis of lexical taxonomies: the case of WordNet top-level. In: Proceedings of FOIS 2001, pp. 285–296 (2001). https://doi.org/10.1145/505168.505195
8. Guizzardi, G., Almeida, J.P.A., Guarino, N., Carvalho, V.A.: Towards an ontological analysis of powertypes. In: Proc. Joint Ontology Workshops 2015 Episode 1: The Argentine Winter of Ontology. CEUR Workshop Proceedings, vol. 1517. CEUR-WS.org (2015)
9. Paulheim, H., Gangemi, A.: Serving DBpedia with DOLCE – more than just adding a cherry on top. In: Arenas, M., et al. (eds.) ISWC 2015. LNCS, vol. 9366, pp. 180–196. Springer, Cham (2015). https://doi.org/10.1007/978-3-319-25007-6_11
10. Ravin, Y., Leacock, C.: Polysemy: Theoretical and Computational Approaches. OUP (2000)
11. Wetzel, L.: Types and Tokens: On Abstract Objects. MIT Press, Cambridge (2009)
12. Wikidata: Help:items – Wikidata (2021). https://web.archive.org/web/20210127110938/. https://www.wikidata.org/wiki/Help:Items. Accessed 2 May 2021

Social Aspects of Conceptual Modeling

A Sustainability Requirements Catalog for the Social and Technical Dimensions

Diogo Albuquerque[1], Ana Moreira[1(✉)] [iD], João Araujo[1] [iD], Catarina Gralha[1] [iD], Miguel Goulão[1] [iD], and Isabel Sofia Brito[2,3] [iD]

[1] NOVA LINCS, School of Science and Technology, NOVA University of Lisbon, 2829-516 Caparica, Portugal
dh.albuquerque@campus.fct.unl.pt,
{amm,joao.araujo,catarina.gralha,mgoul}@fct.unl.pt
[2] UNINOVA-CTS, 2829-516 Caparica, Portugal
[3] Polytechnic Institute of Beja, 7800-295 Beja, Portugal
isabel.sofia@ipbeja.pt

Abstract. Sustainability poses key challenges in software development for its complexity. Our goal is to contribute with a reusable sustainability software requirements catalog. We started by performing a systematic mapping to elicit and extract sustainability-related properties, and synthesized the results in feature models. Next we used iStar to model a more expressive configurable catalog with the collected data, and implemented a tool with several operations on the sustainability catalog. The sustainability catalog was qualitatively evaluated regarding its readability, interest, utility, and usefulness by 50 participants from the domain. The results were encouraging, showing that, on average, 79% of the respondents found the catalog "Good" or "Very Good" in endorsing the quality criteria evaluated. This paper discusses the social and technical dimensions of the sustainability catalog.

Keywords: Sustainability requirements modeling · Non-functional requirements · Sustainability requirements catalog · Goal modeling

1 Introduction

Sustainability implies *development that meets the needs of the present without compromising the ability of future generations to meet their own needs* [6]. This challenge calls for the integration of social equity, economic growth, and environmental preservation, considering also their effects on each other. These three dimensions have been integrated in a multidimensional line of thought that also encompasses an individual and a technical dimension [24]. Each dimension addresses different needs (e.g., improve employment indicators, reduce costs, reduce CO_2 emissions, promote high agency, and easy system evolution) and impacts on the others and respective stakeholders. Therefore, sustainability-aware systems differ from other types of systems in that their functionality must explicitly balance the trade-offs between these dimensions.

© Springer Nature Switzerland AG 2021
A. Ghose et al. (Eds.): ER 2021, LNCS 13011, pp. 381–394, 2021.
https://doi.org/10.1007/978-3-030-89022-3_30

Despite lacking a common definition in Software Engineering, existing works in software development handle sustainability as a non-functional requirement (e.g., [27]). We follow the view that sustainability is "an emergent property of a software system" [30]. As an emergent property, sustainability cannot be added to a specific part of the software system during later activities of software development nor should it be looked into in isolation. In this work, we look at sustainability as a complex composite quality attribute, formed of five complex aggregates of quality attributes, one for each dimension, which, in turn, is composed of the quality attributes relevant for that dimension. Given the complexity of sustainability and the lack of approaches to help with the identification and analysis of sustainability requirements and their integration with other system's requirements, reusable artifacts can contribute to alleviate this complexity.

Our goal is to develop a reusable sustainability catalog that can be configured for different contexts and purposes. Our stating point was a systematic mapping study to gather from the existing body of knowledge the fundamental sustainability properties. The extracted concepts of each sustainability dimension were synthesized using feature models [15], to represent common and variable features (or concepts). Given that feature models lack the means to represent certain types of concepts and relationships needed for sustainability, we mapped their features and relationships to iStar 2.0 [11], a goal-based requirements description language, and specified the missing information. The iStar framework provides means to support (i) a clear separation between elements such as goals, qualities, tasks and resources and (ii) different types of relationships, such as contributions. Finally, we implemented an extension to the piStar tool [26], offering configuration operations (e.g., add, select, project/filter, export) to extract subsets of the catalog according to the problem domain needs and stakeholders' preferences.

We qualitatively evaluated the sustainability catalog and its guide regarding their readability, interest, utility and usefulness. We sent a questionnaire to 89 participants, including the authors of the selected primary studies from our mapping study. 16 out of 50 respondents are among those authors. 79% of the respondents "Agree" or "Strongly agree" that the catalog fulfills the quality criteria. This paper focuses on the social and technical sustainability dimensions.

This paper is structured as follows. Section 2 summarizes the results of a mapping study aiming at collecting sustainability concepts and relationships and synthesizes the results in feature models. Section 3 refines the various concepts and models them using an iStar goal model. Section 4 discusses the implementation of the tool support, and Sect. 5 discusses the results of the qualitative evaluation performed. Finally, Sect. 7 presents related work and Sect. 8 draws the conclusions and offers ideas for future work.

2   Sustainability Concepts and Relationships

This section summarizes the results of a systematic mapping study and finishes with a feature model synthesizing the information found. A mapping study process consists of planning, conducting, and reporting [25]. The planning phase defines the research questions, the search and study selection strategy, and the data extraction form. The conduction phase shows the execution of the search while presenting the results for each research query. The reporting phase analyzes and presents the results given in the previous phase.

2.1 Eliciting Concepts: Planning and Conduction

We started by formulating the research questions and respective search string to run in the DBLP digital library, as it compiles a large amount of publications from different sources (e.g., IEEEXplore, ACM, Science Direct, Springer-Link). The general research question *What are the requirements that contribute or relate to sustainability?* was derived after a PICOC analysis. With variants of the keywords in the research question, we built the search string *(method OR process OR technique OR model OR tool OR approach OR framework OR catalog OR catalogue) AND (sustain* OR green) AND (requirement OR attribute)*. The inclusion and exclusion criteria (typical ones) were defined to help selecting the relevant studies for analysis and data extraction. The search was performed automatically, and then manually, via forward and backward snowballing.

We run the search string on DBLP which indexes the relevant fora in computer science, retrieving 169 candidates. First, papers were select based on title and abstract reading and then the selected studies were fully read for data extraction, resulting in 7 papers [2,3,7,8,10,12,28]. After snowballing, 5 more articles [19,20,22,24,27] more studies were added to the final list of papers.

2.2 Discussion and Synthesis of Results

Primary studies discussing software sustainability and its importance [2,3,7,8, 12], models and frameworks [19,24,28], requirements and sustainability relationships [10] were essential for this part of our work. Sustainability has often been equated with environmental issues, but it is clear that it requires simultaneous considerations of social and individual well-being, economic prosperity and the long-term viability of technical infrastructure [2,24]. Thus, a sustainable product should balance the goals of these dimensions. This is hard due to intra- and inter-dimension relationships among properties within one dimension and across different dimensions. The set of selected papers provided valuable information about relationships (some also available in [4,9,17]).

The synthesis of the results are expressed in a feature model [15], representing sustainability properties as features and relationships as constraints between features. Each model offers a view of each dimension and captures information about common and variable features at different levels of abstraction. Even though our study is broader and includes the environmental and economic dimensions, we chose to discuss in this paper, the social and technical dimensions.

Social Dimension. The social dimension relates to societal communities and the factors that erode trust in society [3]. It can also be seen as the well-being of humans living in such society [20]. This dimension is related to notions such as, honesty, transparency, communication, security and safety [3]. This dimension is divided into *satisfaction* (of the stakeholder), *security* (of the system) and (social) *safety*. Satisfaction can be linked with *usefulness* (the achievement of pragmatic goals), *trust* (confidence in the company), and *fairness* (regarding equality and honesty) [10,13]. Security is an important requirements of the social dimension [10], as systems' data and information cannot be compromised, hence divided into *confidentiality, authenticity, integrity,* and *accountability* [14]. Safety is divided into *freedom from risk* (i.e., mitigation of the potential risk to people [13]) [10] and *legislation* [22] (compliance with the laws and legislation). A few relationships were also elicited. In particular, security increases trust of stakeholder (represented by a *requires* relationship), since a secure system is one that inspires trust to the user [13]. A system's authenticity requires both its integrity and its accountability [14]. However confidentiality may be prejudicial for accountability [14], since it could be harder to trace the origin of the data, due to possible anonymity. The feature model in Fig. 1 expresses the decomposition of the dimension and the various relationships among features, where optional operators were used to allow flexibility to the decision maker.

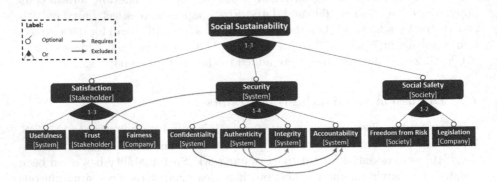

Fig. 1. Feature model for the **social** dimension.

Technical Dimension. This dimension has the central objective of long-time usage of systems and their adequate evolution with changing surrounding conditions and respective requirements. It refers to maintenance and evolution, resilience, and the ease of system transitions [3], and is divided into *functionality, maintainability, compatibility* and *reliability* of the system. Functionality is linked with *functional appropriateness* (everything works as intended) and *functional correctness* (lower possibility of occurring internal errors and/or failures) [10]. Maintainability is important to guarantee how well a system is maintained, and it is divided into *testability* (effectiveness and efficiency with which test criteria can be established [14]), *modularity* (components may be separated and recombined, often with the benefit of flexibility and variety in use, with minimal impact on other components [14,16]), and *modifiability* (changes to a software system can be developed and deployed efficiently and cost effectively [14]). Compatibility is divided into *adaptability* (ability to adapt to constant changes) and *interoperability* (ability to couple of facilitate interface with other systems). Finally, reliability [3] is divided into *availability* (the system is able to function during "normal operating times" [14]), *recoverability* (in the event of an interruption or a failure, the data can be recovered and the desired state of the system is re-establish [14]), and *fault tolerance* (continue normal operation despite the presence of hardware or software faults [14]). Regarding relationships, adaptability of the system helps its modifiability because an adaptable system is one that is easily modifiable [18]. If a system is robust and has a good component of fault tolerance, then it will perform its tasks normally, leading to an increase of its availability [14]. If we define a set of criteria (functional- or performance-like) for the system to meet, we will help the system to function properly and as desired [13]. Finally, if we correctly maintain a system, in what concerns the correct usage of its components, it will lead to an increase of its reliability resulting in a long-lasting, healthier system [10]. Figure 2 expresses these decomposition and the relationships among features, once more allowing for configuration.

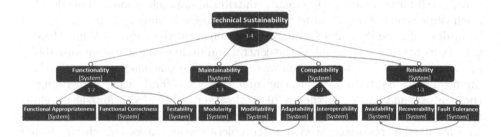

Fig. 2. Feature model for the **technical** dimension.

Inter-relationships. Sustainability dimensions are inter-dependent [3], affecting each other positively or negatively and sharing some key requirements [10,22,27]. Here, we limit the discussion to the effects between the social and technical dimensions (even though the study also elicited economic and environmental properties). If a product has diverse functionalities and is reliable and provides interoperability, it may impact positively on the user satisfaction (social sustainability). Society can also have a positive impact on the technical side of a product by providing feedback and suggest new functionalities. The constant and ever evolving needs of the society can be seen as one of the main boosters of technology, which will ultimately result in better and more advanced products. Figure 5 depicts two of those relationships, for example, the help contribution between Functionality (of the system from the Technical Sustainability dimension) and Satisfaction (of the stakeholder from the social dimension).

3   Modeling Sustainability Catalog

Despite the feature model benefits, its constructors are not expressive enough to specify different types of properties (e.g., goals and qualities) as well as positive and negative level of effects among them. Also, as our plan for the near future is to refine those properties to the operationalization level to capture in the catalog possible solutions, a more expressive modeling notation is required. We chose the iStar framework as it provides the needed semantics and offers a good base for trade-off analysis [11].

We mapped the elements of the feature models (the source models) representing the notions of sustainability into elements of the iStar framework (the target model). Sustainability is composed of several dimensions and each dimension is an aggregate of several qualities that have effects on qualities of the same dimension and qualities of other dimensions. To obtain a cohesive catalog, we opted for mapping each dimension to a quality and sustainability to a root quality aggregating the various quality dimensions. Additionally, non-functional requirements identified in the mapping study, were also mapped to qualities dependent of the corresponding quality dimension. These were further refined in the iStar model, using the iStar links (e.g., refinement, contribution, qualification and neededBy). Each dimension catalog is, in fact, an SR (Strategic Rationale) iStar model that complies with the iStar 2.0 standards. We perceived the catalogs themselves as the actors of our models, and as the central and main element, the sustainability of each dimension (a quality), then was refined in various qualities. Finally, these main qualities relate to a set of other qualities, goals (and tasks), depending on the context, and can be further refined. However, we settled a four-level refinement as a maximum, to reduce the size of the whole catalog. The final step was to add possible resources needed to complete certain tasks (which we do not show here due to lack of space).

Lets take as an example the social dimension and some of its requirements (see Fig. 3). The central quality is social sustainability. As discussed in Sect. 2.2, social sustainability relates to three different features: security, safety and satisfaction. These features, which in the iStar model are qualities, all link to the social sustainability via contribution links of type make. The third level focuses on the satisfaction (of the stakeholder), for instance. We know that satisfaction relates to the usefulness of the system, the stakeholder's trust and the fairness of the company. They are all qualities. Given each refinement, we should look for possible relationships. For example, the system's security helps stakeholders increase their trust on the system. Thus, such relationship is a help link contribution. We can further refine the usefulness, trust and fairness qualities. To assist this process, we applied known information about these refinements, which are presented in other NFR catalogs, such as [9]. Considering *usefulness* as an example, a useful system should accomplish its proposed functionalities, mapped into an iStar goal [14]. This goal (in a different color) can be named "accomplishment of proposed functionalities [system]". The final catalog is then obtained by creating links (e.g. contribution links) between model elements from different dimensions.

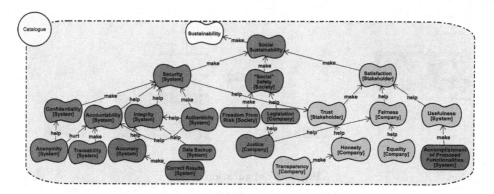

Fig. 3. Social dimension of the sustainability catalog.

4   Catalog Implementation and Tool Support

Our goal was to develop a reusable catalog. Thus, the tool should support configurability and modifiability. Configurability lets the user select a set of requirements across any combination of dimensions, obtaining only the sustainability requirements needed for her domain. Modifiability, on the other hand, lets the user modify the catalog according to his/her needs or knowledge. Also, the ability to save and load a custom catalog are basic functionalities. Finally, the tool includes functionalities to enhance the user experience, such as labels (e.g., labels for colors of model elements).

Among the existing tools supporting the iStar framework, we chose the open source piStar tool [26] because it is compliant with the iStar 2.0 standard, it is simple to use, produces valid and visually appealing iStar 2.0 models, and supports extendibility and customizability. We implemented three plugins for piStar[1]: configurability of the catalog; color label; and element label. The implementation uses JavaScript and HTML. The plugins, on the GUI, are clickable buttons that when clicked, perform the specified function. The configurability plugin is the main one and implements the configuration of the catalog, allowing the user to select the wanted features and getting the corresponding model. Even if we ideally want a fully sustainable system, in many situations the best we can do is to try to maximize a subset of dimensions by combining some properties of some dimensions to achieve partial sustainability.

The user has full freedom to choose the more suitable sustainability requirements for his domain and the catalog will shape accordingly. For instance, if we have a project that only focuses on two dimensions of sustainability, we can abstract from the other dimensions. We can configure and filter the catalog according to specific needs, selecting a checkbox associated with the main qualities of each dimension. The selected qualities will be displayed to the user. For instance, Fig. 4 shows the configuration steps leading to the resulting catalog model after selecting all the qualities of social and technical dimensions.

---

[1] These plugins are available from [1], in the *tool* tab.

Fig. 4. Configuration steps.

Figure 5 shows the outcome of the configuration, a custom catalog according to the selected dimensions and respective features.

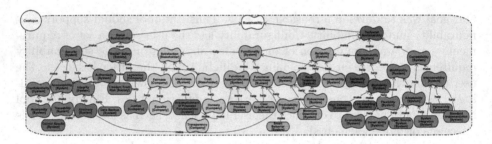

Fig. 5. Result of the catalog configuration.

The color and element labels facilitate the understanding of the catalog. Their purpose is purely for consulting information, so that one can check the color typology of the catalog (for the color label) or the semantics of each of its elements (for the elements label). Each element of a dimension has a respective color, so that the identification of a certain element would be easier to the user. A color for each dimension was defined. If an element relates to two or more dimensions, its color will result from the mixing of the colors of each dimension that it relates to. The catalog's color labels are shown in Fig. 6.

5   Preliminary Evaluation

5.1   Instrument Design and Participants Recruitment

We built a guide for the catalog and a questionnaire to perform an early assessment of the sustainability catalog. We evaluated the catalog in terms of clarity, readability, relevance, usefulness, and the extent to which it offers a general and concise idea about sustainability requirements. We also assessed the guide for

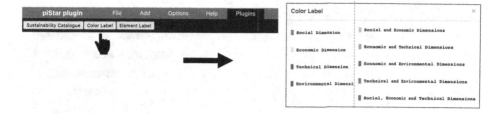

Fig. 6. Color label.

the catalog. We conducted this assessment through a survey composed of closed 5 points Likert-scaled questions. The survey included two additional open-end questions where participants commented on the most relevant or positive aspects of the catalog and identified opportunities for improvement. We collected basic demographic information on our participants. The guide, catalog, survey, and raw data included in this preliminary evaluation are available in this paper's companion site [1]. We chose the exact wording of the guide and the questions to make them accessible to novices and experts. We created the survey instrument with Google Forms. It has 5 sections: introduction, personal data, guide questions, catalog questions and open feedback questions. We collected respondents contacts to discern the experts from novices and make the survey results available to those who requested them. That said, we omit the contact information from the shared raw data to preserve respondents anonymity.

We recruited survey participants through convenience sampling, leveraging authors lists of related work papers on sustainability and personal contacts. This recruitment strategy allowed us to gather feedback from experts and novices with respect to sustainability. We invited 89 participants (41 experts and 49 novices) and received a total of 50 responses (16 experts and 34 novices) corresponding to a global answer rate of about 56% (34% for experts and 71% for novices). 26% of our participants hold a BSc, 34% have a MSc, and 40% hold a PhD.

5.2 Results

We organize the presentation of the results into the closed questions about the guide and the catalog, followed by the open questions about the catalog. For each question, we present the results concerning novices, experts and all of them combined. Figure 7 summarizes the answers collected with the questionnaire.

Guide Questions. The two first questions assess the *perceived usefulness* and *understandability* of the guide. Most novices and half of the experts expressed a positive perception about the guide's *usefulness*, while the remaining were neutral about it. Concerning *understandability*, 78% of the respondents expressed a positive perception, while 18% expressed a neutral one and the remaining 4% (1 novice and 1 expert) had a negative perception. One of our novice participants did not answer this question.

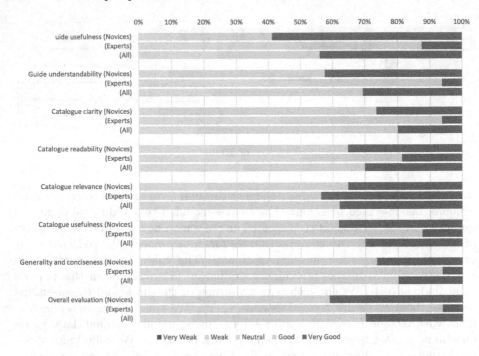

Fig. 7. Summary of the qualitative evaluation of the sustainability catalog.

Catalog Questions. The last 6 questions, summarized in Fig. 7, assess the *clarity of the concepts in the catalog*, the *readability of the catalog*, the extent to which the *catalog is relevant, useful, general and concise* and, an overall evaluation of the catalog. The perceptions expressed by participants are positive, both for novices and experts, albeit novices have a more positive perception than experts in 5 of the questions. The exception is the perceived relevance of this catalog, which collected more positive answers from experts than from novices. The number of participants expressing negative feedback (*Weak*) was, at most, 3 (out of 50). Although the *Very Weak* category was also available as an alternative, our participants did not select it in any of the questions. The least positive perceptions concerned the catalog *readability*, where 68% of our respondents ranked it as *Very Good* (30%) or *Good* (38%), 26% were *Neutral*, and the remaining 6% considered it *Weak*.

We asked an additional closed question concerning the participant's willingness to use this catalog as a basis for future projects related to sustainability. 50% answered *Yes*, 48% *Perhaps*, and 2% (1 expert) answered *No*.

Open Questions. We collected feedback from participants on relevant or positive aspects, as well as points for improvement, comments and suggestions.

The most mentioned **relevant or positive aspects** were: *understandability, simplicity, configurability* and *completeness* of the catalog. Regarding *under-*

standability, some respondents enjoyed *"the visual representation of the concepts and the ability to see clear relationships"*, the *"perspective on inter-dependencies"* and the fact that *"it provides a general understanding of software sustainability requirements"*. In what concerns *simplicity*, participants liked *"the possibility to clearly visualize the interactions between the attributes and the goals in various different areas"*, as well as *"the organization in multiple layers and the support for fast-creation of sustainability concerns"*. Regarding *configurability* respondents mentioned the value of *"being able to be applied to nearly all projects"* and that *"(...) it can be tailored to user's need"*. Finally, in terms of *completeness*, participants referred *"the concept of a taxonomy that software developers can go to in order to make sure that they have addressed the most important sub-domains of sustainability"*.

About the **points for improvement**, the *color palette* and the *need for a use case or an example*, were the most cited ones. Respondents said *"maybe you could also use some colors for links since there may be positive and negative contributions"*, and *"you could use less saturated colours"*. One respondent suggests *"maybe some example could illustrate the benefit of the catalog"*, and *"it gives an impression of completeness and generality, while the focus should be on domains and examples"*. We agree that more examples are needed.

On **comments and suggestions** we had compliments about the importance and completeness of our work. One participant commented *"this is a good piece of work providing especially novice software requirement engineers or developers an understanding of sustainability in software development"*. We had some respondents asking if they could access the final work once finished, and various suggestions to make our work fully open-source and accessible to anyone.

6 Threats to Validity

Internal Validity. A threat to our survey is that we might not have asked the correct questions, or the questions might be ambiguous. To mitigate this, a segmentation of the questionnaire was performed so we clearly separate different evaluation topics and we were very careful on the wording and structure of the questions (validated among the authors). Furthermore, the participant may not have enough knowledge to answer the questions. Thereunto, we constructed a guide for our work. However, it may be too complex for the participant, or it may fail passing the adequate information. We made an effort to write the guide as succinct as possible and easily readable with the aid of visual illustrations.

Construct Validity. Our catalog is based on the results obtaining from the mapping study. Therefore, its completeness and correctness depends on how well the mapping study was conducted. One threat of the mapping study is concerned with the search string not including all the relevant keywords. This was mitigated by validating it among the authors and also by performing an evaluation of the catalog with external participants through a questionnaire, where each question is directly related to an evaluation criterion (in a 1:1 mapping).

External Validity. We performed a preliminary qualitative evaluation with 50 participants, including 16 experts. A larger sample of participants is required for an extended external validity. The participants' answers may be biased, since the answer is directly linked to their familiarity with the topic. To mitigate this issue we produced a guide document explaining the contents of the catalog.

Conclusion Validity. Even though DBLP compiles a vast amount of publications from different sources covering the most relevant *fora* in Computer Science, we may have missed relevant information in our mapping study. To mitigate this, we performed backward and forward snowballing.

7 Related Work

Some related works exist. We will summarize each and comment of the differences to our work. A sustainability design catalog to help developers and managers eliciting sustainability requirements is discussed by Oyedeji et al. [20]. It is based on the Karlskrona manifesto principles and the sustainability indicators. Positive and negative effects of software on the environment can be identified by using the approach. However, the inter-dependencies between dimensions are not covered. Paech et al. [21] present an approach to support the elicitation of sustainability requirements, by providing a checklist of general and IT-specific details for the sustainability dimensions and a checklist of general influences between the dimensions. Such checklists can be used to refine the requirements of a software application, in an iterative way, with sustainability aspects from the different dimensions. The use of checklists could be incorporated in our tool to configure our catalog. In Saputri and Lee [29], a goal-based approach is proposed to specify sustainability requirements, allowing the analysis of sustainability properties to evaluate impact and trade-off analysis of those requirements. The authors do not make use of a catalog to help the sustainability requirements identification. Brito et al. [5] define a model for sustainability concepts plus their relationships, as well as conflicts between sustainability dimensions or between those and other system requirements. For conflict management, a multi-criteria decision making method is used to rank, stakeholders and effects between requirements. This approach does not provide a catalog, but a multi-criteria method could be integrated into our work. In Penzenstadler et al. [23], an approach is proposed to identify successful sustainability interventions using leverage points (LPs), i.e., system locations where a change can impact significantly system-wide. Compared to ours, they do not provide a catalog to support their approach.

8 Conclusions

The sustainability catalog was defined based on the available published literature. It is domain independent and can be configured, using a web-based tool, to accommodate a subset of the whole set of properties (requirements and relationships). Even though this is a preliminary catalog, the results of the qualitative evaluation involving authors, teachers and students, are encouraging. The questionnaire was carefully thought to inquire about readability, interest and usefulness, and included a question about intention of use in future projects. A total of 50 respondents, from different ages, degrees, and academic experience, rated the catalog positively (rating 4.1 out of 5) and 98% of the participants stated they would use, or consider using, it in future projects.

We need to address the remaining sustainability dimensions: environmental, economic and individual. We collected some initial information for the first two and initiated their conceptualization. Also, the catalog's configurability needs to allow selection of refined qualities, not only the first level properties of each dimension. We plan to develop a sustainability web-application portal, and integrate a configured model with specific problem domain models. This web-application could then offer new adaptive labels, working sessions, and ease of look-ups, for example. Finally, we will apply the catalog to the UBike project[2], and hope to use it in several other cases studies. Offering a set of examples to illustrate the benefit of the catalog scenarios.

Acknowledgment. We thank NOVA LINCS (UIDB/04516/2020) for the financial support of FCT – Fundação para a Ciência e a Tecnologia, through national funds.

References

1. Albuquerque, D., et al.: A sustainable requirements catalogue for software modelling - companion site. https://sites.google.com/fct.unl.pt/sustreqscatalogue/. Accessed April 2021
2. Becker, C., et al.: Requirements: the key to sustainability. IEEE Softw. **33**(1), 56–65 (2016)
3. Becker, C., et al.: Sustainability design and software: the karlskrona manifesto. In: Engineering, ICSE 2015, vol. 2, pp. 467–476. IEEE Press, USA (2015)
4. Boehm, B., In, H.: Identifying quality-requirement conflicts. IEEE Softw. **13**(2), 25–35 (1996)
5. Brito, I., et al.: A concern-oriented sustainability approach. In: 2018 12th International RCIS, pp. 1–12. IEEE (2018)
6. Brundtland, G.H.: Our common future: development that meets the needs of the present without compromising the ability of future generations to meet their own needs. World Commission on Environment and Development [WCED] (1987)
7. Calero, C., Piattini, M.: Puzzling out software sustainability. Sustain. Comput.: Inf. Syst. **16**, 117–124 (2017)
8. Chitchyan, R., et al.: Sustainability design in requirements engineering: state of practice. In: 2016 IEEE/ACM 38th ICSE-Companion, pp. 533–542 (2016)
9. Chung, L., Nixon, B.A., Yu, E., Mylopoulos, J.: Non-functional Requirements in Software Engineering, vol. 5. Springer, Heidelberg (2000). https://doi.org/10.1007/978-1-4615-5269-7
10. Condori-Fernandez, N., Lago, P.: Characterizing the contribution of quality requirements to software sustainability. JSS **137**, 289–305 (2018)
11. Dalpiaz, F., et al.: iStar 2.0 language guide (2016). https://arxiv.org/abs/1605.07767v3

---

[2] https://jleal687.wixsite.com/u-bike.

12. Easterbrook, S.M.: Climate change: a grand software challenge. In: of the FSE/SDP WS on Future of Software Engineering Research, FoSER 2010, pp. 99–104. ACM (2010)
13. Glinz, M.: On non-functional requirements. In: 15th IEEE International Requirements Engineering Conference (RE 2007), pp. 21–26. IEEE (2007)
14. ISO/IEC: ISO/IEC 25010:2011(en), Systems and software engineering - Systems and software Quality Requirements and Evaluation (SQuaRE) - System and software quality models
15. Kang, K., et al.: Feature-oriented domain analysis (FODA) feasibility study. Technical report CMU/SEI-90-TR-021, Software Engineering Institute, Carnegie Mellon University, Pittsburgh, PA (1990)
16. Landtsheer, R.D., van Lamsweerde, A.: Reasoning about confidentiality at requirements engineering time. In: 10th ESEC, pp. 41–49. ACM (2005)
17. Mairiza, D., et al.: Towards a catalogue of conflicts among non-functional requirements. ENASE **2010**, 20–29 (2010)
18. Miller, R.E.: The Quest for Software Requirements. Mavenmark Books (2009)
19. Naumann, S., et al.: The greensoft model: a reference model for green and sustainable software and its engineering. SUSCOM **1**(4), 294–304 (2011)
20. Oyedeji, S., Seffah, A., Penzenstadler, B.: A catalogue supporting software sustainability design. Sustainability **10**(7), 2296 (2018)
21. Paech, B., et al.: Towards a systematic process for the elicitation of sustainability requirements. In: RE4SuSy@ RE (2019)
22. Penzenstadler, B.: Infusing green: requirements engineering for green in and through software systems. In: CEUR WS Proceedings, vol. 1216, pp. 44–53 (2014)
23. Penzenstadler, B., et al.: Software engineering for sustainability: find the leverage points! IEEE Softw. **35**(4), 22–33 (2018)
24. Penzenstadler, B., Femmer, H.: A generic model for sustainability with process-and product-specific instances. In: WS on Green in/by SE, pp. 3–8 (2013)
25. Petersen, K., et al.: Systematic mapping studies in software engineering. In: EASE 2008, pp. 68–77. BCS Learning & Development Ltd., Swindon (2008)
26. Pimentel, J., Castro, J.: piStar tool - a pluggable online tool for goal modeling. In: 26th International Requirements Engineering Conference (RE), pp. 498–499 (2018)
27. Raturi, A., et al.: Developing a sustainability non-functional requirements framework. In: 3rd International WS on Green and Sustainable Software, pp. 1–8. ACM (2014)
28. Roher, K., Richardson, D.: A proposed recommender system for eliciting software sustainability requirements. In: 2013 2nd International WS on User Evaluations for Software Engineering Researchers (USER), pp. 16–19, May 2013
29. Saputri, T.R.D., Lee, S.-W.: Incorporating sustainability design in requirements engineering process: a preliminary study. In: Lee, S.-W., Nakatani, T. (eds.) APRES 2016. CCIS, vol. 671, pp. 53–67. Springer, Singapore (2016). https://doi.org/10.1007/978-981-10-3256-1_4
30. Venters, C.C., et al.: Software sustainability: the modern tower of babel. In: CEUR WS Proceedings, vol. 1216, pp. 7–12. CEUR (2014)

Conceptual Modeling of Gender-Inclusive Requirements

Inês Nunes(✉)📵, Ana Moreira📵, and João Araujo📵

NOVA LINCS, NOVA University of Lisbon, Lisbon, Portugal
ir.nunes@campus.fct.unl.pt, {amm,joao.araujo}@fct.unl.pt

Abstract. As technologies revolutionize the way we live, overlooking gender perspectives in the development of digital solutions results in gender-biased technology that, instead of advancing gender inclusion, creates new barriers in achieving it. This paper proposes a conceptual model for gender inclusion in software development. We started by performing a systematic mapping study to gather the relevant concepts from the existing body of knowledge. This served as groundwork for the definition of a conceptual model of gender-inclusive requirements.

Keywords: Gender issues · Gender-inclusive · Conceptual model · Requirements engineering · Software development

1 Introduction

Gender issues refer to "all aspects and concerns related to women's and men's lives and situation in society, to the way they interrelate, their differences in access to and use of resources, their activities, and how they react to changes, interventions and policies" [11]. Over the last decades, research and assessment have made it possible to understand where and when gender issues occur specifically, enabling the development of measures that contribute to significant progress for equal rights, responsibilities, and opportunities [40]. Yet, intersecting forms of discrimination are still being perpetuated, directly and indirectly, by social norms, practices, and gender-based stereotypes [22]. Such is the case of the technology field: women comprise only 3% of ICT graduates worldwide [45], hold just 24% of all digital sector jobs [26], and represent only between 2% to 4% of open source developers [46]. Unfortunately, women still face gender-based prejudice and hostility when joining the field [21] and encounter inequalities in the workplace that reinforce existent gender bias that excludes them [26]. The under-representation of women and gender imbalance in positions of power in the software industry suggest that software products might not be inclusive.

Although gender issues emerge early during software development, there are very few approaches for addressing them. Thus, our goal is to study how gender issues have been addressed in software engineering. The first step towards fulfilling this goal was to conduct a systematic mapping study on gender issues in software engineering. The results confirmed the hypothesis that gender plays

© Springer Nature Switzerland AG 2021
A. Ghose et al. (Eds.): ER 2021, LNCS 13011, pp. 395–409, 2021.
https://doi.org/10.1007/978-3-030-89022-3_31

a significant role in the users' attitudes toward software and software systems developed in male-dominated environments and teams favor characteristics statistically associated with men. Differences in characteristics, such as experiences, opportunities, roles, responsibilities, and levels of access and decision-making imply distinct needs and expectations from software technologies [17,21,37]. However, software is assumed to be gender-neutral [48], but design techniques such as the I-methodology [6], which models users' behaviors based on that of development teams, leads to gender issues in systems. For instance, software is designed expecting users to learn new features through tinkering. However, female users are statistically less likely to do so compared to male users [9]. When explicitly addressed, confusion and misconceptions about gender and assumptions about women and girls as an homogeneous group can inadvertently integrate harmful stereotypes into the software. In particular, the 'shrink it and pink it' practice [36] creates pink, simplified technologies, such as fashion and wedding video games [18], that impose and reinforce traditional notions of femininity [6]. From the mapping study we gathered a comprehensive overview of the state of the art on gender issues and developed a conceptual model of gender-inclusive software to support requirements engineers in integrating a gender perspective in software development. The conceptual model is then illustrated with an example.

In summary, the contributions of this paper are twofold: i) A mapping study to identify existing approaches to handle gender issues in software engineering from which the results served as the conceptual baseline for the development of the model, ii) a conceptual model to enable the elicitation of gender-inclusive requirements grounded in the conceptualization of gender as a social construct.

Section 2 describes the mapping study used for the creation of the conceptual model of gender-inclusive requirements presented in Sect. 3. Section 4 presents an example and a brief discussion of the model. Section 5 concludes this paper.

2   Gender Issues in Software Engineering

A systematic mapping study [33] was performed to understand how gender issues have been addressed in software engineering. The research method consists of planning, conducting, and reporting.

2.1   Planning and Conducting

Planning Phase. Planning involves the formulation of the research question, the definition of the search and study selection strategies, the establishment of the quality assessment criteria, and lastly, the specification of the data collection and extraction strategy. The research question is: *How have gender issues been addressed in software engineering?* It was decomposed into four sub questions: **RQ1.** How are gender and gender issues understood in software engineering? **RQ2.** What are the software application domains where gender issues were addressed? **RQ3.** What gender issues impact software users? **RQ4.** What approaches have been proposed to address gender issues in software development?

Conducting Phase. The conducting phase follows the research protocol defined in the previous phase and it is consists of applying the search process, selecting the relevant studies according to the inclusion and exclusion criteria and the quality assessment, and performing the data extraction and synthesis.

The **search strategy** aims to find the most complete and consistent set of studies according to the research purpose [50]. The search string was built with the key terms of the research questions:

("gender issues" OR "gender diversity" OR "gender bias" OR "gender stereotype" OR "gender inclusive" OR "gender equality" OR "gender gap" OR "gender difference") AND ("software engineering" OR "requirements engineering")

The search string was run automatically on July 11, 2020, on Google Scholar, yielding 729 candidate studies that were saved in a bibliography tool. Snowballing was used on the final set of selected papers to find applicable studies.

The **inclusion and exclusion criteria** were defined during the planning phase to avoid bias when evaluating and selecting the relevant studies that answer the research questions. The evaluation was performed in two iterations: (i) analyzing and reading the title and the abstract of the 729 studies, and excluding the studies that met at least one of the exclusion criteria, which decreased the number of studies to 60; (ii) reading the 60 studies in full, resulting in 31 selected studies. The **quality criteria** focused on the number of citations considering the year of publication and the CORE Rank. Snowballing was applied to the 31 studies and 5 more were selected for data extraction, totaling 36 studies.

A **data extraction** template records the content of each selected study to ensure that the selected papers are subjected to the same extraction criteria. The template was designed as a form and it consisted of a section for the metadata of the study and a data extraction section for the gender conceptualization (RQ1), the application domain (RQ2), a description of the gender issues identified (RQ3), and the respective proposed approach to address them (RQ4).

2.2 Reporting the Results

RQ1. How are gender and gender issues understood in software engineering? To answer this question we extracted information concerning the gender definition from the selected studies. We devised four categories of gender conceptualizations and classified the studies according to them: *Binary (categorical view of gender), Binary and Social Context, Social Construct,* and *Intersectional.*

The studies of the first category assumed a binary view of gender [3–5,8,15,17,19,21,25,30,32,44,47,49], focusing on individuals who either identify themselves as female or male, and assuming one's biological sex corresponds to one's gender. Most studies did not discuss their model of gender and used the concept as a statistical variable to analyze differences between women and men in the use, preferences, adoption, or interaction with software. The studies from the second category understood gender as a self-described attribute influenced by social roles [13,14,16,18,20,23,24,28,29,34,37,41,48]. However, they tackled gender as binary. In the third category, the studies conceptualize gender as a social construct and discuss the limitations of assuming gender binary approaches [2,7,9,27,35,36,42]. As a social construct, gender is a spectrum in which individuals align themselves by expressing their gender identity, independently of biological sex. Thus, differences in attitudes towards software are related to differences in gender expressions that result from internalized gendered behavior from a given social context. Yet, these differences in needs and expectations are not being considered and software is statistically privileging male users, placing female individuals at a disadvantage when using them [3,8,15,23,28,32,48]. Lastly, the fourth category presents "intersectionality" where approaches seek to explain how gender intersects with other social identities (e.g., race, culture), and how these intersections form multiple, layered identities [6,39]. Hence, social and cultural context are fundamental gender factors to consider when developing software. In summary, the following three main gender issues were identified.

Software is Gender-Neutral. Predominantly male technology development teams assume software technologies as exclusively technical and gender-neutral. Mostly, they assume their own needs and values are universally applicable. Also, there is a lack of knowledge from those involved in software development about the concept of gender and its impact, predominating the idea that these are unrelated, or that gender does not impact software.

Binary Conceptualization of Gender. If gender is addressed, it is typically simplified to a statistical binary category, sometimes associated with biological sex. This highlights the existence of gender differences. However, it does not fit them in a social context to understand why they exist, and therefore, does not provide any information about how to solve them. Moreover, a strict female/male binary approach can embed gender stereotypes in the software.

Lack of Approaches. When awareness is raised, there is a lack of support to address gender issues during the software development process, namely common and practical definitions of gender, and tools and guidance for integrating them in software. In the absence of a concrete method, gender-based stereotypes and assumptions can be made and left unquestioned by the development team, leading to a biased system that can harm its users.

RQ2. What are the software application domains where gender issues were addressed? A broad set of software application domains address gender issues. From the selected studies, *Human Computer Interaction* was the domain with more papers [2,6,9,16,27,34–36,42,48] (10 out of 36), providing evidence of gender differences in the interaction and performance in computing tasks and presented a concrete focus on the inclusion of gender perspective in the technology design. The second application domain was *End User Applications* [3–5,8,15,19,44], where gender issues were found in problem-solving software, with 7 studies. The third was *Open Source Software* [7,13,21,28] which contributed with 4 studies, mainly in participation and contribution to project development. Furthermore, the application domains *Web Applications* [17,29,41], *Mobile Applications* [25,32,37] and *Game Development* [14,18,49] included the same number of articles, with 3 out of 36, followed by *Machine Learning* with 2 studies [20,23], sharing the common goal of preventing algorithms from perpetuating gender stereotypes. The application domains in which gender issues have been least addressed are *Social Networking Services* [30], *Requirements Engineering* [47] and *Smart Cities, Mobility & IoT* [24] with 1 study each. With the exception of the *Machine Learning* domain, where gender issues refer to bias in datasets and the creation of algorithms, empirical research on significant gender differences in attitudes toward software was presented across software domains.

RQ3. What gender issues impact software users? Statistically, female and male users present differences in attitudes toward software: female users are motivated to use technology as a tool to accomplish a goal, exhibit a comprehensive processing style, have low self-efficacy, show aversion to risk, and are process-oriented learners [9]. Male users see technology as a source of entertainment, are more selective, exhibit high self-efficacy, are risk-tolerant, and learn by tinkering [9]. However, software itself is not supportive of all users, but rather favors the attitudes typically associated with males, disadvantaging users with female characteristics [9]. Additionally, the *Characteristics* are interrelated and mutually influenced. Self-Efficacy is positively correlated to Perceived Ease of Use for female users [19] and related to Willingness to Learn [3] and Tinkering [4]. Motivation for using the system is also related to the Willingness to Learn different features [19], which may be lower for female users [15], and to the interaction Environment, where female users are more motivated by a collaborative Environment, rather than a competitive one [5]. The perceived Cost-Benefit of learning may also be higher than a male user's perceived cost to learn the same feature [44]. Moreover, perceived Ease of Use is more important for female users, while male users are more influenced by perceived Usefulness [24]. Regarding Visual Design, Sense of Belonging and consequent Motivation for using the software system are impacted negatively when user interfaces are driven by gender-biased design choices in aesthetics, images, and language [29]. Although female users were more affected by the stereotypical images, male users were also affected, and both benefited from the gender-inclusive design [29]. Visual Design is also more important and impacts levels of Credibility for female users [32]. Moreover, they are more accurate in assimilating and decoding verbal and nonverbal Cues [29,41]. If the Language or Communication Style of an interface or online community is not gender-inclusive (e.g., masculine gender-exclusive language, such as using "guys" when referring to a group or "he" as default, "boy's club", sexist language) their Sense of Belonging, Willingness, Self-efficacy, and Motivation to engage decreases [13,29]. The online programming community StackOverflow negatively affects women's participation through its male-oriented design, culture of criticism, and unwelcoming, competitive, and hostile environment [13,28]. Furthermore, users with female characteristics are more concerned about Privacy [37] and are more socially oriented [25] therefore prefer technology that enables them to be available and connect to others, specially with people they already know [30]. They also have less Access to digital resources [24], less previous technological experience [13], are more sensitive on cost of purchasing [25], and have less Time available to interact with the system and can be discouraged if it compromises too much time to learn [14,49]. Thus, the compatibility of the system with their everyday Routine is essential for its use [24]. The set of characteristics that influence attitudes towards software are shown in Table 1.

Table 1. Characteristics that influence attitudes towards software

Characteristic	Description	Concept
Risk	Perception of possible outcomes when using a software [9]	Perceptions
Financial cost	Perception regarding the financial cost of a software [25]	Perceptions
Ease of use	Perception that using the technology will be effort-free [19]	Perceptions
Usefulness	Perception that using the technology will provide utility [19]	Perceptions
Credibility	Level of credibility attributed to a software [32]	Beliefs
Trust	Belief in the reliability and trustworthiness of a software [25]	Beliefs
Privacy	Concerns and behavior for privacy when using a software [37]	Beliefs
Cost-benefit	Earned benefit compared to the cost of trying a software [44]	Beliefs
Self-efficacy	Belief in the ability to use software in varied situations [9]	Beliefs
Sense of belonging	Feeling of fitting in with an online culture or community [29]	Beliefs
Linguistic & communic. style	Linguistic and communication styles in an online community/website interface/software [29]	Preferences
Visual design	Aesthetics of the software interface, including imagery, colorfulness, complexity, and fonts [32]	Preferences
Cue detection	Cue detection in interface design, language, and community norms of a particular software [32]	Skills
Information processing style	Strategies for processing new information and solving problems in a software task [9]	Skills
Awareness	Previous experiences and knowledge about a software [13]	Skills
Willingness to learn	Desire to acquire knowledge about a software [3]	Motivations
Motivation	Reasons behind one's behaviors towards software [9]	Motivations
Tinkering	Exploratory behavior when using a software [9]	Motivations
Time commitment	Time one has available for using a software [14]	Responsibilities
Routine integration	Software compatibility with one's habits, behavior, patterns, and environments [24]	Responsibilities
Social interaction	Type and quantity of social interaction provided by an online community/software [25]	Environment
Environment	Conditions for interacting with the software [5]	Environment
Community	Size, culture, and environment of an online community [13]	Environment
Access	Access to technological resources [24]	Access

RQ4. What approaches have been proposed to address gender issues in software development? Very few existing works propose approaches to address gender issues during the system's development. One of these works is GenderMag [9], a method for detecting and fixing gender inclusivity bugs in software through a systematic process that evaluates its features. The process is based on a set of personas that represent a range of distinct users structured around five underlying gender differences in problem solving skills: motivation, information processing style, computer self-efficacy, risk aversion, and tinkering. Results showed that applying GenderMag improved the software's inclusiveness and eliminated the gender gap in the software's design [16]. IT&me [27] uses gender-sensitive personas in the design process of software to ensure the diversity of female perspectives. Personas were developed with an agile, iterative approach model that involved potential users, preventing the integration of stereotypical gender assumptions in the software platform design [27]. In [24], a conceptual model that relates gender differences in daily mobility patterns and social roles with user acceptance of smart mobility technologies is proposed with the aim of considering the needs of all users during development. Another study [44] proposed an end-user profile formation approach, 'RULES', to be used in behavioral modeling implementations, consisting of five behavioral attributes influenced by the user's gender, namely risk, usefulness, and ease of use perception, learning willingness, and self-efficacy. Yet another work [18] proposed an integrative approach to understand and evaluate gender inclusiveness in game development through a framework that guides the design of gender inclusiveness in games. Lastly, [47] uses a modified coherence method to overcome gender differences in communication patterns by adding a structure to requirements elicitation and allowing clear information transfer in interviews between mixed gender users and analysts.

Threats to Validity. The threats to validity to this is study is discussed as follows. *Construct validity.* The completeness and correctness of the conceptual model depends on how well the mapping study was conducted. One threat concerns the search string not including all the relevant keywords. This was mitigated by validating it within the authors and an external reviewer. *Internal validity.* To minimize the threat of not including all the relevant information for this study, we attempted to gather all the keywords' synonyms that represent the research questions and tested several search strings based on the number of relevant results they retrieved, and chose the most optimal. However, since the number of studies was high, we could have missed some relevant work due to exhaustion. *External validity.* To ensure we did not miss relevant research work regarding our purpose, we opted to perform the automatic search in Google Scholar, which provides a very large set of publications in Software Engineering, to ensure we cover the maximum results possible. Additionally, we used the Snowballing approach. However, we did not consider Non-English or unavailable studies. *Conclusion validity.* We saved the retrieved studies in the Google

Scholar's bibliography management tool at the time of the review, and used the data extraction form to structure the data necessary to answer each RQ.

2.3   Related Work

Stumpf et al. performed a conceptual review on gender-inclusive HCI design that provides an overview of the motivations, the state of the art, and possible future work for this area [43]. Díaz et al. observed differences between women and men in effort and accuracy of elicited requirements, and concluded that mixed teams yield the most optimal results [10]. In addition, Aksekili et al. showed that organizational support and policies for women's advancement improves team work quality and performance of agile software development teams [1]. The work presented here addresses the relationship between gender concepts and the software development process and how it impacts the developed software and how users interact with it, based on the systematic mapping study we conducted.

3   A Conceptual Model for Gender-Inclusive Requirements

The conceptual model for gender-inclusive requirements was constructed as a UML class diagram, shown in Fig. 1. For clarity, we omitted the characteristics where gender differences where identified and their interrelations (see Table 1). The development process was based on the methodologies proposed in [12,31]. The domain of the conceptual model concerns the intersection of gender with software technologies, exploring the mutually influencing relationship between gender and software development and software itself. Its purpose is to find and mitigate gender issues from the beginning and throughout the software development life cycle and support requirements engineers in the elicitation of gender-inclusive requirements that, if satisfied, will make software systems inclusive for every user. We resorted to the findings of the systematic mapping study to identify and define the concepts and relationships that compose the conceptual model. We used the domain classification criteria to define its scope of application and the categories *Social Construct* and *Intersectional* for its gender conceptualization. Next we present a description and a brief discussion for each of the five main concepts of the model: *Human Actor*, *Gender*, *Sociocultural context*, *Characteristics*, and *Software System*.

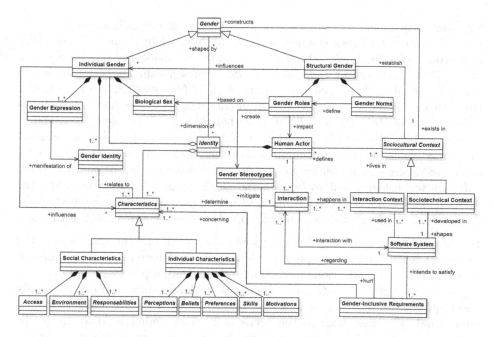

Fig. 1. Conceptual model of gender-inclusive requirements

Human Actor. This represents all types of users and developers of the *Software System*. The *Human Actor* lives in a particular *Sociocultural context* and has a unique *Identity* that is characterized by their *Individual Gender* and *Characteristics*. The *Characteristics* of the *Human Actor* determine their *Interaction* with the *Software System*. These interactions can happen in various *Interaction Contexts*, which can be distinct from the *Sociotechnical Context* where the *Software System* was developed and where the *Human Actor* may or may not have participated. The *Human Actor* expects the *Software System* will be inclusive and support their *Individual Characteristics* and *Social Characteristics* for a successful *Interaction*. The 'quality of pluralism' from [2] was used to represent the *Human Actor* in our model. This conceptualization seeks to recognize the complex and unique identities of users across *Sociocultural contexts* to foster engagement with diversity and to challenge the homogeneous points of view that underpin the assumptions made about users in the early stages of development.

Gender. We conceptualize gender both as a structural feature of society and as a complex part of an individual's *Identity*. The first, *Structural Gender*, represents the normative societal attributes and opportunities constructed around the binary female/male based on the perceived *Biological Sex* of the *Human Actor*, including *Gender Norms* and *Gender Roles* [35]. These are defined and reinforced in a particular *Sociocultural Context* through social expectations and interactions, creating gendered power asymmetries in society and establishing gendered systems that perpetuate inequality. Consequently, the belief that only two mutually exclusive categories of gender exist is normalized. In this context, *Gender Stereotypes* emerge and are internalized by *Human Actors* that perpetuate them by conforming to the expected behavior and reinforcing it to others [7,20]. The second, *Individual Gender*, represents the *Human Actor*'s self-identified gender [35], which is one part of their *Identity* [39]. We represent it through the individual's experience of gender, their *Gender Identity*, which is independent of their *Biological Sex*, and their *Gender Expression*, the manifestation of their *Gender Identity*. Both *Gender Identity* and *Gender Expression* are conceptualized as a continuum where the *Human Actors* can align themselves to describe how gender shapes diverse behaviors and attitudes towards software technologies and go beyond the gender binary [42]. Furthermore, the *Human Actors* can vary their *Gender Identities* according to the context of the *Interaction*, which allows the construction of fluid and complex identities [36].

Sociocultural Context. This represents the social and cultural factors and events of a particular time period. *Gender* is constructed within a *Sociocultural context* and institutionalized through socialization processes and systems, represented by *Structural Gender*. The software development process, especially the requirements engineering phase, is shaped by a range of social factors and contextual influences, such as the needs and values, represented in the model as *Characteristics*, of development teams, stakeholders, organizations, and communities, which are represented by the *Sociotechnical Context*. This context is defined by a very narrow subset of the population: it is overwhelmingly male and with high levels of education and income [23,48]. Software systems are developed in male-dominated environments where acknowledging different contexts is overlooked under the assumption of technical neutrality and thus, embody and reflect the masculine culture and identity of its creators [34,35], at the expense of underrepresented perspectives who have been historically excluded [39]. In contrast, the *Human Actors* who interact with the *Software System* can be highly diverse in behavior, preferences, and needs, constituting the *Interaction Context*. Since the *Software System* is the product of the values and priorities of its *Sociotechnical context*, the historical patterns of gender discrimination, the consequent lack of gender diversity, and limited decision-making power from underrepresented *Human Actors* restricts the discussion of different viewpoints, which may introduce *Gender Stereotypes* about female perspectives into the *Software System* [39]. Therefore, we emphasize the distinction between the two contexts to provide a clear understanding of how ignoring the *Sociotechnical context* of software during development may unintentionally lead to systems that replicate the existing structures of gender inequality in society.

Characteristics. Represent part of the *Identity* of the *Human Actor* and determine their *Interaction* with a *Software System*. These characteristics are influenced by the *Individual Gender* of the *Human Actor*, creating gender differences in the *Interaction*. The majority of the studies from where these differences were collected were previously classified as *Binary* or *Binary, Social Construct*. However, because we conceptualize *Gender Identity* as a spectrum, we do not expect a *Human Actor* to be consistent with one gender for all the *Characteristics* but rather vary because these are the result of complex individual experiences and social attributes, opportunities, and relationships. For example, a *Human Actor* can be characterized with an information processing style statistically more prevalent among female users while showing attitudes towards risk more prevalent in male users. Thus, we can consider diverse groups of *Human Actors* and account for behavioral diversity among them. Furthermore, we organized the *Characteristics* that are influenced by *Gender* (see Table 1) as either *Individual*, representing the personal attributes of a *Human Actor*, or *Social*, representing the *Characteristics* that are established in relation to others. This classification facilitates the selection of the most suitable *Characteristics* for the type of *Software System*. *Individual Characteristics* include *Perceptions* (Perceived Risk, Perceived Financial Cost, Perceived Ease of Use, and Perceived Usefulness), *Beliefs* (Credibility, Trust, Privacy, Cost-benefit, Self-efficacy, and Sense of belonging), *Preferences* (Linguistic and Communication Styles and Visual Design), *Skills* (Cue Detection, Information Processing Style, and Awareness), and *Motivations* (Willingness to learn, Motivation, and Tinkering). *Social Characteristics* include *Responsibilities* (Time commitment and Routine integration), *Social Environment* (Social Interaction, Environment, and Community), and *Access* (Access to technological resources).

Software System. This represents the *Software System* the *Human Actor* interacts with in a *Interaction Context*. The *Software System* intends to satisfy the *Gender-Inclusive Requirements* regarding the *Interaction*. Therefore, it is first necessary to acknowledge that because software is the product of decisions made in exclusionary contextual settings, the *Socio-technical context*, it is not neutral. The *Gender-Inclusive Requirements* concern the multiple and diverse *Characteristics* of *Human Actors*. Thus, an analysis of whose *Characteristics* are being prioritized and which ones are being neglected is required to assess whether the decisions being made discriminate against users that are underrepresented during the software development process. The *Gender-Inclusive Requirements* are not intended to be fixed and separate requirements, but rather capture the needs and perspectives of diverse users and integrate them into the functional and non-functional requirements according to the *Software System* domain. Furthermore, the construction of the *Identity* of potential users with focus on *Gender* takes into account evidence-based gender differences, conceptualized as *Characteristics* and the underlying context that shapes them to challenge binary assumptions and gender stereotypes and encourage the representation of diverse perspectives so that all users benefit equally from the system to be.

4 Application and Discussion of the Conceptual Model

The *Car-sharing System* [38] allows users to rent cars via a web or mobile application, and charges based on the rental period, distance, and car model. The conceptual model provides a representation of how gender issues may arise in the software development process and how they can be mitigated by taking a gender perspective that stem from an understanding of the gender concepts and the system domain. The use of the model should be specified according to the organization and system's goals, but the following criteria should always be satisfied: i) address historical patterns of gender discrimination; ii) identify and mitigate gender stereotypes; iii) incorporate multiple perspectives, preferences, and needs; iv) account for behavioral diversity within groups of different genders. The aim of the model is to make the impact of gender on software development explicit, facilitate communication, and improve decision-making and documentation regarding gender-inclusive goals for guiding requirements engineers in the elicitation of gender-inclusive requirements that will benefit all users.

Consider for example that the system will be developed in a technology company where the development and management team are predominantly male. Due to the ubiquitous nature of the car-sharing system, the *Interaction context* can be complex, unexpected, and highly gender-diverse. The gender gap between the *Sociotechnical context* and the *Interaction context* will be significant. Therefore, requirements engineers must carefully plan the elicitation process to mitigate gender issues such as unequal status and decision-making power in the company that results in masculine perspectives being prioritized [48] and the possibility of *male hegemonic identity* [34] where women adopt the mainstream culture of the company for integration avoiding introducing gender perspectives in group sessions. Thus, diverse groups of stakeholders should be consulted, including those who have substantially less power or influence, and specifically elicit information from women through individual interviews or group sessions where they are the majority. Inclusive language should be adopted, for instance, by avoiding binary language such as "both genders" or describing users as opposites to each other, but rather using they as default pronouns.

The contextualization of the *Interaction* is captured during the elicitation process through the specification of its influencing factors: the diverse *Characteristics* of the *Human Actors* and the underlying influence of *Gender* on them. The actors are the individuals that provide their cars and those who rent them. The system is intended to be used in the everyday personal and professional life of its users. Hence, an understanding of the pervasiveness of *Structural Gender* in their *Sociocultural context* is fundamental to help discovering the needs that must be met for the system to be gender-inclusive. In this system, *Gender Roles* represent the gender division of labor that translates into different needs and motivations for using this alternative mobility system. These shall be identified by the requirements engineers through the specification of the appropriate *Characteristics* for the system domain and that will mirror real-life behavior of the users. As a result of uneven socioeconomic conditions between women and men, different daily mobility patterns emerge in their routines, with the women's being more complex in activities and responsibilities [24], and thus requirements engineers should select *Routine Integration* and *Perceived Financial Cost* as relevant *Characteristics* to support the elicitation of this information in semi-structured interviews, questionnaires, or creativity techniques. Requirements engineers should act as facilitators in the use of *Gender Identity* as a component of the users' *Identity* to elicit information that would otherwise be missed, rather than categorizing users, and encourage the stakeholders to engage with diversity and think of more complex and realistic users.

The conceptual model provides a starting point for the integration of a gender perspective in software development and a way to analyze requirements processes in light of gender-inclusion goals. It is meant to be used as a tool in established practices of organizations from the beginning and throughout the software development to create systems that satisfy gender-inclusive requirements.

5   Conclusions

The systematic mapping study on gender inclusiveness in software engineering confirms three issues: software is assumed to be exclusively technical and neutral; software development ignores the complex sociocultural implications of gender and constructs it as static and binary; the limited existence of approaches for integrating gender as a complex facet of the identity of users during software development. To address this gap, the key gender-related concepts from the study served as the foundation for the proposal of a conceptual model for gender-inclusive requirements. An illustration example shows the use of this model.

We are creating a framework based on the conceptual model that offers a set of guidelines with concrete goals for integrating a gender perspective in the existing practices of requirements engineers and in people management. It includes reusable checklists with a set of questions related to each concept of the model to guide interviews and brainstorming sessions. In the near future we will empirically evaluate this framework with junior and senior experts and will develop a web-based tool to support the documentation of its activities.

Acknowledgment. We thank NOVA LINCS (UIDB/04516/2020) for the financial support of Fundação para a Ciência e a Tecnologia.

References

1. Aksekili, A.Y., Stettina, C.J.: Women in agile: the impact of organizational support for women's advancement on teamwork quality and performance in agile software development teams. In: Przybyłek, A., Miler, J., Poth, A., Riel, A. (eds.) LASD 2021. LNBIP, vol. 408, pp. 3–23. Springer, Cham (2021). https://doi.org/10.1007/978-3-030-67084-9_1
2. Bardzell, S.: Feminist HCI: taking stock and outlining an agenda for design. In: SIGCHI Conference on HCI, pp. 1301–1310 (2010)
3. Beckwith, L., et al.: Effectiveness of end-user debugging software features: are there gender issues? In: SIGCHI Conference on HCI, pp. 869–878 (2005)
4. Beckwith, L., et al.: Tinkering and gender in end-user programmers' debugging. In: SIGCHI Conference on HCI, pp. 231–240 (2006)
5. Beckwith, L., Burnett, M.: Gender: an important factor in end-user programming environments? In: VL/HCC, pp. 107–114. IEEE (2004)
6. Breslin, S., Wadhwa, B.: Exploring nuanced gender perspectives within the HCI community. In: India Conference on HCI, pp. 45–54 (2014)

7. Brooke, S.: "Condescending, rude, assholes": framing gender and hostility on stack overflow (2019)
8. Burnett, M., et al.: Gender differences and programming environments: across programming populations. In: ACM-IEEE ESEM, pp. 1–10 (2010)
9. Burnett, M., et al.: GenderMag: a method for evaluating software's gender inclusiveness. Interact. Comput. **28**(6), 760–787 (2016)
10. Díaz, E., et al.: Are requirements elicitation sessions influenced by participants' gender? An empirical experiment. Sci. Comput. Program. **204**, 102595 (2021)
11. European Institute for Gender Equality, E.U.: Effectiveness of institutional mechanisms for the advancement of gender equality (2014)
12. Fernández-López, M., et al.: METHONTOLOGY: from ontological art towards ontological engineering (1997). https://www.aaai.org/
13. Ford, D., et al.: Paradise unplugged: identifying barriers for female participation on stack overflow. In: ACM SIGSOFT International Symposium on FSE, pp. 846–857 (2016)
14. Gao, G., et al.: Gendered design bias: gender differences of in-game character choice and playing style in league of legends. In: CHI, pp. 307–317 (2017)
15. Grigoreanu, V., et al.: Can feature design reduce the gender gap in end-user software development environments? In: VL/HCC, pp. 149–156. IEEE (2008)
16. Hilderbrand, C., et al.: Engineering gender-inclusivity into software: tales from the trenches. arXiv preprint arXiv:1905.10361 (2019)
17. Hsu, C.C.: Comparison of gender differences in young people's blog interface preferences and designs. Displays **33**(3), 119–128 (2012)
18. Ibrahim, R., et al.: deGendering games: towards a gender-inclusive framework for games. In: IADIS International Conference on GET (MCCSIS), pp. 127–130 (2010)
19. Katerina, T., Nicolaos, P.: Examining gender issues in perception and acceptance in web-based end-user development activities. Edu&IT **23**(3), 1175–1202 (2018)
20. Kay, M., et al.: Unequal representation and gender stereotypes in image search results for occupations. In: ACM Conference on HCI, pp. 3819–3828 (2015)
21. Kuechler, V., Gilbertson, C., Jensen, C.: Gender differences in early free and open source software joining process. In: Hammouda, I., Lundell, B., Mikkonen, T., Scacchi, W. (eds.) OSS 2012. IAICT, vol. 378, pp. 78–93. Springer, Heidelberg (2012). https://doi.org/10.1007/978-3-642-33442-9_6
22. Latz, I., et al.: Equal rights for women and girls in the world's constitutions (2014)
23. Leavy, S.: Gender bias in artificial intelligence: the need for diversity and gender theory in machine learning. In: Workshop on Gender Equality in SE, pp. 14–16 (2018)
24. Lenz, B., Kolarova, V., Stark, K.: Gender issues in the digitalized 'smart' mobility world – conceptualization and empirical findings applying a mixed methods approach. In: Krömker, H. (ed.) HCII 2019. LNCS, vol. 11596, pp. 378–392. Springer, Cham (2019). https://doi.org/10.1007/978-3-030-22666-4_28
25. Liu, D., Guo, X.: Exploring gender differences in acceptance of mobile computing devices among college students. IseB **15**(1), 197–223 (2017)
26. Mark West, R.K., Chew, H.E.: I'd blush if I could: closing gender divides in digital skills through education. EQUALS and UNESCO (2019)
27. Marsden, N., et al.: Developing personas, considering gender: a case study. In: 29th Australian Conference on Computer-Human Interaction, pp. 392–396 (2017)
28. May, A., et al.: Gender differences in participation and reward on stack overflow. Empir. Softw. Eng. **24**(4), 1997–2019 (2019)
29. Metaxa-Kakavouli, D., et al.: Gender-inclusive design: sense of belonging and bias in web interfaces. In: HCI, pp. 1–6 (2018)

30. Muscanell, N., et al.: Make new friends or keep the old: gender and personality differences in social networking use. Comput. H.B. **28**(1), 107–112 (2012)
31. Noy, N.F., et al.: Ontology development 101: a guide to creating your first ontology (2001). http://protege.stanford.edu/publications
32. Oyibo, K., et al.: Gender difference in the credibility perception of mobile websites: a mixed method approach. In: UMAP, pp. 75–84 (2016)
33. Petersen, K., et al.: Systematic mapping studies in software engineering. In: EASE 2008, p. 68–77 (2008)
34. Ramos, A.M.G., Rojas-Rajs, T.: Inclusion of gender perspective in design and it environments. In: HCI, pp. 1–4 (2016)
35. Rode, J.A.: A theoretical agenda for feminist HCI. Interact. Comput. **23**(5), 393–400 (2011)
36. Rode, J.A., Poole, E.S.: Putting the gender back in digital housekeeping. In: 4th Conference on Gender & IT, pp. 79–90 (2018)
37. Rowan, M., Dehlinger, J.: Observed gender differences in privacy concerns and behaviors of mobile device end users. Proc. CS **37**, 340–347 (2014)
38. Saputri, T.R.D., Lee, S.W.: Addressing sustainability in the requirements engineering process: from elicitation to functional decomposition. JSEP **32**(8), e2254 (2020)
39. Schlesinger, A., et al.: Intersectional HCI: engaging identity through gender, race, and class. In: Conference on HCI, pp. 5412–5427 (2017)
40. UN Secretary-General: Special edition: progress towards the sustainable development goals (2019)
41. Simon, S.J.: The impact of culture and gender on web sites: an empirical study. DATABASE Adv. Inf. Syst. **32**(1), 18–37 (2000)
42. Spiel, K., et al.: How to do better with gender on surveys: a guide for HCI researchers. Interactions **26**(4), 62–65 (2019)
43. Stumpf, S., et al.: Gender-inclusive HCI research and design: a conceptual review. Found. Trends® HCI **13**(1), 1–69 (2019)
44. Tzafilkou, K., et al.: Gender-based behavioral analysis for end-user development and the 'rules' attributes. E&IT **22**(4), 1853–1894 (2017)
45. UNESCO: Cracking the code: girls' and women's education in science, technology, engineering and mathematics (stem) (2017)
46. Wang, Z., et al.: Competence-confidence gap: a threat to female developers' contribution on github. In: 40th IEEE/ACM ICSE-SEIS, pp. 81–90. IEEE (2018)
47. Warkentin, M., Malimage, N.: Overcoming mixed-gender requirements misspecification with the modified coherence method (2012)
48. Williams, G.: Are you sure your software is gender-neutral? Interactions **21**(1), 36–39 (2014)
49. Winn, J., Heeter, C.: Gaming, gender, and time: who makes time to play? Sex Roles **61**(1–2), 1–13 (2009)
50. Zhang, H., et al.: Identifying relevant studies in software engineering. Inf. Softw. Technol. **53**(6), 625–637 (2011)

Usability of Open Data Datasets

Solomon Antony[1]([⊠]) [iD] and Dharmender Salian[2]

[1] Murray State University, Murray, USA
santony@murraystate.edu
[2] University of the Cumberlands, Williamsburg, USA
dsalian0302@ucumberlands.edu

Abstract. 'Open data' is the term used to describe the concept that data is available freely for anyone to use for analysis and research. Most democratic governments in the world have taken steps to publish public data under the 'Open data' umbrella. While it is a welcome step that can enable data analysis by citizen scientists, the quality and accessibility of open data datasets makes the process a bit challenging for those not trained in data management. Using concepts of structuredness of data, a dataset usability measurement is developed. Using a randomly selected set of datasets from a popular open data portal, an instrument is developed, validated, and applied. The paper ends with elaborating future research directions and listing recommendations for publishers of open data datasets.

Keywords: Open data · Normal forms · Usability

1 Introduction

In December of 2007, thirty individuals who can classified as thinkers and information activists met in Sebastopol, north of San Francisco, California. Their main agenda was to come up with a list of 10 principles of open government. One of their major recommendation was the idea of 'open public data'. A year later the US President signed memoranda which included 'open data' as an important pillar of open government. The idea behind open data is that public data must be published online before they can be claimed by third parties. Subsequently, in May 2009 the Data.gov portal was opened. One of the main aspects of Open Government Data Act was that government data is required to be made published in machine-readable format. Not only it was a commendable effort to make the data public and machine readable, but the individual agencies were also free to choose any format of data. Currently the datasets can be found in fifty formats including HTML, XML, JSON, PDF, TIFF, GIF, DOC etc. While a large amounts of government decisions are based on numerous perspectives such as policy, politics, welfare, the Open Government Act expressed the intent to move towards evidence-based decision making. To make evidence-based decisions, the data sets must be amenable to be used by data analysis software programs. This paper aims to understand the level of structuredness of open data.

Section 2 of the paper summarizes relevant literature that deals with quality of open data datasets. Section 3 describes the sampling approach and data coding method.

A. Ghose et al. (Eds.): ER 2021, LNCS 13011, pp. 410–422, 2021.
https://doi.org/10.1007/978-3-030-89022-3_32

Section 4 goes over development an instrument to measure the usability of the datasets. Then in Sect. 5, we provide outline of future studies and guidelines for potential users of open data dataset and for publishers of open data datasets.

2 Literature Survey

Global economy is data centric, and governments are becoming responsive to open data. Open data are publicly available datasets structured to be available and consumable [8]. In addition to the initiatives by the US government, the UK government created Data.gov.uk to provide access to non-personal UK government data so that entrepreneurs and other entities can use data published by local authorities, central government to be useful for building products and services. The Indian government created Data.gov.in for supporting open data. Chile created its open data portal in in 2011 and Denmark in 2012 [9]. For a list of government initiatives from around the world, see Appendix.

It is laudable that many governments are making efforts towards creating open data portals, but efforts are required for ensuring data quality. Open data datasets originate from different organizational units and it is likely that the organizational units have different standards for data quality [9]. While statistical agencies have stricter standards for data quality, municipalities have data which is more likely to be incomplete, inaccurate, or incorrect [13]. Open data datasets that are of poor-quality will hamper their effective use [11].

There are many dimensions to the metrics of data quality - accuracy, applicability, understandability, relevance, availability, timeliness, and primacy [3]. Typically, accuracy of data, or understandability of data are determined at the time of use by the data analyst. While these are important attributes for a user, a dataset must have appropriate structure *before* it can be used. For example, the keys of the data records must be non-empty, and the formats must be machine readable [12]. Also, there is a need for consistency of structure of datasets between different time periods [14].

Bad formatting, missing values, redundant information, inconsistencies within a column (e.g. inconsistent date formats) will require extensive data cleansing operations [6]. Cleansing the data can be expensive [1]. When using such data, citizen data analysts with inadequate data cleansing knowledge may end up with incorrect conclusions (i.e., garbage-in-garbage-out). Hence, it important that open data datasets be assessed for structural usability. The assessment instrument may employ criteria that are based on concepts of Normal forms, functional dependencies, pivot tables, and data summaries. This paper aims to develop and demonstrate such an instrument for assessing the structural usability of open data datasets.

Most of software programs for data analysis accept text files, spreadsheet, database tables, comma separated values (CSV), XML-based files (XML), and rich text formats (RTF) as inputs [2]. This study will review CSV or xls format files and focus on the structural accuracy of the data.

3 Sampling the Datasets

The objective of this study is to develop an instrument and metric that assesses the usability of open data datasets for analytics. Most popular analytics software programs accept both comma separated values (CSV) and Excel file formats for inputs[1]. The US government's data.gov portal was used for selecting sample datasets. The portal provides access to more than 272,000 datasets of which a majority (more than 90%) are datasets from the Federal Government agencies and organizations. The entire catalog is more than 14,000 web pages long and it is accessible page by page. From the 14,000 page catalog, a random list of 1000 pages were chosen to collect sample datasets. The contents of each page were programmatically scanned and hyperlinks that lead to a csv or xls file were extracted. Following those links that lead to an actual CSV or Excel file, 765 files were downloaded. For all practical purposes, these data files can be considered truly a random sample of csv data files from an open data portal. A word cloud generated using the words in the file names is shown in Fig. 1.

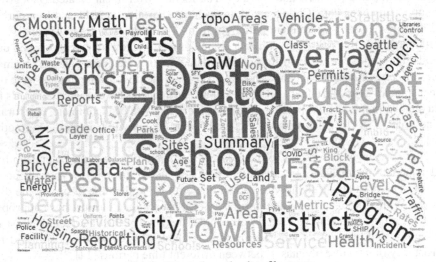

Fig. 1. Words from the data file names

On a review of these files, some patterns discovered. Those patterns are used to identify characteristics to develop a metric for data usability. The details of the patterns are described next.

4 Developing a Metric for Dataset Usability

Common set of operations a data analyst would perform on a dataset includes (i) descriptive statistics, (ii) inferential statistics and (iii) predictive statistics. To use the data analysis tool's standard interface the data must meet certain minimum qualifications. (a) It must be rectangular in shape, (b) There must be column headers, and (c) entries under a column must have the same data types.

4.1 Developing the Instrument Items

Most files we sampled have headers and a rectangular shape, (e.g., see Fig. 2).

---

[1] https://data.wu.ac.at/.

	A	B	C	D	E	F	G	H	I	J	K	L	M	N	O	P	Q
1	OBJECTID	ZONEID	ZONING	ZONELUT	CONTRAC	ORDINAN	EFFECTIVE	HISTORIC	PEDESTRI	SHORELIN	OVERLAY	LIGHTRAIL	OLDZONE	GEO	Shape__A	Shape__Length	
2	1	542	NC3-65	NC3		119218	9.13E+11						295		4784.087	289.0667	
3	2	543	NC3-65	NC3		119218	9.13E+11						295		17315.45	602.9217	
4	3	544	NC3-65	NC3		119218	9.13E+11						295		6379.147	321.0795	
5	4	545	NC3-65	NC3		119218	9.13E+11						295		66107.36	1223.271	
6	5	546	NC3-65	NC3		119218	9.13E+11						296		230985.4	1992.594	
7	6	547	NC3-65	NC3		119218	9.13E+11						295		22115.59	603.0409	
8	7	548	NC2-40	NC2		119218	9.13E+11						297		163047.8	1664.546	
9	8	564	NC2-40	NC2		119218	9.13E+11						0		136523	1534.243	
10	9	566	NC2-40	NC2		119218	9.13E+11						0		26363.38	653.6977	
11	10	567	NC1-30	NC1		119218	9.13E+11						0		35982.19	847.7322	
12	11	568	NC3-65	NC3		119218	9.13E+11						0		87869.27	1550.567	
13	12	580	NC3-65	NC3		119235	9.14E+11						172		151907.7	2062.465	

Fig. 2. A Usable dataset

While these expectations are commonplace, we did find datasets that do not meet these requirements. See Fig. 3 for an example of inconsistent datatype in the same column. In this image, the data type in the second column is missing and inconsistent.

	A	B	C	D	E	F	G	H	I	J	K
1	the_geom	OBJECTID	Name	DOCKET	ORDINAN	DESCRIPTION	WEBLINK				
2	MULTIPOLYGO	36144	Middle Harriso	81	2014	Middle Harrisc	http://czo.nola.gov/Article-18#18-26				
3	MULTIPOLYGO	36193	HU-B1A Use Re	81	2014	HU-B1A Use Re	https://czo.nola.gov/article-18/#18-18				
4	MULTIPOLYGO	36199	HU-B1A Use Re	81	2014	HU-B1A Use Re	https://czo.nola.gov/article-18/#18-18				
5	MULTIPOLYGON (((-89.855162640037	30.153397633056,	-89.855143725037	30.152345971397,	-89.854956751457	30.152148839795,	-89.8549625509				
6	6729422959 30.	-89.996774424;	-89.997024162;	-89.9970688850	-89.99721	-89.997335740	-89.99745	-89.99757	-89.99766	-89.99769	-89.99793 -
7	MULTIPOLYGO	36238	HU-B1A Use Re	53	2020	HU-B1A Use Re	https://czo.nola.gov/article-18/#18-18				
8	MULTIPOLYGO	36154	HU-B1A Use Re	81	2014	HU-B1A Use Re	https://czo.nola.gov/article-18/#18-18				
9	MULTIPOLYGO	36227	HU-B1A Use Re	1	2017	HU-B1A Use Re	https://czo.nola.gov/article-18/#18-18				
10	MULTIPOLYGO	36142	Magazine Stree	81	2014	Magazine Stre	http://czo.nola.gov/article-18/#18-20				
11	MULTIPOLYGO	36103	CT Corridor Tra	81	2014	CT Corridor Tra	http://czo.nola.gov/article-18/#18-16				

Fig. 3. Dataset with inconsistent column datatypes

Some datasets may contain column headers that are repeating. They are pivots of a particular dimension e.g., 2012 population, 2013 population, 2014 population, etc. While, such a dataset passes the minimum qualifications, structuring data by grouping them make it harder for the analyst to compute growth statistics across the years. However, some software tools (e.g., Power BI) have features to unpivot the data and normalize the data. See Fig. 4 for an example of a dataset whose columns are repeating. A Level

	A	B	C	D	E	F	G	H	I	J	K	L	M	N	O	P	C
1	DBN	Grade	Year	Demogra phic	Number Tested	Mean Scale Score	Num Level 1	Pct Level 1	Num Level 2	Pct Level 2	Num Level 3	Pct Level 3	Num Level 4	Pct Level 4	Num Level 3 and 4	Pct Level 3 and 4	
2	01M015	3	2006	ELL	4	s	s	s	s	s	s	s	s	s	s	s	
3	01M015	3	2006	EP	35	671	0	0	10	28.6	19	54.3	6	17.1	25	71.4	
4	01M015	3	2007	ELL	8	668	0	0	1	12.5	6	75	1	12.5	7	87.5	
5	01M015	3	2007	EP	23	674	2	8.7	2	8.7	16	69.6	3	13	19	82.6	
6	01M015	3	2008	ELL	6	670	0	0	0	0	6	100	0	0	6	100	
7	01M015	3	2008	EP	31	668	0	0	6	19.4	23	74.2	2	6.5	25	80.6	
8	01M015	3	2009	ELL	9	664	0	0	1	11.1	8	88.9	0	0	8	88.9	
9	01M015	3	2009	EP	24	669	0	0	3	12.5	20	83.3	1	4.2	21	87.5	
10	01M015	3	2010	ELL	4	s	s	s	s	s	s	s	s	s	s	s	
11	01M015	3	2010	EP	22	673	5	22.7	11	50	5	22.7	1	4.5	6	27.3	
12	01M015	3	2011	ELL	9	669	4	44.4	3	33.3	2	22.2	0	0	2	22.2	
13	01M015	3	2011	EP	19	672	6	31.6	10	52.6	3	15.8	0	0	3	15.8	
14	01M015	3	2012	ELL	3	s	s	s	s	s	s	s	s	s	s	s	
15	01M015	3	2012	EP	18	679	2	11.1	9	50	7	38.9	0	0	7	38.9	
16	01M015	4	2006	ELL	6	610	3	50	3	50	0	0	0	0	0	0	

Fig. 4. Dataset with repeating columns

dimension is used as pivot to show repeating groups of Num and Pct Level columns. Although, the table is flat to view, the data have orthogonal dimensions.

Some datasets may have subtotals as a column or row entry for a group of columns or records. For example, the dataset may have population by states and states could be grouped by region they belong to, and the regional sub-totals may be included in the dataset. See Fig. 5 for an example of subtotals within groups of rows.

Grade	Year	Category	Number T	Mean Scal	Level 1 #	Level 1 %	Level 2 #	Level 2 %	Level 3 #	Level 3 %	Level 4 #	Level 4 %	Level 3+4	Level 3+4 %
3	2006	Asian	9768	700	243	2.5	543	5.6	4128	42.3	4854	49.7	8982	92
4	2006	Asian	9973	699	294	2.9	600	6	4245	42.6	4834	48.5	9079	91
5	2006	Asian	9852	691	369	3.7	907	9.2	4379	44.4	4197	42.6	8576	87
6	2006	Asian	9606	682	452	4.7	1176	12.2	4646	48.4	3332	34.7	7978	83.1
7	2006	Asian	9433	671	521	5.5	1698	18	4690	49.7	2524	26.8	7214	76.5
8	2006	Asian	9593	675	671	7	1847	19.3	4403	45.9	2672	27.9	7075	73.8
All Grades	2006	Asian	58225	687	2550	4.4	6771	11.6	26491	45.5	22413	38.5	48904	84
3	2007	Asian	9750	706	156	1.6	402	4.1	3886	39.9	5306	54.4	9192	94.3
4	2007	Asian	9881	704	209	2.1	564	5.7	3968	40.2	5140	52	9108	92.2
5	2007	Asian	10111	700	211	2.1	626	6.2	4257	42.1	5017	49.6	9274	91.7
6	2007	Asian	9808	694	343	3.5	778	7.9	4356	44.4	4331	44.2	8687	88.6
7	2007	Asian	9779	685	333	3.4	1220	12.5	4255	43.5	3971	40.6	8226	84.1
8	2007	Asian	9734	681	466	4.8	1537	15.8	4661	47.9	3070	31.5	7731	79.4
All Grades	2007	Asian	59063	695	1718	2.9	5127	8.7	25383	43	26835	45.4	52218	88.4
3	2008	Asian	9951	707	67	0.7	275	2.8	4809	48.3	4800	48.2	9609	96.6

Fig. 5. Dataset with subtotals and repeating columns

Some datasets have groupings of columns that appear to describe the same entity. Such groupings can indicate multiple dependencies among columns. Multiple dependencies among the columns is equivalent to having transitive dependency in Normal form terms. Having multiple dependencies will not hamper data analysis. However, not having transitive dependencies will prevent running summary statistics on one of the dependent columns. Consider the dataset shown in Fig. 6. There is dependency between Vendor, and Vendor City. Suppose the user wishes to compute frequency counts of vendor cities. Using this data directly instead of separating the FD's first and then running frequency counts will lead to more accurate counts. The analyst must be cautious when using dataset with multiple dependencies.

ContractT	ContractDesc	Vendor	Vendor Address Line 1	Vendor Addr	Vendor City	Vendor St	Ve
Open Soli	Recreation Instr	1st & Life Inc	168 W Main St, Unit 33		New Market	MD	
Bridge Co	Street Sign Resu	3M Company	3M CENTER BUILDING	424-1E-04	ST PAUL	MN	
Open Soli	Recreation Instr	480 Club LLC	10003 Wedge Way		Montgomery Villa	MD	
Informal -	Moving and Recc	495 Movers, Inc.	640 Lofstrand Lane		Rockville	MD	
Non-Com	Provide capital ir	7TH GENERATION FOUND	12640 ROLLING RD		POTOMAC	MD	
Open Soli	Road Equipment ir	A & C PLOWING	25409 Jarl Dr		Gaithersburg	MD	
RFP - Non	Contract for Cont	A Morton Thomas and As	800 King Farm Blvd, 4th Floor		Rockville	MD	
Non-Com	To provide adult	A Plus Adult Medical Day	50 W Gude Dr Ste 52, 50 W GUDE DR,	Rockville	MD	
Non-Com	Provides for renc	A Wider Circle Inc	4808 Moorland Ln Ste 802		Bethesda	MD	
Non-Com	Support for the V	A Wider Circle, Inc.	4808 Moorland Lane, Suite 802		Bethesda	MD	
Non-Com	Remodeling and	A Wider Circle, Inc.	4808 MOORLAND LN STE 802		BETHESDA	MD	
Open Soli	Road Equipment	A. Marquez Trucking Inc	1101 Ednor Road		Silver Spring	MD	
RFP - Non	Water Resources	A. Morton Thomas & Assc	12750 Twinbrook Pkwy, Ste 200		Rockville	MD	
RFP - Non	Multi-Disciplinar	A. Morton Thomas and A:	800 King Farm Blvd, 4th Floor		Rockville	MD	
Bridge Co	Engineering Serv	A. Morton Thomas and A:	800 King Farm Blvd	4th Floor	Rockville	MD	
IFB - Non-	HVAC Systems Pi	AAA Complete Building S	5151 WISCONSIN AVENUE, N.W., SU	Washington	DC	
Open Soli	Recreation Instr	Aaron Kaufman	100 Fallsgrove Blvd, APT 2203		Rockville	MD	
Informal -	PREA Audit Servi	AB Management and Con	2310 Victoria Crossing Lane		Midlothianv	VA	

Fig. 6. Groupings of columns

Some datasets are based on summary of values from a transaction system. Such reports would have the dimensions folded into columns and the summaries of values are shown as columns. These datatypes would rate high on the usability scale. For example, in Fig. 7 the totals for Year, Cohort category and Demographic are the dimensions, and the remaining columns are the fact summaries.

	A	B	C	D	E	F	G	H	I	J	K	L	M	N	O
	Cohort Year	Cohort Category	Demographic	Total Cohort Num	Total Grads Num	Total Grads Pct of cohort	Total Regents Num	Total Regents Pct of cohort	Total Regents Pct of grads	Advanced Regents Num	Advanced Regents Pct of cohort	Advanced Regents Pct of grads	Regents w/o Advance d Num	Regents w/o Advance d Pct of cohort	Regents w/o Advance d Pct of grads
	2001	4 Year Jur	Asian	9,807	6,501	66.30%	5,261	53.60%	80.90%	3,277	33.40%	50.40%	1,984	20.20%	30.50%
	2001	5 Year	Asian	9,807	7,377	75.20%	5,618	57.30%	76.20%	3,369	34.40%	45.70%	2,249	22.90%	30.50%
	2001	6 Year	Asian	9,807	7,599	77.50%	5,691	58.00%	74.90%	3,380	34.50%	44.50%	2,311	23.60%	30.40%
	2002	4 Year Jur	Asian	10,554	7,082	67.10%	6,062	57.40%	85.60%	3,601	34.10%	50.80%	2,461	23.30%	34.80%
	2002	5 Year	Asian	10,554	8,054	76.30%	6,554	62.10%	81.40%	3,743	35.50%	46.50%	2,811	26.60%	34.90%
	2002	6 Year	Asian	10,554	8,260	78.30%	6,632	62.80%	80.30%	3,754	35.60%	45.40%	2,878	27.30%	34.80%
	2003	4 Year Jur	Asian	10,403	7,467	71.80%	6,568	63.10%	88.00%	4,274	41.10%	57.20%	2,294	22.10%	30.70%
	2003	5 Year	Asian	10,403	8,372	80.50%	7,062	67.90%	84.40%	4,410	42.40%	52.70%	2,652	25.50%	31.70%
0	2003	6 Year	Asian	10,408	8,569	82.30%	7,150	68.70%	83.40%	4,420	42.50%	51.60%	2,730	26.20%	31.90%
1	2004	4 Year Jur	Asian	10,897	8,075	74.10%	7,188	66.00%	89.00%	4,729	43.40%	58.60%	2,459	22.60%	30.50%
2	2004	4 Year Aug	Asian	10,897	8,455	77.60%	7,414	68.00%	87.70%	n/a	n/a	n/a	n/a	n/a	n/a
3	2004	5 Year	Asian	10,891	8,999	82.60%	7,719	70.90%	85.80%	4,860	44.60%	54.00%	2,859	26.30%	31.80%

Fig. 7. Summary report as a dataset

In Fig. 8, End quarter date and Facility name are dimensions, and the remaining columns are fact summaries. Star-schema datasets is desirable, and not having a star schema will not hinder usability.

	A	B	C	D	E
	End Quarter Date	Facility Name	Average Inmate Population	Average Number of Permanent Beds	Inmate Population Density
	6/30/2019	Bridgeport	709	879	80.7
	6/30/2019	Brooklyn	454	456	99.6
	6/30/2019	Cheshire	1315	1560	84.3
	6/30/2019	Corrigan-Radgowski	1101	1304	84.4
	6/30/2019	CRCI	1461	1512	96.6
	6/30/2019	Enfield	0	740	0
	6/30/2019	Garner	574	750	76.5
	6/30/2019	Gates	0	1139	0
)	6/30/2019	Hartford	930	1035	89.9
	6/30/2019	MacDougall/Walker	1948	2218	87.8
2	6/30/2019	MYI	320	704	45.5
3	6/30/2019	New Haven	711	769	92.5
	6/30/2019	Northern	193	577	33.4
5	6/30/2019	Osborn	1330	1505	88.4
5	6/30/2019	Webster	0	584	0
7	6/30/2019	Willard-Cybulski	1146	1148	99.8

Fig. 8. Star-schema formatted dataset

Some datasets appear to be generated by exporting the logs from transaction or accounting systems or as star-schema output. Such datasets too are usable to an extent.

See Fig. 9 for an example. In this dataset, column F is the financial figure and other columns represent some dimension of business accounting.

A	B	C	D	E	F	G
Fund	Department	BCL Code	BCL Name	BCL Purpo	2013 Expenditure	Allowance
General Subfund	Finance General	2QA00	Appropriation	The purpc	57706023	
General Subfund	Finance General	2QD00	Reserves	The purpc	36818259	
General Subfund	Finance General	2QE00	Support to Op(	The purpc	293281640	
General Subfund	A	CZ000	City Budget Of	The purpc	4085671	
Drainage and Wastev	Seattle Public Utiliti	N100B-DV	Administratior	The purpc	5135857	
General Subfund	Seattle Fire Departn	F1000	Administratior	The purpc	7369739	
General Subfund	Law Department	J1100	Administratior	The purpc	1893005	
Solid Waste Fund	Seattle Public Utiliti	N100B-SW	Administratior	The purpc	4536121	
Water Fund	Seattle Public Utiliti	N100B-W(	Administratior	The purpc	9563508	
General Subfund	Seattle Fire Departn	F2000	Resource Man;	The purpc	10901977	
General Subfund	Seattle Fire Departn	F3000	Operations	The purpc	140454281	
General Subfund	Seattle Fire Departn	F5000	Fire Preventio	The purpc	7174837	
General Subfund	Seattle Fire Departn	F6000	Grants & Reim	The purpc	389234	
General Subfund	Legislative Departm	G1100	Legislative De;	The purpc	12066489	
General Subfund	Department of Neig	I3100	Director's Offi(	The purnc	470249	

Fig. 9. Transaction logs as dataset

Another desirable characteristic is that each row of the dataset is unique. The uniqueness can be assured if there is an identifier column in the dataset. See Fig. 10 for a data set with Town code as the identifier column.

	A	B	C	D	E	F	G	H	I	J	K	L	M
1	Town Code	Town	Residenti al	Commerc ial	Industrial	Public Utility	Vacant Land	Land Use	10 Mil Forest	Apartme nts	Total Real	Total Real Property Tax Exemptio ns	Net R Prope
2	1	Andover	2.17E+08	4509200	1068300	616800	5715260	628920	0	1536000	2.31E+08	1175900	2.3E
3	2	Ansonia	6.51E+08	78406900	15386600	33000	0	3180	115880	15401400	7.6E+08	5875149	7.54E
4	3	Ashford	2.25E+08	12664800	0	0	10252600	3079110	9700	9243600	2.6E+08	1017175	2.59E
5	4	Avon	1.97E+09	2.61E+08	32007780	322590	4635590	258670	0	32453520	2.31E+09	4345060	2.3E
6	5	Barkhams	2.46E+08	11609096	4324720	0	2726010	33858540	0	2173380	3E+08	1022790	2.99E
7	6	Beacon Fa	3.58E+08	14013620	30697430	313640	13336720	177810	0	732140	4.18E+08	3286346	4.14E
8	7	Berlin	1.39E+09	2.55E+08	1.23E+08	3005200	25562750	10853450	0	168100	1.8E+09	5568297	1.8E
9	8	Bethany	4.53E+08	24959070	4823080	0	3319640	242590	0	311720	4.87E+08	1974115	4.85E
10	9	Bethel	1.27E+09	1.88E+08	79222670	0	36010240	5518570	0	20778950	1.6E+09	5232160	1.59F

Fig. 10. Dataset with an identifier column

Some datasets have groups of columns that describe a certain entity. Such a dataset would be considered a relational table with transitive dependencies, and they are also usable to a certain degree. See Fig. 11 for an example. Column M has the identifying code for Column N.

The issues addressed so far are primarily syntactic issues. Semantic issues – such as "Are columns easy to interpret?", and "Are numeric units specified?" are also important.

	A	B	C	D	E	F	G	H	I	J	K	L	M	N	O	P	Q
	OBJECTID	MNL_FEA _KEY	MNL_CM PNT_KEY	MNL_UPS FEATUR E_KEY	MNL_DN S_FEATU RE_KEY	MNL_EQ NUM_ID	MNL_UPS _ENDPT_I D	MNL_DN S_ENDPT _ID	MNL_MN LPT_ID	MNL_MA P_AREA_I D	MNL_SSC 2001_ID	MNL_NP DES_ID	MNL_FEA TYPE_CO DE	MNL_FEA TYPE_TEX T	MNL_OW NER_COD E	MNL_OW NER_NA ME	MNL_PA RALLEL_C ODE
	1	2156440	-29052	15346	15366		209-457	209-252	209-457 2(	209	LC82-1		STB	Stub	RWW	Ronald W	NA
	2	2156451	-28936	548	547		203-102	203-003	203-102 2(	203	LC1571-1		STB	Stub	RWW	Ronald W	NA
	3	2156477	174336	9678	9684		208-061	208-062	208-061 2(	208	LC1540		MNL	Mainline	RWW	Ronald W	NA
	4	2156488	174861	11978	11933		209-195	209-197	209-195 2(	209	LC1525		MNL	Mainline	RWW	Ronald W	NA
	5	2156489	174853	11855	11837		209-191	209-192	209-191 2(	209	LC1831		MNL	Mainline	RWW	Ronald W	NA
	6	2156496	-28990	3838	3869		209-418	209-026	209-418 2(	209	LC58		STB	Stub	RWW	Ronald W	NA
	7	2156513	-29008	8474	8500		209-445	209-181	209-445 2(	209	LC258		STB	Stub	RWW	Ronald W	NA
	15	2156542	175063	16717	16710		209-298	209-297	209-298 2(	209	LC1505		MNL	Mainline	RWW	Ronald W	NA
	16	2156544	-29045	13447	13444		209-469	209-273	209-469 2(	209			STB	Stub	RWW	Ronald W	NA

Fig. 11. Dataset with transitive dependency

Most portals provide a separate 'dictionary' like text file along with each dataset. While one can assume that those accompanying text files will have adequate description of the columns, and unit of measures and other meta-data entries, we deem it important to include the semantic aspect an important issue. To assess the sematic aspect, we can inspect if the column titles are made up of complete words. Since the study uses the data.gov of the USA, we can include "Are most of the column titles made up of complete English words?" as a criterion. See Fig. 11 for an example of dataset where the majority of column titles are not made with complete English words. See Fig. 10 for an example, where the majority of column titles are made up of English words.

Based on the analysis of sample of datasets, we recommend that each dataset be evaluated using these questions. The questions and direction of impact on Usability are show in Table 1.

Table 1. Data set characteristics and their impact on usability

No.	Criteria question	Impact on usability		Weight
		Answer yes	Answer no	
1	Is the dataset a rectangular table?	Positive	Negative	20%
2	Do all values for each column have the same data type?	Positive	Negative	17%
3	Are there any sub-totals or totals of groups of rows or groups of columns?	Negative	Positive	13%
4	Are there any groupings of rows?	Negative	Positive	10%
5	Are there any groupings of columns?	Negative	Positive	10%
6	Is there an identifier for each row?	Positive	Negative	10%
7	Is the table a star schema, with fact columns and multiple dimensions?	Positive	Neutral	10%
8	Are there multiple dependencies among the columns?	Neutral	Positive	7%
9	Are most of the column titles made up of complete English words?	Positive	Negative	3%

These items are to be used to evaluate the usability of datasets. The items are listed in decreasing order of importance. A potential weighting scheme is also shown. The weighting scheme is based on somewhat arbitrary assumption that having a rectangular table is approximately seven times as important as having complete English words in the title. The weights are of the remaining items are approximate multiples of 3%.

The usability computation process is a two-step process. In the first step, each dataset in the sample must be coded against each criteria question. While it is possible to develop an automated tool to answer each criteria question, the study used a more traditional approach of human coders.

Human coders may differ in their interpretation of the questions. To test if the interpretation of the questions are the evaluation of a dataset against these questions are implementable, the two authors coded 22 datasets independently. The overall agreement was 0.76. The initial distribution of percentage of agreement is shown in Fig. 12. Distribution of agreement. One of the datasets was interpreted differently by the two coders and that resulted in 0.25 agreement. The disagreement was traced to two reasons: (i) The dataset did not have 'rectangular' shape, because it had a report header and many blank rows. (ii) the headers were not variable names, were instead variable values. These two aspects of the dataset were interpreted differently by the two coders, resulting in low agreement. After this was corrected, the agreement measure went up to 0.78.

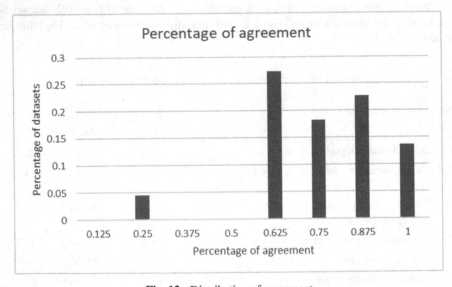

Fig. 12. Distribution of agreement

Next, the extent of how well the sample datasets fared on the Usability assessment is presented.

4.2 Evaluating the Usability of the Datasets

A summary of question-wise results is shown in Table 1. As evident from the table, majority of the datasets have high usability (95% are rectangular shaped). There are some with inconsistent datatypes within each column which can be corrected by most analysis software programs. Few of them have row sub-totals and column sub totals and may require special scripts to extract data. Datasets with groupings of column will require some processing to detect Functional Dependency patterns among the rows.

Table 2. Summary of dataset evaluations

	Question	Desirable answer	Proportion (Yes)
1	Is the dataset a rectangular table?	Yes	95%
2	Do all values for each column have the same data type?	Yes	91%
3	Are there any sub-totals or totals of groups of rows or groups of columns?	No	14%
4	Are there any groupings of rows?	No	14%
5	Are there any groupings of columns?	No	9%
6	Is there an identifier for each row?	Yes	86%
7	Is the table a star schema, with fact columns and multiple dimensions?	Yes	0%
8	Are there multiple dependencies among the columns?	No	27%
9	Are most of the column titles made up of complete English words?	Yes	84%

Since each question has a weight associated with it (see Table 1), one can compute a weighted sum score for each dataset in the sample. If a dataset has "Yes" for Question #1, it will get 0.20 points for Question 1. If it has "No" for Question #1, it will get −0.10 for Question 1. The sum of the question points is defined as the Usability Score of the dataset. Using this method, the usability scores of the sample datasets were computed. The summary statistics of the usability measure are shown in Table 3.

The highest usability score a dataset can get is 1.0 and the lowest is −0.5. As can be seen in Table 3, most datasets have high scores (Median = 0.825, Mean = 0.731). There are a small number of very low scoring datasets (Skewness = −1.99).

Table 3. Summary statistics of usability scores

Mean	0.731
Standard Error	0.046
Median	0.825
Mode	0.950
Standard Deviation	0.283
Kurtosis	4.592
Skewness	−1.985
Range	1.250
Minimum	−0.300
Maximum	0.950
Sample size	38

5   Limitations of This Study

Globally, many governments have open government data initiatives but data usability varies depending on quality and evaluation requirements [7]. Several open data communities have developed suggestions and applications around open government data initiatives [10]. Value of this data is immense but additional issues also are important like discoverability, harvesting, community engagement and interoperability [5]. Here we did not discuss data discovery or data visualization. Data discovery deals with end users able to find required dataset and data visualization refers to whether initial understanding can be obtained of dataset so to decide to probe further [12].

This research considered only datasets available through the open data portal of the USA government. The diversity of organizations at the federal, state, county and city levels may imply that sample datasets too are diverse in quality, but this was not verified in this paper. Future studies will include open data portals from other countries as well. Worldwide, there are numerous open data portals (280 or more according to https://data.wu.ac.at/portalwatch/portalslist) and by sampling datasets from those portals would provide a more diverse and more accurate picture of usability of datasets from all open data portals.

6   Future Research Directions and Implications for Practitioners

So far, research in usability of open data dataset has been largely focused on the quality and timeliness of data. Discussions on data structure as a dimension of data quality were limited to whether the data was in 1NF or 2NF. This research project peels back the cover over the structure of data and reviewed the shape, and nature of columns and rows. The logical next phase of research would focus on developing an automated tool for grading samples of datasets from more open data portals. Another line of research will focus on the human aspect of usability of open data datasets. Using controlled experiments, the assessment instrument will be empirically validated. We will explore variables such as speed (how quickly users can analyze the data), satisfaction (how satisfied they are with the datasets), and effectiveness (have they achieved goals).

Authors and agencies that generate datasets for open data portals can ensure usability of their datasets by following these guidelines. (i) Ensure each row has a unique identifier. (ii) Ensure that values under each column have the same data type. (iii) Do not include sub-totals, row totals, or column totals the data file, and move them to a separate summary file. (iv) While publication of datasets with grouped columns is not discouraged, it is highly recommended that the same data be published as unpivoted format as well. For a complete list of recommended guidelines, refer to Table 2. Publishing open data that use these guidelines for structuring the data will lead to easier usage by citizen scientists and analysts.

Appendix: Open Data Portals from Selected Countries

Country	Portal
Abu Dhabi	https://addata.gov.ae/
Australia	http://data.gov.au/
Canada	https://open.canada.ca/en/open-data
Denmark	http://www.odaa.dk/
European Union	https://data.europa.eu/en
France	http://data.gouv.fr/
Germany	https://www.govdata.de/
India	http://Data.gov.in
Japan	https://www.data.go.jp/
Russia	http://opengovdata.ru/
South Africa	https://southafrica.opendataforafrica.org/
Spain	https://datos.gob.es/
Sweden	https://www.dataportal.se/en
Ukraine	http://data.gov.ua
United Kingdom	http://data.gov.uk/
Uruguay	http://datos.gub.uy

References

1. Atre, S.: Rules for data cleansing. Computerworld **32**(10), 69–72 (1998)
2. Barlas, P., Lanning, I., Heavey, C.: A survey of open source data science tools. Int. J. Intell. Comput. Cybern. **8**(3), 232–261 (2015). https://doi.org/10.1108/IJICC-07-2014-0031

3. Enable quality assessments of open data (2016). Open data handbook. https://opendatahand book.org/solutions/en/Enable-Quality-Assessment/
4. Immonen, A., Ovaska, E., Paaso, T.: Towards certified open data in digital service ecosystems. Softw. Qual. J. **26**(4), 1257–1297 (2017). https://doi.org/10.1007/s11219-017-9378-2
5. Janssen, M., Charalabidis, Y., Zuiderwijk, A.: Benefits, adoption barriers and myths of open data and open government. Inf. Syst. Manag. **29**(4), 258–268 (2012)
6. Kirchner, K., Zec, J., Delibašić, B.: Facilitating data preprocessing by a generic framework: a proposal for clustering. Artif. Intell. Rev. **45**(3), 271–297 (2015). https://doi.org/10.1007/s10462-015-9446-6
7. Máchová, R., Lnenicka, M.: Evaluating the quality of open data portals on the national level. J. Theor. Appl. Electron. Commer. Res. **12**(1), 21–41 (2017). https://doi.org/10.4067/S0718-18762017000100003
8. NSF. Open data at NSF (2016). https://www.nsf.gov/data/
9. OGP. Open government partnership (2015). www.opengovpartnership.org/. Accessed 28 June 2017
10. Petychakis, M., Vasileiou, O., Georgis, C., Mouzakitis, S., Psarras, J.: A state-of-the-art analysis of the current public data landscape from a functional, semantic and technical perspective. J. Theor. Appl. Electron. Commer. Res. **9**(2), 34–47 (2014). https://doi.org/10.4067/S0718-18762014000200004
11. Sadiq, S., Indulska, M.: Open data: quality over quantity: SSIS. Int. J. Inf. Manag. **37**(3), 150 (2017)
12. Slibar, B., Oreski, D., Klicek, B.: Aspects of Open Data and Illustrative Quality Metrics: Literature Review. Varazdin Development and Entrepreneurship Agency (VADEA), Varazdin (2018)
13. Susha, I., Grönlund, Å., Janssen, M.: Organizational measures to stimulate user engagement with open data. Transforming Gov. People Process Policy **9**(2), 181–206 (2015)
14. Sutton, C., Hobson, T., Geddes, J., Caruana, R.: Data diff: interpretable, executable summaries of changes in distributions for data wrangling. In: Proceedings of the 24th ACM SIGKDD International Conference on Knowledge Discovery and Data Mining, pp. 2279–2288. ACM (2018)

Author Index

Printed in the United States
by Baker & Taylor Publisher Services